VISUAL PERCEPTION

VISUAL PERCEPTION

PHYSIOLOGY, PSYCHOLOGY, AND ECOLOGY
3RD EDITION

Vicki Bruce

Department of Psychology, University of Stirling, UK

Patrick R. Green

Department of Psychology, University of Nottingham, UK

Mark A. Georgeson

School of Psychology, University of Birmingham, UK

Psychology Press
An imprint of Erlbaum (UK) Taylor & Francis

Copyright © 1996 by Psychology Press,
an imprint of Erlbaum (UK) Taylor & Francis Ltd.

Psychology Press, Publishers
27 Church Road
Hove
East Sussex, BN3 2FA
UK

British Library Cataloguing in Publication Data
A catalogue record for this title is available from the British Library

ISBN 0-86377-450-4 (Hbk)
ISBN 0-86377-451-2 (Pbk)

Subject index by Christine Boylan
Printed and bound by BPC Wheatons Ltd., Exeter, UK

To Michael
and
To the memory of Rodney Green
and
To Joel and Luke

Contents

Preface to the First Edition

Our primary aim in writing this book has been to present a wide range of recent evidence and theoretical developments in the field of visual perception to an advanced undergraduate readership. The material covered is drawn from three areas: the neurophysiological analysis of vision, the "computational" accounts of vision that have grown out of traditional experimental approaches and artificial intelligence, and work on vision that shares at least some of J.J. Gibson's "ecological" framework.

In the first part of the book we discuss the evolution of different types of eye, the neurophysiological organisation of visual pathways, particularly in mammals, and contrasting theoretical interpretations of single-unit responses in visual systems.

We turn in the second part to psychological and computational models of the interpretation of information in retinal images, discussing perceptual organisation, the perception of depth and of movement, and pattern and object recognition. The contribution of David Marr's work to these problems is emphasised.

In the third part we discuss how extended patterns of light can provide information for the control of action and to specify events; topics covered are the visual guidance of animal and human locomotion, theories of the control of action, and the role of vision in animal social behaviour and human event perception.

We have assumed that our readers will have some prior knowledge of basic neurophysiology (for Part I of the book) and experimental psychology (for Parts II and III), such as might have been gained from an introductory psychology course.

Our choice of topics differs in some respects from that of most textbooks on visual perception. Some topics are excluded. In particular, we do not discuss sensory physiology and psychophysics in as much detail as other texts. We do include material on animal perception that would usually be found in an ethology text, and consider in detail research on human and animal reactions to patterns of optic flow. Our choice of topics is governed by a consistent theoretical outlook. We have been committed to the value of an ecological approach in its wider sense; that espoused by David Marr as much as by James Gibson, who both argued for the need to consider the structure of the world in which an animal or person lives and perceives. It is this commitment that has guided the overall plan of the book.

We have attempted to go beyond exposition of theoretical and empirical developments in each of our three areas, and to discuss promising issues for further research and to present an analysis and critique of the theories we discuss. We have been most speculative about future possibilities for the ecological approach in Chapters 11 and 12, and address global theoretical issues most fully in Chapter 13. Our final conclusion is that an ecological perspective offers valuable insights, but that a "direct" theory of perception is not adequate.

These are exciting times in the study of visual perception, and we believe that there is much to be gained by cross-fertilisation between research areas. There are real and important issues dividing different theoretical camps, which must continue to be debated vigorously, but it is also worthwhile to mark out some potential common ground.

Although the readers we have in mind are advanced psychology students, we have designed the book to be useful also to zoology students specialising in neurophysiology and in animal behaviour, and particularly to students in the increasingly popular courses that combine zoology and psychology. We hope that research workers may also find the book useful; although it will surely be superficial in their areas of primary interest, it may be helpful in approaching the literature in adjoining areas.

Our manuscript has been improved considerably as a result of critical comments from

a number of people. Our colleague Alan Dodds read the entire manuscript, and Robin Stevens read parts. A number of anonymous reviewers furnished further comments. We would like to thank all these people most sincerely. They spotted blunders, and suggested ways of making points more clearly, which would not have occurred to us alone; any remaining errors are, of course, our own responsibility. Mike Burton helped us with our own, and other people's, mathematical reasoning. He was also one of several people who introduced us to the mysteries of word-processing; Chris Blunsdon, Roger Henry, and Anne Lomax are the others.

Roger Somerville (WIDES Advertising and Design) drew all those figures not otherwise acknowledged, and thus contributed enormously to the text. Sam Grainger took many photographs, and E. Hildreth, D.H. Hubel, Fergus Campbell, John Frisby, and Paul Ekman all provided photographs for us to use. Penny Radcliffe typed endless letters and helped in many other ways when we ourselves were flagging. Mike Forster and Rohays Perry encouraged us to see this project through, and gave us editorial help.

Preface to the Second Edition

As the first edition went to press in 1984, research on visual perception was progressing rapidly in a number of areas. The second wave of research inspired by Marr's work was just developing; research into the computation of optical flow was already accelerating; and the connectionist revival was gathering momentum. We have tried to mention all these developments in our new edition by including three (largely) new chapters. In Chapter 5, we bring our earlier discussion of Marr and Hildreth's theory of edge detection together with the more recent work of Watt and Morgan to review approaches to raw primal sketch computation. Chapter 9 is entirely new, and in it we show how "connectionist" modelling can be applied to the problems raised in the second part of the book. Finally, Chapter 13 considers accounts of how the optic flow field, so central to the third part of the book, could actually be computed by the visual systems of different species.

In addition to these new chapters, we have reorganised the second half of Part III somewhat, and have considerably expanded our discussion of imprinting and face perception in the resulting Chapter 16. We have updated other material throughout the text, and particularly in Chapter 3 where we have brought our treatment of the physiology of vision up to date. We have also emphasised the recent convergence between theoretical developments and physiological evidence at a number of points in Parts II and III.

Our thanks are due again to all those who helped us with the first edition, and additionally to those who reviewed or otherwise commented on the text after its publication; they have done much to encourage us to embark on this revision. We thank Mark Georgeson and Roger Watt for their expert scrutiny of our draft second edition; their suggestions have helped us to improve the accuracy and thoroughness of our new material. We also thank Mark Georgeson for providing a valuable illustration. Our thanks are due again to Mike Burton, who gave us considerable help in interpreting the connectionist literature. Any errors remaining after help from these colleagues are, of course, entirely our own reponsibility. Finally, we thank Mike Forster, Rohays Perry and Melanie Tarrant for their support and editorial work, which has made production this time as smooth as last time.

Preface to the Third Edition

Six years have passed since the publication of the second edition of this book, and the field has continued to flourish. In preparing this extensively updated edition, the two authors of the earlier editions are very pleased to include Mark Georgeson as an additional author. Mark was an enthusiastic reviewer of earlier versions, and has been able to add considerable expertise in early visual processing mechanisms to this new edition.

In this third edition, the chapter topics and overall structure are largely unchanged from the second edition. The one exception is that we have moved the chapter on motion processing from Part III to Part II, where it sits more easily given its strong computational flavour. In some individual chapters, however, the treatment of material is radically different from that in previous editions. The structure of Chapter 3 has changed considerably to accommodate an updated account of the primate visual pathway, and in Chapters 5, 6, 7, and 8 recent advances in psychophysical analysis and computational modelling of early visual processing have made major revisions necessary. Throughout these chapters, we have aimed to provide the fuller explanation of basic principles such as spatial and space-time filtering, which are needed to understand recent advances in the field. As a result, some material in Parts I and II is more technically demanding than before, but

we think more useful as a result. We have tried always to provide verbal descriptions alongside any equations, so that those for whom mathematical expressions are a hindrance rather than a help should be able to skip the formulae but retain the sense.

In preparing the final version we have been helped by careful comments from several reviewers, including George Mather and Mike Harris, and by suggestions from many colleagues, including John Wann. We thank them sincerely for their efforts, but the blame for remaining imperfections lies with us. We are also grateful to the many colleagues in our three institutions whose efforts maintain the e-mail links on which we have relied so heavily in preparing this book. It is a pleasure to thank Mike Forster, Rohays Perry, Tanya Sagoo, and Caroline Osborne for their editorial support, which has ensured that production of the book has gone just as smoothly as before. We would also like to thank David Burr for supplying Figure 5.18. Finally we thank our long-suffering families, friends and dog, who have been deprived of company, food and walks during long hours of writing. The new author is grateful to Jan Georgeson for tea and (some) sympathy over the months of midnight oil, and dedicates his efforts on the book to Joel (9) and Luke (7), the students of the future who may one day read it.

Part I

The Physiological Basis of Visual Perception

1

Light and Eyes

All organisms, whether bacteria, oak trees, or whales, must be adapted to their environments if they are to survive and reproduce. The structure and physiology of organisms are not fixed at the start of life; to some extent, adjustments to changes in the environment can occur so as to "fine-tune" the organism's adaptation. One way of achieving this is through the regulation of growth processes, as when plants grow so that their leaves face the strongest available light. Another way, which is much more rapid and is only available to animals, is movement of the body by contraction of muscles.

If the movement of an animal's body is to adapt it to its environment, it must be regulated, or guided, by the environment. Thus the swimming movements of a fish's body, tail, and fins are regulated so as to bring it into contact with food and to avoid obstacles; or the movement of a person's throat, tongue, and lips in speaking are regulated by the speech of other people, linguistic rules and so on.

In order for its movement to be regulated by the environment, an animal must be able to detect structures and events in its surroundings. We call this ability *perception*, and it in turn requires that an animal be sensitive to at least one form of energy that can provide information about the environment. One source of information is provided by chemical substances diffusing through air or water. Another is mechanical energy, whether pressure on the body surface, forces on the limbs and muscles, or waves of sound pressure in air or water. Further information sources, to which some animals are sensitive but people probably are not, are electric and magnetic fields.

An animal sensitive to diffusing chemicals can detect the presence of nearby food or predators, but often cannot pinpoint their exact location, and cannot detect the layout of its inanimate surroundings. Pressure on the skin and mechanical forces on the limbs can provide information about the environment in immediate contact with an animal. Sound can provide information about more distant animals but not usually about distant inanimate structures.

Sensitivity to diffusing chemicals and to mechanical energy gives an animal considerable perceptual abilities, but leaves it unable to obtain information rapidly about either its inanimate world or about silent animals at a distance from itself. The form of energy that can provide these kinds of information is light, and consequently most animals have some ability to perceive their surroundings through vision. The only large animals able to move about rapidly without vision are bats, dolphins and other cetaceans, which use an echolocation system based on ultrasonic cries (Griffin, 1958), and some fish species living in murky water, which detect objects in their surroundings by distortions of their own electric fields (Heiligenberg, 1973).

We will begin our discussion of visual perception in animals and people by considering first the physical nature of light and then how the environment structures the light that reaches an observer.

LIGHT AND THE INFORMATION IT CARRIES

Light is one form of *electromagnetic radiation*, a mode of propagation of energy through space that includes radio waves, radiant heat, gamma rays, and X-rays. One way in which we can picture the nature of electromagnetic radiation is as a pattern of waves propagated through an imaginary medium. It therefore has a velocity, 3×10^8m/sec in a vacuum, and a wavelength, which ranges from hundreds of metres in the case of radio waves to 10^{-12} or 10^{-13}m in the case of cosmic rays. Only a very small part of this range is visible; for human beings, radiation with wavelengths between 400 and 700 nanometres (1nm $= 10^{-9}$m) can be seen (Fig. 1.1).

For some purposes, however, the model of electromagnetic radiation as a wave is not appropriate and we must instead treat it as a stream of tiny wave-like particles called photons travelling in a straight line at the speed of light. Each photon consists of a quantum of energy (the shorter the wavelength of the light the larger the energy quantum), which is given up as it strikes another particle. We need these two conceptions of the nature of electromagnetic radiation because nothing in our experience is analogous to the actual nature of it and we must make do with two imperfect analogies at the same time.

These problems are of no concern in understanding how light is propagated around the environment. For these purposes we can think of light as made up of rays, which vary in both intensity and wavelength. Rays are emitted from light sources and would, in a vacuum, travel in a straight line without attenuation. A vacuum is not a congenial environment for animals, however, and the fate of light rays travelling through natural habitats is more complex.

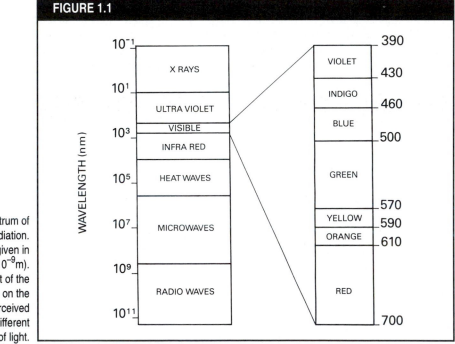

FIGURE 1.1

The spectrum of electromagnetic radiation. Wavelengths are given in nanometres (1nm $= 10^{-9}$m). The visible part of the spectrum is shown on the right, with the perceived colours of different wavelengths of light.

First, as light passes through a medium, even a transparent one such as air or water, it undergoes *absorption*, as photons collide with particles of matter, give up their energy and disappear. Absorption is much stronger in water than in air and even in the clearest oceans there is no detectable sunlight below about 1000 metres. Longer wavelengths are absorbed more strongly, so that available light becomes progressively bluer in deeper water.

Second, light is *diffracted* as it passes through a transparent or translucent medium. Its energy is not absorbed, but instead rays are scattered on striking small particles of matter. Diffraction of sunlight by the atmosphere is the reason why the daytime sky is bright; without an atmosphere, the sky would be dark, as it is on the moon. The blue colour of the sky arises because light of shorter wavelengths is scattered more, and so predominates in the light reaching us from the sky.

Third, the velocity of light is lower when it passes through a transparent medium than when it passes through a vacuum. The greater the optical density of the medium, the lower is the velocity of light. When rays of light pass from a medium of one optical density to a medium of a different density, this change of velocity causes them to be bent, or *refracted* (unless they strike the boundary between the two media perpendicularly). Refraction therefore occurs at boundaries such as those between air and water, or air and glass, and

we will consider it in more detail when we describe the structure of eyes.

Finally, when light strikes an opaque surface, some of its energy is absorbed and some of it is *reflected*. A dark surface absorbs most of the light falling on it and reflects little, whereas a light one does the opposite. The way surfaces reflect light varies in two important ways. First, a surface may reflect some wavelengths more strongly than others, so that the spectral composition of the reflected light (the relative proportions of wavelengths it contains) differs from that of the incident light. A leaf, for example, absorbs more (and hence reflects less) red light than light of other wavelengths. Note that surfaces do not reflect single wavelengths and absorb all others, but alter the spectral composition of the light reflected from them, increasing the proportions of some wavelengths relative to others.

Second, the *texture* of a surface determines how coherently it reflects light. A perfectly smooth surface such as a mirror reflects light uniformly, but most natural surfaces have a rougher texture, made up of a mosaic of tiny reflecting surfaces set at different angles. Light striking such a surface is therefore reflected in an incoherent way (see Fig. 1.2).

Now that we have described the nature of light and the processes governing its travel through space, we turn to ask how it carries information for animals about their environments. A useful concept

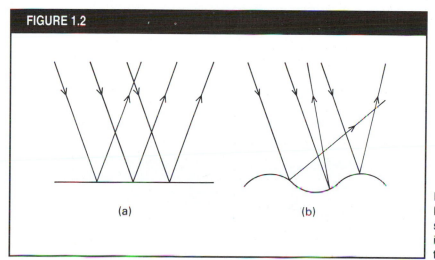

FIGURE 1.2

(a)   (b)

Regular reflection of rays of light from a polished surface such as a mirror (a) and irregular reflection from a textured surface (b).

in understanding this is the *ambient optic array*, a term coined by Gibson (1966). Imagine an environment illuminated by sunlight and therefore filled with rays of light travelling between surfaces. At any point, light will converge from all directions, and we can imagine the point surrounded by a sphere divided into tiny solid angles. The intensity of light and the mixture of wavelengths, or spectral composition, will vary from one solid angle to another, and this spatial pattern of light is the optic array. Light carries information because the structure of the optic array is determined by the nature and position of the surfaces from which it has been reflected.

Figure 1.3 illustrates the relationship between environment and optic array for an imaginary empty environment. At a point just above the ground, there is a simple pattern in the array, with light in the upper part coming directly from the sun or scattered by the atmosphere, and light in the lower part having been reflected from the surface of the ground. The array is therefore divided into two segments differing in the intensity and spectral composition of light arriving through them. The boundary between these two areas specifies the horizon.

Each of these two segments can be further subdivided, and so finer levels of spatial pattern in the optic array carry further information. The upper segment contains a region in which light of very high intensity arrives from the sun, and its position relative to the horizon specifies time of day. In the lower segment, the rays of light reflected from the textured ground surface will differ in intensity and wavelength from point to point in the array. In other words, there will be a fine structure in the optic array, characteristic of the surface from which the light has been reflected. A sandy surface and a stony surface, for example, would give rise to different patterns of fine structure in the optic array.

If we add objects to this simple environment (Fig. 1.4) we get an optic array with a more complex spatial pattern. It is divided into many segments, containing light reflected from different surfaces, and differing in the average intensities and spectral compositions of light passing through them. The boundaries between these segments of the optic array provide information about the three-dimensional structure of objects in the world. Again, at a finer level of detail, each segment of the array will be patterned in a way determined by the texture of the surface that its light is reflected from.

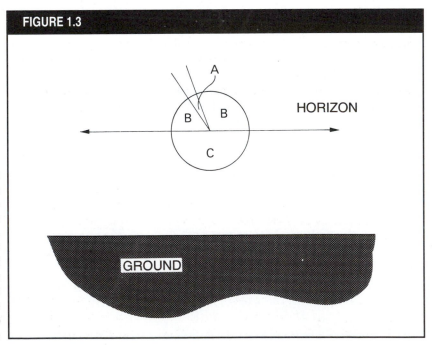

FIGURE 1.3

Two-dimensional section through the spherical optic array at a point above the ground in an open environment. In angle A incident light arrives directly from the sun, in angle B it has been scattered by the atmosphere, and in angle C it has been reflected from the ground. The arrows point to the distant horizon.

FIGURE 1.4

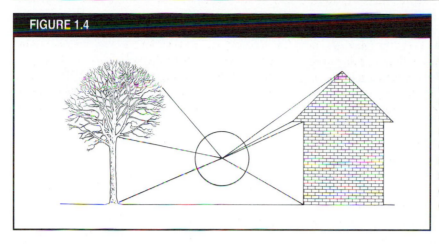

Section through the optic array at a point above the ground in an environment containing objects. The optic array is divided into segments through which light arrives after reflection from different surfaces. Each segment has a different fine structure (not shown) corresponding to the texture of each surface.

At this level, the optic array can carry information about further properties of objects and terrain.

So far, we have considered how a static optic array provides information about the world. Most natural environments contain movement, however, and most animals need to detect it. Any movement in the environment will be specified by a change in the spatial pattern of the optic array. Some movement in nature is slow, such as the daily movement of the sun across the sky. The optic array in Fig. 1.3 will change with the movement of the sun, not only in the position of the segment of rays arriving from the sun but also in the spectral composition of light from different parts of the sky.

Rapid movement, such as that of other animals, will be specified in short-term fluctuations in the spatial pattern of the optic array. If one of the objects in Fig. 1.4 moves, the boundaries of some segments in the optic array will move relative to the others. This spatiotemporal pattern in the optic array can carry further information about the direction, speed, and form of movement involved.

We have been looking at simple optic arrays in daylight in open terrestrial environments, but the same principles apply in any illuminated environment. At night, the moon and stars illuminate the world in the same way as does the sun, although with light that is many orders of magnitude less intense. In water, however, there are some differences. First, refraction of light at the water surface means that the segment of the optic array specifying "sky" is of a narrower angle than on land. Second, light is absorbed and scattered

much more by water than by air, so that information about distant objects is not specified in the pattern of intensities and wavelengths in the optic array. Third, in deep water, light from below is not reflected from the substrate but scattered upwards (Fig. 1.5).

These examples all illustrate one important point: the spatial and temporal *pattern* of light converging on a point in a land or water environment provides information about the structure of the environment and events occurring in it. The speed of light ensures that, effectively, events in the environment are represented in the optic array instantaneously. Only in deep oceans and completely dark caves is no information at all available in light, although the phenomenon of *bioluminescence*—the emission of light by organisms—means that even in these habitats light may carry information about the biological surroundings.

Up to this point we have considered a point just above the ground, or in open water, and asked what sort of information is available in the optic array converging on that point. Now we must put an animal at the centre of this optic array and ask how it can detect the information available in it. If it is to detect any information at all, it must first have some kind of structure sensitive to light energy, and our next topic is the evolution of such structures among animals. How do different kinds of light-sensitive structures allow light energy to influence the activity of animals' nervous systems, and what scope do these structures have for

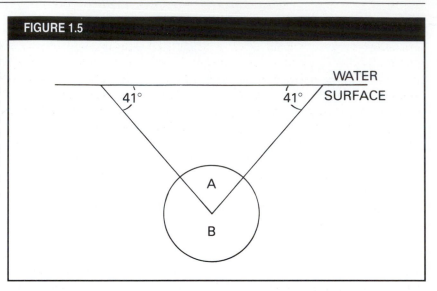

FIGURE 1.5

Section through the optic array at a point below the water surface. Because light rays from the sky and sun are refracted at the air–water boundary, they are "compressed" into an angle (A) of 98°. Incident light in angle B has been scattered by water or reflected from underwater objects.

detecting the fundamental information-carrying features of optic arrays: spatial pattern and changes in spatial patterns?

THE EVOLUTION OF LIGHT-SENSITIVE STRUCTURES

Many biological molecules absorb electro-magnetic radiation in the visible part of the spectrum, changing in chemical structure as they do so. Various biochemical mechanisms have evolved that couple such changes to other processes. One such mechanism is photosynthesis, in which absorption of light by chlorophyll molecules powers the biochemical synthesis of sugars by plants. Animals, on the other hand, have concentrated on harnessing the absorption of light by light-sensitive molecules to the mechanisms that make them move.

In single-celled animals, absorption of light can modulate processes of locomotion directly through biochemical pathways. *Amoeba* moves by a streaming motion of the cytoplasm to form extensions of the cell called pseudopods. If a pseudopod extends into bright light, streaming stops and is diverted in a different direction, so that the animal remains in dimly lit areas. *Amoeba*

possesses no known pigment molecules specialised for light sensitivity, and presumably light has some direct effect on the enzymes involved in making the cytoplasm stream. Thus, the animal can avoid bright light despite having no specialised light-sensitive structures.

Other protozoans do have pigment molecules with the specific function of detecting light. One example is the ciliate *Stentor coeruleus*, which responds to an increase in light intensity with a reversal of the waves of ciliary beat that propel it through the water. Capture of light by a blue pigment causes a change in the membrane potential of the cell, which in turn affects ciliary beat (Wood, 1976).

Other protozoans, such as the flagellate *Euglena*, have more elaborate light-sensitive structures, in which pigment is concentrated into an eyespot, but *Stentor* illustrates the basic principles of *transduction* of light energy that operate in more complex animals. First, when a pigment molecule absorbs light, its chemical structure changes. This, in turn, is coupled to an alteration in the structure of the cell membrane, so that the membrane's permeability to ions is modified, which in turn leads to a change in the electrical potential across the membrane.

In a single cell, this change in membrane potential needs to travel only a short distance to influence processes that move the animal about. In a many-celled animal, however, some cells are specialised for generating movement and some for detection of light and other external energy. These are separated by distances too great for electrotonic spread of a change in membrane potential, and information is instead transmitted by neurons with long processes, or axons, along which action potentials are propagated.

In many invertebrates, particularly those with translucent bodies, the motor- and interneurons, which generate patterns of muscle contraction, contain pigment and are directly sensitive to light. This sensitivity is the basis of the diffuse "dermal" light sense of various molluscs, echinoids, and crustacea, which do not possess photoreceptor cells but nevertheless are sensitive to light, and particularly to a sudden dimming of light caused by an animal passing overhead (Millott, 1968).

Most animals sensitive to light possess *photoreceptor* cells, specialised for the transduction of light into a receptor potential. Photoreceptor cells may be scattered over the skin, as in earthworms, or may be concentrated into patches called *eyespots*, such as those along the mantle edge of some bivalve molluscs.

An animal with single receptor cells or patches of cells in eyespots cannot detect the spatial pattern of light in the optic array, because a single receptor cell samples the *total* light reaching it from all directions. It can, however, detect changes over time in total intensity, and invertebrates with a dermal light sense or simple eyespots probably do no more than this. For an aquatic animal, a sudden reduction in light intensity is likely to mean a potential predator is passing overhead, and clams and jellyfish respond to such dimming with defensive responses.

If any spatial pattern in the optic array is to be detected, an animal's photoreceptors must each be sensitive to light in a narrow segment of the array. In practice, any photoreceptor cell has some such directional sensitivity. The way pigment is arranged in the cell makes it more sensitive to light from some directions than from others, and further directional sensitivity is achieved in simple eyespots by screening the receptor cells with a layer of dark pigment.

An animal with eyespots distributed over its body, each screened by pigment, therefore has some ability to detect spatial pattern in the light reaching it (see Fig. 1.6). It would, for example, be able to use the pattern of activity in its eyespots to maintain its swimming orientation by keeping the source of greatest light intensity above it, or to orient defensive responses according to the rough direction of approach of a predator.

FIGURE 1.6

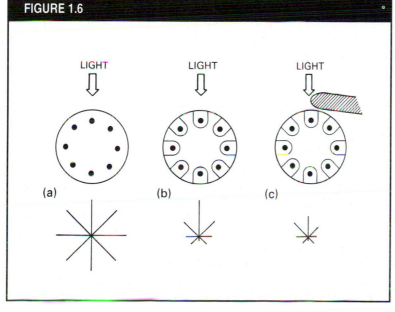

A hypothetical transparent disc-shaped animal with patches of photoreceptor cells around its edge. The lengths of the bars in the lower diagrams represent the intensities of light falling on each patch. In (a) each patch is sensitive to light through 360° and so each receives the same amount of light. In (b) and (c), screening of the patches by pigment reduces the angle through which they are sensitive to light. The amounts of light striking each receptor now differ, and the pattern of differences captures information available in the optic array specifying the direction of the water surface (b) or an overhead object (c).

The evolution of greater complexity in eyes can be thought of as the invention of various ways of improving directional sensitivity. One simple way of doing this is to sink a patch of receptor cells into the skin to make an "eye-cup" or *ocellus* (Fig. 1.7). Many invertebrates possess eye-cups, particularly coelenterates, flatworms, molluscs, and annelid worms. Eye-cups vary in the detail of their structure: some are open to the water, others are filled with gelatinous material, and many contain a crystalline lens.

The receptor cells in an eye-cup are clearly sensitive to light from a narrower angle than if they were on the surface of the skin, and the presence of a refractile lens further helps to reject light rays at a large angle from the axis. An animal with eye-cups distributed over its body can, because of this greater directional sensitivity, detect finer spatial pattern in the optic array than can the animal in Fig. 1.6 with its eye-spots. Some molluscs have rows of regularly spaced eye-cups along the body—examples are the marine gastropod *Corolla* and some bivalves with eye-cups along the mantle edge—and these animals are potentially able to detect nearby moving objects through successive dimming of light in adjacent eye-cups.

Because the angles through which eye-cups are sensitive to light are wide, and overlap a good deal, the degree of directional sensitivity achieved by an animal with many eye-cups is not great. Further directional sensitivity requires the possession of a true *eye*. The eye-cups of molluscs appear to be miniature eyes, but their function differs from that of eyes in a crucial way. A true eye forms an *image* on a layer of photoreceptor cells. When an image is formed, all light rays reaching the eye from one point in space are brought together at one point in the image, so that each receptor cell in the eye is struck by light coming from a different narrow segment of the optic array.

As we will see later in this chapter, a lens provides one means of forming an image. However, the lenses in most mollusc eye-cups do not form an image on the layer of photoreceptors (Land, 1968), and so spatial pattern in the optic array is not mapped on to the array of receptors in a single eye-cup. Instead, following the principle illustrated in Fig. 1.6, it is mapped onto the array of eye-cups over the body. In a sense, it is the whole animal that is an eye. To build a true eye requires *both* the concentration of photoreceptor cells into one part of the body *and* some apparatus for forming an image on them. We next describe the two basic structural plans of true eyes, the compound and the single-chambered eye.

The compound eye

A compound eye can be constructed by continuing the process of making eye-cups more directionally sensitive, while at the same time making them smaller and grouping them all together into a single structure. Eyes of this kind have evolved in some bivalve molluscs (e.g. *Arca*) and in the marine annelid *Branchioma*, but the most elaborate eyes based on this principle are those of crustaceans and insects. A compound eye is made up of a number

---

FIGURE 1.7

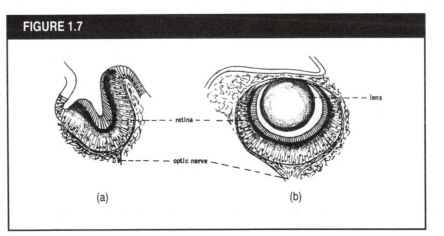

Examples of eye-cups, from the limpet *Patella* (a) and the snail *Murex* (b). Reproduced from Barnes (1974) by permission of the publishers. Copyright © 1974 by Saunders College Publishing, a division of Holt, Rinehart and Winston Inc.

of *ommatidia*; each one is a small, elongated eye-cup with a crystalline cone at the tip and the light-sensitive *rhabdom* below it. Transparent cuticle—the cornea—covers the whole array of ommatidia (Fig. 1.8a).

Compound eyes vary in several ways around this basic plan. The number of ommatidia varies greatly, and the structure of the cone differs in the eyes of different insect groups, some eyes not having a cone at all. A particularly important kind of variability in the compound eye is the degree of optical isolation between adjacent ommatidia. This is greatest in the *apposition* type of eye, characteristic of some crustaceans and of diurnal insects, in which the rhabdoms and cones touch and there is absorptive screening pigment between the ommatidia. These two features reduce the amount of light that can reach a rhabdom from cones other than the one above it and so keeps the angle of acceptance of light of each ommatidium low.

At the other extreme is the *superposition* eye, which has less pigment between ommatidia and a clear space between the layer of cones and the layer of rhabdoms, so that there is more opportunity for light to reach a rhabdom from neighbouring cones. The difference in structure between apposition and superposition eyes reflects an important difference in the means by which they form an image on the layer of rhabdoms. In the apposition eye, light striking the cone of an ommatidium from outside its narrow angle of acceptance does not reach the rhabdom, but is either reflected or absorbed. This mechanism yields an image in bright light, but has the disadvantage that, in dim light, each ommatidium cannot gather sufficient light to stimulate the receptors.

In a superposition eye, on the other hand, light rays from one point in space striking *many* adjacent cones are brought to a focus on the same rhabdom. Three different types of superposition eye have been identified, which use different optical arrangements to focus light rays in this way, and their details are described by Nilsson (1988). The result in all three cases is that each rhabdom gathers light over a wide area of the eye without losing directional sensitivity. Superposition eyes can therefore provide vision in dimmer light than can apposition eyes, and accordingly are commonly found in nocturnal insects and in marine crustacea.

So far, we have seen how the structure of a compound eye ensures that each rhabdom samples a small segment of the optic array. How do the

FIGURE 1.8

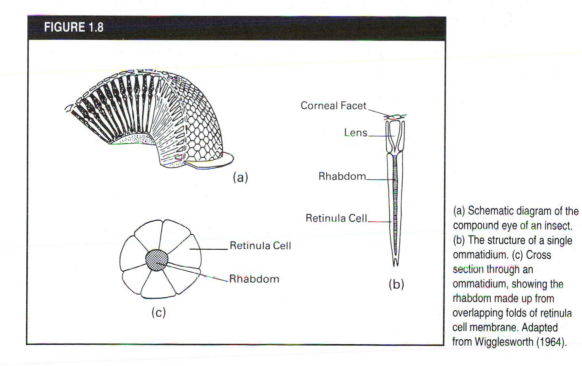

(a)

Corneal Facet

Lens

Rhabdom

Retinula Cell

(b)

Retinula Cell

Rhabdom

(c)

(a) Schematic diagram of the compound eye of an insect. (b) The structure of a single ommatidium. (c) Cross section through an ommatidium, showing the rhabdom made up from overlapping folds of retinula cell membrane. Adapted from Wigglesworth (1964).

rhabdoms transduce the light striking them into electrical changes in nerve cells that can ultimately modulate behaviour? Figure 1.8b,c shows the structure of a typical rhabdom, made up of between six and eight *retinula* cells arranged like the slices of an orange. The inner membrane of each retinula cell is folded into a tubular structure called the *rhabdomere*.

The rhabdomeres contain molecules of *rhodopsin* pigment. The rhodopsins are a family of light-sensitive molecules, each made up of two components linked together: a protein, opsin, and a smaller molecule, retinal. The shape of retinal changes when it absorbs light, and this change is coupled to an increase in membrane conductance and consequently a wave of depolarisation. The size of this *receptor potential* is proportional to the logarithm of the intensity of light striking the cell.

Most diurnal insects and crustaceans possess more than one type of retinula cell, each type having a pigment with a different relationship between wavelength of light and the probability of absorption, or *absorption spectrum*. Commonly, there are three types of pigment, with peak absorption at different points in the range of wavelengths from yellow through blue to ultraviolet. As we will see later, possession of two or more pigments with different absorption spectra makes colour vision possible.

The response of single retinula cells does not depend only on the wavelength and intensity of light striking them; they are also sensitive to the *plane of polarisation* of light. Unpolarised light is made up of waves vibrating in all planes around the direction of propagation. If light is absorbed or diffracted in such a way that some planes of vibration are represented more than others, the light is said to be polarised. One piece of information that the plane of polarisation of light from the sky can provide is the position of the sun, even when completely blocked by cloud, and bees make use of this information in navigating.

Single-chambered eyes

The second basic structural plan for eyes is that of the single-chambered eye, which can be derived by enlargement and modification of a *single* eye-cup rather than by massing eye-cups together.

Figure 1.9 shows three devices—a pinhole camera, a concave mirror, and a convex lens—that can form an image, and all three designs can be achieved by modifying an eye-cup in different ways.

A pinhole camera can be made from an eye-cup by nearly closing off its opening, and the cephalopod *Nautilus* possesses an eye of this kind. The design has not been a popular one in the animal kingdom because the aperture of a pinhole camera must be small to form an image and so can admit only small amounts of light.

A concave mirror can be made by coating the back of an eye-cup with reflecting material and moving the photoreceptors forward to the image plane. The eyes of the scallop *Pecten* are arranged in this way, with a silvery layer of guanine crystals at the back of the eye forming an image at the level of the retina (Land, 1968). This is also a rare tactic, and only one other animal, the deep-sea ostracod crustacean *Gigantocypris*, is known to adopt it.

By far the most evolutionarily successful type of single-chambered eye uses a convex lens, as a camera does, and is found in the vertebrates and the cephalopod molluscs (octopus and squid). This type of eye has evolved by the enlargement of the eye-cup so that the image formed by the lens falls on the receptor cells and not behind them. Intermediates on the evolutionary route from eye-cup to single-chambered eye can be seen in gastropod molluscs such as *Pterotrachea* and in the alciopid annelids.

For the moment, we will only outline the basic structure of the vertebrate eye, before looking at it in detail in the next section. Figure 1.10 shows the important components of this kind of eye—the cornea, iris, lens, and retina—and also the remarkable degree of convergent evolution of the eye in two unrelated groups of animals, the cephalopods and the vertebrates (a convergence so close that dilation of the pupil of the eye signals sexual arousal in cuttlefish just as in people).

The structure of the retina, the mat of photo-receptors at the back of the eye, does differ in the two groups. Cephalopod photoreceptors are built on the same rhabdomeric plan as those of the arthropods, but vertebrate receptors are of the *ciliary* type, in which the layers of membrane containing light-sensitive pigment are stacked in

FIGURE 1.9

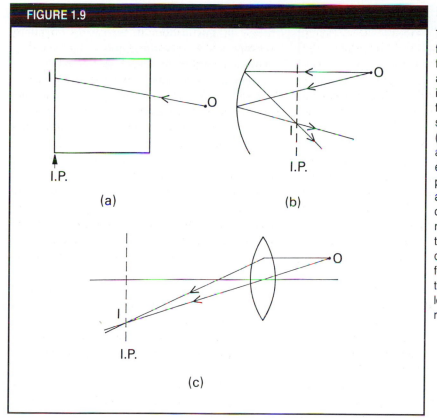

(a)

(b)

(c)

The optics of image formation. An image is formed when rays of light arriving at one point I in the image plane (I.P.) all come from the same point O in space. In the pinhole camera (a) this occurs because the aperture is so small that each point in the image plane is illuminated by light arriving through a narrow cone. A concave mirror (b) reflects light in such a way that all rays striking it from one point are brought to a focus at the same point in the image plane. A convex lens (c) achieves the same result by refraction of light.

an outer segment of the cell. There are two types of ciliary receptor, rods and cones, and they have differently shaped outer segments (Fig. 1.11). Rods and cones are packed into the retina with their long axes parallel to the direction of incident light, and a layer of absorptive pigment behind, which reduces internal reflection. Whereas receptors in the cephalopod eye are arranged sensibly, facing the light from the lens, the vertebrate retina is "inverted", that is, the rods and cones are in the layer of the retina furthest from the lens, with their outer segments pointing away from it, so that light must pass through a layer of cells to reach them (for further details, see Ch.2, p.28).

FIGURE 1.10

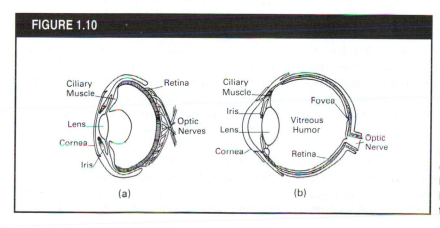

(a)

(b)

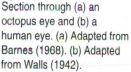

Section through (a) an octopus eye and (b) a human eye. (a) Adapted from Barnes (1968). (b) Adapted from Walls (1942).

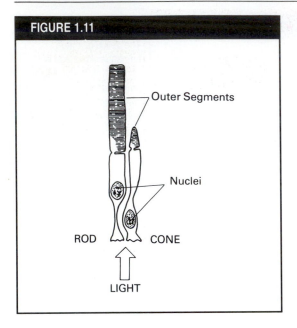

FIGURE 1.11

Outer Segments

Nuclei

ROD   CONE

LIGHT

Structure of rod and cone in the vertebrate retina. The outer segments contain folded layers of membrane packed with light-sensitive pigment. Adapted from Uttal (1981).

The pigments in rods and cones belong to the rhodopsin family, and transduction begins in the same way as in the retinula cells of insects: photons absorbed by the retinal part of the rhodopsin molecule cause it to change in shape and to detach from the opsin part. This change triggers a cascade of enzymatic processes in the outer segment that result in the breakdown of cyclic guanosine monophosphate (cGMP). This in turn causes the conductance of a channel in the cell membrane, gated by cGMP, to fall, and the membrane is hyperpolarised. In darkness, cGMP is resynthesised and the membrane potential returns to its resting level. The details of these biochemical processes are described by Pugh and Cobbs (1986); note that the overall effect of light striking a rod or cone is to cause a hyperpolarising receptor potential (in contrast to the depolarisation of a rhabdomeric receptor).

Conclusions
The pattern of evolution of light-sensitive structures in animals, as we have outlined it, is summarised in Fig. 1.12, and the interested reader will find further details in Land (1981). The central theme in this pattern is increasing directional sensitivity of photoreceptors and therefore increasing ability to detect spatial pattern and movement in the optic array. At one extreme, a jellyfish can detect dimming of the total light reaching it in order to escape from an overhead predator, and at the other a hawk can spot a mouse running through grass many metres below.

As we have seen, increased directional sensitivity has been achieved in a variety of ways, through the evolution of two quite differently constructed eyes, and the modification of each type to form an image in more than one way. It would be mistaken to attempt to rank these different types of eye in order of merit, or to think of the vertebrate eye as an evolutionary pinnacle. Although most vertebrate eyes achieve greater directional sensitivity than any compound eye, this does not imply that the former is intrinsically a better eye. For optical reasons, a single-chambered eye small enough to fit an insect's head would not have any greater directional sensitivity than a compound eye of the same size (Kirschfeld, 1976). The two optical designs are suited to animals of different sizes, and neither is more "advanced" than the other.

THE ADAPTIVE RADIATION OF THE VERTEBRATE EYE

In the remainder of this chapter we examine in more detail the workings of the vertebrate eye and particularly the differences between the eyes of different species. In the course of evolution, many variations on the basic single-chambered plan have evolved and, to some extent, these variations are related to the demands of each species' environment and way of life. This kind of evolutionary modification of a basic structure is called *adaptive radiation*.

Focusing the image
The fundamental job of a single-chambered eye is to map the spatial pattern in the optic array onto the retina by forming an image; all light rays striking

FIGURE 1.12

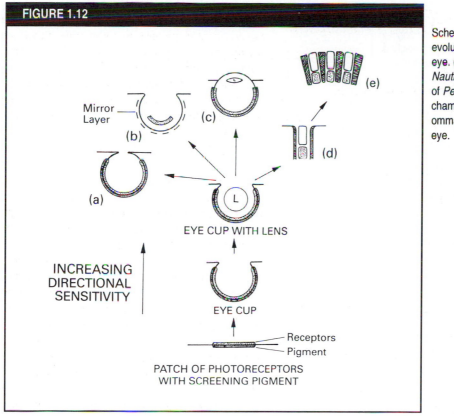

Schematic diagram of the evolution of different types of eye. (a) "Pinhole" eye of *Nautilus*; (b) Reflecting eye of *Pecten*; (c) Single-chambered eye; (d) Single ommatidium; (e) Compound eye.

the eye from one point in space are brought to a focus at one point on the retina. What influences how efficiently vertebrate eyes do this?

The ability of a person or animal to detect fine spatial pattern is expressed as *visual acuity*. This can be measured by the use of a *grating*, a pattern of parallel vertical dark bars equal in width and separated by bright bars of the same width. As the dark and bright bars are made narrower, there comes a point when an observer is no longer able to *resolve* the grating, that is, to distinguish it from a uniform field of the same average brightness. As the width of the bars at which this happens will depend on how far the observer is from the grating, we do not measure width as a distance but as a *visual angle*, the angle that a bar subtends at the eye. Figure 1.13 shows how size, distance, and visual angle are related. Under optimal lighting conditions, the minimum separation between the centres of adjacent dark and bright bars that a person can resolve is about 0.5min of arc.

Visual acuity is limited by several processes. The first is the efficiency with which the optical apparatus of the eye maps the spatial pattern of the optic array onto the retina. The second is the efficiency with which receptor cells convert that pattern into a pattern of electrical activity; and the third is the extent to which information available in the pattern of receptor cell activity is detected by the neural apparatus of retina and brain. For the moment, our concern is with the first of these processes, and the important consideration is how sharply the eye focuses an image on the retina. As an image becomes more blurred, spatial pattern in the optic array is smoothed out in the pattern of light at the retina and the detection of fine differences is compromised.

Before considering how the eyes of different species achieve optimal focusing, we need to explain in more detail the optical principles governing the formation of an image by a single-chambered eye. An image is formed because light

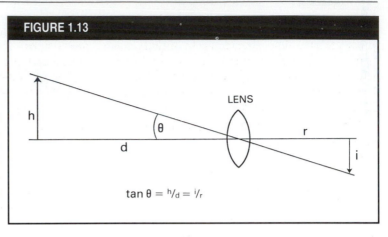

FIGURE 1.13

The formula relating visual angle θ subtended by an object to its height *h*, and its distance from a lens *d*, and also to the height *i* of its image on a projection plane at a distance *r* from the lens. For small visual angles, the retinal surface approximates to a projection plane, and *r* is the diameter of the eye and *i* the height of the retinal image. For larger visual angles, the curvature of the retina is significant, and the relationship tan θ = i/r does not hold.

is bent, or refracted, at the boundary between two transparent media of different optical densities, such as air and glass. The degree of bending of light is determined by the difference in refractive index of the two media. In a convex lens, the two air-glass boundaries are curved in such a way that parallel rays of light are bent through a greater angle the greater their distance from the axis (Fig. 1.9c). Rays of light from one point on an object at optical infinity, arriving at the lens in parallel, therefore converge to the focal plane of the lens. The distance of the focal plane from the centre of the lens is its focal length, f.

The greater the degree to which a lens bends parallel light rays to converge at the focus, the shorter its focal length. A convenient measure of a lens' performance is its *power*, defined as the reciprocal of its focal length (power is measured in dioptres if focal length is measured in metres).

An image of an object at infinity is therefore formed at a distance f from the lens, and we say that the *image plane* lies at this distance. If the object is brought closer to the lens, the relationship between its distance *u* from the lens and the distance *v* of the image plane is given by:

$$\frac{1}{f} = \frac{1}{u} + \frac{1}{v}$$

As the object comes nearer to the lens, the image plane will therefore move further back from it, so that the image formed on a surface located in the focal plane will be blurred. In a camera, the image is kept focused on the film as object distance varies by changing the distance between the lens and the

film. As we shall see, the vertebrate eye solves the problem in a different way.

In a vertebrate eye, there are four refracting surfaces as light passes from external medium to cornea to aqueous humour to lens to vitreous humour. The refracting power of each surface is determined both by its curvature (a fatter lens is more powerful) and by the difference in refractive indices (RIs) of the media on either side of it. For an animal living in air, there is a large difference in RI between the external medium (RI = 1) and the cornea (RI = 1.376 in the human eye), and this surface has considerable refracting power. Accordingly, the eyes of land vertebrates have a flattened lens contributing little to the total refracting power of the eye (in the human eye, the front surface of the cornea provides 49 out of a total of 59 dioptres).

For aquatic vertebrates, however, none of the refracting surfaces has such a large difference in RIs, as the RI of water is similar to that of the cornea. A strongly curved surface is therefore needed somewhere, and it is provided by a near-spherical lens, not only in aquatic vertebrates but also in squid and octopus. Also, the lens of a fish eye is of a higher refractive index than that of the human eye.

Now, if the power of the lens-cornea combination, and its distance from the retina, are both fixed, then a sharply focused image will only be formed of objects lying at a certain range of distances from the eye. This range is called the *depth of field*, and is the distance over which the object can move to and from the eye without the image plane falling outside the layer of retinal receptors. For a human eye focused at infinity, this range is from about 6 metres to infinity. The reason why we can focus on objects less than 6 metres from the eye is that its optics can be adjusted by a process called *accommodation*.

Three different mechanisms of accommodation are known in vertebrate eyes. One is to alter the radius of curvature of the cornea, a mechanism used by some bird species (Schaeffel & Howland, 1987). The second, used by fish, amphibians, and snakes, is to move the lens backwards and forwards to keep the image plane on the retina, and the third, used by other reptiles, birds, and mammals, is to alter the power of the lens by changing its shape. In the human eye, contraction of the *ciliary muscles* attached to the lens causes it to thicken, increasing its curvature and therefore its power, so that nearby objects are brought into focus. When the ciliary muscles are fully relaxed, the lens takes on a flattened shape and the eye is focused at infinity.

In this way, the power of the human lens can be adjusted over a range of up to 15 dioptres, a figure that falls with age. The ability to accommodate over a wide range is clearly useful to human beings and to other primates, which characteristically examine the detail of objects at close range, but may not be so important to other vertebrates. Because light is scattered and absorbed by water, there is no need for the eyes of fish and other aquatic animals to focus on distant objects, and so they can be somewhat myopic (unable to bring an object at infinity into focus) without missing out on any information available in the optic array.

In contrast, the need for accommodation is especially great for animals that live both on land and in water, and need to achieve acuity in two media of different refractive index. Diving birds, seals, and amphibious fish and turtles show a fascinating variety of adaptations in eye structure and function to solve this problem (Sivak, 1978). Various mechanisms for increasing the range of accommodation of the lens are found in otters, turtles, and diving birds. In diving ducks, the lens is flexible, and contraction of the ciliary muscles causes it to bulge through the pupil in a rounded shape. As a result, accommodation of up to 80 dioptres is possible, and this is enough to compensate for the loss of refractive power when the cornea is immersed in water (Sivak, Hildebrand, & Lebert, 1985).

Another solution to the problem, used in the eyes of penguins and the flying fish *Cypselurus*, is to flatten the cornea so that it has little or no refractive power in air or water, and to rely largely on the lens for refraction. Still another tactic is to divide the eye into separate image-forming systems with different optical properties. Such eyes are found in the "four-eyed" fish *Anableps*, which swims at the surface with the upper part of the eye, adapted for vision in air, above the surface, and the lower part, adapted for vision in water, below it. Finally, a fourth solution is found in the eyes of seals, which have a spherical lens suitable for underwater vision, but a narrow slit pupil that closes in air to form small apertures acting as pinhole cameras, so that the lens no longer forms the image.

Even when an eye is optimally focused, there is a certain degree of blur in the image caused by optical imperfections. For several reasons, lenses do not bring light rays to a focus in the ideal way we have described so far. First, parallel rays may be brought to a slightly different focus depending on how far from the axis they strike the lens (spherical and comatic aberration) or depending on their orientation relative to the lens (astigmatic aberration). The refractive index of a medium varies with the wavelength of light, so that different wavelengths are brought to a focus in slightly different planes (chromatic aberration). Finally, scattering of light in the fluids of the eye and in the retinal layers overlying the receptors further blurs the image.

A boundary between two segments of the optic array differing in intensity is therefore spread out on the retina to some extent, even with optimal focus. Given the figure for the acuity of the human eye mentioned earlier, however, the impact of these aberrations is not great, at least in optimal conditions. One way in which some sources of aberration, particularly spherical aberration, can be reduced is by constricting the pupil so that light only enters the lens through a narrow aperture. This means of reducing aberration, however, is not available in dim light.

Vision in bright and dim light

If an eye is optimally focused, the spatial pattern in the optic array is transformed into a pattern of light intensity on the retina with a minimum degree of blur. The second constraint on an animal's or a person's visual acuity now comes into play: the efficiency with which this pattern of light on the retina is transformed into a pattern of electrical activity in receptor cells.

One factor that will influence this efficiency will clearly be the density of packing of receptor cells in the retina. The more densely receptors are packed, the finer the details of a pattern of light intensities that can be transformed into differences in electrical activity. If acuity were limited by receptor spacing and not by optical factors, the minimum distance between adjacent dark and bright bars for a grating to be resolved would be equal to the average distance between adjacent receptors (assuming receptors are packed in a rectangular array). The difference in acuity between people and falcons is the result of a difference in receptor packing. The photoreceptors in the falcon's eye are packed three times more densely than in the human eye, and the falcon can resolve a grating with a spacing of 0.2min of arc, as compared with the figure for a human observer of 0.5min (Fox, Lehmkuhle, & Westendorff, 1976).

A second factor, which we need to dwell on at more length, is the intensity of light striking the retina. It makes a difference to the detectability of a spatial difference in light intensity on the retina whether two neighbouring cells are being struck by 5 and 10 photons per second or by 5000 and 10,000. The reason is that, even under constant illumination, the rate at which photons strike a receptor fluctuates around an average value, and this variability increases as the square root of the average value. If light intensity is high, so that the average rates of photon flux striking two adjacent receptors are also high, then the difference between the two rates will therefore be large relative to the fluctuation in each.

As the light reaching the eye becomes dimmer, the difference in photon flux at adjacent receptors eventually becomes comparable to the extent of fluctuation, and so is detectable only if the two rates of flux are averaged over a period of time. Now, if this difference is caused by a moving boundary in the optic array, the difference in photon flux may not be present in any part of the retina long enough to be detected. As light becomes dimmer, the maximum speed of movement in the optic array that can be detected will fall.

One solution to this problem would be to increase the cross-sectional area of receptor cells so that each sampled a larger segment of the optic array and so received a larger flux of photons. Alternatively, the outputs of neighbouring receptors could be "pooled" by connection to one interneuron, so that they effectively acted as a single receptor. Either solution would increase the *sensitivity* of the eye, but, as we discussed earlier, they would both decrease its *acuity*. The design of an eye is therefore subject to a trade-off between sensitivity and acuity. What are the implications of this constraint for the evolution of vertebrate eyes?

Many vertebrate species use only part of the daily cycle for their activities, being either nocturnal or diurnal. Nocturnal animals need eyes with high sensitivity in dim moon- and starlight, and this is true also of deep-sea fish. Diurnal animals, on the other hand, can have eyes with high acuity. Even so, it is unusual for a species' vision to operate in a very narrow band of light intensities. The intensities encountered by either a diurnal or a nocturnal animal vary over several orders of magnitude (see Fig. 1.14), and so in either case vision must be adapted to operate in a *range* of light intensities. Strict specialisation is likely to be found only in animals such as deep-sea fish and bats living in dark caves by day.

The most striking way in which the vertebrate eye is adapted for vision in a range of light intensities is in the structure of the retina. We noted earlier the two kinds of vertebrate photoreceptor—rods and cones—and saw that a rod has a deeper stack of pigment-filled layers of folded membrane in its outer segment than has a cone. A photon passing through a rod therefore stands a lower chance of coming out at the other end than one passing through a cone, and so the membrane potential of a rod will be influenced by levels of light too low to affect a cone.

It is therefore not surprising that there is a correlation between the ratio of rods to cones in an

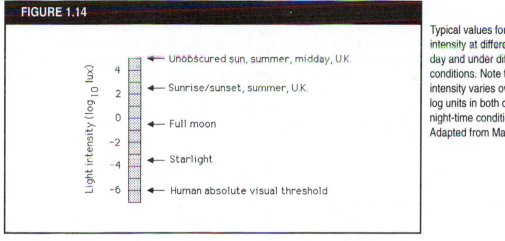

FIGURE 1.14

Typical values for light intensity at different times of day and under different conditions. Note that intensity varies over several log units in both daytime and night-time conditions. Adapted from Martin (1985).

animal's retina and its ecology. Diurnal animals have a higher proportion of cones than do nocturnal animals, although pure-cone retinas are rare, found mostly in lizards and snakes. Pure-rod retinas are also rare, found only in animals—deep-sea fish and bats—that never leave dark habitats.

A further adaptation of the retina in animals active in dim light is the presence of a silvery *tapetum* behind the retina, which reflects light back through it and so gives the rods a second bite at the stream of photons, although at the cost of increasing blur through imperfect reflection. The glow of a cat's eyes in the dark is caused by reflection of light by a tapetum behind its retina.

A possibility exploited by a few nocturnal animals is to use infrared (IR) radiation, which can provide information about the environment in the absence of visible light, subject to some limitations. First, IR is rapidly absorbed by water, and therefore only potentially useful on land. Second, the IR radiation emitted by an endothermic (warm-blooded) animal would screen any radiation it detected, and so we would only expect sensitivity to IR in exothermic (cold-blooded) animals. Third, it could only be used to detect objects differing in temperature from the rest of the environment.

The one group of vertebrates that does detect information carried by IR radiation is a group of snakes, the pit vipers, which hunt for small birds and mammals at night. The cornea and lens of the vertebrate eye are opaque to IR, and so a different

kind of sensory organ is required. These snakes have specialised organs alongside the eyes, acting as pinhole cameras to form an IR image of their surroundings, which enable them to detect the location of nearby exothermic prey, such as mice.

So, a retina containing only rods or only cones adapts an animal for vision in a narrow range of light intensities. How is retinal structure adapted for vision over a wider range? Imagine that we start with an animal that is basically diurnal but needs to be equipped with some night vision. We add rods to the pure-cone retina, scattering them about evenly among the cones. We discover, though, that to capture much light at night, we need a great many rods. In the human eye, for example, there are 120 million rods as opposed to only 7 million cones.

Now, if we have added the rods evenly over the retina, we would find the distances between the cones are now much larger than when we started and that acuity in daytime vision is reduced. The way out of this problem in many vertebrate eyes is to divide the retina into two regions. One small area is rich in cones, with little or no pooling of the outputs of adjacent receptors, whereas the other, larger, area is rich in rods, with considerable pooling of outputs. The cone-rich region provides high acuity vision in bright light, whereas the rod-rich area provides high sensitivity vision in dim light.

This pattern is found especially in birds and in primates, where the cone-rich area is usually circular, and sometimes contains a pit-like depression in the retina, called a *fovea*. Some bird species possess two such areas in each eye, one corresponding to the frontal and one to the lateral visual field (Nalbach, Wolf-Oberhollenzer, & Remy, 1993). The cone-rich area of the human eye, the *macula lutea*, contains a fovea. There are only cones in the centre of the fovea, and their proportion and density of packing decrease further out into the retina. At more than about 10° from the centre, outside the macula, there are few cones, and the peripheral part of the retina contains almost all rods.

There are other ways in which vertebrate eyes are adapted to operate over a range of light intensities. One is movement of cells containing pigment, and sometimes also the receptor cells, in the retina. These *retinomotor* responses are found in fish, and in some reptiles and birds, and act to screen the rods with pigment in bright light and to expose them in dim light.

A second mechanism, rare in fish but more common in birds and especially mammals, is dilation and constriction of the pupil by the muscular tissue of the iris. In diurnal mammals, the pupil is usually round, and its function is to reduce the aperture of the lens in bright light and so reduce blur of the retinal image due to spherical and other optical aberrations. In dim light, when sensitivity and not acuity is at a premium, the pupil opens to admit more light. Mammals active in both day and night often have a slit pupil, which, for mechanical reasons, can close more completely than a round one. A cat's eye has a retina adapted for nocturnal vision and a slit pupil which allows it to operate in the daytime.

A third process, known as *adaptation*, occurs in the retinas of many animals to adjust the sensitivity of photoreceptors and interneurons to varying intensities of light. In the human eye, the iris does not play a major role in regulating the intensity of light reaching the retina, and so adaptation is the main means by which sensitivity is adjusted. We can see over a range of approximately seven log units of light intensity (a 10^7-fold range), but at any one time our vision is effective over a range of only one or two log units, and this range can shift

upwards (light adaptation) or downwards (dark adaptation). We return to adaptation in Chapter 2.

To conclude, vertebrate eyes are subject to the basic physical constraint that greater sensitivity in dim light can only be won at the cost of reduced acuity. Different species strike different bargains between these two factors, depending on their ecology, but many manage to operate over a range of light intensities. Human beings are an example of a basically diurnal species with acute *photopic* (bright light) vision and some degree of low acuity *scotopic* (dim light) vision. We are fairly adaptable, although not as much as cats!

Sampling the optic array

An animal with simple eye-cups distributed over its body can detect light reaching it from any direction, and so, at any instant, can sample the entire optic array. Once an animal's photoreceptors are concentrated into a pair of eyes at the front of the body, this is no longer possible, although it is nearly achieved by some insects, such as dragonflies, which have large compound eyes wrapped almost completely around the head.

The angle through which light striking a single vertebrate eye is focused onto the retina can be as great as 200°, and so nearly panoramic vision can be achieved by placing the eyes *laterally*, on either side of the head, with their axes approximately perpendicular to the body. This arrangement is common among vertebrates, and can enable an animal to detect predators approaching from any direction. In mallard ducks, and some other birds with laterally placed eyes, the visual fields of the two eyes cover the entire celestial hemisphere and there is no blind area above or behind the head that a predator could exploit (Martin, 1994a).

Laterally placed eyes give the maximum ability to detect predators, but other, competing demands on vision have resulted in the eyes of some species being swung forwards. If the axes of the two eyes are parallel, or nearly so, they are said to be *frontally* placed. In owls and other birds of prey, the eyes are in an intermediate position between frontal and lateral placement. These birds need high acuity in order to detect small, distant prey, and this is achieved in part through the magnification of the retinal image caused by the large size of their eyes. Just as in a telephoto lens, however, this magnification is won at the cost of narrowing the angle through which the eye accepts light, and more frontal placement of the eyes is therefore necessary to prevent a blind area forward of the head.

Another advantage of a frontal eye position is that it increases the size of the *binocular field*, the segment of the optic array sampled by both eyes simultaneously. The binocular field is narrow in animals with laterally placed eyes, and largest in those such as cats and primates where the axes of the eyes are approximately parallel. A human eye accepts light through an angle of about 150°, but the large degree of binocular overlap means that the angle for two eyes is not much greater. When the same information is obtained from the optic array by two eyes, greater accuracy can be achieved in discriminating spatial and temporal pattern from noise in photon flux and in photoreceptor responses (Jones & Lee, 1981). Also, for reasons that are explained in Chapter 7, information about the distances of objects can be obtained.

More frontal eye placement therefore offers a number of advantages, but at the price of losing the ability to obtain information from a large segment of the optic array at one time. This constraint can be overcome by movement of the head, eyes, or both, to change rapidly the segment from which light is accepted. Head and eye movements are also important for animals that possess a fovea, as the segment of the optic array they can sample with high acuity is no more than a few degrees wide, and must be frequently moved relative to the retina.

Most vertebrates can move their eyes to some extent, although few can move them through large angles. The chameleon is a striking exception; its angle of vision is small, and, as it searches for prey, its two laterally placed eyes swivel about quite independently, giving a distinctly creepy impression! The chameleon apart, the eyes of primates make the largest, most rapid, and most precisely controlled eye movements. The human eye is held in position by a dynamic balance between three pairs of antagonistic muscles, and

instability in this balance causes a continuous small-amplitude *tremor*. As a result, the image on the retina is in constant motion, any point on it moving by about the distance between two adjacent foveal cones in 0.1sec.

Sampling of the optic array is achieved by three kinds of eye movement. First, rapid and intermittent jumps of eye position called *saccades* are made in order to fixate an object with foveal vision. As a person reads or looks at a picture, the eyes make several saccades each second to scan the page or screen. Once an object is fixated, *pursuit* movements keep it in foveal vision as it moves, or as the observer moves. If the distance of an object from the observer changes, *convergence* movements keep it fixated by the foveas of both eyes. As an object comes closer, convergence movements turn the direction of gaze of both eyes towards the nose. If an object comes within a few inches of the face, further convergence is impossible and "double vision" occurs (we say more about convergence and stereoscopic vision in Chapter 7). Whereas saccades are sudden, intermittent changes of eye position, both pursuit and convergence are smooth and continuous.

To summarise, at any instant the human eye samples a relatively large segment of the optic array (the *peripheral* field) with low acuity, and a much smaller segment (the *central*, or *foveal* field) with high acuity. Smooth and saccadic eye movements shift this high-acuity segment about rapidly, so that acute vision over a wide angle is achieved. Further details of human eye movements, their anatomical and neural mechanisms, and models of their control may be found in Carpenter (1988).

This highly specialised way in which we sample the optic array makes it difficult for us to appreciate the different ways in which other animals do so. We are used to detecting what other people are looking at from the direction in which their eyes are pointing, but this direction may mean something quite different in other species. A horse, sheep, or rabbit does not need to look straight at something in order to see it, and the angle of a bird's head may be related to what it is looking at in quite a different way depending on whether it is fixating monocularly or binocularly. It is only when watching animals such as cats and apes looking that we are on familiar ground!

Detecting wavelength

A vertebrate eye maps not only the pattern of light intensities in the optic array onto the retina but also the pattern of different spectral compositions of light. We have already seen that the spectral composition of light in a segment of the optic array can carry information about the kind of surface the light was reflected from. Imagine a bird or a monkey searching for insect prey or fruit among dense foliage. The pattern of intensity of light reflected from the scene will be a patchwork of bright and dark regions, depending on the orientation and reflectance of leaves and stems, and on the effects of shadow. Against such a background it will be nearly impossible to detect the patch of light reflected from the target on the basis of its intensity. The task will be much easier, however, if the animal is also sensitive to differences in the spectral composition of light reflected from different surfaces, and so can detect differences in *colour*. This ability is therefore particularly important to species that need to find food or other targets against a dappled background such as foliage (Mollon, 1989).

In order to detect differences in the spectral composition of light, an animal must possess at least two sets of receptor cells, containing pigments with different absorption spectra (see p.12). A single receptor type is not enough; a difference in the spectral composition of light falling on two neighbouring receptors containing the same pigment will cause a difference in their electrical response, but a difference in just the intensity of light can have exactly the same effect. In a retina containing only one type of receptor cell, the pattern of receptor potentials therefore cannot carry information about the patterns of intensity and of spectral composition in the optic array independently, and an animal with such a retina would be incapable of colour vision.

We have already seen that insects usually possess three types of retinula cell, each with a different pigment. In any one vertebrate species, all rods in the retina contain the same pigment type, and so animals with pure-rod retinas cannot detect wavelength and intensity differences independently. This need not be a handicap; for deep-sea fish, the spectrum of available light is narrow, and such fish usually have a pure-rod retina in which the peak of the absorption spectrum of the pigment matches the blue light available.

Species capable of colour vision may have cones with a pigment different from that in the rods, or they may have two or more types of cone, each with different pigments. The cones of birds and some reptiles contain coloured oil droplets through which light must pass to reach the outer segment, and these coloured filters will further differentiate the wavelength sensitivities of cones. In human beings and other primates, the retina usually contains three groups of cones with different pigments. In the case of the human retina, these pigments have peak absorption at 419, 531, and 558nm (Fig. 1.15), and presumably cones containing these pigments have corresponding peaks in their sensitivity spectra. In photopic conditions we are able to distinguish colours because of this differential sensitivity of cones, whereas in scotopic conditions, when only rods are stimulated, we have no colour vision.

This *trichromatic* basis for primate colour vision is only one of a number of arrangements found among vertebrates. Most other mammals are *dichromatic*, possessing two cone types (Jacobs, 1993), whereas many birds have four and possibly more (Maier & Bowmaker, 1993). This implies that two surfaces reflecting light of different spectral compositions could appear the same colour to humans (if they excite each of the three cone types equally), but could be discriminated by a bird. Many bird species possess a type of cone sensitive to ultraviolet light and so, like bees and other insects (see p.12), are able to discriminate surfaces such as flowers and plumage on the basis of differences in ultraviolet reflectance that are invisible to us (Bennett & Cuthill, 1994). Many vertebrates (but no mammals) are also sensitive to the plane of polarisation of light (see p.12), although the photoreceptor mechanism involved is different from that in insects (Cameron & Pugh, 1991).

FIGURE 1.15

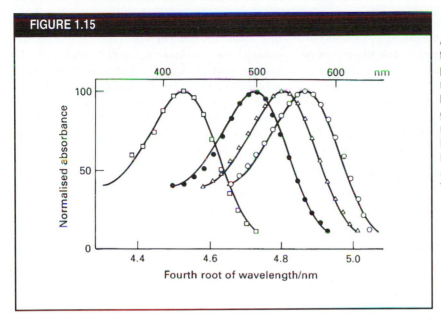

Absorption spectra of the four types of human photoreceptor. From left to right, curves are for: blue-sensitive cones, rods, green-sensitive cones, and red-sensitive cones. Reproduced from Dartnall, Bowmaker, and Mollon (1983) with permission of The Royal Society.

We have explained how the possession of photoreceptors with two or more pigments differing in their absorption spectra is a necessary precondition for colour vision, and we deal further with this topic in Chapter 3 (pp.60–61). A full introduction to psychophysical studies of human colour vision, and to the relationships between their findings and the properties of cone pigments, is given by Mollon (1982).

CONCLUSIONS

We have followed the workings of the vertebrate eye from the entry of light through the cornea to the formation of a pattern of receptor potentials in the receptor cells of the retina. We have seen how the eye is adapted in different ways in different species to maximise the amount of information in the optic array captured in this pattern of excitation, and that the extent to which this can be achieved is constrained by various factors, especially the amount of available light. A more detailed account of the adaptive radiation of the vertebrate eye is given in Walls' (1942) classic work, and a modern treatment of the topic, concentrating on the eyes of birds, can be found in Martin (1994b). A thorough introduction to the anatomy, physiology, and optics of the human eye is given by Barlow and Mollon (1982).

In order to understand the workings of eyes, it is necessary to understand the physical properties of light, and the biochemistry of its absorption by photoreceptors. This does not mean, however, that visual perception is about seeing *light*; instead, it is about seeing objects, surfaces, and events in the world around us. Light provides the *means* of achieving this, because its spatial and temporal pattern is determined by the layout of the surrounding world. The formation of an image on the retina, and the transduction of light in photoreceptors, ensure that at least some of this pattern is captured in a pattern of electrical activity in the retina.

A camera works in a similar way to an eye, capturing the spatial pattern of light at a point in space in a pattern of chemical change in the light-sensitive grains of a film. The camera is therefore a useful analogy for understanding the optics of the eye, but it is important not to stretch the analogy too far. There are a number of design features of the eye that would be highly undesirable in a camera. The image has a yellowish cast, particularly in the macular region, and it contains a shadow of the dense network of blood vessels overlying the layer of receptor cells in the retina. Also, the movements of the eye consist not just of a series of fixations, during which the image is static, but of smooth movements and tremor, causing the image to move continually. A camera that moved in this way would produce blurred photographs.

In principle, as these factors cause predictable distortions of the retinal image, it would be possible to correct for them and to recover an image comparable to a photograph. To think in terms of "cleaning up" the retinal image in this way implies, however, that the role of the eye is to take a snapshot of the world at each fixation and to send a stream of pictures to the brain to be examined there. This conception of the eye's role betrays a second, more serious, limitation to the analogy between camera and eye. The purpose of a camera is to produce a picture to be viewed by people, but the purpose of the eye and brain is to extract the information from the changing optic array needed to guide an animal's or a person's actions, or to specify objects or events of importance. Although this could be achieved by first converting the retinal image into a neural "image" of photograph-like quality and then extracting information from this second image, such a process seems implausible on grounds of economy; it would be wasteful.

Apart from blur caused by optical factors, the imperfections of the retinal image do not result in any loss of information about spatial patterns and their changes. It therefore seems likely that the visual system extracts important variables embedded in the spatiotemporal pattern of electrical activity in rods and cones, without first correcting distortions in it. As we show in Chapter 2, the extraction of information about pattern begins in the retina itself, and the optic nerve does not transmit a stream of pictures to the brain, as a television camera does to a television set, but instead transmits *information* about the pattern of light reaching the eyes.

2

The Neurophysiology
of the Retina

Information is available to animals, in the spatial and temporal pattern of the optic array, to specify the structure of their surroundings and the events occurring in them. Compound and single-chambered eyes map this spatiotemporal pattern onto an array of light-sensitive receptor cells, so transforming it into a pattern of electrical activity in these cells. This pattern of receptor cell activity must in its turn be transformed so that information needed to guide the animal's actions is made available.

These further transformations take place in the central nervous system, and one way of studying them is to record the electrical activity of single nerve cells in retina, optic nerve, and brain in response to stimulation by light. The ultimate aim of this approach is to understand how information important to an animal is detected by networks of nerve cells and represented in patterns of neural activity. For all but the simplest animals, this is a distant goal indeed, and our knowledge does not yet extend beyond the early stages of neural transformation of patterns of light. In this chapter we describe the first of these stages, the transformation that the pattern of receptor cell activity undergoes in the retina. We consider first a

relatively simple example, and then go on to the more complex retina of vertebrates.

THE RETINA OF THE HORSESHOE CRAB

The horseshoe crab *Limulus* has two compound eyes placed laterally on its shell, each made up of several hundred ommatidia (see Fig. 1.8, p.11). Each ommatidium contains 10 or more retinula cells, and their axons form a bundle, the optic nerve, which runs to the brain. What information passes down these axons when light falls on the eye? The first step in answering this question was taken by Hartline and Graham (1932), who recorded the activity of single axons in the optic nerve while shining a spot of light onto the corresponding ommatidia. They established that action potentials (impulses) pass down an axon at a rate roughly proportional to the logarithm of the intensity of light falling on its ommatidium. As we saw in Chapter 1, transduction of light by a rhabdomeric receptor causes a depolarisation of the membrane, which is proportional to the logarithm of light intensity, and so this result simply implies that the impulse rate follows depolarisation in a linear way. The resulting *logarithmic coding* of stimulus intensity is a common feature of many sensory systems, and is necessary in order to compress a wide band of physical stimulus intensity (such as the intensity of natural light) into a narrower band of impulse rates.

So far, it seems that the pattern of light intensity over the eye of *Limulus* is reproduced faithfully in the pattern of activity of optic nerve axons, each one reporting light intensity in one part of the optic array. In fact, things are by no means so simple, and both the temporal and the spatial pattern of light undergo transformation in the retina.

Transformation of temporal pattern

Impulse frequency in a receptor cell axon does not follow changes in light intensity in a simple way, but shows the phenomenon called adaptation that we mentioned in Chapter 1. At the onset of a spot of light, impulse rate rises rapidly to a peak and then falls, after a second or so, to a steady level maintained while the light is on (Fig. 2.1a). Both the peak rate and the steady level are related logarithmically to the intensity of light (Fig. 2.1b). This process is called *light-adaptation*, and it means that a high impulse rate signals a sudden *increase* in light intensity and not a steady bright light.

Second, if a receptor is adapted to light and then left in darkness, its sensitivity to light gradually rises. The impulse rate generated in response to a test flash of light increases rapidly over the first few minutes in darkness, and then more gradually, to reach a maximum after about an hour. This process of *dark-adaptation* is the much slower converse of light-adaptation. It means that the activity of an axon does not signal absolute light intensity but intensity *relative* to the degree of dark-adaptation of the receptor.

The effect of these two processes is that the output of a photoreceptor is quite stable over a wide range of light intensities, but that this stability can be disturbed by a sudden change in intensity. The temporal pattern of the output is therefore a transformation of the temporal pattern of the input: slow changes in light intensity are filtered out whereas rapid ones are not.

Transformation of spatial pattern

In their first experiments, Hartline and Graham used spots of light small enough to illuminate only one ommatidium at a time. What happens when, as in real life, light falls on all the ommatidia of the eye? Is the pattern of activity in the optic nerve simply the sum of the responses of individual photoreceptors to light, or do the signals from ommatidia interact with one another?

In a classic experiment, summarised in Fig. 2.2a, Hartline, Wagner, and Ratliff (1956) demonstrated that the outputs of ommatidia do indeed interact with one another, through a process of *lateral inhibition* between neighbouring photoreceptors. Each cell inhibits the firing rate of those in a roughly circular area around it. The strength of the inhibition rises with increasing

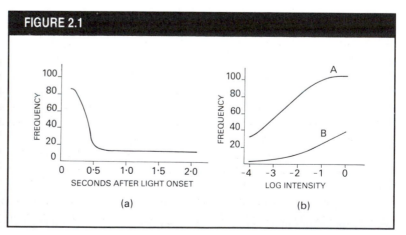

FIGURE 2.1

(a) The response of a single ommatidium to light. The frequency of discharge of impulses rises rapidly to a peak and then falls to a steady level within 0.5sec. (b) The peak response (A) and the steady response (B) of a single ommatidium to a flash of light at different light intensities. Note the logarithmic relationship between intensity and response. Adapted from Hartline and Graham (1932).

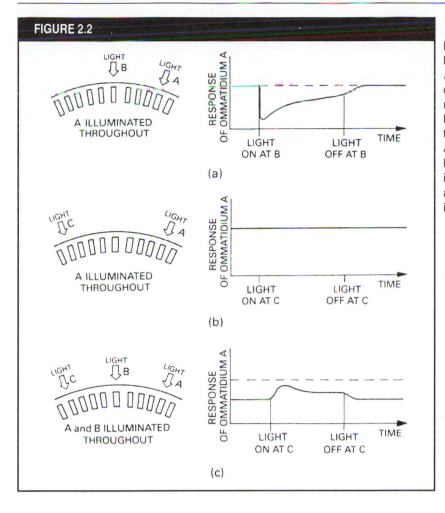

FIGURE 2.2

(a)

(b)

(c)

Experiments demonstrating lateral inhibition in the eye of *Limulus*. (a) Light falling on ommatidium B inhibits the response of ommatidium A to light. (b) Ommatidium C is too far from A for it to inhibit A's response. (c) Even so, light falling on C causes an inhibition of B's response and therefore lifts the inhibition imposed by B on A.

intensity of light falling on the inhibiting ommatidium, and falls with increasing distance between the ommatidia. Lateral inhibition is mutual, each photoreceptor being inhibited by its neighbours, which it in turn inhibits. Also, each photoreceptor inhibits its own activity, a process in part responsible for light-adaptation.

This model successfully predicts the effects of more complex patterns of light falling on the eye. For example, the inhibition imposed on ommatidium A by illumination of another, B, can be reduced by illumination of a third ommatidium, C, on the far side of B from A (Figs. 2.2b and 2.2c). This is disinhibition; cell C inhibits B and in so doing reduces B's inhibition on A. The neuroanatomical basis of lateral inhibition is in collateral branches spreading sideways from each receptor cell axon in a layer just below the ommatidia, making inhibitory synaptic contacts with other nearby cells (Purple & Dodge, 1965).

Just as adaptation in receptors causes a transformation of the temporal pattern of light at the eye, so lateral inhibition causes a transformation of its spatial pattern. If the whole eye is evenly and diffusely illuminated, excitation of receptor cells by light will be largely cancelled by inhibition from neighbouring cells. The activity of optic nerve axons will therefore be low and will vary little with changes in light level. Consider next what happens if there is a sharp boundary between a brightly and a dimly lit area of the retina. The output of those ommatidia lying just inside the bright area will be less inhibited, as their neighbours to the dim side are less active, whereas the output of those just across the boundary will be more inhibited, as their neighbours on the bright side are more active. The result is shown in Fig. 2.3: there will be a marked peak and trough in the firing pattern at the location of the edge. Lateral inhibition therefore gives prominence to rapid *spatial* changes in light intensity, in the same way as adaptation does for rapid changes over time. We will see in the next section that the retina of the vertebrate eye works in a similar way to filter out slow changes in light intensity over time and space, and will discuss later in the chapter why this should be a general property of visual systems.

THE VERTEBRATE RETINA

In Chapter 1 we described the vertebrate retina simply as a carpet of rods and cones covering the back of the eye. However, there are also several layers of nerve cells between the photoreceptors and the vitreous humour filling the eye, and these contain cells of four kinds: *horizontal*, *bipolar*, *amacrine*, and *ganglion* cells. Dowling (1968) established by electron microscopy that there is a

common pattern, across many vertebrate species, of synaptic connections between these neurons, and Fig. 2.4 summarises his findings. Receptors synapse in the *outer plexiform layer* with both horizontal cells and bipolar cells, and bipolars synapse in the *inner plexiform layer* with both amacrine and ganglion cells. Some ganglion cells receive input directly from bipolars, whereas others are driven only by amacrines. The axons of ganglion cells run over the surface of the retina to the blindspot, where they are bundled together into the optic nerve, which runs to the brain.

Although the vertebrate retina is more complex than that of *Limulus*, there is a basic similarity in structure. In both cases there are nerve cell pathways running in two directions at right angles to one another: a receptor-brain pathway and a lateral pathway. The first pathway is represented in the *Limulus* retina by the axons of receptor cells, but in the vertebrate retina it consists of a series of cells linking the receptors through the bipolars and amacrines to the ganglion cells.

Whereas in *Limulus* each receptor cell axon runs from one photoreceptor unit, the outputs of vertebrate photoreceptors are pooled together, so that a group of receptors acts as a functional unit.

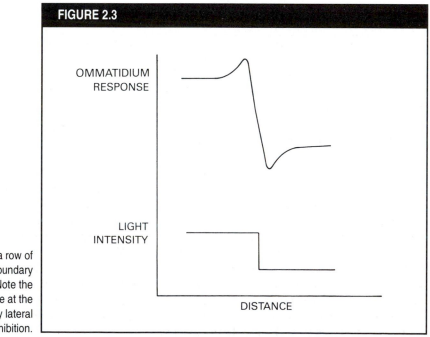

FIGURE 2.3

OMMATIDIUM RESPONSE

LIGHT INTENSITY

DISTANCE

The responses of a row of ommatidia to a dark–light boundary falling on the eye. Note the sharpening of the response at the boundary caused by lateral inhibition.

FIGURE 2.4

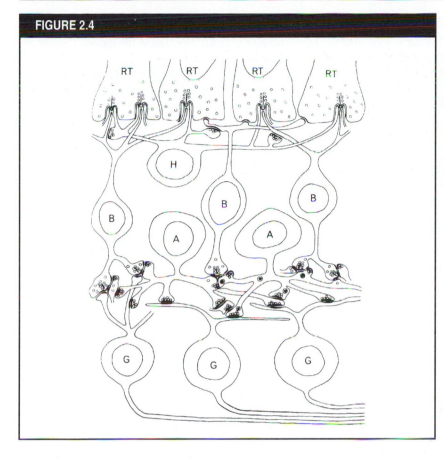

The structure of the vertebrate retina:
RT – receptor terminals
H – horizontal cells
B – bipolar cells
A – amacrine cells
G – ganglion cells
Reproduced from Dowling (1968) with permission of The Royal Society.

This occurs in two ways: through direct excitatory synaptic contact between neighbouring rods and cones, and through convergence of a number of receptor outputs to a single bipolar cell. The number of receptors pooled reflects the trade-off between acuity and sensitivity discussed in Chapter 1. In a primate eye, each bipolar cell in the fovea connects to one or two cones, whereas in the periphery, a bipolar may connect to many rods. The ganglion cell axons leading from the fovea therefore have the potential to carry information about fine detail in the pattern of receptor excitation, whereas those leading from the periphery sacrifice this potential in order to achieve greater sensitivity to dim light.

The lateral pathway is also simpler in the retina of *Limulus*, and consists of the collaterals of receptor cell axons. In vertebrates, it is made up of two systems, the processes of horizontal cells ramifying in the outer plexiform layer and the processes of amacrine cells in the inner plexiform layer. The anatomy of the vertebrate retina therefore suggests that transformations of spatial pattern similar to those in *Limulus* are carried out, but also hints that these patterns are likely to be more complex.

The first step in analysing the transformations of pattern taking place in the vertebrate retina is to establish the relationship between its input and its output: the pattern of light falling on it and the rate at which ganglion cells fire impulses. The first experiments of this kind were just like Hartline's on the *Limulus* retina, using small spots of light as stimuli. These demonstrated that each ganglion cell has a *receptive field*, a region of the retina, usually roughly circular, in which stimulation affects the ganglion cell's firing rate. Many different kinds of receptive field have been identified, but one type—the *concentric* field—is probably common to all vertebrates.

Concentric receptive fields

Concentric receptive fields were first discovered by Kuffler (1953) in a study of the responses of cat ganglion cells. Kuffler found that the effects of a spot of light depend on whether the light falls in a small circular area in the centre of the field, or in the ring-shaped area surrounding the centre. Some cells respond with a burst of impulses to either the onset of a spot of light in the centre of the field, or to the offset of a spot of light in the surround; this is called a *centre-on* response. Other cells show the converse, *centre-off* response: offset of a spot of light in the centre of the field or onset in the surround causes a burst of impulses (Fig. 2.5). Kuffler's experiments therefore demonstrated that light falling in the two regions of the receptive field has opposite effects, and so the centre and surround are said to be *antagonistic* to one another. When the intensity of light falling in the "on" region increases or decreases, the strength of the cell's response changes in the same direction. An increase or decrease in light intensity in the "off" region causes the response to change in the opposite direction.

Further progress in understanding concentric receptive fields was made by Enroth-Cugell and Robson (1966) in experiments using sinusoidal gratings as stimuli. We will describe their methods in detail, because they have subsequently been widely used in research on the responses of single cells to light. Like the gratings described in Chapter 1 used to measure visual acuity, a sinusoidal grating is made up of parallel bright and dark bars. Their edges have a blurred appearance, however, as the brightness of the pattern varies sinusoidally with distance rather than changing sharply at the boundaries of the bars (see Fig. 2.6). The intensity of light reflected from the grating therefore follows a sine wave, in just the same way as the sound pressure near a vibrating tuning fork varies sinusoidally with time. One cycle of the grating is the distance spanned by a light bar and the adjacent dark bar. A grating is described by the parameters of: *spatial frequency*, expressed as the number of cycles per degree of visual angle; *contrast*, expressed as the difference between maximum and minimum intensities in the pattern, divided by their sum; and *phase* of the pattern

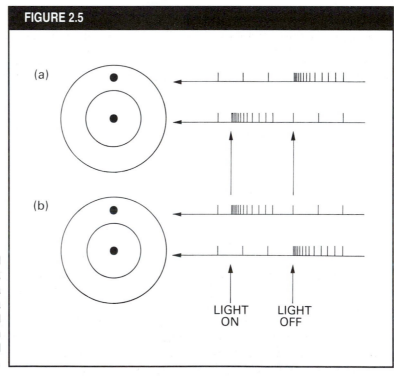

FIGURE 2.5

(a)

(b)

LIGHT ON   LIGHT OFF

The responses of cat retinal ganglion cells to spots of light. A centre-on cell (a) responds with a burst of impulses to the onset of a spot of light in the centre of its field or to the offset of a spot of light in the surround area. A centre-off cell (b) responds in the opposite fashion.

FIGURE 2.6

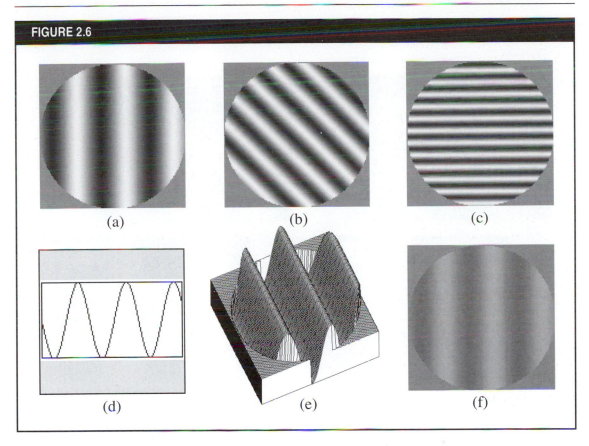

(a)   (b)   (c)

(d)   (e)   (f)

Sinusoidal gratings varying in orientation and spatial frequency, from a fairly low frequency (a) through medium frequency (b) to a higher frequency (c). The luminance profile (d) is a graph of intensity against position, and for these gratings it is a sine wave. In general, image intensity varies in two dimensions (x,y) and can be visualised as a surface (e). The grating shown in (f) has the same frequency as (a) but lower contrast. The luminance (or intensity) (L) of a sinusoidal grating as a function of position (x) is:

$$L(x) = L_0 + L_0.c.\sin(2\pi fx - \Phi)$$

where L_0 is the mean luminance and f is the frequency of the grating. Contrast (c), ranging from –1 to +1, controls the amount of luminance variation around L_0. Changes in phase (Φ) shift the position of the grating without altering anything else.

relative to a fixed point, expressed in degrees or radians.

Enroth-Cugell and Robson exposed an area of retina to a diffuse field of light alternating at regular intervals with a sinusoidal grating of the same average light intensity. What responses would be expected at onset and offset of the grating by cells with concentric receptive fields? Figure 2.7 shows the distribution of light intensity over the receptive field of an on-centre cell when it is illuminated by a grating whose bar width matches the diameter of the receptive field centre. In Fig. 2.7a, where the peak of the grating falls on the centre of the field, a burst of impulses will occur at the onset of the grating, because the centre becomes brighter than the surround. If the phase of the grating relative to the centre of the field is shifted by 180° (Fig. 2.7b), there will be a *decrease* in response at grating onset, when the centre becomes dimmer than the surround. If the phase is shifted by 90° in either direction (Fig. 2.7c,d), however, there is no net change of light intensity over either the centre or the surround at grating onset or offset.

FIGURE 2.7

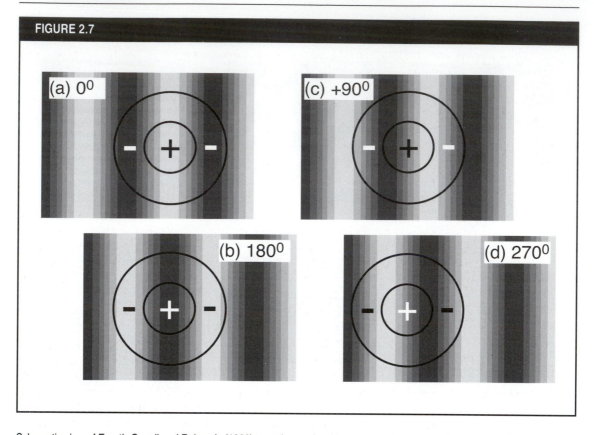

Schematic view of Enroth-Cugell and Robson's (1966) experiments in which cat retinal ganglion cells were tested with sine-wave gratings presented at different spatial phases (a–d), relative to the centre of the cell's receptive field (+).

If the response of a ganglion cell is determined by the difference between light intensity in centre and surround, we would therefore expect to find two *null positions* as the phase of the grating relative to the field centre is changed through a full 360°. At these positions, in both on- and off-centre cells, there will be no response to onset or offset of a grating, because an increase of light in one half of the field is balanced by a decrease in the other. Enroth-Cugell and Robson found that some ganglion cells, which they called *X cells*, behave in exactly this way. They are said to have a *linear* response because, in order to balance at the null-point, the summation of light-evoked signals across the centre and surround regions must be occurring in a linear (additive) fashion. Others, called *Y cells*, behave differently, however. With these, no null position of a grating can be found, and the cell responds with a burst of impulses to on- and offset of the grating whatever its phase.

A related distinction between X and Y cells is in their response to moving gratings. As a sinusoidal pattern of light moves over an X cell's field, the cell's impulse rate rises and falls with the peaks and troughs of the pattern. The response of Y cells, on the other hand, shows a constant elevation to a drifting grating, on which is superimposed a modulation in phase with the grating. This test also shows that the response of a Y cell to the pattern of light in its receptive field is *nonlinear*; it cannot be predicted by algebraic summation of excitatory and inhibitory influences from centre and surround.

These early experiments on the retinal ganglion cells of cats serve to illustrate the basic properties of concentric receptive fields, and the concept of linear spatial summation. X and Y cells work in a broadly similar way to those in the retina of

Limulus, as they filter out slow changes in light intensity over time and space, and respond best to contrast between a region of the retina and the area around it. We will discuss later the general significance of these processes, and will next look briefly at the mechanisms within the retina that produce concentric receptive fields.

Retinal mechanisms underlying concentric fields

We can think of photoreceptors as measuring light intensity in each small part of the retina, and of these measurements being combined and transformed in the network of retinal cells and their synaptic connections. Here we discuss briefly the ways in which the neural "wiring" of the retina produces concentric receptive fields.

It is important first to emphasise that it is an over-simplification to see receptors as simply measuring light intensity. Even before receptor signals pass to horizontal and bipolar cells, transformation of the input pattern occurs, as the response of rods and cones to light is not a simple function of intensity. Instead, the cones show adaptation in the same way as the photoreceptors of *Limulus*. An example can be seen in intracellular recordings made by Normann and Werblin (1974) from photoreceptors of the amphibian *Necturus*. They found that cones respond to light with a hyperpolarisation proportional to the logarithm of light intensity over an intensity range of 3.5 log units. The centre of this range continually shifts, however, to match the current background illumination. Figure 2.8 shows the intensity-response curves for cones adapted to three different background intensities. Note that the cell's response does not signal absolute light intensity, but intensity relative to the current level of adaptation.

Even at this early stage, we see that receptors respond to changes in light intensity and not to absolute intensity. Diurnal animals are active in a wide range of light levels, and adaptation ensures that cones have maximum sensitivity to changes around whatever the current background light level may be. The situation is different with rods, where Normann and Werblin (1974) found that the operating range does not shift far above the dark-adapted level. Rods do not show as large a degree of adaptation because they are specialised for detecting a narrow range of low light intensities.

It should be noted that adaptation of the vertebrate visual system to variation in light level involves other processes in addition to adaptation of rods and cones. Light falling on one receptor causes the response of nearby receptors to adapt, showing that some further process must operate in the neural circuitry of the retina to adjust its sensitivity to light. The mechanisms involved are not yet fully understood, and a review of current theories can be found in Green (1986).

What processes in the retina bridge the gap between the responses of rods and cones and the receptive fields of ganglion cells? The response of an X-cell can be described by the model shown in Fig. 2.9 (Enroth-Cugell & Robson, 1966). The output of the cell is determined by the algebraic

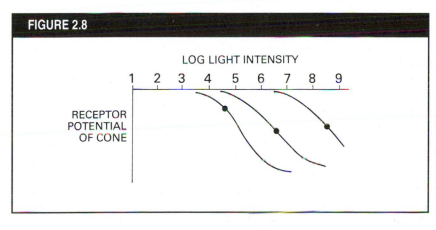

FIGURE 2.8

LOG LIGHT INTENSITY

1 2 3 4 5 6 7 8 9

RECEPTOR POTENTIAL OF CONE

The relationship between log light intensity and receptor potential of a cone. The circles mark the light level around which each curve was obtained and to which the receptors were adapted. Adapted from Normann and Werblin (1974).

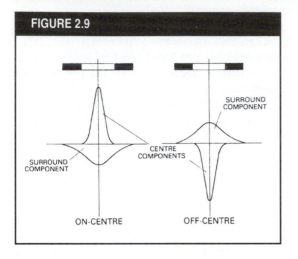

FIGURE 2.9

Enroth-Cugell and Robson's (1966) model of the organisation of X cell fields. The strength of the centre component depends on the light falling in the centre of the field and the strength of the surround component on light falling throughout the field. In both cases, the contribution of light intensity is weighted by a Gaussian function. The response of the cell is determined by the difference between the two components.

sum of a centre and a surround component. Each component sums the total light falling in a circular area, and the contribution of each part of the area to the sum is weighted according to its distance from the centre of the receptive field. The relationship between weighting and distance follows a bell-shaped *Gaussian* curve (see Fig. 2.9), and the effect of light on the weighted sum therefore falls rapidly with distance from the field centre. The curve obtained by taking the difference between the centre and the surround Gaussians describes the antagonistic organisation of the field.

What neural mechanisms perform this computation on the pattern of receptor signals over the retina? Werblin and Dowling (1969) made intracellular recordings from the retinal neurons of *Necturus*, and found that bipolar cells have centre-on or centre-off concentric fields. The linear spatial summation necessary to establish centre-surround organisation therefore occurs in the outer plexiform layer; the centre component is generated by the summed input of a group of neighbouring receptors to a bipolar cell, and the surround component by the input from a wider

circle of receptors, mediated by horizontal cells. The two inputs act in an opposing way to generate a sustained slow potential in the bipolar cell. In *Necturus*, some ganglion cells are driven directly by bipolars, and therefore have concentric fields comparable to those of cat X cells.

One approach to explaining the more complex, nonlinear properties of Y cells is to add an extra component to the model of linear spatial summation. Victor and Shapley (1979) propose that Y cells receive two kinds of synaptic input from bipolar cells. One is a direct input, just like that to X cells, which the response of the Y cell follows in a linear way. The other is indirect, via amacrine cells: a Y cell receives a large number of these inputs, each of which is driven by light from a small sub-region of the receptive field. At the bipolar-amacrine synapses, the bipolar signal is rectified (rectification is a nonlinear operation in which only the positive or only the negative part of a signal is passed). In an on-centre Y cell, the rectified outputs of bipolar cells add to the linear component of the centre response at light onset, but do not subtract from the surround response at light offset (and vice versa in an off-centre cell). As a result, the Y cell responds to the onset and offset of light, whatever its spatial pattern.

There is evidence that the nonlinear inputs to Y cells in Victor and Shapley's (1979) model may extend far beyond the boundaries of the conventional receptive field, as retinal ganglion cells can be influenced by light falling on the retina *outside* the receptive field centre and surround. This was first shown by McIlwain (1964), who found that a cell's threshold for responding to a dim spot of light falling in its field centre was lowered if a dark spot moved over the retina up to 90° or more away from the field centre. Further experiments on this *periphery effect* demonstrated that ganglion cells, especially Y cells, would respond to moving patterns located far from the receptive field (e.g. Ikeda & Wright, 1972). Clearly, some long-range process within the retina must be responsible, and as the spatiotemporal properties of the periphery effect are very similar to the nonlinear mechanism of Y cells (Derrington, Lennie, & Wright, 1979), it is reasonable to conclude that a spatially extensive network of nonlinear inputs from amacrine cells influences the behaviour of many ganglion cells.

The models of neural circuitry in the retina that we have described so far assume that the basic processes involved are linear, and that nonlinearities can be explained by adding extra mechanisms to them. This assumption has been challenged by Gaudiano (1994), who points out that adaptation in photoreceptors means that the first stage of retinal processing is not linear, and therefore the linear spatial summation exhibited by X cells must rely on some *further* nonlinearity to "correct" for the effects of adaptation. In Gaudiano's model of retinal circuitry, this occurs in the interaction between bipolar and ganglion cells, which no longer involves simple linear pooling of signals. An important feature of the model is that it can generate *either* X-like *or* Y-like responses in ganglion cells driven by the same kind of retinal circuit, depending on the relative sizes of field centre and surround.

Further details of the model can be found in Gaudiano (1994), but the approach illustrates an important general principle. The responses of X cells arise from an operation on the input to the retina that, overall, is approximately linear, but there is evidence that some of the component stages of this operation are markedly nonlinear. The possibility that neural systems in the visual pathway may be designed to perform a linear operation by combining nonlinear processes in complex ways is intriguing, although controversial, and we will note it again in Chapter 3 (p.56). In the next section, however, we will return to the description of retinal ganglion cell responses, concentrating now on findings from monkeys, which are the animals with a visual pathway most like our own.

Retinal ganglion cells of monkeys

Most retinal ganglion cells of monkeys have concentric on- or off-centre receptive fields. These fall into two distinct categories, and we begin our description of them by considering differences in their responses to colour patterns (de Monasterio & Gouras, 1975). One of the types shows a property called *colour-opponency*; by using spots of monochromatic light (light of a single wavelength) as test stimuli, it can be shown that the receptive fields of these cells have antagonistic centre and surround regions, and that the peak sensitivities of the two regions are at different wavelengths. If such a cell is tested with spots of white light, which excite centre and surround about equally, it will show the same centre-surround antagonism as a cat X cell. On the other hand, if a patch of *coloured* light filling the whole receptive field is used, spatial antagonism will not occur, as centre and surround are differently excited, and the cell's response will be a function of the wavelength of the light. Its firing will be excited at some wavelengths and inhibited at others (see Fig. 2.10). The response of a colour-opponent cell therefore carries information about both the wavelength of light in its field and differences in light intensity (or luminance) between centre and surround.

The second type of cell identified by de Monasterio and Gouras (1975) lacks colour-opponency, as the peak sensitivities of centre and surround are at the same wavelength. In consequence, such a cell responds little to monochromatic light filling the receptive field, but strongly to a difference in luminance between centre and surround across a broad band of wavelengths.

Because of these different responses to colour stimuli, the two cell types have been called "colour-opponent" and "broad-band", but they are now more commonly called P and M cells, respectively, because they make connections with "parvocellular" and "magnocellular" areas in the brain (these are described in Chapter 3, p.44). The differences between P and M cells in their responses to colour arise from differences in their synaptic connections in the retina. Recall that primates have three types of cone, with different absorption spectra (p.22). In an M (broad-band) ganglion cell, the receptive field centre and surround receive input (via bipolar, horizontal, and amacrine cells) from the same type (or types) of cones, whereas for a P (colour-opponent) cell, the type (or types) of cone driving the two parts of the receptive field are different. We will return to colour opponency and the specific combinations of cones driving P cells in the next chapter (p.45).

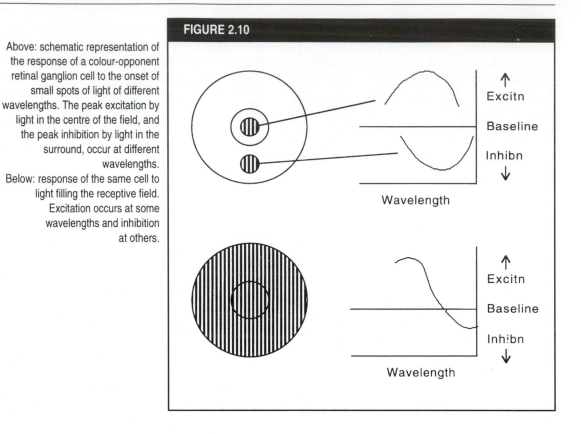

FIGURE 2.10

Above: schematic representation of the response of a colour-opponent retinal ganglion cell to the onset of small spots of light of different wavelengths. The peak excitation by light in the centre of the field, and the peak inhibition by light in the surround, occur at different wavelengths.
Below: response of the same cell to light filling the receptive field. Excitation occurs at some wavelengths and inhibition at others.

De Monasterio and Gouras (1975) demonstrated a number of other differences between M and P cells. First, P cells give a *tonic* (or *sustained*) response to a stimulus, continuing to fire impulses while it is present in the receptive field, whereas M cells show a *phasic* (or *transient*) response that fades quickly if the stimulus does not change. Second, M cells have thicker axons than P cells and so conduct impulses more quickly. Third, the receptive field centres of M cells are larger than those of P cells. The fields of both types increase steadily in size with eccentricity (the distance from the fovea, measured in degrees of visual angle), but at all eccentricities the population of M cells has distinctly larger field centres than their P cell neighbours (see also Croner & Kaplan, 1995). Leventhal, Rodieck, and Dreher (1981) matched M and P cells to two types of ganglion cell with differently shaped dendritic trees, and found that the diameters of these trees vary in just the way that would be expected: the dendritic spread of both types increases with eccentricity, and that of M

cells is always greater than that of P cells at the same eccentricity.

A final important difference between M and P cells is in their sensitivity to patterns of light of low contrast. The *contrast sensitivity* of a cell can be measured by projecting a grating onto its receptive field and then varying the contrast of the grating to determine the threshold contrast required to evoke a response. When M and P cells are compared in this way, the contrast threshold of M cells is about 10 times lower than that of P cells (Kaplan & Shapley, 1986). In other words, M cells have much higher contrast sensitivity than P cells.

It is worth noting that M and P retinal ganglion cells in monkeys do not correspond straightforwardly to the X and Y cells of cats. When Enroth-Cugell and Robson's (1966) tests are applied to monkey ganglion cells, virtually all P cells and the majority of M cells show linear spatial summation (like X cells), whereas a minority of M cells behave in the same nonlinear way as Y cells (Shapley & Perry, 1986). There are several possible patterns of evolutionary homology between ganglion cell types in cats and monkeys. One, favoured by Shapley and Perry, is that the two types of M cell correspond to cat X and Y cells, whereas P cells are a primate specialisation with no equivalent in cats.

A number of theories to account for the marked two-way division of the visual pathway from the primate retina have been proposed, and we will discuss them in the next chapter, after following the pathway into the brain. To complete this summary of the properties of monkey retinal ganglion cells, it should be noted that not all fall into the M and P classes. Some cells do not have concentric receptive fields, but respond to light onset, offset, or both, in any part of the field, or may respond only to moving spots of light (de Monasterio & Gouras, 1975). Others have colour-opponent responses but without a concentric field (de Monasterio, 1978), and these have recently been found to form a distinct third pathway to the brain (Hendry & Yoshioka, 1994; see p.45). There is a similarly diverse group of non-concentric cells in cats, known as W cells (Cleland & Levick, 1974; Stone & Fukuda, 1974).

THE RETINA AS A FILTER

At several points in this chapter, we have described the retina as a *filter*, and have introduced the idea that adaptation, lateral inhibition, and centre-surround antagonism filter out slow changes in light intensity over time and space. In this section, we will introduce some concepts that allow filtering operations of this kind to be described in more precise ways, before looking at their application to retinal processing.

Imagine some physical quantity that varies over time, for example, the pressure propagated through the air from a sound source. If the source is a tuning fork, which produces a pure tone, then pressure will vary sinusoidally with time (see Fig. 2.11a). If the sound is a note played on a musical instrument, the variation of air pressure with time will be more complex, because multiples of the fundamental frequency, or *harmonics*, are also produced and add to the fundamental (see Fig. 2.11b,c). It is easy to see that such a waveform can be described either as a pattern of variation of intensity with time, or as a set of component sinusoidal waveforms added together. In order to convert the second description back into the first, we would need to know the frequency and amplitude of each component, and also their phase relationships— how they are to be "lined up" before being added together.

FIGURE 2.11

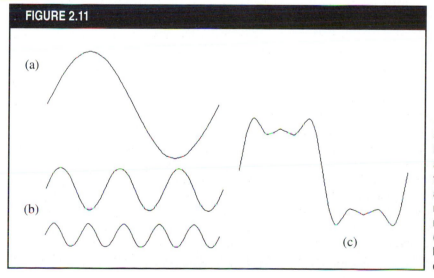

(a) a sinusoidal waveform and (b) its third and fifth harmonics. The relative amplitudes of the fundamental and harmonics are similar to those that might be produced by a musical instrument.
(c) the waveform produced by adding the three components together.

This way of converting a sound pressure waveform into a description of its component frequencies is a simple example of a mathematical operation called *Fourier analysis*. Both descriptions contain exactly the same information about the pattern of change of pressure over time, but represented in different ways that can be changed back and forth between one another. The next step in understanding the general importance of Fourier analysis is to see that *any* waveform can be analysed in the same way; it need not be made up of a fundamental frequency and harmonics, and need not even be periodic. In general, the Fourier description of a waveform will not be a small set of frequencies (as in the simple case of a musical tone), but a continuous function of amplitude and phase against frequency.

So far we have used patterns of sound pressure varying over time to illustrate Fourier analysis, but there is nothing at all special about either sound pressure or time. The same principles can be applied to the variation of any quantity over time, such as the fluctuating light intensity falling on a photoreceptor, or to the variation of a quantity over *space*. The light intensity reflected from the grating shown in Fig. 2.6 varies sinusoidally along one spatial dimension, and Fourier analysis would yield a single component at a particular spatial frequency. More complex gratings could be made by adding harmonics to the fundamental spatial frequency. As higher and higher harmonics were added, the grating would come to resemble a square-wave grating more and more closely. Finally, Fourier analysis can be applied not only to patterns of light intensity that vary along one spatial dimension, but also to images, in which it varies along two dimensions. The only difference is that amplitude and phase are now functions not only of spatial frequency but also of orientation. An example of Fourier analysis of an image is given in Fig. 2.12.

The concept that temporal and spatial patterns of light intensity can be described in frequency terms provides us with a means of describing filtering operations in a precise, quantitative way. The input and output of a filter are related by a *transfer function*, which specifies how effectively different frequencies pass through the filter. For example, in high-pass and low-pass filters, only the temporal or spatial frequencies above or below some value are transmitted, whereas in a band-pass filter only those frequencies within a particular band of values are transmitted. An illustration of the results of passing an image through low- and high-pass spatial filters is shown in Fig. 2.13. A more detailed introduction to the concepts of Fourier analysis and frequency filtering, which requires only a modest background in mathematics, can be found in de Valois and de Valois (1990). We will make extensive use of the key concepts outlined above in later chapters, but now turn to consider their application to retinal processing.

The retina is just one of a series of filters that operate on the optic array. Before photoreceptor signals pass to the retinal circuitry, the processes of image formation and transduction of light described in the previous chapter have already filtered out high spatial and temporal frequencies. Optical formation of a retinal image and the pooling of light across each receptor aperture both act as low-pass spatial filters (see p.18), and the probabilistic nature of photon capture implies a low-pass temporal filter, which can be significant at low light intensities (see p.18). These early filters are then followed by the neural circuits of the retina, which in general act as high-pass temporal and spatial filters, through the processes of adaptation and lateral inhibition (centre-surround antagonism), respectively, although the spatial summation of light responses within receptive field centres is another low-pass operation, akin to the blurring imposed by the optical filtering in the eye.

If we consider the information that animals need from natural optic arrays, and the intensities of light involved, we can understand why the filtering out of low temporal and spatial frequencies should be a general feature of the first stage of visual processing in animals. In order to interact with its surroundings, an animal needs information about relatively rapid changes from one part of the optic array to another (specifying the structure of objects) and about rapid changes over time in those spatial changes (specifying movement). The scale of these changes in intensity is determined by the range of variation in the reflectance of natural

FIGURE 2.12

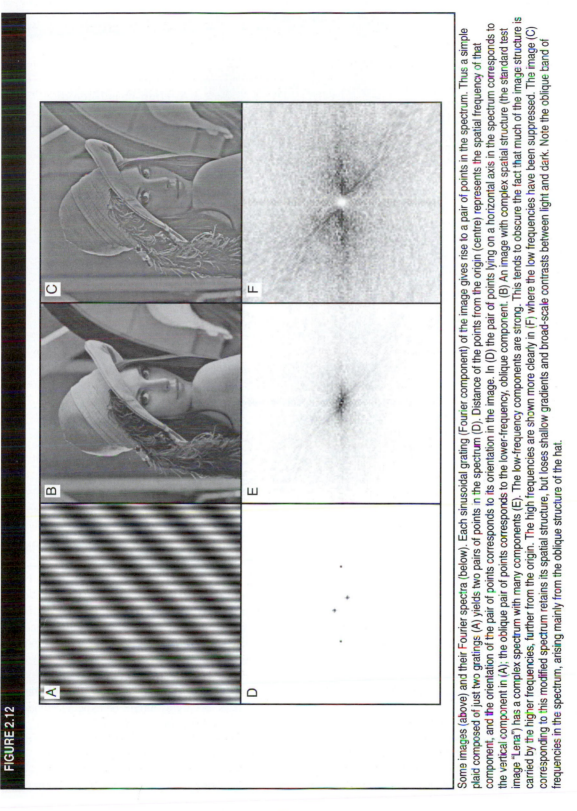

Some images (above) and their Fourier spectra (below). Each sinusoidal grating (Fourier component) of the image gives rise to a pair of points in the spectrum. Thus a simple plaid composed of just two gratings (A) yields two pairs of points in the spectrum (D). Distance of the points from the origin (centre) represents the spatial frequency of that component, and the orientation of the pair of points corresponds to its orientation in the image. In (D) the pair of points lying on a horizontal axis in the spectrum corresponds to the vertical component in (A); the oblique pair of points corresponds to the lower-frequency, oblique component. (B) An image with complex spatial structure (the standard test image "Lena") has a complex spectrum with many components (E). The low-frequency components are strong. This tends to obscure the fact that much of the image structure is carried by the higher frequencies, further from the origin. The high frequencies are shown more clearly in (F) where the low frequencies have been suppressed. The image (C) corresponding to this modified spectrum retains its spatial structure, but loses shallow gradients and broad-scale contrasts between light and dark. Note the oblique band of frequencies in the spectrum, arising mainly from the oblique structure of the hat.

FIGURE 2.13

Spatial filtering of an image. (A) A high-pass filtered version of the original (B), with low frequencies suppressed, as in Fig. 2.12C. (C) The complementary, low-pass filtered image, with high frequencies suppressed. In fact, (C) was produced by blurring the image directly, to average or smooth out the higher frequencies, and (A) was formed by subtracting the low frequencies (C) from the original (B), i.e. B = A + C. Graphs show the intensity profile of a horizontal slice through the centre of each image. Note the smoothness of (C) and the lack of large-scale differences in (A).

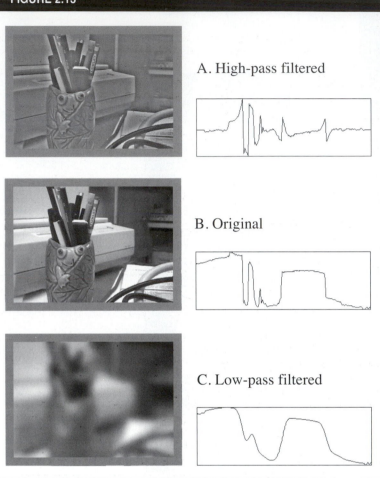

A. High-pass filtered

B. Original

C. Low-pass filtered

surfaces. Under the same light source, the brightest natural surfaces reflect light with an intensity about 20 times greater than that reflected by the darkest surfaces (de Valois & de Valois, 1990, p.160), and so the retina must transmit changes in intensity over this range. Now, the diurnal variation in the illumination of natural environments (see p.18) means that these variations are superimposed on a roughly 10^9-fold variation in light intensity. If the retina did not perform any filtering, but coded absolute light intensities in the firing rates of ganglion cells, the spatial and temporal changes that provide useful information about the world would be swamped by largely irrelevant variation in light with the time of day, as well as weather and shadow conditions. By filtering out low temporal

and spatial frequencies, the visual systems of animals minimise this problem.

It is important to note that this broad generalisation about the function of retinal filtering omits many differences in detail between different animal species. For example, there is evidence that primate ganglion cells with concentric receptive fields do not carry out as important a *spatial* filtering operation as this general account suggests. The response of monkey ganglion cells does not fall off as steeply as would be expected when the spatial frequency of a grating is reduced, because the contribution of the surround component to the cell's response is only about half of the centre response even at low frequencies (Croner & Kaplan, 1995). The receptive field profile and

FIGURE 2.14

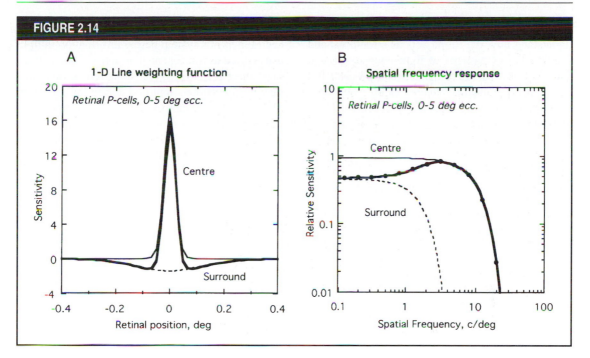

"Typical" ganglion cell receptive field in central vision of the monkey. (A) Line response profile represents the responsiveness of the cell to a long, thin, bright line presented at different positions across the receptive field. The curve was generated from median values of experimental data on P cells in central vision (Croner & Kaplan, 1995), using Gaussian profiles for centre and surround (thin lines). (B) Spatial frequency response to gratings of different spatial frequencies. Note that both the centre and surround act as low-pass filters, but their net effect (centre minus surround) is a broadly tuned, band-pass filter. Attenuation at low frequencies is mild, because the surround is weaker than the centre.

spatial frequency response of a "typical" ganglion cell in the monkey's central retina are shown in Fig. 2.14. Note in panel A that the inhibitory surround is relatively weak compared to the receptive field centre, and so there is correspondingly modest attenuation of the cell's responsiveness at low frequencies. This means that the ganglion cell's response does not accentuate sharp luminance changes as much as is often supposed.

It may therefore be that in monkeys and other mammals (such as cats) only mild spatial filtering occurs at the level of the retina (Robson, 1983), and more diverse and selective filtering occurs in the striate cortex (see Chapters 3 and 5). The situation in other vertebrate groups seems quite different: cells lacking concentric receptive fields, and with nonlinear responses to complex stimulus patterns, are more common in nonmammals, such as frogs (Lettvin, Maturana, McCulloch, & Pitts, 1959) and pigeons (Maturana & Frenk, 1963). These differences between vertebrate species in the proportions of different ganglion cell types suggests that more complex operations are carried out in the retinas of simple animals such as frogs than in those of monkeys. Variations between species in the complexity of synaptic connections in the retina also lend support to this view (Dowling, 1968), and suggest a general evolutionary trend among vertebrates from complex to simple retinal processing, in parallel with an opposite trend in the complexity of processing in the brain.

CONCLUSIONS

Beginning with the pioneering work of Hartline and of Kuffler, research on the properties of retinal cells has reached a point where some general principles of retinal function are clear. We understand how the retina acts as a temporal and spatial filter of patterns of light intensity and, in some species, of wavelength. Much progress has been made towards understanding how the network of cells in the retina is organised to achieve these functions, and there is a real prospect for the future of being able to understand retinal processing of patterns of light in terms of neurophysiology and neurochemistry. Even in animals as simple as the horseshoe crab, however, many further stages of processing must occur in the central nervous system before information in light can be used to control and plan actions. As we have seen, there is evidence that some retinal functions may have become simplified during the evolution of mammals, perhaps to allow more complex and flexible processing in the brain. In Chapter 3, we will complete our survey of the physiology of vision by following the optic nerves into the vertebrate brain.

3

Visual Pathways in the Brain

The neural circuitry of the retina transforms a fluctuating pattern of light into a pattern of neural activity in the cells making up the optic nerve. The information carried by this pattern is then transmitted along the optic nerve to the brain, where many further operations take place on it, with the eventual result that the actions of the animal are controlled appropriately. A great deal is known about the first few of these operations, and in this chapter we will outline the main findings and theories. We will begin with a short general description of the pathways from eye to brain in vertebrates, and then go on to consider the visual pathway of primates in more detail.

In exothermic vertebrates, the axons of retinal ganglion cells making up the optic nerves project to the *optic tectum*, a structure in the midbrain. Their projection is orderly, with axons maintaining the same topographic relationship to each other as that of their receptive fields on the retina. This order is maintained in the tectum, where cells are arranged in layers called *retinotopic maps*, in which the positions of cells relative to one another correspond to the relative positions of their fields on the retinal surface. In mammals, some retinal ganglion cells project in a similar way to the paired *superior colliculi* (see Fig. 3.1), structures in the midbrain that are homologous to the optic tectum and contain a number of layered retinotopic maps

of the contralateral visual field. In the monkey superior colliculus, cells in the three superficial layers respond to moving stimuli but are not selective for direction of movement or for the form of a stimulus (Wurtz & Albano, 1980).

The majority of mammalian ganglion cells project to the dorsal part of the two *lateral geniculate nuclei* (LGN) of the thalamus (see Fig. 3.1). Their axons terminate at synapses with LGN cells, which are arranged in layers, or laminae. Each layer contains a retinotopic map of half of the visual field, those in the right LGN having maps of the left side of the visual field and those in the left LGN having maps of the right side. In animals with laterally placed eyes, this is because there is complete crossing over of the optic nerves at the optic chiasm to run to opposite sides of the brain. In animals with binocular overlap, there is a partial crossing over, or *decussation*, of the optic nerves at the chiasm. The axons of ganglion cells in the left halves of each retina (carrying information about the right half of the visual field) run to the left LGN, and conversely for axons from the right halves of each retina, as illustrated in Fig. 3.2. This pattern of connections means that images of the same object formed on the right and the left retinas can be processed together in the same part of the brain. The axons of LGN cells in turn form the optic radiations (see Fig. 3.1) and project to the visual

FIGURE 3.1

Schematic diagram of the primary visual pathway of a primate. Adapted from Gluhbegovic and Williams (1980).

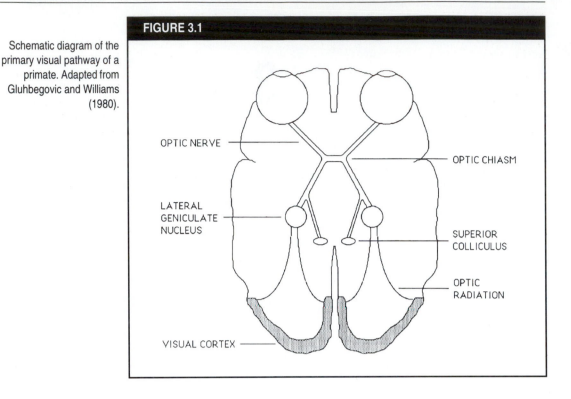

OPTIC NERVE

OPTIC CHIASM

LATERAL GENICULATE NUCLEUS

SUPERIOR COLLICULUS

OPTIC RADIATION

VISUAL CORTEX

cortex, a part of the highly folded sheet of nerve cells that forms the outer layer of the cerebral hemispheres.

Other ganglion cell axons run to various structures such as the hypothalamus, tegmentum and ventral LGN, but little is known of these pathways. The two main paths for visual information to the mammalian brain are therefore the projections from retina via LGN to the visual cortex (the geniculocortical path), and from retina to superior colliculi (the retinotectal path). In people, the first must be intact for conscious experience of vision to be possible, and people with damage to the visual cortex will report complete blindness in part or all of their visual field. Even so, they will show some ability to locate or even identify objects that they cannot consciously see (Weiskrantz, 1986), suggesting that, although most visual functions rely on the "primary" geniculocortical path, the "secondary" retinotectal path can carry enough information to guide some actions in an unconscious way. It should be noted, however, that the two pathways do not function independently in the intact brain, as there is a

corticotectal path providing the superior colliculi with input from the cortex.

THE LATERAL GENICULATE NUCLEUS

Our first step in adding more detail to the broad sketch given earlier will be to describe the structure and function of the primate LGN. In Old World monkeys, the LGN contains six layers of cells, three receiving input from one eye and three from the other. As in other mammals, each layer maps the contralateral visual field, and all six maps are aligned in precise register. There is a striking difference in cell size between the lower two and the upper four layers. Because cells in the former are larger, they are called the *magnocellular* layers, and the latter are called the *parvocellular* layers. Most M retinal ganglion cell axons project to the magnocellular layers, and the rest to the superior colliculi, whereas all P ganglion cells project to the parvocellular layers (Leventhal et al., 1981); it is this pattern of connections that gave M and P

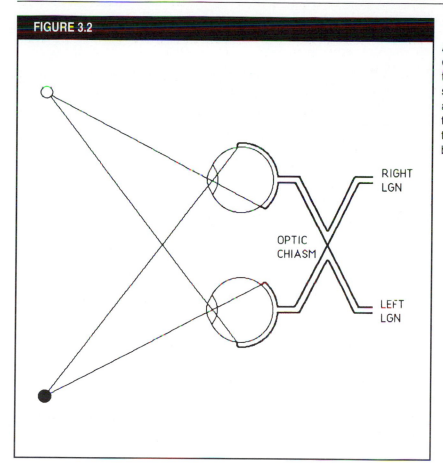

FIGURE 3.2

An illustration of the decussation of optic nerve fibres at the optic chiasm, showing how information about objects in one side of the visual field is transmitted to the opposite side of the brain.

RIGHT LGN

OPTIC CHIASM

LEFT LGN

ganglion cells their names. In addition, a third division of the LGN has recently been identified (Hendry & Yoshioka, 1994). This consists of "interlaminar" populations of cells below each of the six major layers, which receive input from retinal ganglion cells with colour-opponent but nonconcentric receptive fields (see p.37).

The receptive fields of LGN cells are generally similar to those of the retinal ganglion cells that drive them, and the differences between M and P ganglion cells in colour opponency, contrast sensitivity, and linearity described in the last chapter (p.35) also apply to M and P cells in the LGN (Derrington & Lennie, 1984). The colour-opponent responses of P cells fall into just four categories (Derrington, Krauskopf, & Lennie, 1984). The two most common categories of cell are driven by antagonistic inputs from red- and green-sensitive cones (see p.23) and are either

excited by red light and inhibited by green (+R–G cells) or vice-versa (+G–R cells). In the other two cell types, one part of the field is driven by both red- and green-sensitive cones, in varying combinations, while the other is driven by blue-sensitive cones. These +B–Y and +Y–B cells show blue-yellow opponency and are less common than the red-green opponent types. Figure 3.3 illustrates the responses of all four types, and shows how the transition between excitation and inhibition of their response is independent of light intensity. Where a patch of light fills its receptive field, P cells therefore carry information about its wavelength independently of its intensity, a property that is necessary for colour vision (see p.22).

The close similarity between the receptive fields of retinal ganglion cells and the LGN cells that they drive suggests that little further filtering takes place

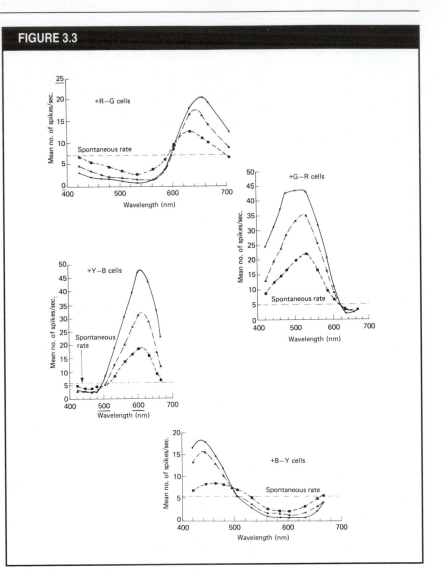

FIGURE 3.3

The relationship between wavelength of light and response for the four classes of P cell in the monkey LGN, each at three different levels of light intensity. The dashed lines show the cell's spontaneous firing rate in the absence of light stimulation. Reproduced from De Valois, Abramov, and Jacobs (1966), *Journal of the Optical Society of America, 56,* pp.966–977.

in the LGN, and that it acts as a relay between retina and visual cortex. However, it is important to note that axons also run from the visual cortex back to the LGN. This feedback may have some influence on the activity of the LGN that is not apparent in anaesthetised animals, and so the "relay" model may be wrong. We will return to this problem later when we discuss feedback pathways in the visual system (p.65).

The main focus of research on the LGN has been the remarkably strict segregation between M and P pathways, maintained from the retina straight through to the input to the visual cortex. Are the functions of the two pathways just as distinct? One influential theory was put forward by Livingstone and Hubel (1988), who argued that M and P cells are the first stages of a two-way division of function continuing much further through the visual system. They proposed that M cells are the first stage of a system responsible for extracting information from the changing optic array about the large-scale spatial layout of the surroundings and about movement, whereas P cells carry out the first steps in extracting information about colour and fine spatial structure. This theory was based in part on the receptive field properties of LGN cells, and particularly the colour-opponency of P cells and the higher contrast sensitivity of M cells. It was also based on experiments in human vision using "equiluminant" patterns, in which colour varies but luminance does not. The fact that it is often difficult to perceive motion or spatial structure in such patterns supports Livingstone and Hubel's (1988) theory, if it is assumed that equiluminant patterns stimulate only P and not M cells. However, there is controversy about whether this assumption is correct, and a review of the arguments can be found in Schiller and Logothetis (1990).

Another way of exploring the functions of M and P cells is to lesion the appropriate layers of the LGN and then test monkeys on a range of different visual tasks to determine which ones are impaired. Experiments of this kind have led to a rather different picture from that first suggested by the receptive field properties of single cells. Schiller, Logothetis, and Charles (1990) found that monkeys with a lesion of the P layers had clear deficits in a number of tasks when stimuli were presented in the affected part of the visual field; these included discriminations of colour, texture, fine shape, and pattern.

Contrary to Livingstone and Hubel's (1988) theory, however, lesions of the M layers did not interfere with the discrimination of large-scale spatial patterns, and tasks of this kind could be performed normally when the P layers alone were intact. Magnocellular lesions affected only the abilities to detect motion in a complex display, and to discriminate a rapidly flickering stimulus from a steady one. This deficit in flicker detection was later found to occur only with a relatively low-contrast stimulus (Merigan & Maunsell, 1993). A further problem for the theory came with evidence that magnocellular lesions do not abolish motion perception altogether, but only reduce the visibility of moving stimuli (Merigan, Byrne, & Maunsell, 1991).

Another important finding from these lesion experiments is that, in most circumstances, monkeys' thresholds for detecting contrast were affected by lesions of the P but not of the M layers (Merigan, Katz, & Maunsell, 1991; Schiller et al., 1990). This seems surprising, because we have seen that individual M cells have higher contrast

sensitivity than P cells. However, the results are consistent, and illustrate the risks involved in jumping from knowledge of single cell responses to conclusions about the functions of those cells in the visual system as a whole. There are about eight times as many P cells as M cells per unit area, and so it may be that the P cell *population* yields greater sensitivity than the M population, despite the lower sensitivity of individual cells. Information provided by M cells is presumably important in other contexts, such as the detection of moving low-contrast patterns.

Overall, the results of lesion experiments imply that the contribution of the P pathway to the visual control of behaviour is larger, and that of the M pathway is smaller, than Livingstone and Hubel's (1988) theory proposed. Broadly speaking, it seems that most visual tasks can be performed with little deficit when the P layers alone are intact, and that M cells have a specialised role in transmitting information about fast motion. This accounts for the transient responses and high-contrast sensitivity of M cells, their importance for the detection of low-contrast flicker, and the finding that lesions in the M layers only affect behavioural contrast sensitivity for fast-moving stimulus patterns (Merigan et al., 1991).

A more general message provided by these results is that we should be cautious about trying to identify the M and P pathways with *psychologically* distinct visual functions, as it seems that some of these functions can use information transmitted along both pathways. It is safer to describe the functions of cells at this level of the visual pathway in terms of the frequency characteristics of the temporal and spatial patterns that they transmit. The P pathway can be described as a channel carrying information about patterns of light at all spatial frequencies, but only at low to medium temporal frequencies, whereas the M pathway "fills in" by transmitting in a region of high temporal and low spatial frequencies (Derrington et al., 1984; Merigan & Maunsell, 1993). In addition, the nature of colour-opponency implies that the P pathway acts as a channel for transmitting information about luminance contrast at high spatial frequencies, and about wavelength (chromatic contrast) at low spatial frequencies.

THE STRIATE CORTEX

Like other regions of the cerebral cortex, the visual cortex is a folded sheet of neurons about 2mm thick. It has a distinctive striped appearance in cross-section, caused by the arrangement of cells in layers of different densities (see Fig. 3.4), and for this reason it is also known as the *striate* cortex. Below these layers is the white matter, made up of the axons which connect the striate cortex to other areas of the cortex, and to the LGN and other sub-cortical structures. The axons of LGN cells terminate at synapses with cortical cells in most layers, although their most abundant connections are in layer IVc, where M and P cells terminate in separate sub-layers, and in layers II and III, where interlaminar cells terminate. Cortical cells form a complex network in which fibres run both vertically between layers and horizontally within them (Lund, 1988), and both the number of different cell types, and the complexity of the connections between them, are much greater than in the retina.

The first recordings from single cells in the striate cortex were made in cats (Hubel & Wiesel, 1959, 1962), and the first results from monkeys were obtained by Hubel and Wiesel (1968). Some cells, including all those in layer IVc, have concentric fields similar to those in the LGN, but others have a quite different kind of receptive field organisation, in which elongated excitatory and inhibitory areas lie adjacent and parallel to each other. In some cells, there is just one excitatory and one inhibitory area, whereas in others there are three or more parallel antagonistic areas (see

FIGURE 3.4

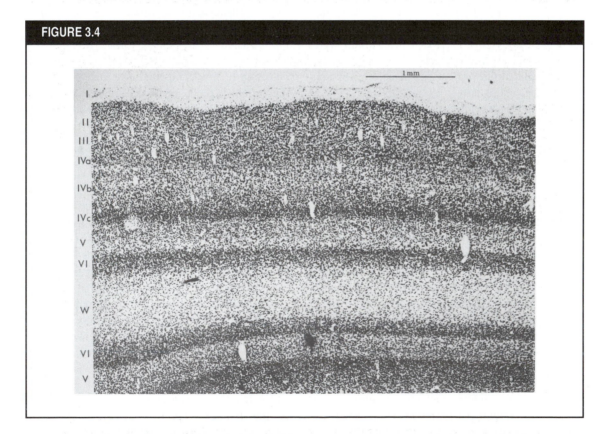

Section of monkey visual cortex stained to show cell bodies. The outer surface of the cortex is at the top, and the layers are numbered I to VI down to the white matter (W). The lowest layers of a fold of cortex can be seen below the white matter. Reproduced from Hubel and Wiesel (1977) with permission of The Royal Society.

Fig. 3.5). Hubel and Wiesel (1968) classified all these as *simple* cells. Like the X retinal ganglion cells of cats (see p.32), they perform a linear spatial summation of light intensity in their fields, and so are sensitive to the contrast and position (or phase) of a grating. Because of the elongated shape of their receptive fields, they also have a distinctive property absent in the retina or LGN: they respond most to a particular orientation of a bar, edge or grating (see Fig. 3.6). This *orientation preference* is quite narrow, and turning the stimulus through more than about 20° from the preferred orientation greatly reduces the cell's firing rate.

Simple cells have a variety of other properties. The majority are selective for wavelength (Thorell,

De Valois, & Albrecht, 1984), some having colour-opponent responses like those of P cells in the LGN. Others have more complex properties, such as "dual-opponency", in which different regions of the receptive field show opposite colour-opponent responses (e.g. +R–G in one region, +G–R in another) (Livingstone & Hubel, 1984; Michael, 1978, 1981; T'so & Gilbert, 1988). Simple cells respond weakly to stationary stimuli, and often have direction-selective responses to moving patterns. Finally, some show "end-inhibition", responding more strongly to a short bar or edge that ends within the receptive field than to a long one that extends across the whole field.

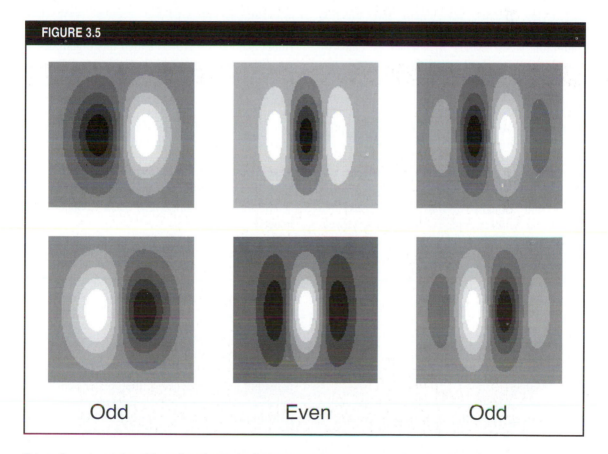

FIGURE 3.5

Odd   Even   Odd

Schematic representation of the variety of receptive field structures discovered for simple cells in the striate cortex. The number of excitatory (light) and inhibitory (dark) regions may be 2, 3, 4, or more, and the orientation of the field might be at any angle, not necessarily vertical. The receptive field may be symmetrical (even) or anti-symmetrical (odd), or may be asymmetrical (not shown). Receptive field size also varies widely from cell to cell, and increases greatly in peripheral vision. The somewhat idealised fields shown here are Gabor functions (discussed in the text, p.56; see also Glossary).

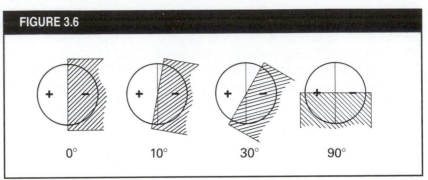

FIGURE 3.6

The orientation preference of a simple cell. A light–dark edge falling on the vertical boundary between excitatory and inhibitory areas evokes a strong response. As the edge is rotated, less of the excitatory and more of the inhibitory area is illuminated and the response is reduced.

Another group of cells in the striate cortex were classified by Hubel and Wiesel as *complex* cells. These have many properties in common with simple cells, including orientation preference and, to varying extents, wavelength and direction selectivity, and end inhibition (those showing end inhibition were termed *hypercomplex* cells by Hubel and Wiesel). The critical difference is that the receptive field of a complex cell cannot be marked out into excitatory and inhibitory regions, and a suitably oriented stimulus will elicit a response no matter where it lies in the receptive field. A complex cell can be most easily distinguished from a simple cell with a "drifting" grating, moving through the receptive field. The response of a simple cell will rise and fall as the peaks and troughs of the grating pass the boundaries between regions of the field, whereas the response of a complex cell remains at a steady high level (De Valois, Albrecht, & Thorell, 1982). Like the Y retinal ganglion cells of cats, complex cells therefore have marked nonlinearities in their responses. It should be stressed, however, that there is no simple correspondence between complex cells and those M cells in the LGN that have nonlinear responses; the large majority of complex cells are driven by both M and P cells, or by P cells alone (Malpeli, Schiller, & Colby, 1981).

This brief account of cells in the striate cortex has described only the main characteristics of simple and complex cells. Full descriptions of the many sub-types within each class can be found in Schiller, Finlay, and Volman (1976), and theories and physiological evidence about the cortical "wiring" responsible for these cells' responses is reviewed by Ferster and Koch (1987).

Functional architecture in the striate cortex

We have seen that the striate cortex is organised into layers, parallel to its surface, in which cells have different properties. It is also organised, in an astonishingly precise and regular way, into *columns* running at right angles to the surface. Hubel and Wiesel (1962) called this organisation the *functional architecture* of the cortex, and revealed it by relating the responses of single cells to their positions in the cortex, as reconstructed from electrode tracks. This technique was later supplemented by a range of methods for staining cells chemically according to their activity, or according to their connections with different parts of the LGN. More recently, optical methods have been developed that allow rapid changes in the activity of neurons in cortical tissue to be directly imaged.

The most basic feature of functional architecture is an orderly retinotopic mapping of the visual world onto the surface of the cortex, just like that in the laminae of the LGN, with the left and right halves of the visual field mapped onto the right and left cortices, respectively. The map is not metrically accurate, as the cortical area devoted to the central part of the visual field is proportionally much larger than that devoted to the periphery. This is mainly a consequence of the greater density of retinal ganglion cells in the central retina. As in the retina, the receptive fields of cells in the centre of the visual field are smaller than those of cells with peripheral fields.

In layer IVc of the cortex, where most axons from the LGN terminate, cells respond to a stimulus presented in one eye only, just as cells in the LGN do. In other layers, however, cells have *binocular fields*: they respond to their optimal stimulus if it is presented to either eye. Even so, they often respond more strongly to stimuli in one eye than in the other, and are said to show *ocular dominance*. Cells sharing the same ocular dominance are grouped together into bands, and these form an alternating pattern of right- and left-eye bands running across the cortex. As Fig. 3.7 illustrates, these can be made visible with appropriate staining techniques (LeVay, Hubel, & Wiesel, 1975). Note that there is a good deal of overlap in the receptive fields of nearby cortical cells, and so the pattern of ocular dominance columns does not imply that alternating stripes of visual space are represented in the cortex by input from only one eye.

A third feature of functional architecture was discovered by staining the striate cortex so as to reveal levels of the enzyme cytochrome oxidase (CO), which are greater in cells that are more metabolically active. This technique revealed a regular array of dark blobs of tissue rich in CO (Wong-Riley, 1979), visible most clearly in layers II and III, but absent in layer IV. There are many other biochemical differences between cells in these blobs and those in the "inter-blob" regions (see e.g. Edwards, Purpura, & Kaplan, 1995), and Horton and Hubel (1981) showed that the blobs are aligned along ocular dominance stripes (see Fig. 3.8).

Despite much research, it is not entirely clear whether blob and inter-blob cells have different roles in processing visual information. Livingstone and Hubel (1988) proposed that the functional separation they suggested between P and M pathways in the LGN (see p.46) continues in the striate cortex. They argued that the blob cells are part of a pathway processing colour information, whereas the inter-blob cells have a role in processing information about spatial structure and motion. Support for this model has been equivocal. The anatomical connections are not as specific as it would predict, as P cells connect to both blob and inter-blob cells, whereas M cell input is concentrated on the blobs (Edwards et al., 1995). Data from single-cell recordings provide some support for the model; Livingstone and Hubel (1984) reported that blob cells are selective for wavelength but not orientation, whereas inter-blob cells have the opposite properties. On the other hand, other researchers have not found this difference in wavelength selectivity (Lennie, Krauskopf, & Sclar 1990). Finally, a general problem in distinguishing the functions of blobs and inter-blob regions is that the boundaries between them are not distinct. Both the biochemistry of cells and their responses to visual stimuli vary smoothly between the two regions (Edwards et al., 1995).

A fourth aspect of functional architecture emerged when the orientation preferences of cells were related to their position. Hubel and Wiesel (1974, 1977) had found from single-cell recordings that the orientation preferences of cells changed

FIGURE 3.7

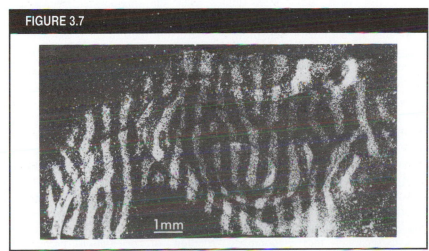

1mm

The pattern of ocular dominance columns in the visual cortex revealed as alternating light and dark bands by autoradiographic methods. Reproduced from Hubel and Wiesel (1977) with permission of The Royal Society.

FIGURE 3.8

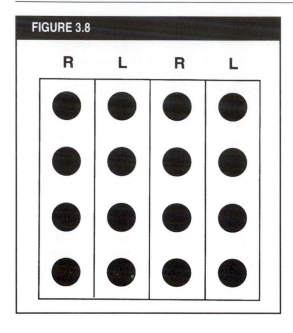

R   L   R   L

Schematic diagram of a small region of the surface of the visual cortex, showing alternating bands of right- and left-eye dominance, and CO blobs (dark circles) lying along them.

systematically, and linearly, with position across the cortex for distances of 0.5–1mm. After some distance, say 1mm, where cells had shown a systematic clockwise stepping of their orientation preferences, the sequence would reverse to anticlockwise. There were also discontinuities in this "sequence regularity", and regions of no orientation preference. Hubel and Wiesel therefore suggested that orientation-selective cells are organised in columns or "slabs", in which all cells have the same preferred orientation, and that adjacent slabs represent adjacent orientations. They also concluded that the orientation slabs tended to be at right angles to ocular dominance bands.

However, it is very difficult to derive a complete 2-D map of orientation preference from 1-D probes with a microelectrode. Much more powerful, direct evidence comes from recent studies by Blasdel and colleagues who used an optical imaging method to photograph directly the patterns of activation across a region of monkey cortex, in response to gratings of different orientations. By presenting stimuli to the left and right eyes separately they could relate the patterns of orientation preference to the structure of ocular dominance columns. Sophisticated image-processing methods were used to draw the underlying structures out of related sets of response images. In Fig. 3.9a we show a sample of results from Obermayer and Blasdel (1993). The heavy lines are the boundaries between left and right ocular dominance bands, and the lighter lines are iso-orientation contours. Along each of these contours the orientation preferences of cells should be constant (but recall that single cells are not recorded individually here). The iso-orientation contours radiate out from "singularities" that tend to lie along the centres of left and right eye bands; the contours then tend to run parallel to each other, cross the ocular dominance boundaries at right angles and converge to another singularity. A complete circuit around each singularity represents a rotation from 0° to 180° (not 0–360°), either clockwise or anticlockwise.

In Fig. 3.9b we offer a schematic view, which we think captures the major aspects of Blasdel's very extensive findings, and suggests some functional interpretations. The basic, repeating unit of structure is the set of iso-orientation contours radiating from each singularity. The radii bend around to meet their partners from the adjacent left (L) or right (R) eye band. At the ocular dominance border, then, we find the parallel "slabs" and sequence regularity described by Hubel and Wiesel, and the intersection of slabs and bands at right angles. Near the singularities (which are probably the centres of CO blobs) we find instead a "pinwheel" structure (described by Bartfeld & Grinvald, 1992). In order for orientations to match across the L/R border, the singularities must have opposite rotational signs (+ and −). Cells in the L/R border region tend to be driven by both eyes, and this pattern of organisation ensures that the two monocular inputs are well matched in orientation, a feature that is presumably important for stereoscopic vision (see Chapter 7). Sequence regularity requires at least two adjacent singularities of the same sign within L and R bands. As singularities are about 350mm apart (Obermayer & Blasdel, 1993), we can see why a complete rotation of orientation preference

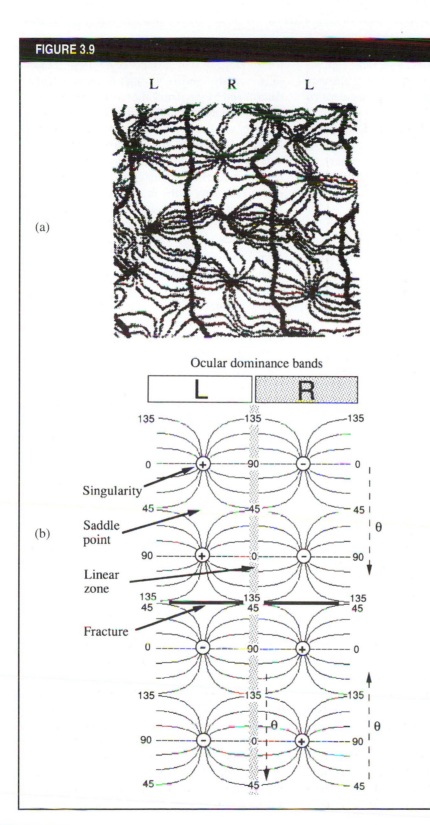

FIGURE 3.9

L R L

Ocular dominance bands

Singularity

Saddle point

Linear zone

Fracture

(a) Sample of results from Obermayer and Blasdel (1993) showing the relationship between ocular dominance bands and the organisation of orientation selectivity in the monkey's visual cortex. Heavy lines mark the boundary between bands of cortical tissue dominated by input from the left eye (L) and the right eye (R). These bands are about 0.5mm wide. Thinner lines are "iso-orientation contours". Along each contour, cells would have the same "preferred" or optimal orientation. Adjacent contours represent orientations 11.25° apart. Note how the contours tend to radiate from "singularities" lying along the centres of the L and R bands, but cross the L–R border at right angles. Adapted from Obermayer and Blasdel (1993), with permission of the Society for Neuroscience.

(b) Our schematic summary of Blasdel's findings (see a). Orientation rotates either clockwise (+) or anticlockwise (−) around each singularity, but the iso-orientation contours bend around to cross the L/R boundary in parallel bands. Orientation changes more slowly in the regions between two singularities of the same sign (saddle points), but changes very abruptly between singularities of opposite sign (fractures).

(0–180°) takes about 700mm in the "linear zone". Halfway between singularities of the same sign we meet a "saddle point" where orientation changes much more slowly. Halfway between singularities of opposite sign within an L or R band we meet a "fracture"—a discontinuity in sequence regularity. This whole pattern (Fig. 3.9b) suggests that both a radial arrangement and a linear arrangement of orientation preferences are important, possibly for different visual functions (see Blasdel, 1992, for further ideas).

Spatial filtering in the striate cortex

It is clear that a complex transformation of the input from the LGN takes place in the striate cortex, but what part does this transformation play in achieving the eventual goal of using information from light to control behaviour? Whereas the functions of retinal processing are relatively easy to understand, this is a much more difficult question, and we should say at the outset that the answers available are tentative and incomplete.

An early view of the function of the visual cortex (e.g. Barlow, 1972) was that it creates a representation of the visual world in terms of features, such as the edges and corners of objects. Simple and complex cells were regarded as feature detectors, each signalling the presence of a specific geometric feature by firing impulses. One problem with this theory, which we will discuss further in Chapter 5, is that detecting the edges and other features of natural objects in an image is a great deal more difficult than was first thought. Another problem, more relevant here, is that the firing rate of a simple or complex cell is determined by many parameters of the spatiotemporal pattern of light in its field, including contrast, phase, orientation, wavelength, and motion. The firing rate is therefore *not* a useful signal for the presence of a particular feature, such as an oriented edge or a corner. Instead, a cell in the striate cortex acts as a *filter* for multiple dimensions of the image falling in its receptive field (Van Essen, Anderson, & Felleman, 1992).

In this section, we will deal in more detail with just one aspect of the filtering function of striate cells: their role in filtering spatial patterns of light intensity. We saw in Chapter 2 (p.40) that retinal

ganglion cells respond to sinusoidal gratings over a wide range of spatial frequencies. Their response falls steeply above a high-frequency cut-off determined by the size of the receptive field centre, but is maintained at low frequencies because of the relative weakness of the surround component. Retinal ganglion cells therefore respond to a grating across a broad range of spatial frequencies, and this breadth can be measured by the *bandwidth* of the cell. This is the ratio of the frequencies at which half the maximum contrast sensitivity (see Ch. 2, p.36) is obtained, measured in octaves (Fig. 3.10). An octave is a doubling of frequency, e.g. from 2 to 4 cycles/degree (c/deg) or 4 to 8c/deg; 2 octaves is a quadrupling of frequency and so on. The bandwidths of LGN cells are typically 5 octaves or more.

Cells in the striate cortex have much narrower bandwidths, averaging 1.5 octaves, and so can be regarded as band-pass filters, sharply "tuned" to particular spatial frequencies. Furthermore, striate cells vary greatly in their spatial frequency tuning, the optimum frequency ranging from 2 to 8c/deg in the region corresponding to the foveal visual field (De Valois et al., 1982; see Fig. 3.11). The spatial frequency tuning of a cell is determined by both the size and number of receptive field regions or "lobes" (see Fig. 3.5). Smaller lobes yield a higher optimum frequency, whereas a greater number of lobes (of alternating sign) gives a narrower spatial frequency bandwidth.

These findings suggest that the visual cortex may be organised to analyse the spatial pattern of light in each of many small regions, or "patches", of the retinal image into its spatial frequency components. If so, then the firing rate of a cell provides a measure of the amplitude of the frequency component to which the cell is tuned, at its preferred orientation. The fact that there are cells with all combinations of spatial frequency and orientation-tuning further supports the theory that the striate cortex performs a "patch-wise" Fourier analysis of the retinal image, each patch being transformed by a small block of cortical tissue containing cells with overlapping receptive fields and a full range of frequency and orientation tunings (De Valois & De Valois, 1990; Robson, 1983).

FIGURE 3.10

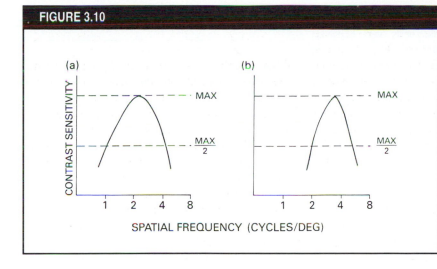

(a) (b)

CONTRAST SENSITIVITY

SPATIAL FREQUENCY (CYCLES/DEG)

Measurement of the selectivity of a cell for spatial frequency.
Cell (a) has peak sensitivity at 2.3 cycles/degree and a bandwidth of $\log_2 (4/1) = 2$ octaves.
Cell (b) has peak sensitivity at 3.2 cycles/degree and a bandwidth of $\log_2 (5/2) = 1.3$ octaves.

According to this theory, simple cells might represent a sub-system in which the phases of spatial frequency components are encoded, whereas complex cells represent a parallel sub-system in which absolute phase information is discarded, although relative phase could be preserved (recall that only simple cells have receptive fields with excitatory and inhibitory subregions, and so are selective for the phase of a grating). The information provided by simple cells could be used in tasks such as the precise location of objects, and the outputs of complex cells could be used for purposes such as the discrimination of different texture patterns.

There is some evidence that the blocks of cortex that transform each patch of the image may be centred on CO blobs. Blob cells are tuned to low spatial frequencies, whereas inter-blob regions contain cells that are tuned to a wider range of frequencies (Born & Tootell, 1991; Edwards et al., 1995; Tootell, Silverman, Hamilton, Switkes, & De Valois, 1988). A closer study of the relation between CO density and spatial frequency preference revealed some very close correlations (Silverman, Grosof, De Valois, & Elfar, 1989), suggesting that in moving from blob to inter-blob regions the preferred spatial frequency of cells increases systematically. We have already seen that on any single (curved) radius (Fig. 3.9b) preferred orientation is constant. There is therefore a strong possibility that blobs are the centres of blocks of cortex (see Fig. 3.9b) that serve to represent a Fourier-like transform of small patches of the retinal image (De Valois & De Valois, 1990).

FIGURE 3.11

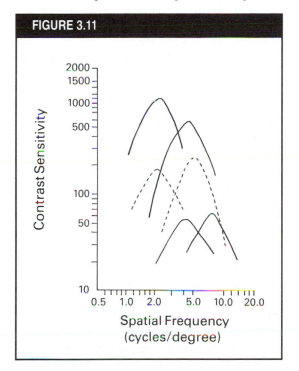

Contrast sensitivity of individual cells in the same region of visual cortex to sinusoidal gratings of different frequencies. Reproduced from De Valois et al. (1982) with kind permission from Elsevier Science Ltd., UK.

Jones and Palmer (1987) showed that the receptive fields of simple cells can be well described as *Gabor functions* (Fig. 3.5)—the product of a sine-wave multiplied by a smooth bell-shaped (Gaussian) envelope (although other mathematical descriptions can also be used). Making the Gaussian wider introduces more lobes into the receptive field, and makes it correlate better with a grating of a particular spatial frequency; in other words, the receptive field is more specifically tuned to that frequency. Thus, for a fixed frequency, the wider the spatial receptive field the narrower is its frequency bandwidth and vice-versa. There is an inevitable trade-off here between specificity for spatial location and for spatial frequency. To be perfectly location-specific, the receptive field should be the size of a single receptor, and to be perfectly frequency-specific it should be an extended sine wave. The Gabor function is a localised wave-packet that partly satisfies both these demands. Simple cell receptive fields thus approximate an optimum balance between the opposing demands of coding spatial frequency and spatial location. Shapley and Lennie (1985) review other evidence relevant to this issue, and suggest that approximately linear filtering is achieved by simple cells, in part through nonlinear mechanisms. We have already noted a similar possibility in the case of spatial summation in the retina (see p.35).

Further theoretical analysis by Field (1987) suggests that the 1.5 octave bandwidth of striate cells may represent an efficient visual coding strategy that exploits statistical redundancies present in natural images, and optimises the way in which image information is shared out across a range of filters tuned to different frequencies. However, our understanding of the significance of the patchwise Fourier transformation remains incomplete. Along with spatial frequency filtering, simple and complex cells also act as filters for other variables, such as colour, motion, and stereoscopic depth (see Ch. 7). This suggests we should view the striate cortex as an unspecialised, multidimensional filter that could provide parallel input to a number of other filters, each specialised for particular stimulus properties. We will see in the next section evidence that this may indeed be its role.

BEYOND THE STRIATE CORTEX

Many regions of the cerebral cortex surrounding the striate cortex also contain neurons that respond to visual input. Some of these "visual areas" in the *extrastriate* (or *prestriate*) cortex can be marked out straightforwardly, as they contain retinotopic maps of the visual field similar to that in striate cortex. In others, the map is partial, disorderly, or both, and so the identification of some areas and their boundaries is difficult (Van Essen, 1985), and a definitive list cannot be made. In the macaque monkey, there are at least 30 visual areas, covering a large region of the occipital, temporal, and parietal cortex (Fig. 3.12). The deep folding of the cortex means that some areas, lying within folds (or *sulci*), are not visible from the exterior.

The pattern of connections between these areas is by no means a simple chain from one area to the next. Instead, each area sends output to several others, and most if not all connections are matched by reciprocal connections running in the opposite direction. In all, there are more than 300 neural projections linking extrastriate visual areas, and almost all can be classified according to the cortical layers in which they arise and terminate as either ascending (leading away from the striate cortex) or descending (leading towards the striate cortex). When pathways are classified in this way, it is possible to organise visual areas into a hierarchical scheme, in which they are placed at different levels according to their distance from the striate cortex, or V1 (Maunsell & Newsome, 1987; see Fig. 3.13). As we will see later, this roughly hierarchical pattern of anatomical connections between visual areas is not necessarily matched by a clearly hierarchical mode of operation.

There is also evidence that extrastriate areas segregate into two main pathways after area V2. A "dorsal" pathway runs via V3 and V3A to the middle temporal area (MT, also known as V5), then to the medial superior temporal area (MST) and finally to area 7a in the parietal lobe, and a "ventral" pathway runs to V4, then to the posterior and anterior inferotemporal areas (PIT and AIT) in the temporal lobe. As Figure 3.13 shows, the segregation between these pathways is by no

FIGURE 3.12

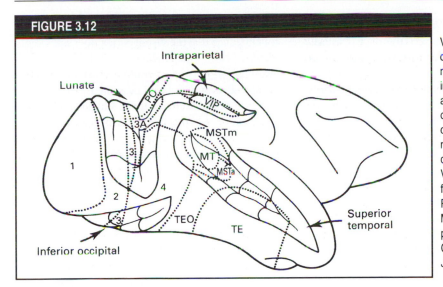

View of the right side of the cerebral cortex of a macaque monkey. The four sulci (folds in the cortex) marked with arrows have been opened out to reveal parts of the cortical surface that are normally hidden. Numbers denote visual areas V1, V2, V3, V3A, and V4. Redrawn from an original drawing by Professor A. Cowey, from Martin (1988) with the permission of Professor Cowey and Elsevier Trends Journals.

means clear-cut: there is a degree of overlap and interconnection between them, and some areas do not fit clearly into the scheme. Despite these complications, however, there are several sources of evidence for an underlying separation into two pathways. By tracing neural connections back from the posterior parietal and the inferior temporal cortex (the supposed destinations of the dorsal and ventral pathways), Baizer, Ungerleider, and Desimone (1991) found a striking segregation of the two sets of connections into different parts of extrastriate areas. A very different approach,

FIGURE 3.13

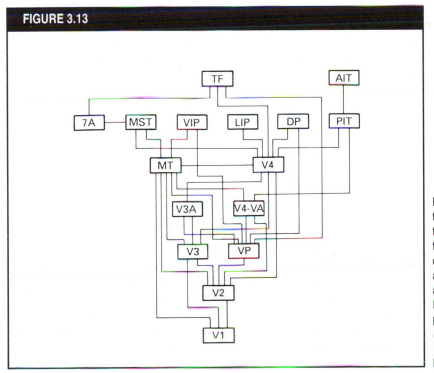

Extrastriate visual areas in the macaque monkey. Only the best-known areas, and the most prominent connections between them, are shown. From Maunsell and Newsome (1987). Reproduced, with permission, from the *Annual Review of Neuroscience, Vol.10.* © 1987, by Annual Reviews.

adopted by Young (1992), has been to analyse mathematically the connectivity of extrastriate areas, and this has also shown a distinct segregation into two systems.

Although a map of connections between areas, such as Fig. 3.13, suggests that the two pathways divide after V2, the internal structure of V1 and V2 reveals that the division can be traced further back, into V1 itself. When V2 is stained for cytochrome oxidase activity, a pattern of stripes appears, quite different from the blobs in V1. Dark, CO-rich stripes alternate with pale inter-stripes, and the dark stripes themselves are alternately thick and thin. The outputs of V1 blob and inter-blob cells to V2 are segregated, connecting to thin stripes and to inter-stripes, respectively (Livingstone & Hubel, 1983), whereas thick stripes receive input from layer 4B in V1. In turn, thin stripes and inter-stripes send output to V4, whereas the thick stripes connect to MT (DeYoe & Van Essen, 1985).

The organisation of connections through V1 and V2 to later areas shows that the division between dorsal and ventral pathways begins in V1 itself, albeit with some cross-connection between the pathways within V1 and V2, just as there are cross-connections between areas at later stages. Livingstone and Hubel (1988) took this evidence a stage further, arguing that the dorsal and ventral pathways are direct continuations of the subcortical M and P pathways, respectively. This model of two streams of visual processing remaining distinct from the retina straight through to extrastriate cortex has been influential, but is undoubtedly too simple. One difficulty is the evidence that M and P pathways merge in the visual cortex (p.50). Another is the effect of blocking activity in M and P layers of the LGN on responses of cells in V4. The model would predict that V4 activity would be reduced only when P layers are blocked, but Ferrera, Nealey, and Maunsell (1992) showed that blocks in both layers are equally effective. On the other hand, there is evidence that input to the dorsal pathway is largely from the M system, as the reduction in MT activity is much greater following blocks in M than in P layers (Maunsell, Nealey, & DePriest, 1990).

More evidence about the relationships between subcortical and cortical pathways is reviewed by

Merigan and Maunsell (1993), and the safest conclusion is that the visual cortex does not simply provide two independent conduits for visual information, but rather combines and reorganises M and P inputs into a new two-way division between dorsal and ventral pathways. Our next question is whether these two pathways have separate functions, extracting in parallel different kinds of information from the pattern of activity of striate cells. In the next section we will outline the physiological evidence relevant to this issue.

Separate functional pathways in the extrastriate cortex

Drawing on evidence from the effects of brain lesions on vision, Ungerleider and Mishkin (1982) proposed that high-level visual functions are carried out independently by two separate cortical systems. One system, in the parietal lobe, is responsible for extracting information about the spatial layout of the environment and about motion, and another, in the temporal lobe, extracts information about the form, colour, and identity of objects. Loosely speaking, the two systems are responsible for determining where an object is, and what it is, respectively.

Evidence in support of Ungerleider and Mishkin's (1982) theory has been obtained from people, using techniques such as positron emission tomography (PET), which allow the activity of the brain to be imaged in conscious subjects. Haxby et al. (1991) obtained PET scans while people performed either a spatial or a face-matching task. In both cases, activity in the occipital cortex increased relative to a control condition, but there were also differences between the two tasks. Activity increased in the temporal lobe during the face-matching task, but in the parietal lobe during the spatial task (Fig. 3.14). Similar results have also been obtained by Zeki et al. (1991) by comparing scans of subjects watching motion and colour displays.

Turning to evidence from monkeys, the pattern of connections between extrastriate areas is consistent with Ungerleider and Mishkin's (1982) hypothesis. Inputs to areas in the parietal cortex (in the dorsal pathway) arise from regions within

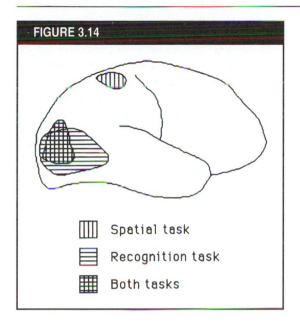

FIGURE 3.14

|||| Spatial task

≡ Recognition task

▦ Both tasks

View of the right side of a human brain, showing the areas in which cerebral blood flow increased during a spatial task and an object recognition task. Adapted from Haxby et al. (1991).

earlier extrastriate areas (such as V2), where cells have peripheral receptive fields, whereas inputs to the inferotemporal cortex (in the ventral pathway) come from regions representing the centre of the visual field (Baizer et al., 1991). These findings suggest that the ventral pathway has the role of analysing information obtained during the fixation of objects, whereas the dorsal pathway handles information about large-scale movements in the periphery of the visual field.

Functional specialisation of the dorsal and ventral pathways has also been examined by testing animals with lesions in extrastriate areas on various visually guided tasks. The evidence for specialisation of the dorsal pathway in motion processing is relatively clear-cut: lesions in MT cause specific deficits in motion perception while leaving pattern discrimination unaffected (Newsome & Paré, 1988). In the ventral pathway, V4 lesions do affect the ability to learn colour and pattern discriminations (e.g. Heywood & Cowey, 1987), but other findings suggest a more complex role for this area. Schiller and Lee (1991) found that monkeys trained to shift their gaze towards the

"odd" element in a display performed poorly after V4 lesions, but only if the odd element was less conspicuous than the others. This was so not only for size and brightness discrimination tasks, but also for a motion task. The implication is that V4 has a critical role in controlling attentional strategies, and is not only a stage in the processing of colour and shape. Supporting this interpretation, Baizer et al. (1991) found that V4 was one of only two extrastriate areas where connections from temporal and parietal cortex mix appreciably, suggesting that its function does not fit easily into the theory of two pathways.

Overall, the lack of experiments directly comparing V4- and MT-lesioned animals on the same visual task makes it hard to draw firm conclusions, but the lesion evidence for a specialised visual processing role in MT and the dorsal pathway is stronger than that for V4 and the ventral pathway. Using a different method, Salzman, Murasugi, Britten, and Newsome (1992) provide further evidence that MT is specialised for motion processing. They trained monkeys to discriminate the direction in which a patch of dots was moving, varying the difficulty of the task by mixing the dots with others moving in random directions. The display was placed so that its retinal image fell on the receptive fields of a group of neighbouring MT cells sharing the same preference for direction of motion. On some trials, these cells were electrically stimulated, and the result was a strong and consistent effect on behaviour: the monkeys were more likely to respond as if motion was in the direction to which the stimulated cells were sensitive. Their perception of motion appeared to have been shifted in a specific direction by increasing the cells' activity.

The responses of single cells in different extrastriate areas provide another source of information about functional differences. As we have seen, cells in V1 act as multidimensional filters, selective for many different stimulus parameters at once. If the dorsal and ventral extrastriate pathways have separate functions, then we would expect that single cells in them would be selective for fewer stimulus dimensions, and that cells in different areas would be selective for different dimensions.

There is some evidence for this kind of differentiation of single cell properties within V2. Wavelength-selective cells are most common in thin stripes and in inter-stripes, whereas orientation selectivity is most common in thick stripes, although these differences are only in relative numbers, and all cell types are found in all regions (DeYoe & Van Essen, 1985). At later stages, the evidence is that cells continue to be multidimensional in their selectivity. Cells in both MT (Malonek, Tootell, & Grinvald, 1994) and V4 (Desimone & Schein, 1987) are selective for orientation and most other parameters for which V1 cells are selective. There are differences in the relative numbers of different cell responses; direction selectivity is rare in V4 but common in MT, whereas the opposite is true for wavelength selectivity (Zeki, 1978). Even so, it is not clear just what the functional significance of such differences in the proportions of different responses might be.

Hierarchical processing in extrastriate pathways

Clearer evidence for functional specialisation of extrastriate areas has been obtained by looking not for specific restrictions in the stimulus dimensions to which cells are sensitive, but instead for increases in the complexity of the dimensions concerned. Imagine, for example, that we found an extrastriate area where cells were selective for wavelength, direction of motion, contrast, and so on, but also for complex properties of geometric patterns, such as the number of corners possessed by a shape. If we could establish that V1 cells were not selective for such properties, then we would have evidence that the area concerned was part of a pathway responsible for hierarchical processing of information about shape.

There is strong evidence that cells in MT and MST are selective for more complex properties of motion than just its direction, supporting the view that the dorsal pathway is specialised at least for motion processing. We will discuss the details of this evidence in Chapter 8 when we deal with the computation of motion in general, and for now will consider only the ventral pathway. One piece of evidence that the ventral pathway has a specialised

role in identifying objects is that the responses of cells become progressively less selective for the spatial location of a stimulus. Receptive field sizes in V4 are typically 30 times the area of those in V1, whereas in AIT they are up to 100 times larger. Fields of IT cells often extend across the right and left visual fields, and always include the foveal region. These findings are consistent with the hypothesis that the ventral pathway is specialised for identifying objects, without encoding information about their position in the visual field.

Two further properties of cells in V4 and IT have been studied extensively, and provide more evidence for hierarchical processing of colour and shape information. First, Zeki (1980) argued that cells in V4 have greater selectivity for wavelength than those in V1, and that their preferred wavelengths cover a wider range of the spectrum. Zeki's conclusion that further analysis of colour is carried out in V4 has been criticised, however, on the grounds that retinal ganglion cells have the same wavelength selectivity and distribution of preferred wavelengths as those in V4 (de Monasterio & Schein, 1982).

In further experiments, however, Zeki (1980) made the important discovery that some V4 cells show *colour constancy*. This term refers to the fact that we perceive a surface as having a constant colour despite changes in the spectral composition of light reflected from it. An everyday example of colour constancy occurs when we move from daylight into an artificially lit room. The composition of light from an electric bulb is markedly different from that of sunlight, and is relatively richer in long wavelengths. The same surface will therefore reflect more long wavelength light under a light bulb than in sunlight, and, if our perception of colour depended on wavelength alone, it would appear redder. In fact, the colour we perceive remains largely constant; a white sheet of paper, for example, does not appear orange indoors or bluish outdoors (note that colour constancy is not perfect, as those with a good eye for colour know when choosing clothes under artificial light).

A powerful demonstration of colour constancy is provided by experiments in which two surfaces reflect light of identical spectral composition but are seen as having different colours (Land, 1977). In a typical experiment, a patchwork display of differently coloured surfaces is illuminated by mixed light from projectors with red, blue, and green filters. The intensities of light from the three projectors are first adjusted to some arbitrary values—for example, so that the spectral composition of their mixed light falling on the display is equal to that of daylight—and the composition of light reflected from one surface, A, is measured. Now, by adjusting the intensities of the three projectors, it is possible to make the spectral composition of light reflected from another surface, B, equal to that reflected from A in the first stage. When this is done, B is *not* seen as having the same colour as A did in the first stage, as would be expected if perceived colour is determined by the spectral composition of reflected light alone. Further discussion of how the visual system might achieve this compensation for variation in ambient light, and more detailed descriptions of experiments, can be found in Land (1977) and Mollon (1982). For the moment, the important point is that the perception of colour depends on some kind of comparison between the spectral composition of the light at one point in an image and that of light in the surrounding area.

Returning to area V4, Zeki (1980) reported a number of cells that responded selectively to a surface of a particular colour, and that maintained this response as the spectral composition of light illuminating the surface changed. Under these circumstances, the composition of light falling in the cell's field changed, but its response, just like an observer's perception of colour, remained constant. Zeki (1983) compared the responses of cells in V1, and found no evidence of colour constancy; instead, all the cells studied were selective for wavelength alone. A possible explanation for this result is that the smaller receptive fields of V1 cells did not sample a sufficiently wide range of different colours in the patchwork display and therefore could not show colour constancy (Jacobs, 1986).

Zeki's findings demonstrate that some process takes place either in V1 or between V1 and V4 that converts wavelength-selective responses into ones selective for the more abstract property of perceived surface colour. Desimone and Schein (1987) suggest that the large "suppressive" surrounds of the fields of V4 cells are important in colour constancy. Stimulation of the surround alone has no effect on a cell's response, but a response to a colour or pattern stimulus in the field centre is suppressed if the same stimulus is present in the surround. It is possible that this could form part of the mechanism for making spectral comparisons that is required for colour constancy.

Another body of evidence for hierarchical organisation of the ventral pathway is provided by the finding that some cells in the inferotemporal (IT) area are selective for quite elaborate geometrical shapes. By systematically simplifying shape stimuli until a cell's response disappeared, Tanaka (1993) was able to identify the "minimum" shape for a cell's response, and to show that cells sensitive to similar shapes are grouped together in columns in IT.

Another approach to studying shape selectivity in IT has been to use complex, natural images as stimuli and to determine what variations in them affect a cell's response. For example, Perrett, Rolls, and Caan (1982) found that 10% of a sample of IT cells showed a preference for *faces*, of either people or monkeys. These were defined as cells that responded more than twice as vigorously to faces than to any of a wide variety of other simple or complex stimuli. Perrett et al. (1982) found that the responses of these cells were unaffected by transformations of faces that do not affect their recognition by people, such as changes in distance or colour, although their responses were reduced if faces were turned from a front to a profile view. The cells were also selective for the spatial configuration of features making up a face, giving weaker responses to scrambled photographs of facial features. Further work (Perrett et al., 1986), has shown that some cells are selective for the *identity* of faces, responding most strongly to the faces of specific individual monkeys or people, or for the *view* from which a face is seen (see Ch. 16, p.343).

There is no doubt that these IT cells are selective for more abstract properties than are V1 cells, and that hierarchical processing is taking place in the ventral extrastriate pathway. However, do these cells act as "face detectors" of the kind that Barlow (1972) argued might be found at higher levels in visual pathways? Does a monkey possess a single IT cell for each monkey or person it knows, and does activity of that cell uniquely signal the presence of that monkey or person? There are two reasons why we cannot draw these conclusions. First, the same face excites many cells, meaning that its presence is not signalled by a unique cell. Second, the same cell is excited by more than one face, and so its activity does not uniquely specify a particular face. Although some cells discriminate more sharply between faces than do others (Baylis, Rolls, & Leonard, 1985; see Fig. 3.15), none is known to respond only to a single face.

This evidence implies that recognition of a face is coded not by a single cell but by a specific *pattern* of activity in a *population* of cells. Further analysis of face-selective cells in IT suggests that a fairly small population of cells may be sufficient to generate a pattern of activity coding uniquely for a particular face (Young & Yamane, 1992). In Chapter 10, we will return to this concept of population-coding, and discuss theoretical models in which the recognition of complex objects is based on the distributed activity of many simple units.

RECENT DEVELOPMENTS

So far in this chapter we have discussed a range of problems in interpreting how visual pathways in the primate brain function, and we have compared different points of view on such questions as the functions of M and P pathways, the role of CO blobs, and the extent of parallel processing in the extrastriate cortex. Throughout we have taken for granted three widely held assumptions about the principles by which the visual pathway is organised.

The first assumption is that properties of the spatiotemporal pattern of light reaching the eye are coded in the activities of single cells, measured as the average rate of firing of impulses over some short period (on the scale of hundreds of milliseconds). If this is so, then the functions of single cells can be deduced by measuring their average firing rates while stimulus parameters are varied.

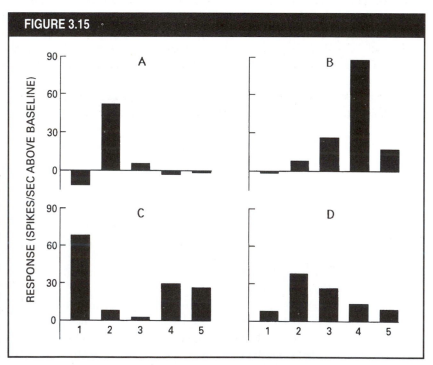

FIGURE 3.15

The responses of four different face-selective cells (A–D) in the inferotemporal cortex to five different face stimuli (1–5). Cell A is strongly selective for face 2. Cells B and C are selective for faces 4 and 1, respectively, but less strongly. Cell D shows weak selectivity between faces. Adapted from Baylis et al. (1985).

The second assumption is that the activities of single cells code *local* properties of the pattern of light (except in IT and other high-level extrastriate areas). This seems an obvious implication of the existence of relatively small, stable, and clearly defined receptive fields.

Third, the various pathways between the retina and high-level extrastriate areas are assumed to be one-way channels, carrying out a sequence of transformations of patterns of neural activity, in which the pattern of activity at each stage is determined by the one before. A more general assumption underlying this one is that the visual pathway can be treated as a separate "module" of the brain, operating independently to deliver one (or perhaps several) representations of the surrounding world, which are then used to control the animal's actions.

In this last section, we will describe some recent findings that challenge all three of these assumptions, and which suggest that we may still have much to learn about the fundamental principles by which the visual pathway works.

How do single cells code information?

The assumption that the nervous system codes information about the world only in terms of the average firing rates of single cells has recently been questioned. Could it be that the fine temporal pattern of impulses fired by a cell, smoothed out when average firing rates are measured, contains important variables? In particular, could the *rhythmic* pattern with which many neurons fire be significant? In area 17 of the cat cortex (which is similar physiologically to the striate cortex of monkeys), the firing rate of cells oscillates with a rhythm of 40–60Hz, and there is some evidence that this rhythm is important for the coding of visual information.

Gray, König, Engel, and Singer (1989) found that firing rhythms of area 17 cells were more strongly synchronised the closer the cells' receptive fields were to one another, and the more similar their orientation preferences were. They then recorded from pairs of cells with the same orientation preference and with "co-linear" receptive fields (see Fig. 3.16). When the cells were stimulated with bars moving in opposite directions, firing was not synchronised, but with bars moving in the same direction, there was weak synchronisation (Fig. 3.16a,b). However, a single bar extending across both receptive fields elicited strong synchronisation (Fig. 3.16c). The striking feature of these results is that, in the second and third conditions, the patterns of light within the two receptive fields are identical, and it is the global pattern of light across a wider area that is responsible for the stronger synchronisation.

The results obtained by Gray et al. (1989) suggest that synchronisation of rhythms of firing

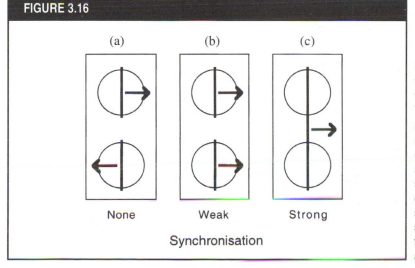

FIGURE 3.16

(a)   (b)   (c)

None   Weak   Strong

Synchronisation

Synchronisation of rhythms of firing in V1 cells. The receptive fields of two cells are shown. The fields are nearby but not adjacent, and both cells respond strongly to a vertical bar. The degree of synchronisation is shown when vertical bars are swept through the fields in opposite directions (a) and in the same direction (b), and when a single bar is swept across both fields (c). Adapted from Gray et al. (1989).

in cells at different points in the cortex may be a means of coding for the presence of large-scale patterns of light, which are too extended spatially to be coded in the activity of single cells with restricted receptive fields. Such a mechanism could explain an important feature of visual perception that we will discuss in detail in Chapter 6: the visual system rapidly and "automatically" groups together in a pattern small elements that are similar in properties such as orientation, and so separates out objects from their backgrounds. Perhaps synchronisation of cell activity at early stages in the visual system is the process responsible for this grouping of image elements.

The evidence for synchronisation of neural activity within V1 has been taken up and extended by Tononi, Sporns, and Edelman (1992) in an ambitious model of cortical processing of visual information, in which signals within and between different extrastriate areas act to synchronise and bind together processing of different aspects of an image, such as colour, shape, and motion, so as to form a coherent percept. There is some evidence for this kind of neural synchronisation between separate cortical areas: Bressler, Coppola, and Nakamura (1993) found an increase in coherence between neural activity in the striate and motor cortex at specific phases in the performance of a discrimination task. On the other hand, failures to replicate results such as Gray et al.'s (1989) in monkeys have been reported (Bair, Koch, Newsome, & Britten, 1994; Young, Tanaka, & Yamane, 1992), and the latter authors also question the statistical basis of some of the conclusions from cats. The significance of synchronisation of rhythmic firing for visual processes remains an open question, and a review of experiments on the topic can be found in Singer and Gray (1995).

Dynamic cell assemblies

By demonstrating that the activity of cortical cells is influenced by stimuli lying outside the receptive field (see Fig. 3.16c), Gray et al.'s (1989) results also challenge the classical view that the receptive fields of cells in visual areas are stable and clearly defined. There is considerable evidence from other experiments for effects of this kind, quite independently of any evidence for synchronisation of firing; we have already seen one example in the "periphery effect" in retinal ganglion cells (p.34). In the visual cortex, the responses of cells to an oriented bar are often altered when a second bar is projected into nearby areas, outside the receptive field. The effect may be to increase or reduce the cell's response, or to alter its orientation preference (Gilbert & Wiesel, 1990). Note that this is not a case of centre-surround antagonism like that in the LGN, as the stimulus outside the receptive field has no inhibitory effect on firing by the cell when presented alone. Instead, it is more akin to the effects of the suppressive surrounds of V4 cells (Desimone & Schein, 1987).

It is likely that effects of this kind are caused by long-range horizontal connections within the visual cortex, extending much further than the width of a receptive field and specifically linking cells with similar ocular dominance and orientation preference (Malach, Amir, Harel, & Grinvald, 1993). Interactions between cells through these connections may cause large-scale "ensembles" or "assemblies" of cortical cells to emerge and re-form in continually changing patterns, as the pattern of input from the LGN changes. Using optical methods for visualising neural activity, Grinvald, Lieke, Frostig, and Hildesheim (1994) have shown that stimulation with a moving grating of a small site in V1, 1° square, is followed within 200msec by spreading of neural activity over distances much greater than predicted from receptive field sizes. The neural interactions that cause this large region to be activated appear to be "invisible" to conventional single-cell recording techniques

By blocking LGN input to a small region of visual cortex, Gilbert and Wiesel (1992) obtained further evidence for the dynamic formation of cell assemblies. They found that the receptive fields of cells surrounding the affected area immediately increased in size. As these changes occur within minutes, they cannot be the result of new growth of neural connections, and the implication is that cortical receptive fields are not a stable property of local patterns of neural connections, but emerge from dynamic interactions between cells over wide areas.

Whether cell assemblies in visual areas form and dissolve through changes in synchronisation of firing rhythms, or through some other mechanism, it is certainly possible that they are involved in analysing large-scale structure in patterns of light. Evidence supporting this hypothesis has been obtained by testing orientation-selective cells with elongated bars to which they are sensitive, but which have a gap corresponding to the cell's receptive field. Consequently, bars are only actually present on either side of the field, and are co-linear. In both V1 (Grosof, Shapley, & Hawken, 1993) and V2 (von der Heydt, Peterhans, & Baumgartner, 1984), cells respond as if the bar passed through the receptive field (cf. the discussion of "illusory contours" in Chapter 5, p.96). The rapid formation, over a wide region of cortex, of an assembly of active cells sharing the same orientation preference provides an explanation for these findings.

Feedback effects in visual pathways

Are the various pathways between retina and extrastriate visual areas one-way channels for the processing of visual information? We have already seen that, beyond the LGN, almost all neural connections between visual areas are matched by reciprocal "feedback" connections. What is the function of these feedback connections, and does their existence imply that "one-way" models of visual processing are incorrect? There is evidence that the feedback loop between V1 and the LGN operates in a positive fashion to increase the gain of cell responses, and to "lock the system on" to particular spatial patterns of light. Sillito, Jones, Gerstein, and West (1994) found that the correlation of responses of pairs of LGN cells was greater when they were stimulated by a drifting grating, extending over both receptive fields, than by separate stimuli, even though the pattern of light in both cells' fields was identical. This effect disappeared if feedback from V1 was blocked, implying that feedback boosts the activity of those LGN cells that drive a common set of V1 cells, and so in turns strengthens the response in V1. Essentially, the suggestion is that a dynamic cell assembly emerges, which is extended over two

"stages" in the pathway rather than being confined to a single one.

If all feedback connections worked in this way, then the concept of one-way processing channels through the visual system would not be seriously affected. It could still be argued that new properties of single cell responses are generated at each stage, and that the role of feedback is only to enhance or modulate these responses. However, there is evidence that "feedback" connections may have more significant effects than this model can accommodate. Mignard and Malpeli (1991) showed that the orientation preference of cells in layers 2 and 3 of V1 is not affected by blocking LGN input, and that connections from V2 are responsible for maintaining it. If orientation selectivity can be derived equally well from either LGN or V2 input, then what grounds are there for describing one input as "feedforward" and the other as "feedback"?

There is also older evidence difficult to reconcile with a role for V1 as a straightforward input channel to cortical visual pathways. The responses of many simple and complex cells in area 17 of the cat are influenced by nonvisual stimuli, including the location of a sound source (Fishman & Michael, 1973) or the angle of tilt of the animal's body (Horn & Hill, 1969). This selectivity for dimensions of auditory and vestibular stimulation must rely on other inputs besides those from the LGN.

Finally, single-cell recordings in V4 and IT, made while monkeys perform visual tasks, provide further important evidence on this issue. If the ventral extrastriate pathway works sequentially to transform the pattern of light on the retina into some abstract representation of the identities of objects in the visual field, then we would not expect an animal's behavioural state (apart from head and eye movements) to affect the responses of cells. In fact, powerful effects of this kind have been found, and we will describe two examples to illustrate.

Moran and Desimone (1985) asked whether the responses of V4 cells were affected by changes in animals' attentional state. For each cell, they first determined the boundaries of the receptive field and then the stimuli to which the cell responded. Both an effective and an ineffective stimulus were then presented together at different locations within the receptive field. If the monkey had previously been trained to attend to the location of the effective stimulus in order to detect a signal of some reward, the cell responded strongly. If, however, it had been trained to attend to the location of the ineffective stimulus, the response was much weaker, even though the pattern of light falling in the receptive field was identical in the two conditions. As Moran and Desimone put it, it was "almost as if the receptive field had contracted around the attended stimulus". About half of V4 cells showed this kind of attentional control.

In area AIT, many cells have properties suggesting that they are involved in memory processes. Miller, Li, and Desimone (1993) gave monkeys a task in which a "sample" picture was flashed in the field of an AIT cell (recall that these fields are very large). After a delay, the same picture was presented, accompanied by another, and the correct response was to shift gaze towards the picture matching the sample. During the delay period, Miller et al. (1993) tested the responses of cells to various pictures. In about half the cells tested, the response that would normally be observed to a picture was suppressed if that picture was the sample. In other words, the response was not just to a particular visual pattern, but to that pattern if it was unexpected in the context of the task.

Many other results demonstrating these attention and memory effects in the ventral pathway have been reported (for a review and theoretical interpretation, see Desimone & Duncan, 1995). They clearly imply that extrastriate pathways do not function independently of other brain processes to deliver a representation of the visual world, but that their operation, beyond the earliest stages, is strongly influenced by processes responsible for attention, memory, and the organisation of behaviour. Presumably these influences rely in part on the feedback connections between extrastriate areas. As we discuss in later chapters, there is much psychological evidence to show that a perceiver's expectations and knowledge influence perception, and so there must be an interaction between such information and that from the retina at some stage in the brain.

CONCLUSIONS

We have now given a brief sketch of current knowledge of the structure and function of those regions of the primate brain known to be involved in analysing the pattern of light falling on the retina. The organisation of some individual areas, such as V1, is becoming clear, although recent findings, such as the dynamic properties of receptive fields, have provided surprises along the way. However, it is fair to conclude that the general principles by which the extrastriate visual pathways are organised remain mysterious. Although there is good evidence for a degree of independent parallel analysis of different attributes of the changing retinal image, we cannot safely assume that these pathways are organised as sequential stages leading to some abstract, central representation of the visual world. On the other hand, we do not yet have a satisfactory set of principles to replace this model. In the remaining chapters, we will turn to the analysis of the mechanisms responsible for visual perception using evidence from behaviour and conscious experience.

Part II

Processing Retinal Images

4

Approaches to the Psychology
of Visual Perception

In Part I of this book we introduced you to some of the developments and theories that have emerged from the study of the neurophysiology of vision. The study of the neurophysiological level has uncovered some important properties of cells in the visual pathway, but a proper understanding of the jobs that these cells are doing requires that we consider the process of visual perception at a different, more "computational" level. This was an argument put most forcefully by Marr (1976, 1982) whose work will be discussed extensively within this section.

Marr argued that three different levels of theory must be distinguished if we are to understand a complex information-processing task such as visual perception. For any process (and vision consists of very many processes), we should first formulate a *computational* theory, which describes what is being computed and why. Next we may consider the *algorithms* for achieving the computation, and the *representations* that form the input to and output from these algorithms. Finally we may describe the *implementation* of the algorithm, whether in neural tissue or in a computer. In this part of the book we turn to the level of computational theory, representation, and

algorithm in order to understand better the problems and processes of visual perception. These higher levels of theory are essential to make sense of some of the physiological findings we encountered earlier, and to allow us to explore aspects of perception where neural mechanisms are as yet unknown. It is to the psychology, rather than the physiology, of vision that we must now turn.

In this part of the book we consider how the perception and recognition of three-dimensional objects might be achieved as a result of the processing of one or more retinal images. The retinal image has been seen in almost all accounts of visual perception as the input on which later processes operate. We are thus primarily concerned with those findings and theories that have emerged within this "traditional" approach to visual perception. The focus of much of this research has been on human perception, and this is undoubtedly due at least in part to the historical underpinnings of psychology in philosophy of mind. Before embarking on the details of the topics in this section, we feel we should outline very briefly how such theories of visual perception have evolved.

It is only relatively recently that a separate science of "psychology" has emerged. During the

17th and 18th centuries, scholars interested in natural philosophy made discoveries about light and eyes, and discussed epistemological issues in ways that were to colour subsequent thinking about visual perception well into this century. On the physical side, an understanding of image-formation by lenses, and the observation by Descartes of a retinal image formed on the back of a bull's eye, led to a long-standing belief that the eye functions much like a camera (or camera obscura in the days of da Vinci and Kepler), and that the starting point for vision is an image. However, it was obvious that the images produced by cameras and by eyes are clearly lacking in many of the qualities that we perceive in the world. Images are flat, static, and meaningless. Visual perception reveals a solid, mobile, and meaningful world. It seemed that perception must therefore involve processes that go beyond the information present in the image. On the philosophical side, the empiricists such as Locke (1690) and Berkeley (1709) argued that perception was somehow constructed from more primitive sensations through a process of learning through association. Although nativist philosophies were also voiced, in which knowledge of the entities of "space", or "time" were considered inborn, or divinely given, it is probably not too much of an overgeneralisation to say that it is the empiricist tradition that has dominated modern thinking in psychology. We will not delve here into the controversy between the "nativists" and the "empiricists", but simply agree with Boring (1942, p.233) that:

No simple exposition of this great and largely fruitless controversy can, however, be adequate to its complexities. For one thing, almost every protagonist turns out, whatever he was called, to have been both nativist and empiricist. Everyone believed that the organism brought something congenitally to the solution of the problem of space; everyone believed that the organisation of space may be altered or developed in experience.

The dominant empiricist position in the 19th century led to the attempted analysis (often using introspective methods) of perceptions into their component sensations by the structuralists, and considerable debate about which elements or attributes should be considered as fundamental (see Boring, 1942). By analysing elementary sensations it was hoped that ultimately the complexities of human thought could be unravelled, as all complex ideas must ultimately have been derived through sensory experience. The mechanisms whereby perceptions were constructed from sensations, through reference to knowledge previously acquired through learning, were also discussed, most notably by Helmholtz (1866), whose idea of perception involving unconscious inference or conclusions is still echoed by contemporary theorists (e.g. Gregory, 1973, 1980). Compare their statements:

… such objects are always imagined as being present in the field of vision as would have to be there in order to produce the same impression on the nervous mechanism … The psychic activities that lead us to infer that there in front of us at a certain place there is a certain object of a certain character, are generally not conscious activities, but unconscious ones. In their result they are equivalent to a *conclusion* … (Helmholtz, 1866, trans. 1925, pp.2–4).

… we may think of sensory stimulation as providing *data* for *hypotheses* concerning the state of the external world. The selected hypotheses, following this view, are perceptions (Gregory, 1973, pp.61–63).

Thus a view of perception as indirect and inferential persists today, although the methods used to study vision have become more sophisticated, and some rather different ideas about perception have been voiced in the years between Helmholtz and Gregory. We will mention some of these landmarks in method and theory very briefly.

Towards the end of the 19th century, the content of perception was commonly studied using the methods of analytic introspection—although Fechner's psychophysical methods (1860) saw the beginning of a more "objective" way to study the senses. However, introspectionist methods were largely abandoned in the United States, following J.B. Watson's lead in 1912. Watson put forward his case for behaviourism (Watson, 1913, 1924), in which mentalistic notions such as "sensations" and "perceptions" were replaced by objectively observable "discriminative responses". The behaviourists argued that we can never know how animals, or other people, experience the world, and hence should only observe their behaviour, to examine how their responses are related to variations in the stimuli presented. Ironically, although classical behaviourism provided the methodological tools for the comparative study of perception, it considered it illegitimate to explain any observed differences in the perceptual capabilities of different species in terms of internal processes. The methods of contemporary psychology are still influenced by the behaviourist tradition, although students of perception, on the whole, now regard subjects' verbal reports of their perceptual experience as legitimate "responses" to be recorded and analysed.

At much the same time as Watson was developing behaviourism, the European Gestalt psychologists reacted against the structuralist assumptions that perception could be reduced to sensations. They retained an introspective, although phenomenological approach. They were nativist in philosophy, maintaining that perceptual experience was the result of certain dynamic field forces within the brain. We discuss Gestalt ideas further in Chapter 6.

Gestaltists apart, most other movements in the psychology of perception have been empiricist in flavour, and most have implicitly or explicitly assumed that perception should be regarded as some process of interpretation or construction from the incomplete information provided by the retinal image. Two movements, closely related to each other, that emphasised such complexities of human perception flourished transiently during the 1940s and 1950s. The first of these, "transactional functionalism" (Kilpatrick, 1952), rested on the demonstrations of Ames (Ittelson, 1952). Ames' displays included a trapezoidal window that looked rectangular, a collection of sticks that could be seen as a chair, and perhaps best known, a curiously constructed room, which (when viewed statically and monocularly) appeared room-shaped but did strange things to the apparent sizes of people standing or walking within it (see Fig. 4.1).

FIGURE 4.1

The Ames room. The room is perceived as being of conventional shape, with right-angled corners and rectangular windows. The people standing inside the room appear to be of very odd sizes. In fact, it is the room that is oddly shaped—the people are both of normal height. Photograph copyright © Eastern County Newspapers Ltd.

Such demonstrations were used to illustrate the apparently infinite number of objects that could give rise to any single retinal image, and to emphasise the probabilistic and inferential nature of seeing. What one sees will be what one expects to see, given one's lifetime of perceptual experience. Whereas transactional functionalism stressed the individual's history as important in determining his or her perception, the "new look" (e.g. Bruner & Goodman, 1947) stressed the importance of individual differences in motivation, emotion, and personality in influencing what the person might see. Cantril (in Wittreich, 1959) for example claimed that one observer, whose husband walked across the Ames room, persisted in seeing him remain constant in size, whereas the stranger accompanying him shrank or grew. Wittreich confirmed this observation with some of the married couples he tested.

During the 1960s, associationist explanations of perceptual learning and discriminative responding gave way to a new "cognitive psychology" of perception, attention, and memory. Attempts were made to describe the stages that intervened between stimulus and response. The revolution in information technology provided a new metaphor for psychology, in which information from the senses was seen to be processed in ways not unlike the processing of information in a computer. Processes of sensory coding, storage, and retrieval of information were all discussed, and the development of computer models of some of these processes was seen to be a legitimate goal of psychological theorising. If a machine could be designed that could "see", its computer program could constitute the implementation of a theory of how seeing is achieved by humans. (See Boden, 1987, or Garnham, 1987, for introductions to the field of artificial intelligence [AI]). Marr's (1982) theory represents perhaps the most sophisticated attempt yet to explain the information-processing operations involved in vision within a framework that cuts across the boundaries between physiology, psychology, and artificial intelligence.

In this very cursory discussion of the history of visual perception there has been one notable omission. We have mentioned theories that have taken an "impoverished" retinal image as the starting point for perceptual processing. In Part III of this book we describe a quite different—controversial—theory, which was first proposed by J.J. Gibson (1950a, 1966, 1979). This theory suggests that the "input" to a perceptual system is structure in the entire optic array, and trans-formations over time in that structure. Gibson denies that perception involves construction, interpretation, or representation, and his theory thus stands apart from those that we have mentioned here. (Although, paradoxically one can draw some parallels between some of Gibson's ideas and those of both the Gestaltists and the behaviourists—two diametrically opposed schools. We shall have more to say about this in Chapter 11.) In this part of the book, however, we are concerned to explore how far we can explain the perceptual accomplishments of people and animals when these perceptual activities *are* seen as the end-products of the processing of retinal images. This is the mainstream of theories of visual perception, and we defer any challenge to it for the moment.

A unifying principle in the psychology of visual perception has been that unless the perceiver makes assumptions about the physical world that gave rise to a particular retinal image, perception just is not possible. The only dispute has been over how specific such assumptions need to be. For some contemporary theorists, these assumptions are thought to be quite specific and may be learned through an individual's lifetime experience—for example the assumption that windows or rooms are rectangular. For others, the assumptions may be more general and hard-wired (that is, built into the central nervous system and not dependent on learning), such as the assumption that similarly oriented texture elements should be grouped together (see Chapter 6). Many theorists have argued that perceptual parsimony is achieved (at the cost of occasional error or illusion) by making use of specific world knowledge to infer, from sensory data, what it is that gave rise to those data. Thus tentative "object hypotheses", obtained by accessing stored information in memory, may constrain and guide the interpretation of incoming sensory data. Such perceptual theories may be described as involving a strong "top-down" or "conceptually driven" component. Many AI models of perception fall into this category and some of these will be discussed in Chapters 6, 7, and 9. Other models (e.g. Marr, 1976) have been developed largely along "bottom-up" or "data-driven" lines. In such theories very general constraints are incorporated within each stage of information-processing, but specific world knowledge is only employed in the act of seeing when relatively low-level stages of information-processing produce ambiguous results. One of Marr's many achievements is his demonstration that a great deal of the processing of images can be achieved without recourse to specific world knowledge (e.g. Marr, 1976).

OVERVIEW OF MARR'S THEORY OF VISION

In each of the chapters that follow in this part, we describe some of the ideas that have been important historically, including a description of Marr's theory of the topic under discussion. Of those theories that have emerged within the "information-processing" tradition, Marr's is the most compatible with our aim to account for animal, as well as human, perception. Although his aim has been to provide a theory that may be applicable to human perception, and hence he relies at least in part on human psychophysical evidence to support his statements, he stresses that the same kind of analysis could be applied to visual perception in other species. Most importantly, his level of "computational theory" demands that we always consider what is being computed from light, and why. Ecological as well as physiological considerations would allow us to tailor a theory in the spirit of Marr to the beast in question (Marr, 1982, p.32).

> Vision, in short, is used in such a bewildering variety of ways that the visual systems of different animals must differ significantly from one another. Can the type of formulation that I have been advocating, in terms of representations and processes, possibly prove adequate for them all? I think

so. The general point here is that because vision is used by different animals for such a wide variety of purposes, it is inconceivable that all seeing animals use the same representations; each can confidently be expected to use one or more representations that are nicely tailored to the owner's purpose.

Because Marr's theory is of some importance to this section of the book, but appears dotted around the different chapters contained here (which also discuss the work of people other than Marr), we take this opportunity to provide a brief summary of the important points that he makes.

An image, the input for visual processing, represents intensity over a huge array of different locations. This array of intensity values is created by the way in which light is reflected by the physical structures that the observer is viewing, and focused by the observer's eye (see Chapter 1). The goal of early visual processing is to create from the image a description of those structures—the shapes of surfaces and objects, their orientations and distances from the viewer. This is achieved by constructing a number of distinct representations from the intensity values in the image. The first representation is the *primal sketch*. The primal sketch describes the intensity changes present in the image and makes more global structures explicit. The first stage in this process is to locate discontinuities in light intensity because such "edges" will often coincide with important boundaries in the visual scene. In Chapter 5 we describe how a description of all these intensity changes, the *raw primal sketch*, is formed. The raw primal sketch consists of a set of statements about the edges and blobs present, their locations, orientations, and so on. From this complex and rather messy representation, larger structures— boundaries and regions—can be found through the application of grouping procedures. This more refined description is known as the *full primal sketch*, and in Chapter 6 we describe how it can be derived.

The full primal sketch captures many of the contours and textures within an image, but a description of an image is only one aspect of early visual processing, where the goal is to describe surfaces and shapes relative to the viewer. Marr sees the culmination of early visual processing as a *viewer-centred* representation, which he calls the $2\frac{1}{2}$-D sketch. This is obtained by an analysis of depth and motion and shading, as well as the structures assembled in the primal sketch. We describe some of the processes that contribute to the formation of the $2\frac{1}{2}$-D sketch in Chapter 7. The analysis of image motion plays a role in these processes, and in Chapter 8 we describe the advances made since Marr's work in understanding motion processing.

The $2\frac{1}{2}$-D sketch describes the layout of structures in the world from a particular vantage point. We need such a representation to guide any action we may need to take, whether simple eye movement or complicated locomotion. However, a further, and equally essential, aspect of vision is the recognition of objects. In order to recognise what object a particular shape corresponds to, a third representational level is needed—one centred on the object, rather than on the viewer. This third level Marr terms the *3-D model representations*, and these we describe in Chapter 9. It is at the stage of formation of the 3-D model representations that a stored set of object descriptions is contacted. As far as possible, previous stages of visual processing proceed in a bottom-up fashion, making use of general constraints rather than any specific object "hypotheses."

Thus Marr's theory involves a number of distinct levels of representation, each of which is a symbolic description of some aspect of the information carried within the retinal image. A variety of different processes have been proposed by Marr and recent advocates of his philosophy to transform one representation to another, and we describe some of these processes in the chapters that follow.

Marr's theory sees vision as proceeding by the explicit computation of a set of symbolic descriptions of the image. Object recognition, for example, is achieved when one of the descriptions derived from an image matches one that has been stored as a representation of a particular, known object class. Recently, there has been increasing interest in a rather different kind of computational model, in which "concepts" are represented as activities distributed over many elementary processing units. Such connectionist models provide convenient ways of implementing certain kinds of algorithm. We conclude this part of the book by introducing connectionist models and describing how they have been applied to problems of depth perception and object recognition.

5

Images, Filters, and Features: The Primal Sketch

In this chapter we consider the early stages of visual processing, the nature of the initial representations built from a retinal image, and the algorithms that produce them. In Chapter 1 we explained how light provides information about the visual world, through the relationship between the spatial structure of the optic array and surrounding surfaces and objects. A promising starting point for processing the retinal image, which is a projection of the optic array, is therefore to create a representation of it that makes its spatial structure explicit, specifying where the most significant changes occur in the intensity and spectral composition of light. Note that we are making a simplifying assumption here, treating the retinal image as static and ignoring change in its structure over time caused by movement of the perceiver or of objects. In later chapters, we will return to the question of how motion in a retinal image can be processed and represented.

Light, surfaces, and vision

Clearly there is a relationship between the places in an image where light intensity and spectral composition change, and the places in the surroundings where one surface or object ends and another begins, but this relationship is by no means a simple one. We cannot assume that every intensity or spectral change in an image specifies the edge of an object or surface in the world. Although the edges of objects do give rise to intensity and spectral changes in an image of a scene, these changes will also arise for a host of other reasons, for example where the edge of a shadow is cast on a surface by another object. Clearly when referring to "edges" we must take care to indicate whether we are referring to features of the scene or the image of it. These are two separate domains, and the formidable task of vision is to derive a description of the former from the latter.

Intensity changes also arise from variations in the angle between the surface and the direction of incident light. The intensity of reflected light is at a maximum if the surface faces towards the light source, and falls as it turns away. For an ideal, diffuse Lambertian surface the luminance (L) of the surface is proportional to the cosine of the angle (θ) between the direction of illumination and the surface normal, and is independent of the viewing direction or viewing distance. Thus:

$$L = I.R.\cos(\theta)$$

where I is the intensity of illumination and R is the reflectance, a fixed property of the material itself that indicates the proportion of incident light that is reflected. (See Nayar & Oren, 1995, for an interesting discussion of the physics of surface reflection, and why the moon looks flat.) As we saw in Chapter 1 (p.5), reflectance generally varies with wavelength, but most of our discussion here centres on spatial variations in image intensity (luminance), leaving aside spectral variations.

The simple equation for image luminance given above tells us a great deal about the problem of vision. Three different aspects of the visual world (lighting, surface material, surface orientation) are confounded in one variable, luminance. Mathematics tells us that it is impossible to solve an equation to recover three unknowns (I, R, θ) with only one given (L), yet that is the task apparently faced by the visual system. It is tempting to appeal for help from additional variables such as colour, motion, or binocular vision, but as human observers cope very well with single, stationary, black-and-white photographs it is clear that in some sense vision does achieve the impossible. It can only do so by applying plausible assumptions or "constraints" that reduce the ambiguity inherent in the optical image of a scene. In situations where these assumptions are incorrect we suffer illusions (but see also Morgan, 1996).

WHAT IS AN IMAGE ?

We have seen that image luminance varies with variations in illumination, such as those caused by dappled lighting, and with variations in surface orientation, which occur over curved surfaces or at creases, bumps, and folds in a surface. The *luminance profile* of an image (Fig. 5.1A,B) thus has a complex waveform across space, not unlike a sound wave. Furthermore, almost all natural surfaces are textured (see Ch.1, p.5), and so give rise to complex local variations in intensity and spectral composition within small regions of the image.

The complex relationship between natural surfaces and the intensity of light reflected from them is illustrated in Fig. 5.1A,B, which shows the intensity of light measured along a line across a natural image. Figure 5.1C,D illustrates the full, two-dimensional variation, as a "landscape" whose peaks and valleys are the highs and lows of image intensity. The contour map (E) is also a useful plot of the intensity variation. Where contour lines bunch together the intensity is varying most steeply across space, and this may define the locations of edges, as we shall see later. Notice that intensity varies in a complex fashion everywhere—within the face, and within the background. The boundary between head and background is not particularly special or salient in the luminance profile. In Fig. 5.1, or almost any natural image, the changes in light intensity and spectral composition associated with the edges of objects are embedded in a mass of changes caused by surface texture, surface shape, shadows, and the layout of light sources. A fuller discussion of all these factors can be found in Watt (1988, Chapter 1 & 1991, Chapter 3), but the implication for present purposes is that there is no simple correspondence between the edges of objects in a natural scene and the intensity changes in an image.

THE PRIMAL SKETCH

Recent theories have recognised the complexity of the relationship between the structure of natural scenes and the structure of images, and have proposed that the task of describing the structure of the image must come before the task of interpreting the image in terms of objects and events in the world. The first task (image description) has been broken down into two main stages. The first stage is to make local changes in light intensity explicit, in a representation that Marr (1982) terms the primal sketch. This name was introduced in the context of a particular model described by Marr and Hildreth (1980), but has come to be used generically to refer to the early stage of feature representation in vision. In the second stage of Marr's scheme, larger structures and regions are

FIGURE 5.1

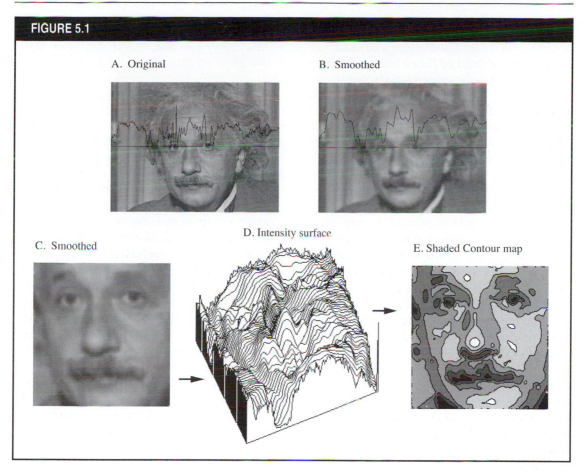

A. Original

B. Smoothed

C. Smoothed

D. Intensity surface

E. Shaded Contour map

Images—the raw data for vision. (A) The complex distribution of intensity across an image is shown by the graph superimposed; it plots the intensity values along the horizontal line through the eyes. (B) As A, after a smoothing operation has been applied to the image. In general, an image (C) has a complicated variation of intensity that can be visualised as a surface (D) or as a contour map (E). How is spatial structure found in this elaborate "landscape" of intensity?

identified by other algorithms taking the primal sketch as their input, and we consider this further in Chapter 6. This approach has the advantage that the information about intensity changes in the primal sketch can also be used as input for other processes working in parallel that compute depth and motion in the retinal image. These are described in Chapters 7 and 8.

Before we consider particular algorithms, it is important to make clear what task they are required to perform. They must take as their input a *grey-level* representation of the retinal image and transform it into an output that describes local image features—the primal sketch. A grey-level

representation of the image is obtained by measuring light intensity in each of a large number of small regions of the image, called *pixels* (from picture elements). This representation is therefore simply a two-dimensional array of light intensity values, of the kind illustrated in Fig. 5.1. Such an input representation corresponds to that available to the visual pathway, with each pixel and its associated intensity value corresponding to a photoreceptor and its receptor potential.

The primal sketch must specify where in the image significant changes in intensity occur, and what those changes are like. To do this requires a computational theory of what is to be computed, coupled to a model of how this computation is to be carried out. In the last 25 years a large number of algorithms has been published for edge detection in computer vision; for general introductions to this topic see Jain, Kasturi, and Schunk (1995), Schalkoff (1989), or Winston (1984). We shall describe and compare several of the more enduring ones, and those that have received most attention as models for human visual processing.

Algorithms for edge detection

The work of Marr and Hildreth (1980) was important and influential because it combined a well-motivated computational theory about what is to be detected with an implementation that was plausible in terms of known physiology and psychophysics. The key idea was this: edges in an image are those points at which the luminance is changing most steeply across space. Note that this is a theory that defines what an edge is, rather than an empirical fact about images. If we consider a simple one-dimensional intensity profile I(x), then the steepness of the profile at any given point is the *first derivative* or *gradient*, dI/dx. It can be approximated by the difference (δI) in intensity between adjacent pixels, divided by their separation (δx). That is, δI/δx approximates the true derivative dI/dx. If dI/dx is positive, the luminance at that point is increasing from left to right; if negative, it is decreasing. Now, Marr and Hildreth's theory (like others before it) states that edges are to be found at gradient peaks. This could be done directly by scanning through the values of dI/dx to find those that are larger than their neighbours on either side. Alternatively, a standard method of elementary calculus is to consider slope values again. At a peak the slope is zero, and so to find peaks in dI/dx we can look for zeros in *its* derivative. The derivative of dI/dx is d^2I/dx^2, the second derivative of the image luminance I(x), meaning that we apply the derivative operation twice in succession. In summary (Marr & Hildreth, 1980, p.192):

> Wherever an intensity change occurs, there will be a corresponding peak in the first

directional derivative, or equivalently, a zero-crossing in the second derivative of intensity.

Effective exploitation of this principle has to face several important difficulties. First, images are two-dimensional, not one-dimensional, so that edges may occur at any orientation. Second, images are noisy, containing unwanted or irrelevant variations that are exaggerated by derivative operations. Third, edges exist at a variety of spatial scales, from large (blurred edges) to small (sharp edges). For blurred, large-scale edges the gradient is shallow and local differences become very small and unreliable.

The problem of edge orientation is illustrated in Fig. 5.2B, which shows the result of taking the partial derivative ($\partial I/\partial x$) of an image (A) in a horizontal direction. Peaks of gradient (light bands in Fig. 5.2B) capture vertical and near-vertical, dark-to-light edges quite nicely, and conversely the dark bands mark vertical light-to-dark edges. Note, however, that horizontal edges (e.g. on the collar) are missed by this ($\partial/\partial x$) operator. A 1-D operator is not sufficient for a 2-D image. An obvious, standard solution is to take derivatives in two or more directions (e.g. $\partial/\partial x$ and $\partial/\partial y$) and combine the results. This is quite compatible with the variety of orientation-specific cells found in visual cortex and with some recent psychophysical evidence (Georgeson, 1992) but an efficient simplification was introduced into Marr and Hildreth's (1980) model by combining these multiple orientations into one circular filter. Recall that peaks in dI/dx are just those places where the values of the 2nd derivative d^2I/dx^2 pass through zero, i.e. *zero-crossings*. Marr and Hildreth's operator simply summed two operators at right angles to each other, to form what is known as the Laplacian operator, ∇^2 (pronounced "del-squared", defined as $\partial^2/\partial x^2 + \partial^2/\partial y^2$). It is a nonoriented, 2nd derivative operator.

Gaussian smoothing (G) is required to combat noise, and so when combined with the Laplacian the final operator can be expressed as: $\nabla^2 G$ or ($\partial^2 G/\partial x^2 + \partial^2 G/\partial y^2$), the Laplacian-of-Gaussian

FIGURE 5.2

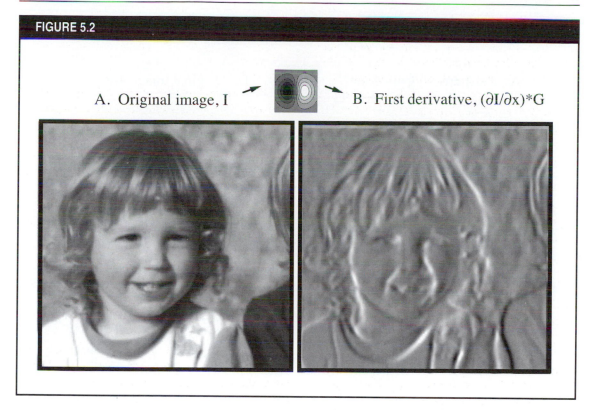

A. Original image, I → → B. First derivative, $(\partial I/\partial x)*G$

Edges and gradients in images. (A) Original image. (B) Filtered image that highlights the places that have a steep gradient in a horizontal direction. Light points have a steep positive gradient; dark points have a steep negative gradient. Notice how these points are associated with vertical or near-vertical edges in the original. The filter's receptive field (inset, enlarged × 4) combined two operations—smoothing by a Gaussian filter (G) and differentiation (d/dx).

(LoG) operator. The receptive field of the LoG operator is shown inset in Fig. 5.3, and it has a circular, centre-surround form analogous to the receptive fields of retinal ganglion cells (see Ch.2, p.30), LGN cells, and some cells in the input layers of V1 (see Ch.3, p.48). The pattern of zero-crossing (ZC) locations produced by this filter is shown in Fig 5.3A, and is seen superimposed on the original image in Fig. 5.3B.

Although the ZC pattern produced by this filter does capture much of the edge structure of the image, it is clearly not perfect. Some ZCs seem to wander off course, terminate too soon, or miss fine structure that is visible to the eye. Such a ZC pattern is only a starting point for a more comprehensive theory of edge representation. Perhaps the main limitation in our example is that the filter had a

single, fixed size. This means that it will average out smaller details that we actually wish to preserve, and will be unreliable for much larger, blurred features that present the receptive field with a shallow gradient and hence a very weak signal.

Marr and Hildreth's (1980) proposed solution to these limitations, inspired by the evidence for multiple filters in human vision ("spatial frequency channels", discussed further later, see pp.84–86), was to incorporate several filter sizes operating on the image at the same time. Figure 5.4 shows Einstein's face filtered through circular, LoG filters of four different sizes, each differing from the next by a factor of two in width. The receptive fields used are shown to scale, attached to each image. Note how the image information is de-composed, and distributed across the four scales. The coarsest

FIGURE 5.3

A. Zero-crossings in 2nd derivative, $(\partial^2 I/\partial x^2 + \partial^2 I/\partial y^2)*G$

B. Original image + ZCs

(A) illustrates Marr and Hildreth's principle for edge detection, using the circular "Mexican-hat" receptive field (Laplacian-of-Gaussian, LoG). This image marks zero-crossings (ZCs) in the 2nd derivative of the original (Fig. 5.2A) after smoothing. These ZC points are associated with steep gradients in any direction. (B) ZCs are superimposed on the original image, to illustrate the association between ZCs and edges.

scale captures the broad contrasts between different image regions, while smoothing out all fine detail. The reverse is true for the smallest scale, where only fine, local contrasts are preserved. Larger regions are reduced to a mean grey value, implying little or no response from the filter. Information is not lost, however, but distributed across scales. The image formed by averaging across the four scales (adding the four image intensities, pixel by pixel, and dividing by four) is very similar to the original. In other words, the spatial frequency content of the original image is split into four adjacent, overlapping bands, and when these bands are summed together the original image can be reconstructed.

In the Marr–Hildreth model, zero-crossings (ZCs) are extracted separately for each filter size (Fig. 5.5), and we should think of the ZCs only as candidate edges. Whether a ZC location is written into the primal sketch as an edge segment depends on the relation between ZCs at adjacent scales. The *spatial coincidence assumption* proposed that an edge existed in the image only if ZCs at the same position and orientation existed in at least two filters of adjacent sizes. Figure 5.5 reveals that the number and density of ZCs increases with the fineness of the filter. At each scale there will therefore be many ZCs that are not supported by partners in the next larger scale, but may be supported by those at a finer scale. This proposal, however, was never fully elaborated or tested, and the problem of combining information across spatial scales remains a difficult one for all approaches to edge detection.

The primal sketch is proposed as a symbolic representation of the image in terms of four different tokens—edge-segments, bars, terminations and blobs—denoting four different kinds of

FIGURE 5.4

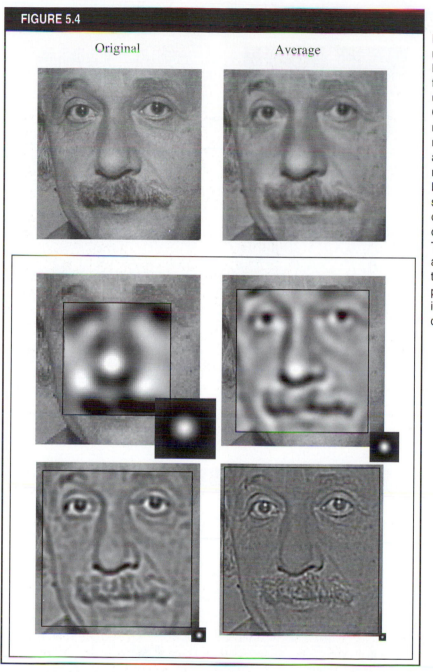

Original

Average

Example of spatial filtering at multiple spatial scales. Top left: Original image. Below: four filtered images obtained using circular, Laplacian-of-Gaussian, centre-surround receptive fields. The receptive fields, shown attached to each image, ranged from large to small. Note that the filter output is shown only within the black outlines. Top right: average of the four filtered images. The similarity between this and the original image shows that multiscale filtering can preserve all the image information, even though any one scale does not.

intensity change, illustrated in Fig. 5.6. These basic elements of the primal sketch are derived by grouping and combining the ZCs. For example, edge segments are found by examining the coincidence of ZCs across filter scales (as just described) and bars are found where there are nearby, parallel edge segments of opposite polarity. Blobs are asserted where ZCs form small closed contours. As the example in Fig. 5.6 shows, this "raw" primal sketch does not selectively pick out the outlines of objects, as the tokens also represent texture elements and markings within surfaces. In

FIGURE 5.5

The results of passing an image (upper left) through $\nabla^2 G$ filters of three different widths. Upper right, lower left and lower right: zero-crossings obtained with a narrow, an intermediate, and a wide filter. Reproduced from Marr and Hildreth (1980) with permission of The Royal Society.

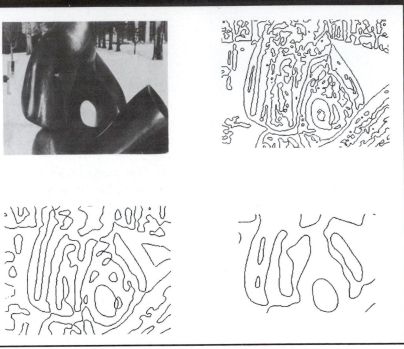

FIGURE 5.6

The zero-crossings obtained from a picture of a plant behind a wire mesh fence, using (a) a narrow and (b) a wide $\nabla^2 G$ filter. These are combined to give the raw primal sketch; the locations of blobs, edge segments, and bars are shown in (c), (d), and (e). Reproduced from Marr and Hildreth (1980) with permission of The Royal Society.

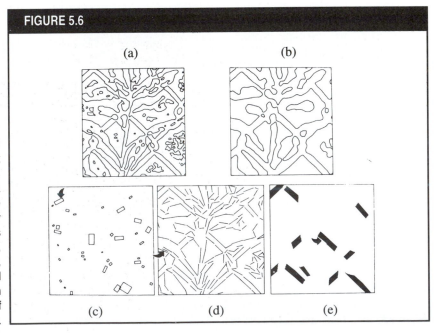

Chapter 6 we describe Marr's proposals for further grouping algorithms that take the raw primal sketch as input and recover the boundaries of objects. The aim at this first stage is just to extract from a noisy image a symbolic representation of the significant gradients of light intensity.

Implementation: Derivative operators as spatial filters

Marr and Hildreth (1980) argued that the first stage of computing the primal sketch is carried out in the visual pathway from retina to striate cortex, and that the role of simple cells is to measure the positions, strengths, and orientations of zero-crossing segments. Simple cells do not detect edges, as the feature detection theory held (see Ch.3, p.54), but instead measure parameters from which the locations of edges can later be obtained. According to Marr and Hildreth, the known properties of the visual cortex take us only to an early stage in visual perception—the computation of oriented zero-crossing segments (Fig. 5.7). How these are combined into the primal sketch by the nervous system is not known, although cells with "end-inhibition" (Ch.3, p.49, discussed further later) may be involved in the detection of terminations and blobs.

It is worth noting that derivative operations can be equivalently described in terms of spatial filtering by receptive fields. The inset in Fig. 5.2 shows (enlarged ×4) a map of the receptive field used in filtering A to produce B. Canny (1986) proved mathematically that to detect a step edge (a simple light–dark edge) reliably in a noisy image the optimal filter is very like the one shown in Fig. 5.2. The adjacent positive and negative regions effect a local differencing operation, while the size of each region serves to smooth the image somewhat by local averaging of pixel values. The receptive field, which is quite like that of many simple cells in the visual cortex (see Ch.3, pp.48–49), thus carries out two operations—differentiation and smoothing. Smoothing works by replacing each pixel value by a weighted average of pixels in that neighbourhood, thus reducing fine, local variations (noise). If the weighting of adjacent pixels drops away smoothly with distance, according to a bell-shaped Gaussian function (G), this is known as Gaussian smoothing, or Gaussian blurring. The receptive field that combines Gaussian smoothing with differentiation is thus a *Gaussian derivative operator*, $\partial G/\partial x$. The idea that cortical simple cells act as 1st, 2nd, and higher Gaussian derivative operators has received close attention from Koenderink and van Doorn (1987) and Young (1985, 1987; Young & Lesperance, 1993). Interestingly, Young (1985) has shown that $\partial G/\partial x$ operators can be approximated rather well

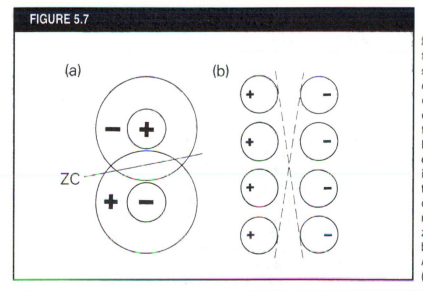

FIGURE 5.7

(a) (b)

ZC

Marr and Hildreth's scheme for the detection of zero-crossing segments by cortical simple cells. In (a) the fields of an on-centre and an off-centre LGN cell overlap. If both are active, then a zero-crossing ZC must lie between them, and an AND gate connected to them would detect it. In (b) an AND gate connected to parallel rows of on- and off-centre cells (field surrounds not shown) will detect a zero-crossing segment falling between the dashed lines. Adapted from Marr and Hildreth (1980).

by subtracting one Gaussian from an adjacent one, rather as in the model of Fig. 2.9, but offset from each other by as much as 1–2 standard deviations. These "difference of offset Gaussian" (DOOG) functions are not only convenient to implement in computer programs, but would also be a simple and robust way for biological systems to carry out calculus operations, even with higher-order (2nd, 3rd, 4th ...) derivatives. The next section looks more closely at the evidence for these cortical filters, and their role in spatial vision.

MULTIPLE SPATIAL FILTERS

A central feature of Marr and Hildreth's theory is its use of 2nd derivative operators at several spatial scales. Thus it assigns a functional role to cells in the visual cortex tuned to a range of different spatial frequencies (De Valois et al., 1982; see Ch.3, pp.54–56). Coarse-scale filters, with large receptive fields, respond selectively to low spatial frequencies, whereas fine-scale filters (with small receptive fields) respond to high spatial frequencies. As well as this physiological evidence, studies of the ability of observers to detect low-contrast gratings and other spatial patterns also imply that there are multiple spatial frequency-tuned filters in the human visual system.

Sub-threshold summation

Campbell and Robson (1968) and Graham and Nachmias (1971) discovered that contrast thresholds for detection of compound gratings (composed of two sinusoidal gratings with spatial frequencies f and 3f, e.g. 3 and 9 cycles/degree) were almost the same as those for the detection of the components presented individually. These studies at very low contrast suggested that visual input is processed in multiple, independent channels, each analysing a different band of spatial frequencies. The basic rationale of *sub-threshold summation* is that if adding two patterns together improves sensitivity then the two patterns must be summing their effects in a common channel or filter; if not, they must be passing through separate channels. Actually, the visibility of a two-

component pattern may be slightly higher than a single grating, because when two channels are weakly stimulated the observer has two chances to detect a channel response, rather than one. The same would be true if a weak stimulus were presented twice instead of once. This small improvement is known as *probability summation*. The visibility of a compound pattern whose two components differ widely in spatial frequency or orientation is no better than would be expected by probability summation alone. Thus, for the combination of gratings of 3 and 9c/deg, or of 0° and 90° orientations, the data favoured independent detection by separate filters.

More recent evidence suggests that at higher contrasts the channels interact with each other (e.g. through mutual inhibition) more than one would suspect from threshold studies. Thus, although spatial filters in human vision are probably not entirely independent, there is wide agreement that multiple spatial filters exist. For a very full treatment of this research, consult Graham's (1989) monograph.

Contrast adaptation and masking

Spatial frequency channels have been analysed in detail by measuring contrast thresholds for detecting sinusoidal gratings before and after exposure to gratings of higher contrast (Blakemore & Campbell, 1969). If an observer views a high-contrast grating at a spatial frequency of (say) 5c/deg for 5 minutes, then the ability to see a low-contrast 5c/deg grating is much reduced for a few minutes afterwards. The process resulting in temporary loss of sensitivity is termed *contrast adaptation*. It is quite distinct from local adaptation to the mean light level (light adaptation), because eye movements or pattern movements sufficient to average out local light adaptation do not eliminate the observed contrast adaptation (Jones & Tulunay-Keesey, 1980; Kelly & Burbeck, 1980).

Testing the same observer with a grating of 10c/deg or 2c/deg after adaptation to 5c/deg would produce little or no change in sensitivity, showing that adaptation is specific, or "tuned", to spatial frequency. The bandwidth of the tuning curves is about 1.4 octaves (Georgeson & Harris, 1984), the same as the median bandwidth of cortical cells

(Ch.3, p.55), but the bandwidth of both adaptation and cortical cells decreases systematically with increasing spatial frequency (Fig. 5.8). Adaptation is also tuned to orientation, producing little effect when the adapting and test patterns are more than 30–45° apart in orientation (Movshon & Blakemore, 1973; Snowden, 1992). Finally, if the adapting stimulus is given to one eye and then the other eye is tested, loss of sensitivity still occurs in the same "tuned" fashion but its strength is reduced by about 30% (Bjorklund & Magnussen, 1981; Blakemore & Campbell, 1969). Adaptation is therefore occurring at binocular site(s) in the visual system. This whole cluster of results compellingly argues that contrast adaptation, and the oriented spatial frequency filters implied by it, reside in primary visual cortex, V1.

Analogous reductions of contrast sensitivity occur if the test grating is masked by a superimposed, higher-contrast, masking pattern. Many of the properties of masking turn out to be similar to those of adaptation (Foley & Boynton, 1993; Georgeson & Georgeson, 1987). Wilson et al. (1983; also Wilson, 1983) have interpreted the spatial frequency tuning of masking in a model with six independent channels tuned to different spatial frequency bands, with peak sensitivities

ranging from 0.7 to 15c/deg (Fig. 5.9). Note that six is the minimum number of filters required to account for the masking data. There may be more and, given the huge number of cells in the visual cortex, it may even be reasonable to think of a continuum of filters spanning the visible range of spatial frequencies.

Filter bandwidths and spatial derivatives

The bandwidths of spatial filters derived from contrast adaptation and masking, and from monkey V1 cells, are compared in Fig. 5.8. The agreement is remarkably good. It is evident that filters tuned to high spatial frequencies are *more specific* to their preferred spatial frequency, and so presumably have a greater number of alternating positive and negative lobes within their receptive fields (see Ch.3, p.56). De Valois, Thorell, and Albrecht (1985) obtained direct evidence for this by measuring both the bandwidth of cat and monkey V1 cells and the number of cycles of a grating that produced the cells' greatest response. For simple cells, those with broad bandwidth (1.2 to 2 octaves) were most activated by rather few bars (1–2 cycles of a grating at the optimal frequency), whereas narrow-band cells (0.5 to 1.1 octaves) preferred to have many more bars in their receptive fields,

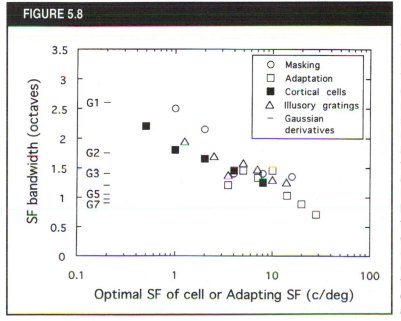

FIGURE 5.8

Estimates of the tuning of spatial frequency filters (expressed as bandwidth, in octaves) obtained from single-cell recordings in striate cortex (De Valois et al., 1982; solid squares) and from psychophysical studies of contrast adaptation and masking (open symbols). The single-cell data are averages, and the wide spread of values around each mean value is not shown. Horizontal dashes (left) mark the bandwidth of Gaussian derivative filters, from 1st (G1) to 7th (G7) derivative. Illusory grating data (open triangles) are from Georgeson (1980); masking data (open circles) from Wilson et al. (1983); adaptation data recalculated from Blakemore and Campbell (1969).

FIGURE 5.9

Spatial frequency tuning curves of the six spatial filters derived from contrast masking data via a mathematical model of contrast detection. Comparison with Fig. 2.14B shows that these filters are much more sharply tuned than retinal ganglion cells, but are similar to the tuning of cortical cells (Fig. 5.8) Replotted from Wilson et al. (1983).

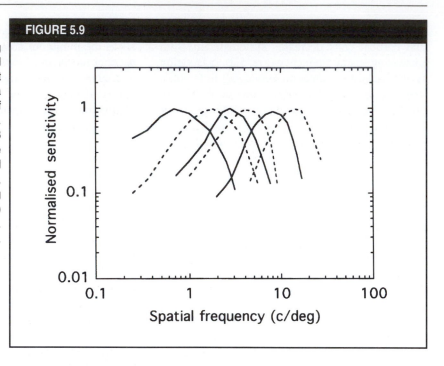

ranging from 2 to 5 cycles of the grating pattern. The presence of very narrow-band simple cells (0.5 to 1 octave) was confirmed in the cat's striate cortex by Robson, Tolhurst, Freeman, and Ohzawa (1988), and von der Heydt, Peterhans, and Dursteler (1992) similarly found that the narrow-band "grating cells" of monkeys tended to be tuned to higher spatial frequencies (8–16c/deg), as already implied by Fig. 5.8.

The bandwidth of cells thus describes their spatial filtering effect, and has implications for the underlying receptive field structure and for the idea that visual cells act as Gaussian 1st and 2nd derivative operators (Canny, 1986; Marr & Hildreth, 1980). No matter whether they are of large or small scale, derivative operators have a fixed bandwidth (in octaves), and the bandwidth decreases with increasing derivative number (1st, 2nd, 3rd ...). It is worth listing the first few (from Young, 1985). The first seven derivatives have bandwidths of 2.6, 1.77, 1.42, 1.22, 1.09, 0.99, 0.92 octaves, as shown at the left of Fig. 5.8. It is clear that bandwidths from physiology and psychophysics fall well below the 2nd derivative bandwidth (G2, 1.77 octaves) at medium and high spatial frequencies. We must therefore conclude

that although some filters may well serve as 1st and 2nd derivative operators, many cannot do so, especially at the higher frequencies, because they are too narrowly tuned. In other words, Marr and Hildreth's (1980) theory does not provide a role for the spatial filtering properties of many cortical cells, especially those responsive to fine detail.

There must therefore be other roles played by spatial filters in vision. Recall that to describe the image usefully, the primal sketch must not only locate the positions of edges, but also describe their properties, such as blur, contrast, length, and orientation. Georgeson (1994), for example, reported psychophysical evidence consistent with a role for 3rd derivative operators in encoding the blur (and possibly contrast) of edges. While the location of edges may be given by zero-crossings in the 2nd derivative output, their blur can be recovered from the ratio of 1st to 3rd derivative values taken across the edge; see Kayargadde and Martens (1994a,b) for more detailed computational analysis along similar lines. Nevertheless, the role of the narrow-band filters in vision remains largely unknown. Several recent approaches that diverge from Marr's paradigm, and explore other routes from filters to features, are described next.

OTHER ROUTES TO THE PRIMAL SKETCH

One alternative to Marr and Hildreth's edge-finding algorithm was developed by Pearson and Robinson (1985), who had been disappointed with the results obtained when it was applied to the problem of automatic sketching of images of faces. Pearson's group was faced with the applied problem of compressing moving images of faces into a form economical for transmission down telephone lines to provide video-phones, particularly useful for deaf people to communicate at a distance using sign language. An implementation of Marr and Hildreth's algorithm led to a cluttered, unusable sketch. This setback led them to consider in detail the nature of the edges that it was important for their artificial visual system to sketch.

Pearson and Robinson (1985) noted that the face is not a flat pattern (see also Bruce, 1988, and Chapters 9 and 16) but is a bumpy surface. The places where an artist draws lines in order to sketch the face correspond to places where the surface of the face turns sharply away from the line of sight, in addition to places where there is a sharp contrast such as at the hairline. Subject to certain lighting constraints, the former surface feature gives rise to a luminance *valley* in an image (see Fig. 5.10), whereas the latter gives rise to a luminance discontinuity (a step edge). Pearson and Robinson devised a "valley-detecting" algorithm that found just these kinds of intensity changes in an image. It first applies a filter of the shape shown in Fig. 5.10 to the image, and is able to use a single width of filter because the input images are always of faces and of a standard size. The problem of intensity changes occurring over different scales therefore does not arise. Note the similarity between this filter and the even-symmetric simple cell or Gaussian 2nd derivative. Rather than detecting zero-crossings in the output of this filter, as Marr and Hildreth's (1980) model does, Pearson and Robinson's algorithm then looks for the *peak* responses of the filter. The particular filter they use responds most strongly when it finds a luminance valley in the image. It will also respond, although less strongly, to a step edge. Valleys and edges at

different orientations are found by separately applying filters oriented to detect horizontal, vertical, and diagonal valleys.

Figure 5.11 shows examples of a line drawing of a face produced by Pearson and Robinson's system, next to an artist's sketch of the same face. The "automatic" sketch blacked in blocks of hair, eye-brows, etc. using a simple procedure to darken any area whose mean intensity falls below some criterion. The result is an automatic sketch that bears a striking resemblance to that produced by the human artist.

An interesting additional feature of the "valley-detecting" algorithm is that it provides an account of why it appears more natural to the visual system to present a cartoon drawn in black on a white background, than one drawn in white on a black background, and why photographic negatives of human faces appear so difficult to

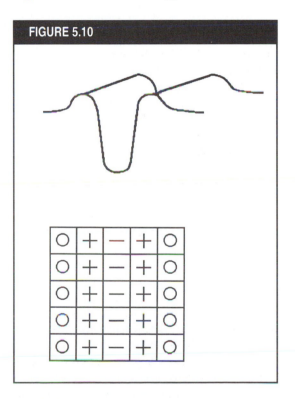

FIGURE 5.10

Top: a luminance valley. Bottom: an oriented "valley detector" mask that computes differences in intensity across different image regions. Adapted from Pearson, Hanna, and Martinez (1986).

FIGURE 5.11

Left: a cartoon produced by a human artist. Right: a cartoon produced automatically by the algorithm described in the text. Reproduced from Pearson et al. (1986) with permission of the publishers, Cambridge University Press.

recognise. An account of edge detection based on zero-crossing location does not predict the asymmetry between positive and negative images, but this is easily accounted for in terms of the valley-detecting routine. A black-on-white cartoon reproduces the locations of luminance valleys from the original picture, whereas in a white-on-black cartoon these valleys have been turned into ridges. A black-on-white cartoon will pass through the valley detecting algorithm unaltered, whereas white-on-black cartoons and photographic negatives suffer distortions to the locations of facial features when passed through the same filter (Pearson, Hanna, & Martinez, 1986).

Pearson and Robinson's cartoon-drawing algorithm is thus based on a similar initial step to Marr and Hildreth's (1980) algorithm, although it works at only a single spatial scale. The difference lies principally in what is detected from the output of the filter—peaks rather than zero-crossings, to locate lines rather than edges.

Watt and Morgan (e.g. Watt, 1988; Watt & Morgan, 1985) have also pointed out difficulties for the "zero-crossing" theory of edge detection, and have produced an alternative theory of the derivation of the primal sketch that bears some similarity to the scheme of Pearson and Robinson. The detection of zero-crossings is useful for locating edges but there are other kinds of intensity change that the visual system might need to describe (see examples in Fig. 5.12). Watt and Morgan's (1985) MIRAGE algorithm allows other changes in intensity to be described and also claims to give a better account of human psychophysical data than is given by theories based on the detection of zero-crossings in the second derivative. How does MIRAGE work?

The first stage of the MIRAGE system is the same as that of Marr and Hildreth's model—the image is convolved with a range of circular, "Mexican hat" (Gaussian 2nd derivative) filters of different sizes. However, MIRAGE then differs from Marr and Hildreth's algorithm in the way that information is combined from different filter sizes. In the Marr scheme, ZCs are found at each scale, and the multiple ZCs are interpreted to make assertions about the presence of edges. In MIRAGE, the outputs of all the filters are combined very early, in a *fixed* way that keeps the positive and negative portions of the functions separate. Positive and negative parts of the filter outputs are separately *summed* to yield two signals, the S+ and S– signals (see Fig. 5.13). The locations of edges, bars, and luminance plateaux are then determined from measurements made on the S+ and S– signals, as follows.

FIGURE 5.12

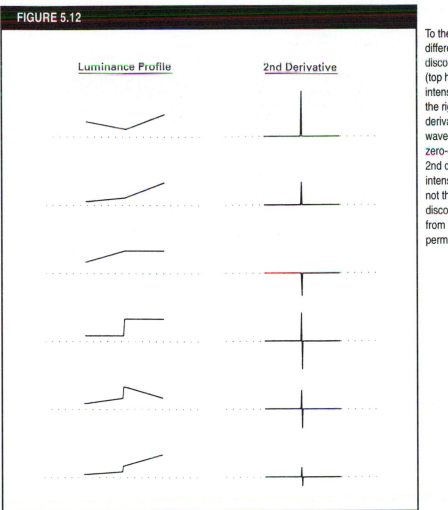

Luminance Profile   2nd Derivative

To the left are shown different profiles with discontinuities in gradient (top half of the figure) or intensity (bottom half). To the right are shown the 2nd derivatives of these waveforms. Note that zero-crossings arise in the 2nd derivatives of the intensity discontinuities, but not the gradient discontinuities. Reproduced from Watt (1988) with permission.

Each of the S+ and S− signals contain sections (Z) that are zero and response regions (R) that depart from zero (see Fig. 5.14, third row). The R regions are "zero-bounded masses" and an example is marked in Fig. 5.14. Thus there are just two kinds of "primitive", Z and R, that describe the signals. The spatial sequence of Z and R regions can be used to interpret the intensity changes present. Edges give rise to one kind of sequence and lines give rise to another. The rules (Watt & Morgan, 1985) are quite simple: (1) *Null rule*: A Z region of zero response is a luminance plateau; (2) *Edge rule*: An R region with a Z on only one side (and therefore an R of opposite sign on the other) marks the boundary of an edge; (3) *Bar rule*: An R region with a Z on both or neither side is a light or dark bar, depending on the sign of R.

Additionally, the position, mass, and spread of the response regions are measured. The chevrons in Fig. 5.14 (fourth row) mark the "centroids" (mean positions) of these zero-bounded masses and these play a particularly important role in locating and describing an intensity change, in contrast to the zero-crossings of Marr and Hildreth's scheme. In Fig. 5.14, the height and width of each chevron represents the mass and spread of each zero-bounded response. The masses and their spreads can be used to describe the contrast and blur of edges and the width of bars (see Watt, 1988; Watt & Morgan, 1985). This scheme

FIGURE 5.13

A luminance profile (resulting from two sets of stripes of different widths) is passed through $\nabla^2 G$ filters of two different widths. The output from the smaller filter has numerous zero-crossings, whereas the output from the larger filter has few. At the bottom is shown the result of separately summing the positive and negative portions of these filter outputs. Reproduced from Watt (1988) with permission.

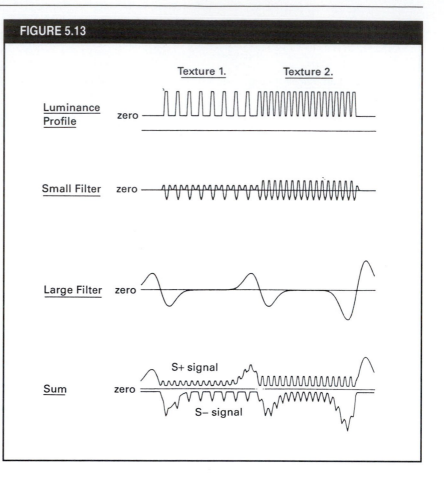

gives a good qualitative account of the appearance of various luminance profiles, including several well-known illusions of brightness.

Turning to quantitative results, Watt (1988) summarises a considerable amount of psychophysical evidence to argue that the MIRAGE algorithm provides a good account of feature representation in human vision. One example comes from an experiment by Watt and Morgan (1983), who asked subjects to say which of two edges looked more blurred. Watt and Morgan measured the smallest difference in blur that could be detected between the test and reference edges for different amounts, and different types of blur. Discrimination of different types of blur was consistent with a mechanism in which peaks and troughs in the 2nd derivative output were localised and compared. Thus a *metric*, or internal code, for blur could be the separation between

peaks and troughs, or between centroids, in the filter response around an edge.

Figure 5.15 (p.92) plots the blur difference thresholds obtained for Gaussian blur against the variation in blur of the reference edge, and also shows the predicted functions that should be obtained from filters of different sizes. The data give a very good fit to the theoretical curve from the largest filter size. As Fig. 5.15 shows, however, a system that could independently access the outputs of the smaller filters should be capable of greater sensitivity to differences in low degrees of blur (at less than 1 minute of arc in Fig. 5.15). The observation that human observers cannot do any better than would be predicted from the largest-scale filter is taken as evidence that the visual system cannot access the different filter outputs independently (Watt, 1988). This is a bold conclusion, but it is also worth sounding a note of

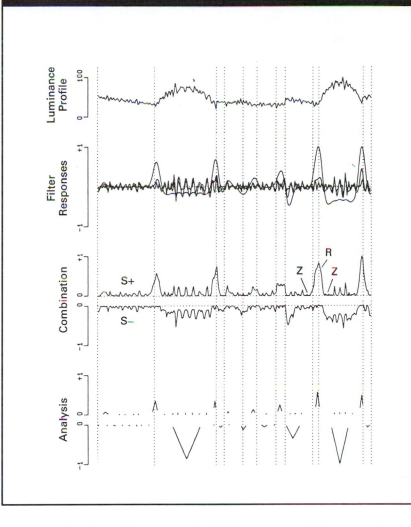

The MIRAGE algorithm. A luminance profile (top) is passed through $\nabla^2 G$ filters of three different widths (second row). The positive and negative portions of these filter outputs are separately summed (third row). The zero-bounded masses in these combined filter outputs are analysed and the apexes of the chevrons in the bottom row mark the locations of the centroids of these masses. Reproduced from Watt (1988) with permission.

caution. The predictions of Fig. 5.15 were based on assumptions about the factors that limit blur discrimination. Specifically, it was assumed that the internal blur metric (let us call it B) is subject to Weber's Law, which states simply that the just noticeable difference (ΔB) is proportional to the stimulus value, B: that is, $\Delta B/B = K$, a constant. In other words, in order to see a change there needs to be a fixed percentage change in the stimulus value. Weber's Law is an empirical finding that often holds approximately in sensory experiments. The predictions in Fig. 5.15 assumed that Weber's Law holds for the blur code (B), and that the constant (K) would be the same for all filters. If different

assumptions were made, either about these factors or about the relative sensitivity of the filters, the pattern of predictions could be quite different.

Further evidence consistent with the use of centroids as descriptive primitives in MIRAGE comes from the data of Watt and Morgan (1984) who examined how accurately people could localise edges of different contrasts. Subjects were asked to decide whether or not two edges were aligned, and their accuracy as a function of contrast was compared with theoretical curves based on the detection of peaks and zero-crossings from the 2nd derivative, and the detection of centroids of zero-bounded masses in S+ and S− signals. As

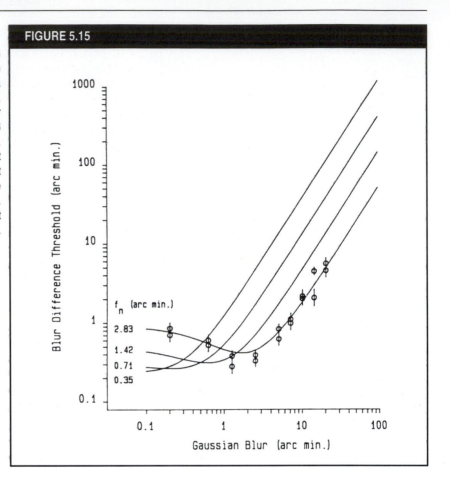

FIGURE 5.15

Solid lines show the predicted variation in the threshold for detecting a difference in Gaussian blur, as a function of blur, for four different filter sizes (2.83 down to 0.35 minutes of arc). The data points from Watt and Morgan (1983) clearly fit the prediction from the largest filter size. Reproduced from Watt (1988) with permission.

Fig. 5.16 shows, the data give a much better fit to the curve predicted by centroid measurement than to the one predicted by measurement of peaks or zero-crossings (although only the *shapes* of the curves should be compared, not their vertical positions). But again, as so often in science, this success depends partly on ancillary assumptions that are not central to the theory. In this case the assumption concerns the internal "noise" or variability of neural responses. The comparison drawn between theory and data in Fig. 5.16 presumes that the internal signal-to-noise ratio in a filter is proportional to stimulus contrast. Although this simple assumption is not implausible, it is not necessarily correct. We can see that relating vision models to experimental data is a difficult and uncertain business.

MIRAGE remains an interesting model, especially in its ideas on how a set of interpretive rules (mentioned earlier) is applied to the filter outputs to describe a localised set of image features (Watt & Morgan, 1985). Finally, keeping in mind the important distinction between an algorithm and its implementation, we can begin to see a possible convergence of the MIRAGE and Marr–Hildreth approaches. For MIRAGE, an edge lies between two masses of opposite sign. It could locate the edge by averaging the two centroid locations (the "centroid of centroids"; Watt, 1988). We can also view this as a robust way of finding the zero-crossing—an implementation for the zero-crossing algorithm. It is not so different from the AND-ing of adjacent on- and off-cell responses (see Fig. 5.7) suggested by Marr and Hildreth themselves. Psychophysical evidence on the shift of perceived edge location with increasing contrast lends support to this view (Mather & Morgan, 1986).

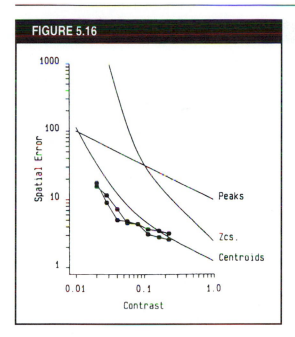

FIGURE 5.16

The data points (from Watt & Morgan, 1984) show the random error associated with judgements of edge location as the contrast of the edge is varied. The solid lines show theoretical predictions based on the detection of peaks, zero-crossings, and centroids. Reproduced from Watt (1988), with permission.

ENERGY MODELS FOR FEATURE DETECTION

The models considered so far have used multiple scales of filter, but restricted themselves to one type of filter—usually with even symmetric receptive fields (like $\nabla^2 G$ or d^2G/dx^2). Since the early days of Hubel and Wiesel (1962, 1968) it has been recognised that simple-cell receptive fields can be even symmetric (like Fig. 5.10), or odd symmetric (like $\partial G/\partial x$, inset to Fig. 5.2). By definition, in an even symmetric shape the right half is a simple reflection of the left half, whereas in an odd symmetric shape the right half is an *inverted* reflection of the left half (cf. Fig. 3.5). An early suggestion based on supporting psychophysical studies was that these two sub-types of cells acted as "bar detectors" and "edge detectors", respectively (e.g. Kulikowski & King-Smith, 1973). Certainly an odd symmetric field will show a peak of activity at the location of a step edge,

whereas an even one will show a peak of activity at the location of a line or bar. Unfortunately this simple idea is inadequate because, as we have seen, the even filter also shows a peak (and trough) adjacent to an edge—hence the need for rules to *parse* or interpret the pattern of responses in models such as MIRAGE and the Marr–Hildreth model.

Local energy from odd and even filters

A more recent approach that has emerged from the interplay of studies in biological and machine vision uses both the even and odd filters together to overcome this problem. It is based on the concept of *local energy* or *contrast energy*, and is very easy to describe but less easy to appreciate why it works. Suppose first that there are matched pairs of even and odd filters that have the same preference and tuning for orientation and spatial frequency. Pollen and Ronner (1981) found cell pairs of this kind in the cat's cortex. Given an intensity image, I(x), let the output signal from the even filter be e(x) and that from the odd filter be o(x). The energy function E(x) is then defined as:

$$E(x) = e(x)^2 + o(x)^2$$

We can see immediately that energy (E) is always positive and that it will have a high value where either e(x) is high or o(x) is high, or both. Figure 5.17 shows an example of responses of odd (row B) and even (row C) filters to edges and lines (row A). The response to a thin bright line (third column) reveals the shapes of the two receptive fields. Both are multi-lobed, and so the response profiles have several peaks and troughs across space. The energy response, however (plotted here as amplitude, $\sqrt{E(x)}$), has just a single peak at the location of the line. Why? The even and odd receptive fields can each be expressed as a Gabor function (see Fig. 3.5), which is simply a sine-wave oscillation at some frequency (f), tapered by a bell-shaped, Gaussian envelope, G(x). We have seen that Gabor functions provide a good general description of most simple cell profiles (Ch.3, p.56). Thus the even field can be written as:

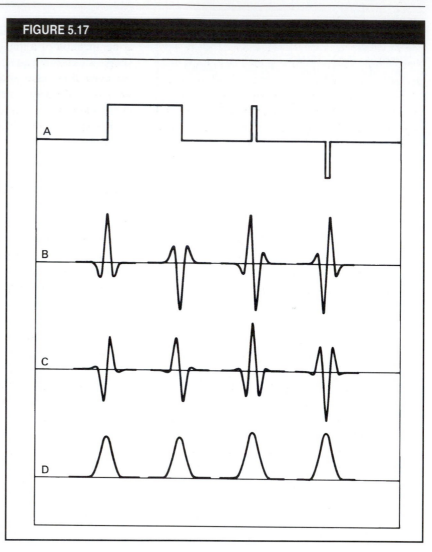

FIGURE 5.17

Energy model for localising line and edge features. Intensity profile (A) containing two edges and two lines gives rise to response profiles of odd-symmetric (B) and even-symmetric (C) spatial filters. Energy profile (D) has simple peaks at the locations of lines and edges. Redrawn from Heitger et al. (1992), with kind permission from Elsevier Science Ltd., UK.

$$G(x).\cos(2\pi fx)$$

and the odd field as:

$$G(x).\sin(2\pi fx)$$

The energy response to a line is therefore:

$$E(x) = [G(x).\sin(2\pi fx)]^2 + [G(x).\cos(2\pi fx)]^2$$
$$= [G(x)]^2$$

because $\sin^2(\ ) + \cos^2(\ ) = 1$. The amplitude $\sqrt{E(x)}$ of this combined response thus simplifies to $G(x)$,

the smooth single-peaked curve shown in Fig. 5.17D. Much the same is true for the edge response (first and second columns), although it would be more elaborate to show this mathematically. A good intuition to hold in mind is that at any given location (x) the energy response reflects the *amount* of image contrast present within the receptive field aperture centred at x. Thus the energy response (row D) peaks at points of high contrast, but does not reflect the fine structure of the image at that point. More formally, the energy response preserves amplitude, but throws away phase information. Conversely the ratio o(x)/e(x) represents local phase but not amplitude.

Applying these signal-processing concepts to vision, Morrone and colleagues pioneered the idea that visual features are detected specifically at peaks of local energy (Morrone & Burr, 1988; Morrone & Owens, 1987; Morrone, Ross, Burr, & Owens, 1986). Going beyond simple lines and edges, they showed that energy peaks also coincided with the location of a variety of other features, including triangle waves and features whose luminance profile was intermediate between that of a line and an edge. Figure 5.18 (from Burr & Morrone, 1990) shows the energy model doing a good job of feature extraction on a natural image. The energy peak could also account quantitatively for the well-known illusory features ("Mach Bands") seen at the junction between a luminance ramp and a plateau (Ross, Morrone, & Burr, 1989). It should be obvious from Fig. 5.17 that the energy peak itself does not identify the *type* of feature, and it is suggested that the system could consult the $e(x)$ and $o(x)$ signals at the energy peak location. If the even signal also has a peak the feature is a bar, but if the odd signal has a peak it is an edge. Thus the "contrast energy" theory interprets the linear filter output in the same way as the early feature detector models, with the crucial difference that energy peaks select the locations to be interpreted. This removes the need for the more elaborate parsing rules of the Marr and MIRAGE methods.

Malik and Perona (1992, Section IV) analysed energy models more generally, showing that they are well-suited for the task of detecting composite edges. These occur quite frequently in natural images, and consist of two superimposed luminance profiles, such as an edge and a line, or an edge and a ramp. For 2-D images the energy calculation must be done at a number of different orientations, as any odd-symmetric filter cannot be circular and so must be orientation-specific. Malik and Perona's rule for finding features in 2-D images is, for each pixel location, to find by interpolation the orientation at which energy is maximum, then to determine whether that pixel location is also a spatial peak of energy. The performance of this algorithm was claimed to surpass that of the Canny (1986) system based on finding points of maximum gradient, but the comparison between the two approaches was not extensive.

Experimental evidence: Energy computations in physiology and psychophysics

The energy-peak proposal is simple and attractive in itself, and also has strong physiological support. The energy computation $[e(x)^2 + o(x)^2]$ has been widely accepted as a model for the behaviour of cortical complex cells (Adelson & Bergen, 1985; Emerson, Bergen, & Adelson, 1992; Heeger, 1992a). Complex cells are tuned for orientation and spatial frequency, as simple cells are, but do not show distinct lobes of excitation and inhibition within the receptive field (see Ch.3, p.50). Our earlier calculations show how computing energy

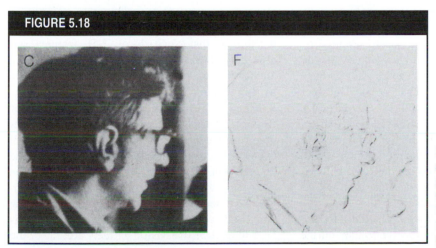

FIGURE 5.18

Left: Profile of a vision scientist. Right: Energy peaks (dark points) map the major features of the image. From Burr and Morrone (1990). Reprinted by kind permission of the authors.

E(x) eliminates the alternating spatial structure of the simple cell. If a line is drifted across a complex cell's field, the response rate just rises and then falls, reflecting only the envelope G(x) (Pollen, Gaska, & Jacobson, 1988). Similarly, when a grating is drifted across the complex field the most common response is a uniform increase in firing rate (Movshon, Thompson, & Tolhurst, 1978; Skottun et al., 1991). Simple cells, on the other hand, modulate their response in time with the passage of light and dark bars across the field. This is diagnostic of a linear filter underlying the behaviour of the cell, as in a linear system a sine-wave input gives sine-wave output at the same frequency. Complex cells clearly do not do this and so they, and the energy computation, are *nonlinear* operators, but they do exhibit the spatial and orientation tuning passed on to them by simple (or simple-like) linear units.

How comprehensive is the energy model as a description of human feature extraction? This is hard to say, as the number of psychophysical studies is small, but the intrinsic nature of the energy function suggests that a full description of spatial structure may need both energy-peak detection and zero-crossing detection operating in parallel. Recall that the energy function E(x) follows the *envelope* of local contrast variation in the filtered image (illustrated in Fig. 8.8). For a sine-wave input, sin(fx), the paired outputs e(x) and o(x) are of the form k.sin(fx) and k.cos(fx), respectively. Therefore $E(x) = k^2$, a constant, with no peaks at all; the local energy profile is flat. This would imply that a sine-wave grating is featureless, which seems implausible, to say the least. Moreover, Georgeson and Freeman (reported by Georgeson, 1994) found that subjects could accurately adjust the blur of a single edge (possessing a strong energy peak) to match the blur of edges in a sine wave (with no energy peak), implying that a similar edge description is derived in both cases. They also found that the number of edges seen in two-component gratings (with frequencies f and 3f) was six per cycle, as predicted if zero-crossings are detected, rather than two as predicted from energy peaks.

On the other hand, positive evidence for the use of energy peaks comes from experiments on the perceived location and movement of "contrast blobs" —i.e. patches of a grating whose luminance profile is a Gabor function. Subjects can accurately align the positions of such "blobs" even when the underlying frequencies or orientations are different. This could not be done on the basis of local ZC features, and suggests that the peak of the envelope is available from an energy-type computation (Hess & Holliday, 1992). Similarly, the perceived movement of such blobs can, under appropriate spatial and temporal conditions, be seen to follow the movement of the envelope rather than the internal features of the blobs (Boulton & Baker, 1993). Under other conditions (at inter-stimulus intervals shorter than 40msec) perceived movement follows the internal structure of the blobs instead. These complementary lines of evidence suggest that parallel analyses are applied, using both the "first-order" linear filter outputs and the "second-order" energy profile. This important distinction is discussed further in Chapters 6 and 8 in the contexts of texture segmentation and motion perception.

ANOMALOUS CONTOURS, OCCLUSION CUES, AND END-STOPPED CELLS

Both the styles of contour analysis just discussed aim to make explicit the location, orientation, and contrast of lines and edges in the image. Neither makes explicit the location of important events along a contour—such as line-ends, corners, or points of high curvature. It has long been recognised that such local 2-D features are especially informative about the shape of a boundary and about the occlusion of one surface by another lying in front of it.

Figure 5.19A,B,C illustrates three varieties of "illusory contour" that are generated by configurations of line-ends and interrupted edges. Such contours seem to be created especially when the arrangement of line-ends is consistent with the presence of one surface occluding another. However, the term "illusory" presumes that the only "real" contour is a luminance boundary. It is becoming clear that vision extracts accurately the

FIGURE 5.19

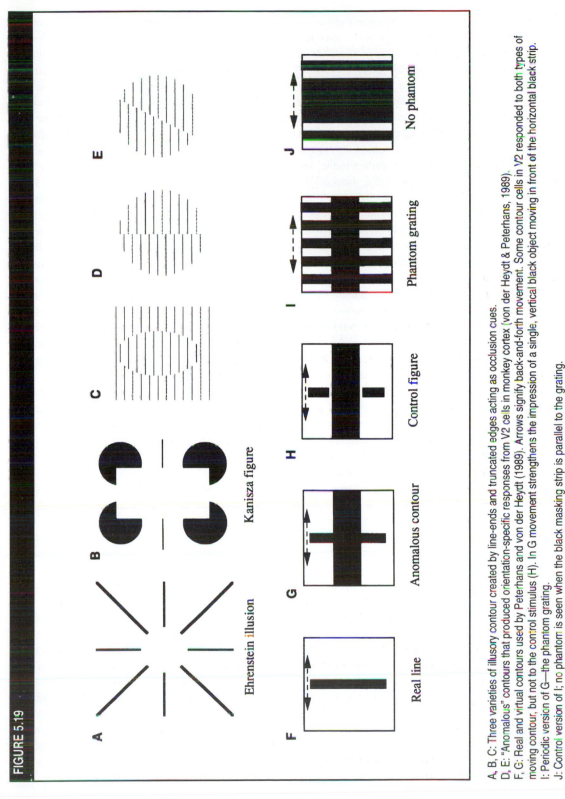

A, B, C: Three varieties of illusory contour created by line-ends and truncated edges acting as occlusion cues.

D, E: "Anomalous" contours that produced orientation-specific responses from V2 cells in monkey cortex (von der Heydt & Peterhans, 1989).

F, G: Real and virtual contours used by Peterhans and von der Heydt (1989). Arrows signify back-and-forth movement. Some contour cells in V2 responded to both types of moving contour, but not to the control stimulus (H). In G movement strengthens the impression of a single, vertical black object moving in front of the horizontal black strip.

I: Periodic version of G—the phantom grating.

J: Control version of I; no phantom is seen when the black masking strip is parallel to the grating.

location and orientation of a wide variety of spatial discontinuities in image properties, that is, boundaries where there is a relatively sharp change in colour, texture, or motion (e.g. Regan & Hamstra, 1992; Sary, Vogels, & Orban, 1994), and so the lack of a luminance edge does not make a border "illusory". However, such semantic issues matter less than the questions of how contours in general are detected and represented by visual processes. To be consistent with earlier usage, we shall continue to refer to the visible boundaries created by occlusion cues as "illusory" or "anomalous", while bearing in mind that from a wider perspective they are no less "real" than other visible contours. Their "reality" is reinforced by recent physiological and psychophysical findings that point to common pathways in early vision processing "real" and "illusory" contours.

Von der Heydt and Peterhans (1989) studied the responses of V1 and V2 cells in alert monkeys to "anomalous" contours of different orientations (Fig. 5.19D,E). Almost no V1 cells responded to these contours, although they responded to the line gratings from which they were constructed. In contrast, about 40% of the V2 cells sampled were classified as "contour neurons" because they showed an orientation-specific response both to "real" lines (Fig. 5.19F) and to anomalous contours (Fig. 5.19D). The preferred orientation, orientation bandwidth, and degree of direction selectivity tended to be very similar for the two types of contour. The orientation of the anomalous contour can be varied separately from the orientation of the lines that create it (compare Figs. 5.19D and E) and it was found that orientation-tuning depended mainly on the orientation of the anomalous contour, but the response rates were typically higher when the grating lines were at right angles to the contour. This may correspond to the perceptual finding that illusory contours (as in Fig. 5.19A) are seen more vividly when the inducing lines intersect the illusory contour at right angles than at other angles (Kennedy, 1978).

A model for "illusory contours"

What neural mechanisms might underlie this apparent ability of "contour neurons" to encode the orientation of such different types of contour?

Nothing in the basic model for simple and complex cell fields would produce this behaviour, but the "end-inhibited" hypercomplex cells described in Chapter 3 (pp.49–50) are especially sensitive to truncated gratings, lines, or edges. At one or both ends of the receptive field (which may be simple or complex) there is an inhibitory zone that suppresses the cell's response when the stimulus line or edge is longer than the length of the main (central) receptive field. Heitger et al. (1992) pointed out that energy peaks from oriented filters locate luminance contours, but do not isolate the 2-D *key points* such as line-ends and T-junctions. They extended the energy model for complex cells described in the previous section to include the property of end inhibition, by applying a further stage of spatial differentiation *along* the preferred orientation of the complex filter. The 1st derivative served to model cells with one end-zone and the 2nd derivative modelled those with two. To isolate the key points more precisely further inhibitory interactions were added between cells to suppress responses to elongated contours.

By linking together several line-end-sensitive mechanisms, a reliable means of detecting anomalous contours can be obtained. Peterhans and von der Heydt (1989) proposed this as a model for the detection of both real and anomalous contours by "contour neurons" in V2 (see Fig. 5.20). In this model, two distinct mechanisms converge onto a common path. The simple or complex oriented unit responds selectively to (say) vertical lines or edges, whereas the group of end-stopped units (tuned to horizontal orientation) responds well to a vertical alignment of line-ends such as that in the abutting grating stimulus of Fig. 5.19D. The contour neuron thus responds in a similar orientation-specific way to both kinds of contour and (presumably) to their combination.

Peterhans and von der Heydt (1989) also tested V2 neurons with stimuli derived from the well-known Kanisza (1976) figures (Fig. 5.19B). When patterns such as Fig. 5.19G move, human observers see especially strong illusory contours, as shown by Tynan and Sekuler (1975) who studied a spatially periodic version known as the "phantom grating" (Fig. 5.19I). The phantom grating is seen to "fill in" across the black strip where there is no

FIGURE 5.20

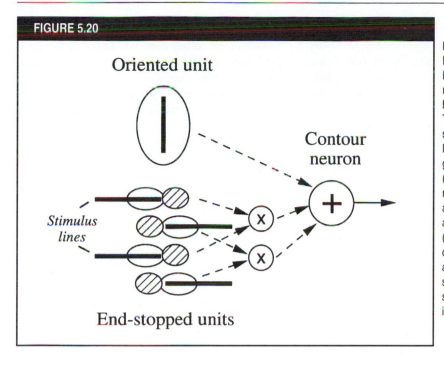

Oriented unit

Contour neuron

Stimulus lines

End-stopped units

Model proposed by Peterhans and von der Heydt (1989) for detection of real and anomalous contours by contour neurons in V2. The oriented unit responds selectively to (say) vertical lines or edges, whereas the group of end-stopped units (tuned to horizontal lines) responds well to the vertical alignment of line-ends in the abutting grating stimulus (Fig. 5.19D). The two types of input mechanism are actually superimposed in space. Not all V2 neurons show evidence for this dual input.

luminance contrast, and to move along with the real grating. Interestingly, the phantoms are not seen if the central black strip is parallel to the bars (Fig. 5.19J). Note the absence of "key points" (line-ends, corners) in this case. Some 30% of V2 cells appeared to respond to these contours (Fig. 5.19G) as well as to "real" contours (Fig. 5.19F), whereas V1 cells appeared not to do so. We say "appeared" because the interpretation is more difficult in these experiments. If the conventional receptive field overlapped the "real" parts of the phantom figure then the responses would be unsurprising. The control for this was to break the continuity of the phantom figure, as shown in Fig. 5.19H. This tends to eliminate the illusory contour and so a "contour neuron" should reduce its response in this case. Some cells did this, but others did so rather little, or even increased their response. Overall, though, the evidence in favour of a model like that of Fig. 5.20 is now substantial. These V2 neurons appear to be an important step towards the goal of object recognition, as they abstract orientation while generalising across at least two very different types of image discontinuity. Such generalisation (or "cue invariance") is vital in the task of shape recognition and (ultimately) object constancy.

Convergence of cues in orientation coding

The convergence of mechanisms that process the orientation of "real" and "illusory" contours is also implied by studies of the *tilt aftereffect* (TAE). Inspection of lines or gratings tilted (say) 15° off vertical makes a subsequent vertical pattern seem tilted a few degrees in the opposite direction. This classic aftereffect of adaptation (Gibson & Radner, 1937), like other aftereffects such as contrast adaptation (p.84), is widely used as a tool for probing visual mechanisms. The fact that the TAE is orientation-specific immediately implies that it is of cortical origin, and this is confirmed by the finding of inter-ocular transfer. If one eye is adapted and the other is tested, the TAE is still observed, showing that adaptation is at least partly at a binocular site where the two eyes can interact.

Such transfer of an effect from one condition to another can be exploited to test for the convergence of pathways. What would happen if we adapted to a "real" contour, and then tested with an "illusory" contour, or vice-versa ? A failure of the TAE to transfer from one kind to the other would support independent processing whereas complete transfer would imply common processing. In fact, several studies have confirmed the transfer of TAE between real and illusory contours, and vice-versa, implying common processing (Berkley, DeBruyn, & Orban, 1994; Paradiso, Shimojo, & Nakayama, 1989; Smith & Over, 1975, 1977). Moreover, there was almost 100% inter-ocular transfer of the TAE for an illusory contour (like Fig. 5.19D) whereas there was only partial transfer for a real contour. This suggests that the illusory contour arises at a higher cortical site that is more completely driven by binocular input, and is indicative of V2 rather than V1 (Paradiso et al., 1989).

A similar conclusion was drawn from the effects of *binocular rivalry* on the TAE. Rivalry occurs when two very different images are presented to the two eyes, such that normal binocular fusion (see Chapter 7) is impossible. Fragmented parts of each image may be seen, or a strong image in one eye may partly or completely suppress a weaker one in the other eye. If an adaptation effect is reduced by rivalry suppression then we may conclude that its site is at or after the site of rivalry. Van der Zwan and Wenderoth (1994) found that the presence of binocular rivalry during the period of adaptation suppressed the TAE for an illusory contour, but not for a real contour. Several earlier studies had also found that the aftereffects of contrast adaptation (thought to be in V1) were unaffected by rivalry (e.g. Blake & Overton, 1979). These findings imply that illusory contours arise at a higher site (perhaps V2) than the first site of adaptation to real contours (V1). Most importantly, the transfer of aftereffect between different types of contour implies common processing of different edge cues at the higher site.

In fact, this convergence of information from different contour cues may be even more extensive, involving luminance contours, line-ends, colour, and motion. Berkley et al. (1994) found that adapting to contours defined by real lines or by line-ends or by a reversal in motion direction could in each case produce a TAE on test contours of all three types. This suggests the sort of convergence of cues sketched in Fig. 5.21. Furthermore, Flanagan, Cavanagh, and Favreau (1990) examined the TAE using gratings defined by colour contrast (e.g. red-green or blue-yellow) or luminance contrast. Adapting to *pairs* of luminance and colour gratings tilted +/–15° from vertical in opposite directions revealed aftereffects *specific* to luminance or colour contrast. That is, after such dual adaptation a vertical test grating seemed tilted one way if it was defined by luminance contrast, but the opposite way if defined by colour contrast. This suggests that there are different oriented units specific to colour and to luminance contrast. Conversely, adapting to single gratings showed considerable transfer of the TAE between colour and luminance conditions. These two results are not contradictory, and suggest two stages of orientation selective mechanism: at the first stage (Fig. 5.21) units are specific to colour or luminance contrast and mediate the colour- or luminance-specific TAE, and the second stage receives converging input from colour and luminance units and explains the generalisation of the TAE between colour and luminance conditions (Flanagan et al., 1990). In short, the concept of converging cues (Fig. 5.21) unifies quite a wide range of psychophysical and physiological findings on the encoding of oriented features in images. We shall return to this when we consider depth cues in Chapter 7.

CONCLUSIONS

We began this chapter by considering the *primal sketch* theory of Marr (1982). The core of this theory is that a description of local intensity changes or *features* in the image forms the gateway to later descriptions of image regions, object surfaces, and object shapes. Some alternative approaches, such as MIRAGE or the energy model, share the same broad aims but differ at the level of algorithm and implementation. All these models filter the retinal image through receptive fields that are sensitive to luminance contrast, and then employ nonlinear operations to derive features from the filter outputs. All agree on the importance of multiple scales (sizes) of filter, but differ in their use of this information. Detailed study of the filters themselves has shown that at small scales (high spatial frequency) the filters are much more tightly tuned for spatial frequency (and orientation) than any of these models would require, and leaves open

FIGURE 5.21

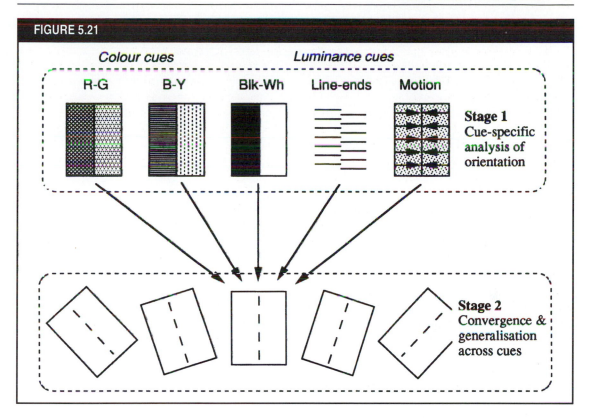

Summary of orientation coding derived from physiological and psychophysical findings. Both types of evidence suggest that cue-specific analysis may be more closely associated with area V1, whereas the convergence of cues occurs at a higher, more completely binocular site (V2 or beyond).

many questions about their role. One possibility is that the whole set of filters, tuned jointly to different orientations and spatial frequencies, delivers a Fourier-like transform of local patches of the image. Such transforms are being used widely in digital applications for compact, efficient coding, storage, and transmission of image data. Perhaps the functional architecture of V1 serves the same very general purpose, whereas the encoding of features is done mainly at later stages. We saw

evidence that V2 begins to abstract contour orientation while generalising across a variety of "cues" or types of image discontinuity. Parallel processing of luminance contrast, colour, and motion might be better thought of as occurring before the feature representation rather than after it as in Marr's scheme. The complexity of known neural pathways (see Chapter 3) allows for many possibilities.

6

Perceptual Organisation

In Chapter 5 we considered how the primal sketch—a description of edge and line segments, terminations and other key features—may be derived from an array of intensities in the retinal image. In this chapter we turn to consider how such low-level descriptions may be organised into larger perceptual "chunks". When we view the world we do not see a collection of edges and blobs—unless we adopt a very analytical perceptual attitude—but see instead an organised world of surfaces and objects. How is such perceptual organisation achieved? How do we know which parts of the visual information reaching our sensory apparatus belong together? These are the questions addressed in this chapter. The first part of the chapter concentrates on human perception, because it was through the study of this that many of the principles of perceptual organisation became established. We

return to the broader perspective of animal vision when we consider how such perceptual principles may be exploited in natural camouflage and advertisement. In the final part of the chapter we turn to artificial intelligence approaches to perceptual organisation.

As we discussed in Chapter 4, the psychology of human visual perception during the late 19th and early 20th century was dominated by associationism. It was assumed that perception could be analysed in terms of its component sensations, and that complex ideas were the result of associating together simpler ones. However, as the Gestalt psychologists pointed out, an analysis of perception into discrete sensations overlooks some important aspects of form and structure. Each of the arrangements shown in Fig. 6.1 possesses the quality of "squareness" despite being composed of

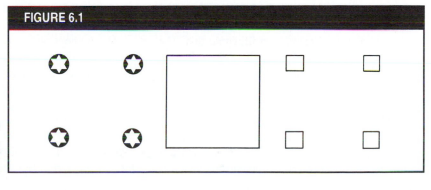

FIGURE 6.1

Each of these three forms is seen as being square, despite being composed of quite different elements.

quite different elements. A tune is recognisable despite being played in a different key or at a different speed. The spatial and temporal relationships between elements are as important as the absolute size, location, or nature of the elements themselves, and a sensation-based account of perception fails to capture this.

Even Wundt (1896) recognised that a simple structuralist analysis failed to capture certain perceptual phenomena (Wundt, 1896, trans. 1907, p.368):

> A compound clang is more in its ideational and affective attributes than merely a sum of single tones.

But it was the Gestalt psychologists, notably Koffka (1935), Köhler (1947), and Wertheimer (1923), with whom the catch-phrase "the whole is greater than the sum of its parts" became identified. We will first describe the Gestalt ideas about perceptual organisation, and then consider more recent accounts.

AMBIGUOUS PICTURES

The world that we view appears to be composed of discrete objects of various sizes seen against a background of textured surfaces. We usually have no difficulty in seeing the boundaries of objects, unless these are successfully camouflaged (see later), and there is generally no doubt about which areas are "figures" and which comprise the "ground". However, it is possible to construct pictures in which there is ambiguity about which region is "figure" and which "ground". Edgar Rubin, one of the Gestalt psychologists, used the face–vase picture (Fig. 6.2) to illustrate this. The picture can be seen either as a pair of black faces in profile, or as a white vase, but it is impossible to maintain simultaneously the perception of both the faces and the vase. The contour dividing the black and white regions of the picture appears to have a one-sided function. It "belongs" to whichever region is perceived as figure. People viewing this picture usually find that their perception of it shifts

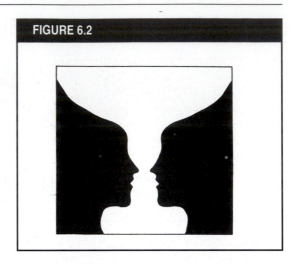

FIGURE 6.2

This picture, devised by E. Rubin in 1915, can be seen *either* as a pair of faces in silhouette, *or* as a white vase.

from one interpretation to the other, sometimes quite spontaneously. The artist M.C. Escher exploited this principle of perceptual reversibility when he produced etchings in which there is figure/ground ambiguity (see Fig. 6.3).

It is also possible to construct pictures so that the internal organisation of a particular figure is ambiguous. Jastrow's duck–rabbit picture (Fig. 6.4a) may be seen as a duck (beak at the left), or a rabbit (ears at the left), but not both simultaneously. Even a figure as simple as a triangle turns out to be perceptually ambiguous, as Fig. 6.4b shows (Attneave, 1971). The triangles appear to "point" in any one of the three possible directions, and when they appear to change direction they all change together, implying some spatially extended organising process that is applied to all the individual triangles simultaneously (Palmer, 1992). Some abstract and "op"-art may be perplexing to view because no stable organisation is apparent (see Fig. 6.5).

The perception of such ambiguous displays is interesting in its own right, and psychologists have investigated the factors influencing which organisation of an ambiguous display will be preferred, and the factors determining perceptual reversals (for example see Attneave, 1971; Hochberg, 1950; Pheiffer, Eure, & Hamilton, 1956). In all these examples, the perceptual "data" remain the same, but the interpretation varies. It

FIGURE 6.3 (top); FIG. 6.4 (bottom left); FIG. 6.5 (bottom right)

M.C. Escher's "Circle Limit IV".

Fig. 6.4 (below left)
(a) Duck or rabbit? This ambiguous picture was introduced to psychologists by J. Jastrow in 1900.
(b) Triangles as ambiguous figures. Note how the whole group of triangles appears to point in one, then another of the three possible directions. After Attneave (1971).

Fig. 6.5 (below)
"Supernovae" 1959–1961 by Victor Vasarely.

(a)

(b)

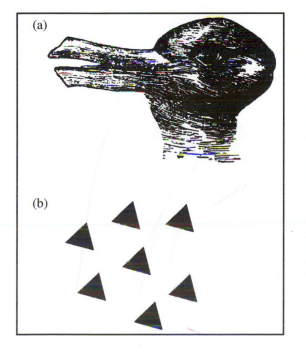

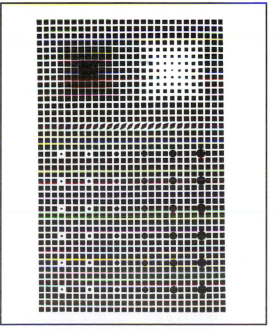

seems as though there must be a strong "top-down" component in such perceptions. Higher levels of perceptual interpretation appear to be continually constraining and guiding the lower levels of image analysis.

However, these ambiguous pictures have been cleverly constructed, and our perception of them is not necessarily typical of normal processing. Ambiguity generally does not arise in the real world, nor in most pictures. Rather than having constantly shifting interpretations, we usually see a stable and organised world. For example, viewing Fig. 6.6a in isolation, most people would report seeing a hexagon, whereas those viewing Fig. 6.6b report seeing a picture of a three-dimensional cube, even though Fig. 6.6a is an equally legitimate view of a cube, viewed corner on. Figure 6.7 is seen as a set of overlapping circles, rather than as one circle touching two adjoining shapes that have "bites" taken out of them. Why, given these possible alternative perceptions, do we see these pictures in these ways?

GESTALT LAWS OF ORGANISATION

The Gestalt psychologists formulated a number of principles of perceptual organisation to describe how certain perceptions are more likely to occur than others. Some of their principles were primarily to do with the grouping of sub-regions of figures, and others were more concerned with the segregation of figure from ground. However, as sub-regions of a figure need to be grouped in order for a larger region to be seen as "belonging

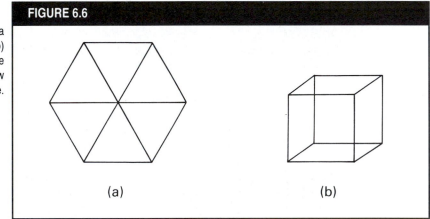

FIGURE 6.6

The form at (a) looks like a hexagon, whereas that at (b) looks like a cube. Of course (a) is also a legitimate view of a cube.

(a)   (b)

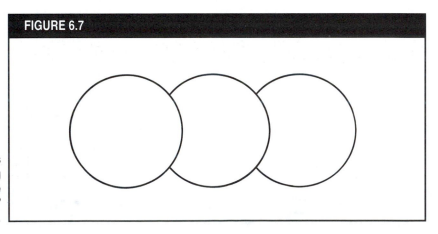

FIGURE 6.7

Most people would see this as a set of overlapping circles, although two of the shapes might have "bites" taken out of them.

together" as a figure, we will discuss all these principles together.

Proximity

One of the most important factors determining the perceptual organisation of a scene is proximity of the elements within it. Things that are close together are grouped together. In Fig. 6.8a the perception is of columns, because the horizontal spacing of the dots is greater than their vertical spacing. In Fig. 6.8b we see rows, because the horizontal spacing of the dots is the smaller, and Fig. 6.8c is ambiguous: the dots are equally spaced in both directions. Proximity in depth is a powerful organising factor. The central square in a Julesz random-dot stereogram (see Ch.7, p.144) is not visible until the two halves of the stereo pair are viewed in a stereoscope. Dots with the same disparity values are then grouped together and the square is seen as a distinct figure floating above its background.

Similarity

Things that look "similar" are grouped together. The examples shown at the top of Fig. 6.16 (p.112) appear to consist of two distinct regions, with a boundary between them. The elements on one side of this boundary have a different orientation from those on the other. In Fig. 6.9 the perception is of columns, even though the proximity information suggests rows, illustrating that similarity may override proximity information. The question of *how* similar items must be in order to be grouped together is an empirical one to which we will return.

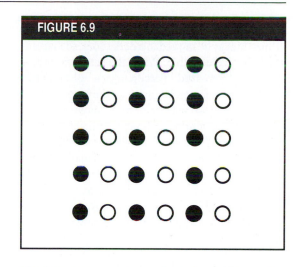

FIGURE 6.9

This picture is seen as columns. Similarity in brightness of the dots overrides proximity.

Common fate

Things that appear to move together are grouped together—think of a flock of birds or a school of fish. A camouflaged animal will remain well-hidden only if it remains stationary. As soon as it moves it is easier to see. Gibson, Gibson, Smith, and Flock (1959) illustrated grouping by common fate with a simple demonstration. They sprinkled powder on two sheets of glass, and projected an image of the powder onto a screen. While the sheets were held still a single collection of powder was seen. As soon as one sheet was moved across the other, viewers saw the powder segregated into two independent collections, by virtue of the movement in the display. Johansson (1973) has produced an even more dramatic demonstration of the power of movement to confer organisation. He attached

FIGURE 6.8

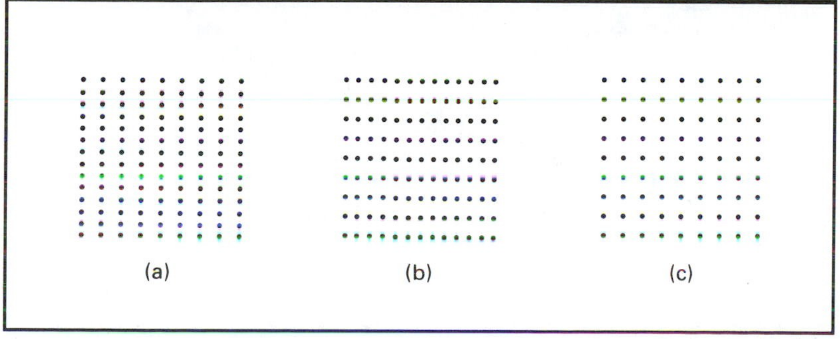

(a)   (b)   (c)

The dots in (a) form columns because they are closer vertically than horizontally. At (b) we see rows, the dots here are closer horizontally; (c) is ambiguous, the dots are equally spaced in both directions.

lights to the joints of a darkly clothed actor and filmed him as he moved in a dark room, so that only the lights were visible. When the actor was at rest, observers reported perceiving a disorganised collection of points. As soon as the actor walked, their perception was that of a moving human figure, whose actions, gait, and even gender could be discerned from the pattern of moving points. Johansson's demonstrations suggest that "common fate" involves much more than simply grouping together elements that have a common speed and direction, and we shall return to discuss the perceptual organisation of such complex displays in Chapter 15.

Good continuation

In a figure such as Fig. 6.10, one tends to perceive two smooth curves that cross at point X, rather than perceiving two irregular V-shaped forms touching at X. The Gestaltists argued that perceptual organisation will tend to preserve smooth continuity rather than yielding abrupt changes. Quite dissimilar objects may be perceived as "belonging together" by virtue of a combination of proximity and good continuity (see Fig. 6.11). Good continuation may be considered the spatial analogue of common fate.

Closure

Of several geometrically possible perceptual organisations, that one will be seen which produces a "closed" rather than an "open" figure. Thus the patterns on the left and right of Fig. 6.1 are seen as squares rather than as crosses, because the former are closed. The Gestaltists suggested that the stellar constellation "the plough" might be seen as a plough because of closure and good continuation.

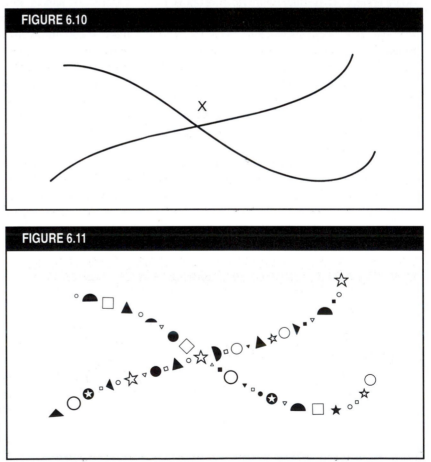

FIGURE 6.10

This is seen as two smooth lines crossing at X, rather than as two V-shapes touching at X.

FIGURE 6.11

Quite dissimilar shapes may be grouped together through a combination of proximity and good continuation.

Relative size, surroundedness, orientation, and symmetry

Other things being equal, the smaller of two areas will be seen as a figure against a larger background. Thus Fig. 6.12a will tend to be perceived as a black propellor shape against a white background because the black area is the smaller. This effect is enhanced if the white area actually surrounds the black as in Fig. 6.12b, because surrounded areas tend to be seen as figures. However, if we orient the figure so that the white area is arranged around the horizontal and vertical axes then it is easier to see this larger area as a figure (Fig. 6.12c). There seems to be a preference for horizontally or vertically oriented regions to be seen as figures. Also note that both these sets of patterns are symmetrical. Symmetry is a powerful perceptual property, and may be more salient perceptually than nonreflected repetition (Bruce & Morgan, 1975). Examples of symmetry and repetition are shown in Fig. 6.13. Symmetrical areas will tend to be perceived as figures, against asymmetrical backgrounds. Figure 6.14 shows how relative size, orientation, symmetry, and surroundedness may all operate together so that it is difficult if not impossible to see anything other than the black areas as the figures in this picture. The reader will note the perceptual stability of this picture compared with the ambiguity of Fig. 6.2, where the relative sizes, surroundedness, and symmetries in the display favour neither the "faces" nor the "vase" particularly strongly.

The Law of Prägnanz

For the Gestalt psychologists, many of these laws were held to be manifestations of the Law of Prägnanz, introduced by Wertheimer. Koffka (1935, p.138) describes the law:

> Of several geometrically possible organisations that one will actually occur which possesses the best, simplest and most stable shape.

Thus an organisation of four dots arranged as though they were at the corners of a square (Fig. 6.1, right) will be seen as a "square" because this is a "better" arrangement than, say, a cross or a triangle plus an extra dot. The square is a closed, symmetrical form, which the Gestaltists maintained was the most stable.

Although the Gestaltists accepted that familiarity with objects in the world, and "objective set", might influence perceptual organisation, they rejected an explanation solely in these terms. A major determinant of perceptual organisation for them was couched in terms of certain "field forces" that they thought operated within the brain. The Gestaltists maintained a *Doctrine of Isomorphism*, according to which there is, underlying every sensory experience, a brain event that is structurally similar to that experience. Thus when one perceives a circle, a "circular trace" is established, and so on. Field forces were held to operate to make the outcome as stable as possible, just as the forces operating on a soap bubble are such that its most stable state is a sphere.

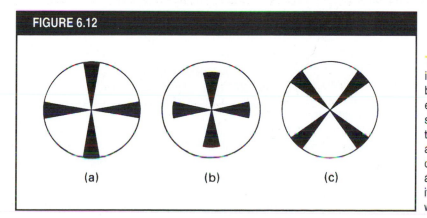

FIGURE 6.12

(a)   (b)   (c)

The preferred perception of (a) is a black propeller on a white background. This preference is enhanced if the white area surrounds the black, as at (b). If the orientation of the forms is altered, so that the white area is oriented around the horizontal and vertical axes, as at (c), then it is easier to see the larger white area as a figure.

FIGURE 6.13

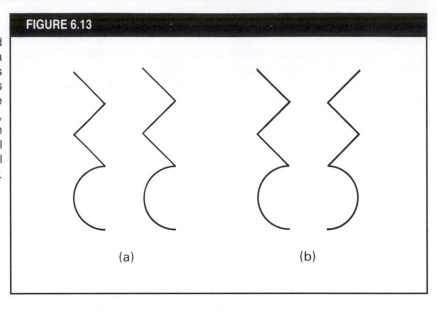

At (a) one form is repeated without reflection around a vertical axis. This arrangement is not as perceptually salient as the arrangement shown at (b), where repetition with reflection around the vertical axis produces bilateral symmetry.

(a)   (b)

FIGURE 6.14

This picture clearly shows black shapes on a white background. The black shapes are vertically oriented, symmetrical, small (relative to the background), and surrounded by the background.

Unfortunately, no evidence has been provided for such field forces, and the physiological theory of the Gestaltists has fallen by the wayside, leaving us with a set of descriptive principles, but without a model of perceptual processing. Indeed, some of their "laws" of perceptual organisation today sound vague and inadequate. What is meant by a "good" or a "simple" shape, for example? Recently workers have attempted to formalise at least some of the Gestalt perceptual principles.

RECENT APPROACHES TO PERCEPTUAL ORGANISATION

Hochberg and Brooks (1960) tried to provide a more objective criterion for the notion of "goodness" of shape by presenting subjects with line drawings (Fig. 6.15) and asking them to rate the apparent tridimensionality in these figures. They argued that as the complexity of the figures

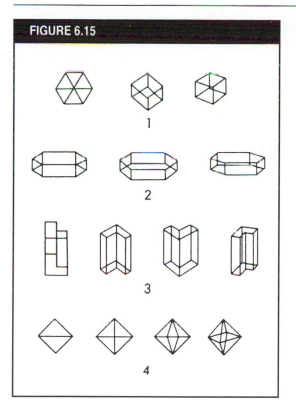

FIGURE 6.15

1

2

3

4

Examples of the forms used by Hochberg and Brooks (1960). In each of rows 1–4, the figure at the right is most likely to be seen as three-dimensional. From Julian E. Hochberg, *Perception*, 2nd edn., p.142. Copyright © 1978. Prentice-Hall Press, New York.

was the number of continuous lines. This reflects the discontinuity present, as the more continuous lines there are, the more discontinuities must be present between each. Thus the more complex, asymmetrical, and discontinuous the 2-D pattern, the more likely it was to be perceived as the projection of a 3-D figure. Hochberg and Brooks then applied their measures to a set of new figures and found they correlated well with the perceived three-dimensionality in these.

Thus it is possible to express Gestalt ideas such as "good shape" more precisely. In similar vein we now consider recent attempts to tackle the problem of grouping by similarity. How similar must items be before they are grouped together? It is unlikely that they must be identical, because no camouflage can ever perfectly match its surroundings, yet we know that camouflage can be remarkably successful. But if identity is not required, what are the important variables that determine grouping by similarity? This has been investigated by seeing how easily two different regions of a pattern, or more naturally textured image, segregate perceptually from each other. The logic of this is that the more the elements in two different regions cohere with one another, by virtue of the perceptual similarity that exists between them, the less visible will be the boundary between these two regions.

Olson and Attneave (1970) required observers to indicate where the "odd" quadrant lay within a circular display of simple pattern elements (see Fig. 6.16). They found that the quadrant was most easily spotted if the elements within it differed in slope from those of the rest of the display (e.g. < ∨) and was most difficult to find if the elements differed in configuration, but not in the slopes of their component parts (e.g. > <). Similar conclusions were reached by Beck (1972) who asked his subjects to count elements of one type (e.g. <) that were distributed randomly within a display containing elements of a different type (e.g. >). Again he reasoned that the more the odd elements stood out from the background elements, and grouped with each other rather than with the background, the easier they would be to isolate and count. Like Olson and Attneave, Beck found that slope differences led to faster counting than configurational differences.

as two-dimensional line drawings increased, so there should be a tendency for the figures to be perceived as though they were three-dimensional objects. They made a number of measurements on the figures and looked for those that correlated well with perceived three-dimensionality. The best measure was the number of angles in the figure. This measure seems to represent "complexity". The more angles the figure contains, the more complex it is in two dimensions, and the more likely it is to be perceived as a representation of a "simpler", three-dimensional object. A second measure that correlated well was the number of differently sized angles. This reflects the asymmetry in the 2-D figure, as a figure in which many of the angles are of the same size is more likely to be symmetrical than one in which many differently sized angles are present. A final measure

FIGURE 6.16

Some of the displays used by Olson and Attneave (1970) to investigate grouping by similarity. In the displays marked 1, 2, and 3, the lines in one region are of a different orientation to the rest, and the odd region is easy to spot. In display 4, odd elements are curved, and the odd region is reasonably evident. In displays 5 and 6, the configurations, but not the slopes, of the elements differ from one region to the next. Here it is much harder to spot the odd quadrant. Reprinted from Olson and Attneave (1970). Copyright © 1970 by the Board of Trustees of the University of Illinois.

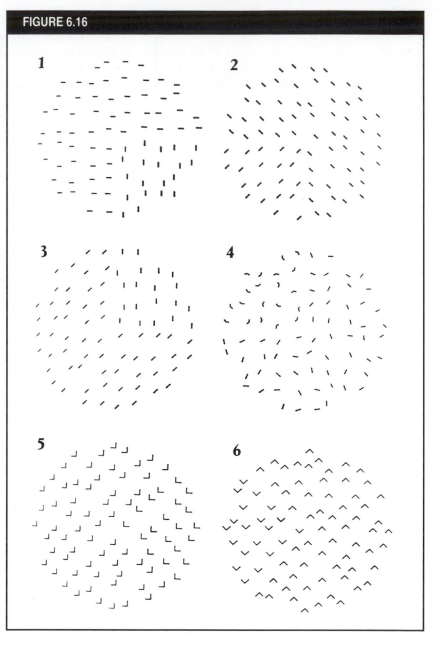

Such findings are interesting because they demonstrate that the variables that influence grouping by similarity are not necessarily the same as those that would influence the judged *conceptual* similarity of the same elements viewed individually by humans. Thus L and ⟨ might be considered more similar (both letter L, with one example tilted) when viewed as a single pair, than would L and ⌐ . However, when large numbers of these elements are combined, it is the difference in the common orientations of two populations that is perceptually more salient than the difference between the conceptual identity of the individual members. Julesz (1965) stresses that in similarity grouping we are looking at spontaneous, pre-attentive visual processing, which precedes the identification of patterns and objects, and which is quite different from deliberate scrutiny. In some textures it is possible to discern that an odd region is present by carefully examining and comparing individual pattern elements, just as one can find a camouflaged animal by careful inspection. Such processes of scrutiny, however, are at a much higher level than the grouping mechanisms we are discussing here. These "pre-attentive" grouping mechanisms appear to be implemented at a relatively early stage of processing; indeed, De Yoe, Knierem, Sagi, Julesz, and van Essen (1986) have observed cells in areas V1 and V2 of the monkey cortex that respond if texture elements differ in orientation between the centre and surround of their receptive fields.

Julesz (1965, 1975) extended the study of grouping by similarity to include more naturally textured images in which brightnesses and colour were varied as well as slope and configuration of elements. First, and most simply, he noted that two regions would be segregated if there was a clear brightness or colour difference between them, and that brightness and colour grouping appeared to operate by "averaging" rather than taking detailed account of statistical differences in the brightness distributions. If two halves of a pattern are constructed so that one half contains mostly black and dark grey squares (with a few light grey and white ones), and the other contains mostly light grey and white squares (with a few dark grey and black ones), then a clear boundary is seen between the two regions. If, however, one region contains mostly black and light grey squares, and the other contains mostly dark grey and white ones, then no clear boundary is perceived even though the composition of the two pictures in respect to the relative frequencies of the different types of square is still quite different. Here it is the average brightnesses in the two halves of the pattern that matters, not the details of the composition of these average brightnesses. Similarly, if a region is composed mostly of red and yellow squares (with a few blue and green ones) and the adjacent area is mostly green and blue (with a few red and yellow squares) then good segregation is achieved. If one region is mostly red and green, and the other mostly yellow and blue, then the segregation is not as clear.

Julesz (1965) proposed that the perceptual system imposes a "slicer" mechanism. A region of similar brightness or similar wavelength could be grouped together as distinct from another region where the "average" brightness or wavelength differed from the first.

However, the spatial distribution or "granularity" of different regions is also important. If two regions have the same overall average brightness, but with the pattern elements distributed differently, so that they are spaced apart in one region and clumped together in the other (see Fig. 6.17), a perceptual boundary will be evident. Finally, in other work on region discrimination, Julesz confirmed the findings of Olson and Attneave, and Beck, in demonstrating the importance of differences in slope in perceptual segregation.

Julesz tried to tie together a number of observations on perceptual grouping in terms of the formal statistical properties of the patterns being viewed. He initially made the strong claim that two regions can not be discriminated if their first- and second-order statistics are identical (Frisch & Julesz, 1966; Julesz, Frisch, Gilbert, & Shepp, 1973). Differences in the first-order statistics of patterns capture differences in their overall brightness. Differences in second-order statistics capture differences in granularity and slope.

Julesz's initial attempts to capture the variables determining similarity grouping in formal mathematical terms were thwarted by counter-examples, and this led him to devise his theory of "textons" (e.g. Julesz, 1981). Julesz suggested that texture discrimination depended on whether or not differences could be detected in local *features*, where these features or "textons" were the basic elements of pre-attentive (i.e. early) vision. Textons are elongated blobs or line segments (with associated parameters such as aspect-ratio and orientation) and their terminators, and thus correspond to the representation in the primal sketch as conceived by Marr and others. Julesz (1981) suggested that textures would only be discriminable where there were differences in the first-order statistics of the textons. For example, two regions of texture containing different elements with the same numbers of terminators

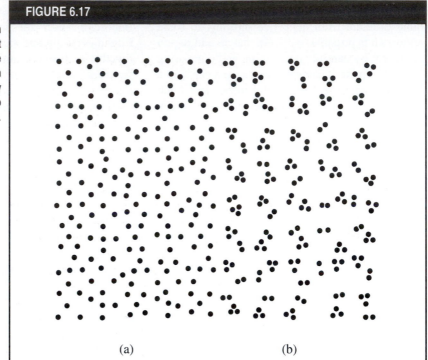

FIGURE 6.17

The average brightness in region (a) is the same as that in (b), but the dots in (b) are clumped together more than those in (a). A clear boundary is seen between the two regions.

(a)   (b)

(see Fig. 6.18) do not segregate; only the number of textons (elongated features and terminations) seems to be important, whereas their spatial arrangement, and plausible candidate features such as closure and connectivity, appear to be unimportant.

The pre-attentive visual system, evidently, cannot determine the location of terminators, but can count their numbers (or density) or their first-order statistics (Julesz, 1981, p.95).

The work of Julesz and associates emphasises that pattern elements need not be identical in order to be treated together by grouping processes. Such grouping processes seem to operate between elements of similar brightness, wavelength, slope, and granularity. These properties correspond to those that we know are extracted early on in visual processing (see Chapters 2 and 3), and correspond to the properties captured by the descriptions in the primal sketch (Chapter 5). We return to consider Marr's work towards the end of this chapter.

Thus we have seen how recent work in the area of perceptual grouping has quantified the Gestalt principles of "good shape" and "similarity". All the work described earlier has made use of artificial patterns and textures, however. Can these laws of perceptual organisation be demonstrated in more natural settings?

CONCEALMENT AND ADVERTISEMENT

In this section of the chapter we return to the broader perspective of animal vision, to demonstrate how the Gestalt principles can give some insights into the ways in which the colouration and shapes of animals can help to conceal or to reveal them. The study of camouflage in nature also provides us with a way of exploring the ways in which perceptual grouping processes in other species may be similar to, or differ from, our own.

Animals that remain concealed from predators have a greater chance of surviving and

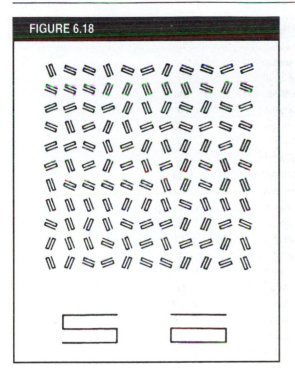

FIGURE 6.18

At the top is shown a texture made up of two different regions. The larger region is composed of "S-shaped" elements, with a smaller region composed of "10-shaped" elements. The odd region cannot be discriminated without close scrutiny, showing that if the number of lines and number of terminators agree, their exact positions are ignored. From Julesz (1981). Reprinted with permission from *Nature* (Vol.290, pp.91–97). © Macmillan Magazines Limited.

reproducing, and a predator also stands a better chance of obtaining food if it is not easily visible to its own prey. In order to remain concealed an animal should not stand out as a figure against its background, but needs instead to blend with it. On the other hand, for the purposes of breeding or defending territory, animals may need to be conspicuous to potential mates or competitors. Under such circumstances the animal may need to stand out as a distinctive figure against its surroundings. Whether an animal will be camouflaged or conspicuous depends on its behavioural needs and the habitat in which it lives. Some animals may need to remain hidden for much of the time but have the potential of occasionally giving a highly distinctive display or warning sign. This can be achieved by temporarily revealing distinctive surface features that are normally hidden beneath wings or tails, or by changing skin colour, coat, or plumage to meet changing circumstances. Thus, to understand why a creature is coloured in a particular way we need to consider ecological factors as well as perceptual ones.

Merging and contrasting

An animal that needs to be hidden should avoid standing out as figure against its background. An animal that needs to be seen should stand out as a figure distinctly from its background. The way in which this is achieved will depend on the nature of the background habitat.

An animal can blend with a uniform background by being of similar average colour and brightness. Many species are coloured fairly simply to match the habitat in which they live—for example, tropical tree-snakes are green and polar bears are white. Some animals show seasonal variation in their colouration to match their changing habitats. The Arctic fox is white in winter and brown in summer. In other species, different animals may be coloured differently in differing environments. The peppered moth is darker in urban than in rural areas, for example.

A more radical way to prevent standing out as a figure, and one that is more effective against nonuniform habitats, is to break up the perceptual cohesiveness of the surface of the body by *disruptive colouration*. Dissimilar surface areas are less likely to be grouped together as a single figure. If some of the patches of surface colour are in turn similar to elements in the background this leads the animal's surface to be grouped together with its habitat. Disruptive colouration along with *background picturing* is an efficient method of camouflage where the habitat contains different coloured and shaped elements and variations in light and shade. The tree frog shown in Fig. 6.19 is a good example of a creature whose surface markings incorporate these features. An artificial example is the green, brown, and black mottled pattern painted on tanks and combat jackets to achieve camouflage for military purposes.

In these examples of camouflage we see exploitation of the principle that grouping by similarity (with the background habitat) may

FIGURE 6.19

This African frog is well camouflaged when seen against the bark of the tree on which it habitually rests. Its asymmetrical markings show disruptive colouration along with background picturing. However, the shadow cast by the frog's head on the bark could reveal it. Photograph by P. Ward. Copyright © P. Ward/Bruce Coleman Ltd. Used by permission.

override grouping by proximity (of adjacent parts of the animal's surface). Effective disruptive colouration must match the background in terms of average brightness, colour, and density of markings. Where the background texture elements have some intrinsic orientation, as in Fig. 6.19, surface markings must be similarly oriented.

Conversely, in order to be conspicuous, an animal needs to have high brightness or colour contrast with its background. The all-black crow is a distinctive form against grass-land or stubble field. In addition, the outline of an animal's body or of significant signs or structures can be enhanced by *outlining*. Many butterflies have contrasting borders around the edges of their wings, and some fish may have black edges to emphasise their distinctive fin shapes. Because flat structures are less conspicuous as figures than solid ones (see later), and solid bodies have no single contour line (the particular contour that will correspond to the animal's outline in an image of it will depend on vantage point), it makes sense that only "flat" structures such as butterfly wings or fish fins should be outlined in this way (Hailman, 1977). More frequently we find local outlining to emphasise the shape of a patch that serves as a courtship or warning signal. Such patches are often outlined in white or black in fish and birds.

Symmetry and regularity

Symmetrical forms stand out more readily as figures against their backgrounds than do asymmetrical ones. As animals are bilaterally symmetric, those that need to be hidden must reduce their apparent symmetry. Camouflaged snakes may rest in irregular coils so that the symmetry of surface markings is not evident. The frog in Fig. 6.19 has asymmetrical markings that make it less visible as separate figure. Conversely, symmetry and repetition may be employed to enhance an animal's outline or internal features. Butterflies with dramatic markings on their wings become highly salient symmetrical figures when their wings are spread. Signal patches can also be made conspicuous by virtue of their shape. Regular geometric forms such as circles, squares, and triangles are perceptually salient figures, and they are also rare in the habitats of animals, so that surface markings that are geometrically regular will be additionally distinctive due to their dissimilarity to background elements. Hailman (1977) suggests that the common use of circular signal patches may be because they are regular, and hence unusual, rather than functioning as eye mimics. Triangular patterns can be seen on the breeding plumage of some male birds such as peacocks, and rectangular patches are found on the wings of some ducks. In many birds and fish we find another kind of regularity in the form of repeated markings—the series of tail spots on cuckoos and head stripes on sparrows, for example.

Counter-shading and reverse counter-shading

A creature might be well camouflaged in terms of matching the colours and contrasts in its background, but could still be apparent as a distinct figure by virtue of its solidity. There will be a distinct depth difference between the upper part of a cylindrical body and the surface on which it rests, which may be revealed to an observer by stereopsis or motion parallax (see Chapter 7). This will lead to grouping by proximity in depth and by common fate, just as central regions of texture can be revealed in random-dot stereograms (see Chapter 7). Many birds use sideways movements of their heads to reveal prey by motion parallax. A solution to this problem is to be as flat as possible, either behaviourally, by crouching, or structurally, by becoming flat during the course of evolution. Moths and flatfish, by virtue of their flat shapes, are at minimal depth differences from the surfaces on which they rest. Crouching also reduces the likelihood that an animal will be revealed by the shadow it casts. The head of the frog in Fig. 6.19 casts such a shadow on the bark.

Creatures that inhabit environments where there is a strong light source have the additional problem of unequal illumination of their surfaces, leading to self-shading, which again will tend to reveal. This can be compensated for by *counter-shading*. A counter-shaded animal has its darkest surface areas where the most light strikes its body, and is lighter where less light is incident (Thayer, 1918). The zebra's stripes may in part serve a counter-shading function. The black stripes are at their broadest (and hence the coat on average is at its darkest) where the body receives most light.

The clearest examples of counter-shading are found among fish, who often have dark dorsal and light ventral regions. This means that they are relatively concealed from air-borne predators where their darker backs will be seen against the murk of the water, and also concealed when viewed by a predator swimming beneath them, as their light undersides are now seen against the brighter

sky above. The counter-shading evident in an animal can usually be explained in terms of the direction of the habitual light source and the shape of its body. Caterpillars that live on the undersides of leaves have counter-shading, with their undersides, which receive the most light, darker than their backs.

If appropriate counter-shading can serve to conceal an animal then *reverse* counter-shading could act to reveal it. There are some animals, who lead their lives in upright posture, who are lighter dorsally and darker ventrally. In the male bobolink (a kind of blackbird) reverse counter-shaded plumage, in which the head and back are white, is adopted for the breeding season, where the bird needs to be distinctive, but discarded during winter when the bird's plumage is darker dorsally (Hailman, 1977).

Immobility and camouflage

However well concealed a stationary animal may be, grouping by "common fate" would tend to reveal it if it moved. It therefore benefits a camouflaged animal if it can remain still for a large proportion of the time. In many species, the adults may be brightly coloured for courtship or aggressive purposes, whereas the young may have quite different plumage or coats that merge with their backgrounds. Whether the young of a species are camouflaged or not will depend on the habitat in which the nest or den is sited, and on the behaviour of both young and parents. For example, if the nest is on open ground, and both parents leave it to forage, then camouflage of the young is more important.

However, as Cott (1940) pointed out, although immobility is advantageous to concealment, it is not essential. A green tennis ball is harder to follow on a grass court than a white one. Thus, even if an animal is active, it will be harder to spot or track if it merges with its background. Some creatures have markings that appear to make it harder to track their movement. Many snakes that flee in defence (Jackson, Ingram, & Campbell, 1976), and some fish, have longitudinal stripes that may deceive observers because they appear to remain still as the animal moves forward. Of course, movement is one of the easiest ways for an animal to reveal itself when it needs to be conspicuous. Some make use of temporal redundancy by making repetitive or stereotyped movements of their bodies in their displays, and others repeatedly flash signal patches beneath their tails or wings.

PERCEPTUAL ORGANISATION IN OTHER SPECIES

These examples of animal colouration thus illustrate how the Gestalt laws may be useful to help understand camouflage and concealment principles, at least when assessed by human vision. However, a successful camouflage for a particular species is not necessarily that which prevents its detection by a human visual system. It is the properties of the predator's, the prey's, and the conspecific's visual systems that are important. Some species may not appear well-hidden to us because their colours are different from those of their habitats. However, provided they need to be hidden from colour-blind species, only the brightness levels are important. Conversely, crab spiders, which match the flowers on which they live, may be well concealed to our eyes and to the eyes of many of their predators, but they may be detectable to any insect prey that have good sensitivity to ultraviolet radiation (Eisner, Silberglied, Aneshansley, Carrel, & Howland, 1969). How can we find out whether an animal's colouration is having its apparent (to our eyes) effect of hiding the animal or making it conspicuous?

It is possible to examine how accurate our own perceptual intuitions are about the relative degrees of concealment attained by camouflaged animals by observing the "success" that different surface markings confer to an animal in terms of its survival. This can be done through natural observation or through experiment. For example, a radical change in the predominant colouration of the peppered moth has been observed in areas where industrial pollution is present. At one time, darker members of the peppered moth species were rare. Over the last 200 years or so, in areas where

buildings and trees are polluted with soot and grime, the predominant colouration in the moths has changed. Darker members are much more frequent than lighter ones, whereas in rural areas the lighter moths are still common. This suggests that the avian predators that feed on such moths find light moths distinctive on dark backgrounds in the same way that we do. In industrial areas the gene for darker colouration has conferred an advantage on those possessing it, whose chances of surviving and reproducing have therefore been enhanced (Kettlewell, 1973).

As well as such "natural" experiments, it is possible to conduct controlled experiments in which members of a prey species are placed against different backgrounds and then exposed to predators. The success of a particular camouflage can be assessed in terms of the number of prey that survive! Sumner (1934), for example, reared mosquito fish in differently coloured tanks. These are fish that, in common with many others, adjust their colours to tone in with their surroundings. After seven to eight weeks those fish reared in a black tank were very dark, whereas those raised in a white tank were a much paler buff or grey. Equal numbers of the "black" and "white" fish were transferred into experimental tanks that were painted black or pale grey, and exposed to the Galapagos penguin as predator. Of the fish that were appropriately colour-adapted 32% were eaten, as compared with 68% of those that were inappropriately colour-adapted. Thus the Galapagos penguin seems to find fish with high contrast to their background more easily than those with low contrast, again in agreement with our own perceptions. More dramatic experiments can involve artificially colouring the prey species before exposing them to predation (e.g. Croze, 1970).

Experiments such as these are not always ethically acceptable (most people would be unhappy if the prey used in such studies were mammals or birds rather than fish or insects). A further experimental way of assessing degree of concealment without the sacrifice of too many animals is illustrated by Pietrewicz and Kamil (1977). They conducted operant conditioning experiments in which blue jays were trained to detect moths in colour slides. Interestingly they showed that the birds were sensitive to the orientation of the moths (whether their heads were pointing up, down, or horizontally), as well as to the degree of visual similarity existing between the moth's markings and those of the bark against which it was photographed. Only the latter aspect is noticeable to us. Similarly, Dittrich, Gilbert, Green, McGregor, and Grewcock (1993) trained pigeons to respond to photographs of wasps and then tested their transfer to photographs of various hoverfly species with black and yellow striped markings. The pigeons' ranking of hoverflies in terms of their similarity to wasps was different from that made by humans.

Observing the "success" of various surface markings is, of course, not the only way to study perceptual organisation in other species. Hertz (1928, 1929), for example, describes some delightful experiments with jays and bees in which she investigated aspects of their figural perception directly as they searched for food from arrangements of objects. She concluded that for the jay birds (though not for the bees), perceptual organisation was very similar to our own. To appreciate fully the adaptive significance of animal colouration requires continued research along these lines.

WHY DO THE GESTALT LAWS WORK?

We have shown that many of the Gestalt laws are useful descriptive tools for a discussion of perceptual organisation in the real world, but we are still some way from having an adequate theory of *why* the principles work and *how* perceptual organisation is achieved. We mentioned earlier how the Gestalt psychologists themselves attempted to answer both these points with their model of brain field forces. What alternative answers would contemporary theorists provide?

Marr's (1976, 1982) approach to vision emphasises that we should always consider what general assumptions about the world can be brought to bear on visual processing to constrain the range of possible interpretations for any particular image. The Gestalt principles of organisation may work because they reflect a set of sensible assumptions that can be made about the world of physical and biological objects. Because the same kind of surface reflects and absorbs light in the same kind of way, the different sub-regions of a single object are likely to look similar. Because matter is cohesive, adjacent regions are likely to belong together, and will retain their adjacency relations despite movement of the object. The shapes of natural objects tend to vary smoothly rather than having abrupt discontinuities, and many natural objects (at least those that grow) are symmetrical. A solid object stands on (and hence is at a different depth from) the surface on which it rests, and objects tend to be small compared with the ground. A perceptual system that made use of such assumptions to interpret natural images would generally achieve correct solutions to perceptual organisation, unless deceived by a camouflage exploiting these very same assumptions. It is perhaps not surprising that in our perception of unnatural displays (such as the patterns used by experimental psychologists or the authors of textbooks), we employ the same set of assumptions that serve us well in interpreting natural images.

However, having a set of descriptive principles, even if we know why they work, is still only a starting point for a full information-processing theory of grouping processes. We need to know how such principles can be applied to primitive elements recovered from images—edges, blobs, and so on—in order to recover the potentially significant structures present. It is research in artificial intelligence (AI), which has attempted to provide such a *process* theory of perceptual organisation, that is much more powerful than a purely *descriptive* theory, such as that of the Gestaltists or more recent workers like Julesz. Marr's (1976) early visual processing program implemented such a process theory and made extensive use of Gestalt principles to achieve perceptual organisation. Before describing Marr's work, we digress briefly to introduce other research in AI that has attempted to formalise organisational processes by making use of a rather different set of constraints.

ARTIFICIAL INTELLIGENCE APPROACHES TO GROUPING

Scene analysis programs

Many researchers in AI during the 1960s and 1970s attempted to solve what became known as the "segmentation problem". This is the problem of dividing a visual scene into a number of distinct *objects*. Most researchers avoided the complexities of natural images, and restricted their programs to a world of matt, white prismatic solids that were evenly illuminated. Figure 6.20 shows a line drawing of the outlines of such a collection of objects. Viewed analytically, Fig. 6.20 is just a collection of straight lines in a variety of orientations. However, our spontaneous perception of such a scene is more likely to be of a collection of distinct objects. Thus this scene is readily described by our visual apparatus as being made up of two blocks and a wedge, with one block partially occluding the other two structures. Here again we have an example of perceptual organisation. Somehow we know that the regions labelled a, b, and c belong together as one structure, distinct from d, e, and f, which belong to another. The Gestalt psychologists might argue that the perception of regions a, b, and c as belonging to a "cube" provides a closed, simple, and symmetrical interpretation, but this does not really address the question of how such a solution is achieved by visual processing.

This was the kind of problem tackled by Guzman (1968), Clowes (1971), and Waltz (1975), among others, who set out to produce computer programs that could "see" objects from collections of lines such as these. The common principle in all their work was a consideration of the *junctions* present in these figures. A junction is a point where two or more lines meet. Different junction types have different implications for the possible arrangement of surfaces within the picture. Thus Guzman suggested that the presence of an *arrow* junction would generally imply that the edges that formed the fins of the arrow belonged to a single body, whereas a T junction generally implied that the shaft and the cross-bar of the T belonged to different bodies. Figure 6.20 shows how these principles apply in our example.

Guzman's program SEE considered only junctions, and incorporated his own informal

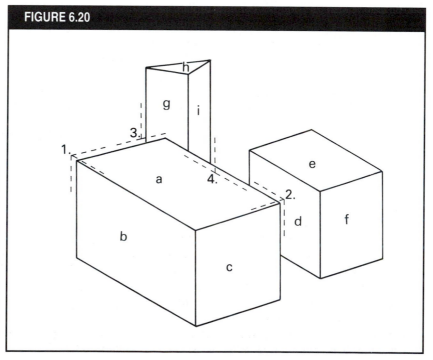

FIGURE 6.20

We have no difficulty in seeing that regions a, b, and c belong together (likewise d, e, and f; g, h, and i). Guzman's program SEE interpreted pictures like this by examining the junctions present. Examples of arrow junctions are shown at 1 and 2, and T junctions are shown at 3 and 4. What other kinds of junction are there in this picture?

intuitions about the interpretations of different junction types. Clowes tackled the problem of junction specification more systematically, and employed a more sophisticated notion of how different junction types in the image relate to the organisation of *objects* in the "scene" depicted. This was achieved by considering the nature of the *edges* depicted by the junction lines (Clowes, 1971; Huffman, 1971), as well as the nature of the intersection of these lines. Edges may be convex, concave, or occluding (see Fig 6.21). Only certain combinations of edge types are compatible with a particular configuration of lines at a junction. By ensuring that edges were consistently labelled along their entire length, Clowes' program OBSCENE was able to interpret pictures successfully provided that no more than three lines met at a single junction. The program was also able to "reject" certain pictures as "impossible" (see Fig. 6.22, for example), whereas SEE would simply accept such examples as objects.

The most elegant example of work of this type was that of Waltz (1975), who introduced a fourth edge type, the crack, and whose program accepted pictures of scenes containing shadows. Once shadows are introduced, the possible labellings for a particular type of junction increase dramatically, as a number of different types of edge can now be present. Nevertheless, Waltz's program was able successfully to parse scenes containing shadows. His work illustrates how adding more information in the form of light and shading may actually aid the interpretation of a scene by providing additional local constraints.

Although such A.I. programs are intrinsically interesting, and point out the complicated processing that may underlie our everyday ability to perceive patterns such as these, they are of limited importance. The programs work by incorporating the constraints of their visual worlds, but the particular constraints employed are specific to the world of white prismatic solids—an artificially manufactured world for whose perception our visual systems did not evolve. The principles embodied within these segmentation programs would fail to recover the significant structures in natural images. Natural objects may have internal markings, texture, and shading (see

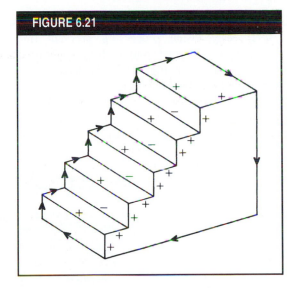

FIGURE 6.21

Three different kinds of edge are shown: concave (–), convex (+), and occluding (>).

Ch.5, p.76). Straight lines and angular junctions are rare. Indeed, A.I. segmentation programs of the type described either start with a line drawing as input, or make use of initial programs to find the edges in images of prismatic solids by using the assumption that edges are straight, along with higher-level knowledge about "likely" places to find lines (e.g. Shirai, 1973).

Marr's program

Of more interest to our discussion is a processing model that aims to recover structures from natural images of everyday objects and surfaces, despite

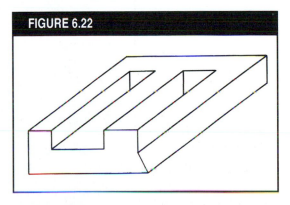

FIGURE 6.22

An impossible object. Reprinted from Clowes (1971) with kind permission of Elsevier Science, The Netherlands.

their noise, texture, and shadow. Marr's (1976, 1982) early visual processing program finds occluding and internal contours from images such as those shown in Fig. 6.23. We have already considered some of Marr's ideas in Chapters 4 and 5. He proposed that cells in the retina and visual cortex of mammals function to locate *zero-crossings* (see pp.78–82) in the spatially filtered retinal image, which serve as the first step towards recovering information about edges in the world. A comparison of the zero-crossings found by sets of cells with different receptive field sizes leads to a set of assertions about the "features" present at each location in the image. This set of assertions is the raw primal sketch.

The primitives in the raw primal sketch are edges, bars, blobs, and terminations, which have the associated attributes of orientation, contrast,

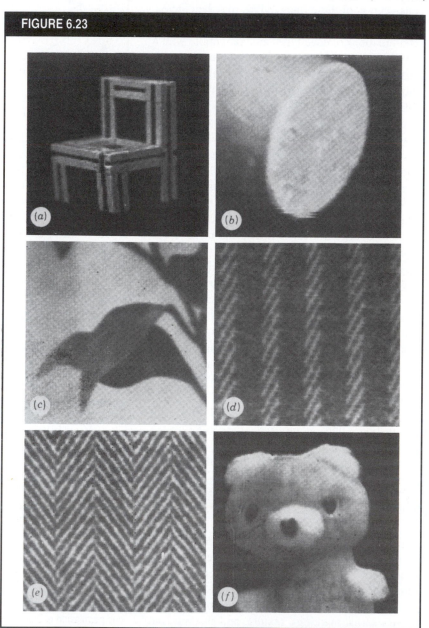

FIGURE 6.23

Examples of the images analysed by Marr's (1976) early vision program: (a) a chair; (b) a rod; (c) a plant; (d) and (e) textures; and (f) a teddy bear. Reproduced from Marr (1976) with permission of The Royal Society.

length, width, and position. The representation of a straight line would consist of a termination, then several segments having the same orientation, then a final termination. The raw primal sketch is a very complex, messy affair (see Fig. 5.6), from which we need to recover global structures as well as internal structures and surface texture.

Marr proposed that this is achieved in the next stage of early visual processing by the recursive assignment of *place tokens* to small structures, or aggregations of structures, in the raw primal sketch. These place tokens are in turn aggregated together to form larger units, in a cyclical manner. Place tokens can be defined by the *position* of a blob, or of a short line or edge; by the *termination* of a longer edge, line, or elongated blob; or by a small *aggregation* of tokens. Aggregation of these place tokens can proceed by clustering nearby place tokens on the basis of changes in spatial density (see Fig. 6.24), by curvilinear aggregation, which produces contours by joining aligned items that are near to one another (see Fig. 6.25), and finally by theta aggregation. Theta aggregation involves the grouping of similarly oriented items

in a direction that relies on, but differs from, their intrinsic orientation. Theta aggregation can, for example, be used to recover the vertical stripes in a herring-bone pattern where all the individual texture elements are oriented obliquely (see Fig. 6.26).

The grouping together of place tokens thus relies on local proximity (adjacent elements are combined) and similarity (similarly oriented elements are combined), but more global considerations can also influence the structures detected. For example, in curvilinear aggregation, a "closure" principle could allow two edge segments to be joined even though the contrast across the edge segments differed due to illumination effects (see the image in Fig. 6.27). Marr's theory therefore embodies many of the Gestalt principles that we discussed at length earlier.

The grouping procedures use the construction of tokens at different scales to locate physically meaningful boundaries in the image. It is essential that different scales are used in order to recover different kinds of surface properties.

FIGURE 6.24

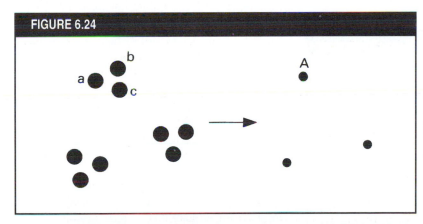

Place tokens corresponding to small dots can be grouped together by proximity to yield higher-order place tokens. Here, place tokens at a, b, and c are grouped to yield a place token at A, and likewise for the other dots in this figure.

FIGURE 6.25

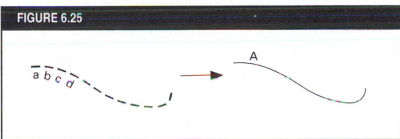

Curvilinear aggregation will group place tokens at a, b, c, d, and so on to yield a single structure A.

FIGURE 6.26

Theta aggregation can recover the vertical orientation of the stripes of a herring-bone pattern.

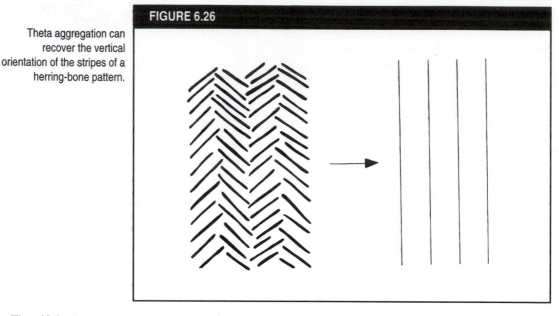

Thus if the image was a close-up view of a cat, the raw primal sketch might yield descriptions mostly at the scale of the cat's hairs. At the next level the markings on its coat may appear ... and at a yet higher level there is the parallel stripe structure of these markings (Marr 1982, p. 91).

FIGURE 6.27

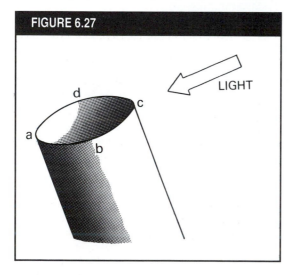

Curvilinear aggregation along with the application of a closure principle could reveal the contour a-b-c-d, despite the different contrasts of the edge segments along this contour. This pattern of shading might arise if a tube was illuminated in the direction shown.

In a herring-bone pattern we know that the "bones" are short parallel segments oriented at 45°, and that, at a larger scale, these form vertical stripes (Fig. 6.26).

Boundaries arising from changes in surface material (where two different objects overlap, for example), or from abrupt changes in surface orientation or depth, can be revealed in two ways. First, boundaries may simply be marked by place tokens. The elliptical boundary perceived in Fig. 5.19C, for example, could be produced by the curvilinear aggregation of the place tokens assigned to the termination of each line. We saw earlier (Fig. 5.20) how complex cells in V2 may be organised to link such line-ends to implement the kind of aggregation process that Marr had in mind. Second, texture boundaries may be revealed by discontinuities in parameters that describe the spatial organisation of an image. Changes in the local density of place tokens, their spacing, or their overall orientation structure could all be used to reveal such boundaries. Although the boundary in Fig. 6.29 is not defined by the spacing of place tokens, it is revealed by discontinuity in the spatial distribution of orientations of the small elements in the image.

This last example also illustrates how Marr's theory can be applied to the problem of texture and region discrimination tackled by Julesz (see

FIGURE 6.28

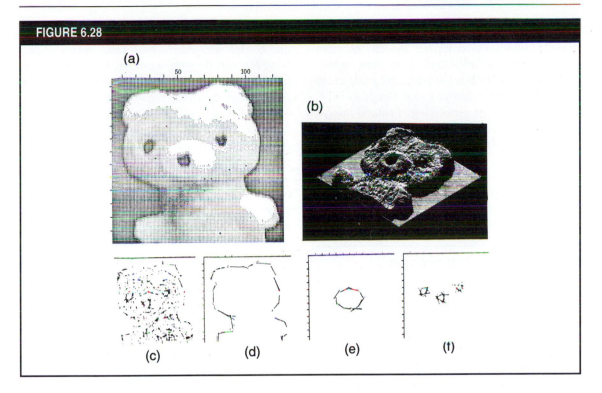

The image of a teddy bear (Fig 6.23f) is printed at (a), and shown as an intensity map at (b). The location of all the small edge segments in the raw primal sketch is shown at (c). The structures that emerge after grouping operations are shown at (d), (e), and (f). Reproduced from Marr (1976) with permission of The Royal Society.

pp.113–114). Julesz tried to arrive at a universal mathematical formula to explain why some texture boundaries were perceptually evident, although others were invisible without scrutiny, but Marr provided a process theory that offered a more powerful explanation. Julesz's explanation was purely descriptive; Marr showed how a set of descriptive principles could be used to recover texture and larger structures from images.

The success of these organising principles in Marr's (1976, 1982) early visual processing program can be judged by its ability to recover the occluding contours from realistic images such as the teddy bear (see Fig. 6.23f), and to reveal the internal contours of the bear, which correspond to eyes, nose, and muzzle outlines (Fig. 6.28). Such structures are recovered without recourse to high-level knowledge. The program knows nothing of the usual shape of a teddy bear's head, and does not find the contours that correspond to its eyes because it "expects" to find them. Marr's

FIGURE 6.29

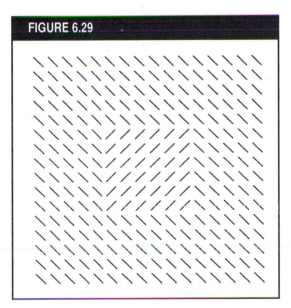

Example of texture segmentation, defined by "orientation contrast". The centre and background regions have the same mean luminance but differ in element orientation.

theory of early visual processing thus contrasts strongly with some computer models, or more general theories of visual perception where expectations and "object-hypotheses" guide every stage of perceptual analysis (e.g. Gregory, 1973; Roberts, 1965). The processing of natural images by Marr's program works because the program embodies grouping principles that reflect general properties of the world. Things that are oriented similarly, or lie next to each other, are more likely to "belong together" than things that are oriented dissimilarly and spaced far apart.

ENERGY MODELS FOR TEXTURE SEGMENTATION

In Marr's scheme, local oriented features are found first, then subjected to a variety of grouping operations, described earlier. Recent thinking about texture segmentation in the context of spatial filtering has suggested, on the other hand, that boundaries between regions differing in texture may be detected rather more easily and directly than previously suspected. Consider the image of Fig. 6.29 in which the centre square and background regions are defined only by a difference in element orientation. A spatial filter tuned to right-oblique orientation would respond strongly to the centre region, but rather little to the background, as illustrated in Fig. 6.30A. At this point, the texture border has been transformed into a boundary between low- and high-contrast areas in the filter's response pattern. How might this boundary be found? A simple, but important idea is to do further processing that converts this contrast difference into an intensity difference, and then to find that intensity edge by standard methods (cf. Chapter 5).

To convert the contrast difference into an intensity difference requires a *nonlinear* operation, and there are several, roughly equivalent, possibilities that the modeller, or evolution, could select. To get the flavour of this, let us suppose that the filter response values of Fig. 6.30A were either +10 or −10 (arbitrary units) in the centre region and +1 or −1 in the background. The mean response is

0 in each region, and so local averaging would lose the border altogether. *Full-wave rectification*, however, will do what we want. By definition, a full-wave rectifier sets negative values to positive. All values in the centre region would then become +10, and the surround values would be +1. Contrast difference has been converted to intensity difference as required. *Half-wave rectification* sets negative values to zero, leaving positive values unchanged. The centre responses would then become 0 or 10 (mean 5), while the background values were 0 or 1 (mean 0.5). Again a mean intensity difference emerges, but accompanied by greater variability of local values. A third option is *squaring* of the filter responses. As in the full-wave case, all values go positive, but in addition high values are emphasised relative to low ones. Centre responses would go to +100, and surround values to +1. These nonlinear, rectifying operations are both simple and physiologically plausible. Figure 6.30B shows an example of the effect of full-wave rectification on the pattern of filter responses. A mean intensity difference is clearly achieved, but with some residual variation at a fine scale. An appropriate degree of spatial smoothing in the edge-detection operator allows this variation to be ironed out (Fig. 6.30C) before the boundary is located (Fig. 6.30D).

In summary then, the foundation for several recent *energy models* of texture segmentation (Bergen & Adelson, 1988; Bergen & Landy, 1991; Bovik, Clark, & Geisler, 1990; Malik & Perona, 1990) is a chain of simple ideas: (i) regions that are differently textured necessarily differ in their spatial structure; (ii) if we apply a bank of spatial filters to the image, at different orientations and different scales, then at least some of those filters will be more strongly activated by one texture than the other; (iii) the difference in activation can be converted into a simple intensity difference in response energy across space; (iv) this energy difference is greatest at the texture boundary and can be found by procedures already familiar from the detection of luminance edges. In short, spatial filtering (step ii) and a suitable nonlinearity (step iii) can convert the problem of texture segmentation into a much simpler problem of edge detection.

FIGURE 6.30

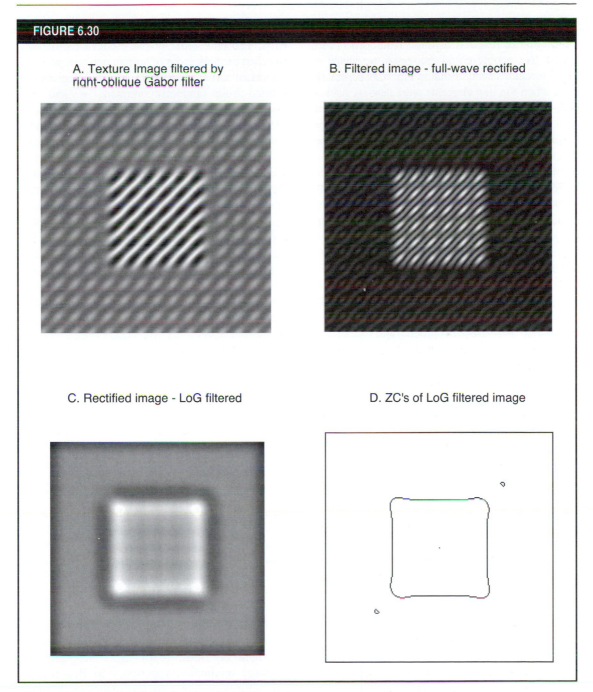

A. Texture Image filtered by right-oblique Gabor filter

B. Filtered image - full-wave rectified

C. Rectified image - LoG filtered

D. ZC's of LoG filtered image

Worked example of the energy approach to finding texture boundaries. The input image is a texture with the centre region defined by orientation contrast (Fig. 6.29). (A) Output image from a small, right-oblique filter. Note large response to right-oblique lines, as expected. In A and C, large positive and negative responses are represented by light and dark, respectively; zero response is mid-grey. (B) Filter output (as A) after full-wave rectification, i.e. negative values in A set to positive. This converts the difference in contrast to a difference in mean intensity of response. Zero response is black in this plot. (C) Rectified image (as B) after a second stage of filtering by a smoothing, second-derivative filter (LoG; see Figs. 5.3, 5.4). This image should have zero-crossings at the texture edges, and this is confirmed by the zero-crossing contour shown in D.

How well does this approach fit with human perception of textured regions? Nothdurft (1985) found that people could recognise the shape of texture regions such as that in Fig. 6.29 especially well when the line elements were densely packed and relatively long. Short lines, sparsely spaced, yielded no visible shapes at all. Shape discrimination also improved with the difference in orientation between lines in the "figure" and lines in the background, being fairly poor for a 10° difference and much better for differences of 30° or 90°. All of these factors would be expected to enhance the differential activation of filters between the two regions, and so the energy models are broadly consistent with Nothdurft's results. Furthermore, we can ask whether the *edge* is vital in segmentation or whether we need consider only the general difference in activation between the regions. Nothdurft (1985) offers a demonstration suggesting that the edge is crucial, and specifically that *orientation contrast* at the boundary is the important factor. When element orientation changed abruptly at the region boundary, segmentation was very clear, but when the same elements were redistributed within the centre and background regions, segmentation disappeared. When the variability of orientations in the background increased, the orientation change at the boundary also had to be increased to maintain segregation (Nothdurft, 1991). The importance of feature contrast at boundaries also seems to hold for segmentation based on changes in motion direction and colour (Nothdurft, 1993).

These principles for finding texture boundaries were applied in a full, multi-channel model by Malik and Perona (1990). Their model used both circular and oriented filters at a range of spatial scales, in order to capture the variety of textural differences that might occur in images. Interestingly, they argued in favour of half-wave rectification rather than full-wave or squaring, and for the use of only even-symmetric filters, not odd-symmetric; see their paper for details. The model also incorporated some inhibitory interactions between filter responses to accentuate the larger values, followed by smoothing and edge detection, as described earlier. The model performed well when tested against a variety of

texture pairs for which good psychophysical data exist. The rank order of the model's predictions matched the rank order of human performance. An important test case is where adjacent regions are formed from randomly oriented "+" and "L" elements. The two regions have the same mean luminance, and the line segments have the same length and the same (random) distribution of orientations. As segmentation is very clear for this texture pair, Julesz (e.g. 1984) argued that line-intersections (in the "+" elements) acted as one of the primitive atoms ("textons") of texture vision. The success of filter-based energy models on this and related tasks clearly challenges the need for texture vision to make features or textons explicit (Bergen & Adelson,1988; Malik & Perona, 1990).

Bergen and Landy (1991) developed a model with a similar flavour to the Malik and Perona model, specifically aimed at segmentation by orientation differences. We sketch their model in Fig. 6.31, because it incorporates several additional mechanisms of wider interest in early vision. Its first stages—squaring and smoothing of oriented filter outputs—were discussed earlier. The next stage is *opponency*, taking the difference between energies in channels tuned to orthogonal orientations (horizontal-vertical, H-V; left-right oblique, L-R). Opponency is a well-known feature of colour vision (see Ch.2, p.35), and probably motion analysis too (Adelson & Bergen, 1985; see Chapter 8). Its function in the model is to improve the orientation-coding properties of the system by enhancing the difference in energies between regions. There is physiological evidence for opponency between orientations, as V1 cells can be inhibited by stimuli oriented at right angles to their preferred one (Morrone, Burr, & Maffei, 1982) and corresponding effects are observed in the electrical response of the human visual cortex (Morrone & Burr, 1986). This supports the proposed orientation opponency in Bergen and Landy's model. At the contrast-gain control stage (see Bonds, 1991; Heeger, 1992a), the outputs of the opponent mechanisms, (H-V) and (L-R), are each divided by the sum (H + V + L + R) of the response energies from the four oriented channels. This normalises the response values, making them independent of the overall luminance contrast of

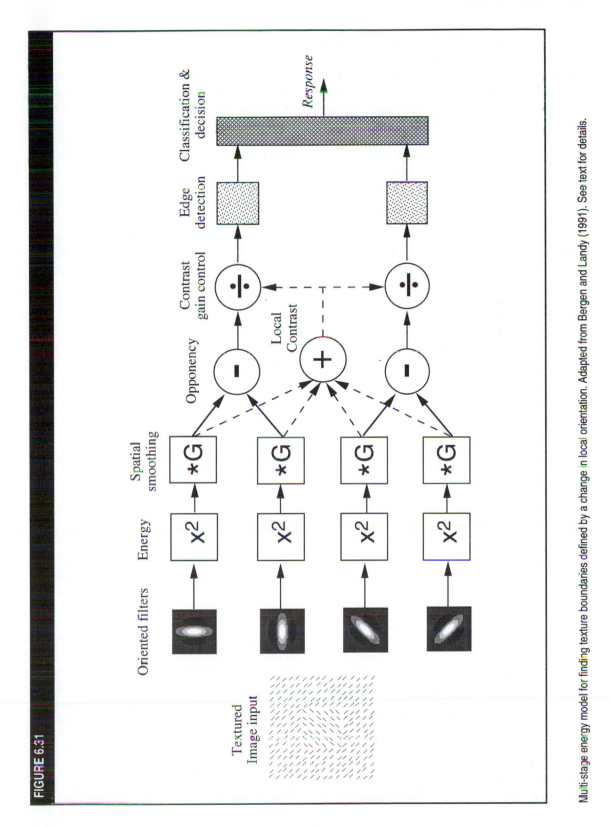

FIGURE 6.31 Multi-stage energy model for finding texture boundaries defined by a change in local orientation. Adapted from Bergen and Landy (1991). See text for details.

the stimulus pattern. It also suppresses weak responses in one channel when responses are strong in the other channel. The full model was able to give a good account of psychophysical data on shape discrimination for textured regions defined by orientation difference (Bergen & Landy, 1991). We shall see many of its features reappear in our discussion of motion analysis (Chapter 8).

In summary, spatial contrast in the magnitude or "energy" of filter responses may be adequate to account for much of texture segregation. The spatial selectivity of the filters achieves a grouping by similarity of orientation or size, without having to represent the texture elements individually. This makes good sense for natural surfaces such as bark (Fig. 6.19) or skin, which have readily identifiable texture, but where it is not clear that individual "elements" even exist. Another Gestalt "law"—proximity—can be seen in the same light, as more closely packed elements increase the intensity and uniformity of the filter outputs after the nonlinear stage. For example, in the classic "rows and columns" demonstration (Fig. 6.8), closer packing in the columns will activate vertical filters more strongly than horizontal ones, and vice-versa for rows. When vertical and horizontal filters are equally activated (Fig. 6.8c), the organisation is ambiguous. The grouping and linking of explicitly derived local features—in the Marr and Julesz traditions—is therefore not the only basis for more global levels of perceptual organisation.

BEYOND FILTERS: TO CONTOURS AND SURFACES

It would be wrong to conclude from these texture studies, however, that fairly simple post-processing of filter outputs provides a complete account of perceptual organisation. The energy models are relevant to the effects of proximity and similarity, but give little information about structural factors such as symmetry, closure, or "good form". We round off our discussion with several lines of recent experimental evidence pointing to further organising processes: first, that the Gestaltists' "good continuation", or

equivalently Marr's notion of "curvilinear aggregation", is implemented by cooperative processes across the image; second, that elongated contours are segmented into parts that correspond to the parts of objects; and finally, that textural grouping and segmentation may depend on the representation of surfaces in depth, and not just on image-processing operations of the kind sketched in Fig. 6.31.

Perceptual linking along straight and curved paths

Simple demonstrations of "good continuation", such as Figs. 6.10 and 6.11, are amenable to a spatial filter approach, because oriented receptive fields that spanned several elements could automatically pick up the dominant orientation along the curve, and at the intersection of two curves. The experiments of Field, Hayes, and Hess (1993), however, cannot be explained so easily, and point to a more active linking process. Their observers were presented with large arrays of 256 small, randomly scattered striped patches (Gabor patches), and within this large set of randomly oriented distractors a sub-set of just 12 patches was arranged along an undulating, snake-like path. The observer's task was to determine which of two such arrays contained the "snake", as a function of various parameters such as the "wiggliness" of the snake (path angle), and the degree to which the path elements were aligned or misaligned along the direction of the path (Fig. 6.32a). Straight paths, with elements aligned along the path, were most easily detected. Much more surprising was the finding that very jagged, undulating paths, which changed direction by up to 40–60° with every step, were still highly detectable, provided the elements were *aligned* along the path. As the path contains elements in all orientations, it cannot be distinguished from the distractors by applying any single oriented filter. Instead it was the alignment of orientations along the curve that was important. Misalignment by +/–15° reduced performance, and misalignment by +/–30° made the path almost undetectable. In contrast, alignment or misalignment of spatial phase had no effect. Field et al. (1993) interpret these findings in terms of an "association field", suggesting "a localised linking

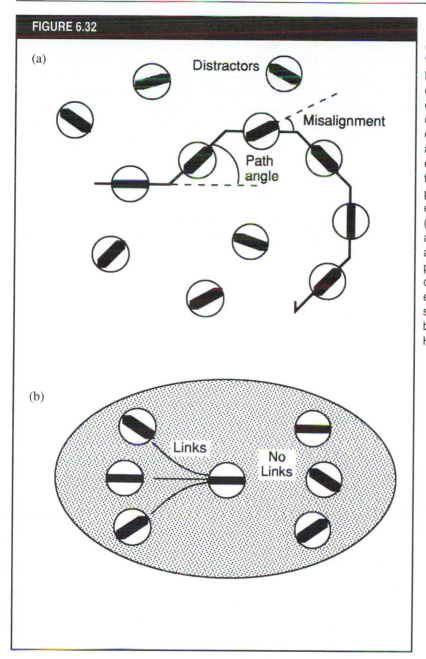

FIGURE 6.32

(a) Display used for research on "good continuation". Subjects had to detect the presence of a continuous path of elements embedded in a field of randomly oriented distractors. The path changed direction by a given angle from step to step, and elements might be misaligned from the local direction of the path. Lines joining the path elements were not present. (b) Association field proposed to account for the finding that alignment of elements along the path was the crucial factor in detecting its presence. Adjacent elements would be "linked" if a smooth curve could be drawn between them. After Field, Hayes, and Hess (1993).

process or association between the responses to the elements in the path according to a specific set of rules" (p.185). Their scheme for this linking process is shown in Fig. 6.32b, indicating that links will be made between two adjacent stimulus elements if both their orientation and position are such that they would lie on a simple smooth curve passing through both elements. This is more specific than the idea that elements are grouped if they are close and/or similarly oriented. The association field could serve to build a chain of linked elements representing a continuous contour, or a "flow" of texture in the image (Field et al., 1993).

Further evidence for spatially extended linking of local responses comes from experiments of Polat and Sagi (1993, 1994). Their experiments tested a very basic visual task—the forced-choice detection of very low-contrast patches of sinusoidal grating—with and without the presence of two adjacent "masking" patches of higher contrast. One might guess that contextual and grouping effects would be minimal in this kind of task, but it was not so. When the masking patches were superimposed on the test patch they made it harder to see. This is conventional masking, discussed in Chapter 5 (p.85). However, when the masking patches were adjacent to the test patch they tended to improve its detection; contrast thresholds were lower than in the baseline condition without a mask. This is *facilitation*, and the forced-choice method ensures that it is a genuine improvement in visual performance, and not an artefact of guessing or reporting bias. Facilitation was greatest when the masking patches had the same spatial frequency and orientation as the test (Polat & Sagi, 1993), and were co-axially aligned with it (Polat & Sagi, 1994). The spatial range of facilitation was extensive: it remained quite strong even when the masks were displaced from the test patch by as much as six spatial periods of the test grating. Unlike the "snake" detection experiments discussed earlier, facilitation did not seem to extend along smoothly curved paths, but was greatest for collinear alignment (Polat & Sagi, 1994). Even so, both types of study suggest that "local" spatial filters in vision actually interact across fairly long distances, in ways that serve the detection and representation of elongated contours. Facilitatory interactions across space have been found both psychophysically (e.g. Cannon & Fullenkamp, 1993) and physiologically (Nelson & Frost, 1985). Anatomical studies have revealed long-range connections across the visual cortex, linking cortical columns with a common orientation preference that may mediate these interactions (Gilbert, 1995), and the process of linking may well be associated with the selective synchronisation of cells across the cortex, discussed in Chapter 3 (pp.63–64).

Segmenting parts for recognition

Marr's (1976) program showed how an object's occluding contour and internal markings could be assembled from the collection of more primitive descriptions comprising the raw primal sketch, on the basis of assumptions that generally hold true in the world of natural objects. More recently, other researchers have shown how similar general assumptions can be used to segment a complex occluding contour into different "part" components—a problem reminiscent of that originally tackled by Guzman and others with artificial objects.

For example, Hoffman and Richards (1984) provided a formal computational analysis of the role played by concavities in contour segmentation. They discussed *the transversality regularity*: distinct parts of objects intersect in a contour of concave discontinuity of their tangent planes. At any point around this intersection, a tangent to the surface of one part forms a concave cusp with the tangent to the surface of the other part (concave means it points into the object rather than into the background; see Fig. 6.33). This transversality regularity means that in an image of a complex shape, "concavities" mark the divisions between the contours of distinct parts. Concavities can be detected in contours of smooth shapes by seeking places where there is greatest negative curvature (see Fig. 6.35).

Hoffman and Richards provided some compelling demonstrations as evidence for the importance of these concavities in our segmentation of shapes. They examined a number of classic ambiguous "reversing" figures, such as the Schröder staircase (Fig. 6.34) and the faces–vase figure (Fig. 6.2), and showed how reversals of these figures are related to the possible alternative part segmentations. In the Schröder staircase (Fig. 6.34), for example, according to the partitioning scheme, "parts" of the figure must be "steps", as each of the steps is bounded by two lines of concave discontinuity. When the staircase is seen in such a way that the plane marked "x" in Fig. 6.34 appears to face upwards, then the steps that are defined by concave discontinuities pointing into the staircase are such that planes "x" and "y" are seen to belong together as faces of the same

FIGURE 6.33

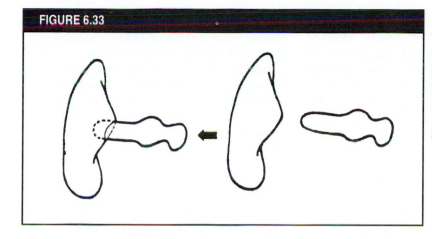

The "transversality regularity": When two surfaces interpenetrate they always meet in concave discontinuities. Reprinted from Hoffman and Richards (1984) with kind permission of Elsevier Science, The Netherlands.

FIGURE 6.34

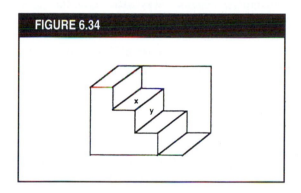

The Schröder staircase shows how part boundaries change as the figure and ground reverse. Reprinted from Hoffman and Richards (1984) with kind permission of Elsevier Science, The Netherlands.

FIGURE 6.35

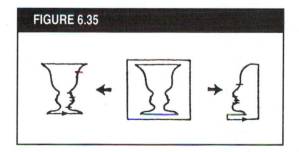

The faces–vase figure. When the vase region is taken as figure, then the concavities (minima of curvature) divide the vase into a base, stem, etc. When the faces regions are taken as figure, the concavities reveal parts corresponding to forehead, nose, etc. Reprinted from Hoffman and Richards (1984) with kind permission of Elsevier Science, The Netherlands.

step. But when the figure reverses, so that the staircase now lies in the upper right of the picture, and plane "x" appears to face downwards, the concavities pointing into the body of the staircase define a different set of steps; planes "x" and "y" now form faces of different, adjacent steps. In the faces–vase figure (Fig. 6.35), when the figure is seen as the vase, then concavities pointing into it define its parts as the base, stem, and bowl. When the figure is seen as a pair of faces, then the concavities pointing into them define parts as forehead, nose, and so forth. This demonstration shows how the same contour can be "recognised" as two distinct objects: what matters is the way in which the contour is partitioned prior to recognition, and this in turn seems to involve a simple search for concavities referred to the centre of whichever region is seen as the figure.

Hoffman and Richards (1984) have shown how the kind of occluding contour that might result from the application of the Gestalt grouping principles may be resegmented into its parts. As we will see in Chapter 9, such segmentation forms an essential stage in Marr's theory of the analysis and recognition of occluding contours, and at that point we will return to the part structure of objects.

Perceptual grouping and the representation of surfaces

Marr (1982) did not regard his early visual processing program as solving the "figure-ground" or "segmentation" problem as traditionally conceived. The goal of early visual processing is not to recover the "objects" present within a scene—for the division of a scene into component objects is an arbitrary and ambiguous affair. Which should we regard as the "objects" to be recovered—a crowd of people, each individual person, or the eyes, ears, and nose of each? Such consideration depends on the use to which the information is to be put. The recovery of the full primal sketch, in which some potentially significant structures such as occluding edges may be found, is only one aspect of early visual processing. Marr saw the goal of early visual processing as describing the surfaces present in the image. In recent years, Nakayama and colleagues have marshalled experimental evidence supporting the view that many early vision operations, such as texture segmentation and motion correspondence, take place at the level of surface representation, and not in the 2-D image domain.

Of particular relevance to this chapter are the experiments of He and Nakayama (1994) on texture segmentation. The task was to discriminate a target region containing white L-shaped elements from a background region containing white vertical bars, or vice versa (Fig. 6.36A). Thus target and background regions are distinguished by the presence or absence of horizontal bars. This relatively simple task could therefore be done by grouping features in the primal sketch, or by a filter-based scheme of the kind discussed earlier. Next, by manipulating stereoscopic cues (see Chapter 7), He and Nakayama (1994) made the "L" and "bar" elements appear to be an array of white rectangles occluded by nearer, black rectangles (Fig. 6.36B). In these circumstances, perceived texture segmentation was weak, even though the same low-level cues were present as in control conditions. In the control conditions, where segmentation was strong, occlusion of surfaces was not perceived, and the elements were seen simply as "L"s and "bars".

These results certainly present a strong challenge to both the filter-based and

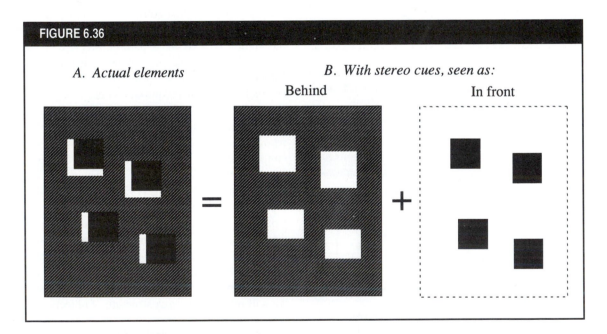

FIGURE 6.36

A. Actual elements   *B. With stereo cues, seen as:*

Behind   In front

Schematic illustration of the displays used to show that an easy texture discrimination could be eliminated by creating the appearance of two homogeneous surfaces, one occluding the other. Segmentation of regions containing white bars and Ls was initially strong (the experiments used many more elements than shown here). But when the white elements appeared to be a uniform field of white squares, partially occluded by nearer black squares, segmentation was weak. After He and Nakayama (1994).

feature-grouping accounts. In the first case, they perhaps imply that the secondary stages of smoothing and edge detection in models like Fig. 6.31 occur much later than has been supposed. In the second case, they suggest either that feature-grouping must operate at a relatively high level, at which 3-D surfaces and the occlusions between surfaces are represented, or that feature-grouping can be controlled by those higher levels of representation. It is to the representation of surfaces in depth that we turn in Chapter 7.

CONCLUSIONS

The Gestalt psychologists, through the study of perception of simple patterns, gave us insights into the organisational principles that may apply to the perception of the world. The study of natural camouflage and concealment shows that these principles fare well in describing the utility of various surface markings of animals. Marr showed how such principles might be incorporated within a processing model that reveals the structures hidden in the messy data obtained from natural images. Recent research has begun to uncover some of the basic mechanisms underlying this recovery of "global" structure by human and animal visual systems. At a relatively low level, nonlinear transformations of the outputs of spatial filters can convert higher-order structures, such as texture boundaries, into simpler intensity edges whose detection is relatively well understood. But in addition, experiments confirm the existence of active processes linking elements across visual space, and the work of He and Nakayama implies that at least some of these processes take place at a fairly high level where a representation of surfaces in depth has been established.

7

Perceiving Depth

Towards the end of the previous chapter we described how Marr's early visual processing program recovers aspects of the structure of images from an initial array of intensities. As we pointed out, Marr saw the outcome of early visual processing as a description of the surfaces being viewed by an observer. The recovery of occluding and internal contours is one aspect of this, but the full primal sketch is still essentially a description of the *image*, rather than of the *world*. The visual world that we view consists of surfaces extending away into the distance, and solid objects resting on them at different distances and with their surfaces inclined differently towards us. In addition, the pattern of light reaching the retina is never static. The eyes, heads, and bodies of observers move, and objects and animals in the scene being viewed also move. In this chapter we consider some of the optical information available to animals that allows them to perceive the layout of surfaces in the world and the relative distances of objects from themselves.

Perceiving the third dimension
The psychology of perception has been dominated by the apparent paradox of three-dimensional vision. As we discussed in Chapter 1, the eye can for some purposes be thought of as a camera, with

the cornea and lens acting to focus light onto a mosaic of retinal receptors. At any instant of time, therefore, one can conceive of the pattern of excitation of retinal receptors as a "picture", curved around the back of an eyeball. Although curved, the image is essentially two-dimensional, and yet our perception is of a three-dimensional world. How might depth be recovered ?

The problem of how we recover the third dimension was tackled resolutely by the British empiricist philosophers, notably by Berkeley (1709). Berkeley's views have come to dominate our thinking on many aspects of perception. The British empiricists rejected any notion that ideas were implanted in the mind at birth, saying instead that all complex ideas had to be built up by the association of simpler ones. As all information is received via the organs of sense, ultimately all knowledge must be achieved by the associating together of simple sensations. It was assumed that the third dimension must be perceived by associating together visual "cues" with the position of objects felt by touch.

Convergence and accommodation
The primary cues that Berkeley suggested could become associated with the felt positions of objects were the different angles of inclination of the eyes

FIGURE 7.1

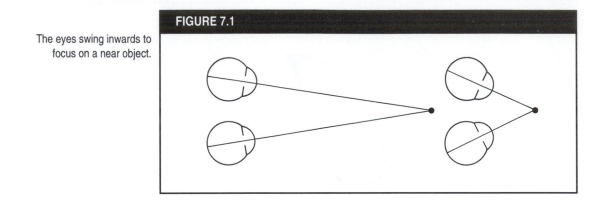

The eyes swing inwards to focus on a near object.

(see Fig. 7.1), different degrees of blurring of the image, and different degrees of strain in the muscles around the lens.

Today we would refer to the different angles of inclination of the eyes as the degree of *convergence* and we would include both blurring and strain under the heading of the accommodation of the lens (see Fig. 7.2 and Ch.1, pp.16–17). Convergence and accommodation are often listed in introductory texts as "physiological" cues to depth. As the degree of convergence or accommodation is only a single value, these cues could at best provide information about only one distance at a time. Most research has concluded that in practice they are minor sources of depth information (e.g. Foley, 1980). Blur, on the other hand, is a visual cue that varies over the whole image, as a function of objects' distances from the plane of clearest focus. Pentland (1987) has shown that blur could in principle be used to compute an accurate depth map, and he gave evidence that humans do use it to some extent. There is, however, a much more important and accurate visual source of information about relative distance for creatures with binocularly overlapping fields of vision—stereopsis.

BINOCULAR STEREOPSIS

Animals with overlapping visual fields have stereoscopic information available to them from a comparison of the images obtained at the two eyes. Each eye sees a slightly different view of the world due to the horizontal separation of the two eyes. You can confirm this by alternately opening and closing each eye. Objects at different distances will appear to move together, or apart, reflecting the *horizontal disparity* between the two views. This binocular view must surely be of high value, because it is gained only by losing the 360° panoramic view enjoyed by animals with side-facing eyes, such as fish, rabbits, or horses (see Ch.1, p.20).

Figure 7.3A shows how the geometry of binocular vision gives rise to slightly different images in the two eyes. If the two eyes are fixating on a point P, then the images cast by P fall at the centre of the fovea in each eye. Now consider a second point Q. If the image of Q fell (say) 5° away from the fovea in both eyes we should say that Q stimulated corresponding points in the two eyes, and that Q had zero disparity. If instead the image

FIGURE 7.2

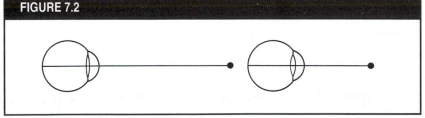

The lens accommodates, by becoming thicker, when the eye focuses on a near object.

FIGURE 7.3

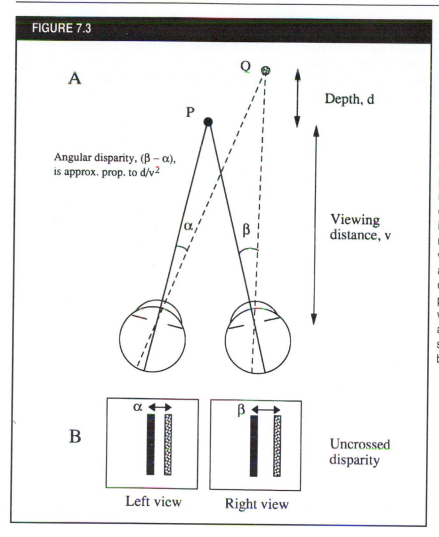

A

Q

Depth, d

P

Angular disparity, $(\beta - \alpha)$,
is approx. prop. to d/v^2

α β

Viewing
distance, v

B

α β

Uncrossed
disparity

Left view   Right view

Geometry of binocular vision. The eyes fixate point P, whose image thus falls on the centre of the fovea in each eye. Point Q, further away than P, is imaged on noncorresponding or disparate points in the two eyes. The disparity $(\beta - \alpha)$ produced by point Q is measured by the discrepancy between the two image locations, and is measured in degrees of visual angle. Disparity is approximately proportional to depth, d, but inversely proportional to the squared viewing distance. (A) shows a plan view, from above; (B) shows the field of view seen by each eye.

was located 6° away from the fovea in one eye but 5° away in the other, we should say that Q stimulated disparate, or noncorresponding points and that Q produced a disparity of 1°. In general, if Q's image falls α degrees from the fovea in the left eye and β degrees from the fovea in the right eye then the binocular disparity is $(\beta - \alpha)$, measured in degrees of visual angle. The amount of disparity depends on the physical depth (d) of Q relative to the fixation point P. In fact, disparity is approximately proportional to this depth difference divided by the square of the viewing distance (v). Thus disparity increases with the amount of depth, but decreases rapidly with increasing viewing distance.

Disparity has both a magnitude and a sign. A point Q further than the fixation distance creates *uncrossed disparity*. That is, the right eye's view of Q is shifted to the right relative to the left eye's view $(\beta > \alpha$; see Fig. 7.3B). Points nearer than the fixation distance create *crossed disparity* (right eye's view is shifted more to the left; $\beta < \alpha$; not shown). If the brain can compute the sign and magnitude of disparity this will give precise information about the relative distances of objects in the world. For most people this is so, but some 2–5% of people show stereo-anomalous or stereo-blind performance and appear to lack the mechanisms for processing either crossed or uncrossed disparities (Richards, 1971).

Because disparity decreases with squared distance, the value of stereo vision must be greatest in the near space around an animal. For example, increasing an object's distance from 2m to 20m decreases the disparity by a factor of 100. Hence far objects will tend to yield disparities that are too small to be detected. Also, to interpret image disparity in terms of real depth (in metres, or feet and inches), the distance must be taken into account, because a given disparity for a far object represents a much greater depth than for a near object. The convergence cue referred to earlier may play an important supporting role here in *scaling* disparity information to recover real depth.

Encoding disparity and depth

How might disparity be sensed? It requires a comparison of information from the two eyes, and so retinal cells clearly cannot do it. Left and right eye information remains segregated in different layers of the LGN, and the earliest stage of processing that shows binocular responsiveness is the primary visual cortex (V1), where many simple and complex cells are driven by input from both eyes (see Ch.3, pp.50–51). Among these cells, some respond maximally when their optimal stimuli fall on disparate areas of the two retinas (e.g. Blakemore, 1970; Hubel & Wiesel, 1970). A cell selective for disparity would respond most strongly to a stimulus lying at a particular distance, or within a range of distances, from the eyes, and so could help to code depth information.

Early evidence suggested that selectivity for disparity was found only in V2 (Hubel & Wiesel, 1970), but it is now established that disparity-selective cells do exist in the primary visual cortex of both cats (Clarke & Whitteridge, 1977) and monkeys (Poggio & Poggio, 1984). The experiments of Poggio and Fischer (1977) were especially important in establishing the depth sensitivity of cortical cells recorded from trained, alert monkeys. The animals were presented with moving-bar stimuli on a screen placed at different real distances and four patterns of response were identified. Tuned excitatory cells responded vigorously to appropriate stimuli at or close to the fixation distance and were often inhibited by further or closer stimuli. Tuned inhibitory cells

responded to a wide range of depths but were inhibited around the fixation distance. Near cells were excited by stimuli nearer than the fixation distance, but inhibited beyond it, and Far cells showed the opposite pattern to Near cells.

As a code for disparity, the firing rate of a single V1 or V2 cell is ambiguous because it varies with factors such as contrast and speed, as well as disparity. However, a comparison of the activity within a population of such depth-sensitive cells could serve to encode disparity unambiguously. To see how the different factors in a cell's response might be disentangled, let us take a simplified example. Suppose a Far cell's response R_{Far} was proportional to (1 + disparity), but scaled by various other factors (contrast, speed, etc.), whereas a Near cell's complementary response was proportional to (1 − disparity) and other factors. Thus:

$$R_{Far} = (1 + \text{disparity}) \times (\text{other factors})$$
$$R_{Near} = (1 - \text{disparity}) \times (\text{other factors})$$

If we take the ratio of responses, the other factors cancel out, and disparity can be recovered. Simple algebra then shows us that:

$$\text{disparity} = (R_{Far} - R_{Near})/(R_{Far} + R_{Near})$$

In this schematic example, disparity is recovered as the contrast between the two cell's responses. In general, the required computation will depend on the particular relation between disparity and response, but the point is that appropriate comparisons between cells can recover unambiguous information, even though individual cells have many pieces of information contributing to their response level. This is an important point that applies to any domain of sensory coding.

Stereopsis and single vision

Turning now to psychological evidence, the importance of disparity information for the perception of depth can easily be demonstrated. It is possible to create strong depth impressions from pictures by sending to each eye separately the view that the eye would see if an actual object in depth were presented. Wheatstone (1838) is usually attributed with the invention of the first *stereoscope*, shown in Figure 7.4A. He drew the view of an object as it appeared to each eye (Fig. 7.4B), and then with an arrangement of mirrors sent the left-eye view to the left eye of an observer and the right-eye view to the right eye. The result was that the observer saw a "solid" object, in depth.

It is possible to arrange such stereo demonstrations in a number of ways, all of which depend on separating out the left- and right-eye views, and then sending these separately to each eye. A common technique is to use anaglyphs where one view is drawn in red and one in green, and the two superimposed. The viewer looks through glasses containing a red filter for one eye and a green filter for the other, so that only one of the images is passed to each eye. The resulting perceptions of solid objects in depth are of course illusory. No actual solid object exists, but the

disparities that would exist if an object were present have been captured in the anaglyphs. The brain thus receives the information that it would receive if an actual 3-D object were presented, and the phenomenal impression reflects this. Frisby (1979) provides numerous examples of anaglyphs and his book is well worth consulting.

In this book, we present various stereograms for "free fusion". A stereo pair of images is presented side-by-side, as in Fig. 7.4B, and by converging the eyes in front of the page, the right eye can fixate the left image while the left eye fixates the right. Some practice is needed to acquire this trick of cross-eyed fusion, but for students of vision it is a skill worth acquiring. In the early stages, fix your gaze on a pencil held in front of the page, and vary its distance from the page until fusion is achieved. One sign of this is seeing three images: a central fused one, flanked by the two monocular views. Ignore the monocular views.

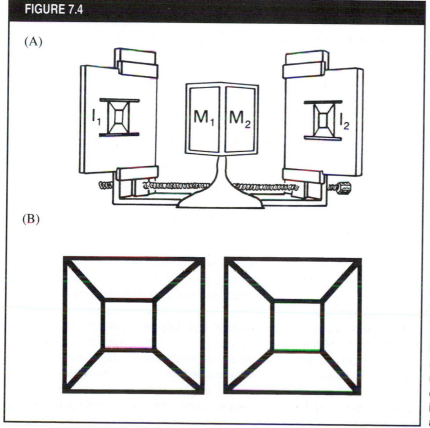

FIGURE 7.4

(A)

(B)

(A) Wheatstone's stereoscope (1838). A picture of an object is drawn as it would appear to the left eye (I_1) and to the right eye (I_2). If these two images are sent to each eye separately, via mirrors M_1 and M_2, an observer sees a single object in depth. Adapted from Boring (1942).
(B) Stereogram of the type used by Wheatstone. With cross-eyed fusion (see text) it should appear in depth as a truncated pyramid.

Although it seems relatively easy to appreciate how disparity in the images to the two eyes might be computed, and there is evidence that cells in the cortex may indeed measure disparities, it is less easy to appreciate why our phenomenal impressions of objects in the real world, or of illusory forms in a stereoscope, are of *single* objects. If you focus on a pen held near your eyes, you will experience double images ("diplopia") of more distant objects, but within a certain range of distance a single view is seen, known as "fusion" or single vision. If the eyes fixate a given point, the region of space within which single vision is possible is known as Panum's fusional space, and the corresponding range of disparities over which single vision holds is Panum's limit. The classical value for Panum's limit is a disparity of about 0.1°. This means that if a point or line is at the fovea in one eye, and we shift its partner more than 0.1° off the fovea in the other eye, single vision will give way to diplopia. This limit is all the more surprising when we translate it into real depth. When viewing an object at 57cm (about arm's length), the fusional space has a depth of only +/–9mm! Taken at face value, this would imply that almost all views of a 3-D scene should appear as double. Why does the visual world not fall apart in this way? Several factors play a part in our current understanding.

- *Attention*. We fixate on, and attend to, the object of interest. Perhaps we simply do not notice the diplopia present elsewhere? This might be so, but there are also more specific structural and dynamic effects at work.
- *Retinal eccentricity*. Panum's limit is larger in peripheral vision than in central vision (Ogle, 1964), probably reflecting the larger size of receptive fields in the periphery, and so the fusional space is also larger away from the fovea.
- *Image size*. The classical experiments on Panum's limit were done with very small targets—dots or thin wires—for which the limit is indeed small. However, recent research has revealed an important *size-disparity correlation*. The disparity limit for fusion is much larger for broad, fuzzy targets (low spatial frequencies) than it is for narrow targets

containing much higher spatial frequencies. Indeed, for bars wider than about 10min arc the disparity limit for fusion increases in direct proportion to the width of the target (Schor, Wood, & Ogawa, 1984). The minimum disparity that will just produce a sense of depth also increases with width in the same way (Schor & Wood, 1983).

The size-disparity correlation was recently confirmed by experiments evaluating contrast sensitivity for stereopsis. Smallman and MacLeod (1994) measured the lowest contrast at which disparity (and presumably depth) could just be discriminated, for a series of spatially filtered textures. They found that for large disparities (10–20min arc) sensitivity was greatest for coarse, low spatial frequency textures (1c/deg), whereas for small disparities (1–5min arc) sensitivity peaked at increasingly high spatial frequencies (5–10c/deg).

These relations between size (spatial frequency) and disparity can be understood in the context of a multi-scale or multiple-filter model, with receptive fields of different sizes at the same retinal location (Freeman & Ohzawa, 1990). If receptive field disparities (discussed earlier) are roughly proportional to receptive field size then the system will be able to handle much larger disparities for large, fuzzy targets because they are processed by larger receptive fields. Ferster (1981) found evidence of this kind in the cat's visual cortex. This multi-scale aspect plays an important part in current models of stereo vision, discussed later.

- *Dynamic factors*? The classical Panum's limit was measured with targets that were not only narrow, but also stationary. Until fairly recently, it was thought that the range of disparities for which single vision holds can be much larger if disparity is slowly increased from a small, fused value. That is, Panum's limit *stretches* over time (Fender & Julesz, 1967). The effect appeared to be important for natural vision where we look from one object to another at a different distance. If the first object is seen as fused (single vision), and we change our convergence to fixate a second object then the disparity of the first object increases but fusion of it may be maintained as Panum's limit supposedly stretches. This dynamic effect would serve to extend the range of fusion in normal viewing conditions.

Unfortunately for this neat theory, careful work by Erkelens (1988) implies that the stretching effect does not exist. He confirmed that the fusional range was indeed larger for increasing disparity than for decreasing disparity, but he added a vital control condition. The fusional range for increasing disparity was no bigger than for stereograms simply switched on at a fixed disparity. This leaves no room for a dynamic stretching effect. The greater difficulty in the decreasing condition appeared to be caused by the period of binocular rivalry that preceded re-fusion.

Nevertheless, fusion and stereopsis do have important temporal characteristics: human vision is poor at picking up rapidly changing disparity. Schor and Tyler (1981) used line stimuli whose disparity (and perceived depth) oscillated back and forth over time. They found that Panum's limit for single vision was much smaller for disparities that changed rapidly (above about 0.5 cycles/sec) than for slower changes. In the language of filtering, the fusion process behaves as a low-pass temporal filter. Perceived stereoscopic motion in depth is restricted to slow changes in rather the same way.

How is binocular matching achieved?

Most theories of stereo vision have argued that in analysing binocular disparity the visual system must determine which parts of one eye's image correspond to particular parts in the other eye's image. Measuring the sign and magnitude of disparity seems relatively easy once the *correspondence problem* has been solved, but we shall see later that "correspondenceless" algorithms have also been developed.

It used to be thought that the spatial forms presented to each eye were recognised independently and then the images were matched and fused. For example, Sherrington (1906, p.380) suggested:

During binocular regard of an objective image each uniocular mechanism develops independently a sensual image of considerable completeness. The singleness of binocular perception results from the union of these elaborated uniocular sensations. The singleness is therefore the product of a synthesis that works with already elaborated sensations contemporaneously proceeding.

However, not all agreed with this—particularly given the strange results that could be obtained using stereoscopes. For example, Darwin received a communication from A.L. Austin in New Zealand (Galton, 1907, p.227).

Although a perfect stranger to you, and living on the reverse side of the globe, I have taken the liberty of writing to you on a small discovery I have made in binocular vision in the stereoscope. I find by taking two ordinary carte-de-visite photos of two different persons' faces, the portraits being about the same sizes, and looking about the same direction, and placing them in a stereoscope, the faces blend into one in a most remarkable manner, producing in the case of some ladies' portraits, in every instance, a *decided improvement* in beauty.

Darwin passed this information on to Galton, who confirmed these observations. Ross (1976) suggests that Galton disagreed with the monocular combination explanation because the binocular perception of two different faces was so unlike an "optical" combination of the faces.

A more serious challenge to contemporary versions of the recognition and fusion theory (e.g. Ogle, 1964) came with the important work of Bela Julesz in the 1960s, summarised in his 1971 book. Julesz developed *random-dot stereograms* as a tool to explore the processes of stereopsis.

A random-dot stereogram is shown in Fig. 7.5. Both members of the stereo pair consist of a uniform, randomly generated texture of black and white dots. There is no recognisable form present in either member of the pair. However, if the

FIGURE 7.5

A random-dot stereogram of the kind devised by Julesz. If this pair were viewed in a stereogram, a square would be seen floating above the background. Photograph courtesy John Frisby.

stereogram shown in Fig. 7.5 is viewed in a stereoscope, or with free fusion (described earlier), the viewer sees a central square of texture floating above the background. This is because the stereogram in fact contains disparate "forms" camouflaged by the background texture. Each half of the stereogram contains identical background elements. The central regions, corresponding to the perceived square, also match, but are displaced sideways as shown in Fig. 7.6. The gaps that remain after this lateral shifting are then filled in with more texture. Thus the eyes are presented with the disparities that would be present if an inner square of texture were actually held above the background texture.

This important demonstration makes it difficult to maintain any theory of stereopsis that depends on the recognition and fusion of global monocular contours. It could be argued that local patterns or clusters of black and white dots are detected and matched, but Julesz (1971) argued against this. For example, fusion can be achieved from stereograms in which one member of the pair is blurred, reduced in size, or has "noise" added to it such that local patterns are disrupted. Julesz proposed instead that stereopsis proceeds on a point-by-point comparison of dots of the same brightness polarity (white or black). He argued that polarities must be the same because fusion cannot be achieved if one member of a random-dot stereo pair is reversed in contrast, i.e. if black dots in one image correspond to white dots in the other.

The idea that individual dots are the basis of binocular matching leads to an enormous

FIGURE 7.6

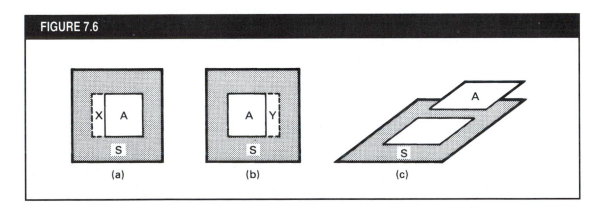

(a)   (b)   (c)

(a) and (b) are the two halves of a random-dot stereogram shown in simplified form. Both have the same surrounding texture (S). A central region (A) has been shifted to the right in (a) and to the left in (b). The gaps left have been filled in with more texture (X and Y). If such a stereogram were constructed, and viewed in a stereoscope, the central square would be seen floating above the background, as shown at (c). Adapted from Julesz (1965).

correspondence problem. Any given dot in one eye might be matched with tens or hundreds of dots in the other eye. To see just how big a problem this creates, consider a small array of 4 dots in each eye. As Fig. 7.7 shows, each dot in one eye might be matched with any of the 4 dots in the other eye, yielding 16 possible locations in space from which the images could have arisen. Four are "true", the other 12 are "ghosts" or "false fusions". The correspondence problem is in principle much worse than this, however, as we should also consider the number of different *arrangements* of dots that might be chosen as a solution. For each dot in the left eye there are four choices in the right eye. Thus, in the absence of further constraints, the number of different matching arrangements is $4 \times 4 \times 4 \times 4 = 256$ solutions to the correspondence problem for only four dots. For a modest 10×10 array of 100 dots there would be 10^{10} solutions for each row, implying no less than 10^{100} different possible solutions, and even more if vertical disparities were allowed. In practice observers all

reach the same, simple solutions to such stereoscopic puzzles, and so there is either a very powerful mechanism for solving the correspondence problem, or the problem is rendered less severe by adopting other constraints on what can be matched. For example, if we allowed any dot to enter into only one pairing (the *uniqueness constraint*, see below) the four-dot problem would reduce from 256 to $4 \times 3 \times 2 \times 1 = 24$ solutions.

Julesz (1971) proposed that the correspondence problem is solved by a *global stereopsis* mechanism, which selects a match based on the most uniform set of disparity measurements (p.150):

Thus, to obtain local stereopsis of a few edges or dots, one can visualize how the binocular disparity units will maximally fire for similar receptive fields in the two retinae of the same shapes, orientations and retinal co-ordinates. On the other hand, for complex textured surfaces, another level of neural

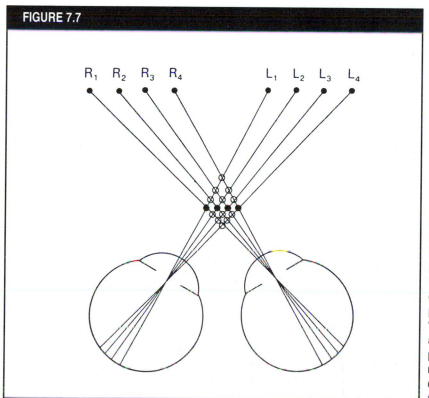

FIGURE 7.7

Both eyes look at four dots, but the correspondence between the two retinal projections is ambiguous. Each of the dots L_1 to L_4 could match any of the four projections of dots R_1 to R_4. "False" matches are shown as open circles in the projection field. Correct matches are shown as solid circles. Adapted from Marr and Poggio (1976).

processing has to be evoked that evaluates the possible local solutions and selects the densest firing units of the same disparity. This processing I will call global stereopsis, and it is on another level of complexity from the commonly quoted local stereopsis of the textbooks.

Julesz (1971) outlined a mechanism for global stereopsis, couched in mechanical terms, where neural units for the left and right eyes were represented by two arrays of magnets, coupled laterally by springs. The model was ingenious, but qualitative and untested. However, the idea that arrays of units cooperate to achieve global binocular matching was influential, and was taken up by Marr and Poggio (1976), who developed a stereo algorithm based on cooperativity between units. In their theory, they took the crucial further step of considering what constraints could be provided by physical properties of the world and used in a theory of stereopsis (Marr, 1982, p.112).

(1) A given point on a physical surface has a unique position in space at any one time and (2) matter is cohesive, it is separated into objects, and the surfaces of objects are generally smooth in the sense that the surface variation due to roughness, cracks, or other sharp differences that can be attributed to changes in distance from the viewer, are small compared with the overall distance from the viewer.

These physical considerations give rise to three constraints in the matching of stereo images. First, a pair of candidate image elements to be matched must be physically similar if they are to have originated from the same point on an object's surface (the compatibility constraint). Second, any item in one image should match only one item in the other image (the uniqueness constraint). Finally, the disparity should vary smoothly almost everywhere in an image (the continuity constraint).

These matching constraints can be successfully embodied within an algorithm that can "solve" random-dot stereograms (Marr & Poggio 1976). The solution gradually drops out of a network of excitatory and inhibitory connections that take account of these three constraints simultaneously. We describe the operation of this network in more detail in Chapter 10, where we use it to introduce a particular class of connectionist models.

Marr and Poggio's (1976) algorithm provided a particularly clear example of how a proper understanding of the nature of a visual processing problem can lead to a workable solution to that problem. However, the particular algorithm proposed does not provide a complete account of human stereo-matching, because it fails to account for a number of psychophysical observations. For example, Julesz and Miller (1975) showed that high spatial frequency "noise" added to stereograms did not disrupt stereopsis obtained from lower spatial frequency components, provided there was no overlap in the spatial frequencies of the noise and the stereo image. This was one of a number of demonstrations that stereo matching may proceed within independent spatial-frequency tuned channels. Marr and Poggio (1979) produced a second stereo algorithm in which they attempted to account for such findings by suggesting that the image is analysed by a set of channels of successively finer resolution. This algorithm solves the problem of eliminating false stereo matches essentially by evasion.

The inputs to this stereo matching algorithm are the zero-crossings obtained using $\nabla^2 G$ filters of different widths (see Chapter 5). To satisfy the compatibility constraint, candidate matches must be zero-crossings of the same sign and orientation. The broadest-width filters produce relatively sparse zero-crossings because finer structure is blurred out. Provided that matches are tolerated only up to a disparity limit equal to about half the width of the filter, then because the zero-crossings are sparse, the probability of false matches is small. The scheme thus exploits the size-disparity correlation (see earlier, p.142) to minimise the ambiguity of matching.

Matching in this scheme proceeds from coarse to fine. Once a match has been achieved within a low spatial frequency channel, this controls vergence movements of the eyes, reducing the disparity and causing finer channels to come into correspondence. Interim results are held in a temporary memory, termed the "2½-D" sketch. The model was implemented and tested very extensively by Grimson (1981), who also extended the model by adding processes that would interpolate a smooth *surface* description from the sparse ZC points at which disparity was measured. Even without surface interpolation the model performed well on many natural and random-dot images. Importantly, it succeeded on those stereograms where one image was blurred or partly restructured (discussed earlier) that had led Julesz to propose global, cooperative stereopsis. In a multi-scale, coarse-to-fine model then, cooperativity between disparity-sensing units may not be essential to stereo matching.

Mayhew and Frisby (1981; also Frisby & Mayhew, 1980) developed a rather different computational model, in which the process of stereo matching was seen as intimately linked with the elaboration of edge descriptions in the raw primal sketch. This contrasts with Marr, who viewed stereopsis as a more-or-less separate module of visual information processing. The constraints that Mayhew and Frisby made use of are rather different from Marr's. Perhaps the clearest difference lies in their inclusion of a *figural continuity* constraint. For each zero-crossing in one eye's image, candidate matches are established from the other eye's image. Such candidates must be within a certain disparity, and they must be zero-crossings of the same sign and similar orientation to the target. If there are several candidate matches, most can be eliminated by checking whether other zero-crossings in the near vicinity of the candidate bear the same *figural* relationship to it as those in the near vicinity of the target. Such a procedure successfully eliminates false matches from natural and random-dot stereo pairs. Mayhew and Frisby's (1981) algorithm also incorporated a rule that looked for correspondences between the different-sized filter channels, just as Marr and Hildreth's (1980) edge-detecting algorithm looked for coincident zero-crossings between different channels (see Chapter 5). Like others (e.g. Pearson & Robinson, 1985; Watt & Morgan, 1984; see Chapter 5), however, Mayhew and Frisby argued that use of zero-crossings alone did not give a good account of human computation

of intensity changes, and they suggested that peaks as well as zero-crossings were used.

Pollard, Mayhew, and Frisby (1985) proposed an alternative stereo algorithm ("PMF") that ensures figural continuity via a somewhat different route. The algorithm was developed to accommodate experimental findings of Burt and Julesz (1980) who found that human binocular fusion is limited not simply by an upper limit on the disparity of individual points, but by an upper limit on the *gradient* of disparity across space. The disparity gradient is closely related to the slant of a surface in space, relative to the observer's line of sight. If the slant in depth is too steep, fusion is not possible. Burt and Julesz found that observers could not achieve fused, single vision of two points in space if the disparity gradient between them (defined as the difference in disparity divided by the mean angular separation between the points) was greater than about 1. Pollard et al. (1985) argued that a binocular combination rule that tolerates matches up to a disparity gradient of 1 would preclude false matches and implicitly satisfy the constraints of surface continuity that we have discussed earlier.

Disparity from spatial phase

Almost all models of stereo vision share the broad view that some set of "things" (dots, edges, or in the 19th century complete objects) is located in the left and right images, a correspondence is established between the two sets, and then the distance (disparity) between corresponding things is measured. An alternative concept has emerged in recent years, based on the idea already touched on several times in this book, that cells in early vision act as spatial filters. The approach is quite radical, as the locations of "things" are not made explicit, and distances as such are not measured.

The heart of the new idea is that even- and odd-symmetric receptive fields (described earlier; Fig. 3.5) can be used together to sense changes in the position (or phase) of an input signal. To see how, consider Fig. 7.8 in which even and odd fields centred on a fixed position (P) are shown superimposed on a grating stimulus. In panel A the grating bar is centred at position P, and the even

FIGURE 7.8

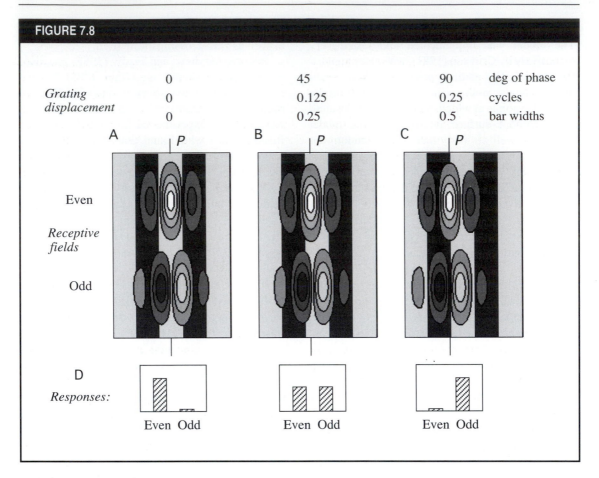

Grating displacement	0	45	90	deg of phase
	0	0.125	0.25	cycles
	0	0.25	0.5	bar widths

How binocular disparity can be recovered from phase information, using even and odd receptive fields. (A) The even field is stimulated best when a grating bar is centred on it. (B, C) The even response drops, and the odd response rises, when the grating is shifted to the right by up to half a bar width (a 90° phase shift; cf. Fig. 2.7). The odd field is stimulated best when an edge is centred on it. (D) The balance (and ratio) of the two responses varies smoothly with the position (phase) of the grating. If such a position code was extracted separately for the left and right eyes then the binocular disparity could be given by the difference between the codes for each eye at corresponding points P.

field is stimulated strongly, whereas the odd field's response is zero (panel D, left). If we shift the grating by a quarter or half a bar width to the right (panels B, C), the even field's response drops and the odd field's response increases. Thus the balance between the even and odd responses (panel D) varies directly with the displacement of the grating. Moreover, a particular ratio of responses specifies the position (phase) of the grating relative to point P. Although the even and odd responses would both increase with the stimulus contrast, this conveniently cancels out in the ratio, making it depend on position but not contrast.

Binocular disparity is a shift in image position between the eyes, and so a simple algorithm for recovering disparity at any point P is to extract the position codes (response ratios) for each eye separately, and then compare them by subtraction (Sanger, 1988). In symbols, if the even and odd filter responses at any position x are $e_L(x)$, $o_L(x)$ for the left eye and $e_R(x)$, $o_R(x)$ for the right eye, then the monocular phases $\Phi_L(x)$, $\Phi_R(x)$ are given by

$$\tan[\Phi_L(x)] = o_L(x)/e_L(x),$$
$$\tan[\Phi_R(x)] = o_R(x)/e_R(x),$$

and phase disparity = $\Phi_R(x) - \Phi_L(x)$. The difference in phase between the two eyes is proportional to the spatial disparity; for example, a 90° phase difference represents a spatial disparity of half a bar width.

The idea of stereo from phase disparity has two main advantages. First, matching features or items do not have to be identified, and so there is no correspondence problem. Second, the computation can be carried out at all locations, not just at zero-crossings or peaks of filter output, so that a dense, rather than sparse, set of disparity values tends to be produced, leading more easily to a surface description.

One may wonder whether the logic of computing stereo from phase disparity holds for natural vision where the input is a complex image rather than a periodic grating. Computational experiments and analysis suggest that, although there are complications (e.g. Langley, Atherton, Wilson, & Larcombe, 1990; Fleet, Jepson, & Jenkin, 1991), the approach can still be applied. Because the spatial filters in the visual cortex respond best to a particular orientation and spatial frequency, the output of a given filter in response to a complex image is actually much more periodic and "grating-like" than its input (cf. Fig. 5.2), so that the local phase of the output is usually well-defined and can be recovered from the ratio of odd and even filter responses, as required.

To test this approach, Sanger (1988) implemented a multi-scale algorithm for phase disparity using Gabor filters of three or four different sizes. Each filter delivered its own disparity estimates, but the weight or confidence attached to these estimates varied across space and across filters. For example, in a blurred region of the image, the larger filters would be given greater weight. Each filter has a disparity limit proportional to its receptive field size—i.e. the size-disparity correlation (p.142) appears again. The final output was a confidence-weighted average of the estimates taken across all filter sizes. This worked well on a variety of random-dot stereograms and natural images, but like other models it had difficulty where changes in depth were very steep. This is because at steep depth edges, parts of a rear surface are seen by one eye

but not the other, and so disparity cannot be defined in these regions. The role of such occlusions in stereo vision is discussed later (p.152).

We saw earlier that psychophysical work strongly supports a multi-scale model of stereopsis, and some of that evidence bears on the idea of phase disparity. Several studies have found that the smallest disparity for which depth can be discriminated with sinusoidal gratings represents a constant phase shift of about 4–6° (1 to 1.5% of the grating period), at spatial frequencies below about 3c/deg (Legge & Gu, 1989; Schor & Wood, 1983). Likewise the largest disparity for which single vision held good was about a 90° phase shift for frequencies below 3c/deg (Schor et al., 1984). On the other hand, for higher spatial frequencies these disparity thresholds were approximately a constant spatial (not phase) displacement. Thus the little evidence so far is rather mixed, and more crucial tests have yet to be conducted.

Nevertheless, the role of phase disparity must be taken seriously, because physiological evidence for this type of coding is now strong. First, we know that cortical simple cells can be well described as Gabor filters (see Chapter 5) and that filters with a 90° phase difference tend to co-occur at a given cortical location (Pollen & Ronner, 1981). Second, R.D. Freeman and colleagues (DeAngelis, Ohzawa, & Freeman 1991; Freeman & Ohzawa, 1990) have plotted very accurately the spatial receptive field structure of binocular simple cells in the cat. Whereas some cells have nearly identical fields for both eyes (Fig. 7.9, Cell 1), other cells have fields of similar size, orientation, and periodicity, but with clearly different phases in the two eyes (Fig. 7.9, Cell 2). For cells tuned near to vertical the interocular phase disparities ranged from 0° to almost 180°, whereas cells with near-horizontal receptive fields had disparities close to zero. This suggests that vertically tuned cells play the greatest part in encoding horizontal disparities for stereo vision. These disparity-sensitive simple cells probably feed on to complex cells, possibly in several stages that serve to reduce the cells' dependence on other factors such as position and contrast, and make responses more specific to disparity *per se* (Ohzawa, DeAngelis, & Freeman 1990). Freeman and Ohzawa (1990)

FIGURE 7.9

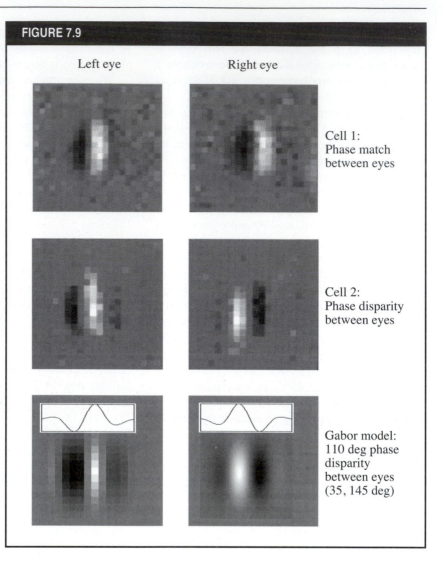

Left eye   Right eye

Cell 1:
Phase match
between eyes

Cell 2:
Phase disparity
between eyes

Gabor model:
110 deg phase
disparity
between eyes
(35, 145 deg)

Phase Disparity. Receptive fields of binocular simple cells plotted separately with stimuli given to the left and right eyes. Top: a cell for which the receptive fields were well-matched in size, orientation, and phase of the receptive field's on and off sub-regions. Middle: receptive fields were well matched in size and orientation but differed in phase. Thus this cell exhibited a *phase disparity*. Data from Freeman and Ohzawa (1990). Bottom: shows how the phase and phase disparity can be quantified. Taking a Gabor function to model the receptive field (see Fig. 3.5), the best-fitting phase of the underlying sine wave can be found. Inset: the profile of the Gabor function. On the left the Gabor model has been quantised into large pixels to match the sampling of the real data above.

argue that the Near, Far, and Tuned cells of Poggio and colleagues (see earlier, p.140) can be better interpreted as cells with different interocular phase disparities and different spatial scales. This way of describing binocular cells copes better with the existence of cells whose properties are intermediate between the Near, Far, and Tuned "types" (Ferster, 1981; LeVay & Voigt, 1988).

Are these physiological findings consistent with the computational models of phase disparity coding? At first glance it might seem not, as the models combine even and odd filters *within* each eye to make monocular phase explicit, and then compare phase between the eyes, whereas

binocular simple cells appear to combine even and odd filters *between* the eyes first. Thus it does not seem likely that the hierarchy of cortical cells follows the same steps as the model. However, this is a nice example of the need to distinguish between an algorithm and its implementation (Marr, 1982). The computational goal is to recover phase difference, and in fact it is straightforward to show that from a common starting point—the assumption of even and odd filters for the left and right eyes—the same result can be calculated in several different, but equivalent, ways. The physiological results of Ohzawa et al. (1990) strongly suggest that a chain of calculations is carried out by the simple-to-complex cell sequence that does not make monocular phase explicit but could readily compute phase difference. In short, the computational theory of stereo from phase difference is supported, and a specific implementation is suggested by the physiological findings.

The task of computing positional change is common to stereopsis and motion analysis, and there are many parallels to be drawn between the two processes. In Chapter 8 we consider in more detail how the sequence of simple and complex cells may use even and odd filters to compute direction and speed of motion in a way that is closely allied to the computation of disparity discussed here.

Stereo depth and occlusion cues

Having surveyed a variety of well-developed models for stereopsis, we now turn to the relation between stereo and other cues for depth. Many of the computational accounts we have discussed assume that stereopsis is achieved prior to, or in parallel with, the elaboration of the features present in the image, and is therefore a relatively low-level process. The clarity of depth in random-dot stereograms, where familiarity and all other depth cues are eliminated, encouraged the view that stereo vision operates as an independent module, uninfluenced by other processes.

However, several demonstrations show that other factors can override stereo information. In "pseudoscopic" viewing the left and right eyes' views are interchanged by optical means. This reverses all the disparities, and so one might expect perceived depth always to reverse. This is true for random-dot stereograms, and for simple depictions of wire-frame objects, but if a photographed scene is shown pseudoscopically one rarely sees trees, cars, and buildings inside-out. Stereo vision is being overridden here, either by other depth cues such as occlusion, perspective, and shading (see later), or by the knowledge we have of familiar objects. Gregory's (1973) "hollow face" illusion (see Fig. 7.10) is similar. If a hollow mask of a face is viewed from a distance of a few feet, the impression is of a normal face, with the nose nearer to the observer than the forehead. Only at very

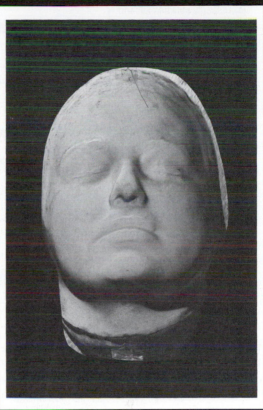

FIGURE 7.10

This is a picture of a hollow mask, illuminated from behind. In real life, as in this photograph, we see a normal face, with the tip of the nose nearer to us than the eyelids. Photograph by Sam Grainger.

close range indeed does the stereoscopic information dominate, to make the mask look hollow. Hill and Bruce (1993, 1994) have shown experimentally that both the familiarity of faces and a general preference for convexity tend to favour the illusory, face-like interpretation of the hollow mask.

There is also increasing evidence that other processes can not only veto stereopsis but also cooperate with it. Harris and Gregory (1973) and Ramachandran and Cavanagh (1985) produced stereograms in which each eye was stimulated with disparate *illusory contours* (Fig. 7.11; cf. Ch.5, Fig. 5.19). When the inducing edges had crossed disparity (hence stood forward) illusory contours were observed completing the gaps between the

FIGURE 7.11

(a) Disparity between left and right illusory contours can produce a stereoscopic image of a square floating above its background. When the illusory contours are superimposed on a repeating "wallpaper" pattern, the floating square "captures" the pattern. (b) The same "capture" occurs even when the background is of continuous lines. The stereoscopic fusion of the disparate *illusory* contours overides both the continuity and zero disparity of the background lines. From Ramachandran and Cavanagh (1985). Reprinted with permission from *Nature* (Vol. 317, pp.527–531) © 1985 Macmillan Magazines Limited.

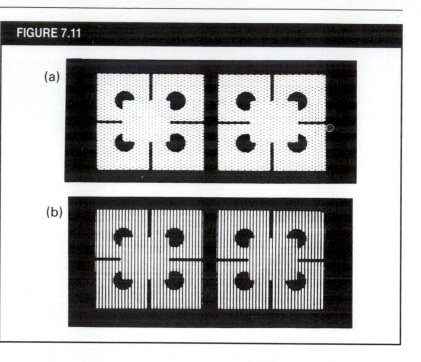

sectors. Subjects could see the illusory square floating above its background but did not see it as readily if the disparity suggested it should be behind the background. This supports the view that these subjective contours occur specifically as representations of *occluding contours*. They can be evoked by monocular occlusion cues such as the terminations of lines and edges, and they appear to be reinforced by disparity cues consistent with the occlusion interpretation, but suppressed by the opposite disparity cues.

The representation of stereo depth and of occlusion appear to be intimately linked. We saw earlier that all models of disparity processing have difficulty with *unpaired* regions of an image. These occur where one eye sees part of a surface, but the other eye's view is blocked by another surface in front—an occluding surface. Although their disparity is undefined, unpaired regions are perceived as lying in the same plane as the more distant surface. Shimojo and Nakayama (1990) realised that the geometry of occlusion imposes a particular relation between the monocular (unpaired) and binocular regions. At a step edge in depth (Fig. 7.12A), if the nearer surface lies to the right of the rear surface then an unpaired region is

seen by the left eye, but if the nearer surface lies to the left, the unpaired region is seen by the right eye. Both these situations are valid in terms of ecological optics, as they arise from viewing a 3-D world. On the other hand, if an unpaired region is seen by the right eye in the first situation (nearer surface to the right), then this is invalid and cannot arise from viewing an arrangement of surfaces in depth. Shimojo and Nakayama (1990) found that valid unpaired regions were seen at the depth of the rear surface and suffered little binocular rivalry or suppression, whereas similar invalid regions appeared in front of the rear surface and were frequently suppressed by rivalry. A demonstration of these stereo effects is given in Fig. 7.12B. The grey crescents are unpaired regions, and for cross-eyed fusion the upper left and lower right crescents are the valid ones. They should appear stable and not subject to rivalry, unlike the other two crescents.

The finding that rivalry takes account of occlusion relations implies that there is more to stereopsis than the process of binocular matching and disparity analysis. It has only recently been realised that the analysis of half-occlusions (unpaired regions) is an important component of

FIGURE 7.12

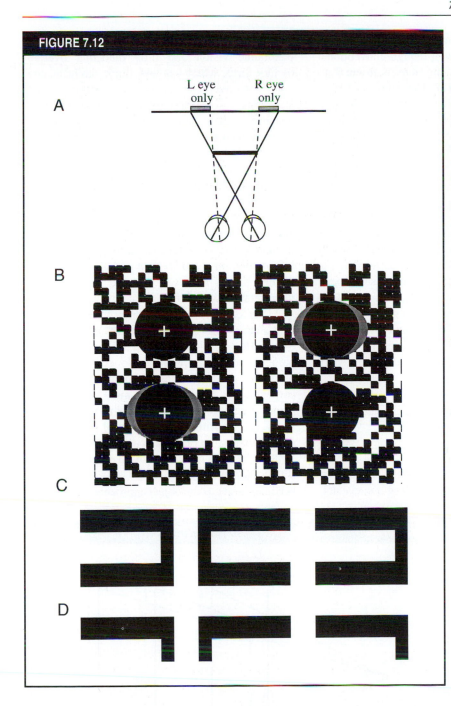

(A) When one surface is viewed behind another, parts of the rear surface are seen only by the left eye, or only by the right eye. These are "half-occlusions". A "valid" unpaired region seen only by the right eye lies to the right of a step edge in depth where the nearer surface forms the left-hand side of the edge, and vice versa for the left eye.

(B) Stereo pair of images arranged for cross-eyed fusion. The grey crescents are unpaired regions, but only two of them are "valid" (see text). These regions appear stable, lying in the rear plane. The depth of "invalid" crescents is less clear and they suffer binocular rivalry. After Shimojo and Nakayama (1990).

(C, D) Stereopsis from occlusion cues, without matching features. Cross-eyed fusion of the centre and left images creates a white rectangle floating in front of a dark one. Fusing the centre and right images reverses the (implicit) disparity and makes the white rectangle float behind a dark aperture. After Liu et al. (1994).

binocular stereopsis. Anderson (1994) argues that disparity and occlusion are complementary sources of information: "While disparity provides relative depth information about surface features visible to both eyes, half-occlusions provide information to segment the visual world into coherent objects at object boundaries" (p.365). Further discussion of this is given by Anderson and Nakayama (1994), and Fig. 7.12C,D gives even more striking demonstrations of occlusion relations playing a part in stereopsis itself. In C, the geometry of the binocular stimulus is entirely consistent with a white rectangle floating in front of a larger black one. This is perceived, even though conventional disparity analysis of matching edges is absent (Liu, Stevenson, & Schor, 1994). The centre and right pair in C and D take a little more thought, because when cross-fused a white rectangle appears behind, not in front. Where is the occlusion here? Closer inspection reveals the answer. The white rectangle appears as if behind an aperture cut in the white page, but *in front* of a dark space that lies beyond the aperture. The binocular geometry is consistent with this perception. Occlusion-based stereo vision is at work in both cases, but at present little is known of the mechanisms through which occlusion and disparity interact in stereopsis.

This account of stereopsis has necessarily been selective. The interested reader is advised to consult more detailed treatments of stereo given by Julesz (1971), Gulick and Lawson (1976), Poggio and Poggio (1984), Howard and Rogers (1995) and the relevant sections of Kaufman (1974) and Marr (1982).

PICTORIAL CUES TO DEPTH

One-eyed humans can be accurate at gauging distance (as you will see if you close one eye and try reaching for objects), and creatures with panoramic vision and little binocular overlap include birds, which can take flight, navigate, and land. Convergence, accommodation, and stereopsis can work only over relatively short distances. There must therefore be sources of information other than disparity to tell animals about the distances of objects in their world. Given the "flat" retinal image, what can these sources be?

As well as the physiological and binocular cues, there are the "pictorial" cues to depth, so called because artists since the Renaissance have employed them to convey an impression of depth in their work. If certain features can give depth information on a canvas then perhaps those same features may be used by the brain in its interpretation of the "flat" retinal picture.

Many of these pictorial cues are varieties of *perspective*. They arise from the way in which a 3-D world is projected onto a 2-D retina, from a particular viewpoint. Consider for convenience the properties of images cast by objects on a plane perpendicular to the line of sight, the "frontal plane" (see Fig. 7.13). We can think of such an image as capturing the geometrical properties of retinal images, ignoring the curvature of the latter.

The size of an image cast by an object is smaller if the object is far away, as at C in Fig. 7.13, and becomes larger as the object approaches the frontal

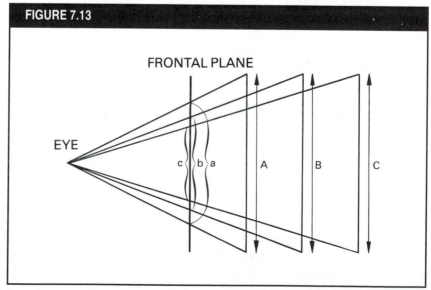

FIGURE 7.13

The size of the image cast by an object decreases with increase in distance.

plane, as at A in Fig. 7.13. Thus the size of an image depends on the object's size and distance. Let us consider a naturally occurring surface, slanting away from the frontal plane and consisting of large numbers of roughly similar texture elements. The image cast by such a receding plane will contain a *gradient of image size*, also called a texture gradient, or texture perspective. As we will see in the third part of this book, the notion of a gradient is central to some approaches to space perception, but for the moment we are treating it as a "cue" for the perception of distance.

Linear perspective is perhaps the best-known pictorial cue to depth. The horizontal separation of images cast by a pair of railway tracks is larger for the nearer portions of the tracks and smaller for the more distant portions. The images cast by parallel lines at the frontal plane converge as the lines recede horizontally from the observer.

Because our eyes are elevated above the ground that supports us and other objects, there are also differences in the *height* in the visual field of images cast by objects at different distances. Further objects are imaged higher in the visual field. The "cues" of relative size, perspective, and relative height are all simple consequences of the geometry of the retinal image, and all three operate together whenever objects are viewed by the human eye (see Fig 7.14).

Shading is an important aspect of pictures (or images) that conveys an impression of solidity and depth, and in the previous chapter we described how animals may be counter-shaded to counteract

this. One of the most basic facts about the visual world is that lighting comes from above (sun, sky), and not from the ground. Because most surfaces reflect light diffusely, the intensity of light (luminance) reflected from a surface is greatest when the surface faces the light source, and decreases as the surface slants or curves away from the lighting direction (see Ch.5, p.75). Thus the pattern of intensity variation (shading) across a surface carries information about the 3-D surface shape of the object. At its simplest, the direction of shading can distinguish between convex "bumps" and concave "dents". In Fig. 7.15, we see "bumps" on the left but "dents" on the right. This is surprising when we realise that those on the right are identical to the left ones, but turned upside down. Turn the book upside down, and the dents will become bumps and vice versa. This surprising and robust effect means that the human visual system *assumes lighting comes from above*, or at least is strongly biased towards this assumption. With this ecologically valid constraint, direction of shading can be interpreted. Shading from light to dark downwards implies a convex surface (its upper part catches the light more), whereas the reverse shading implies a concave "dent" (its lower part catches the light more). This accounts for the perceived depth and depth reversal in Fig. 7.15 and many other similar demonstrations. Without some constraint of this kind the shading is ambiguous, but such ambiguity is rarely perceived. Indeed, this lighting constraint is deeply and unconsciously embedded into early visual processing, as it is tied

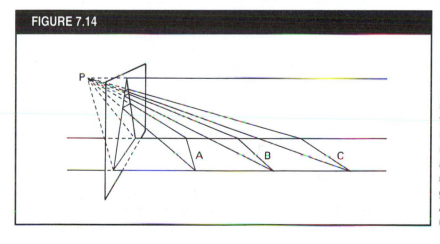

FIGURE 7.14

In this diagram, an observer at P looks at a set of square units on the ground (paving slabs, perhaps). The image formed at the frontal plane illustrates how the "cues" of relative size, perspective, and relative height are all simple consequences of the geometry of image formation. Adapted from J.J. Gibson (1950a).

FIGURE 7.15

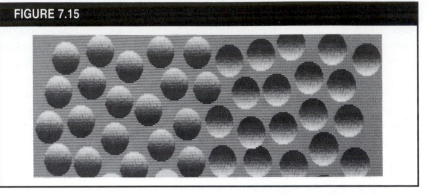

The shapes on the left are usually seen as bumps, but those on the right are usually seen as dents, consistent with an overhead light souce. From Ramachandran (1988). Reprinted with permission from *Nature* (Vol.331, pp.163–166). © 1988 Macmillan Magazines Limited.

to retinal (or head) orientation, not external or gravitational orientation. Try viewing Fig. 7.15 with various combinations of tilted book and tilted head to confirm this.

A number of machine vision algorithms have been developed to recover *shape-from-shading* (cf. Horn & Brooks, 1989), with the aim of describing the 3-D surface shape given only the pattern of reflected light intensities. Because the problem is inherently ambiguous or "under-constrained", all algorithms have to adopt strong assumptions or constraints to arrive at a solution. These may include assumptions about the nature of the lighting, or about the reflective nature of the surfaces, or about the smoothness of the surface shape. For example, one might assume matt surfaces of uniform reflectance, like a plaster sculpture. Needless to say, such constraints are powerful if correct (when applied to aerial photographs of a desert, for example) but may go hopelessly wrong. Unlike a desert the human face, for example, is neither matt nor of uniform reflectance.

Pentland (1989) identified an intriguing simplification that could in principle be implemented by human vision. Provided that the lighting direction is not too close to the line of sight, it turns out that the depth profile of a surface (of uniform reflectance) is approximately a linear transformation of the intensity image received by the camera (or retina). Any linear transformation can be expressed as a filtering operation, involving changes in Fourier amplitude and phase, and so if the visual system implemented the inverse filtering operation (which is fairly straightforward, given

our current knowledge of visual filtering at multiple scales, orientations, and phases) it would recover the surface shape. Pentland's algorithm worked well on pictures of low-relief surfaces, and tolerably well on a photograph of a face and a cartoon line drawing.

Although human vision clearly uses shape-from-shading rules, it is less clear that it uses shading in a quantitative manner. It may be used qualitatively in conjunction with other cues such as texture variation, surface contours, and the shape of occluding (boundary) contours (Ramachandran, 1988). Knill (1992) gives some very nice examples in which the same shading pattern is interpreted as two quite different corrugated surfaces according to the shape of contours "painted" on the surface.

Atmospheric perspective

Not only are the images cast by objects smaller when they are at a distance, but over long distances they are also less clear, less bright, and have slightly different spectral properties. This is because light is scattered and absorbed by particles in the atmosphere—and different wavelengths are scattered to different degrees (see Chapter 1). Figure 7.16 gives a powerful impression of depth because of the way in which the light reflected by the distant hills has been scattered—although there are also other cues, such as relative size and occlusion, operating here.

Occlusion

Most natural scenes are cluttered with a variety of objects, such as trees, plants, and rocks, lying at different distances. The view of one object is often

FIGURE 7.16

The image of the near hills is brighter and clearer than the image of the distant ones, from which the light has been scattered by the atmosphere. Photograph by Mike Burton.

partially obscured by a nearer one, producing the cue of *interposition* or occlusion. It provides information about ordering in depth, but no measure of relative or absolute distance. As a very simple example, Fig. 7.17A is seen as circles, with one on top of another. This is not the only possible interpretation; we might see the drawing as representing adjacent shapes, one circular and the others with "bites" taken out of them. Usually, however, we interpret the irregular images as representing a "good" shape (cf. Gestalt principles discussed in Chapter 6) that is partially covered by another good shape. On this view, detecting occlusion requires a high level of shape representation, but another view is that line-ends and T-junctions in an image are low-level features from which an occlusion interpretation may be derived (see Ch.6; Fig. 6.20). For example, Fig. 7.17A shows that at T-junctions the leg of the T belongs to the occluded surface but the crossbar of the T belongs to the occluding surface.

These occlusion cues are features in an image that point to the description of one surface lying in front of another. They are pictorial cues equally visible to both eyes. This is rather different from our earlier discussion of stereopsis (Ch.7, p.152) where features visible to one eye but not the other served as "half-occlusions", with the implication that those features lie on the occluded surface. Thus, when one object partially obscures another, it yields both monocular and binocular cues to occlusion, as well as conventional stereo disparity cues, and disparity can either reinforce or countermand the pictorial (monocular) cues, as cross-fusion of Fig. 7.17A will show.

Occluding objects may fragment the image of an occluded object into several separate regions, and to maintain the structure of that object the fragments must remain linked or grouped together, as belonging to a single object. Figure 7.17B shows that the grouping of parts is more effective when the occlusion cues are more evident (upper row). When the occlusion cues are reinforced by disparity, the grouping of the occluded parts seems even more robust, as free fusion of Fig. 7.17B should confirm. Conversely, when occlusion cues were countermanded by disparity, grouping and recognition of occluded objects was much more difficult (Nakayama, Shimojo, & Silverman, 1989).

DEPTH FROM MOTION

So far we have considered a static observer viewing an unchanging scene. Most natural scenes, however, are alive with the movements of animals, plants, clouds, water, and so on. Movement in the optic array arises not only because external objects move, but also because the observer's head and body move, generating "optic flow" (see Part III of this book). Image movement on the retina is further complicated by the fact that the eyes move in the head, even when head and body are stationary. Thus, in addition to physiological, binocular, and pictorial cues to depth, recent research has considered how movement of an observer, or of objects, can produce information about relative

FIGURE 7.17

Stereo cues can reinforce, or countermand, occlusion cues in depth interpretation. In A and B, with cross-eyed fusion of the centre and right images the cues reinforce each other. Similar fusion of the left and centre images puts stereo depth and occlusion in opposition to each other. Images in B are adapted from Nakayama et al. (1989). Perceptual grouping and recognition of objects fragmented by occlusion are much more effective when occlusion cues are strong.

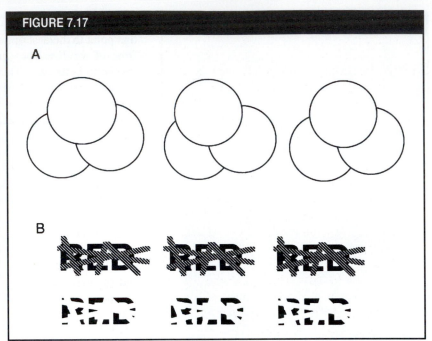

distance through *motion parallax* or *motion perspective*.

In Fig. 7.18 we see an eye viewing two objects at different distances. As the eye moves laterally, the image cast by the nearer object B travels further across the retina than that cast by object A. Similarly, if the eye were still and objects A and B moved across the line of sight at equal speed, the image of the nearer object would travel further and faster across the retina than the image of the more distant one. In fact, the ratio of speeds is inversely proportional to the ratio of distances from the observer: if A were twice as far away as B it would move at half the speed, and so on. Relative speed

FIGURE 7.18

Motion parallax. The observer looks at two objects (A and B) at different distances. If the observer moves (as in the left diagram), or the objects move at equal speed (as in the right diagram), the image of the nearer object B moves further across the retina ($b_1 - b_2$) than does the image of A ($a_1 - a_2$).

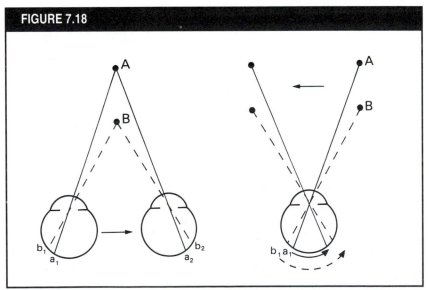

of motion of different portions of the retinal image could therefore signal relative depth.

If we consider a stationary, textured 3-D surface, instead of just two points, then the entire field of relative motions produced by the observer's movement conveys very detailed information about the 3-D structure of the surface. One way to appreciate this fact is to realise the close geometric connection between the motion parallax cue and binocular disparity (also known as binocular parallax). If a single eye moves laterally through (say) 6cm then the changes in image structure between the start and finish of the movement are just those that could be picked up simultaneously by having two eyes separated by 6cm. Motion parallax and stereo cues therefore represent temporal and spatial samplings of the same 3-D information. The experiments of Rogers and Graham (1979, 1982) were instrumental in showing that human vision does in fact exploit the motion cue to convey a sense of depth as rich as that obtained from binocular stereopsis. Observers were shown random-dot patterns (on a flat screen) in which the pattern of relative movements were those that would have been produced by a variety of corrugated 3-D surface shapes. With no motion the surface (not surprisingly) looked flat, but with the motion cue the different surface shapes (sine wave, triangle wave, square wave) were clearly and reliably recognised (Rogers & Graham, 1979). The ability to recognise depth from motion declined as the surface corrugations became narrower (higher spatial frequency), and a similar restriction applied to stereo vision tested under similar conditions (Rogers & Graham, 1982). Peak sensitivity to depth from stereo or motion occurred for fairly broad corrugations of 0.2–0.4c/deg. This contrasts markedly with sensitivity to luminance contrast that peaks at spatial frequencies of 2–5c/deg in foveal vision, and extends to much higher spatial frequencies. Perhaps shading cues (from luminance contrast) convey finer details of surface structure, whereas motion and stereo carry information about larger-scale surface shape. In Part III of this book we consider in greater detail how motion information may inform an animal or person about the layout of the world and their own movements within it.

In summary, although the optical projection of a 3-D world onto a 2-D retina contains many inherent ambiguities, various signs, cues, or clues available in the retinal image are correlated with distances in the world and allow the "lost" third dimension to be recovered by the observer. At least some aspects of depth perception appear to be innate rather than learned, even in humans, who are not independently mobile at birth, and we will be considering some of this evidence in Chapter 13. It does not seem as though all the cues to depth need to be learned through associating visual information with the felt positions of objects.

INTEGRATING DEPTH CUES

Modules and cue integration

We have seen that depth information is obtained from a variety of sources or cues, including stereo disparity, motion, texture, occlusion, perspective, and shading, and Marr (among others) proposed that these cues are processed initially by separate, parallel modules. Such a view of visual processing is consistent with the evidence that cortical pathways processing visual information are organised into separate "streams", dealing with form, colour, depth, motion, and so on (see Ch.3, pp.56–62). Yet we do not see multiple objects from these multiple cues; we do not see separately a stereo surface, a motion surface, and a shaded surface. The simple fact that we see one object, or one surface, suggests that the multiple cues are integrated in some way. We have also seen that information is lost in the projection from 3-D to 2-D, and that each cue is an ambiguous indicator of distance, depth, and surface structure. The ambiguity might be reduced by combining information from several cues. For example, if one cue says that the state of the world is either a, b, or c, and a second cue is compatible with states c, d, or e, then a logical combination of the cues is unambiguous (c). A number of different theorists suggest that it is the act of recognising a particular object at a particular location that knits together the separate descriptions, and we consider one such theory in Chapter 10 when we discuss the work of Feldman (1985). For converging perspectives from experimental psychology, the reader should consult the work of Treisman leading to her feature integration theory (Treisman, 1988).

Cue integration: The 2½-D sketch

Marr (1982) proposed that the goal of early visual processing is the production of a description of the visible surfaces of the environment, so that their dispositions and layouts are described with respect to the viewer. This description he termed the 2½-D sketch, and it serves to integrate the multiple depth cues. Stereopsis, the analysis of motions present in the image, and the contour, texture, and shading information available from the full primal sketch all contribute to the 2½-D sketch, which acts as a buffer store in which partial solutions can be stored as processing proceeds. The label "2½-D" reflects the idea that the sketch captures a great deal about the relative depths and surface orientations, and local changes and discontinuities in these, but is viewer-centred rather than object-centred and does not make explicit the 3-D structure of spatial forms. The latter involves parts of an object that may not be visible in any single view, and involves 3-D descriptive primitives (concerned with axes and volumes) that are not part of the surface description.

Marr sees the representation in the 2½-D sketch as a set of vector-like primitives, which may be depicted as a set of "needles" (Fig. 7.19). The length of each needle describes the degree of *slant* of that part of the surface, and the orientation of each needle describes the *tilt* or direction in which the surface slants. In addition, the relative distance from the viewer to each point on the surface could be represented very roughly by a third, scalar quantity (not shown in Fig. 7.19).

Marr's concept of the 2½-D sketch is a computational theory of visual representation. It set out a programme of research in computer vision, and provided a possible model for human vision. Whether human vision actually works in this way is an experimental issue, to which we now turn. What experimental evidence do we have that human vision integrates depth cues to form a surface representation? There are really two questions here, about integration and about surface

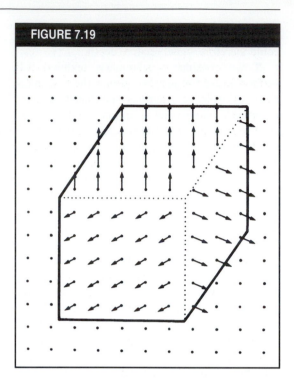

FIGURE 7.19

The 2½-D sketch of a cube. The surfaces of the cube are represented by a set of vector primitives, like needles. The length of each needle represents the degree of slant of the surface, and the orientation of the needle represents the direction in which the surface slants. From *Vision* by Marr (1982). Copyright © 1982 by W.H. Freeman and Company. Used with permission.

representation, and we shall concentrate on the first.

To investigate the interaction of depth cues, researchers need to be able to manipulate different depth cues independently, and then to investigate situations where cues are either in conflict, or in accord with each other. Pseudoscopic vision (interchanging the left and right eye's views; see p.151) is one example of cue conflict, where stereopsis is often suppressed by contrary pictorial cues. The Ames room (see Fig. 4.1) offers conflict between different pictorial cues. Natural vision, however, does not generally involve such gross conflict of cues, and the study of concordant cues may be more informative.

Manipulating depth cues separately was hard to do until the advent of computer-generated displays. Braunstein (1968) was one of the first to examine the interaction of texture gradients and velocity gradients in the perception of surface slant, using computer-simulated objects. A given display contained a random-dot texture consistent with a slant of 0°, 20°, 40°, or 60°. The same display also contained a velocity (motion parallax) gradient indicative of 0°, 20°, 40°, or 60° slant. All 16 combinations of texture and velocity gradients were tested, and the results showed that both cues influenced perceived slant, but the weight assigned to motion was more than twice as great as that assigned to texture. The idea that perceived depth is just a weighted average of the depth provided by a variety of cues is surprisingly simple, but receives support from more recent research.

Current computer graphics technology can render precisely shaded, textured, moving stereograms and has enabled much more sophisticated studies of this kind, linked to a renewed interest in theories of cue integration (e.g. Bülthoff & Mallot, 1988; Johnston, Cumming, & Parker, 1993). Stevens and Brookes (1988) examined the perception of slant of a simulated surface on which a square grid of lines was drawn. The monocular cues to surface slant (linear perspective, and foreshortening of the squares) were controlled independently of the disparity gradient across the surface. Most surprisingly, it was found that the monocular cues to slant dominated over the stereo information. In a further experiment, Stevens and Brookes found that this dominance was peculiar to *plane* surfaces, and that stereo was much more effective when *curved* surfaces were tested. Thus they concluded that "stereo depth derives most effectively from disparity contrast; when disparity varies linearly it is dramatically less salient" (p.382), and further that "the effective stereo features correspond to places where the second spatial derivatives [of disparity] are non-zero" (p.385), at points of curvature in depth.

Consistent with these findings, Johnston et al. (1993) found that for a textured stereogram of a curved, cylindrical surface (Fig. 7.20A) the contribution of texture information to depth was significant, but small in comparison to the strength of stereo depth. Moreover, their data support the theory of linear, weighted averaging of cues: as the

texture cue increased in its implied depth, so the stereo depth cue had to be decreased linearly to maintain a constant perceived shape in depth. But the weighting (relative importance) given to texture was only 10–20%, with the remainder (80–90%) given to stereo. Most of the contribution from texture came from the shape compression that occurs when viewing a slanted surface element (e.g. circular blotches on a surface are imaged as ellipses), rather than from changes in the imaged area or density of surface elements (Cumming, Johnston, & Parker, 1993). In a related study, Young, Landy, and Maloney (1993) studied the interrelation of texture and *motion* cues in the portrayal of a cylindrical surface. Overall, texture and motion were more nearly equal partners in determining the 3-D shape of the surface. The linear combination model was again supported, and it was found that the perceptual weight assigned to a cue decreased if that cue was rendered more "noisy" or unreliable.

In summary, the model emerging from these recent studies on the integration of stereo, texture, and motion cues to surface depth is sketched in Fig. 7.20B, and it is broadly consistent with Marr's original concept. Depth values (e.g. surface slant or curvature) are computed by relatively independent modules, and a weighted average of these values determines perceived depth. Note that the stereo module computes disparity values, and to convert these to depth values requires additional information about viewing distance—an example of "cue promotion". Such information could come from binocular convergence or the motion module, or both. It may be that this simple averaging model applies only when the various cues are not too discrepant. Where cue-conflict is gross there can be other outcomes, but the averaging model may be more relevant to natural vision. In a further test, Johnston, Cumming, and Landy (1994) found evidence for the linear summation of stereo and motion cues. That is, as the depth implied by motion was increased, the depth implied by stereo had to be decreased (and vice versa) to maintain a constant perceived shape—the "apparently circular cylinder". Their results are summarised in Fig. 7.20C, as the relative weights given to the two cues. Note that the weight given to stereo was less

FIGURE 7.20

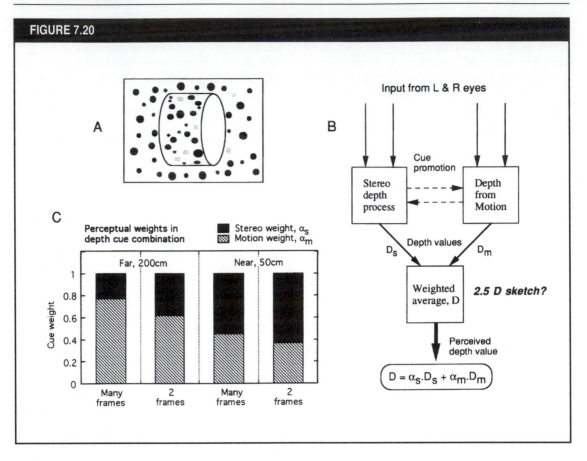

(A) Schematic view of the textured cylinder and background used in experiments on integration of depth cues. Black outlines were not present, and the cylinder was portrayed by a combination of stereo, motion parallax, and texture cues. The implied depth of the cylinder could be varied independently for each cue, allowing the effects of cue combination to be studied. (B) Linear model of depth cue averaging implied by the experiments (see text). This model may hold only for moderate discrepancies between cues. Cue promotion refers to the idea that cues such as disparity and motion parallax may have to be rescaled by other information such as convergence in order to yield depth values as output. (C) The relative importance assigned to depth cues in perceptual averaging can vary with circumstances. The weight given to motion parallax (in combination with stereo disparity) decreased with only two frames in the movie sequence, and the weight assigned to stereo increased at a nearer viewing distance. Data from Johnston et al. (1994).

at a far distance (where disparities in the real world are smaller), and when the motion cue was stronger (many frames in the movie sequence). Reducing the movie sequence to two frames decreased the role of motion in depth perception, but increased that of stereo. Thus the integrative device (2.5-D sketch?) of Fig. 7.20B may serve to optimise perception by weighting the cues according to the validity and reliability they have under different circumstances. This points to a rather intelligent perceptual process.

SPATIAL VISION DURING EYE MOVEMENTS

In this section, we step beyond our main theme of depth perception to consider the wider implications of eye movements for spatial vision. The eyes themselves are never at rest. We can distinguish a number of different types of human eye movement, characterised by different sizes, latencies, and speeds, and these were described in Chapter 1 (p.21). The role of saccades is to direct the gaze to different points in the scene, in order that the high acuity of the fovea can be used to analyse the region of interest. Pursuit (tracking) movements serve a similar purpose of locking the gaze onto moving objects. Unlike the image motions produced by head and body movement, those produced by eye rotation within a stationary head are not informative about depth and 3-D structure. This is because the viewpoint does not change significantly, so that the image movements are almost pure translation, without distortion or change of structure, i.e. without motion parallax.

The fact that large saccadic eye movements are very frequent raises important questions about how we perceive a stable visual world, and these are discussed later. In addition, the eye also undergoes small movements (tremors, flicks, and drifts) even during "stationary" fixation, and there is evidence that these small movements are essential for perception. This has been revealed by experiments that examined perception without eye movements, using the technique of *stabilised retinal images*.

Image stabilisation can be achieved in a number of ways. One early method was by attaching to the cornea of the eye a contact lens on which was mounted a miniature projector. As the contact lens, and hence the projector, moved with the eye, the images of objects presented to the eye remained focused on constant retinal positions. Loss of perception of colour and contour occurs within seconds of stabilisation (Heckenmuller, 1965) and pattern vision gives way to a diffuse luminous "fog". Pritchard (1961) claimed that form perception is disrupted in a rather interesting manner. He presented observers with patterns, pictures, and words and his subjects reported that they disappeared, and sometimes reappeared, in fragments, such that "meaningful" chunks were preserved. Thus the stimulus word BEER might be reported as PEER, BEE and BE at different times. Although this might suggest a role for "top-down" processes, the reappearances may have been produced by occasional slippage of the lens system (Cornsweet, 1970), whereas the meaningful nature of the fragments may have resulted from reporting bias on the part of the observers.

More recent work by Kelly (1979a,b) and Tulunay-Keesey and Jones (1980) used better stabilisation methods, and quantified the degree of image fading by the change in grating contrast sensitivity that takes place. It turned out that fading is substantial but not actually complete, for contrast sensitivity is low but not absent after stabilisation. Fading takes about 2–3sec for a low-contrast pattern, increasing to as much as 10–20sec for patterns of high contrast and high spatial frequency (Tulunay-Keesey, 1982). Fragmentary reappearance of images was not reported. A very strong negative afterimage is seen when the faded pattern is turned off, suggesting that the fading is probably caused by local adaptation of retinal elements (see Ch.2, p.33) at or before the level of retinal ganglion cells (Burbeck & Kelly, 1984). Kelly's (1979b) experiments showed that normal contrast sensitivity could be restored by imposing a slow (0.15deg/sec) drift on the stabilised pattern, akin to the slow drifts of eye position that accompany normal fixation. The general conclusion from the stabilised image experiments is that small movements of the image across the retina are vital for the maintenance of perception over time. Local adaptation processes allow each region of the retina to adapt to the average luminance level in that region, but small eye movements prevent pattern contrasts within a region from fading out.

The larger saccadic and tracking eye movements raise several important problems for our understanding of spatial perception and movement perception. How do we know where things are in space? When image movement occurs how do we know whether it is due to object movement or eye movement? The retinal image moves or jumps every time the eyes move, and yet perceived position of objects does not change or jump about. Retinal position and movement *alone* are evidently no guide to an object's location and movement in external space. This implies either that absolute retinal position is unimportant (a position adopted by Gibson, 1966, 1979) or that the eye movements are somehow taken into account (a view held most notably by Helmholtz).

Distinguishing movement of the eyes from movement in the world

Consider a stationary eye viewing an isolated object as in Fig. 7.21. As the object moves across

FIGURE 7.21

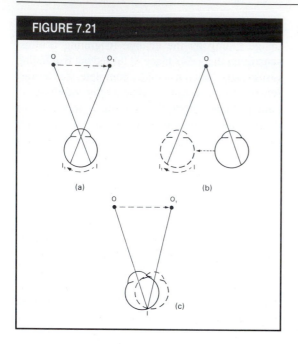

(a)

(b)

(c)

At (a), a stationary eye views a moving object O. As O moves to O_1, its image I moves across the retina to I_1. At (b) the same image movement ($I - I_1$) is produced when the eye moves but the object remains stationary. At (c) the eye moves to track the movement of the object. O moves to O_1, but its image remains at the same place, I.

the line of sight, the image it casts will move across the retina—it will be cast on different receptors as it travels. In this situation we correctly perceive ourselves as still and the object as moving. Now suppose we move the eye, but the object remains stationary. Again the image will move across the retina—but this time we will perceive the object at rest and ourselves as moving. Finally, consider what happens when the eye tracks a moving object. The image is cast on the same part of the retina, just as when the eye and the object were stationary, but now movement *is* perceived.

It appears that the information contained within the retinal image is ambiguous. In order to perceive correctly what is moving and what is at rest, the visual system may take into account information about the way the eyes are moving. Following Helmholtz, Gregory (1972) suggested that two systems must be involved in movement perception—the image-retina system and the eye-head system. For a stationary head, Fig. 7.22 illustrates how an object's lateral (angular) position is the sum of its position in the visual field (i.e. relative to the fovea) and the direction of gaze (eye position in the head). If internal estimates were available for both these quantities, or their

FIGURE 7.22

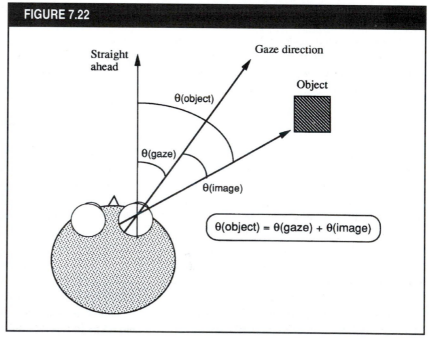

For a stationary head, the angular position of an object relative to the observer's straight ahead direction is the algebraic sum of the position of the object in the visual field, θ(image), and the direction of gaze, θ(gaze). The same holds for angular velocities (the time-derivatives of the angular positions).

Straight ahead

Gaze direction

Object

θ(object)

θ(gaze)

θ(image)

$$\theta(\text{object}) = \theta(\text{gaze}) + \theta(\text{image})$$

time-derivatives (angular velocities), they could be summed to compute the object's true lateral position or movement. Several experimental phenomena imply that an "extraretinal eye position signal" (EEPS) is indeed available for use in judgements of position and movement. If a moving light is tracked by the eyes in a dark room it appears to move smoothly even though its retinal position is (nearly) stationary. When a small afterimage is viewed in total darkness and saccades are made to the left and right, the afterimage is seen to change position accordingly (Grusser, Krizic, & Weiss, 1987), even though its retinal position cannot change. Perceived movement must in both cases come from the eye-head system (EEPS) alone.

Although saccades are very rapid movements, up to 500deg/sec, it is evident that the EEPS is a sluggish or low-pass filtered version of the actual saccadic movement. Grusser et al. (1987) found that the apparent extent of afterimage displacement decreased progressively as subjects were asked to make faster saccadic alternations of gaze direction. The perceived displacement decreased with increasing frequency of movement, even though the actual eye displacement did not decrease. This is the sign of a low-pass filter that cannot follow high-frequency changes. At a sufficiently high rate (around 3.5 saccades per second) the afterimage appeared stationary in space, even though the eyes were moving. The sluggishness of the EEPS is confirmed by very different experiments on the judged position of spots of light flashed in darkness at different times during a saccade (Honda, 1991; Matin, 1976). Suppose, for example, that a saccade was made to the right. Targets flashed up to 100msec before, or in the early part of, the saccade were perceived too far to the right (compared with their true position), whereas later target spots, up to 150msec after the saccade, were seen too far to the left. This confirms that the EEPS is a temporally blurred (low-pass filtered) version of the real saccadic displacement (Fig. 7.23), running ahead of the saccade in the early phase, but lagging behind it in the later stage of the movement. The pattern of errors was more complicated when the target spots were flashed against a dimly visible background, reflecting additional influences of relative visual position (Honda, 1993).

Because the EEPS is a blurred replica of the actual eye position, we might expect position perception to be very unstable. With every saccade, objects would appear to lurch to the left and right before settling down. This does not happen, and so it may be that the EEPS is not used continuously to derive object position from retinal position. If it were used intermittently, between saccades, the position code would be more accurate but sampled discontinuously over time. This view is reasonable, because visual information received *during* a saccade is of very poor quality, and actively suppressed. The high speed of saccades means that information is grossly blurred or smeared by temporal integration (like "camera-shake" in photography). This rapidly moving blur or smear is not usually seen, because it is masked by the strong, clear images received during fixation before and after the saccade (Campbell & Wurtz, 1978; MacKay, 1970). The properties of such *forward masking* and *backward masking* have been intensively studied in laboratory experiments (see Breitmeyer, 1984, for a review).

In addition to suppression by visual masking, *saccadic suppression* also occurs via some neural process that actively inhibits visual detection during saccades and eye blinks (Riggs, Merton, & Morton, 1974; Riggs, Volkmann, & Moore, 1981). Saccadic suppression appears to affect the magnocellular pathway (see Ch.3, pp.44–51) most strongly, because the loss of sensitivity is greatest at low spatial frequencies (Burr, Holt, Johnstone, & Ross, 1982; Volkmann, Riggs, Moore, & White, 1978), and because chromatic patterns, detected by the parvocellular system, do not suffer saccadic suppression (Burr, Morrone, & Ross, 1994). We should remember, though, that in natural viewing all patterns would be degraded during saccades by temporal smear, and suppressed by forward and backward masking. In summary, it is surprisingly reasonable to think of vision as a sequence of discrete "snapshots" obtained during periods of fixation, with the EEPS being employed discontinuously to update the encoded position of objects across a sequence of saccades in which image position is changing.

What is the source of the EEPS? Eye movements could be taken into account in one (or

FIGURE 7.23

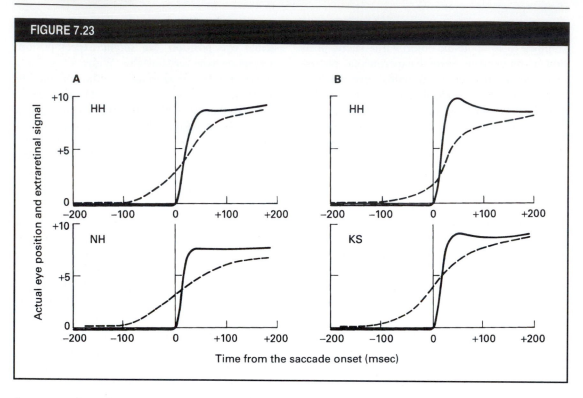

Comparison of the time-course of a saccadic eye movement (solid curves) with the time-course of the extra-retinal eye position signal (EEPS; dashed curves). The EEPS was deduced from data on the misperception of the position of dots flashed during a saccade. Note that the EEPS is a sluggish, temporally blurred version of the real saccade. Thus errors arise when the EEPS is combined with image position information (see Fig. 7.20) to compute the objective position of a target. A: vertical saccades. B: horizontal saccades. Redrawn from Honda (1991), with kind permission from Elsevier Science Ltd., UK.

both) of two ways. Sherrington (1906) originally proposed the *inflow* theory in which afferent (sensory) signals from the eye muscles are taken into account when movement in the retinal image is interpreted. Helmholtz (1866) proposed instead the *outflow* theory where motor commands sent to the eye muscles (described by Helmholtz as an "effort of will") are used in interpreting image movement. Early evidence seemed to favour Helmholtz's theory. If the eye is moved passively by pressing on the side of the eyeball, the visual world appears to move, as the reader can easily confirm. Here an eye movement is not accompanied by the normal oculomotor command (outflow). If sensory signals from the muscles were being processed, such passive movement (it was argued) should still be compensated, but it appears not to be. The converse condition (motor command present, without actual eye movement) would

provide a crucial test of the outflow theory. This is the "paralysed eye experiment" that has had a long and somewhat chequered history.

Several attempts were made to immobilise the eye using paralysing drugs or a mechanical wedge (Brindley & Merton, 1960; Mach, 1914), and subjects reported that the visual world appeared to move in the direction of the attempted eye movement. Here it appears that the commands to the muscles are being taken into account despite the fact that no actual change in the muscles results. Unfortunately, it seems unlikely that these experiments actually immobilised the eye. The only study to do this successfully was by Stevens et al. (1976), who went to the extreme of whole body paralysis to stop any eye movement. Following an attempted saccade, their heroic subject reported a kind of displacement, or relocation of the visual world *without* movement.

Stevens et al. suggest that a spatial system compares information from the retina with commands sent to the muscles, in the way suggested by Helmholtz, but that this system is responsible for maintaining a perceptually stable spatial world without being involved in motion perception. Two further systems were suggested by Stevens et al. to account for their effects: an *eye position system*, which uses afferent information from the eye muscles, and a *pattern system*, which analyses motion in the retinal mosaic.

Normally there will be a great deal of information from the background against which any object appears that can disambiguate the interpretation of image movement. Following Gibson (1966), Stevens et al. suggest that movement in part of the retinal mosaic is interpreted as movement of an object in the world, whereas movement of the whole mosaic is interpreted as an eye movement, without any need to involve efferent information at all. When a large structured background is present, the system appears to rely more on an object's position and motion relative to the background, and to give less weight to the EEPS (Pelz & Hayhoe, 1995). This illustrates how some apparent ambiguity in the retinal image may disappear when one considers the information available in the entire mosaic, rather than a restricted portion of it, a point to which we will return later in the book.

Integrating information from successive fixations

The 2½-D sketch as conceived by Marr is still a very early stage of vision, and indeed Marr argues that it must be based on a *retinocentric* frame (Marr, 1982, p.284):

> If one used a frame that had already allowed for eye movements, it would have to have foveal resolution everywhere. Such luxurious memory capacity would be wasteful, unnecessary, and in violation of our own experience as perceivers, because if things were really like this, we should be able to build up a perceptual impression of the world that was everywhere as detailed as it is in the centre of gaze.

However, in order to integrate information from successive fixations to form a representation of the scene that is stable *across* eye movements requires going beyond the representation envisaged by Marr for the 2½-D sketch. In this section we consider how this might be achieved.

We saw earlier that humans and other animals sample their visual worlds with a series of discrete fixations, separated by saccades. No visible blur is apparent when our eyes dart from location to location and processing during a saccade is suppressed by several means. Somehow we must be able to integrate these successive "snapshots" to produce our perception of a stable visual world.

The problem of integrating successive slightly different retinal images is analogous to the problem of fusing two disparate images when stereopsis is achieved. In both cases the brain must discover which aspects of the retinal image *correspond* to the same objects and match them accordingly. We hope that the earlier discussion of stereopsis will have indicated that the correspondence problem is not trivial. It is no easier to solve when one considers integrating successive fixations.

If a view from one discrete sample of the visual world is to be matched with a second slightly different view obtained at a later time, there must be some sort of *memory* to preserve the first view for comparison with the second. Information-processing psychologists have identified one such short-lived visual memory system, which at first might seem a likely candidate to mediate the integration of successive glimpses. This short-lived visual memory system is known as *iconic memory* (named by Neisser, 1967). Its properties were first described in a classic paper by Sperling (1960); see Humphreys and Bruce (1989) for a review.

Could iconic memory be the system that serves to integrate successive views as observers fixate different portions of a scene? Hochberg (1968) and Turvey (1977b) argue strongly that it could not, because iconic memory is tied to anatomical, specifically retinal, coordinates. Thus, like Marr's 2½-D sketch, it can serve no useful integrative function, because we have just replaced the problem of comparing different retinal snapshots with that of comparing different iconic snapshots.

It seems that a memory system at a more abstract level than the iconic would be needed to serve this integrative function.

There is considerable, converging evidence for a post-iconic visual store that seems to play a role in visual imagery as well as in visual perception. For example, Phillips (1974) describes some elegant experiments in which he directly compared the properties of iconic memory with those of the short-term visual store (STVS). Iconic memory may be masked by the presentation of a bright light or pattern immediately after the test stimulus, is tied to anatomical coordinates, and is not affected by pattern complexity. STVS is not disrupted by masking, not tied to anatomical coordinates, but is affected by pattern complexity. In STVS, less is retained from complex than from simple patterns. These observations suggest that STVS is a limited-capacity short-term store at a more "schematic" level than iconic memory.

Hochberg (1968) implicated such a schematic memory system in the integration of successive views of objects, labelling it a *schematic map*. Hochberg conducted a number of studies in which he mimicked successive local sampling of the entire visual field by revealing partial glimpses of objects to observers, in a technique called *successive aperture viewing*. A line drawing of an object might be displayed section by section through a slit, as shown in Fig. 7.24. Observers were able to recover object structure from these glimpses, see spontaneous reversals in depth, and correctly notice the "impossibility" of certain configurations. Hochberg argued that the partial views were integrated at the level of the schematic map just as they would be if the observer were exploring a complete object with a succession of fixations.

However, Hochberg's schematic map does not serve to combine successive glimpses in a passive, "data-driven" way. Instead, he suggests that one may need previously acquired knowledge about the properties of objects to integrate successive views of them (Hochberg, 1968, p.325):

It seems most plausible to me that they (schematic maps) are built up not only from the successive views of a given object or scene but from *previous experiences* as well.

And elsewhere (Hochberg, 1968, p.324):

A schematic map is a matrix of space-time expectancies (or assumptions).

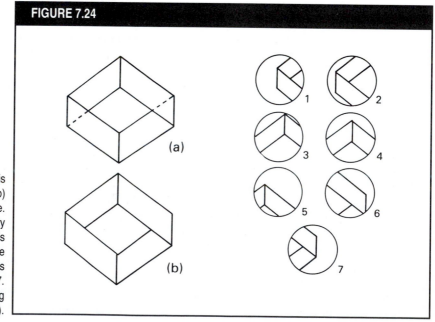

FIGURE 7.24

(a)

(b)

(a) shows a figure that is ambiguous in depth and (b) shows an impossible figure. Observers notice ambiguity and impossibility if a figure is viewed piece by piece through an aperture, as illustrated in frames 1–7. Adapted from Hochberg (1968).

Thus described, Hochberg's idea bears some similarity to Minsky's (1977) notion of "frame systems" (Turvey, 1977b). Minsky (1977) does not explicitly discuss the problem of integrating successive fixations made by the eyes alone, but addresses instead the broader problem of integrating successive views of an object or scene as the whole observer moves around or within it. He suggests that prior knowledge of an object, such as a cube, leads to the establishment of a coherent interlinked system of frames. Each frame corresponds to a symbolic description of one view of the cube. As the observer moves around a cube, different faces of it become visible and others become concealed from view. Minsky suggests that rather than recomputing the description of each viewpoint anew, the correct frames in the system would become available when information about an impending movement became available.

An alternative way to conceptualise the operation of a schematic memory of this kind is to suggest that it reflects a representational level where information is encoded in a coordinate system that is not tied to the retina, but to some frame of reference that remains constant despite eye movements. Possible candidates for such a frame include a head-based "stable-feature" frame (Feldman, 1985) or an environment-based "scene" frame (Feldman, 1985; Pinker, 1984). Physiologically, an area of the cortex has been identified where recoding from a retinal frame to a head-based frame of reference may occur. This is area 7a of monkey parietal cortex, a part of the "dorsal" pathway in extrastriate cortex (Ch.3, pp.56–59). Andersen, Essick, and Siegel (1985) found that cells in this area, like those in other areas, have a receptive field defined by retinal coordinates, but that their responses are also modulated by the position of the eyes. Thus, for a particular eye position, a cell codes the location of a stimulus relative to the head, and Zipser and Andersen (1988; see Ch.10, pp.249–250) have proposed that such cells may provide input to a

further stage in which stimulus location is coded independently of eye position. Contemporary connectionist models provide a way of describing *how* information in a retinotopic frame might be mapped into a frame that would be stable across eye movements, and we will consider such models in more detail in Chapter 10.

CONCLUSIONS

Marr sees the $2\frac{1}{2}$-D sketch as the end-product of *early* visual processing. Although the $2\frac{1}{2}$-D sketch remains to be implemented in a working computer program, the suggestion is that it can be established largely without recourse to downward-flowing information. We still have much to learn about how surfaces are derived from depth cues, but we have seen clear evidence from recent experiments that information from luminance contours, texture, stereo, and motion *is* integrated to form a surface representation, as Marr envisaged. Where one cue is ambiguous or partial, another may supply valid information. Thus when we start from the real input to human vision—which is binocular and dynamic—there may be few ambiguities that cannot be resolved through a full consideration of the products of a number of early visual processing "modules". In Marr's theory, unlike many others contemporary with it, we do not need to know or hypothesise what we are looking at in order to describe at least some aspects of its shape fully. However, to describe the scene being viewed appropriately within a viewer-centred frame is still only an early stage in perception. There must be other processes that allow us to categorise the image of (say) a rubber plant as being that of a "plant" in general and a "rubber plant" in particular. We shall turn to the processes of recognition in Chapter 9, after examining the problem of motion perception.

8

The Computation
of Image Motion

The retinal image is alive with motion from a variety of sources. People and other animals actively explore and sample their visual worlds with eye, head, and body movements, and the motions of things in the world may signal events of interest or danger. In Chapter 7 we saw how the changing view gained by a moving observer ("motion parallax") provides rich information about the 3-D structure of objects and scenes. In Part III of the book we shall see how "optic flow"— the complex pattern of motion throughout the visual field—can provide important information for the control of animals' and people's actions. To use Marr's terms, introduced in Chapter 4 (p.69), all this evidence contributes to a computational theory of the information available in image motion, and the uses to which it can be put. But to understand how this information is obtained, we need to devise algorithms capable of extracting it from a time-varying retinal image and then to ask whether these algorithms are implemented in nervous systems.

In this chapter we therefore discuss some principles of motion computation, along with the visual mechanisms that may carry out these computations. A key idea here is to consider the visual input to be a "space-time image". The analysis of motion can then be tackled with the same concepts that we applied to spatial vision in Chapters 5 and 6. First, we ask how the visual system may recover the velocity (speed and direction) of local image motion, irrespective of the external events that may have caused it. The theory of motion detectors is especially well developed, and we explain how visual filters sensitive to direction of motion are constructed, and how the responses of such filters may be combined and compared to make explicit the velocity of motion. (Readers who want to omit some of the more mathematical detail can skip Boxes 8.1–8.4 without losing the flow of ideas.) We shall also see that there is evidence for several additional strategies or processes of motion analysis, and consider recent accounts of the way in which these multiple cues to motion are extracted and integrated in the brain. We then discuss how local motion information may be combined across space to yield higher-order motion signals that carry information about the components of optic flow, and hence carry information about the spatial structure of the scene and about the observer's own motion. This sets the scene for more extended discussion of the role of optic flow in perception and behaviour in Part III of the book.

FIRST PRINCIPLES: MOTION AS ORIENTATION IN SPACE-TIME

Movement is a change of position over time. It might seem obvious therefore that to perceive movement we must first identify something, note its position, then identify the same thing a moment later and note its position again. The change in position (δs) divided by the time taken (δt) gives the velocity of movement. This simple intuition forms the basis for a class of models of motion perception known as correspondence models, as with this approach the major problem is taken to be that of matching "things" over time. What things should be matched, and how are competing matches resolved? The problem is discussed later in this chapter, and is similar to that encountered in stereoscopic vision (Chapter 7), but with the additional problem of measuring time intervals. However, a different approach holds that simpler measurements made on the time-varying image can recover motion information more directly. Based on extensive experimental evidence, a variety of models for the detection of local motion has been proposed over the last 30 years or more, and these models appear at first sight to differ substantially in the means by which they recover motion

information. Our aim in what follows is to show how motion information can in principle be recovered from the space-time image, and then to show how the various models form a single family, differing not so much in principle, but in the details of their implementation. With a little elementary algebra and calculus we can gain some quite deep insights into this approach.

Let us consider first the simple movement of a rigid pattern to the right at constant speed, V, as shown in Fig. 8.1A. In general, images are of course two-dimensional (2-D), but for simplicity we consider here a one-dimensional (1-D) slice through an image, whose intensity I(X) thus varies in only one spatial direction, say horizontally. Any point at location X within the pattern traces out a path through external space (x) and time (t), and that path is defined by a simple equation:

$$x - V.t = X$$

or

$$x = V.t + X$$

This is the equation of a straight line in the coordinates (t,x) with slope V. All points on a given path have the same intensity I, and as X varies adjacent points trace out parallel paths at different luminances determined by the pattern of intensities I(X) or I(x − V.t). Thus a complete description of the moving pattern is given by its *space-time image* (Fig. 8.1B). A horizontal slice through the space-time image gives us a snapshot of the 1-D spatial pattern at any one instant, and a vertical slice

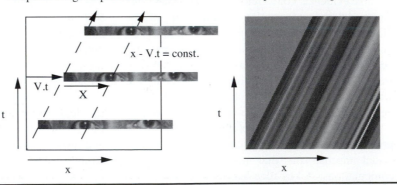

FIGURE 8.1

Two ways of thinking about a moving image: (A) as a sequence of snapshots where the position of any given feature traces out a path through space (x) and time (t). Along that path, (x − V.t) = constant. (B) as a space-time image: an array of image intensities distributed over space and time, whose orientation reflects the velocity V.

A. Spatial image displaced over time

B. Space-time image, I(x,t).

tells us about the temporal fluctuation of intensity at a given spatial position. The tilt of the space-time image away from vertical gives the speed of motion. A vertical space-time image is stationary, a tilted one is moving, a horizontal one arises from a flickering but empty field (a "ganzfeld"). Other, more elaborate space-time patterns can arise from more complex events.

To summarise: *Motion is orientation in space-time*. A moving one-dimensional image can be thought of as a pattern of intensity in space-time (x,t), just as a stationary 2-D pattern is an image in "space-space" (x,y). One of the most basic tasks in motion perception is to recover the velocity V from the time-varying retinal input, and this can be seen as the task of recovering the *orientation* of the space-time image. The idea of a space-time image may at first be unfamiliar, but once assimilated it proves to be a simple and powerful way of thinking about movement and movement analysis. Ideas about spatial image analysis are well developed, and as we can now think of time as if it were a spatial dimension, we can immediately transfer ideas about spatial filtering and orientation detection to the space-time domain. For a more detailed introduction to these ideas see Adelson and Bergen (1985), and for their extension to other visual domains, such as colour and stereopsis, see Adelson and Bergen (1991).

Velocity from space-time gradients

We now proceed to see how velocity V can be recovered by measuring local differences of image intensity in space and time, without explicitly identifying image features or their locations. Velocity corresponds to orientation in space-time, and it can be found from the ratio of temporal and spatial intensity gradients or derivatives. The basic idea is sketched in Fig. 8.2, and derived without approximation in Box 8.1.

The ratio of temporal gradient to spatial gradient thus yields an estimate of velocity V at all points in space and time, except that it cannot be calculated where the spatial gradient $\partial I/\partial x = 0$. In other words, blank, uniform regions carry no motion information. Similarly, the estimate of V would be unreliable where $\partial I/\partial x$ was itself small or noisy, and so we might expect to get best estimates of V at *edges* where the spatial gradient is maximum. This was the insight offered by Marr and Ullman (1981) in extending the theory of edge detection (Marr & Hildreth, 1980) into a theory of motion detection with emphasis on the encoding of direction. Harris (1986) developed the gradient ratio idea further for the encoding of both speed and direction.

To give a concrete example, whose development will be useful later, let us consider a moving sine-wave grating, widely used in visual

---

Box 8.1 Deriving velocity from space-time gradients

We have seen that the intensity of the moving image at any point x and time t is some function $I(x - V.t)$ and so the spatial gradient of the image is the partial derivative:

$$\partial I/\partial x = I'(x - V.t)$$

where $I'(X)$ denotes dI/dX. Similarly, applying the chain rule of calculus, we get the temporal gradient:

$$\partial I/\partial t = -V.I'(x - V.t).$$

Hence, combining the two relations, we get:

$$\partial I/\partial t = -V.(\partial I/\partial x)$$

In words, the rate of temporal change in the image at a given point is proportional to both the speed and the spatial gradient at that point. Clearly, if we can measure both gradients, then V can be recovered directly:

$$V = -(\partial I/\partial t)/(\partial I/\partial x).$$

FIGURE 8.2

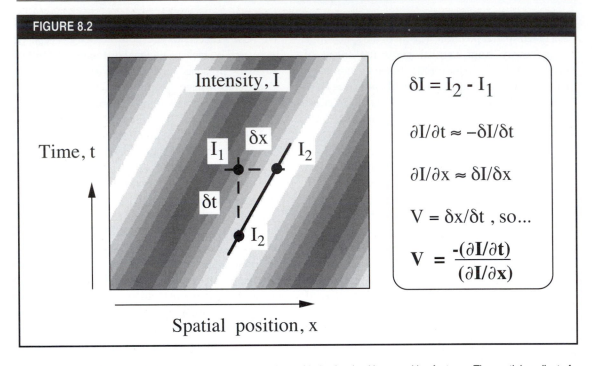

Velocity V can be recovered from spatial and temporal gradients (derivatives), without tracking features. The spatial gradient of intensity $\partial I/\partial x$ is (approximately) the spatial change in intensity (δI) between points δx apart, divided by the separation δx. The temporal gradient $\partial I/\partial t$ is (approximately) the temporal change in intensity ($-\delta I$) at a given position, divided by the interval δt. Because $V = \delta x/\delta t$ it follows that

$$V = (\delta I/\delta t)/(\delta I/\delta x)$$
$$= -(\partial I/\partial t)/(\partial I/\partial x)$$

Velocity is given by (minus) the ratio of temporal to spatial gradients. To exploit this relationship, and encode local velocity, the visual system needs at least two kinds of operators, or receptive fields, that respond to local spatial and temporal differences in image intensity, whose ratio of output values is then proportional to velocity.

experiments. The spatial pattern can be expressed as $\sin(u.X)$ where u is the spatial frequency. It moves at velocity V, and as $X = (x - V.t)$ the space-time image is:

$$I(x,t) = \sin[u(x - V.t)]$$

Examples of space-time images for moving gratings are given in Fig. 8.3A. Note how the tilt in space-time increases with speed, through a lateral shearing of the space-time image (not a rigid rotation). The temporal and spatial derivatives are

$$\partial I/\partial t = -u.V.\cos[u(x - V.t)]$$
$$\partial I/\partial x = u.\cos[u(x - V.t)]$$

and their ratio gives velocity $(-V)$, as expected. It is also worth noting that we can rewrite $I(x,t)$ as $\sin(u.x - u.V.t)$. If we introduce a new term $w = u.V$, then

$$I(x,t) = \sin(u.x - w.t)$$

and we can see that the space-time image not only has a spatial frequency (u) but also a temporal frequency (w). The spatial frequency is the number of bars (cycles) per unit distance, whereas the temporal frequency measures the number of bars (cycles) passing a given point per unit time, in cycles per second, often expressed as Hertz (or Hz). Figure 8.3B illustrates the relationship between spatial frequency, temporal frequency, and velocity

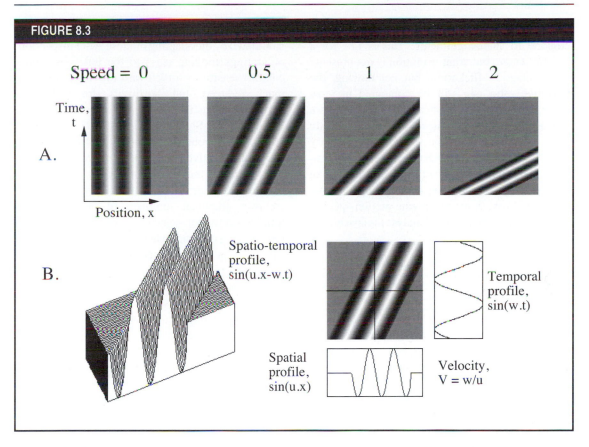

FIGURE 8.3

(A) Space-time image for a moving grating of fixed spatial frequency, at several speeds, V. (B) Cross-sections of the space-time image allow one to visualise the spatial frequency (u) and temporal frequency (w) of the moving grating. Note that for a moving grating, w = u.V, and V = w/u.

for a moving grating. Temporal frequency describes the rate of luminance fluctuation at a given point as the grating moves past it, and the temporal waveform can be seen by examining a vertical cross-section of the space-time image.

Just as spatial acuity in vision is defined by the highest visible spatial frequency—about 40–50 c/deg for human foveal vision—so temporal acuity can be defined by the fastest visible flicker rate—a temporal frequency of about 40–50Hz in ordinary viewing conditions. In general, the visibility of a grating (assessed by contrast sensitivity) depends on both spatial frequency and temporal frequency, as shown by the experiments of Robson (1966) and Kelly (1979b). Human visual sensitivity is greatest at roughly 5c/deg and 5Hz, and there is a pleasing similarity and symmetry in the spatial and temporal properties of contrast sensitivity.

As w = u.V, it follows that for a moving grating, speed V equals the ratio of temporal to spatial frequencies (V = w/u). For example, a grating whose spatial frequency is 2c/deg and whose temporal frequency is 10Hz has a speed of 5deg/sec. It is tempting to think that speed might be encoded by measuring temporal and spatial frequency, and then taking their ratio. This would work for gratings, which are synthetic images created in the laboratory, but would not generalise easily to other patterns that are not periodic and have no dominant spatial frequency. By contrast, obtaining speed from the derivative ratio discussed earlier would apply equally well to all images and so offers an attractive general theory (Harris,1986).

There is, however, an important difficulty in the analysis presented so far. We have assumed that motion is present, and then deduced that its velocity in the x-direction is given by the ratio of temporal to spatial gradients. This is fine for a moving image, but what if motion is not present? If the image is flickering, but not moving, the derivative ratio can still be computed in most places, but obviously it should not be taken as a measure of velocity. This reveals that there are really two problems to be solved in elementary motion analysis: to establish that motion is present, and to compute its speed and direction. The solution adopted by nature, and by computational vision theorists, is to incorporate motion-specific filters or *motion detectors* to analyse the space-time image.

MOTION DETECTORS

We consider first some of the evidence that animal and human visual systems have such direction-selective mechanisms, and use them to represent motion, and then move on to consider how such mechanisms can be built from simpler filters that are not direction-selective. We shall then be able to see how motion detector models can be integrated with the derivative ratio idea both to signal the presence of motion and to compute its velocity.

The motion aftereffect

One of the oldest and most robust observations in the history of vision research is the motion aftereffect (MAE). If you look at a moving pattern for a few seconds or minutes, and then stop the motion, the pattern will appear to be moving in the opposite direction for some time afterwards. The illusory movement of the MAE typically appears slower than the motion that induced it, and the duration of the MAE tends to increase with the duration of inspection. Thus the MAE is a visual aftereffect, like the tilt aftereffect discussed in Chapter 5 (p.99), and hundreds, perhaps thousands, of experimental studies of the MAE have been published this century since Wohlgemuth's (1911) classic monograph.

There is little doubt that the aftereffect results from temporary desensitisation of direction-specific neural mechanisms (motion detectors) stimulated by the adapting motion. After inspection of gratings moving (say) to the left, observers' contrast sensitivity for leftward-moving gratings is much reduced, but sensitivity for rightward moving gratings is only slightly affected (Sekuler & Ganz, 1963; Sharpe & Tolhurst, 1973; Tolhurst, 1973). Thus contrast detection mechanisms are direction-selective, and adapt selectively, provided the speed of movement is greater than about 0.5–1deg/sec (see Graham, 1989, Chapter 12, for a compact graphical summary of the evidence). Similar direction-selective loss of contrast sensitivity is found when a moving grating is *masked* by a superimposed pattern moving in the same direction (Anderson & Burr, 1985; Burr, Ross, & Morrone, 1986). But at slower speeds it appears that the most sensitive mechanisms—those activated at contrast threshold—are not direction-selective.

To see why perceived motion occurs as an aftereffect, let us consider horizontal motion, and suppose that there are some mechanisms or "detectors" specifically responsive to leftward movement, and others responsive to rightward movement. After a period spent adapting to leftward movement, the detectors for leftward movement will be less responsive than those for rightward movement (as first shown by Barlow & Hill, 1963, in the rabbit's retina). Testing with a stationary pattern will then produce a stronger response from the rightward than the leftward mechanisms. To explain the appearance of illusory rightward motion we must suppose that some comparison is made between the activities of different detectors and that when rightward units are more active than others, then motion is seen to the right.

In humans, the motion-sensitive units are almost certainly located in the visual cortex, rather than the retina or LGN. Like the tilt aftereffect, substantial interocular transfer of the MAE is found when one eye is adapted and the other is then tested, implying that binocular cortical units are responsible for much of the effect (e.g. Moulden, 1980). Nevertheless, the MAE has a monocular component too. If the left and right eyes are adapted to opposite motions and then tested separately, each eye sees its own aftereffect (Anstis & Duncan, 1983), implying the existence of monocular, direction-specific mechanisms (Fig. 8.4). These two sets of results suggest that V1 is an important site for the effect, where both monocularly and binocularly driven cells are found. This conclusion is supported by physiological studies in cat and monkey showing that substantial numbers of V1 cells are selective for direction of motion, but cells in the retina and LGN are not, and by the finding that direction-selective cells do in fact adapt to motion by reducing their responsiveness in much the way we would expect from the properties of the MAE (Barlow & Hill, 1963; Hammond, Mouat, & Smith 1986; Vautin & Berkley, 1977).

As it is possible to perceive motion in any spatial direction we might expect there to be cells responsive to many different directions. This is indeed found in cat and monkey cortex, and psychophysical evidence points to the same conclusion. Levinson and Sekuler (1976) devised a novel form of MAE, which we might term the

"directional aftereffect"—a movement version of the tilt aftereffect. Subjects adapted to a random dot pattern drifting at constant speed in a given direction, say +30° from horizontal. They were then tested on a similar pattern drifting horizontally, and asked to judge its perceived direction. There was a large shift of perceived direction, of up to 10° away from the adapting direction. This important result implies that there are different directional units in human vision and that the distribution of activity across different units serves to encode the direction of movement in 2-D (x,y) image space. When the response distribution is biased by adaptation, the perceived direction shifts towards the direction of the unadapted units, away from the adapting direction.

Contrast sensitivity for movement and flicker

Alongside the MAE, several other experimental procedures have contributed to our understanding of early, direction-selective filtering. Experiments on the detectability of low-contrast moving and

FIGURE 8.4

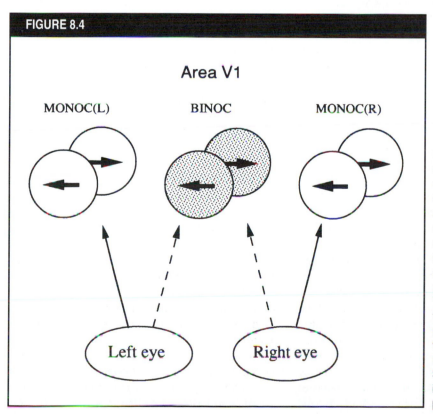

Properties of the motion aftereffect (MAE) imply the existence of different direction-selective motion mechanisms (short arrows), driven by the left and right eyes (MONOC) and by both eyes (BINOC). These units are probably located in primary visual cortex, area V1. Interocular transfer of the MAE demands the presence of BINOC units, whereas eye-specific MAEs require the MONOC units. Such variation in binocularity is consistent with that found physiologically.

flickering gratings have been especially revealing. To appreciate one of the most important results, we need a little basic trigonometry, which will also prove useful later. We introduced the algebraic expression [sin(u.x – w.t)] for a rightward moving grating earlier, and we now give an expression for a flickering grating. If we let the spatial profile be sin(u.x) where u is the spatial frequency of the grating, and the temporal waveform be cos(w.t) where w is the temporal frequency of flicker, then the space-time image, I(x,t), (see Fig. 8.5A, right) is simply their product:

$$I(x,t) = sin(u.x).cos(w.t)$$

and we can now see an important, perhaps surprising, relation between movement and flicker. In words, a flickering grating is the sum of two similar moving gratings drifting in opposite directions. In symbols, the sum of two similar, leftward- and rightward-moving gratings is:

$$F(x,t) = sin(u.x + w.t) + sin(u.x – w.t)$$

and from a standard trigonometric identity it follows that

$$F(x,t) = 2.sin(u.x).cos(w.t)$$

which represents a flickering grating whose contrast is twice that of its moving components. In a kind of shorthand, we might say that (Leftward + Rightward) = 2.(Flicker), as illustrated graphically in Fig. 8.5A. Thus a flickering grating is a space-time plaid, formed from the sum of two oriented (i.e. drifting) sinusoidal components.

Suppose we present one of these moving components at a very low contrast that is barely detectable, and then add to it a similar grating moving the other way. Will the image now be more visible? Because the image contrast is doubled we might intuitively expect sensitivity to double as well. In fact, there is little or no increase in visibility when the second grating is added to the first one (Kelly, 1979b; Levinson & Sekuler,1975; Watson, Thompson, Murphy, & Nachmias, 1980). This key result implies that the two moving components of a flickering grating are detected separately and

independently, by direction-selective mechanisms —"movement detectors". This conclusion has been found to hold for a wide range of spatial and temporal frequencies, again provided that the equivalent speed (V = w/u) is faster than about 0.5–1deg/sec (see Graham, 1989, Chapter 12). Similar psychophysical results have been obtained using monkeys as observers (Merigan et al., 1991).

The detection of time-varying contrast is thus direction-selective, except at slow speeds, and this conclusion is reinforced by experiments that have compared the detection and identification of moving gratings at very low contrasts. When subjects could detect the presence of the moving grating at all, they could also report its direction of movement (leftward or rightward) (Thompson, 1984; Watson et al.,1980). Such results are hard to explain unless the filters operating in these conditions are selective for direction of movement, and also signal that direction perceptually. How might such filters be constructed by the nervous system?

Models of motion detectors: Direction selectivity

As a moving image is oriented in space-time, whereas a flickering image is not, it follows that a motion-specific filter must have a receptive field that is oriented in space-time, in much the same way as filters can be oriented in (x,y) space. In the (x,t) coordinates of Fig. 8.3, a filter oriented clockwise from vertical would respond best to rightward movements, whereas an anti-clockwise orientation would respond best to leftward motion. How could visual systems build such movement-sensitive filters? All attempts to account for the direction selectivity of motion mechanisms involve combining the outputs of pairs of filters that are not themselves direction-selective, but whose receptive fields are displaced in space and time, relative to each other, in order that the combination of the two filters becomes "tuned" to motion.

To start with a simple example, imagine two adjacent receptors, P and Q separated by distance δx. A moving spot of light stimulates P, then stimulates Q after a time lag δt, where $V=\delta x/\delta t$ is

FIGURE 8.5

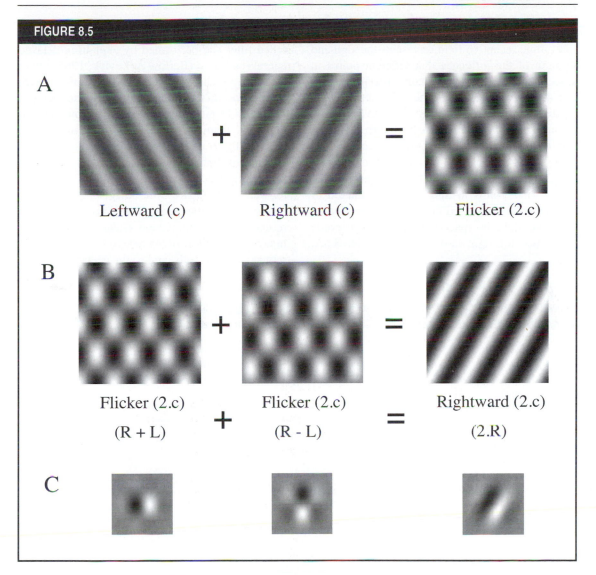

Space-time images. (A) If two drifting gratings, each with contrast c, are superimposed additively, they form a flickering ("counter-phase") grating of contrast 2.c. Mathematically, this follows from application of a standard trigonometric identity: sin(u.x + w.t) + sin(u.x − w.t) = 2.sin(u.x).cos(w.t). (B) The reverse is also true: the addition of two flickering gratings can form a moving grating. In this example, the rightward components of flicker are in phase and so reinforce each other, whereas the leftward components are out of phase, and cancel. (C) Small patches taken from the images of panel B. This shows how an oriented receptive field can be formed as the sum of two nondirectional fields, discussed in Fig. 8.6D.

the speed of movement. A mechanism (let's call it "M" for motion-sensitive) that delayed P's response by δt, then added it to Q's response, would clearly be "tuned" to velocity V, because at that velocity the responses from P and Q would coincide and reinforce each other more than at other velocities. At other speeds the individual inputs to M from P and Q would of course still exist and so the mechanism would not be highly specific for velocity.

The *space-time receptive field* of the hypothetical mechanism M is illustrated in Fig.

8.6A. Just like a spatial receptive field, the space-time receptive field represents the sign and strength of the influence that different points in space and time have on the current response of a cell at a given position. The influence may be positive (excitation, +) or negative (inhibition, −). Because no cell can anticipate the future, all inputs that influence a cell at a given time must come from earlier times. A delayed input is thus represented by a shift *down* the time axis, because it arises from even earlier points in time. The combination of delayed and nondelayed inputs forms an oriented receptive field in space-time, with some crude preference for rightward movement (Fig. 8.6A, right).

Figure 8.6B shows, however, that a more highly tuned filter can be formed by exploiting delayed lateral inhibition (Barlow & Levick, 1965) rather than delayed summation. If the summation device M receives direct excitation (left) and delayed inhibition (right) from points shifted somewhat to the right, then its receptive field is tuned more specifically to rightward motion, and completely suppresses leftward motion. Excitation and inhibition exactly cancel out the response to leftward-tilted space-time images. Barlow and Levick (1965) obtained evidence from the rabbit's retina that this interaction occurs separately in many small regions of the receptive fields of some retinal ganglion cells, and so the cell may sum the

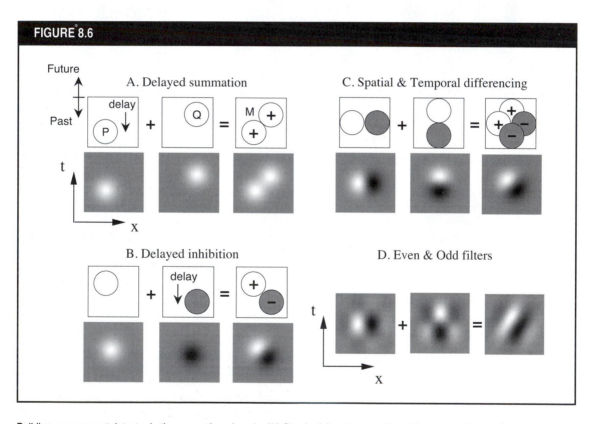

FIGURE 8.6

Building a movement detector in the space-time domain. (A) Simple delayed summation of the output of two adjacent receptors creates an oriented space-time receptive field, but better schemes create greater direction selectivity. (B) Excitation (light blob) combined with delayed lateral inhibition (dark blob) creates an "operator" oriented to the right that suppresses any response to leftward movement. (After Barlow & Levick, 1965.) (C) The *same* oriented (direction-selective) filter can be created as the sum of spatial and temporal differencing (derivative) operations. (After Marr & Ullman, 1981.) (D) Oriented filters can be created by combining receptive fields that have odd and even symmetries in space but even and odd symmetries in time. Note that panel C is a special case of this general strategy. (After Adelson & Bergen, 1985.)

outputs of many units of the kind shown in Fig. 8.6B. The reader may notice from Fig. 8.6B that the Barlow–Levick mechanism is actually computing a space-time derivative, making it sensitive to space-time gradients in a given direction. It can be seen that the goal is to build an oriented space-time receptive field.

A third approach is to start by computing separate spatial and temporal derivatives (Fig. 8.6C), and then adding them. This approach, inspired by the derivative ratio algorithm for velocity (see earlier) is the essence of the Marr–Ullman model (Marr & Ullman, 1981). They attributed the spatial differencing operation to the action of "sustained" X-cells and the temporal differencing to "transient" Y-cells, but later research has not provided great support for that particular implementation, nor for the logical-AND operation that was supposed to combine them. Nevertheless, the general idea could still hold, and it is interesting to note from Fig. 8.6 how similar the outcome of the Barlow–Levick and Marr–Ullman schemes for direction selectivity can be.

Finally, a fourth highly influential model for motion coding was proposed by Adelson and Bergen (1985), based on the "motion sensor" of Watson and Ahumada (1985). It can be seen as a generalisation of the Marr–Ullman scheme, and like all earlier schemes it combines two nondirectional filters to form a directional one (Fig. 8.6D). The underlying logic is illustrated in Fig. 8.5B,C. In brief, the figure shows that just as two flickering patterns can be added together to form a moving one, so two nondirectional, flicker-sensitive receptive fields can be added to form a motion-sensitive (direction-selective) one. This logic is described further in Box 8.2.

Direct evidence that cortical simple cells have space-time receptive fields of this kind (Fig. 8.5D) comes from sophisticated physiological analyses of responses in the cat's visual cortex (McLean & Palmer, 1989, 1994). All the simple cells that were classed as having space-time oriented receptive fields were indeed direction-selective in response to moving bars, and the preferred (optimal) velocity of these cells was well predicted by the space-time orientation of the response field

(McLean, Raab, & Palmer, 1994). Importantly, the spatiotemporal filtering underlying this direction-selectivity does seem to be essentially linear (additive) as our discussion so far has presumed, with nonlinear effects (squaring, or rectification, and contrast gain control) at the output of the cell (Heeger, 1992b).

For some years researchers have attempted to distinguish experimentally between the three or four schemes sketched in Fig. 8.6. Psychophysical experiments discussed so far have implied only the existence of direction-selective filters, and are therefore consistent with any of the schemes. As all the models share the assumption of space-time oriented filters, it might be thought impossible to distinguish them. However, different models arrive at those filters through different stages, and so experiments that could tap into the underlying stages could, in principle, establish the most appropriate model.

Specific support for the gradient scheme (Fig. 8.6C) or its generalisation (Fig. 8.6D) comes from an intriguing variant of the motion aftereffect, discovered by Anstis (1990). The observer inspected a uniform patch of light whose brightness increased smoothly over time, jumped back down, increased smoothly again, and so on. After adapting to this for some time there was a negative aftereffect: a steady patch appeared to grow dimmer over time. This aftereffect suggests that there are visual mechanisms sensitive to the direction of temporal luminance gradient at a given location. Second, and most importantly, a stationary test edge located in the patch appeared to be *moving*, either to the left or right depending on the luminance polarity of the edge, even though the adapting stimulus had not moved at all. This paradoxical motion aftereffect makes good sense in the gradient scheme (Marr & Ullman, 1981), however, because motion is sensed by a combination of spatial and temporal gradient signals. The real spatial gradient given by the test edge and the illusory temporal gradient given by the negative aftereffect of adapting the temporal derivative operator (Fig. 8.6C) combine to signal motion in the usual way. Reversing the sign of one or the other gradient reversed the perceived direction of motion, as the gradient model predicts.

Box 8.2 Creating a direction-selective, space-time oriented filter

We saw in Fig. 8.5A that nondirectional flicker is the sum of rightward (R) and leftward (L) movements; in shorthand: $F_1 = R + L$. Inverting the contrast of (say) the L component creates a second, similar pattern of flicker (F_2), which is shifted in space and time relative to the first one: $F_2 = R - L$. It follows that if we add the two flicker patterns together the L component is cancelled to yield a rightward moving one: $(F_1 + F_2) = (R + L) + (R - L) = 2.R$ (Fig. 8.5B). To create (simulate) receptive fields using this logic, the only further step is to restrict the images to a local "window" in space and time. This can be done by multiplying each of the extended patterns of Fig. 8.5B by a localised Gaussian (or similar) window function. The result is shown in Fig. 8.5C. The essential logic of the operation is preserved, in that the two nondirectional, flicker-sensitive fields respond to both R and L directions; we then add them such that their L responses always cancel, but their R responses reinforce each other, and a direction-selective receptive field is created.

This process can be neatly expressed in one equation. If we let the window function be G(x,t), then the two nondirectional fields are G.sin(u.x).cos(w.t), and G.cos(u.x).sin(w.t). Note that the two spatial profiles are 90° apart in phase (sine vs cosine) and may be described as "orthogonal" to each other, or "in quadrature". The same holds for their temporal profiles. The movement field M(x,t) is their sum:

$$M(x,t) = G.\sin(u.x).\cos(w.t) + G.\cos(u.x).\sin(w.t)$$
$$= G.\sin(u.x + w.t)$$

which defines an oriented receptive field tuned to spatial frequency (u), temporal frequency (w), and speed V = w/u.

ENCODING LOCAL VELOCITY

We now have a framework for thinking about space, time, motion, and direction selectivity. But the evidence for direction selectivity, and the models devised for it, do not tell us how velocity of movement is made explicit. We began with this as a key problem, and we must return to it. McKee, Silverman, and Nakayama (1986) found that perceived velocity of moving gratings, and the ability to discriminate small differences in velocity, was little affected by randomisation of spatial and temporal frequencies, provided that the physical velocity V was preserved. This implies that, at some level, an explicit velocity code is established that allows vision to compare speeds between different spatial and temporal patterns. The simplest general algorithm for velocity is the derivative ratio, $V = -(\partial I/\partial t)/(\partial I/\partial x)$, but in this form it suffers two problems. First, it "blows up" when the spatial gradient $\partial I/\partial x = 0$, and second it makes no use of directional filtering, against all the

experimental evidence. These problems can be overcome, however, by an elaboration of the ratio rule termed the *multi-channel gradient model* (Johnston, McOwan, & Buxton, 1992), outlined in Box 8.3.

The multi-channel model uses both first and second spatiotemporal derivatives to yield a more robust estimate of velocity in an image. For moving images it will always deliver a true estimate of local velocity in the x-direction, up to the limitations imposed by biological or machine implementation of the algorithm. See Johnston and Clifford (1995) for its further extension and success in accounting for three illusions of apparent motion.

We show next that, in order to recover velocity explicitly, the "motion detector" or motion energy model (Adelson & Bergen, 1985) requires further stages of processing. We have seen so far that a quadrature pair of filters can be summed to form an oriented one (Fig. 8.6D). In the full motion energy scheme there are several stages beyond this: the *energy*, *opponency*, and *ratio* stages, summarised in Fig. 8.7. In outline, the four stages

Box 8.3 Multi-channel gradient model:
Encoding velocity via 1st and 2nd derivatives

We saw earlier that the intensity pattern of a moving image can be expressed as some function $I(x - V.t)$. Differentiating with respect to space and time (as indicated by subscript letters, where $I_x = \partial I/\partial x$, $I_{xx} = \partial^2 I/\partial x^2$, $I_{xt} = \partial^2 I/\partial x\partial t$) we can recover velocity V in a variety of ways:

$$I_x = I'(x - V.t) \tag{1}$$
$$I_t = -V.I'(x - V.t) \tag{2}$$
$$\therefore \quad I_t = -V.I_x \tag{3}$$

This restates the simple ratio rule. Differentiating (3) again yields:

$$I_{xt} = -V.I_{xx} \tag{4}$$

Multiplying (3) by I_x and (4) by I_{xx} we get

$$I_x.I_t = -V.I_x.I_x \tag{5}$$

and

$$I_{xx}.I_{xt} = -V.I_{xx}.I_{xx} \tag{6}$$

Adding (5) and (6), and rearranging, we get a new rule for computing velocity:

$$V = -(I_x.I_t + I_{xx}.I_{xt})/(I_x^2 + I_{xx}^2) \tag{7}$$

This expression exploits the simple ratio rule twice by using second derivatives as well as first, and does so more robustly because I_x and I_{xx} tend not to be zero simultaneously, so that the bottom line of the ratio is likely to be greater than zero. The formula can be extended further by including third and higher derivatives too. Combining values within a spatial neighbourhood is also possible and yields greater reliability. The simple gradient ratio is a special case of equation (7), dropping all derivatives higher than the first. As each successive derivative operation is implemented by a different spatiotemporal filter or "channel", the model requires four or more filters, and has been termed the "multi-channel gradient model" of velocity coding. See Johnston, McOwan, and Buxton (1992) for more formal derivation and extensive analysis.

of processing are as follows: (i) the initial, nondirectional filters are combined in pairs to form directional filters; (ii) the outputs of the directional filters are squared and added in pairs to compute *motion energy* for each of the two directions; (iii) the difference between the two energies (*opponent energy*) is a rough measure of the "amount" of movement (and contrast) in the input; (iv) a more accurate *velocity code* is obtained by comparing two energy measures whose ratio varies directly with velocity. Box 8.4 gives further details of these computations, showing that this more complete version of the energy model can recover velocity exactly, and can be equivalent to the multi-channel gradient model. This insight again highlights the family connection between apparently different accounts of motion coding. The merger combines the robustness of the energy model with the velocity specificity of the derivative ratio, and provides an appealing, if somewhat idealised, system for encoding velocity. Johnston and Clifford (1995) say more about versions of the model that are more realistically tuned to experimental data.

FIGURE 8.7

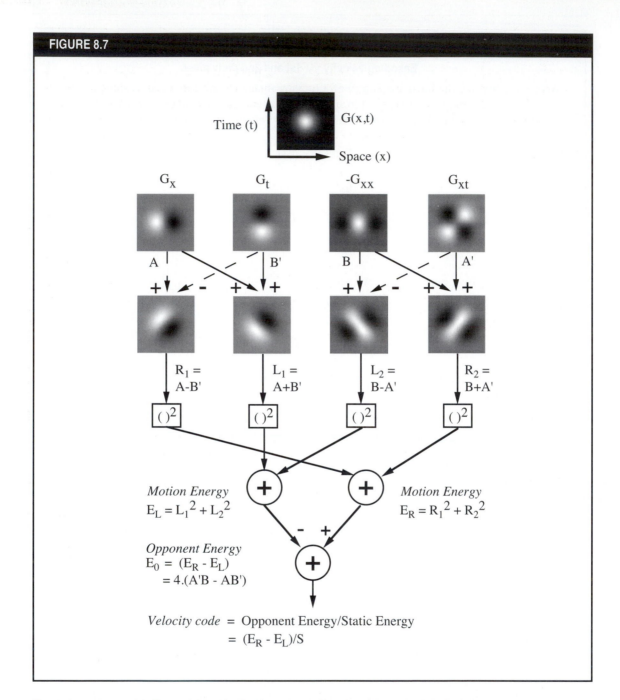

The motion energy model. The model creates direction-selective filters by adding and subtracting the responses of non-directional filters. Each of the outputs A, B, L_1, R_1, etc. should be thought of as a space-time image [A(x,t), B(x,t), etc.] that is the output of a given filter. The outputs are then squared and added to give leftward and rightward energy. Opponent stage takes the difference of the two energy values to eliminate responses to flicker. To encode velocity independently of contrast and other factors, opponent energy must be scaled (divided) by a suitable measure of "static energy". See text for details. This diagram is faithful to the Adelson and Bergen (1985) model, except that it shows a particular choice of input filters designed to produce ideal coding of velocity at the output. These filters have space-time receptive fields that are spatial and temporal derivatives of a Gaussian function, as shown.

Box 8.4 Computing velocity from motion energy

This box explains how nonlinear combination of filter outputs can be used to compute velocity. It should be read in conjunction with Fig. 8.7. There are four nondirectional input units whose responses are denoted by A, B, A', B'(x,t). These are added or subtracted in quadrature pairs to form four directional filters, two leftward and two rightward, whose outputs are denoted L_1, L_2, R_1, R_2(x,t). The leftward (and rightward) pair are 90° out of phase (odd and even) in space-time. In symbols, the outputs are:

$$L_1 = A + B' \qquad\qquad L_2 = B - A', \tag{8}$$
$$R_1 = A - B' \qquad\qquad R_2 = B + A' \tag{9}$$

Motion energy (leftward and rightward) is defined in the same way as local energy or contrast energy (p.93):

$$\text{Leftward energy:} \quad E_L = L_1^2 + L_2^2 \tag{10}$$
$$\text{Rightward energy:} \quad E_R = R_1^2 + R_2^2 \tag{11}$$

The purpose of this step is to deliver a signal that is smooth across space and time, reflecting the pattern of motion flow, rather than the undulating structure of the image in space and time. This emulates the behaviour of complex cells rather than simple cells (see Ch.3, p.50). The next stage is an opponency stage, analogous to that in colour vision, which takes the difference between the two motion energies, to give:

$$\text{Opponent energy, } E_O = (E_R - E_L). \tag{12}$$

After simple manipulation of symbols, omitted here, we get:

$$\text{Opponent energy, } E_O = 4.(A'B - AB') \tag{13}$$

This opponent step enhances direction specificity, and eliminates any response to stationary images or nondirectional flicker. But opponent energy E_O does *not* estimate velocity, partly because it also varies enormously with contrast, being proportional to contrast-squared. Adelson and Bergen (1985) noted that division by a "static energy" signal S would eliminate the contrast dependence, but even this does not guarantee the recovery of velocity unless the various filters are carefully chosen. In an ideal algorithm we would want the motion/static energy ratio (E_O/S) to equal the true velocity, V, for all possible moving patterns, and in principle this can be done. We have seen that A and B are nondirectional spatial filters with the same temporal response, but 90° apart in spatial phase, so let the static energy be:

$$S = 4.(A^2 + B^2) \tag{14}$$

Hence, dividing (13) by (14),

$$E_O/S = (A'B - AB')/(A^2 + B^2) \tag{15}$$

Equation 15 makes an interesting comparison with the gradient model, equation 7:

$$V = -(I_x.I_t + I_{xx}.I_{xt})/(I_x^2 + I_{xx}^2) \tag{7}$$

They are ratios of similar form, and in fact they become identical if we let:

$$A = I_x \qquad\qquad A' = I_{xt} \tag{16}$$
$$B = -I_{xx} \qquad\qquad B' = I_t \tag{17}$$

It follows that with this choice of derivative filters, an energy ratio model will always compute velocity correctly, because equation 7 guarantees that V = E_O/S. Figure 8.7 illustrates the Gaussian derivative filters used in this merger of the Adelson–Bergen and multi-channel gradient models.

In essence, ratio models of this kind encode velocity by comparing the outputs of "fast" and "slow" mechanisms. The velocity tuning of the two mechanisms taken individually is not the critical factor, provided that the ratio of their outputs increases with speed, to give an unambiguous code for velocity. Psychophysical experiments give broad support for this type of ratio model. First, there is evidence from masking, adaptation, and discrimination experiments (Anderson & Burr, 1985; Hammett & Smith, 1992; Hess & Snowden, 1992; Mandler & Makous, 1984) for just two (or at most three) temporal "channels" in human vision, unlike the multiplicity of spatial channels that have been revealed by similar techniques, discussed in Chapter 5. One temporal filter is low-pass, and the other one (or two) are band-pass in the temporal frequency domain. Second, the ratio of the sensitivities of these two channels may depend directly on velocity (Harris, 1980). It is tempting to associate the slow and fast channels with P and M systems, respectively, (see Ch.3, p.47), as the behavioural contrast sensitivity of the monkey is reduced for slow speeds of grating movement after parvo-cellular (P) lesions in the retino-geniculate pathway (Merigan & Eskin, 1986), but sensitivity is lost only at high speeds after magno-cellular (M) lesions (Merigan, Katz, & Maunsell, 1991). The M/P sensitivity ratio may thus depend directly on velocity. Third, adapting to moving gratings influences the perceived speed of subsequently viewed test gratings. Adapting gratings moving faster than the test speed tend to make the test seem slower, and vice versa (Smith & Edgar, 1994; Thompson, 1981). Smith and Edgar (1994) showed that their results were broadly consistent with a ratio model for speed, combined with a subtractive process of adaptation. In summary, then, there is significant support for a fast/slow energy ratio model of velocity coding, and this in turn is compatible with a spatiotemporal derivative approach to motion analysis.

Energy and Reichardt models compared

One of the attractions of the energy model has been that it is consistent with physiological evidence, giving a functional role to direction-selective simple cells (L_1, R_1, etc.) followed by complex cells (E_L, E_R) [cf. equations 8–11, Box 8.4 and Fig. 8.7]. Another important model of motion detection was developed by Reichardt (1969), who used quantitative experiments on the optomotor response of insects (see Ch.12, pp.267–270) to account for the first stage of motion processing in the insect retina. Reichardt's "correlation" model has since been shown by Adelson and Bergen (1985) to be functionally equivalent to the opponent energy model, but without the final ratio stage that encodes velocity. Its output behaves in the same way as the energy model, although it does not have the same linear, direction-selective intermediate stages. The Reichardt model begins with pairs of nondirectional input signals (A,B) along with delayed versions of them (A′,B′), then forms nonlinear, direction-selective responses directly by multiplication (A.B′, A′.B). The final stage takes the difference of these two signals, to give an output equivalent to opponent energy in the Adelson–Bergen model: (A′B − AB′) [see equation 13]. In other words, given the same input filters, the outputs of the two models must be indistinguishable. Experiments on motion perception that give quantitative support to the Reichardt model (van Santen & Sperling, 1984) must equally support the opponent energy model.

We have already discussed the equivalence of the energy ratio and extended derivative ratio models, and so it is tempting to conclude that "all motion models are really the same". Tempting indeed, but also too simple, because each "model" is actually a class of models whose performance will depend on details of implementation, such as the number of stages and choice of filter parameters, as well as the possible inclusion of intensity nonlinearities, and contrast gain controls. What we can say is that the three classes of model overlap interestingly and significantly.

Moreover, even where overall performance is equivalent, the hardware implementation of the models may be distinguishably different. In a detailed analysis of responses in the cat's cortex, Emerson et al. (1992) showed that the behaviour of direction-selective complex cells was nicely consistent with their being the nonopponent motion energy stage of the energy model, but not consistent with any stage of the Reichardt multiplier model. They did not find evidence for an opponent stage in primary visual cortex, but it might be sited at a higher cortical level. It is now very clear that motion processing is incomplete in V1, and that further elaboration occurs especially in the dorsal pathway through V2 to MT, MST, and beyond (see later in this chapter, and Chapter 3).

SECOND-ORDER, NON-FOURIER, AND "LONG-RANGE" MOTIONS

We have so far considered only simple, rigid translation of an image through space and time. Such motions generate luminance contours that are oriented in space-time and can be "picked up" (in Gibson's (1966) terminology, see Chapter 11) by suitably tuned spatiotemporal filters. In a seminal paper Braddick (1974) contrasted this kind of local or "short-range" motion detection with a diverse set of results suggesting that a second kind of "long-range" motion analysis existed. In this section we trace the fate of the "long-range motion" idea, and the rise of ideas about "second-order" or "non-Fourier" motion. The common thread is that motion energy detection is not the only route to motion perception.

Apparent motion

In cinema, television, and video, motion is perceived from a sequence of still frames that are produced by taking successive snapshots or samples of a changing scene at a certain rate. In the cinema the *sample* rate is 24 frames/sec, but when projected each frame is flashed 3 times to increase the *flicker* rate to 72Hz, in order to minimise the distracting appearance of flicker that is invisible beyond 50–60Hz. Perceived motion from a sequence of stills (recall the "flicker books" of childhood) is often termed *apparent motion*, although when the sample rate is high enough there is every reason to believe that "real" (smooth) motion and "apparent" (sampled) motion perception are effectively the same thing. The

small-scale differences between their space-time images are smoothed away by the limited spatiotemporal resolution of the receptors (Watson, Ahumada, & Farrell, 1986).

Motion, however, can be reliably perceived at low sample rates, where the spatial displacement and temporal interval between frames is quite large. Braddick (1980) and Anstis (1980) concluded that there were two qualitatively different kinds of motion analysis. "Short-range" motion was based on the motion detectors discussed in this chapter; "long-range motion" was more loosely defined by exclusion, as that which was not "short-range". It seemed that it could operate across large spatial and temporal gaps, much larger than the likely extent of motion-sensitive receptive fields, could integrate frames presented successively to left and right eyes, and depended on the matching of corresponding visible features or shapes across time. The characteristics of short-range motion, derived mainly from the visual properties of random-dot image sequences, seemed different in every way, requiring short spatial and temporal intervals, monocular presentation, and no prior recognition of coherent contours or shapes in the image (Baker & Braddick, 1985; Braddick, 1974).

Later research has led to a re-evaluation of each of these distinctions, and to the conclusion that long-range motion is not a well-defined category of motion perception (Cavanagh, 1991; Cavanagh & Mather, 1989). For example, as the spatial range of direction-selective fields almost certainly increases greatly with eccentricity and receptive field size, there is no fixed range over which "short-range" motion operates, and so spatial range ceases to be a simple defining characteristic of the two processes. Additional difficulty has been raised by recent experiments on the apparent motion of random-dot patterns, once a standard way of characterising motion detector properties psychophysically. It now seems that the spatial and temporal limits to motion discrimination in these experiments may be determined more by the statistical structure of the stimulus patterns than the properties of the detecting system (e.g. Eagle & Rogers, 1996; Morgan, 1992; see Mather, 1994, for a compact review).

First- and second-order motion

Despite these uncertainties, interest in the idea of multiple routes to motion perception has intensified. Chubb and Sperling (1988) were the first to define clearly several classes of stimulus sequence that did give rise to reliable motion perception, but would not activate the motion energy system described earlier. Consider, for example, a small light square that steps frame-by-frame across a grey background. This is ordinary, "first-order" motion, based directly on luminance contrast and its orientation in space-time. Now suppose that on every step the square reverses polarity, from light to dark, then dark to light, and so on. The average luminance along the path of motion is the same as it is everywhere else—mid-grey. Thus there is no oriented luminance contrast, and the motion energy system should be silent. Nevertheless, motion of a flickering square is seen. As a second example, consider a field of stationary, random, black and white dots. In one region or "window" of the field the contrast is reversing over time at (say) 5Hz. Now let the window containing flicker be moved smoothly over time, while the dots themselves remain stationary. Observers see a region of disturbance or "twinkle" that moves, even though there are no space-time contours, or equivalently no space-time Fourier components, corresponding to this motion. In a final example, let the window define a region of lower-contrast dots, rather than twinkling dots. Again, when the window moves, its motion is reliably perceived. These examples, and there are many others, point to a general class of "second-order" or "non-Fourier" stimuli where spatial structure or motion can be perceived, despite the lack of corresponding structure in the luminance profile. The structure exists, certainly, but it lies in the spatial or spatiotemporal profile of some higher-order property of the image such as local contrast, local flicker rate, and so on.

The role of nonlinearities

We touched on a similar distinction between first- and second-order structure in discussing the perception of texture edges and illusory contours in Chapter 6. In both texture and motion, Chubb and Sperling (1988) and others have emphasised that second-order structure can be readily transformed into a first-order structure by the application of a simple, but suitable, nonlinearity, and can then be detected in well-understood ways. The Bergen and Landy (1991) model for texture segmentation (Chapter 6) was an example of this approach. In our first motion example given earlier, full-wave rectification of contrast (setting negative values to positive) is a nonlinearity that would serve perfectly, because the contrast-reversing square would be rendered as a simple moving square, with positive contrast in every frame. Motion analysis applied after the rectification would obviously yield the correct motion information. Half-wave rectification of contrast (setting negative values to zero) would also be suitable, because it would render the stimulus as an oriented path containing only light spots. This also has strong first-order energy at the true orientation or speed of motion.

Are there special processes in vision devoted to recovering second-order motion, or could it be a by-product of nonlinearities that just happen to be there anyway? This is a key question for theories of motion processing, and the evidence to date seems to favour the "special process" view. Much of the evidence comes from the study of *contrast-modulated* (CM) patterns, illustrated in Fig. 8.8A (right). These are second-order gratings, as it is the *contrast*, rather than luminance, that varies (modulates) sinusoidally across space. This contrast profile imposed on a *carrier* pattern (typically either random dots, or a sine-wave grating) is often called the *envelope* of the pattern. When the envelope is made to drift over time, while the carrier remains stationary, this creates second-order motion whose space-time image is shown in Fig. 8.8B. Observers may be required to discriminate the speed or direction of movement of the envelope. Note that in a naturally moving texture, first- and second-order movements would normally go hand-in-hand, as the carrier and envelope move together. The ability to dissociate them in the laboratory allows us to ask questions about the nature of responses to first- and second-order movements, and particularly whether or not they arise from separate mechanisms.

FIGURE 8.8

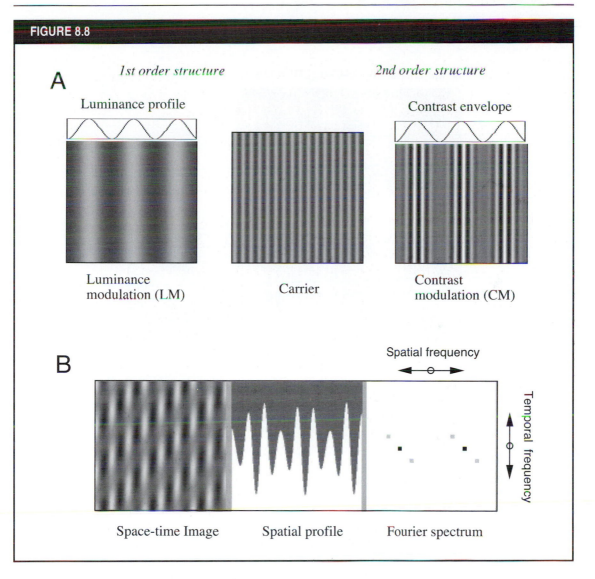

(A) Comparison of a first-order, luminance-modulated grating (LM, left) and a second-order, contrast-modulated grating (CM, right). The CM grating is formed by imposing a low-frequency contrast variation (the *envelope*) onto a high-frequency *carrier* grating. (B) Space-time image for second-order motion stimulus (left), in which the envelope moves while the carrier is stationary. Its Fourier spectrum (right) has energy at the frequency of the carrier (black points), and "sidebands" created by the modulation (grey points), but no energy at the low frequency of the envelope; the centre of the plot, representing lower frequencies, is blank. Thus second-order motion is also called "non-Fourier motion"; the moving envelope has no direct counterpart in the Fourier components of the image.

Fig. 8.9B shows that the Fourier spectrum of a CM pattern contains no salient peaks of energy at the modulating frequency, confirming the second-order, non-Fourier nature of the CM image. This is quite unlike the first-order, luminance-modulated (LM) grating of Fig. 8.9A.

However, Fig. 8.9C shows that half-wave rectification distorts the CM image and its spectrum, creating prominent energy at the modulating frequency. That is, the distorted CM image now contains a first-order grating as well. Fig. 8.9D shows that a compressive (saturating)

FIGURE 8.9

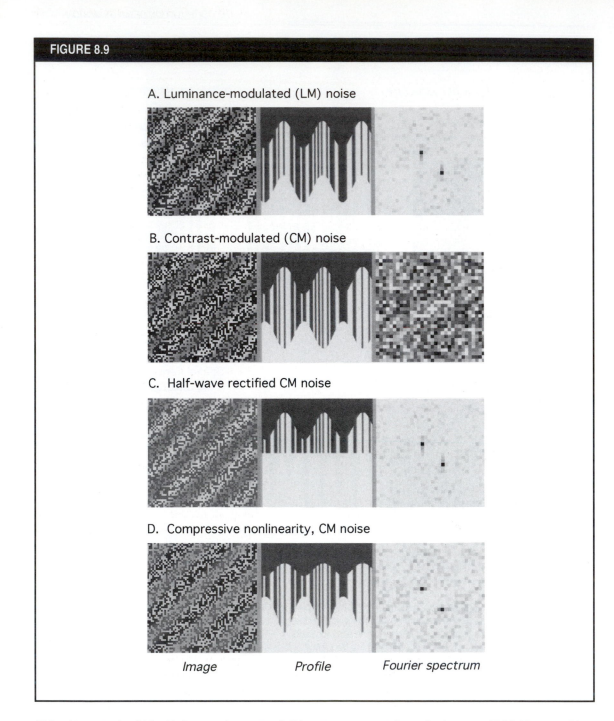

A. Luminance-modulated (LM) noise

B. Contrast-modulated (CM) noise

C. Half-wave rectified CM noise

D. Compressive nonlinearity, CM noise

Image   *Profile*   *Fourier spectrum*

(A) Luminance grating (LM) added to a random pattern (left) has strong energy at the grating frequency (right). The axes of the space-time Fourier spectrum (right) are spatial frequency and temporal frequency, as in Fig. 8.8. (B) Contrast modulation of a random pattern has no prominent energy peaks, but the oriented structure is evident in this spatial image and also when it is presented as a space-time image (as second-order motion). (C) Half-wave rectification distorts the CM image, and introduces energy at the modulation frequency. (D) Compressive transformation of intensity (saturating response at high intensities) also introduces energy at the modulation frequency. Nonlinear processes of this kind (C and D) can be used to recover the second-order structure in spatial and space-time images.

transformation of intensity values does the same. If such nonlinearities occurred early in the chain of processing, and there were no special pathways for second-order motion, then we should expect first- and second-order motion to behave equivalently in a variety of ways. For example, adaptation to first-order patterns should reduce sensitivity for detection of second-order and vice versa. Holliday and Anderson (1994) found that this was not true for rates of movement up to 4Hz, but was true at faster speeds (8 or 16Hz). Similarly Scott-Samuel and Georgeson (1995) found that perception of CM motion could *not* be cancelled by an opposing luminance modulation (LM) at drift rates up to 7.5Hz, but could be cancelled at a fast speed (15Hz). These studies show that responses to CM and LM are not equivalent, at least for slow to medium speeds. If they were equivalent, because of early distortion, we should also be able to see motion in animation sequences composed of alternate CM and LM frames. This has not been found in general (Ledgeway & Smith, 1994; Mather & West, 1993a). Thus, all these results reinforce the idea of a "special process" encoding second-order motion. The exception occurs with fast, high-contrast images where early compressive distortion of the waveform, perhaps at the photo-receptor level, means that CM images produce significant responses in first-order pathways (Holliday & Anderson, 1994; Scott-Samuel & Georgeson, 1995).

When these exceptional conditions are avoided, detection of moving contrast modulation actually involves a much *slower* mechanism than detection of luminance modulation. The sensitivity for CM patterns shows a low-pass characteristic that rolls off at much slower temporal frequencies than LM detection (Derrington & Henning, 1994), implying a sluggish response in the CM process. This is also implied by the finding that the direction of CM motion could be seen only at relatively long durations of presentation, greater than 200msec, whereas the direction of LM motion could be seen at much briefer durations, down to 20–40msec (Derrington, Badcock, & Henning, 1993).

This sluggishness of the second-order mechanism enables it to detect motion over much longer time gaps than the first-order mechanism.

Boulton and Baker (1993) examined perceived direction of motion for a display sequence containing two 100msec flashes of a CM pattern. The entire pattern (carrier and envelope) was spatially displaced in the second flash. When there was no blank time gap between the flashes, perception was evidently dominated by first-order motion because direction of movement became ambiguous when the spatial displacement was about half a cycle of the *carrier grating*. (Note that displacements of a periodic waveform through half a cycle to the left or right are equivalent, and therefore ambiguous in direction.) With a 50–100msec blank gap between the CM flashes, performance was quite different. Direction was correctly perceived over a much greater spatial range, until the displacement reached about half a cycle of the *contrast envelope*. Thus the second-order motion mechanism has a longer "memory" that can span time gaps of 100msec or more. First-order motion gives way to second-order when the time gap is greater than about 40msec (Boulton & Baker, 1993; Georgeson & Harris, 1990).

Second-order mechanisms for motion

Second-order motion perception thus depends on a nonlinear process that recovers the contrast envelope, or "energy profile" of the CM stimulus. The evidence discussed so far, however, does not establish the existence of second-order mechanisms *specific* to motion. Success in the motion tasks might reflect a more general ability to encode the positions of things, and the way those positions change over time. This has sometimes been called "feature-tracking" (Pylyshyn & Storm, 1988) or "attention-based motion perception" (Cavanagh, 1992). A clear demonstration of a second-order motion aftereffect (MAE) would point to direction-specific, second-order detectors, but until recently such an effect has remained elusive.

Now it is becoming clear that second-order MAEs can indeed be found, but only with dynamic or flickering test patterns and not with stationary ones (Ledgeway, 1994; Nishida & Sato, 1995). By contrast, ordinary first-order MAEs can of course be observed on static test images. The reason for this difference remains unclear, but in an ingenious study Nishida and Sato (1995) exploited it to show that separate first- and second-order MAEs can be induced at the same time. They adapted to a carefully designed CM grating sequence, such that the first- and second-order motions were in opposite directions. The perceived direction of MAE on a static test grating was opposite to the first-order adapting direction, whereas on a flickering test grating it was opposite to the second-order direction. This striking experiment shows that separate *motion-specific* mechanisms must exist for first- and second-order information.

Moreover, second-order MAEs observed on flickering test gratings exhibited complete interocular transfer when one eye was adapted and the other was tested, whereas the first-order MAE on a static test grating showed about 50% transfer, as usual (Nishida, Ashida, & Sato, 1994). This result echoes our discussion of the tilt aftereffect (Chapter 5), and suggests again that second-order mechanisms lie at a higher, more completely binocular, cortical site—perhaps areas V2 and/or MT rather than V1. Physiological studies of cat and monkey cortex are beginning to confirm this view, as we now describe.

Zhou and Baker (1993) studied the responsiveness of cat cortical neurons to drifting luminance gratings and to second-order (CM) gratings, where the carrier was stationary and the envelope moved. Very few cells in primary visual cortex (area 17) responded to the contrast envelope of the CM grating, but in area 18 more than half the cells did so. In these cells the preferred direction of movement was the same for LM and CM gratings, but the spatial frequency tuning was different: cells were responsive to lower spatial frequencies of CM than LM. Zhou and Baker argued from these results that first- and second-order processes do not share identical pathways, but run in parallel and converge onto the cells that are responsive to both LM and CM. Such integration of first- and second-order processes is even more evident in the responses of cells in area MT of the monkey. In MT almost all (99%) of cells are direction-selective for movement of first-order, luminance contrast, but 87% of cells tested were also responsive to a moving second-order bar, defined as a twinkling region moving against a stationary background

(Albright, 1992). Again, the preferred direction of movement tended to be the same for both classes of stimulus. This suggests that MT plays a strong role in integrating different cues for motion, and in representing the speed and direction of movement irrespective of the cue(s) that gave rise to it.

This emerging picture of "cue convergence" is similar to our discussion of orientation cues in Chapter 5. The psychophysical and physiological evidence has been incorporated in a well-specified computational model for motion coding proposed by Wilson, Ferrera, and Yo (1992), sketched in Fig. 8.10. After a common stage of oriented, spatial filtering the model embodies separate first- and second-order pathways with separate motion energy mechanisms in each path, as discussed earlier. In the second-order path, the spatial structure of contrast modulation, or other textural variations, is captured by the usual device of rectification or squaring, followed by a second-stage of oriented spatial filtering. The gain control stage in each path is the equivalent of the ratio stage in Fig. 8.7, which minimises contrast dependence and renders the response of each oriented mechanism more nearly proportional to the component of velocity in that direction. The final and crucial stage in the Wilson model is the integrative stage, ascribed to brain area MT, which combines velocity vectors from both paths to compute the final speed and direction of pattern movement in each local area of space.

THE INTEGRATION OF MOTION MEASUREMENTS

Each point in the field of view (or retinal image) can thus be associated with a movement vector that describes the speed and direction of motion at that point. The entire set of such vectors is called the velocity field. To compute the retinal velocity field, the visual system would need to derive two-dimensional velocity vectors at each spatial position, and this raises new problems for our understanding, which has so far been restricted to motion in one spatial dimension. As we shall see, the problems arise when we try to obtain a 2-D

FIGURE 8.10

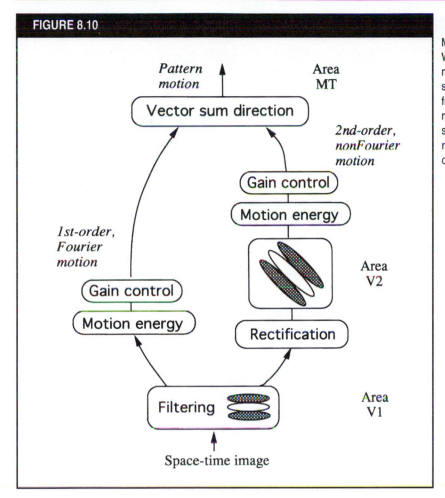

Motion coding model of Wilson et al. (1992). The model combines first- and second-order velocity signals from different directional mechanisms, at a higher stage whose output represents the local velocity of a complex pattern.

vector from 1-D information. This can be the case with long, smooth, moving contours, for which the local speed and direction of movement are ambiguous, and may apply also to individual motion detector systems if they are responsive mainly to one axis of movement in 2-D space.

First let us consider the *aperture problem*, in which an edge or line is observed moving behind a fixed aperture (Fig. 8.11A). In what direction will the line appear to be moving? Almost certainly it will appear to move in the direction of the solid arrow, at right angles to the line. A moment's thought, however, reveals that its actual movement could be quite different. The dashed arrows are two of the possible movement vectors, which could be de-composed into two components, one along and one at right angles to the line. Movement of a line

or edge along itself causes no optical change whatever within the aperture, and so *must* be undetectable. Only the perpendicular component is detectable. The line's actual movement vector is therefore ambiguous, but it must be consistent with the known perpendicular component, even though the component along the line could be anything. It follows that the true velocity vector must have its end-point lying along a *velocity constraint* line, as shown in Fig. 8.11A. Clearly, further information or constraints would be needed to recover the true velocity. Further discussions and illustrations of the problem can be found in Marr and Ullman (1981), Hildreth (1984a,b), and Hildreth and Koch (1987). But as we don't usually look at life through small holes, why is the aperture problem important?

FIGURE 8.11

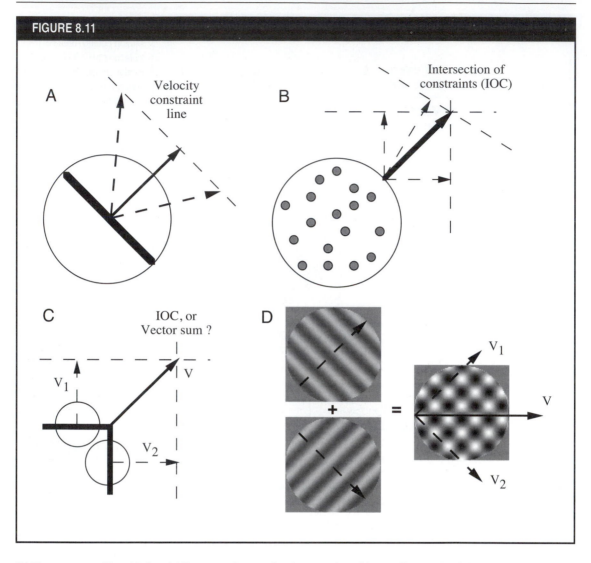

(A) The aperture problem. Motion of 1-D contours in a restricted aperture is ambiguous. The problem is important because the velocity signals of oriented (effectively 1-D) mechanisms may be ambiguous in this way. Velocity constraint line defines the set of motion vectors consistent with the line's observed (perpendicular) component of motion. (B) True velocity vector for a moving 2-D image (bold arrow) can be obtained from the intersection of two or more constraint lines, given by different directional mechanisms. (C) Intersection of constraints (IOC) solution can also be found by combining information from different parts of a moving object. (D) Plaid formed by adding two moving gratings. Component velocities (V_1, V_2) are different from pattern velocity (V). Cells in MT may combine component velocity signals to derive pattern velocity (see text).

Its significance lies in the idea that motion-detecting receptive fields might *always* suffer the aperture problem. They do look at life through a small hole (the receptive field area) and if they are orientation-tuned then they pick up essentially 1-D information even from a 2-D image. This means that individual mechanisms may be capable of sensing only the component of velocity perpendicular to their own receptive field orientation. Fig. 8.11B summarises this problem. Given a moving 2-D texture, containing Fourier components at many different orientations, the motion energy system at a given location may yield a set of velocity vectors from different-oriented mechanisms (dashed arrows) with different lengths and directions. What is the true motion of the pattern? The solution can be obtained unambiguously from the velocity constraint lines introduced in Fig. 8.11A. As there is only one true vector (bold arrow in B) all the constraint lines must be consistent with it. The constraint lines, drawn at right angles to each component vector, intersect in a single point that reveals the true motion vector. Fig. 8.11C shows us that the ambiguity of a moving 1-D contour can also be solved by combining vectors from different locations, provided they belong to the same moving surface or object.

In summary, then, velocity vectors from 1-D mechanisms are ambiguous, but the *intersection of constraints* (IOC) algorithm can, in principle, be used to find the true velocity in two dimensions. The IOC idea came to prominence when Adelson and Movshon (1982) studied the perception of moving plaids, formed as the sum of two sinusoidal grating components moving in different directions (Fig. 8.11D). They found that if the spatial frequencies or contrasts of the components were very different then the motion was seen as incoherent or transparent, with the two gratings sliding over each other. But with reasonably similar contrasts and spatial frequencies, a single coherent motion was seen. This suggested that the visual system does have to combine different 1-D vectors to derive 2-D motion, and that it might implement a version of the IOC algorithm. Note also that the speed (vector length) of the component motions in the plaid is different from the pattern's overall speed. Welch (1989) asked whether speed discrimination (the ability to distinguish small differences in speed) would be determined by the component speed or by the plaid's speed. She found that performance on plaids was limited by the ability to detect differences in the component speeds. This surprising result further supports a two-stage model in which component motions are integrated to extract pattern velocity, and implies that the noise or other factors that limit discrimination lie at the earlier component stage of processing.

These perceptual findings prompted further research to identify the early and later stages of motion processing physiologically. Single-cell recordings from area V1 and MT in primates (Movshon, Adelson, Gizzi, & Newsome, 1985; Rodman & Albright, 1989) revealed that whereas most cells in V1 and some cells in MT responded to the 1-D grating components of a plaid, other cells in MT responded to the direction of pattern movement. For example, a cell responding best to horizontal movement of a vertical grating might also respond best to the horizontal movement of a plaid, even though its components were moving obliquely. Such cells in MT may be integrating the outputs of cells responding to the plaid's components, but whether vision employs the IOC method, or some other algorithm, to achieve this integration is more controversial.

The Wilson model, for example (Fig. 8.10), combines first- and second-order component velocity signals via vector summation rather than IOC. In simple cases the two rules yield the same predicted direction (although not necessarily the same speed) but there are patterns, known as type II plaids, for which the two rules make very different predictions, as shown in Fig. 8.12. The IOC construction always represents the

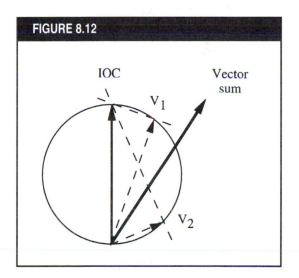

FIGURE 8.12

Velocity vectors in a type II plaid. By definition, the pattern vector (IOC) for the type II plaid does not fall between the two component vectors (V_1, V_2). Thus the IOC and vector sum can be in very different directions, and these two hypotheses about motion component integration can be tested experimentally (see text).

geometrically correct solution for a rigidly moving pattern, and when plaids are presented for durations longer than about 150msec, the perceived direction matches the IOC direction quite closely. Nevertheless, Wilson and colleagues build a persuasive case, supported by detailed modelling of experimental data, that vector summation and not IOC is the rule used at the integrative stage.

First, at brief durations and in peripheral vision, the direction of type II plaids is no longer perceived correctly, and instead they are biased towards the vector sum direction (Yo & Wilson, 1992). This shift is attributed to a reduced contribution from second-order signals in the periphery and to the sluggishness of second-order vision (see earlier, p.191) that reduces its contribution at brief durations (Wilson et al., 1992). According to the Wilson model, first- and second-order signals for type II plaids produce *opposite* errors that normally cancel each other. But when the balance between the two types of signal is disturbed, quite large errors can be revealed. Second, the model predicts that a type II plaid formed from purely second-order (CM) gratings should appear to move in the vector-sum direction, not the IOC direction, because the second-order signals are not now counter-balanced by first-order. This was just the result observed by Wilson and Kim (1994b). In summary, the model of Fig. 8.10 can account for a wide range of normal and illusory perceptions of direction in moving patterns. It also predicts correctly that MT neurons should respond to both first- and second-order motions (Albright, 1992), but its more specific predictions about MT have yet to be tested physiologically.

There are some conditions, however, in which the components of a plaid do not cohere at all, giving the appearance of transparent motion instead. Some psychophysical and physiological studies have suggested that the rules for combining component motions in plaids involve a wide range of cues for the interpretation of occlusion, transparency, and binocular depth (for review, see Stoner and Albright, 1994). In determining whether to integrate early "component" motion signals, visual processes may be evaluating a wide range of evidence about whether the components

arise from a single object surface, or from two superimposed surfaces where one is transparent. The Wilson model has recently been modified to incorporate mechanisms that produce a range of such transparency effects (Wilson, 1994a,b; Wilson & Kim, 1994a). Coherent motion corresponds to a single peak of activity in the set of pattern units, whereas transparency corresponds to two distinct activity peaks in different directions. This enhanced model can account well for the observed effects of relative component contrast on both the emergence of coherence or transparency, and the perceived direction of components when they appear transparent (Wilson & Kim, 1994a).

FEATURE CORRESPONDENCE

We began our discussion of local motion coding by considering the two-process, short-range/long-range theory of Braddick (1974, 1980) and Anstis (1980). The revelation of second-order motion processes has undermined that earlier dichotomy, and has to some extent eclipsed our thinking about "long-range" motion. Nevertheless, it remains quite likely that a third route to the perception of motion lies in the matching of corresponding features across space and time. It is possible to design stimuli that put motion energy detectors and the feature-matching process into opposition. Georgeson and Harris (1990) did this for first-order (LM), and Smith (1994) did so for second-order (CM) image sequences. In both cases, with short or zero time interval between frames motion was seen in the direction predicted by motion energy, but with a 40–60msec time gap between frames motion was seen in the feature-matching direction. Lu and Sperling (1995) have described in greater detail the characteristics of the three motion systems.

This line of evidence supports the 2 × 2 classification of motion processes proposed by Cavanagh (1991), rather than a simple dichotomy. Stimulus information may be first- or second-order, and motion extraction may be based on motion energy or on feature correspondence.

Cavanagh (1992) has associated the latter process with active, attention-driven tracking of feature locations, but as yet rather little is known about the role of attention in motion perception.

The task of matching corresponding features is analogous to the correspondence problem in stereopsis (Chapter 7), and has been tackled in detail by Ullman (1979, p.4):

> The correspondence problem is that of identifying a portion of the changing visual array as representing a single object in motion or in change. The notion of a "correspondence" comes about when the problem is considered (as it is in much of this work) in the context of a sequence of images, such as the frames of a motion picture. The problem then becomes one of establishing a match between parts of one frame and their counterparts in a subsequent frame that represents the same object at a later time.

Ullman argued that correspondences are established on the basis of matches between primitive *elements* of figures such as edges, lines, and blobs, rather than between whole figures. That is, matches are built up between the kinds of descriptive units found in the primal sketch. (Note the similarity between this and the theories of Julesz (1971) and Marr and Poggio (1976, 1979), who established matches between elements, rather than entire patterns, to achieve stereoscopic fusion.) Ullman presents a number of demonstrations to support his case. In one of these, observers were presented with a "broken wheel" display (see Fig. 8.13) in which every other spoke is incomplete. If the "wheel" is rotated by x degrees between successive frames, where x is greater than half the angle between the spokes of the wheel, the observer sees the wheel breaking into three distinct rings. The innermost and outermost rings rotate anticlockwise whereas the middle ring appears to rotate clockwise. This would be expected if matches were established between line segments, but would not be expected if the entire figure were being matched from frame to frame. If figural matching were occurring one would expect to perceive clockwise rotation of the whole wheel.

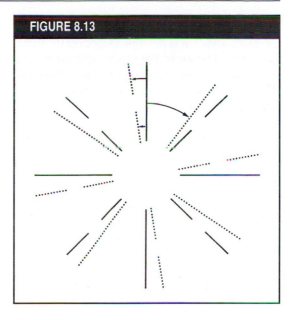

FIGURE 8.13

The solid lines show the first frame of Ullman's "broken wheel" configuration, and the dotted lines show the second frame when it is viewed in apparent motion. Under certain conditions the wheel is seen to split into three rings, with the outer and inner ones moving anticlockwise and the central one moving clockwise, as shown by the arrows. Adapted from Ullman (1979).

Ullman provides an elegant computational account of how correspondence can be achieved by making use of a principle of "minimal mapping". Suppose that one frame of a film consists of elements A and B, and a second frame consists of elements A′ and B′, displaced relative to A and B. The correspondence problem is to establish whether A or B is to be matched with A′. Ullman achieves this by establishing an affinity measure for each possible pairing. The closer together in space, and the more similar in description the two elements in a pair are, the greater will be their affinity (based on the simple assumption that near, similar matches are more likely to belong together than more distant, dissimilar matches). To solve the correspondence process for an entire display of several elements a solution is found that minimises matches with poor affinities and maximises those with strong affinities. A global solution is thus obtained through a set of local measures.

Once the correspondence problem has been solved (although Ullman's solution is not necessarily that used by the human visual system; see Marr, 1982), it is possible to recover the three-dimensional structure that gives rise to a particular set of motions. The kinetic depth effect (Wallach & O'Connell, 1953) provides perhaps the best known example of the recovery of structure from motion. If a shadow is cast by a rotating wire shape onto a screen (see Fig. 8.14), a viewer can readily perceive the shape of the structure behind the screen from the dynamic shadow pattern. Ullman's own demonstration of the recovery of structure from motion involves the images of a pair of co-axial counter-rotating cylinders (see Fig. 8.15). When static, the display looks like a random collection of dots. Once it moves, however, the observer has a

clear impression of one cylinder inside another, with the two rotating in opposite directions. Ullman has shown that it is possible to recover structure from motion if one assumes that the motion arises from *rigid* bodies. Given this rigidity assumption, his structure-from-motion theorem proves that structure can be recovered from three frames that each show four noncoplanar points in motion.

The interested reader is referred to Ullman's book (Ullman, 1979) for a fuller discussion of the processes of establishing correspondences and recovering structure from motion. Throughout his book Ullman, like Marr, attempts to provide a computational account that makes use of general

FIGURE 8.14

The kinetic depth effect (Wallach & O'Connell, 1953). When a wire shape is rotated behind a screen on which its shadow falls, observers see the dynamic shadow pattern as a solid shape in motion.

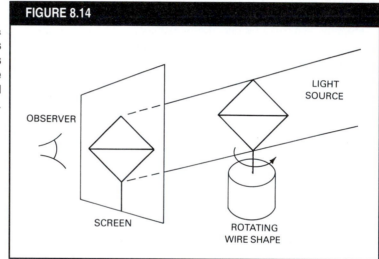

FIGURE 8.15

Illustration of the principles behind Ullman's (1979) counter-rotating cylinders display. The screen shows the pattern of dots that would arise if the images of two, co-axial, glass cylinders covered with dots were projected orthographically onto a screen. As the cylinders are rotated in opposite directions, the pattern of dots on the screen changes. Observers who view a film of the screen can recover the structure of the counter-rotating cylinders from the pattern of apparent motions present.

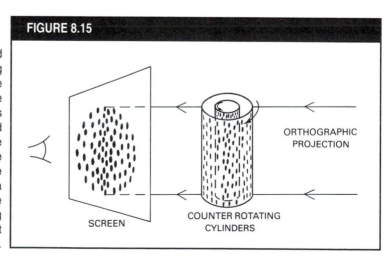

constraints (e.g. assume motion is of a rigid object) rather than knowledge of specific objects. We will return to consider the analysis of structure from motion further in Chapter 15 when we describe the considerable body of work on the perception of biological motion and relative motion that has been conducted by the "ecological" perceptual theorists.

SPATIAL VARIATIONS IN THE VELOCITY FIELD

Where the visual input is sparse, or noisy, or ambiguous because of the aperture problem, there are advantages to be gained by pooling motion information across extended regions of space. There is now a good deal of experimental evidence that perception of global, coherent motion can be seen in displays containing noisy, variable local motions of dots, and that it arises through cooperative processes of spatial integration (Nawrot & Sekuler, 1990; Williams & Sekuler, 1984). The disadvantage of spatial averaging, however, is that it may eliminate genuine spatial variations in velocity. These exist where rigid objects rotate or loom relative to an observer, or where objects deform, as when a tree blows in the wind or a person moves.

To deal with this problem, algorithms have been devised that yield correct velocity fields without presuming velocity to be constant within a region. One approach has been to assume that velocity can vary over images of objects, but that it does so *smoothly*. This is a reasonable assumption for most natural scenes, as the surfaces of objects are smooth relative to their distance from the observer. Sudden changes in distance, and therefore in velocity, will occur only at occluding edges. For example, if a cylinder rotates around its long axis, the velocity of images of elements on its surface varies smoothly from zero at the edges to a maximum along the centre. An algorithm that assumed pure translation would compute uniform velocities over the surface and so would not distinguish a rotating cylinder from a translating one, whereas the smoothness assumption allows the two to be discriminated.

The smoothness assumption does not in itself allow the correct velocity field to be computed, and it is necessary to make a further assumption that some particular measure of velocity variation is minimised. For example, an algorithm that assumes that velocity variation is minimised over areas of the image is described by Horn and Schunck (1981). They show that it computes correct velocity fields for both translating and rotating objects, but also, not surprisingly, that it yields errors at occluding edges where the smoothness constraint does not hold. Another model of this kind is proposed by Yuille and Grzywacz (1988).

An alternative approach is that of Hildreth (1984a,b), who demonstrates that an algorithm minimising variation in velocity along a contour in the image yields correct velocities for objects with straight edges. Evidence that an algorithm of this kind operates in human vision is provided by Hildreth's discovery that the errors it produces for moving curves match a number of visual illusions. Two of Hildreth's (1984b) examples are shown in Figs. 8.16. and 8.17. The computed velocity field for a rotating ellipse differs somewhat from the true field (Fig. 8.16); in particular it has a stronger radial component than it should. Hildreth points out that this corresponds to the illusion of pulsating radial movement seen in a rotating ellipse under some conditions. Similarly, the computed velocity field for a rotating cylinder with a helix on its surface (a barber's pole) shows strong vertical components that are absent from the true velocity field (Fig. 8.17). Again, the same error occurs in human vision, as the rotating barber's pole is seen to move upwards or downwards. Further examples of illusions that seem to reflect a process of minimising velocity variation can be found in Hildreth (1984a,b).

Relative motion and velocity computation

People can see, with great accuracy, oriented contours, shapes and region boundaries that are defined solely by relative motion within fields of random dots (e.g. Regan, 1989; Regan & Hamstra, 1991). Gradients of relative motion also yield surfaces in depth. For example, Rogers and Graham (1979) presented observers with a

FIGURE 8.16

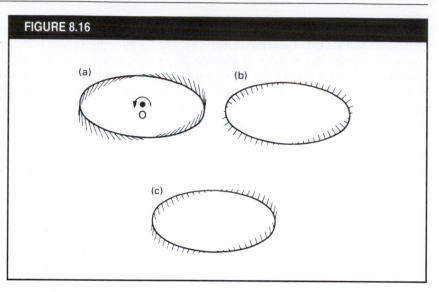

(a) An ellipse rotating rigidly around its centre O. The velocities of points on its edge are shown by straight lines. (b) The components of these velocities perpendicular to the edge. (c) The velocity field obtained from the perpendicular components, which minimises variation in velocity along the edge. Reproduced from Hildreth (1984b) with permission of the publishers, MIT Press.

random-dot pattern in which parallel bands of the pattern moved at different speeds, simulating motion parallax as observers moved their heads. The result was a powerful illusion of a corrugated surface in depth (see Ch.7, p.159). Different profiles of velocity variation across space were seen accurately as different surface shapes. The importance of relative motion for vision leads us to ask at what stage in the processing of image motion it is detected. One possibility is that it is detected relatively late, from a full velocity field representation. Nakayama and Loomis (1974) proposed a model of this kind, in which units with centre-surround organisation are excited by motion in one direction in the field centre and inhibited by motion in the same direction in the surround. A number of these units, with overlapping fields but different direction preferences, are linked to a

FIGURE 8.17

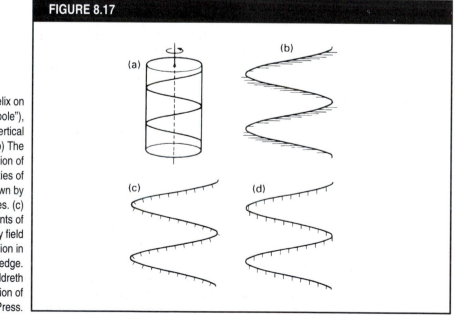

(a) A cylinder with a helix on its surface ("barber's pole"), rotating around its vertical axis. (b) The two-dimensional projection of the helix with the velocities of points along it shown by straight lines. (c) Perpendicular components of velocity. (d) The velocity field that minimises variation in velocity along the edge. Reproduced from Hildreth (1984b) with permission of the publishers, MIT Press.

single "convexity detector" that sums their outputs. Nakayama and Loomis show that the activity of a convexity detector signals the presence of an image velocity boundary passing through its field.

The model of Nakayama and Loomis (1974) appears to receive some physiological support. Cells sensitive to relative motion between a target in the central part of the field and either a similar target or a background texture in the field surround have been discovered in the visual systems of several species, including area MT in the owl monkey (Allman, Miezin, & McGuinness, 1985). The response to motion in a preferred direction in the field centre is facilitated by motion with a different velocity in the surround but suppressed by motion with the same velocity. Cells that have such a suppressive surround, and which therefore respond to relative motion between target and background, are clustered together in patches or columns in MT, distinct from other clusters of cells that show no suppression and appear to collect motion signals over very wide areas (Born & Tootell, 1992). Furthermore, Frost and Nakayama (1983) discovered cells in the pigeon optic tectum that respond to opposite directions of motion in centre and surround, whatever these directions are, as Nakayama and Loomis' (1974) proposed convexity detectors do.

Several psychophysical studies on the detection of second-order, velocity-modulated gratings are also consistent with a direction-specific suppressive surround mechanism. The gratings can be thought of as alternate bands of dots or filtered noise (the carrier), moving in opposite directions. Thus luminance and contrast are spatially uniform, but velocity is modulated with a certain spatial frequency. Subjects' sensitivity to these gratings peaks at fairly low frequency (that depends on the carrier frequency) and shows a decline at even lower spatial frequencies, below the peak. In the detection of luminance contrast, a low frequency decline in sensitivity indicates an inhibitory surround to the receptive field. The same is true here with velocity modulation, but the low frequency decline of *motion contrast sensitivity* indicates a surround mechanism that produces inhibition when stimulated in the preferred direction of the field centre (Watson & Eckert,

1994). This is consistent with the physiological findings above.

Even so, there are some important discrepancies between the physiological evidence and Nakayama and Loomis' theory. The theory assumes a linear summation of velocities in centre and surround, which does not appear to occur in the cells studied. Frost, Scilley, and Wong (1981), for example, found that the response of cells in pigeon tectum to a moving dot in the field centre could be suppressed equally by motion in the same direction in the surround of a dot or of a texture filling the entire field. A linear summation of velocity measurements would cause greater suppression in the second case. Second, the inhibitory surrounds of these cells are often strikingly large, even covering the entire visual field in owl monkey MT (Allman et al., 1985). With a velocity field containing many relative motion boundaries, the inhibitory surround of virtually every cell would therefore contain motion discrepant to that in the centre. With nonlinear summation, all cells would be activated and no information would be available to localise relative motion boundaries in the way that Nakayama and Loomis' model aims to do. These cells do not appear to represent the convexity detectors of this model, and further evidence is needed to clarify their role in the computation of relative motion.

An alternative possibility is that relative motion is computed *before* the velocity field, directly from 1-D component motions. From a theoretical point of view, such a scheme offers a solution to the problem of using smoothness constraints to compute the velocity field. As we have seen, these yield incorrect results at occluding edges where velocity changes abruptly. Hildreth (1984b) suggests that relative motion information obtained from perpendicular components of motion could be used to constrain velocity computation so that variation is minimised only within relative motion boundaries and not across them. The algorithm that she proposes for detecting relative motion in perpendicular components first operates on a number of ranges of orientations of zero-crossings independently. It locates boundaries where the average sign of motion of zero-crossings changes, and then combines the results from all zero-crossing orientations. If such a boundary is present in zero-crossings of more than one orientation, then relative motion is present.

Despite these theoretical proposals, the relationship between computation of velocity and of relative motion in vertebrate visual systems remains unclear at present. Rather more progress has been made in the case of insects, however. Reichardt, Poggio, and Hausen (1983) have developed a model for the computation of relative motion from the outputs of the Reichardt motion detectors described earlier. In this model, the output of each motion detector is inhibited in a nonlinear fashion by the summed outputs of all motion detectors in a region around it. The signals resulting from this interaction are then summed to give an output that controls the insect's turning response. The system has the property of responding to incoherence in the input pattern of motion signals, giving a stronger output the less uniform these are. The fully specified model predicts accurately several properties of flies' responses to textured figures moving against similar backgrounds, such as the fact that the size of the figure has little effect on the strength of the response. Some progress has also been made towards identifying particular classes of cell in the fly visual system that implement this means of detecting relative motion (Egelhaaf, Hausen, Reichardt, & Wehrhan, 1989).

Reichardt et al.'s (1983) model detects relative motion in an image without computing accurate velocity values. Instead, relative motion is computed directly from the outputs of motion detectors that give only the direction of motion reliably. The magnitude of an insect motion detector's output is a function both of image speed and of the spatial structure of the image, which in turn means that the output of the relative motion-detecting system is also influenced by spatial structure. For example, it will respond to a patch of texture moving with the *same* velocity as the background if the spatial components of the textures differ. This apparent weakness of the model may in fact be a strength: an insect does not need to locate accurately all the occluding contours in its visual field, but only to detect small objects moving relative to the background, and usually differing in spatial structure from it. This is discussed further in Chapter 12.

It seems certain that the mechanisms of motion computation that Reichardt and co-workers have identified in insects are much simpler than those operating in human vision or that of other mammals. The fly's visual system is dedicated to processing image motion for a few purposes only, such as figure-ground discrimination or detection of uniform whole-field flow, and so relies on fast, simple mechanisms built for these purposes. In particular, these do not require the computation of the accurate velocity field required to explain human motion perception. One illustration of the difference is that flies are not able to detect a figure and ground oscillating together in antiphase, despite the strong relative motion generated, whereas this form of motion is readily detected by people (Baker & Braddick, 1982). In the final section of this chapter, we examine more complex parameters of relative motion than the simple velocity boundaries we have considered so far, and ask how they are computed in visual systems. Later chapters (12–15) consider how these more complex patterns of motion are used in visual perception and visual guidance of behaviour.

More complex properties of optic flow

Koenderink and van Doorn (1976) show that the pattern of relative motion within any small region of the flow field can be fully described as the sum of an expansion, a rotation, and a deformation (see Fig. 8.18). Each of these simple local transformations can be measured by straightforward differentiation of the flow field and this might be achieved, in a biologically plausible way, by comparing the responses of individual motion detectors responding to neighbouring regions of the field. The main advantage of this analysis is that the expansion and deformation together capture the useful information in the flow field and neither is affected by global rotation. Thus, for example, the rate of expansion can be used to recover time-to-collision (see Ch.12, p.281) and the direction and rate of deformation can be used to recover the tilt and slant of surfaces, respectively. See Harris (1994) for a discussion of these ideas.

FIGURE 8.18

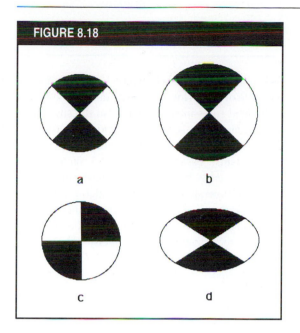

a   b

c   d

A simple pattern (a) subjected to three different transformations: (b) pure expansion, (c) pure rotation, and (d) pure deformation. Any transformation of a patch in the optic flow field can be expressed as a sum of four components: the rates of expansion and rotation, and the rate and axis of deformation. Note that only in (d) does the relative orientation change. Adapted from Koenderink (1986).

Despite its mathematical elegance and apparent biological plausibility, there is, as yet, little evidence that the vertebrate visual system contains mechanisms capable of measuring *local* expansion, rotation, or deformation. Moreover, the required local measures could not be computed when the flow is only sparsely defined, as it will be in relatively untextured regions of the visual field. Koenderink (1986) therefore suggests that visual systems might make use of less general but more robust descriptions of the flow. In particular, there may be a number of mechanisms operating in parallel, each computing one particular property for one particular behavioural purpose. Koenderink further suggests that such computations may not even be based directly on the velocity field. For example, one way to measure deformation is to monitor changes in the relative orientation of texture elements (see Fig. 8.18d), which are available in the output of the visual cortex without any further motion computation.

Single-cell recordings provide some support for the idea that higher levels of motion computation involve multiple processes operating in parallel. One example is seen in the *accessory optic system* (AOS), a region of the vertebrate midbrain to which some optic nerve fibres project (Ch.3, p.43). Cells in the AOS respond to large slowly moving textured patterns and are selective for both direction and speed of motion (Simpson, 1984). These properties suggest that AOS cells are involved in the computation of *global* motion, in contrast to the analysis of *local* motion performed in visual cortex or area MT (see pp.56–57). On the basis of the distribution of preferred directions in AOS cells, Simpson (1984) argues that the function of this structure is to analyse global rotatory movement in the retinal image into three perpendicular components, and thereby contribute to the stabilisation of eyes and head.

In contrast, other regions appear to be involved in the analysis of global translatory motion. Cells in the lateral suprasylvian area of cat cortex are direction selective, and Rauschecker, von Grünau, and Poulin (1987) found that their preferred directions were mainly away from the area centralis. This set of cells would therefore be maximally stimulated by the expanding retinal motion produced by forward movement of the cat. Indeed, some cells in this area show a preference individually for targets moving in depth either towards or away from the animal (Toyama et al., 1985) and are driven by both optic flow and binocular cues to motion in depth. More complex properties of individual cells are seen in the superior temporal polysensory area (STP) of monkey prestriate cortex, where many cells in area MST (which receives strong input from area MT) have very large fields that cover nearly the entire visual field (Bruce, Desimone, & Gross, 1981). Of these, some have different direction selectivities in different parts of the field, responding to motion either towards the area centralis or away from it. Others show selective responses for objects moving in depth that produce either looming or contracting patterns of motion in the field, and others are selectively sensitive to rotary motion (Tanaka & Saito, 1989), or to combinations of expansion and rotation (Duffy & Wurtz, 1991).

There is also psychophysical evidence for a system in human vision that is specifically sensitive to looming and contracting patterns of optic flow. Regan and Beverley (1978) tested observers' thresholds for detecting two types of motion of a luminous square, either oscillating in position or in size. They found that 25mins exposure to an adapting square oscillating in size caused subjects to be about five times less sensitive to small size changes, but scarcely affected their ability to see small positional changes that had equivalent local motions of the edges. Thus adaptation was *specific* to changing size. Regan and Beverley concluded that adaptation must have occured in some higher-level "looming detector" that is sensitive to the specific pattern of relative motion of the four edges. Moreover, the adapting effect is specific to the *direction* of size change (expanding or contracting) and creates *two* negative aftereffects. After adapting to an expanding square, a stationary test square at first seems to be contracting in size and then after a few seconds it appears to be moving away in depth (Beverley & Regan, 1979; for a critical review see Cumming, 1994). From these results Regan and Beverley proposed a three-stage model of motion-in-depth analysis. The first stage contains local, 1-D motion analysers; the second stage combines them in opposing pairs to form filters sensitive to size change, and the third stage represents motion in depth. Importantly, the third stage appears to integrate optic flow and binocular cues, as the depth aftereffect described earlier could be cancelled either by imposing a size change on the test stimulus, or by changing disparity (Regan & Beverley, 1979). This is a further example of cue convergence that we have already met in the contexts of stereo, orientation, and local motion coding. The motion-in-depth stage implied by these experiments integrates (at least) two different cues to motion-in-depth and so is analogous to the integrative, $2\frac{1}{2}$-D sketch stage of Marr's (1982) model, and provides some empirical support for it.

CONCLUSIONS

We considered in some detail how the simplest variable of optic flow—optical velocity—could be computed from intensity values in the space-time image, and have seen that considerable progress has been made on this problem. Several mechanisms, based on first- and second-order motion energy and on feature correspondence, appear to operate initially in parallel, followed by an integrative stage that combines the different cues, and the signals from different directions, to yield a local estimate of velocity. The middle temporal area of the brain (MT or V5) appears to play an important role in this integration of motion signals. For more complex variables, we have seen a variety of models and findings that have yet to fall into a consistent pattern.

One important issue arising from this discussion is the role of the velocity field. We have seen how two lines of argument assume that a representation of optical velocities over the retina has a key role in motion computation. First, work on early motion processing (e.g. Hildreth, 1984b) assumes that a velocity field is the output representation for these processes, and, second, investigations of the higher-order information available in optic flow takes such a representation as given. Although we know that velocity information is computed in the human visual system, we see hints that other analyses computing relative motion, time to contact (Chapter 12), or components of rotation may proceed in parallel, using simpler measurements than the velocity field as their input. These ideas suggest an alternative view, in which the flexibility of human motion processing arises from the operation of many specialised systems together rather than a single general-purpose one. Whether this view eventually proves correct or not, it leads us to consider in Part III the particular purposes of motion computation in perception and in the control of action.

9

Object Recognition

An essential part of the behaviour of animals and people is their ability to *recognise* objects, animals, and people that are important to their survival. People are able to recognise large numbers of other people, the letters of the alphabet, familiar buildings, and so on. Animals may need to recognise landmarks, suitable prey, potential mates or predators, and to behave in the appropriate way to each category.

If we assume that the information available to a person or animal is a static two-dimensional image on the retina, a problem immediately arises in explaining visual recognition. Take the example of a person recognising letters of the alphabet: the problem is that an infinite number of possible retinal images can correspond to a particular letter, depending on how the letter is written, how large it is, the angle at which it is seen, and so on (Fig. 9.1). Yet somehow we recognise all these patterns of light as corresponding to the same letter. Or consider the problem of recognising a friend's face: the image of the face on the retina will depend on the lighting conditions and the distance, angle, and facial expression. Again, all these images are classified together, even though some (such as a full-face and a profile view) are quite dissimilar and more like the same views of different faces than they are like each other (Fig. 9.2).

These are both illustrations of the problem of *stimulus equivalence*; if the stimulus controlling behaviour is a pattern of light, or image, on the retina, then an infinite number of images are

FIGURE 9.1

All these different shapes are classified as the letter A.

FIGURE 9.2

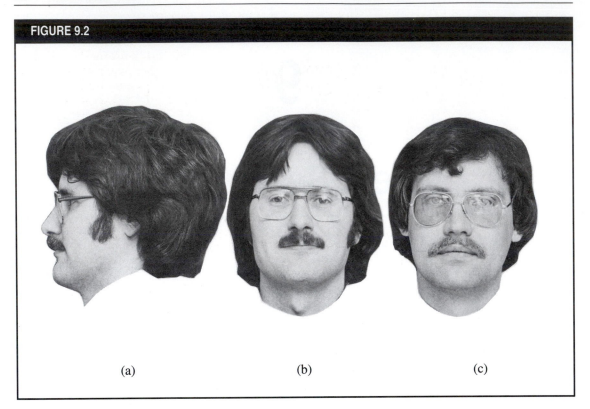

(a)   (b)   (c)

(a) and (b) show two different views of the same person, Patrick Green. View (b) is in many ways more like picture (c), which is of a different person, than it is like view (a). Photographs by Sam Grainger.

equivalent in their effects, and different from other sets of images. Many influential treatments of object recognition assume that all the images corresponding to a particular thing, whether letter of the alphabet or face, have something in common. The problem is to find just what this is and how this thing in common is detected. It is this problem that we will be considering in this chapter.

SIMPLE MECHANISMS OF RECOGNITION

Many animals, particularly simpler ones such as insects and fish, solve the stimulus equivalence problem by detecting something relatively simple that all images corresponding to a particular object have in common. A good example is the three-spined stickleback. Males of this species build nests and defend them against other males by performing threat displays. A stickleback must therefore be able to recognise rival males and discriminate them from other fish and from objects drifting by. The retinal images of rival males will obviously vary greatly, depending on the other fish's distance, angle, and posture, and it seems that classifying these images separately from those of other fish will need elaborate criteria.

In fact, as Tinbergen (1951) discovered, the stickleback manages successfully with quite simple mechanisms of recognition. Tinbergen observed the strength of sticklebacks' aggressive responses to a range of models and found that they would readily attack a crude model of another fish, *provided* it had the red belly colour characteristic of male sticklebacks. Indeed, a crude model with a red belly elicited more attack than an accurate one without (Fig. 9.3).

A feature of an object or animal—such as the red belly of a stickleback—that elicits a response from an animal is called a *key* or *sign* stimulus, and

FIGURE 9.3

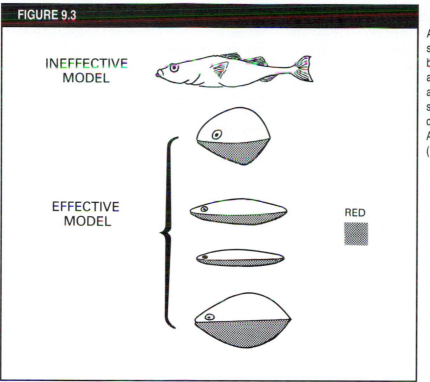

INEFFECTIVE
MODEL

EFFECTIVE
MODEL

RED

An accurate model of a stickleback without a red belly (top) is less effective as a stimulus to elicit aggression from a male stickleback than any of the cruder models below. Adapted from Tinbergen (1951).

it greatly simplifies the problem of recognition. As long as red objects and fish with red markings are rare in the stickleback's environment, it can use the key stimulus to recognise rivals and does not need to use information about another fish's detailed structure and colouration.

The stickleback's recognition of a rival male does depend on more than just the presence of a patch of red of a certain size in the retinal image, as Tinbergen also found that a model with a red patch on its back was attacked less than one with an identical red patch on its belly, and that a model in the "head-down" posture of an aggressive fish was attacked more than one in a horizontal posture. Even so, the presence of this distinctive feature allows a much simpler means of recognition to be effective than would otherwise be the case.

Many other examples are known of key stimuli being important in the recognition by animals of other members of their species, and we will mention two other examples from Tinbergen's work. One is the recognition of female grayling butterflies by males. Tinbergen found that males

would fly towards crude paper models moving overhead and that their response was not affected by the colour or shape of the model. The key stimulus turned out to be the pattern of movement of the model: males would fly towards it if it imitated the flickering and up-and-down movements of a butterfly, but not if it moved in a smooth way. Although butterflies do waste time chasing other males, or butterflies of the wrong species, this simple mechanism of recognition does prevent responses to other kinds of insect.

Another example is the recognition by nestling thrushes and blackbirds of their parents. When the parents bring food to the nest, the young birds turn towards them and gape, opening their mouths wide to be fed. Tinbergen found that gaping is elicited by a moving dark silhouette above the birds' eye level, of any shape and size. Presumably this simple mechanism of recognition is adequate because the chances of anything other than a parent resembling the key stimulus are low.

Key stimuli may also be important in the recognition of prey. Toads feed by snapping at insects flying past them, capturing them with their long sticky tongues, and Ewert (1974) found that they recognise insects by fairly simple criteria, as they will snap at small cardboard squares. Although Ewert's experiments used moving targets, toads will also snap at stationary models (Roth & Wiggers, 1983). Although toads are selective for the size and speed of movement of model prey, these results show clearly that they are not able to recognise insects on the basis of finer details of their appearance.

Thus for some animals the problem of recognising significant objects may be reduced to the problem of detecting localised key stimuli or features that in the natural world are unambiguous cues to appropriate action. Such local features may be quite simple—it is easy to see how a "redness" detector might function in the stickleback, and not too difficult to conjecture how this might be coupled with a rather crude configurational analysis to explain observed preferences for the location of the red patch and the posture of the model. However, such mechanisms are also relatively inflexible, and depend for their success on the predictability of the natural environment. When a scientist introduces a red dummy fish, a paper butterfly, or pieces of cardboard into an animal's surroundings, the assumptions about the properties of mates or prey on which the perceptual mechanism relies are violated.

Other animals, especially primates, have more flexibility in their perception and action and are able to recognise and discriminate on the basis of more complex and subtle criteria. In these cases, as in human perception, the problem of how stimulus equivalence is achieved is a difficult one, as we will see in the remainder of this chapter.

evidence in more detail in Chapter 16. On the whole, however, it is through a process of learning that we come to classify certain configurations as equivalent and distinct from others. The human infant learns to recognise the faces of its parents irrespective of angle, expression, or lighting. A mother will still be "mummy" to her child after she has curled her hair, and a father will still be "daddy" if he hasn't shaved for a few days. Later, the child will learn to distinguish teachers and friends from strangers, family pets from strays, and the long process of formal education enables most to decipher the intricacies of written language. What kinds of internal representations allow for the recognition of complex configurations, and what kinds of processes operate on the retinal image to allow access to these internal representations? These have been the questions posed in the study of human pattern and object recognition.

Much early work on pattern recognition focused on the problem of recognising alphanumeric patterns. There is good reason for such work, as researchers in computer science have had the applied aim of making computers able to recognise such patterns so that they might, for example, achieve automatic sorting of letters with hand-written postal codes. The emphasis on alphanumerics was unfortunate in other ways, because the problem of stimulus equivalence is rather different for alphanumerics than for objects. Letters must be recognised despite changes in their form, but they are only two-dimensional patterns, so that other problems in object recognition are minimised. Nevertheless, the area of alphanumeric recognition is worth discussing briefly because it serves to introduce certain theoretical approaches to the broader area of object recognition.

MORE COMPLEX RECOGNITION PROCESSES

We may speculate that at least some behaviour in humans may be under the control of key stimuli. For example, it has been shown (e.g. Goren, Sarty, & Wu, 1975) that human neonates show innate following of face-like patterns, and we discuss this

TEMPLATE MATCHING

The simplest account that we could offer of how we recognise alphanumeric characters would be that of *template matching*. For each letter or numeral known by the perceiver there would be a template stored in long-term memory. Incoming patterns would be matched against the set of templates, and if there were sufficient overlap between a novel pattern and a template then the pattern would be categorised as belonging to the class captured by that template. Within such a framework, slight changes in the size or angle of patterns could be taken care of by an initial process of standardisation and normalisation. For example, all patterns could be rotated so that their major axes (as discovered by other processing operations) were aligned vertically, with the height of the major axis scaled to unity (see Fig. 9.4). In addition, some pre-processing or "cleaning up" of the image would be necessary. Both humans and other animals (Sutherland, 1973) cope very well with broken or wobbly lines in the patterns they recognise.

Such a template-matching scheme could work provided that such normalising procedures were sufficient to render the resulting patterns unambiguous. Unfortunately this is almost impossible to achieve, even in the simple world of alphanumerics. An "R" could match an "A"

template better than its own, and vice versa (see Fig. 9.5). The bar that distinguishes a "Q" from an "O" may be located in a variety of places (see Fig. 9.6). At the very least we would need more than one template for each letter and numeral, and it becomes difficult to see how children could learn letters and numbers in such a scheme.

Template-matching schemes also fail to account readily for the facts of animal discrimination. Sutherland and Williams (1969) showed that rats trained to discriminate an irregular from a regular chequerboard pattern readily transferred this learning to new examples of random and regular patterns (see Fig. 9.7). As Sutherland (1973) points out, the configuration in Fig. 9.7d should match better with a "template" for pattern 9.7a than for b, but it is treated by the rats as though it were more like b than a. It is also difficult to see how a template-matching model could possibly be applied to the more general area of object recognition, where the problem of stimulus equivalence is magnified. However, a template-matching process can operate

FIGURE 9.4

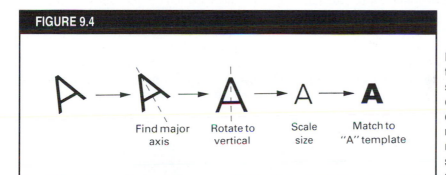

Find major axis   Rotate to vertical   Scale size   Match to "A" template

Before matching to a template, a pattern could be standardised in terms of its orientation and size. This could be done by finding the major axis of the figure, rotating this to vertical, and scaling its size to some standard.

FIGURE 9.5

The bold figures show possible templates for an A (left) and an R (right). The dashed figures show how an R (left) and an A (right) could match another letter's template better than their own.

FIGURE 9.6

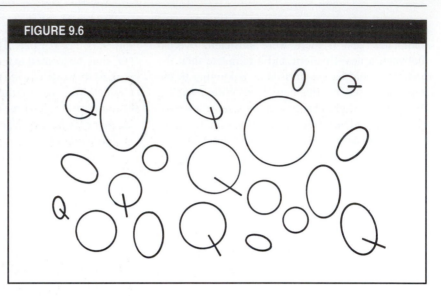

What distinguishes the Qs from the Os? Not the precise form of the circle, nor the precise location or orientation of the bar.

successfully if the form of the characters it must recognise can be constrained. Thus the computer that recognises account numbers on the bottom of cheques matches these to stored templates. The character set has been constrained, however, so that the numerals have constant form, and in addition are made as dissimilar to one another as possible to avoid any chance of confusion. The characters that humans recognise are not constrained in this way.

FEATURE ANALYSIS

When we consider how it is that we know the difference between an A and an R, or a Q and an O, it seems that there are certain critical features that distinguish one from another. The bar that cuts the circular body of a Q is essential to distinguish it from an O, whereas the precise form of the circle

FIGURE 9.7

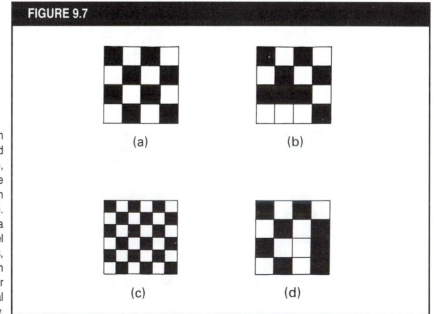

(a)

(b)

(c)

(d)

Rats trained to respond in one way to pattern (a), and another way to pattern (b), later treat pattern (c) in the same way as (a), and pattern (d) in the same way as (b). This is not consistent with a template-matching model (Sutherland & Williams, 1969). Reprinted with permission from the author and the Experimental Psychology Society.

is less crucial. Perhaps a model in which combinations of features were detected would be more successful than one based on templates.

Feature analysis models of recognition were popular with psychologists and computer scientists during the 1960s while physiologists such as Hubel and Wiesel were postulating "feature detectors" in the visual cortex of cats and monkeys (see Chapter 3). Perhaps the most influential model for psychology was Selfridge's (1959) Pandemonium system, originally devised as a computer program to recognise Morse Code signals, but popularised as a model of alphanumeric recognition by Neisser (1967), and Lindsay and Norman (1972). An illustration of a Pandemonium system is shown in Fig. 9.8.

The system consists of a number of different classes of "demon". The most important of these for our purposes are the *feature demons* and the *cognitive demons*. Feature demons respond selectively when particular local configurations (right angles, vertical lines, etc.) are presented. The cognitive demons, which represent particular letters, look for particular combinations of features from the feature demons. Thus the cognitive demon representing the letter H might look for two vertical and one horizontal lines, plus four right angles. The more of their features are present, the louder will the cognitive demons "shout" to the highest level, the decision demon, who selects the letter corresponding to that represented by the cognitive demon who is shouting the loudest. Thus in this system individual characters are represented as sets of critical features, and the processing of any image proceeds in a hierarchical fashion through levels of increasing abstraction. It is this kind of model that Barlow (1972) and others used to interpret the properties of simple cells in the visual cortex (see Ch.3, p.54). Simple cells were thought to be acting as the feature demons in the

FIGURE 9.8

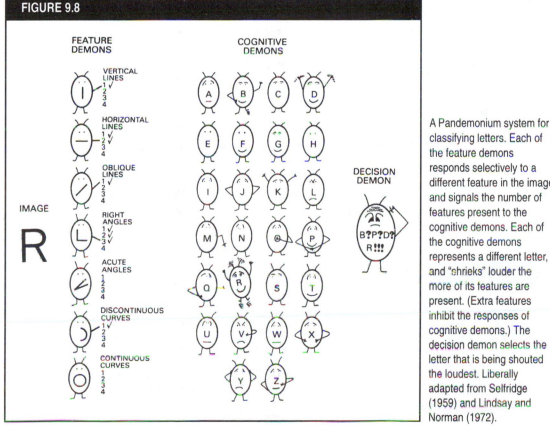

A Pandemonium system for classifying letters. Each of the feature demons responds selectively to a different feature in the image, and signals the number of features present to the cognitive demons. Each of the cognitive demons represents a different letter, and "shrieks" louder the more of its features are present. (Extra features inhibit the responses of cognitive demons.) The decision demon selects the letter that is being shouted the loudest. Liberally adapted from Selfridge (1959) and Lindsay and Norman (1972).

Pandemonium system, passing information on to cells that would supposedly respond to increasingly abstract properties. Such hypothetical cells were dubbed "Grandmother cells" or "Yellow Volkswagen detectors" to express the abstract nature of the stimuli exciting them.

A Pandemonium system can learn to give different weights to different features according to how well these features discriminate between different patterns, and in the next chapter we will consider a number of pattern recognition systems that learn in a similar way, by altering the weights between stimulus and response connections. A system of the Pandemonium type can in principle accommodate certain kinds of contextual effect. These are a ubiquitous feature of human pattern recognition, and Fig. 9.9 shows one example of how context affects the recognition of letters. The same shape can be seen as H or as A depending on the surrounding letters. Within a Pandemonium system we might allow higher-level demons to "arouse" those at lower levels that correspond to particularly likely patterns, so that they would need less sensory evidence to make them shout sufficiently loudly to win over the decision demon. Humphreys and Bruce (1989) give more details of a range of context effects in human pattern and object recognition.

However, as a general model for human pattern and object recognition the Pandemonium system is unsatisfactory. Ultimately it rests on a description of patterns in terms of a set of features, which are themselves like mini-templates. One of the reasons that Pandemonium was so popular was that it seemed consistent with the neurophysiology of the visual cortex; but we have already seen that single cells cannot be thought of as "feature detectors" (see Ch.3, p.54). Although this may not matter for a purely psychological or computational theory of recognition, there are other problems. Feature-list descriptions fail to capture overall structural relations that are captured, but too rigidly, by more global templates. Thus the Pandemonium system depicted in Fig. 9.8 would confuse an F with ⊤ and a T with ⊥ , confusions that humans typically do not make. In addition, the Pandemonium system, in classifying patterns, discards all information that distinguishes different instances of the same pattern. The output of the decision demon would be the same irrespective of the particular version of the letter A shown. We need a way of talking about recognition that allows us to describe the differences between patterns as well as being able to classify together those that are instances of the same type. We need to preserve such differences so that other kinds of classifications can be made. We recognise people's hand-writing, for example, by the particular shapes of the letters they produce. Thus we need a representational format that captures aspects of structure essential for the classification of an item but preserves at some other level structural differences between different instances of the same class.

STRUCTURAL DESCRIPTIONS

A general and flexible representational format for human pattern and object recognition is provided by the language of structural descriptions. Structural descriptions do not constitute a theory of how recognition is achieved, they simply provide the right type of representation with which to construct such a theory. A structural description consists of a set of propositions (which are symbolic, but not linguistic, although we describe them in words) about a particular configuration. Such propositions describe the nature of the components of a configuration and make explicit the structural arrangements of these parts. Thus a structural description of a letter T might look like Fig. 9.10a.

FIGURE 9.9

The same shape may be seen as an H in one context and an A in another (from a demonstration by Selfridge).

FIGURE 9.10

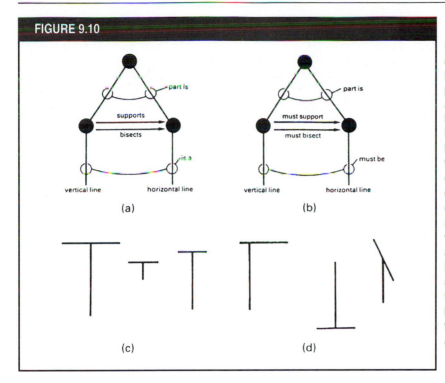

(a)   (b)

(c)   (d)

(a) A structural description for a letter T. The description indicates that there are two parts to the letter. One part is a vertical line, the other a horizontal line. The vertical line supports and bisects the horizontal line. (b) A model for a letter T. This is like the description at (a), but the essential aspects of the description are specified. For something to be a T, a vertical line must support, and must bisect, a horizontal line, but the relative lengths are not important. (c) Shapes that would be classified as Ts by the model. (d) Shapes that would fail to be classified as Ts.

Using the language of structural descriptions it is possible to construct "models" for particular concepts and categories against which any incoming instance can be matched. Such models capture obligatory features of the structure but may be less particular about other details. Thus the "model" for a letter T might look like Fig. 9.10b. It is essential that a horizontal line is supported by a vertical line, and that this support occurs about half way along the horizontal line. But the lengths of the two lines are less important. Figure 9.10c shows examples that would be classified as letter Ts by this model, and 9.10d shows those that would fail.

Structural descriptions are also easier to apply to object recognition than templates or feature representations. A picture of an object can be described by a series of structural descriptions at increasing levels of abstraction from the original intensity distribution. There are thus a number of possible "domains" of description (Sutherland, 1973).

Take for example the two drawings shown in Fig. 9.11. These drawings can be described within a number of distinct domains, which can broadly be grouped together as being either "two-dimensional" or "three-dimensional". The 2-D descriptions describe the picture or image present, and this image can be described in increasingly abstract or global terms. It may be described as a collection of points of different brightnesses, as a collection of lines, or as a group of regions. These different levels of description are reminiscent of the different stages of elaboration of the primal sketch, through the aggregation of small edge segments up to larger contours or aggregated texture regions (see Chapters 5 and 6). Whatever the level of description in the 2-D domain, whether points, lines, or regions, the representations established for these two pictures would look very different. It is within the domain of 3-D description that the equivalence of these two pictures can be established. 3-D descriptions are couched in terms of surfaces, bodies, and objects. The two pictures shown in Fig. 9.11 are equivalent only at the level of an object description that is independent of the vantage point.

The description above again illustrates the thrust of Marr's term "2½-D" sketch for the representation of *surfaces*, from the point of view of the observer. Marr's 2½-D sketch falls

FIGURE 9.11

These two forms are quite different in terms of their two-dimensional description. They are equivalent only in the three-dimensional domain.

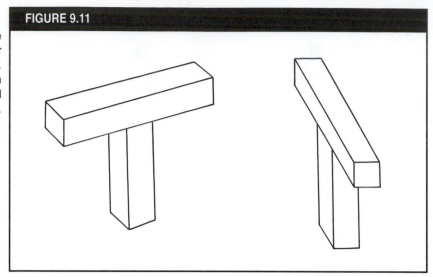

somewhere in between the 2-D and 3-D groups of descriptions in Sutherland's scheme.

Thus two different projections of the same object will have different structural descriptions in the picture domain, but will be equivalent in the object domain (see Fig. 9.11). Provided that structural descriptions are established at all levels simultaneously, we can capture both the equivalences between different views of the same object and their differences. Our problem now is to consider how structural descriptions at the 3-D level can be constructed, stored, and matched, and to examine the extent to which the construction of 3-D representations can proceed in a "bottom-up" fashion.

Winston (1975) provided an early illustration of the use of structural descriptions in object recognition to show how object concepts might be learned by giving examples. His program learns to recognise simple toy block structures such as those illustrated in Fig. 9.12, which contains examples of an "arch", a "pedestal", and a "house".

The computer program is presented with examples of each, as well as "near-misses", in order to build up models for each concept. The procedure for a pedestal might go as follows. First, the program would be presented with an example of a pedestal (Fig. 9.13a) to which it would assign the structural description shown in Fig. 9.14a. Thus a pedestal is described as having two parts, with one part being a "brick" and the other part being a "board", with the former supporting the latter. Then the program would be presented with the sequence of "near misses" shown in Fig. 9.13b–e. For Fig. 9.13b, the description would again show two parts, with one a brick and the other a board, but the

FIGURE 9.12

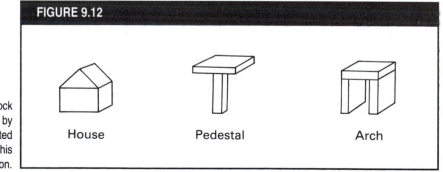

Three of the toy block structures learned by Winston's program. Adapted from Winston (1973) with his permission.

House   Pedestal   Arch

FIGURE 9.13

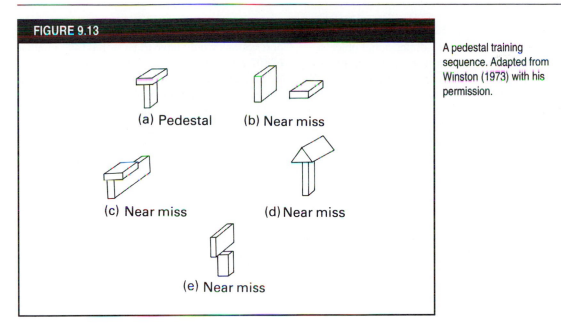

(a) Pedestal   (b) Near miss

(c) Near miss   (d) Near miss

(e) Near miss

A pedestal training sequence. Adapted from Winston (1973) with his permission.

relationship between these is now different. The board is beside the brick, and the program was told that this is *not* a pedestal. By comparing this description of the near-miss with that of the structure labelled pedestal, the program can construct a model for a pedestal in which the support relation is made obligatory. For something to be a pedestal one part *must* be supported by the other. The other examples in the training sequence (Fig. 9.13c–e) further constrain the eventual model for a pedestal (Fig. 9.14b). The eventual model shows that for something to be a pedestal, an upright brick must support a lying board.

Our choice of a pedestal to illustrate this process of learning a structural model from examples was deliberate. The pedestal is like a three-dimensional letter T (see Fig. 9.10), and the structural description for a pedestal is very similar to that described for a T, except that the parts of the pedestal are themselves three-dimensional objects like a brick and a board, instead of the horizontal and vertical lines in the letter T. Thus, this kind of

FIGURE 9.14

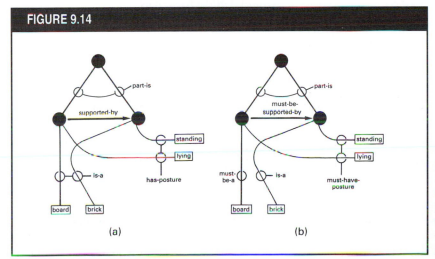

(a)   (b)

(a) A description of the pedestal in Fig. 9.13a. (b) A model for a pedestal built up after training on a sequence of pedestals and near-misses. Adapted from Winston (1973) with his permission.

representation can be used for two-dimensional written characters, or three-dimensional objects.

To return to Winston's program, a process similar to that used for the pedestal can be used to derive a model for a house (Fig. 9.12). Here the eventual model would specify that a brick must support a wedge (the roof). As for the pedestal, both the support relations and the nature of the objects are quite tightly specified. However, in the case of an arch (Fig. 9.12) there is more flexibility. Although the upright structures in the arch model *must* be bricks and *must not* touch each other, the structure they support can be a brick, or a wedge, or maybe even any object at all. An arch is still an arch whatever the shape at the top.

Winston's program is here operating in the object domain. It can accept any projection of a brick or wedge and label these accordingly. However, the structural descriptions for brick and wedge must themselves be specified at a different level of the program. At an even lower level, the line drawing that serves as input must be parsed into separate objects using the procedures described in Chapter 6. The initial stages of the program make use of programs like Guzman's (see Ch.6, p.120) to group regions of the picture together.

The problems with Winston's system are buried within these low-level programs that furnish the descriptions on which the learning program operates. As we noted in Chapter 6, scene analysis programs of the kind developed by Guzman, Clowes, and Waltz work by making use of the constraints inherent in the kinds of scene they describe. But the constraints of the mini-world of matt prismatic solids are not the constraints of the natural world. Although something similar to Winston's learning program might provide a theory of visual object classification, we need a better way of furnishing structural descriptions for such procedures to operate on—one that is not restricted to an artificial world.

To do this, we must return to consider the fundamental problem of object recognition. To recap, the projection of an object's shape on the retina depends on the vantage point of the viewer. Thus, if we relied on a *viewer-centred* coordinate system for describing the object (one in the picture

domain, to use Sutherland's terminology), descriptions would have to be stored for a number of different vantage points. Later in this chapter and in the next one we will consider some recent theories of recognition that do involve the storage of discrete viewpoints, an approach that is now gaining considerable empirical and computational support, at least for certain kinds of recognition task.

However, if we can describe the object with reference to an *object-centred* coordinate system, (i.e. build a structural description in the "object" domain) then it would be possible to reduce the number of object models stored, ideally to only a single one per distinguishable object. This was what Winston attempted to do with an artificial world.

The problem is then to find a way of describing the object within its own coordinate system without confining the discussion to an artificial world, and/or using knowledge of an object-specific kind. If one has to rely at the outset on object-specific knowledge then we would have to know what an object was before we could recognise it—an obvious paradox. However, it seems likely that knowledge of some constraints is essential to parse objects—the question is, how specific are these?

MARR AND NISHIHARA'S THEORY OF OBJECT RECOGNITION

Marr and Nishihara (1978) outlined the foundations for one possible solution to this problem. An object must be described within a frame of reference that is based on the shape itself. To do this, we must be able to set up a canonical coordinate frame (a coordinate frame that is determined by the shape itself) for the shape before the shape has been described.

The appropriate set of descriptive elements (primitives) for describing a shape will depend in part on the level of detail that the shape description is to capture. The fingers of a human hand are not expressed in a system that uses primitives the size of arms and legs. To get around this problem, Marr and Nishihara suggest that we need a modular organisation of shape descriptions with different-sized primitives used at different levels. This allows a description at a "high" level to be stable over changes in fine detail, but sensitivity to these changes to be available at other levels.

First we need to define an *axis* for the representation of a shape. Shapes that are elongated or have a natural axis of symmetry are easier to describe, and Marr and Nishihara restrict their discussion to the class of such objects that can be described as a set of one or more *generalised cones*. A generalised cone is the surface created by moving a cross-section of constant shape but variable size along an axis (see Fig. 9.15). The cross-section can get fatter or thinner provided that its shape is preserved. The class of generalised cones includes "geometric" forms like a pyramid or sphere, as well as natural forms like arms and legs (roughly). Objects whose shape is achieved by growth are often describable by one or more generalised cones, and so we can talk about object recognition in the natural world, rather than an artificial one. In the discussion that follows we will generally be talking about the recognition of shapes composed of more than one generalised cone, so that there will be more than one axis in the representation. For example, a human figure can be described as a set of generalised cones corresponding to the trunk, head, arms, and legs. Each of these component generalised cones has its own axis, and together these form the component axes for a representation of a human.

A description that uses axis-based primitives is like a stick figure. Stick figures capture the relative lengths and dispositions of the axes that form the components of the entire structure. The relative thicknesses of these components (e.g. the human trunk is thicker than a leg) could also be included in the representation, although for simplicity we will omit this detail here. Information captured by such a description might be very useful for recognition as stick figures are inherently modular. We can use a single stick to represent a whole leg, or three smaller sticks to represent the upper and lower limb segments and the foot. At a still finer level, we can capture the details of toes with a set of much smaller sticks. At each level of description we can construct a 3-D model where each 3-D model specifies:

1. A single-model axis. This provides coarse information about the size and orientation of the overall shape described.
2. The arrangements and lengths of the major component axes.
3. Pointers to the 3-D models for the shape components associated with these component axes.

This leads to a hierarchy of 3-D models (illustrated in Fig. 9.16), each with its own coordinate system.

The first "box" in Fig. 9.16 shows the single-model axis for a human body with the relative dispositions of the component axes (corresponding to head, body, legs, and arms). The axis that corresponds to the arm forms the major axis for the "arm model" (next box in the figure), in which the component axes of upper arm and forearm are shown, and so on through to the details of the fingers of a human hand. Such a hierarchy of 3-D

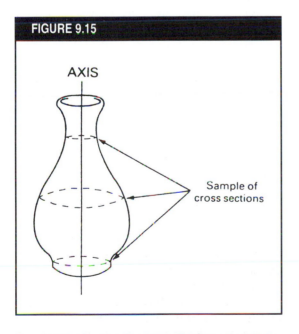

FIGURE 9.15

AXIS

Sample of cross sections

One example of a generalised cone. The shape is created by moving a cross-section of constant shape but variable size along an axis.

FIGURE 9.16

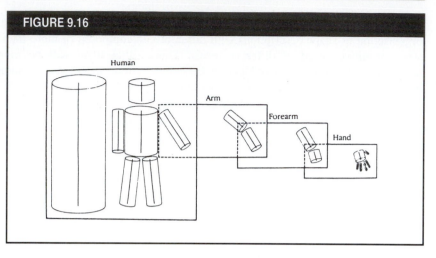

A hierarchy of 3-D models. Each box shows the major axis for the figure of interest on the left, and its component axes to the right. From Marr and Nishihara (1978). Reprinted with permission of The Royal Society.

models is called a 3-D model description. Recognition is thought to be achieved when a match is established between a 3-D model description derived from an image, and one of the stored catalogue of 3-D model descriptions corresponding to known objects. These may in turn be organised hierarchically, in terms of the specificity of their descriptions (see Fig. 9.17). Thus a human figure can be matched to the general model for a biped, or the more specific model for a human. Ape and human are distinguished by the relative lengths of the component axes in the model description for a biped.

At this point we should note that there is some limited evidence for the psychological validity of axis-based representations. For example, Humphreys (1984) asked subjects to decide whether or not two presented objects were the same shape (both elongated triangles or both parallelograms). Humphreys found that when subjects did not know exactly where the second shape would appear relative to the first, judgements were faster if the orientations of the major axis of the shape was preserved, suggesting that this aspect of the shape played a role in the comparison process. Although such results lend some support to Marr and Nishihara's theory, axis-based descriptions do not seem to be constructed when the position of the second shape is known in advance (Humphreys, 1984), nor is there evidence that axis-based descriptions are used for all elongated shapes (e.g. Quinlan & Humphreys,

1993). However, although the evidence for the primary role of axis-based representations is limited, it is also the case that these studies have explored the perception of 2-D shapes rather than the 3-D objects addressed in Marr and Nishihara's theory. Humphrey and Jolicoeur (1993) reported that the identification of line drawings was markedly disrupted when the objects were depicted with their main axis oriented directly towards the viewer so that the main axis appeared foreshortened. This disruptive effect of foreshortening occurred even though the main components of the objects were salient at all viewing angles. Lawson and Humphreys (1996) used a matching task with line drawings of objects rotated in depth. With relatively long intervals between the stimuli there was little effect of the angle between consecutive objects until the to-be-matched stimulus had its main axis foreshortened. These studies lend some support to Marr's theory that object recognition would be disrupted if the major axes of elongation of the object is not visible.

How could such 3-D model descriptions be derived *prior* to accessing the catalogue? The problem is to derive the axes from an image *without* knowing what object it is that the image represents. A possible solution is provided by Marr's (1977) demonstration that we can make use of the occluding contours of an image to find the axis of a generalised cone, provided the axis is not too foreshortened. The only assumption needed is that

FIGURE 9.17

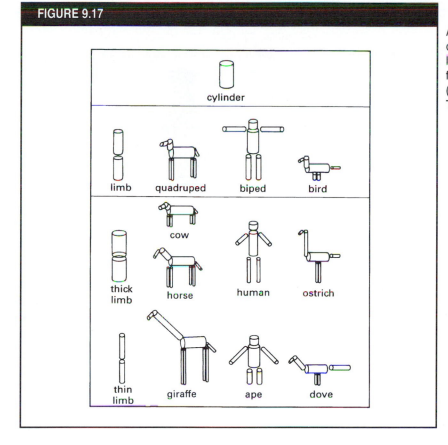

A catalogue of 3-D model descriptions at different levels of specificity. Redrawn from Marr and Nishihara (1978) with permission of The Royal Society.

these contours come from a shape that is comprised of generalised cones.

We have already seen, in Chapter 6, how Marr's early visual processing program derived contour information from an image without knowing what shape it is looking for. Occluding contours in an image are those that show the silhouette of the object (see the outline of the head of the bear in Fig. 6.28, or the donkey in Fig. 9.20). As Marr points out, silhouettes are infinitely ambiguous, and yet we interpret them in a particular way (1982, p.219):

Somewhere, buried in the perceptual machinery that can interpret silhouettes as three-dimensional shape, there must lie some source of additional information that constrains us to see silhouettes as we do. Probably ... these constraints are general rather than particular and do not require a priori knowledge of the viewed shapes.

Let us examine the assumptions that Marr suggests allow us to interpret silhouettes so consistently:

1. Each line of sight from the viewer to the object should graze the object's surface at exactly one point. Thus each point on a silhouette arises from one point on the surface being viewed. We can define the *contour generator* as the set of points on a surface that projects to the boundary of a silhouette (see Fig. 9.18).
2. Nearby points on the contour in an image arise from nearby points on the contour generator on the viewed object.
3. All the points on the contour generator lie in a single plane (see Fig. 9.19).

This third is the strongest assumption, but is necessary in order to distinguish convex and concave segments in the interpetation process. If

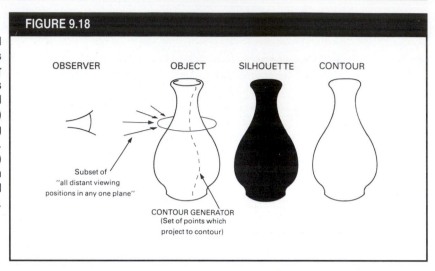

FIGURE 9.18

An object, its silhouette and its contour. The set of points that projects to the contour (the contour generator) is shown. For this figure, all three assumptions (see text) hold for all distant viewing positions in any one plane. Adapted from Marr (1977) and Marr (1982) with permission of The Royal Society.

this assumption is violated, then the wrong conclusion might be reached. For example, the occluding contour in the image of a cube, viewed corner on, is hexagonal (see Fig. 9.19). Because we assume the contour generator is planar, we could interpret such a silhouette wrongly. In the absence of any other information from internal lines or motion, we might interpret the contour as belonging to a spindle shape like one of those drawn, or simply as a flat hexagon. In fact, the points on the cube that gave rise to this contour do not lie in a single plane. It is this assumption of a planar contour generator that may lead us (wrongly!) to interpret the moving silhouette of someone's hands as the head of a duck, or an alligator, while playing shadow games.

Marr has shown that if a surface is smooth, and all the above assumptions hold for all distant

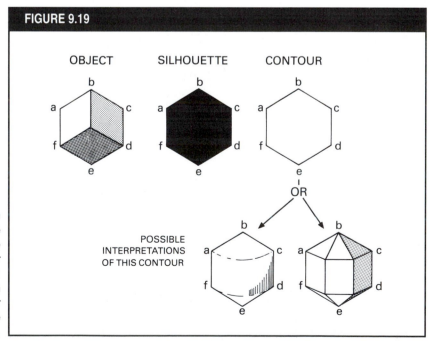

FIGURE 9.19

A cube viewed corner on gives rise to the silhouette and contour shown. The contour generator (a-b-c-d-e-f) is not planar. This silhouette might be seen simply as a hexagon, or interpreted as one of the spindle shapes shown.

viewing positions in any one plane (see Fig. 9.18), then the viewed surface is a generalised cone. Thus shape can be derived from occluding contours *provided* the shape is a generalised cone, or a set of such cones.

Vatan (cited by Marr, 1982) has written a program to derive the axes from such a contour. Figure 9.20 shows how his program derives the component axes from an image of a toy donkey. The initial outline was formed by aggregating descriptions from the raw primal sketch, in the same way as for the teddy bear's head (Ch.6, p.125). From this initial outline, convex and concave segments are labelled and used to divide the "donkey" into smaller sections. The axis is derived for each of these sections separately, and then these component axes are related together to form a "stick" representation for the entire figure.

Now these axes derived from occluding contours are viewer-centred. They depend on the image, which in turn depends on the vantage point. We must transform them to object-centred axes, and Marr and Nishihara (1978) suggested an additional stage to achieve this by making use of the *"image-space processor"*. The image-space processor operates on the viewer-centred axes and translates them to object-centred coordinates, so that the relationships between the different axes in the figure are specified in three, instead of two dimensions. Use may be made of information from stereopsis, texture, and shading to achieve this, but it may also be necessary to use preliminary matches with stored 3-D-model description to improve the analysis of the image. Thus, for recognition, Marr does envisage that there is a continuous interplay between the derivation of an object's description and the process of recognition itself (1982, p.321):

We view recognition as a gradual process that proceeds from the general to the specific

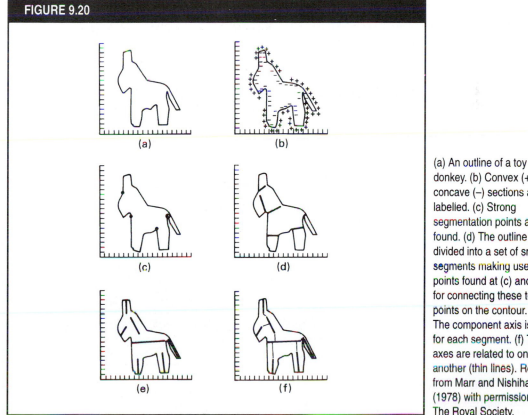

FIGURE 9.20

(a) An outline of a toy donkey. (b) Convex (+) and concave (−) sections are labelled. (c) Strong segmentation points are found. (d) The outline is divided into a set of smaller segments making use of the points found at (c) and rules for connecting these to other points on the contour. (e) The component axis is found for each segment. (f) The axes are related to one another (thin lines). Redrawn from Marr and Nishihara (1978) with permission of The Royal Society.

and that overlaps with, guides, and constrains the derivation of a description from the image.

In summary then, Marr and Nishihara outlined a scheme in which an *object-centred* representation, consisting of an axis-based structural description, could be established from an image and used to access a stored catalogue of 3-D-model descriptions in order for recognition to be achieved. Once an initial match has been established, use may then be made of downward-flowing information to refine the analysis of the image. These ideas of Marr's were speculative; only a few isolated details of these derivation and recognition processes have been specified sufficiently clearly to implement them; and the system itself rests on a number of assumptions and observations about the perception of stick figures and silhouettes that have a rather ad hoc flavour. Nevertheless, in the years since Marr and Nishihara's (1978) theory, there have been a number of developments of these basic ideas.

BEYOND GENERALISED CONES

An important step in the development of Marr and Nishihara's theory was the suggestion that complex occluding contours formed from objects comprising several generalised cones are segmented at regions of sharp concavity. In Chapter 6, we described the work of Hoffman and Richards (1984) who have illustrated the importance of such concavities in segmenting contours to reveal parts for recognition, and thereby have supported one aspect of Marr and Nishihara's theory. However, Hoffman and Richards' scheme is independent of the nature of the "parts" within the image. It will work if these are generalised cones, but it will work too if they are quite different kinds of shapes. Since Marr and Nishihara's theory of recognition was formulated, a number of authors have suggested extensions to their basic approach, to encompass a wider range of shapes among the component parts.

For example, Pentland (1986a) proposed a more flexible system of volumetric representation than can be achieved with generalised cones. Pentland suggests that most complex natural shapes are comprised of *superquadric* components and that these might be the basic components that we recover when analysing images of natural objects. Superquadrics include simple shapes such as spheres and wedges, and all kinds of deformations on these shapes that preserve their smoothly varying form and that do not introduce concavities. Figure 9.21 shows a scene constructed with superquadric components. Pentland's theory is an interesting development for computer vision and graphics, but no evidence has been offered for its *psychological* plausibility.

In contrast, Biederman (1987a) has offered a theory of human object recognition that is clearly related to early ideas of Marr and others, although with some key differences, and which he supports with evidence from a variety of psychological experiments.

In Biederman's theory, complex objects are described as spatial arrangements of basic component parts. These parts come from a restricted set of basic shapes such as wedges and cylinders. Biederman calls these shape primitives

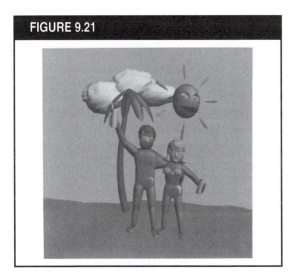

FIGURE 9.21

A scene comprised of superquadrics. Reproduced from Pentland (1987) with permission.

"geons" (a short-hand for the phrase geometric ions), suggesting an analogy with words, which are also constructed from combinations of primitives—phonemes. Like Marr and Nishihara, Biederman suggests that the first stage of object description involves the segmentation of the occluding contour at regions of sharp concavity. This divides the contour into a number of parts, which can then be matched against representations of the primitive object shapes (geons). The nature and arrangements of the geons found can then be matched with structural models of objects. The representation of each known object is a structural model of the components from which it is constructed, their relative sizes, orientations, place of attachment, and so forth (see Fig. 9.22). Where members of the same basic object category (e.g. piano) may have quite different shapes (e.g. grand piano vs upright piano) then more than one structural model would be stored for the object.

The main point of departure of Biederman's theory from Marr and Nishihara's is the suggestion that geons are defined by properties that are *invariant* over different views. According to this theory, it is not necessary to make use of occluding contours to recover an axis-based *three-dimensional shape* description. Instead, each different kind of geon has its own "key" features in the 2-D primal sketch level representation. Thus in Biederman's theory, unlike Marr's, object recognition can be achieved directly from the 2-D (primal sketch) level representation with no need to construct an explicit representation of 3-D shape. Biederman argues that there a number of

"nonaccidental" properties of edges in images that can be used as reliable cues to related properties of edges in the world (cf. Kanade, 1981; Lowe, 1987). The "nonaccidental" principle is an assumption that when a certain regularity is present in an image, this is assumed to reflect a true regularity in the world, rather than an "accidental" consequence of a particular viewpoint. We can illustrate this with the example of a straight line in an image. This will usually result from an extended straight edge in the world, but it *could* result from other "accidental" consequences of viewpoint; for example, a bicycle wheel viewed end-on will give rise to a straight line image, even though it is actually curved. The nonaccidental assumption would lead to the wrong answer in this case, but will usually be correct, and the general assumption is required in order to constrain the interpretation of essentially ambiguous image data. The nonaccidentalness assumption leads to assertions such as that curved lines in images result from curved edges in the world, parallel edges in an image derive from parallel edges in the world, symmetry in the image signals symmetry in the world, and so forth. Nonaccidental properties include collincarity, curvilinearity, symmetry, parallelism, and cotermination (see Fig 9.23).

A geon is identified by a particular set of defining features (such as parallel edges) that can be accessed via these nonaccidental properties. Biederman suggests that the assumption of nonaccidental properties could explain a number of illusions such as the Ames chair (see Ch.4, p.71), and "impossible" objects, where, for example, the

---

FIGURE 9.22

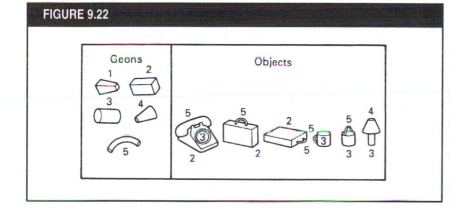

A selection of the volumetric primitives called "geons" (left-hand panel) are used to specify objects in the right-hand panel. The relations between the geons are important, as shown by the difference between a pail and a cup. Reproduced from Biederman (1987b) with permission © 1987 IEEE.

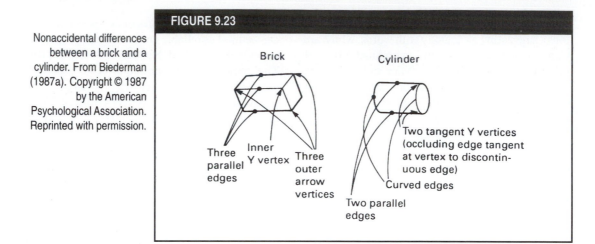

FIGURE 9.23

Nonaccidental differences between a brick and a cylinder. From Biederman (1987a). Copyright © 1987 by the American Psychological Association. Reprinted with permission.

cotermination assumption is violated. Biederman also provides new evidence for the importance of concavities in defining the part structures of objects (cf. Hoffman & Richards, 1984). Biederman (1987a) describes experiments in which objects were presented with regions of contour deleted—either at places where there were concavities in the occluding contour that should help define the parts structure, or from segments between these concavities. Contour deletion had a far greater detrimental effect on recognition when information about concavities was removed than when this was preserved. Biederman and Ju (1988) also produced evidence that supported the proposal that it is *edge* properties, rather than surface or texture properties, that are used to classify objects into basic categories. In Biederman and Ju's experiments object recognition was affected rather little by whether or not appropriate or inappropriate colour was added to line-drawn objects in a recognition test, suggesting that the recognition processes ignore such surface properties.

Biederman has also performed a series of empirical studies that appear to support the geon theory of object recognition. When a picture of an object is presented twice for naming, the naming latency on the second occurrence is much faster than on the first. This speeding up of responses from one presentation to the next is known as *repetition priming*. Biederman and Cooper (1991) investigated how repetition priming is affected by a change in the way a line drawing of an object is

depicted. The amount of priming obtained is reduced when the repeated presentation shows a different exemplar of the category that would access a distinct structural model (e.g. an upright piano followed by a grand piano), compared with the amount of priming shown when the same exemplar is repeated (e.g. another picture of an upright piano). This difference gives a measure of "visual" priming at the level of the structural model itself over and above additional "conceptual" priming that might occur as a result of re-accessing the same object meaning or category label. Biederman and Cooper (1991) showed that the magnitude of this visual priming of object identification was unaffected if the second view of the same object exemplar showed the same object components, represented by complementary but nonoverlapping image edge features. However, visual priming was reduced if the depicted components (geons) themselves were changed from first to second presentation (when different volumetric parts of the same object exemplar are shown on the two occasions). (See Fig. 9.24.)

Further experiments have shown that priming is invariant over other changes that alter the image but preserve its components, such as size, location, and moderate changes in viewpoint. In contrast, these same manipulations do affect memory for line-drawn pictures (Biederman & Cooper, 1992; Cooper, Schacter, Ballesteros, & Moore, 1992; Humphrey & Khan, 1992), suggesting that variations in object components that are irrelevant for

FIGURE 9.24

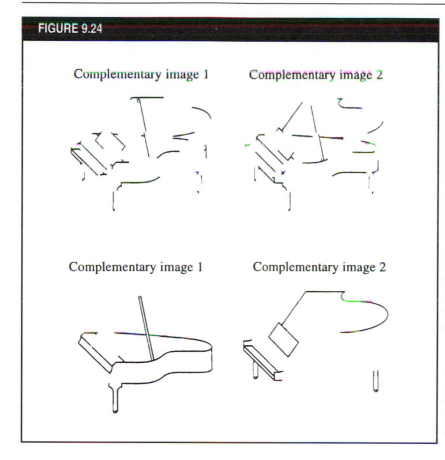

Complementary image 1   Complementary image 2

Complementary image 1   Complementary image 2

Examples of materials used in Biederman and Cooper's (1991) experiment. The top panel shows two complementary images of a piano, created by deleting alternate segments of contour in each image. The amount of visual priming obtained when one member of this pair was followed by the other was as great as when identical images were repeated. The bottom panel shows two complementary images produced by deleting alternate geon components. The amount of priming obtained when one member of such a pair was followed by the other was much reduced and attributed to conceptual rather than visual processes. Adapted from Biederman and Cooper (1991) with permission of the author.

identity may be processed and maintained by other parts of the visual system, perhaps those to do with spatial layout and action. The location of an object in the visual field does not affect its identity, but will affect how an observer reacts to it (e.g. if reaching out to grasp it, or ducking to avoid being hit by it).

Cooper and Biederman (1993; see also Biederman, 1995) furnished other evidence supporting the geon theory. In one study, people were asked to decide whether two objects shown successively were the same or different in name. When objects shared the same name (e.g. both were wine goblets), the two exemplars could differ in terms of the geon shown (e.g. the bowl of the goblet could have rounded or straight sides) or they could differ in a way that did not involve any change in non-accidental properties and hence geons (e.g. the bowl of the goblet could be stretched in the second view compared with the first) (see Fig. 9.25). They found that matching was slowed more (and became more error-prone) by a change in geon than by other metric changes that left the geons unchanged, suggesting that it is the *categorisation* of the shape parts, rather than *holistic or metric* properties of shape, that determines ease of matching.

VIEWPOINT-DEPENDENT RECOGNITION

The theories of object recognition we have discussed here emphasise the recognition of objects irrespective of viewpoint. In fact, there is evidence that not all views of objects are equally easy to recognise. Palmer, Rosch, and Chase (1981) described how each of the different objects they examined appears to have a "canonical" viewpoint, which is often, though not always,

FIGURE 9.25

Examples of the geon-changed (VIC change) and metric-changed shapes used by Cooper and Biederman (1993). Object–name matches were disrupted more by a change of geon than by a metric change even when the metric change was 50% greater (see far-right column) than the amount of metric change that was rated as subjectively equal to the geon change. Reprinted by permission of the author.

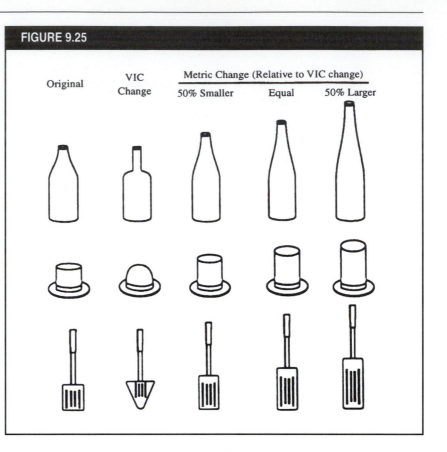

something like a three-quarters view. People asked to imagine such objects report imaging them in their canonical views, and people asked which view they would choose to photograph, or which view of an object is "best", select canonical views. Importantly, Palmer, Rosch, and Chase also found that these canonical views could be named more quickly than other views, suggesting that such views play a privileged role in object recognition.

The advantage of canonical viewpoint could quite easily be accommodated by the theories discussed earlier, even though these stress the recognition of objects independent of viewpoint. Marr and Nishihara (1978) emphasise that certain viewpoints will conceal important major axes that are needed to derive a shape description. For example, a top view of a bucket conceals the axis of elongation, which is probably crucial to its description. For Biederman, certain views may conceal the nonaccidental properties that define the "geons", and other views may reveal them better.

Biederman and Gerhardstein (1993) conducted a series of experiments using the repetition-priming method to investigate whether object recognition was invariant across viewpoint. In their experiments they examined how priming was affected by a change in orientation of the object from the view experienced in the first phase. They found that, provided different viewpoints revealed the same geon components, the amount of repetition priming was affected very little by an angular change of up to 135° between its first and second presentation. If successive viewpoints revealed different geons then the amount of priming was affected more greatly.

Other experiments, however, seem to reveal a much greater dependence on viewpoint than do Biederman's. For example, Bülthoff and Edelman (1992; also Edelman and Bülthoff, 1992) showed that when people were asked to try to recognise rather complex unfamiliar shapes they showed very poor abilities to recognise them in novel viewpoints, even when they had been studied under conditions that ought to have promoted the formation of a 3-D viewpoint-invariant description. There is some dispute about whether such effects of viewpoint-dependence arise only when objects are drawn from a very restricted set within which there are no distinguishing "geons" (see Biederman & Gerhardstein, 1993; and Tarr and Bülthoff, 1995, for discussion). However, effects of viewpoint-dependence have also been found with the kinds of familiar object categories studied by Biederman. For example, Lawson, Humphreys, and Watson (1994) reported experiments in which subjects were required to identify an object from a series of briefly presented pictures. Priming effects were strongly influenced by the visual similarity of successive views, a result that should not be expected if each recognisable view contacts a viewpoint-independent description (see also Lawson & Humphreys, 1996).

A number of authors therefore suggest that our usual ability to recognise objects across a range of viewpoints arises as a result of our experiencing and storing different viewpoints separately, rather than through the recognition of viewpoint-invariant features (Biederman) or the storage of a viewpoint-invariant model (Biederman, Marr). If discrete viewpoints are stored, recognition of novel views may be achieved by alignment of a novel image with one of those stored (e.g. see Bülthoff & Edelman, 1992; Tarr, 1995; Tarr & Pinker, 1989; Ullman, 1989). Theories of viewpoint-dependent recognition of objects are developing rapidly (e.g. see Edelman, 1995). However, it is important to note that object recognition is but one of the tasks accomplished by vision. If recognition can be achieved directly from 2-D features, as Biederman suggests, or through storing a number of viewpoint-specific exemplars (Tarr & Bülthoff, 1995) or "prototypes" (Edelman, 1995), this does not imply that 3-D descriptions of objects are not constructed to guide other actions, such as picking up the object. Different kinds of representation are needed for different kinds of visual task, and even within the task of object recognition it is possible that flexible representational systems are used depending on task demands (see Tarr, 1995, for a discussion).

Whatever the resolution of the rather intense debate about the mechanism by which viewpoint-invariance is achieved, the theories of Marr and Nishihara, and Biederman are all rather limited in scope, because they can only account for the recognition of *basic* categories of object from different configurations of parts. Humans can recognise much more subtle distinctions within classes of objects that share a similar configuration. We can recognise our individual dogs and houses, not just tell a dog from a horse or a house from a church. This ability to recognise objects from within a basic object category is at its most developed when we come to consider recognition of the human face.

DISCRIMINATING WITHIN CATEGORIES OF OBJECTS: THE CASE OF FACE RECOGNITION

Human faces must all be similar in overall configuration because of the other functions of signalling (e.g. expressions) and sensing (e.g. seeing) that they subserve (see Chapter 16). Individual identity must be stamped on this basic configuration. What do we know about the basic form of the representations used to tell one individual face from another?

In contrast to basic-level object recognition, face recognition is not very successful if based on simple "edge" features alone, and seems to require information about surface characteristics such as the pigmentation and/or the texture of skin and hair. One example arises from an experiment by Davies, Ellis, and Shepherd (1978), who showed that famous faces were very poorly recognised from outline drawings that traced the features of faces.

Bruce et al. (1992a) replicated this observation in an evaluation of Pearson and Robinson's (1985) algorithm for sketching images of faces (see Ch.5, p.88). They found that famous faces were quite difficult to recognise when presented as sketches made using Pearson and Robinson's (1985) "valley detecting" algorithm alone, but that the addition of the component that blacks in areas that were dark in the original photograph (see Fig 5.11) restored recognition of these computer-generated sketches to a level comparable to that obtained with the original photographs.

Moreover, Bruce et al. (1994) showed that repetition priming of faces was considerably reduced if there was a change in the image characteristics between the first and second presentation of faces. Priming was reduced if faces were initially seen as photographic images, and then tested as sketches produced by the Pearson and Robinson (1985) algorithm, or vice versa, compared with the amount of priming produced when the format of the images remained constant between the prime and test phases of the experiment. The viewpoint, expression, and face features remain the same between the photographic and sketch versions—what varies is the details of the grey levels across the image. This sensitivity to image format in face priming is in apparent contrast to basic-level object recognition, where Biederman and Cooper (1991) found that priming was insensitive to changes in the image features.

Another observation is difficult to explain if edge features form the basis of the representational primitives used for face recognition. Faces are extremely difficult to recognise from photographic negatives (e.g. Phillips, 1972), although a negative of a face preserves the spatial layout of edges from the original image. Bruce and Langton (1994) were able to show that this impairment of face recognition did not occur when three-dimensional surface shapes of faces were negated (see Fig. 9.26). This finding suggests that the critical factor in the negation effect is the reversal of the relative brightness of pigmented areas such as hair and skin, which are absent from such surface shapes.

These studies of the identification of line-drawn and negated faces suggest that the surface properties of skin and textured areas such as hair—in particular their relative lightness and darkness—play an important role in face recognition. This need not imply that faces are represented in a radically different way from other objects, as object recognition also seems more dependent on surface properties when the task of discriminating within categories becomes more difficult. For example, Price and Humphreys (1989) showed that when objects to be recognised

were drawn from structurally similar categories (such as animals or vegetables), there was a greater advantage in recognising them if they were coloured appropriately rather than inappropriately.

So, one contrast between face recognition (and, perhaps, within-category recognition more generally) and the recognition of basic object types is the extent to which representations preserve information about surface properties. Moreover, a further difference seems to arise in the extent to which different kinds of object discrimination involve decomposing the object shapes into parts, or analysing them more holistically.

The theories of Marr and Nishihara, and Biederman, which we have discussed at length in this chapter, emphasise the decomposition of object shapes into discrete parts, followed by the identification of these parts and their spatial relationships. In contrast to the evidence for a part-based representational scheme for objects, face representation seems to be more "holistic", or at least the relationships between parts (their configuration) seems to be more important in the coding of faces than in that of most objects.

The main observation favouring the holistic processing of faces is that it seems to be difficult or impossible to encode a particular part, or "feature", of an upright face without some influence from other, more distant features. It is not just that the spatial arrangement of face features is important—after all, we have seen that the spatial arrangement of geons is crucial for the definition of an object. For faces, it seems either that the internal description of the parts themselves is influenced by that of other parts, or that parts are not made explicit in the description that mediates face identification. For example, Young, Hellawell, and Hay (1987) took pictures of famous faces and divided them horizontally across the centre. They showed that subjects were able to identify these halves in isolation. When halves of different faces were recombined, however, it became extremely difficult for subjects to name the people who contributed to the composites if these were aligned—new (and unfamiliar) faces seemed to emerge from the combination of the top half of, say, Margaret Thatcher's face and the bottom half of, say, Princess Diana's. However, when the

FIGURE 9.26

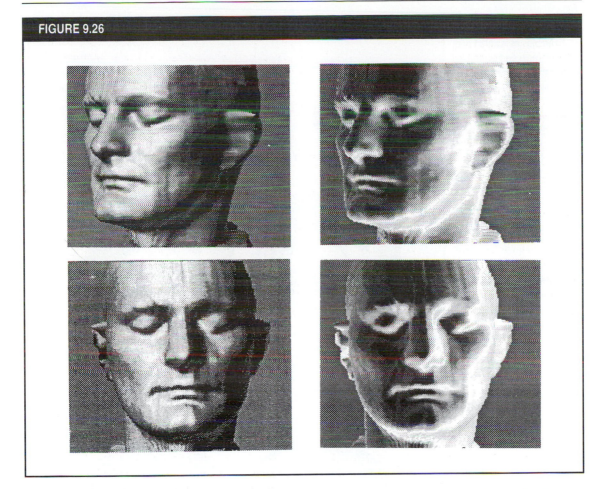

Examples of the surface images used by Bruce and Langton (1994) to explore effects of negation in the absence of surface pigmentation. Positive (left) and negative (right) versions are shown of two of the different viewpoints used in the experiments. Reprinted from Bruce and Langton (1994). © 1994 Pion Ltd. Used by permission.

composite faces were presented upside down, subjects' abilities to identify the halves improved.

Further evidence for the specific use of nondecomposed facial properties in face identification has been obtained by Tanaka and Farah (1993). They asked subjects to learn the identities of individuals constructed from Mac-a-Mug, an electronic "kit" of face features, available for the Macintosh computer. After learning the faces, subjects were asked questions such as "Which is Larry's nose?", where they had to choose the nose that went with the face they had learned to identify as Larry (see Fig. 9.27). Subjects were much better at making this judgement when the noses were shown in the context of the whole

face, then when presented in isolation. However, this advantage for presentations of the whole face was not shown when identities had initially been learned for scrambled faces, upside-down faces, or houses (in the latter case, questions about windows, doors, etc. replaced those about face features such as the nose). These results suggest that memory for intact, upright faces is not based on a representation in which parts are made explicit, in contrast to memory for jumbled or inverted faces. Note, though, that the results do not necessitate the view that facial representations are nondecomposed; the results are also consistent with the idea that memory representations for faces are based on emergent, configural descriptions in

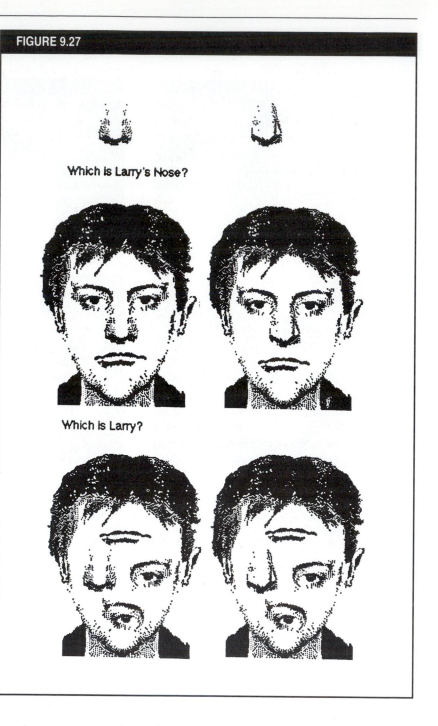

FIGURE 9.27

Examples of isolated part, intact face, and scrambled face test items used by Tanaka and Farah (1993). Subjects in these experiments were better able to distinguish the correct version of a feature (such as Larry's nose) when it appeared in the context of the whole face (centre) than on its own (top row) or in a scrambled face (bottom row). Reproduced from Tanaka and Farah (1993) with permission of the authors and the Experimental Psychology Society.

which parsed features are *no longer* represented independently (Bruce & Humphreys, 1994).

This evidence suggests that, even if face identification does involve part-decomposition, there may be a difference in the relative importance of parts versus their configuration, in the representation of basic kinds of objects versus faces. One theory suggests that the relative emphasis on configural and/or holistic processing of faces emerges as a function of expertise with this object class (e.g. see Carey, 1992), and is orientation-specific. Upside-down faces, which are very difficult to recognise, seem to induce a more parts-based analysis compared with upright faces (see also Bartlett & Searcy, 1993; Rhodes, Brake, & Atkinson, 1993; Young et al., 1987). Diamond and Carey (1986) showed that people who were dog experts also showed dramatic effects of inversion of dog pictures, comparable to the effects of inverting faces, and suggested that the special "configural" mode of processing faces was something that might emerge with expertise within any class of objects sharing the same basic-level configuration. On this argument, face recognition is "special" only in so far as it is a task of within-category recognition at which we are all highly expert, and face recognition can be used to exemplify the more general process of within-category object recognition. (For further discussion and evidence about whether or not face recognition involves specific mechanisms or neural networks not shared with other objects, see Bruce & Humphreys, 1994).

Of course, in Biederman's terms, objects sharing the same overall configuration must share the same geon structural description, and thus some other way of discriminating that which is based on holistic and/or surface properties must be invoked.

However, even within the domain of basic level object recognition, some workers have produced evidence seeming to favour more holistic over part-based object description schemes. Cave and Kosslyn (1993) showed that the identification of objects was severely disrupted by the scrambling of the spatial arrangement of the overall shape, a result that would be expected on a part-based as well as a holistic coding scheme. However, they also found that it mattered rather little how the objects were divided into parts. Dividing objects in ways that coincided with natural part boundaries (i.e. ways that kept geons intact) produced little advantage over dividing them in ways that did not maintain natural part boundaries. It was only when exposure durations were extremely short that there was an advantage for the natural over the unnatural part divisions. Cave and Kosslyn suggest that people can use parts such as geons as the building blocks for recognition but that they do not need to

do so. One problem with Cave and Kosslyn's study, however, is that naturally parsed geons may serve as "objects" for perceptual identification in their own right, which may then compete for identification, thereby disadvantaging the identification of the compound objects. Objects divided in other ways (not into natural parts) would not suffer such competition.

FRACTALS

A further class of objects that are not readily characterised in the simple, part-based way envisaged by Marr and Nishihara, Biederman, and others include naturally rough, crumpled, or branching objects such as trees and clouds, and many textures such as rocky or sandy terrain. Some such "rough" patterns can be described as having a fractal structure (Mandelbrot, 1982). Fractals are patterns that have a fractional dimensionality. For example, a plane is two-dimensional whereas a cube is three-dimensional. A fractal pattern of dimension 2.1 would be almost smooth, like a plane, but with a slightly bumpy surface. As the fractal dimension increased towards 3, the surface would become increasingly craggy. Fractal patterns also have a recursive structure—they look the same at different scales. Figure 9.28 shows some examples of fractal patterns. Pentland (1986b) showed that human perception of the "roughness" of a surface was highly correlated with its fractal dimension as this ranged between 2 and 3 in the way described above, but did not compare the predictive power of fractal statistics with that of any other variable. Cutting and Garvin (1987) showed that ratings of the complexity of patterns like those shown in Fig. 9.28 are well predicted by their fractal pattern statistics, but also found that other variables, such as the number of sides, were equally good predictors of perceived complexity.

Pentland (1986b) describes how fractal-based methods can be used to segment natural images into different regions and objects (cf. Chapter 6), and describes how objects more natural-looking than those shown in Fig. 9.21 can be built by adding

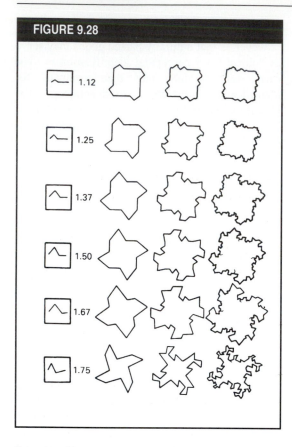

FIGURE 9.28

Examples of fractal patterns derived from different "generators" (left column) whose fractal dimension varies from 1.12 to 1.75. The patterns generated along the rows vary in terms of their depth of recursion—the extent to which the generation process is repeated at different scales. Reproduced from Cutting and Garvin (1987) with permission of the Psychonomic Society, Inc.

together superquadric components using a fractal generation process to roughen the surface. Although this is of considerable interest as a computer graphics application, and shows how a basic "part-based" shape description could be extended so that it could apply to more natural objects, it remains to be seen whether the human visual system makes use of any such system when recognising objects.

CONCLUSIONS

In this chapter we have outlined some of the problems posed by the recognition of objects from retinal images, and have seen how contemporary work in cognitive science has attempted to overcome these problems. We are still a long way from developing a computer program that can recognise everyday objects with the ease that we do, and some way off understanding how we ourselves perform everyday tasks of natural object recognition. The theories of recognition we have discussed in this chapter differ in the extent to which objects are thought to be recognised via abstract models that are viewpoint independent, or by the storage of particular instances or viewpoints seen on distinct occasions. In the next chapter, we will consider how recent connectionist models of object recognition can give a feel for how apparently "abstract" representations might be built up from discrete encounters with objects in the world.

10

Connectionist Models of Visual Perception

Marr's theory of vision, which has provided a unifying framework for this section of the book, sees visual perception as involving the construction and manipulation of abstract symbolic descriptions of the viewed scene. In these terms, for example, an edge-detecting algorithm applied to a retinal image results in a *description* that is rather like a set of sentences describing which edge features are where in the image. In the brain, of course, there can be no such "sentences", but rather there are neurons, or collections of neurons, that are more or less active depending on the inputs they receive from other neurons. In recent years there has been increased interest in building neuron-like models of visual perception (and other sensory and cognitive processes) in which representations of the world are expressed in terms of activities in neuron-like units, rather than in terms of the construction and storage of abstract strings of symbols.

Such "connectionist" models have several apparent advantages over the conventional "symbol processing" model. First, they appear to be more biologically plausible (although, as we will see, some of this apparent plausibility is spurious). They also provide a relatively easy way

to think about *parallel* computations, which can be particularly convenient when a number of different constraints need to be satisfied simultaneously. Connectionist models additionally provide an interesting way of simulating how a system could *learn* to recognise certain categories from a collection of exemplars. This is not unknown in conventional models (e.g. Winston's work, discussed in Chapter 9) but becomes an important central feature of many connectionist models where learning occurs through weight adjustment—the reinforcement of certain excitatory or inhibitory "connections" between the neuron-like units and the weakening of others. Finally, a certain class of connectionist models has the additional property of "distributed" processing. In such models, there is no one-to-one correspondence between a "unit" and a "concept" as there is in more "localist" connection schemes (e.g. Feldman, 1985). Rather, a particular concept is represented in terms of a pattern of activity over a large set of simple units, and different patterns of activity in those same units represent different concepts. Such PDP (parallel distributed processing) versions of connectionist models have some attractive characteristics when applied to pattern and object classification, as we will see later in this chapter.

In this chapter, we introduce connectionist models of three main kinds in order to explore their potential for models of visual processing. First, we show how such models can provide a convenient means of satisfying constraints simultaneously. Second, we show how they can provide a way of *mapping* between different coordinate systems (e.g. retinal, scene-based, object-based). Third, we examine pattern-learning in connectionist models, and in particular we explore the potential of parallel distributed processing (PDP) accounts of object and pattern recognition. We cannot attempt an exhaustive review of this rapidly expanding area. Rather, we aim to introduce the different topics with one or two examples, and the interested reader should consult Ballard, Hinton, and Sejnowski (1983), McClelland and Rumelhart (1986), Rumelhart and McClelland (1986), Hinton (1989), or Morris (1989) for further details and examples.

SATISFYING CONSTRAINTS—MARR AND POGGIO'S (1976) ALGORITHM

Connectionist models provide a particularly effective way to implement an algorithm that has to satisfy many different constraints at once, and we start by introducing connectionist models with a description of their application to stereopsis. Recall from Chapter 7 that Marr and Poggio (1976) suggested that the correspondence problem in random-dot stereograms could be solved through the application of three matching rules that embody constraints of the physical world. Matches must be compatible (black dots with black dots and white with white), unique (a single match for each dot), and continuous (disparity values should only vary smoothly).

The algorithm can be implemented in a competitive neural network where there is a unit for each possible disparity between a feature in one eye's view and another feature in the other eye's view (see Fig. 10.1). Thus each unit in the network

represents a surface feature or patch at a particular depth. Each excited unit can in turn excite or inhibit the activity of other units, and have its own activity increased or decreased in turn by the excitation and inhibition it receives from other units. Marr and Poggio (1976) showed how the matching constraints could be embodied in the patterns of excitation and inhibition in such a network. First, the compatibility constraint means that a unit will only be active initially if it is excited by similar features from both eyes' inputs (e.g. both must be black dots or both white dots in Fig. 10.1). Second, the uniqueness constraint is embodied by inhibition passing between units that fall along the same line of sight—i.e. units that would represent *different* disparities for the *same* features inhibit one another. Finally, the continuity constraint is embodied by having excitation pass between units that represent *different* features at the *same* disparities. Thus unique matches that preserve areas of the same disparities are encouraged. Marr and Poggio showed that a simulation of such a network "solved" random-dot stereograms. For example, if the network was presented with two patterns of random dots, corresponding to the two halves of a random-dot stereogram in which human vision would see a central square at a different depth from its background, the pattern of excitation of the network gradually settled down to a state where adjacent units in a square-shaped region were active at a disparity distinct from that associated with units activated by dots from the background.

Although Marr and Poggio's is a parallel algorithm it was implemented in a serial computer by serial examination of the activity levels of each unit within a number of "rounds" or "iterations" of activity. In each iteration, the amount of excitation or inhibition received by each unit in the network is calculated from the activities present at the end of the previous iteration, and its new activity computed. At the end of that iteration, new activity levels for all the units can be used to compute the amount of excitation and inhibition received by each unit in the next round. These iterations continue until the system reaches a steady state, i.e. one where there is no change in the pattern or amount of activity from one round to the next.

FIGURE 10.1

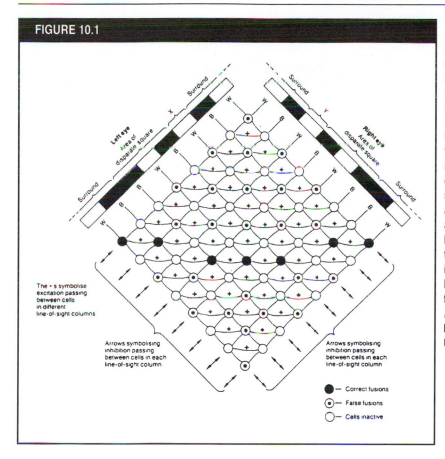

The + s symbolise excitation passing between cells in different line-of-sight columns

Arrows symbolising inhibition passing between cells in each line-of-sight column

Arrows symbolising inhibition passing between cells in each line-of-sight column

● — Correct fusions
◉ — False fusions
○ — Cells inactive

A small slice of a network for solving the correspondence problem in random-dot stereograms in the manner proposed by Marr and Poggio (1976). Black spots have been placed at nodes that are activated by the same features from both eyes' inputs. Bigger black spots mark the nodes whose activation levels are greatest after excitation has passed between nodes representing the same disparity and inhibition has passed down lines of sight. Reproduced from *Seeing: Mind, brain and illusion* by J.P. Frisby, 1979, by permission of Oxford University Press.

This type of parallel algorithm is finding increasing application in a range of applied visual processing tasks where a number of constraints must be satisfied. Other examples can be found in work on such topics as optic flow analysis and shape from shading, and in work on the satisfaction of constraints from multiple sources (e.g. Terzopoulos, 1986).

MAPPING BETWEEN COORDINATE SYSTEMS

In earlier chapters we have discussed how successive stages of visual perception might require that descriptions be built within different coordinate systems. Thus Marr (1982) argued that the primal sketch and 2½-D sketch were based on retinocentric coordinates, whereas the 3-D models were based on object-centred coordinates. Connectionist models can provide a means of mapping between different coordinate systems.

Hinton (1981) presented an early example of how a connectionist architecture could be used to recognise a letter irrespective of its tilt, by implementing a mapping from a particular view of a pattern, to a viewpoint-independent description, without knowing the identity of the letter in advance. This could be achieved by setting up a network of simple units, with some "retina-based" units responding to specific local features falling at particular locations and orientations, and other "object-based" units responding to features oriented and located in respect to a frame centred on the letter rather than on the viewer (see Fig. 10.2). Activation within the retina-based units in turn excites the object-based units, but the degree of excitation will be modified by a separate set of "mapping units", which add in a bias towards a

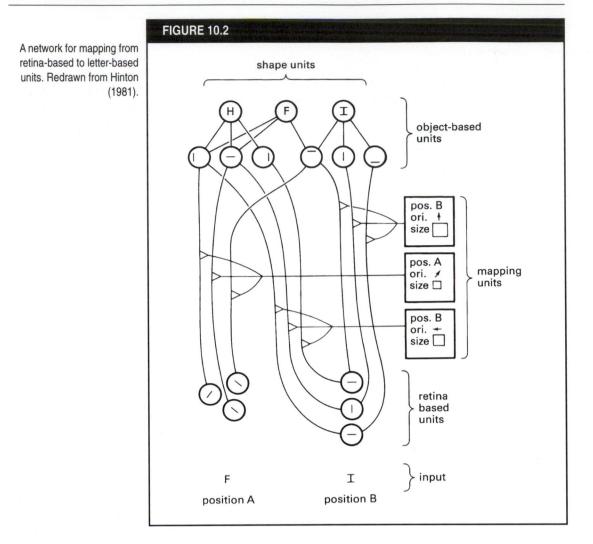

FIGURE 10.2

A network for mapping from retina-based to letter-based units. Redrawn from Hinton (1981).

particular frame. Hinton suggests that there might normally be a bias towards a vertical reference frame, as, in the absence of other information, we would tend to recognise an "I" rather than an "H" from the same features. Hinton's system can be extended to recognise patterns when the mapping rules are not known in advance, because of inbuilt biases from the letter level, which give more weight to combinations of features that define letters irrespective of orientation. Such biases can result in a letter being recognised even if oriented horizontally. Within such a scheme, an object's identity and the frame of reference for its description are recovered simultaneously through the converging pattern of activation.

A more ambitious attempt to describe mappings between different coordinate systems was produced by Feldman (1985). Feldman suggests that visual processing involves establishing representations in four different "frames" of reference—the retinotopic frame, the "stable feature" or head-based frame, the environmental frame, and the "world knowledge formulary" (see Fig. 10.3). The retinotopic frame finds edges, and computes disparity and motion within a retinally based coordinate system. As such, this frame resembles Marr's "2½-D sketch" level. The stable feature frame encodes visual features in a way that is stable across fixations (unlike the retinotopic frame) and thus provides one means of integrating

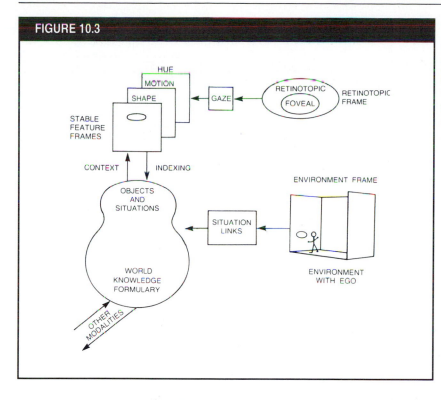

FIGURE 10.3

Four representational frames of reference, and the links between them. Reproduced from Feldman (1985) with permission of the publishers, Cambridge University Press.

across different fixations (see Chapter 7). Features described in the stable feature frame are then used to address "world knowledge" where objects are represented in terms of their "appearance possibilities" (i.e. in viewpoint-dependent rather than view-independent form). The environmental frame maintains a representation of where the recognised objects are located in the space around the viewer.

Feldman offers suggestions about how mappings could be achieved between these different frames. For example, to map from retinotopic to stable feature frame he presents the (deliberately oversimplified) scheme illustrated in Figs. 10.4 and 10.5. The retinotopic frame must be able to sample different spatial regions of the stable feature frame so that the stable feature frame can have foveal resolution across its entire spatial extent. That is, considering a frame of reference based on the head, the eyes can move so that different regions of this space are foveated (brought within the high resolution area of the retina). Knowledge of the current direction of gaze is needed to make the mapping between the

retinotopic frame and appropriate coordinates within the stable feature frame. So, in Fig. 10.4, retinal coordinate 64 maps to ("excites") stable feature frame coordinates 6,5 if gaze direction is 8,8, and retinal coordinate 65 maps to the same stable feature frame position if gaze is 7,8. (Fig. 10.4 shows only a portion of the retinotopic frame. The entire retinotopic frame is seen in Fig. 10.5, which shows how the frame is assumed to have a logarithmic coordinate structure in which fine spatial discriminations are possible in the fovea and increasingly coarse ones towards the periphery).

Feldman suggests that the stable feature frame actually comprises a set of head-based spatial representations that separately describe the depths, motions, hues, and so forth in the current visual scene (see Fig. 10.5). Mappings from the stable feature frame to the world knowledge formulary (catalogue of object appearances) can thus be made on the basis of particular combinations of stable features. For example, Fig. 10.6 shows, greatly simplified, how mappings can be made from features to objects—a golf ball is round (shape), white (colour), and pock-marked (texture),

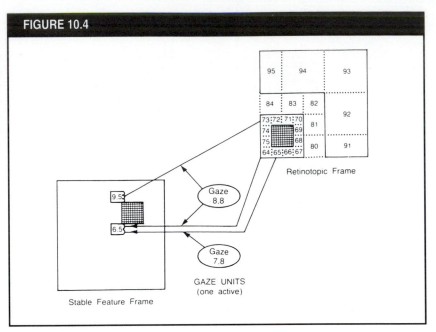

FIGURE 10.4

Retinotopic coordinates map to different stable feature frame coordinates depending on the direction of gaze. Reproduced from Feldman (1985) with permission of the publishers, Cambridge University Press.

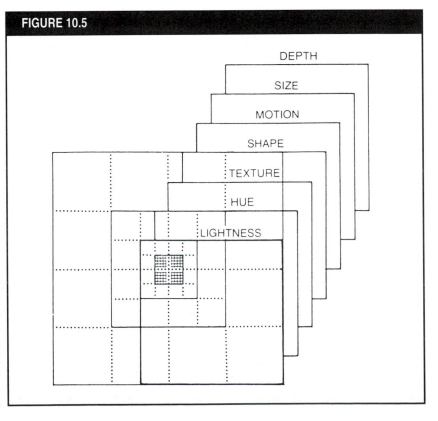

FIGURE 10.5

The logarithmic resolution of the retinotopic frame shown superimposed on the different representational components of the stable feature frame. Reproduced from Feldman (1985) with permission of the publishers, Cambridge University Press.

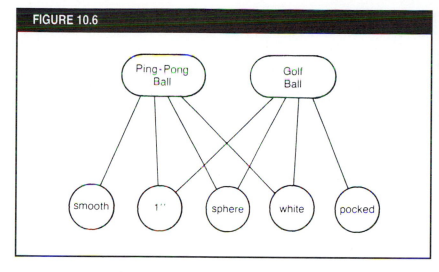

FIGURE 10.6

Mappings between features and objects. Reproduced from Feldman (1985) with permission of the publishers, Cambridge University Press.

whereas a ping-pong ball is round, white, and smooth. As shown in Fig. 10.6, however, such an indexing scheme could lead to false conjunctions between the features of different objects. If a ping-pong ball is small, round, and white, there is nothing to to stop its node becoming active when a scene contains both a tennis ball (large, round, and white) and a marble (small, round, and smooth). Clearly it is important that features at one spatial location are somehow tied together with features at the same spatial location (cf. Treisman, 1988). To achieve this, the features "round", "white", and "pock-marked" must be located in *spatial registration* between the different maps in the stable feature frame, and this would then lead to activation of the "golf ball" node so that a golf ball could be identified at this position. (In fact, Feldman suggests a more elaborate, hierarchical means of achieving this mapping from features at particular locations to "object nodes" by using conjunctions of features as an intermediate mapping. The interested reader should consult his paper for more details.)

As well as objects, the "world knowledge formulary" represents "situations" such as rooms or streets. Knowledge of the current situation is used to help anticipate what particular objects should be seen when gaze is directed to different places, via the fourth frame of the model in Fig. 10.3—the environmental frame. The environmental frame is a representation of how things are arranged in the space around the observer at any time. The idea is that the same system of mappings and mutual excitation can lead to a particular object or building to be expected (or "primed") when an observer's gaze is directed to a known location within a known situation.

Feldman's (1985) framework provides a general idea of how a connectionist model could be developed to build descriptions of objects within different coordinate systems. However, it should be noted that this model still begs all the questions about the basic "primitives" needed to compute disparity or represent objects, questions that are tackled more adequately at the "computational theory" level addressed by Marr. Nor does Feldman address in any detail the question of how these mappings were learned initially.

Hummel and Biederman (1992) produced a computational model of the stages of mapping from retinal features to geon-based object descriptions (see Ch.9, p.223). The model, shown in Fig. 10.7, comprises a series of layers in which units represent increasingly complex image properties, from edges in layer 1 (roughly analogous to Marr's primal sketch level) up to individual objects such as "nuke plant" in layer 7. The challenge in the implementation was to find a way of solving the "binding" problem that is inherent in object recognition theories using part-based structural descriptions. Feldman (see earlier) attempted to tackle one aspect of this

FIGURE 10.7

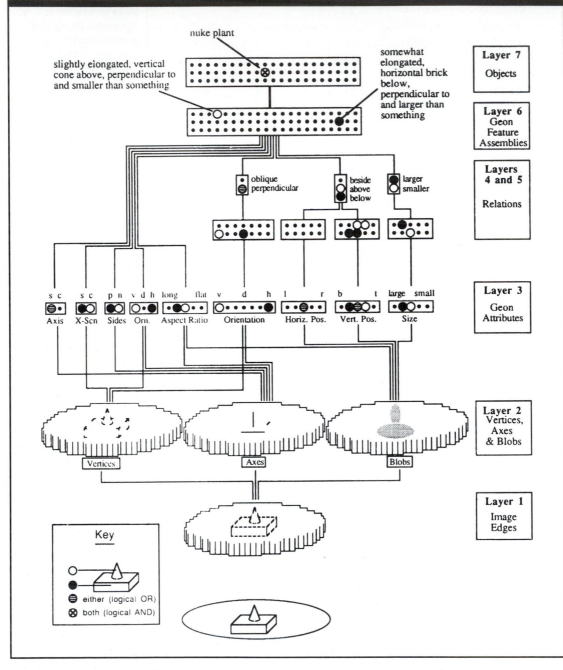

Hummel and Biederman's (1992) neural network model of shape recognition. Distinct representations are activated at each layer, from image edges at layer 1, through to objects (such as "nuke plant") at layer 7. Reproduced from Hummel and Biederman (1992) with permission of the author and publishers. Copyright © 1992 by the American Psychological Association.

binding problem, but avoided much of it by considering only highly simplified "features" of objects. The problem is as follows: if there is a unit that represents a "brick" geon and another one that represents a "cone" geon, other units that represent "above" or "below", and others that represent "horizontal" or "vertical", then we need some way of representing the different spatial relationships between the brick and the cone that characterise different classes of object. We need distinct representations for a "vertical cone above a horizontal brick" (the description that activates the "nuke plant" object in Fig. 10.7) and for "vertical cone above a vertical brick" (a "tree", perhaps), and so on. One way round this would be to store all possible combinations of attributes, but this is both uneconomical and—more importantly— inflexible. The way proposed by Hummel and Biederman is to bind together temporarily conjunctions of items by *synchronising* the activity of independent units that contribute to these conjunctions so that they fire in the same time intervals. (Recall that in Ch.3, p.63 we saw physiological evidence that synchronisation of activity in cortical cells may be important in "binding" features.) In the model, synchronisation is achieved by using a novel kind of connection between different attributes, called a Fast Enabling Link (FEL). FELs are a class of link different from the usual excitatory or inhibitory link, and operate only to synchronise activities between cells. When a unit representing a particular attribute (e.g. "cone") becomes active, an enabling signal travels *very quickly* along its FELs to other units. This enabling signal will make other active units fire in synchrony with each other, by its effect on the refractory component of the cell's activity, but has no effect on inactive units. So, to represent that "above" goes with "cone", "horizontal" goes with "brick", and so forth, the activities of "cone" and "above" are synchronised, and the activity of "brick" and "horizontal" are synchronised, and these temporary conjunctions between units in layers 3, 4, and 5 together activate appropriate descriptions in layer 6 to trigger the recognition of an object such as the "nuke plant" in Fig. 10.7.

Hummel and Biederman trained their model to recognise single views of each of ten different simple objects composed of two or three geons each, and showed that it was able to recognise new instances of these objects in novel locations, sizes, and viewpoints as accurately as the original test images. Recognition performance was reduced as the orientation of the test images was varied in the picture plane (i.e. as objects were shown in different orientations from upright). Human performance in recognising basic-level objects is similar, as it is largely unaffected by size, location, and (to some extent) viewpoint, but is sensitive to orientation. Hummel and Biederman's model thus represents a promising implementation and extension of Biederman's (1987) theory of object recognition. The limitation of the model at present is that it has been tested with a very limited set of objects.

Hummel and Biederman tested their model by training it on the geon feature assemblies of single views of a set of objects and then looking at its ability to generalise to novel instances. The model system is therefore capable of learning new objects, and Hummel and Biederman discuss how novel object categories can be learned through the recruitment of unused object recognition units (an idea also developed in models of face recognition by Burton (1994)). In the next section we consider how connectionist models may be applied to the problems of learning patterns, a question that was very much peripheral to the aims of Hummel and Biederman's (1992) study.

LEARNING TO RECOGNISE PATTERNS

The networks described in the previous section produce mappings between view-specific representations of objects and explicit representations of the defining characteristics of objects that might be view-independent. Neural networks have also attracted considerable attention for their apparent abilities to learn these "defining" or prototypical characteristics of objects from collections of instances, without apparently constructing any explicit representation of the defining characteristics themselves.

WISARD (Wilkie, Stonham, & Aleksander's Recognition Device; e.g. Aleksander, 1983; Stonham, 1986) is a general-purpose pattern classifier constructed to model a neural network (although it is in fact implemented rather differently). In WISARD there is no notion of "reference frame" or "features" at all. The WISARD system demonstrates how a network that stores the responses to a large number of different instances of different pattern exemplars may subsequently be able to classify novel patterns correctly. For example, Stonham (1986) describes how a WISARD system that had been trained on a large number of different views of the faces of each of 15 individuals, was then able to decide which of the 15 faces was shown, without any apparent computation or description of features, reference frames, and so forth. How does the system work?

WISARD takes as its input a large array of pixels, each of which may be either "black" or "white". This pixel array is then sampled by selecting "n-tuples" of pixels so that the entire array is sampled. For example, if there is a 100×50 array of pixels (5000 in total), and "n" is 2, then 2500 pixel pairs will need to be taken to sample the whole image. Pixels within each n-tuple need not be adjacent and indeed are often quite widely separated in the pattern. When an n-tuple is sampled, there are 2^n possible results of sampling. When n = 2, there are $2^2 = 4$ possibilities: the pair of pixels may be both black, both white, the first black and the second white, and vice versa. If n = 3, the number of possible results is $2^3 = 8$. Because of the statistical similarity between different exemplars of the same class, if a number of exemplars of the same pattern were sampled with the same n-tuples, some outcomes would never occur and others would often occur.

For example, consider the pattern "T" shown in Fig. 10.8. If pixel triplets "a" and "b" shown in the figure were among those used to sample this pattern, then imagine what would happen to the results obtained from sampling as different example "T"s were shown. For triplet "a", the three pixels would never all be black if a T was shown; for triplet "b" the pixels will never show more than one black. Now if the same pixels were used instead to sample exemplars of a different pattern, the letter "O" (Fig. 10.8), a rather different pattern of outcomes would be obtained. Now triplet "b", for example, could find three black pixels. WISARD learns different pattern categories by being exposed to many exemplars of each, and storing the results of the pixel sampling process on each occasion. It thereby builds up a representation of the responses obtained when sampling Ts and another of the responses obtained when sampling Os. After training, an unknown pattern may be presented and categorised (as either a T or an O), by seeing whether the response obtained from the same sampling process more closely resembles those stored for Ts or Os. Exactly the same principles are used to recognise faces as those described here for letters. The only difference is

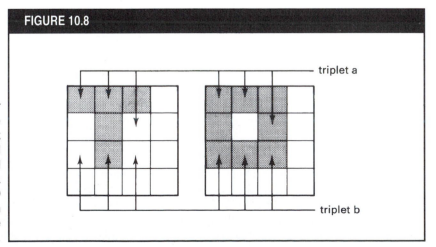

FIGURE 10.8

Pixel triplet "a" would never all be black if a T were shown, but could all be black if an O were shown. Pixel triplet "b" would never find more than one black pixel if a T is shown but could if an O was shown. Redrawn from Humphreys and Bruce (1989) with permission.

that a very large array size is used, and a very large number of instances of each face are sampled in training. At no stage are facial "features" (eyes, lips, etc.) found and measured, or configural relationships between different features determined.

The WISARD system lends itself to a number of applications where, say, industrial parts must be recognised for sorting purposes. In such applications it is possible to ensure that lighting conditions and background surfaces remain the same. A WISARD trained to recognise objects placed against a white background would have problems if the background at test was dark, because the "features" sampled are raw pixel values. There are a number of further limitations to WISARD's powers to generalise to novel views not encountered during training, and these limitations are not characteristic of human vision. WISARD is an interesting and powerful pattern classifier, but it does not appear to be a good model of most *human* object-recognition processes, which are much more independent of viewpoint and lighting than WISARD. Possible exceptions are recognition problems that require the separate identification of shapes within a category sharing the same overall shape, where changes in viewpoint and lighting may have significant effects (e.g. see Hill & Bruce, in press).

In its current implementation, the WISARD system does not depart radically from current conceptions of memory as highly *localised*, because each category that WISARD learns has its own portion of memory assigned to it. In the next section we consider pattern classifiers similarly based on the intensities of individual pixels, but using *distributed* representations.

RECOGNISING PATTERNS IN A PDP NETWORK

An approach that is proving of increasing interest to psychologists uses *distributed* memory networks (Hinton & Anderson, 1981; McClelland & Rumelhart, 1985, 1986; Rumelhart & McClelland, 1986). In such networks, an object category is represented by a pattern of activity across a number of elementary processing units, each of which might, for example, represent a different "feature" in the image. The difference between this scheme and one like Feldman's (see earlier) is that these different "feature" units never activate a discrete "object" node—rather, the object is represented as nothing but a pattern of activity across the more elementary nodes. Successive instances of the same or different categories can be encoded over the *same* set of elementary processing units. This can be achieved if the weights on the connections between units are suitably adjusted, and the particular models differ in the way in which this is achieved.

One class of model makes use of what has been termed a "Hebbian" learning rule (after a suggestion made by Donald Hebb in 1949) to reinforce certain connections at the expense of others. An example is provided by Kohonen's matrix memory model of pattern association (e.g. Kohonen, Lehtio, & Oja, 1981). In this model (see Fig. 10.9) there is a set of input units that are excited by a stimulus, and a set of output units that respond to these input patterns. All input units have connections to each output unit. The task of such a network is to learn to make distinct responses to each of a number of different patterns. This can be achieved if the weights between each input unit and each output unit are adjusted appropriately, becoming either more excitatory or more inhibitory, to reinforce connections that produce the desired responses to certain inputs. A simple Hebbian learning rule adjusts the weights on the connection between each input and output unit in proportion to the product of the input activity to that unit multiplied by its desired output activity. The desired output activity is given by presenting a "forcing stimulus" to the output units along with the input patterns. The network's task is to learn to recreate the different forcing stimulus patterns when later presented with input patterns alone. This completely local learning rule (which adjusts connection weights without taking account of activation anywhere else in the network) can fix the weights so that such a network can discriminate perfectly different input patterns provided these are "orthogonal" (orthogonality is a mathematical

FIGURE 10.9

A set of four input units that encode the stimulus pattern s_j connect to a set of four response units that produce the response pattern r_i according to the matrix of weights (m_{ij}) set on the connections between each input unit and each output unit. These weights are set by associating the stimulus patterns with "forcing stimuli" f_i using a Hebbian learning rule. Adapted from Kohonen et al. (1981).

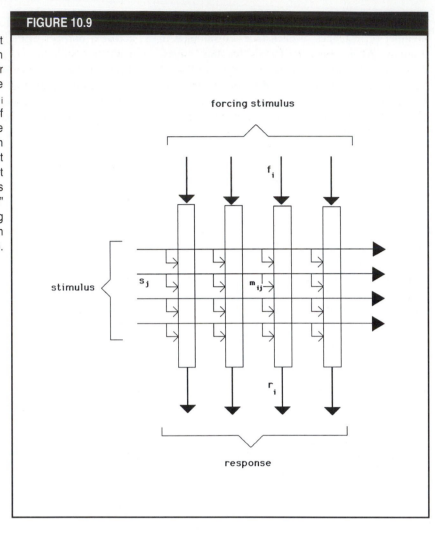

property related to linear independence). Even where patterns are not orthogonal, Kohonen has shown that there is a mathematical approximative technique for fixing the weights on the connections, which can allow such a network to learn different responses to different patterns. This technique is known as *optimal linear associative mapping* and details can be found in Kohonen et al. (1981).

To demonstrate the performance and properties of such a network, Kohonen et al. presented such a network with different views of each of 10 different faces. Each face was represented as a matrix of pixel intensity values, but this two-dimensional matrix was strung out into a single row to provide

a one-dimensional input pattern of intensity values, which could be any one of eight levels of grey. Views of the first face were associated with one response pattern (i.e. a "name" for that face), views of the second face were associated with a second response pattern, and so forth. The network was then tested with novel views of these same 10 individuals, which were within the range of training views but slightly different from any that had been seen. The responses given to these novel views were much more like the "correct" names for each face than they were like any of the other names. The important point here is that the faces themselves were not represented anywhere within the network. Learning consisted of adjusting the weights on connections so that the correct responses were given to test patterns in the future, and a single set of weights thereby encoded all faces.

In that example, each face was associated with a response pattern roughly analogous to a name. However, such networks can also function as "autoassociators" so that each face (or any other input pattern) can be associated with itself (i.e. the forcing stimulus pattern equals the input stimulus pattern). The result of such autoassociative learning is that, given a future input of only part of the stimulus pattern or a noisy version of the stimulus, the "intact" stimulus output pattern will be recreated, and Kohonen et al. (1981) also illustrate this performance using pictures of faces.

Even though such a simple pattern associator, based on "raw" pixel intensities, might seem somewhat implausible as a model of human face memory, recent research by O'Toole, Deffenbacher, Valentin, and Abdi (1994) and Hancock, Burton, and Bruce (1996) has shown that such a model gives a remarkably good account of human performance at recognising face patterns. (In fact, these groups used a technique called "Principal Components Analysis", which is

naturally implemented by such networks.) For example, O'Toole et al. (1994) showed that a pattern associator of this kind trained on Caucasian faces was less able to distinguish between new Japanese faces than between new Caucasian ones; and that faces that humans rated as more distinctive in appearance were better recognised by the network than ones that humans rated as more typical in appearance.

A rather different rule is used to adjust the weights in single-layer nets of the type described by McClelland and Rumelhart (1985), whose network functions in an *autoassociative* fashion. Consider a simple processing module comprising an (artificially) small number of processing units (see Fig. 10.10). Each unit in the network is connected to each other unit. Additionally, there is an input to each unit from the stimulus pattern, and an output or "response" from each unit. Each unit has a "resting" activation level of 0, and nonresting activations can range from −1 to +1. When a pattern is presented to the network (i.e one of a set of values ranging between −1 and +1 is input), each unit calculates its net input, which is the sum of its external input and the inputs it receives from all other units. The input from each other unit equals

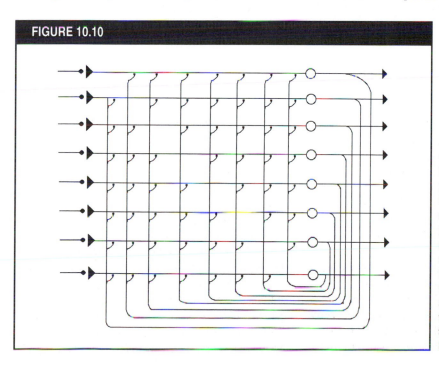

FIGURE 10.10

A set of eight processing units that receive external inputs (from stimulus patterns) and internal inputs from all other processing units. Connections between the units have weights that are set using the delta rule, so that after learning a partial input pattern will tend to recreate the pattern of activation created by the whole input pattern. Adapted from McClelland and Rumelhart (1985).

that unit's activity multiplied by the weight on the connection between that unit and the one whose net input is being calculated. As in all the models we have considered, connections can be positive (excitatory) or negative (inhibitory). When the net input to a unit has been calculated, its activity is updated—positively if its net input is positive and negatively if its net input is negative, although a decay factor also operates to counteract this trend by sending activities back towards zero. The altered activity of the unit will in turn affect the activities of other units in the net and so the network is initially in a fluctuating state. Eventually, however, a network will settle into a state where the activities on the units remain stable from one iteration (cycle of activity summation) to the next.

After this steady state has been reached, the weights on the connections between the units are changed in a direction so that subsequent inputs of part of this stimulus pattern will tend to recreate the entire stimulus pattern. This is done by fixing the *internal* weights to each unit so that the total internal input equals the *external* input from the stimulus pattern. The result is that when the external input to that particular unit is missing (as it might be if a partial pattern was presented) the unit behaves as though it were present. To do this each unit calculates the difference (Δ, or "delta") between its internal and external input, and the weight change from another unit to this one is proportional to the activity of that other unit multiplied by Δ. This learning rule is called the "delta rule".

McClelland and Rumelhart (1985) have shown how, in principle, a network exposed to patterns of features corresponding to different instances of a category could retain distinctions between the two different instances, while also learning the more general characteristics of the category from such examples. The patterns they use are simply sequences of +1s and −1s. If one of these patterns is called "Rover" and the other "Lassie", the problem is whether a network can learn the general characteristics of "dogs" from the examples, while at the same time retaining distinctions between the two "dogs'" identities. (NB. these simulations use hypothetical patterns, not actual pictures of dogs.)

They illustrate their system by describing a simple module of just 24 processing units. One set of units is dedicated to encoding the "object" patterns, another set to the names. For example, to mimic the learning of "dog" prototypes, the first 16 units were given variations on a basic prototype pattern of + and −1s. This prototype pattern was supposed to represent what is common to all dogs, while each presented instance actually learned by the network was some distortion of this basic pattern, which was itself never seen. The remaining eight units were given different (uncorrelated) patterns supposedly corresponding to the name of each of the different dogs that were learned. When later tested with a part of the prototype dog pattern (e.g. the first eight units) it will complete the prototype, i.e. its responses across the remaining eight units will tend to match the pattern for the rest of the prototype.

McClelland and Rumelhart go on to show how, in principle, the same network could learn *different* prototypes. In the example they choose, the network learns some patterns that are distortions around a "dog" prototype, other patterns that are distortions around a "cat" prototype, and a third set of patterns that are distortions around a "bagel" prototype. The dog and the cat pattern prototypes are not completely independent of each other (dogs and cats have some visual characteristics in common), whereas the bagel pattern prototype is completely independent (orthogonal) to that of the dog and the cat. As in the earlier example, the first 16 units were devoted to encoding these object patterns, whereas the last eight units encoded patterns corresponding to the object labels— "dog", "cat", and "bagel". The pattern for each category name was orthogonal to each of the other two, to reflect the fact that although dog and cat visual shapes may be related, their names are not. After training on a series of hypothetical dog, cat, and bagel instances produced from distortions on the dog, cat, and bagel prototypes, the network can be tested by presenting each of the category prototypical visual patterns (the first 16 units) or names (last eight units). The results obtained from such a simulation are shown in Table 10.1, where we see that presenting the pattern or name of each category leads to completion of the appropriate

TABLE 10.1

Pattern Recognition by a PDP Network

	Visual pattern	Name pattern
Prototype Dog:	+ − + + − − − − + + + + + − − −	+ 5 − + − + − + −
Response to dog name:	+ 3 − 4 + 4 + 4 − 4 − 4 − 4 − 4 + 4 + 4 + 4 + 3 + 4 − 4 − 4 − 3	
Response to dog visual pattern:		+ 5 − 4 + 4 − 5 + 5 − 4 + 4 − 4
Prototype Cat:	+ − + + − − − − + − + − + + − +	+ + − − + + − −
Response to cat name:	+ 4 − 3 + 4 + 4 − 4 − 3 − 3 − 4 + 4 − 4 + 4 − 4 + 4 + 4 − 4 + 4	
Response to cat visual pattern:		+ 5 + 4 − 4 − 5 + 4 + 4 − 4 − 4
Prototype bagel:	+ + − + − + + − + − − + + + + −	+ − − + + − − +
Response to bagel name:	+ 3 + 4 − 4 + 4 − 4 + 4 + 4 − 4 + 4 − 4 − 4 + 4 + 3 + 4 + 4 − 4	
Response to bagel visual pattern:		+ 4 − 4 − 4 + 4 + 4 − 4 − 4 + 4

The results of tests after learning hypothetical exemplars of the categories "dog", "cat", and "bagel". The prototype patterns are a series of + or − 1s (shown as + or − without the 1). The decimal points in the responses have been omitted for clarity—an entry of +4 represents an activation of +0.4. Adapted from McClelland and Rumelhart (1985).

pattern of activation in the remaining units, although at decreased strength.

A network of this kind can not only extract the general characteristics of the different categories to which it is exposed ("Lassie", "Rover", "dog") but it also retains sensitivity to the patterns corresponding to particular recent or repeated instances. It will respond strongly to complete the "prototypical" Lassie, but will also respond more strongly to complete a recently or repeatedly encountered view of Lassie than to a novel or less recent view.

This ability both to extract the defining characteristics of concepts and to retain details of particular instances of them is a characteristic of human recognition. Most of the object recognition research we discussed in Chapter 9 concentrated on the problem of how we recognise that an object is, say, a dog, irrespective of its viewpoint. However, people do not just classify the instances of objects they recognise, they can also retain their individuating aspects in memory. For example, in repetition priming experiments, subjects are able to recognise a particular known object at a shorter tachistoscopic exposure, or name it more quickly, if that object has been seen recently (Biederman & Cooper, 1991; Biederman & Gerhardstein, 1993; Warren & Morton, 1982; see Ch.9, p.224). In repetition priming experiments, maximum priming is generally found when identical views of an object are repeated in the test phase, and reduced priming is found when views are different (e.g. Biederman & Gerhardstein, 1993; for related experiments using faces, see also Bruce & Valentine, 1985; Ellis, Young, Flude, & Hay, 1987). An account of object recognition in which prototypical object descriptions emerge from the superposition of all encountered instances might account for such effects. Such "instance-based" models need not be couched in parallel distributed processing terms (e.g. Hintzman, 1986), but it is the PDP versions of instance-based models that have attracted most attention.

However, these simple examples of "single-layer" networks (where there is a single layer of units between input and response) have serious limitations as accounts of human pattern recognition because it can be proved that they cannot learn certain kinds of pattern categories. For example, such nets cannot learn to respond one way if "A" or "B" are present but not if both A and B or neither A nor B are present (the "exclusive or" condition) (Minsky & Papert, 1969). However, networks with more than one layer can overcome these difficulties, provided that suitable learning rules can be devised. The "generalised delta rule", which employs a technique called "back-propagation of errors", provides one solution to this learning problem to allow a multi-layer network, with a layer of "hidden units" between input and output, to learn pattern classifications (Rumelhart, Hinton, & Williams, 1986). In such learning schemes activation from the input layer is generally squeezed through a narrow bottleneck of hidden units, where there are significantly fewer of these than input or output units. Such hidden units acquire interesting properties, appearing to make explicit abstract "features" of their inputs (e.g. Hinton, 1986, 1989). Other solutions for learning in multi-layer nets include competitive learning (Rumelhart & Zipser, 1986) and simulated annealing (Hinton &

Sejnowski, 1986). The interested reader is referred to these papers for details of such systems, which are beyond the scope of this introduction (see also the review by Hinton, 1989; and a review of different connectionist methods applied to face recognition by Valentin, Abdi, O'Toole, & Cottrell, 1994).

The "parallel distributed processing" models of object recognition clearly have some interesting properties that make them attractive as theories of human recognition processes. One weakness of such demonstrations at present is that with some exceptions (particularly with faces) they have generally not been applied to real objects. It is assumed that "Fido" is represented as a set of activities across a set of unknown encoding dimensions or features, and such assumptions beg many of the interesting questions about perception, questions that have been tackled more satisfactorily within the kind of computational framework proposed by Marr. Where distributed memory models have been tested on pictures rather than arbitrary sets of features, they have generally taken as their input raw pixel values (e.g. Kohonen et al., 1981) rather than the oriented edge segments or blobs that seem to be delivered by the early stages of human vision. At the very least we would want to see such simple associative networks accessed by inputs more closely resembling the outputs of early visual processing.

CONNECTIONIST MODELS OF PHYSIOLOGICAL PROCESSES

In recent years there has been a rapid development of connectionist models of the *physiological* organisation of visual pathways in the brain. Although connectionist models are constructed from units and connections that look like neurons and synapses, it is important to treat this similarity cautiously. The models are based on assumptions about patterns of neural connections and the ways synapses are modified, and different models are based on different assumptions (for example, Hebbian and delta learning rules), which cannot yet be properly tested against physiological evidence.

One interesting recent approach, however, has been to set up connectionist models and then compare the properties that model units develop through training with the properties of single cells in a part of the visual system. The reasoning involved is that similarities in the behaviour of units and of cells suggest that the cells are wired up in the way specified by the model.

Linsker (1986a,b,c) investigated a multi-layer network in which there is a basic spatial structure so that inputs to a unit in layer n + 1 tend (according to a Gaussian distribution) to come from nearby units in layer n. An unsupervised Hebbian learning procedure (in which there is no forcing stimulus, so that there is no model response for the system to learn) operates on initially random inputs. After learning, the network produces an impressive range of properties of receptive fields early in the visual system, including centre-surround fields in an early layer and orientation-tuned fields and orientation columns in later ones. The implication is that much of the regularity of structure and function in the visual pathway may arise from the operation of a relatively simple mechanism governing the growth of synapses.

Further support for this hypothesis is provided by Berns, Dayan, and Sejnowski's (1993) connectionist model of the development of disparity selectivity in the visual cortex, in which connections between retinal ganglion and cortical cells develop following a Hebbian learning rule. The model comprised two one-dimensional input layers (the two retinas), with a full set of modifiable excitatory connections, to a single one-dimensional layer of the same size, representing the cortex. The cortical layer also included fixed lateral connections. During training the correlations between the activities within and between each retina were varied. If the model was trained only with activities that were correlated within each retina, then the units in the cortical layer became strongly "monocular"—i.e. excited by units from one or the other but not both retinas. If the model was trained only with activities that were correlated between the two retinas, then the cortical units became strongly binocular, and were activated most by retinal activities of zero spatial disparity. However, if the model was trained first with a phase of within-retina correlations and then with a phase of between-retina correlated activity, then the cortical layer comprised a mixture of "monocular" units, tending to be driven strongly by input from one of the two retinas with nonzero disparities, and "binocular" units, activated by corresponding (zero disparity) units in the two retinas. Berns et al. argue that this two-phase training is analogous to the patterns of correlated activity that would be experienced pre- and post-natally, and that the resulting mixture of monocular and binocular cortical units correspond to the kind of distribution found in the cat primary visual cortex. Obermayer, Sejnowski, and Blasdel (1995) have taken a similar approach, using competitive Hebbian mechanisms to generate cortical topographic maps showing orientation preferences and ocular dominance corresponding to those found in cat visual cortex.

Connectionist modelling has therefore been useful in developing theories of how the organisation of the first stages of the visual pathway is established during development, and it has also been applied to higher levels in the pathway. We saw in Chapter 3 (p.62) evidence that the inferotemporal cortex plays a role in object recognition, and Rolls (e.g. 1987, 1992) has modelled population coding in this area using a pattern recognition net similar to that of Kohonen et al. (1981). An important property of the model is that the selectivity of individual units for input patterns represents a trade-off between two requirements. If selectivity is too low, interference between different inputs arises, whereas if it is too high, generalisation and pattern completion are prevented. This theoretical expectation of units with an optimal intermediate selectivity for patterns is matched, Rolls argues, by the breadth of tuning observed in face-selective neurons (see Ch.3, p.62). Furthermore, Rolls suggests that these units may acquire their properties through a simple, unsupervised competitive learning procedure (cf. Rumelhart & Zipser, 1986).

Two other examples of this approach, using models that incorporate back-propagation algorithms, are provided by Lekhy and Sejnowski (1988) and Zipser and Andersen (1988). In the first study, a network trained to recognise the curvatures of simple geometrical surfaces from patterns of shading in their images generated hidden units that responded to bar and edge patterns and were selective for their orientation, in the same way as cells in the striate cortex. Zipser and Andersen's model was trained to convert an input specifying eye position and the retinal location of a stimulus to an output giving its location in head-centred coordinates. Here the properties of the hidden units came to resemble those of cells in area 7a (Andersen et al., 1985; see Ch.7, p.169).

Demonstrations of this kind provide powerful hypotheses about the organisation and function of regions of the visual pathway, but further physiological evidence is required to test them. In the case of models using back-propagation algorithms, there is the particular problem of finding a way in which these could be implemented physiologically. Although this cannot be done by transmitting error signals back down a nerve cell axon, it is possible that it may be achieved through some mechanism involving the feedback pathways between cortical areas. For example, Becker and Hinton (1992) describe the interesting possibility that back-propagation could be based not on an external "teacher" but on the maximisation of agreement between different signals arising from different processing modules (e.g. vision and audition) or from different units analysing adjacent regions of the same retinal image. They provide an example from stereopsis, constructing a model that can solve random-dot stereograms in this way, by maximising agreement between modules looking at adjacent regions of the input patterns. This is a rather clear example of a connectionist model operating by incorporating general constraints from the world, very much in the spirit of Marr and Poggio's earlier work (see C.7, p.146). Moreover, the cross-module comparisons that they propose in the context of learning are clearly related to other proposals about synchronisation of activity between different processing modules in the visual pathway we discussed in Chapter 3 (p.63).

CONCLUSIONS

Connectionist models are yielding exciting results at present, and we anticipate continuing rapid progress over the next few years. One important wider issue is the relationship between connectionist theories and theories that involve the explicit construction of a *symbolic* representation of the visual world. Whereas some claim that connectionist models pose a fundamental challenge to conventional cognitive science, our own feeling is that developments in connectionist theory will complement (rather than challenge fundamentally) symbol-processing theories such as Marr's. For example, Hummel and Biederman's (1992) connectionist model of Biederman's theory of "recognition by components" is a natural implementation of a model that was originally described at a more abstract level of theory (see Chapter 9). We have also seen how Marr and Poggio's (1976) stereo algorithm is a good example of how a connectionist network might satisfy different constraints simultaneously. In neither of these examples does the connectionist model present a challenge to the symbol-processing perspective that spawned it, and within which issues of computational theory and representational primitives were initially addressed. Similarly, it seems to us that parallel distributed models in particular provide a potentially powerful way to investigate the acquisition of "abstract" structural descriptions for object recognition. Connectionist models complement conventional models by addressing issues at a different level, one that is closer to Marr's notion of the "implementation" level of theory. This view is itself controversial, however, and the debate here focuses on the nature of representations constructed in traditional symbol-processing compared with connectionist modelling, a debate on which we elaborate in Chapter 17.

So far in this book we have analysed how a human or other animal interprets a particular retinal image by constructing from it a representation of the scene being viewed. Most perception, however, particularly in simple animals, has an immediate consequence in terms of the animal's subsequent actions. One attractive feature of the connectionist models we have introduced briefly is that it

becomes quite natural to consider how perception is translated into action as the models themselves are couched in terms of translations between stimuli and responses (e.g. see Tononi et al., 1992). This question of how perceptual processes contribute to the organisation of action is a major theme of the next part of this book.

Part III

Visual Information for the Control of Action

11

Introduction to the Ecological Approach to Visual Perception

In the second part of this book we sketched an explanation of how an account of form, space, and movement perception could be given in terms of the conventional starting point of the retinal image. The impression gained is that visual perception must involve large amounts of computation from instant to instant—building elaborate symbolic descriptions from primitive assertions, inferring distances from a variety of cues, taking account of signals to move eyes, and so on. The slightly different images reaching the two eyes must be combined to form a single three-dimensional percept, and views of the world glimpsed at different moments must also be integrated to result in the perception of a stable world.

In this part of the book we consider a rather different framework for visual perception. The alternative, "ecological", approach emphasises the information that may be available in extended spatial and temporal pattern in the optic array, to guide the actions of animals and people, and to specify events of importance or interest. For the moment, we may regard the two approaches as complementary, with the "ecological" framework operating at a more global level of analysis than the computational accounts we have been considering

until now. However, many of those working within the ecological framework regard their theoretical orientation as antithetical to that of information-processing theorists such as Marr. Inevitably we must confront some of these differences, although we leave the details of the arguments until Chapter 17.

The ecological approach to visual space perception was developed over a 35-year period by J.J. Gibson (Gibson, 1950a, 1966, 1979; see also Reed & Jones, 1982). Gibson's theory of perception takes as its starting point not a "retinal image", which is passively sensed, but the ambient optic array, which an observer actively samples. In Chapter 1 we introduced the notion of an optic array and described how eyes have evolved to detect the spatial and temporal pattern contained within it. Gibson maintains that it is flow and disturbances in the structure of the total optic array, rather than bars, blobs, or forms in an "image", which provide the information for perception that unambiguously informs the observer both about the world and about him- or herself simultaneously. In this ecological approach, perception and action are seen as tightly interlocked and mutually constraining. More controversially, Gibson's is a "direct" theory of perception, in which he maintains that information is "picked up" rather than "processed". Before we embark on an introduction to Gibson's ideas, we should state that we disagree with his notion of "direct perception" in its strong form. Nevertheless, we feel that his theory has been important in inspiring some fascinating research, in which optical variables of higher order than local intensity values have been taken as the input to vision, and shown to provide important sources of information for the control of action (Chapters 12, 13, and 14), and the apprehension of events (Chapters 15 and 16). We think it appropriate to devote this chapter to a description of why and how Gibson developed his theory, before going on to make use of some of his ideas in the remaining chapters of this section.

J.J. GIBSON'S THEORY OF PERCEPTION

During World War II Gibson addressed himself to the problem of how to train pilots quickly, or how to discriminate potentially successful from unsuccessful pilots prior to training. The most difficult, and hence dangerous, aspects of flying are landing and take-off. To land a plane successfully you must know where you are located relative to the air strip, your angle of approach, and know how to modify your approach so that you are aiming for the right position at the right speed. Gibson felt therefore that good depth perception was likely to be a prerequisite of good flying. He discovered, however, that tests based on the pictorial cues to depth, and training measures devised to make people capitalise on depth information, had little success when applied to the problem of training pilots. Here was a clear practical example of the perception of relative distance, and yet attempts to improve "depth perception" were fruitless.

Such observations led Gibson to reformulate his views of visual perception radically. In his 1950 book he began by suggesting that the classical approach to "depth" or "space" perception be replaced by an approach that emphasised the perception of *surfaces* in the *environment*. This

emphasis remained throughout his subsequent books. Gibson's theory emphasises the *ground* on which an animal lives and moves around, or above which an insect, bird, or pilot flies. The ground consists of surfaces at different distances and slants. The surfaces are composed of texture elements. Pebbles, grains of sand, or blades of grass are all elements of texture which, although not identical, possess statistical regularity—the average size and spacing of elements of the same kind of texture will remain roughly constant for different samples. Some surfaces surround objects, and these objects may be attached to the ground (rocks, trees), or detached and independently mobile (animals). Object surfaces, like ground surfaces, have texture. The environment thus consists of textured surfaces that are themselves immersed in a medium (air). Gibson argues that we need an appropriate geometry to describe the environment, which will not necessarily be one based on abstractions such as "points" and "planes", as conventional geometries are. An ecological geometry must take surfaces and texture elements as its starting point.

> A surface is substantial; a plane is not. A surface is textured; a plane is not. A surface is never perfectly transparent; a plane is. A surface can be seen; a plane can only be visualized (Gibson, 1979, p.35).

The structure that exists in the surfaces of the environment in turn structures the light that reaches an observer; we saw simple examples of this in Chapter 1. Gibson argues that it is the structure in the light, rather than stimulation by light, that furnishes information for visual perception. Stimulation *per se* does not lead to perception, as evidenced by perceptual experience in a Ganzfeld (Gibson & Dibble, 1952; Gibson & Waddell, 1952; Metzger, 1930). Diffuse unstructured light, as might be obtained by placing halves of table-tennis balls over the eyes and sitting in a bright room, produces perception of nothingness. To perceive things, rather than no-thing, the light must be structured. In order to describe the structure in light we need an "ecological" optics (Gibson, 1961), rather than a description at the level of the physics of photons, waves, and so on. The physics of photons coupled with the biochemistry of photoreceptor action can be used to explain how light is emitted and propagated and how receptors are stimulated by it, but not how the world is perceived. An ecological optics must cut across the boundaries between physical and physiological optics and the psychology of perception.

Gibson rejected the claim that the retinal image is the starting point for visual processing. Gibson argued that it is the total array of light beams reaching an observer, after structuring by surfaces and objects in the world, that provides direct information about the layout of those surfaces and objects, and about movement within the world and by the observer. Gibson pointed out that the total optic array contains information over space and time that unambiguously specifies layout and events. In Chapter 1 we described how light is structured in the optic array, and here we remind you briefly of the important points.

The ambient optic array at any point above the ground consists of an innumerable collection of light rays of different wavelengths and intensities. Some have been reflected by air particles, others by the surfaces in the world. These rays form a hierarchical and overlapping set of solid angles. The solid angles corresponding to the tiniest texture elements are nested within those that correspond to the boundaries of larger regions or objects. Changes in the pattern or properties of the light from one solid angle to another signal boundaries in the world, where, for example, one object partially conceals or occludes another object, or the ground.

Gibson maintained that the optic array contained *invariant* information about the world, in the form of higher-order variables, where traditional psychologists saw ambiguity and insufficiency in the retinal image. An example of an invariant is given by Sedgwick's (1973) "horizon ratio relation". The horizon "intersects" an object at a particular height, and Sedgwick showed that all objects of the same height, whatever their distance, are cut by the horizon in the same ratio. Further examples of invariants, and a fuller discussion of the concept, can be found in Cutting (1986).

An observer's task is to detect such invariant information by actively sampling the dynamic optic array. For example, the gradient of image size provided by the light reflected from textured surfaces receding away from an observer provides a continuous metric of the visual world. The rate of change of texture density, Gibson claims, can be detected directly, and unambiguously specifies the layout of surfaces in the world. In Chapter 7 we considered gradients of texture as one "cue" for depth perception. For Gibson, they are of more fundamental importance. Figure 11.1 shows examples of how texture gradients (of artificially regular proportions) can give impressions of surfaces receding into the distance. Figure 11.2 shows how the local shape of a surface may be given by the change in texture gradient.

Gibson and co-workers (Beck & Gibson, 1955; Gibson, 1950b; Gibson & Cornsweet, 1952) have shown that changes in phenomenal slant are produced by changes in texture density gradients in viewed images, although the relationship between the two is not straightforward. Phenomenal slant is proportional to, but less than, actual slant. Gibson (e.g. 1975) later criticised these experiments on the grounds that they studied optical slant, i.e. the perceived slant about a plane

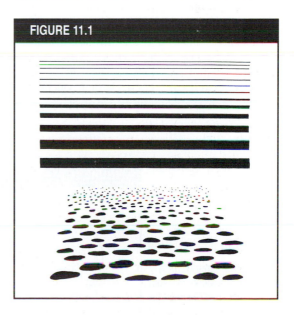

FIGURE 11.1

Examples of texture density gradients.

FIGURE 11.2

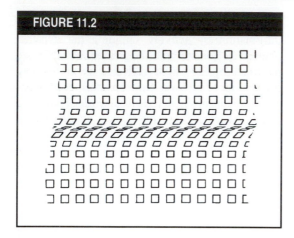

Surface shape and slant can be revealed by texture.

perpendicular to the line of sight, rather than geographical slant—that relative to the ground surface. Hence the observer's task was not ecologically valid.

Surfaces that are flat and receding, or that are curved, are characterised by a number of texture gradients. One is in the *density* of texture elements; in a receding surface, the number of elements per unit of solid visual angle increases with distance. Others are the *perspective* and *compression* gradients, defined by changes in the width and height, respectively, of the projections of texture elements in an image plane. In a receding surface, these both decrease with distance. Perspective and compression gradients have proved to be more important than density gradients in producing the impression of a receding surface in displays, and in distinguishing flat and curved surfaces (Cutting & Millard, 1984).

Gibson originally termed his theory a "ground" theory of perception (Gibson, 1950a) in contrast with traditional "air" theories. In Gibson's view, the perception of objects should never be considered in isolation from the background texture on which they lie. Take the example of an observer viewing an object at a certain distance. Traditional "simplification" of this situation would lead to the schematisation in Fig. 11.3—where we can see that the same image could potentially be cast by an infinite number of objects of different sizes, inclinations, and distances from the observer. Gibson (1950a) called this kind of theory an "air" theory of visual perception because images are discussed as though cast by artificially smooth objects devoid of any background.

Gibsonian optics would depict the situation rather differently. Rather than considering an image cast by, for example, a tree suspended in a perceptual vacuum, Gibson would consider the total array of light reaching the observer. Assuming for the moment a stationary eye and world, the optic array would contain information about a continuous ground receding from the observer in the form of a texture density gradient. The size of this particular tree would be given by the amount of texture it conceals. As a tree itself has texture, the fact that the tree is vertical, rather than inclined away from or towards the observer would also be specified by the lack of change in the texture density in the relevant portion of the optic array, that corresponding to the tree's trunk. Thus this particular pattern of light unambiguously specifies a tree of a particular size at a particular distance.

FIGURE 11.3

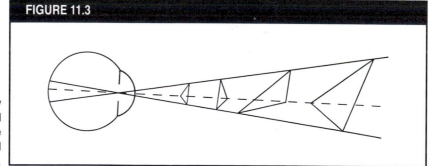

The kind of drawing typically used by students of visual perception to illustrate the ambiguity of the retinal image.

Distance therefore is *not* a line endwise to the eye as Bishop Berkeley thought. To think so is to confuse abstract geometrical space with the living space of the environment. It is to confuse the Z-axis of a Cartesian co-ordinate system with the number of paces along the ground to a fixed object (Gibson, 1979, p.117).

Gibson sees the important information about the layout of surfaces (he rejects the term "space" perception) as coming from a variety of gradients of information in the optic array, and gradients of texture, colour, brightness, and disparity are all mentioned. However, it is misleading to consider the information available to such a "static" observer, as Gibson believes that movement is *essential* for seeing.

What is clear to me now that was not clear before is that structure as such, frozen structure, is a myth, or at least a limiting case. Invariants of structure do not exist except in relation to variants (Gibson, 1979, p.87).

Variants in information are produced by movement of the observer and the motion of objects in the world. The fact that observers *actively* explore their world allows powerful information from *motion* perspective to tell them both about their position relative to structures in the world and about their own movements. When an observer moves (as in Fig. 11.4), the entire optic array is transformed. Such transformations none the less contain information both about the layout and shapes of objects and surfaces in the world, and about the observer's movement relative to the world.

Perception of the world and of the self go together and only occur over time (Gibson, 1975, p.49).

Figure 11.5 shows an example of motion perspective. As an observer walks past a collection of objects at different distances the relative motions present in the changing optic array will be specifically correlated with the layout of such objects. Indeed, as an observer moves in any way

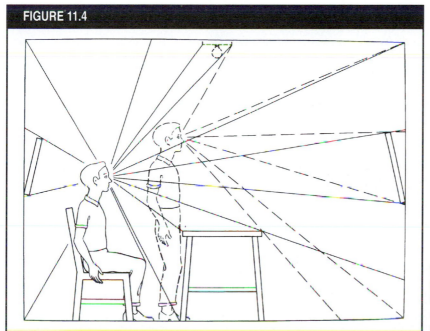

FIGURE 11.4

When an observer moves the entire optic array is transformed. From Gibson (1966). Used by permission of Houghton Mifflin Company.

FIGURE 11.5

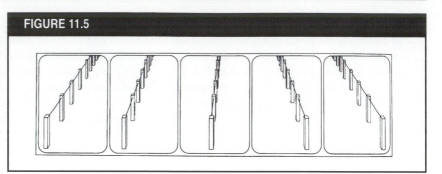

Successive views of a row of fence posts as an observer moves past them. The observer travels from right to left between each of the frames from left to right. From Gibson (1950a). Used by permission of Houghton Mifflin Company.

in the world this locomotion will always be accompanied by *flow* in the optic array. The nature of optic flow patterns is specific to certain types of movement (see Figs. 11.6–11.8). If a pilot is trying to land an aeroplane (Fig. 11.6) there will be streaming in the optic array radiating out from the point at which he is aiming. This point is known as the pole of the optic flow field. The array of optical texture elements (produced by light reflected from the texture elements in the world) expands centrifugally, with elements successively passing out of the bounded visual field of the observer and new elements emerging at the pole. If one was sitting on the roof of a train facing backwards there would be a continuous inward streaming of optical texture elements towards the point from which one

was travelling (Fig. 11.7). If you chose the softer option of remaining seated at a train window the flow pattern would be as in Fig. 11.8.

Gibson (1979) described the relationship between optic flow and locomotion more formally in the following way (abridged from Gibson, 1979, pp.227–229):

1. Flow of the ambient array specifies locomotion and nonflow specifies stasis.
2. Outflow specifies approach and inflow specifies retreat from.
3. The focus or centre of outflow specifies the direction of locomotion in the environment.
4. A shift of the centre of outflow from one visual solid angle to another specifies a change in the

FIGURE 11.6

The optic flow field for a pilot landing an aeroplane. From Gibson (1950a). Used by permission of Houghton Mifflin Company.

FIGURE 11.7

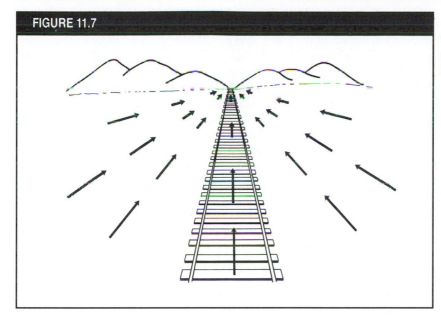

The optic flow field for a person sitting on the roof of a train, facing backwards.

direction of locomotion, a turn, and a remaining of the centre within the same solid angle specifies no change in direction.

That flow in the optic array may be sufficient to specify observer movement is dramatically demonstrated by the fairground amusement called the haunted swing. Here a person is seated in a stationary swing while the room rotates around them. The optical information is identical to that which would be produced if the observer, rather than the room, were being spun, and the subjective impression for the observer is the same—only by closing their eyes can they escape the nauseating sensation of being turned head over heels. In the next two chapters we will discuss in more detail

FIGURE 11.8

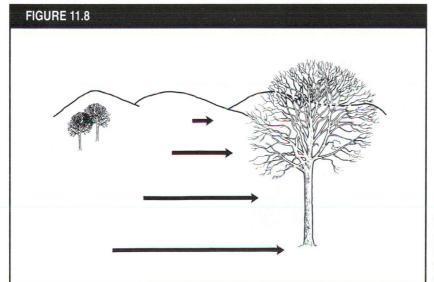

The optic flow field for a person sitting in a train and looking out of the window as they travel from right to left through this terrain.

how optical flow patterns may be used to inform animals and people of their actions in the world.

The fundamental importance of observer movement in Gibson's perceptual theory is reinforced by his notion of perceptual systems to contrast with the traditional "senses". Gibson (1966, 1979) claimed that it was an entire *perceptual system* whose job it is to "see" (1979, p.53).

> Receptors are *stimulated* whereas an organ is *activated* … the eye is part of a dual organ, one of a pair of eyes, and they are set in a head that can turn, attached to a body that can move from place to place. These organs make a hierarchy and constitute what I have called a *perceptual system*.

Movement by the observer, whether of body, head, or eyes, is one way in which variant information is obtained. The other way is through motion or change in objects in the world, i.e. through *events*. Events include objects or animals translating, rotating, colliding or growing, changing colour or disappearing. All such events are accompanied by disturbances in the structure of the optic array. Rigid translation of an object across the field of view involves the progressive accretion, deletion, and shearing of texture elements. An object will progressively cover up (or "wipe out") texture elements in the direction of its movement, uncover (or "unwipe") them from behind, and shear the elements crossed by the edges parallel to its movement (see Fig. 11.9). If the object changes its distance from the observer this change will be accompanied by magnification (if approaching) or minification (if receding) of the texture elements of its own surface, and the covering up or uncovering of texture elements of the background. Texture elements that are covered up by object motion in one direction are uncovered by motion in the reverse direction. The same is true of observer movement. Texture elements that pass out of the observer's view when movement is in one direction will reappear if the movement is reversed. Gibson claims that this principle of *reversible occlusion* underlies the observer's impression of a constant and stable visual world where even those surfaces momentarily hidden are still "perceived".

Once one considers the total array of light there is no ambiguity about whether it is oneself or objects in the world that are moving. Eye movements do not change the structure of the ambient optic array, they simply allow a different portion of the array to be sampled. Movement of the head and body is always accompanied by a systematic flow pattern in the total array. Movement of an object within the world produces local disturbances in the structure of the array. Thus the major distinction between movement within the world or on behalf of the observer can be specified unambiguously by different flow patterns in the optic array. Note that Stevens et al. (1976; see Ch.7, p.166) also discussed how different patterns of motion in the entire retinal mosaic could be used to disambiguate motion perception,

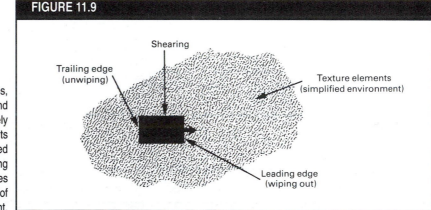

FIGURE 11.9

Shearing

Trailing edge (unwiping)

Texture elements (simplified environment)

Leading edge (wiping out)

As an object moves, elements of background texture are progressively wiped out (covered up) by its leading edge, unwiped (revealed) by its trailing edge, and sheared by edges parallel to its direction of movement.

although the details of their argument are quite different from Gibson's.

Gibson's approach to the psychology of perception became progressively more radical. Whereas in his 1950 book his major aim seemed to be to consider the nature of the visual information in the optic array within a psychophysical framework, in his later work (Gibson, 1966, 1979) he became more interested in defining a totally new approach to perception. In the ecological approach to perception the animal and environment are viewed as intimately interlinked. The end-product of perception is not seen as an internal representation of the visual world—a "percept". Rather the animal is seen as detecting *affordances*. The affordance of some surface or object in the environment is what it offers the animal—whether it can be grasped or eaten, trodden on, or sat on. The notion of an affordance can be traced back to the Gestalt psychologists, and particularly Koffka's idea of the "demand character" of an object (Koffka, 1935, p.7).

> To primitive man each thing says what it is and what he ought to do with it … a fruit says "Eat me"; water says "Drink me"; thunder says "Fear me".

A sawn-off tree trunk of the right flatness and size affords "sitting-on" for a human, or "hopping-on" for a frog; if a surface is flat, extended, and substantial, its property of affording support to terrestrial animals is implicitly given. Gibson makes the strong claim that there is information in the light to specify the affordances of the environment (Gibson, 1979, p.127).

> This is a radical hypothesis, for it implies that the "values" and "meanings" of things in the environment can be directly perceived.

A detailed illustration of the concept of affordance is provided by Warren (1984), who studied people's judgements of whether staircases with differently proportioned steps, depicted in pictures, could be climbed in the normal way or not. Subjects taller and shorter than average differed in their judgements, which proved to be determined by the ratio of step height to the individual subject's leg length. Warren's subjects were therefore sensitive to the affordance of "climbability", but the results cannot tell us whether this is perceived directly or not. Gibson would have argued that an invariant property of the pattern of light reflected from a staircase that specifies "climbability" is picked up directly, but it could equally well be that inferential processes are involved in computing the three-dimensional structure of the steps and in relating their dimensions to information about stride length held in memory.

Although it is relatively easy to appreciate that affordances like "supporting" or "graspable" might be specified in the optic array, it is much less easy to appreciate how qualities such as "eatable" or "writable-with" could be contained within the light. At the point where Gibson claims that a letter-box affords the posting of letters by humans of western culture, his theory is the most controversial. Nevertheless, the concept of affordances provides a powerful way to bridge the gap that exists in more cognitive theories between "perception" and "action". Within the theory of affordances, perception is an invitation to act, and action is an essential component of perception. However, Gibson's claim that all of perception can be understood without appeal to linguistic or cultural mediation is problematic, and we will return to this issue later.

Gibson thus asserts that optical information specifies surfaces of support, falling-off places, impending collision, and so on. And, he claims, affordances are perceived directly, without the need for mediation by cognitive processes. The major task for the ecological psychologist is to discover the invariant information that animals have evolved to detect, and to discover the mechanisms by which they become attuned to this information. Gibson denies the need for "memory" in explaining perception. Incoming percepts are not matched against previously laid down traces, rather the perceptual system has evolved to "resonate" to certain invariant information. The concept of "resonance" is left rather vague by Gibson. For our purposes it is sufficient to stress that the theory suggests that there should be receptors or receptor networks that should be sensitive to variables of higher order than "features" such as lines and edges.

Gibson decries the traditional laboratory experiment in perception in which observers are presented with "stimuli", devoid of context. In such situations the optical information is indeed impoverished but this will only tell us how a human observer copes with artificially impoverished inputs, and may tell us nothing of perception in the optically rich real environment. He denies that ambiguous figures and illusions should be the starting point for a psychology of perception. Although these may be interesting, and may be analysed in terms of the invariant information that they contain, they are not characteristic of normal perception. In the real world such perceptual distortions are rare. Additionally, Gibson regards the perception of *pictures* (the focus of much research in perception) as involving two components—the direct perception of the picture as a picture, i.e. as a flat surface, and the indirect perception of what it is that the picture represents. The picture of an apple, for example, as a flat surface, affords little apart from inspection. The affordances of the object depicted, the fact that it is an apple, can be grasped, thrown, and eaten, are perceived indirectly and without ever fooling an adult observer into actually trying to reach for and eat the picture. Everyday perception is of the "direct", not the "indirect" kind.

Perhaps the best way to illustrate the difference between the approach of Gibson and his students and that of other perceptual theorists is to contrast their explanations of three specific topics. We have already seen how the problem of whether oneself or objects in the world are moving is dealt with by Gibson, but what about other "problems" in perception?

Size constancy

Perceptual constancies have often been used to demonstrate the indirect and inferential nature of seeing. An object at distance $2x$ metres from an observer casts an image on the retina that is half the height of the image cast by that same object at distance x metres from the observer, and we have already seen (in Chapter 7) how relative size of retinal images may be thought of as a "cue" for the perception of depth. However, if you watch a friend walk down the street he or she does not appear to shrink to half size each time their distance from you doubles. Our perception of the sizes of objects is remarkably constant, provided the distances are not too great.

The traditional view of this phenomenon is that the brain must take account of the perceived distance of objects (as given by various cues) and scale perceptual size up accordingly. The consequence of this is paradoxical. Whereas relative image size may act as a cue to distance, the distance thus assessed is then used to judge the apparent size of the viewed object. Gibson views the problem differently. Because, he argues, texture gradients provide a continuous and constant scale for the perception of the world, there is no problem of size-constancy scaling. The size of any object is given by the scale of the background at the point where the object is attached (Gibson, 1950a).

Size constancy breaks down over large distances. In the laboratory, perceived size tends towards image size, but Gibson (1947) showed that in an open, ploughed (and hence textured) field, estimates of the height of a distant stake merely became more variable at great distance rather than the error being in one direction. Size constancy also fails if we view objects from a height, rather than at a horizontal distance. Thus, from the top of a high building people on the pavement below us appear insect-like in their proportions. Traditional theory would explain this in terms of the absence of cues to distance. Gibson would say that when viewing from a height, the absence of the ground removes the continuous scale of texture necessary for accurate size perception.

Stereopsis

In Chapter 7 the reader was introduced to the problems associated with matching two disparate images into single three-dimensional percepts. It was suggested that global stereopsis was achieved on the basis of large numbers of computations and comparisons at a local level. Students of Gibson (e.g. Michaels, 1978) deny that visual perception involves the matching of two distinct images. No one has ever suggested that tactile perception involves such a synthetic step—yet when one feels an object under a cloth, each hand must obtain a quite different tactile impression. It has always been implicitly assumed that we know objects directly by touch, and yet logically the problem of the resulting "singleness" of tactile perception is the same. Therefore, if tactile images need not be compared and integrated, why consider binocular vision to involve the comparison and fusion of two retinal "pictures"? Michaels and Carello (1981) feel that perceptual theory has been misled by the camera metaphor (p.119).

> Just as Gibson took issue with the idea of discrete retinal snapshots, we will take issue with the supposition that the information has two parts, one to each eye, and that these two parts require fusion. And, just as he found it more convenient to consider the information for monocular motion perception to be transformations over a third dimension (time), we might reconsider binocular information in terms of transformations over a third dimension of space … Transformations over time describe the successive order of an optic array and so constitute monocular kinetic information. Similarly, transformations over space describe the adjacent order of two arrays and constitute binocular static information— what will be called the binocular array.

In these terms the task of the ecological perceptual theorist is to understand the invariant information obtained by binocularity, i.e. in the transformations that obtain from one eye's view to the other. It is claimed that invariants can be shown to specify the distances of objects, to remove the ambiguity of monocular shape information, and can specify the shapes and sizes of particular objects (Michaels, 1978).

Motion perception

As we have seen, Gibson's theory puts great emphasis on motion, both of the perceiver and of surrounding objects, as the key to many aspects of visual perception. Gibson's answer to the more basic problem of how motion itself is perceived

also differed strongly from those offered by other contemporary theories. He argued that the transformations in the structure of the optic array that specify motion are the primitive elements for vision, and are directly detected. In contrast, other approaches assumed that features of a static retinal image are primitive, and therefore that processes inside the perceiver are needed to see motion. These include such things as a memory in which to hold information from one retinal "snapshot" to the next, and the ability to recognise and match objects between snapshots. Gibson's aim was to banish all processes of this kind from the act of seeing, whether memory and feature matching from motion perception, or hypothesis testing and scaling from size perception.

The distinction between Gibson's theory of motion perception and image-based theories is perhaps not as clear now as it was several decades ago. By taking a space-time image as the starting point for motion processing, the recent approaches to the computation of image motion presented in Chapter 8 have provided a way of describing changes in images that is close to Gibson's concept of transformation in the optic array. Even so, points of contention still remain. First, models of computation of space-time energy in images do not account for all characteristics of human motion perception, and there is evidence that feature-tracking and attention may play a role in motion perception (see Ch.8, pp.196–199). Any intervention by processes of this kind is obviously at odds with Gibsonian theory. A second problem is whether, from Gibson's perspective, energy models of space-time image processing count as a "direct" or as an "indirect" theory of motion perception. They are certainly far removed from the models of Gibson's day, which proposed mediation by psychological processes of recognition and memory in perception, and are closer to a specification of how networks of cortical neurons might operate, but do they provide a "direct" explanation for motion perception or not? We will return in Chapter 17 to a fuller discussion of the problems involved in defining this key concept in Gibsonian theory.

Gibson's theory in perspective

Gibson's theory is radical indeed. It stands apart from the mainstream of perceptual theory. Some have likened Gibson's ideas to those of the Gestaltists, who took a similar phenomenological approach to seeing. However, the Gestaltists were nativist in philosophy, whereas Gibson sees learning as important; and the Gestaltists sought to explain perceptual phenomena in terms of the physiology of the brain, unlike Gibson. It would be as legitimate to compare Gibson to the behaviourists, who looked at stimuli and responses but did not care to speculate on intervening stages of processing—but the behaviourists saw animals as prodded into action by discrete stimuli or sensations—whereas for Gibson, perception and action are intimately interlinked. Thus Gibson's approach is unique and has until recently been ignored by the vast majority of perceptual psychologists. This is largely because the difference between Gibsonian and traditional accounts of perception is more profound than might be appreciated from the preceding pages. The differences between the two approaches are not just psychological but verge on the philosophical. Traditional perceptual theory holds that perception is indirect and mediated by higher cognitive processes. We do not "just see" the world but actively construct it from fragmentary perceptual data. Gibson is a "direct realist". He holds that perception is direct and unmediated by inference and problem solving. However, at least some of the distinction between a "direct" and an "indirect" theory may be muddied by conceptual and logical confusion (Shaw & Bransford, 1977).

Much of the rest of this book has a distinctly Gibsonian flavour, particularly in Chapters 12, 13, and 14, as we talk about the detection of information from optic flow patterns, and how this might be used to guide the actions of animals and humans in their worlds. However, unlike much of the work in ecological optics, we are concerned to describe physiological and computational models of how this information might be detected. We do not consider it adequate to claim that the observer just "resonates" to "invariants" picked up "directly", although we would concede that for some purposes one can demonstrate how patterns of light may be used to guide action, without detailed enquiry about how the information contained within light is processed. Different levels of analysis suit different purposes, and we return to this in Chapter 17. We also see a distinction between the kinds of visual processing that might be used to guide locomotion through and manipulation of objects in the world, and the kinds of visual processing that might be involved in *understanding* the visual world in conceptual terms. For Gibson (1979), the two kinds of perception apparently do not differ. Thus just as a tree stump affords "sitting on", so a letter-box affords "posting letters" to a human being in a Western culture. In both cases perception is not mediated, in the inferential sense of the word, although humans may have to learn how to use the invariant information in the optic array. However, a fundamental aspect of human cognition is the ability to manipulate symbols and images in order to plan, reflect, and reminisce. It seems likely that such "cognitive" activities are intimately involved in at least some aspects of human perception, and hence in this way too our approach is much less radical than Gibson's. In other animals we may consider how "mental maps" of their environments are established and used. Such considerations appeal to notions of internal representations, "memories" of a kind, that Gibson would not consider appropriate to the subject matter of perception.

Our own aim is to present a pragmatic, rather than a theoretically "pure", account of a variety of perceptual accomplishments, and for many such accomplishments a "weak" version of the Gibsonian approach provides a more comfortable level of analysis than does the "retinal image" approach. In the remaining chapters of this section we will consider aspects of "dynamic" visual perception by animals and humans, but we will not adhere too strictly to a Gibsonian style of analysing these activities. Even so, much of the research we will describe in this section has been conducted by people influenced by, and sympathetic to, Gibson's position, and so the subject matter and the approach of this section will feel very different to that of Part II. In Chapter 17 we tackle these differences explicitly and explore the possibilities for reconciliation and synthesis.

12

Visual Guidance of Animal Locomotion

A crucial part of Gibson's critique of traditional theories of visual perception is his argument that they neglect the relationship between perceiver and environment. It is because of his emphasis on this relationship that Gibson came to describe his own approach as *ecological*. An ecological outlook on vision leads us to ask two kinds of question. First, what information is available in the spatiotemporal pattern of light to specify the structure of the environment and events in it? Second, what information does an animal or person *need* from the pattern of light in order to organise appropriate actions?

We saw in Chapter 11 some of the ways in which Gibson tackled the first question, and in Chapters 12 to 16 we discuss further ways in which the optic array provides information for vision. We attempt to put this problem in the context of the second question, and stress the need to understand the role of visual perception in animals' and people's actions. We begin, in this chapter, by considering how animals use information in light to guide their movement around the solid objects and surfaces that surround them. We will consider first some aspects of the control of flight in insects, and then go on to look at how distance information obtained

from the optic array or optic flow is used to guide animals' actions.

THE VISUAL CONTROL OF INSECT FLIGHT

Steering a straight course

An insect flies by beating its wings rapidly, twisting them as it does so, so that on each downstroke air is driven backwards and downwards. This generates a force on the insect with two components—an upwards force, or lift, and a forward force, or thrust. The aerodynamic principles by which these forces are produced are well understood, at least for larger insects (Pringle, 1974).

Simply beating the wings will not ensure *stable* flight, however. The direction and magnitude of the force produced by the wingbeat must be controlled to prevent the insect rolling, yawing, or pitching (see Fig. 12.1). A degree of stability is provided by insects' anatomy. The abdomen, particularly if it is long, as in the locust, acts as a rudder to counteract pitch and yaw, and in all insects the centre of lift is above the centre of gravity, giving pendulum

FIGURE 12.1

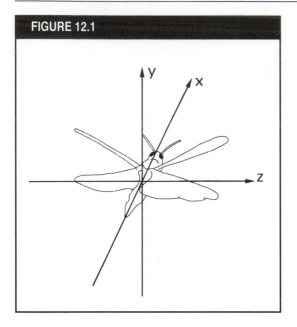

The three orthogonal axes through a flying insect. Rotation around axis x is rolling, around axis y is yawing, and around axis z is pitching.

stability against roll. In these ways, deviation from a stable flight attitude generates a correcting force.

This inherent stability is augmented in all actively flying insects by "active reflexes"—negative feedback loops operating through the insect's nervous system and muscles. Receptors detect information specifying rotation around one of the axes, and the wings, limbs, or abdomen move so as to correct the rotation. One source of information specifying rotation is the pattern of air flow over the insect. In the locust, for example, the rate of air flow over either side of the head during flight is detected by sensory hairs. If the insect yaws, the two rates of air flow differ, and the resulting signals from the sensory hairs cause steering movements of the legs and abdomen (Camhi, 1970). As long as the surrounding air is still, or is moving as a homogeneous mass, this change in the pattern of air flow over the head unambiguously specifies a rotation caused by the insect's own movement, and the corrective movements it triggers will keep the insect on a straight and stable course.

Often, however, an insect flies through air that moves in irregular currents, gusts, and eddies too small for us to detect but large enough to deflect a flying insect. In this situation, air flow over the body provides ambiguous information about the insect's path relative to the environment. An insect that simply regulated its path relative to the air around it would fly in an irregular, "drunkard's walk" path as it was blown about by fluctuating air currents. Such a flight path would be maladaptive for many insects, as they would be unable to fly any distance through the environment in order to reach new food sources.

We would therefore expect insects to be able to detect turns relative to the fixed environment around them as well as relative to the air in which they fly. What information in the optic flow field could specify such turns? Locusts maintain stability in the rolling plane by detecting both the direction from which diffuse light intensity is the greatest and the angle of the horizon relative to the body axis (Goodman, 1965). In a locust's natural environment, these two sources of information unambiguously specify the direction of the force of gravity, whatever the air around the insect is doing.

These two means of ensuring stable flight have their limitations. First, the orientation of the horizon is useful only to insects flying over open country, as locusts do when migrating, but not to insects flying through a cluttered environment of vegetation. Second, neither mechanism can correct yawing turns or prevent an insect flying round and round in circles. A further means by which insects can maintain stable flight, which overcomes both these problems, is through the *optomotor response*.

The first demonstration of the optomotor response (Kalmus, 1949) studied the control of walking rather than flying, and a typical experiment is shown in Fig. 12.2. A fly walks on a platform surrounded by a cylinder with vertical stripes on its inside surface. As the cylinder is turned, the fly turns in the same direction, so that the velocity of flow of optic texture is minimised.

Rotation of the cylinder causes a flow of optic texture in a uniform sideways direction throughout the optic flow field, but what would this pattern of flow specify about a fly's natural environment? It would not specify movement of the environment as, outside an optomotor experiment, the whole

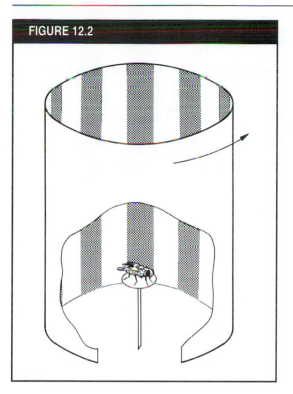

FIGURE 12.2

Experiment to demonstrate the optomotor response of a walking fly.

In an optomotor experiment, a fly detects a pattern of optic flow that specifies its rotation relative to the environment, and makes the appropriate turning movements of its legs to reduce sideways optic flow to a minimum. This ability to detect uniform flow throughout the visual field is also used by many insects to correct turns during flight. The optomotor response can be demonstrated in flight by suspending an insect in the air by a rod glued to its back. In these conditions, it will beat its wings as if flying, and its turning responses to artificial optic flow fields can be measured.

The fruitfly *Drosophila melanogaster* is one example of an insect that shows an optomotor response during tethered flight. It not only responds to a striped pattern moving sideways across its visual field with a yawing turn, but also makes a pitching or rolling turn in response to the rotation of a drum around the other two perpendicular axes (Blondeau & Heisenberg, 1982; see Fig. 12.3). It is important to stress that these rotating striped patterns simulate the optic flow caused by rotation of the insect, whether the rotation arises from its own movement or from an air current or from both. As all these situations require the same corrective manoeuvres, there is no need for an insect to discriminate between them.

It is obvious how these optomotor responses act to maintain stable flight by a fruitfly or other insect, but can they also keep an insect on a straight path through fluctuating air currents? In principle, they can play a part in doing this. Each time the insect is rotated by an air current, flow of texture will cause it to generate an opposing *torque*, or turning force. The insect will therefore keep the direction of its thrust constant relative to the environment. Its actual path will be determined by the resultant of its thrust and the air current, and the insect will therefore follow a zig-zag path. Nevertheless, this path will have a component in a constant direction, and the insect will not fly around in circles.

So far, in discussing the contribution of the optomotor response to stabilising an insect's flight, we have assumed that the optic flow produced by a rotating drum is like that experienced by an insect in natural conditions. This will not usually be so, because the *translatory* motion of the insect

environment would never move in a uniform way (Gibson, 1966). Instead, it would unambiguously specify rotation of the fly due to movement of the surface it is resting on.

An illustration of this point is provided by situations where stationary human observers are presented with uniformly moving texture in a large part of the visual field. Such situations are rare, or must be contrived experimentally (note that forward locomotion does not produce *uniform* flow of texture), but they often cause a powerful impression of self-movement. The reader may have experienced such an effect by standing in shallow water at the seashore and looking straight down. As the water rushes out after each wave, an observer has a strong illusion of moving in the opposite direction. A similar effect can occur at a railway station, when uniform flow created by movement of a train on a nearby platform can be interpreted as movement of the observer's own, stationary train. (We have more to say about control of posture and balance by vision in Chapter 13.)

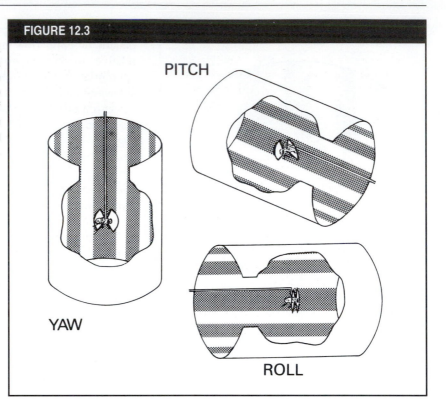

FIGURE 12.3

The optomotor response of a tethered fly to rotation of a drum in all three planes. In each case, the fly turns to minimise velocity of flow of optic texture. Adapted from Blondeau and Heisenberg (1982).

relative to its surroundings will generate a *linear* optic flow field in which optic texture moves everywhere except at the poles (see Fig. 11.6). Unless an insect flies at a high enough altitude to make this linear flow too small to detect, a turn will cause uniform rotary flow to be superimposed on the linear flow field. It might appear that these two components of optic flow need to be detected separately if the insect is to correct a turn, but experiments on the yawing optomotor response (Reichardt, 1969) indicate that this does not happen, and that the optomotor response is determined simply by the sum of motion signals across the retina. As a result, the different patterns of optic flow caused, for example, by a rightwards translation and a clockwise rotation of the insect could elicit the same counter-clockwise turning response.

Does this failure to resolve components of optic flow caused by translation and rotation actually cause any problem for a flying insect? It need not, provided that the same corrective action is required in response to translatory and rotary disturbances

to the flight path. Whether it is blown to the right, or turned clockwise, the appropriate manoeuvre to return an insect towards its original path is a counter-clockwise turn. We will return in Chapter 13 to the resolution of rotary and linear optic flow fields, and will see that it is a more significant problem in human vision.

It should be emphasised that the simple model of summation of motion signals across the retina to generate a turning response is not correct for all insect species. One species with more complex optomotor mechanisms is the hoverfly *Syritta pipiens* (Collett, 1980). The flight performance of hoverflies is one of the most sophisticated among insects, and can easily be observed on a summer day. They can fly forwards, sideways, or obliquely, through grass, flowers, and foliage, hover in a stable position, and fly accurately towards the flowers from which they take nectar.

One component of Collett's model of hoverfly flight control is detection of optic flow over the part of the eye appropriate for the direction of flight. In forward flight, this is the front of the eye, but in sideways flight it is the side of the eye. The optic flow field is regulated so that its pole is kept over one of these areas, and this clearly involves more complex and flexible control than in houseflies. Perhaps similar complexities occur in other insect species, although the ability of the hoverfly to fly with great accuracy in any direction may well mean that its perceptual capacities are unusually elaborate.

The problem of maintaining a stable path or position in a moving medium is faced by other animals besides insects. Being larger and more powerful, birds will not be affected by small air currents, but stronger currents will be important to some species. Hummingbirds hover in a stable position to feed from flowers, and kingfishers, kestrels, and other predatory birds hover similarly before striking at prey. These birds need to detect and correct disturbances of their position by wind in the same way as hoverflies. Fish such as trout also face problems similar to those of airborne insects, in maintaining their position in fast-flowing streams. The study of optomotor processes in fish and birds would present greater difficulty than in insects, but it would be interesting to know whether similar mechanisms are involved.

Flying towards objects

We have seen how the ability to detect rotary optic flow can help an airborne insect to stabilise its flight and to steer a roughly straight course. From time to time, an insect will also need to orient its flight towards particular objects, such as decaying matter on which houseflies feed, flowers from which bees or butterflies take nectar, or potential mates flying nearby. We shall next discuss evidence that insects use optic flow to discriminate such objects from cluttered backgrounds, and to orient their flight towards them.

As well as showing an optomotor response to a revolving striped drum, the housefly *Musca domestica* will turn so as to follow the movement of a single vertical stripe on a drum (Reichardt & Poggio, 1976). As the drum rotates, the fly follows its movement in such a way as to keep the stripe in the centre of its visual field. Reichardt and Poggio found that the yawing torque of a fly in this situation is determined by three factors. One is the

angle between the stripe and the long axis of the fly's body. The second is the angular *velocity* of the stripe. For a given position of the stripe, the fly will turn more quickly if the stripe is moving away from the centre of the visual field more quickly. In this way, the fly has a simple ability to extrapolate from the stripe's rate of movement and predict its future position. Finally, the fly's torque shows small random changes causing it to turn irregularly, which can be observed either when the fly is placed in a homogeneously lit environment, or when it is fixating a stationary stripe.

Land and Collett (1974) were able to show that the same parameters of optic flow control turns when houseflies are in free flight. If two airborne flies come close to each other, they may buzz around in a brief flurry and then separate. Land and Collett filmed encounters of this kind between flies of the species *Fannia canicularis* and found that they take the form of a chase, lasting between 0.1 and 2sec, in which the leading fly is closely followed by the pursuer. The record of one chase (Fig. 12.4) shows how each time the leading fly turns, the pursuer manoeuvres so as to follow it.

Land and Collett were able to reconstruct a pursuing fly's path accurately, given the leading fly's path, by applying two rules governing the pursuer's behaviour. First, as the leader's angular deviation from the pursuer's axis increases, the pursuer turns to reduce the angle. Second, when the leader is within 30° on either side of the pursuer's axis, the pursuer detects the leader's angular velocity and turns to reduce it also. As a result, the pursuer can begin its turn before the leader crosses its midline. These parameters of angular position and velocity are exactly those that Reichardt and Poggio (1976) demonstrated as controlling turns made by tethered flies.

Flies detect two simple optical parameters of optic flow in order to track small nearby targets, and there are at least two possible reasons why this information is useful to a fly. First, Land and Collett (1974) argue that it enables male flies to locate and contact females. How, though, does such a simple form of visual guidance allow males to distinguish females from males, or to discriminate between females of different species? Part of the answer lies in the context of the fly's behaviour;

FIGURE 12.4

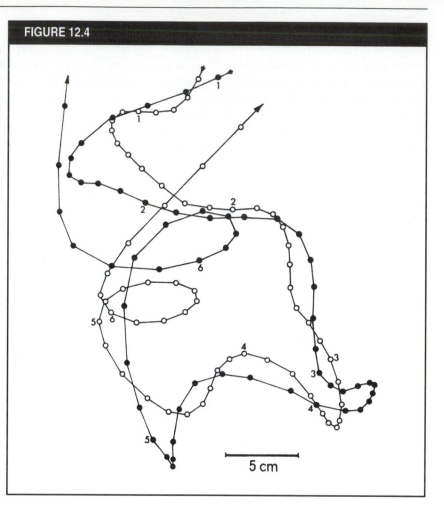

Record of a fly chase. Circles show positions of flies at 20msec intervals (open circles, leader; closed circles, pursuer). Corresponding positions are numbered at 200msec intervals. Reproduced from Land and Collett (1974) with permission of the authors and publishers.

5 cm

Land and Collett suggest that a male fly can fly and turn more quickly than a female, so that a male pursuer can catch up with a female but not with a male. Likewise, a pursuer will be unlikely to catch up with a fly of another species because its aerodynamic properties will differ from those of a female of its own species. If the leader is smaller than a conspecific female and therefore able to turn more quickly, or if it is larger and therefore able to fly faster, the pursuer will fall behind.

Whether the pursuer catches up depends on the size and aerodynamic properties of the two flies. If the leader is a female of the same species, these properties will be matched and the pursuer will catch up and mate. It seems unlikely, however, that this mechanism is foolproof, as flies of other species may well be present that are of the same

size as females of the pursuer's species. Unless they have some further means of discriminating targets at a distance, houseflies will therefore waste some time in pursuit of the wrong target.

A second possible reason why flies track a vertical stripe is that they need to orient towards landing surfaces in order to find food. If a fly passes close to a surface, it will give rise to a patch of optic texture moving rapidly in the flow field. By turning towards this patch, the fly will approach the surface and land on it. If this mechanism is to work in flies' natural environments, however, it must also be sensitive to objects with textured surfaces against similar backgrounds, such as a nearby leaf against a background of foliage. The relative motion of such an object as a fly passes near it will give rise to a boundary in the optic flow field between regions of similar optic texture moving with different speeds.

Reichardt and Poggio (1979) have demonstrated that flies are able to detect and orient towards boundaries of this kind. They presented tethered flies with a vertical stripe of a random-dot texture against a background of the same texture (similar to that illustrated in Fig. 7.5). If both stripe and background either remained stationary or moved together, the flies did not fixate the stripe, confirming that there were no detectable differences in texture between it and the background. *Relative* movement between stripe and background did, however, cause flies to fixate the stripe.

Reichardt et al. (1983) investigated the neural mechanisms underlying this behaviour, and found that they respond in the same way to a difference in spatial structure (such as dot size) between a small patch and its surround as they do to a difference in velocity of motion (see Ch.8, p.202), and so apparently a fly cannot discriminate between the two situations. In the fly's natural environment, however, a nearby object against a cluttered background will give rise to either, or usually both, of these optical features, and so a mechanism built to steer the fly towards a landing surface need not distinguish them. We see here another example of a simple perceptual ability that controls behaviour adequately without delivering a full and accurate description of the environment.

More direct evidence that insects use relative motion to orient towards landing surfaces has been obtained by Srinivasan, Lehrer, and Horridge (1990) from experiments in which honey-bees were trained to feed from a sugar solution on artificial "flowers" consisting of small discs raised above ground level. The bees were easily able to find discs when they and the ground surface below them were both covered with the same random-dot texture. The higher a disc was raised above the ground, the more likely bees were to land on it, and they also showed a strong tendency to land at the edge of a disc, facing inwards. These results suggest strongly that bees find landing surfaces such as flowers by detecting the boundary of a patch of optic texture moving faster than the surrounding texture. Further experiments (Lehrer

& Srinivasan, 1993) confirmed that bees are much more likely to approach and land at a motion boundary where image speed increases suddenly, than one where it decreases.

It is possible that the bees in Srinivasan et al.'s (1990) experiments oriented towards some detailed feature of the edge of a disc, but further evidence in favour of the relative motion hypothesis was obtained by Lehrer, Srinivasan, and Zhang (1990). They made use of the fact, demonstrated in earlier experiments, that the system processing image motion in the bee's visual pathway is "colour-blind", taking its input only from green-sensitive photoreceptors. Lehrer et al. (1990) showed that bees land in the usual way on plain, untextured discs of a different colour to the ground surface. However, if the colours of disc and ground were chosen so that there was no green-contrast between them (and therefore no input to the motion system), bees continued to land on the discs, but without showing their usual preference for landing at edges. These results show that a pathway in the visual system sensitive to colour differences operates alongside one sensitive to relative motion, and that either pathway can control landing manoeuvres. However, the tendency to orient towards the *edge* of a surface depends specifically on the motion pathway.

Sensitivity to small patches of texture moving more quickly than the background provides insects such as houseflies and bees with a robust, general-purpose mechanism for orienting towards landing surfaces, and in bees at least this mechanism works together with another sensitive to colour contrast. But how can this mechanism be compatible with the optomotor response? If an airborne fly turns towards a small object against a textured background, the turn will cause rotary flow of texture in the opposite direction, and it seems that the resulting optomotor response will cancel out the original turn. How can a fly turn towards a potential mate or landing surface lying against a textured background, without being locked into its flight path?

The solution to this problem turns out to be surprisingly simple. Two distinct flight control mechanisms operate in parallel in the housefly (Egelhaaf et al., 1989). First, a "large field" system is sensitive to relatively low-speed image motion over a large region of the retina, and is responsible for the optomotor response. At higher image speeds, caused by oscillating an optomotor drum at a higher frequency, this response to uniform image motion disappears. Second, a "small field" system also generates a yawing turn in response to image motion, but is sensitive to faster motion over a small part of the retina, and is responsible for the tracking of small moving objects described earlier (Land & Collett, 1974; Reichardt & Poggio, 1976). These two systems have been identified with two populations of neurons in the lobula plate, the third stage in the housefly's visual pathway, known as "horizontal" and "figure detection" cells, respectively. Both are linked by way of descending interneurons to motor control centres in thoracic ganglia, and control yaw torque by causing deflection of the hindlegs and abdomen, and differences in wingbeat amplitude (Zanker, Egelhaaf, & Warzecha, 1991).

The critical difference between the "large field" and "small field" systems is in the ranges of image speed to which they are sensitive. When the small field system detects an object, the fly fixates it in a series of fast turns rather than a slow, smooth turn. As a result, image speed is too high to be detected by the large field system, and no stabilising response occurs. In effect, the fly is able to turn to fixate objects by doing so at a speed too high for its flight-stabilising mechanism to respond. The fly's yawing torque is therefore controlled by at least two systems working independently, each designed to work in a particular range of situations without interfering with the operation of the other.

One further mechanism involved in the control of housefly's flight is the one responsible for controlling landing. As a fly approaches a surface, it does not simply crash into it (unless it is made of glass—why should be clear in a moment!) but performs a stereotyped series of landing manoeuvres, in which it decelerates and extends its forelegs forwards. A looming surface straight ahead is specified by centrifugal flow in a wide area of the optic flow field, and this can be simulated by presenting a fly with a rotating disc on which a spiral is painted. Depending on the direction in which the disc is rotated, either inward or outward

movement of edges is generated. If a housefly is suspended in front of a disc rotated so as to produce an expanding pattern, it will immediately give the landing response, whereas a disc rotating in the opposite direction elicits no response (Braitenberg & Ferretti, 1966).

To conclude, houseflies and bees are able to detect the boundaries of surfaces by the relative motion between images of surface and of background, to turn to fixate them, and to adopt a landing posture when they approach a surface closely. It seems likely that other animals moving about through a cluttered environment—a fish swimming through coral, a deer running through a wood, or a squirrel running between branches—also use relative motion in the optic flow field to detect the layout of objects surrounding them. Many manoeuvres of this kind, however, will require information about the *distances* of surfaces from an animal, as well as their positions relative to one another; how do animals obtain this information?

DISTANCE AND THE CONTROL OF BEHAVIOUR

In Chapter 7, we discussed the kinds of optical information that provide human observers with an awareness of depth. Many of these sources of information are also available to animals to control actions such as reaching or jumping, which need to be adjusted according to the distances of objects. In this section, we will consider first the roles of accommodation and binocular disparity, and then the role of image motion, in controlling the actions of animals.

Accommodation and binocular disparity

As the compound eye of insects does not accommodate, this source of distance information is available only to animals with single-chambered eyes. Among these animals, accommodation is potentially more useful the smaller the depth of field of the eye (see Ch.1, p.17). Because depth of field increases rapidly with absolute distance from the eye, accommodation can only provide information about the distances of objects close to it; in general, no more than a few tens of centi- metres away.

The usefulness of binocular disparity in providing information about relative depth also decreases rapidly with absolute distance (see Ch.7, p.139). The maximum distance at which it is useful depends, among other factors, on the distance between the two eyes, and so will generally be greater for vertebrates than for insects. Even so, at least one insect species does detect distance in this way: the extent of a preying mantis' strike at a small insect is determined by the disparity in positions of the image of the target in the two eyes (Rossel, 1983).

These optical considerations suggest that accommodation and binocular disparity will usually not be useful in controlling the locomotion of fast-moving animals, which need information rapidly about the distances of objects several metres away. On the other hand, they are potentially valuable to animals that seize or manipulate objects close to themselves. The use of accommodation and binocular disparity has been demonstrated in several cases where animals make a rapid, ballistic strike at nearby food or prey from a stationary position (a ballistic movement is one not affected by any sensory information once it has begun).

Chameleons, toads, and frogs all capture prey such as insects by orienting towards the target and striking at it with the tongue, the length of the strike being accurately related to the distance of the target. Experiments measuring the errors in strike length caused by lenses or prisms in front of the eyes have shown that the chameleon obtains distance information from the degree of accommodation of its lens when the prey is optimally focused (Harkness, 1977), whereas toads and frogs use both accommodation and binocular disparity (Collett, 1977). There is similar evidence for the use of accommodation by the barn owl to gauge the distance of pecks at food (Wagner & Schaeffel, 1991), and less direct evidence for its use by chickens and pigeons (Schaeffel, 1994).

There are two ways in which an animal could detect the state of accommodation of the lens: by monitoring efferent commands to the muscles that move the lens, or by feedback from sensory receptors (cf. discussion of eye movements, Ch.7, pp.165–166) . One way to distinguish between these alternatives is to use drugs that partially paralyse the lens muscles, so that for a given strength of efferent command the movement of the lens is reduced. If feedback from receptors is monitored, distance estimation will not be affected. In frogs, however, the result is underestimation of distance (Douglas, Collett, & Wagner, 1986), implying that efferent commands to the muscles are monitored rather than the degree of movement that is actually achieved.

Image motion and relative distance

The angular speed of a patch of texture in the optic flow field is equivalent to the speed of its image over a retina. Either parameter depends on the distance of an object from the eye, but also on its angular distance from the direction of motion and on the speed at which the eye is moving relative to the surroundings. These relationships are illustrated in Fig. 12.5.

Often, an animal's speed relative to its surroundings will not be predictable; movement of the air or water, for a flying or a swimming animal, or the slope of the ground, for a running animal, make the relationship between commands to muscles and actual velocity unpredictable. As the animal's velocity cannot be obtained from image movement without knowing the distance of an object, speed of image motion alone cannot, in general, yield *absolute* distance. Differences in speed between images, or motion parallax (see Ch.7, pp.157–158) can, however, provide informa- tion about the *relative* distances of objects.

We saw earlier that honey-bees can detect the presence of motion parallax between a surface patch and its background, and use this information to control landing flight. Further evidence shows that they can detect not only the presence but also the amount of motion parallax between surfaces, and use it to judge their relative distances. Lehrer, Srinivasan, Zhang, and Horridge (1988) trained bees to feed from one of a number of discs mounted above the ground. The disc bearing food varied in size and position, but was always at the same height relative to the others. Lehrer et al. showed that bees

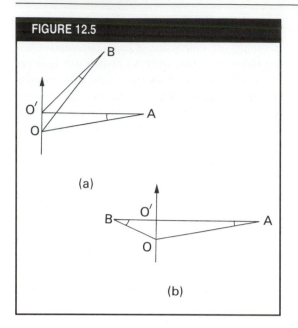

FIGURE 12.5

(a)

(b)

(a) The relation between motion parallax and angular distance from the direction of motion. Objects A and B are equidistant to the eye but B lies at a smaller angle to the direction of motion. As the eye moves in unit time from O to O′, texture reflected from A moves through a greater angle. (b) The relation between motion parallax and object distance. Objects A and B lie at the same angle to the direction of motion, but B is nearer the eye than A. As the observer moves from O to O′, texture reflected from B moves through a greater angle. As the eye moves faster (and the distance from O to O′ in unit time increases), texture reflected from any object moves through a greater angle.

detect the appropriate target from its angular speed relative to that of the other discs as they fly above them.

A second illustration is provided by the "centring" behaviour of honey-bees. When bees fly through an aperture, they follow a path roughly equidistant between the two walls. Kirchner and Srinivasan (1989) demonstrated that they do this by flying so as to equalise image speed on the two sides. They trained bees to fly through a tunnel to a food source, and then moved one of the tunnel walls. If the wall moved in the same direction as the bees' flight, they moved closer to it, whereas if it moved in the opposite direction, they moved towards the other wall (see Fig. 12.6a,b,c). These results could be explained if bees equalised either the speed or the frequency with which stripes passed by on the two sides. Srinivasan, Lehrer, Kirchner, and Zhang (1991) showed that differences in the spatial frequencies of the patterns on the two walls of the tunnel had no effect on bees' flight path (see Fig. 12.6d), confirming that they do use image speed, and not temporal frequency, to gauge relative distance.

Image motion and absolute distance

We have seen that the dependence of image motion on speed of movement prevents it being a general source of information about the absolute distances of surfaces from an animal. Even so, there are a variety of ways in which this problem can be

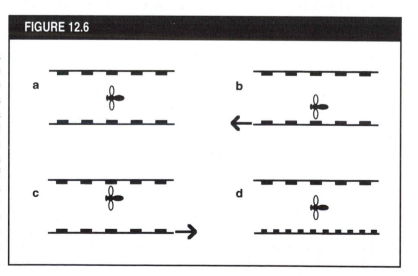

FIGURE 12.6

Schematic view from above of a bee flying along a tunnel with striped walls. (a) Both walls are stationary. (b) The lower wall is moving in the same direction as the bee's flight. (c) The lower wall is moving in the opposite direction to the bee's flight. (d) The walls are stationary but the stripes are of different widths. The bee flies centrally between the walls in (a) and (d), but moves to equalise optical speed of the walls in (b) and (c). Adapted from Srinivasan et al. (1991).

overcome, and all involve making stereotyped movements of the body or head that are at least roughly constant in either their distance or speed. In the first case, the angular distance travelled by an object during the movement gives its absolute distance, whereas in the second case its angular velocity does so. We will next look at examples of stereotyped body and head movements of animals, and at evidence that they contribute to distance perception.

The experiments on honey-bee vision described earlier rely on the ability of bees to learn where they have found food in the past and to return over and over again to these places. They do this not only by associating the characteristics of particular surfaces with food, but also by learning their positions relative to other objects around them. This can be demonstrated by allowing a bee a number of visits to a food source and then moving the array of landmarks around the food a short distance away, removing the food at the same time. The bee will now search for food at the correct place relative to the landmarks, even though none is there. The same behaviour can be observed in other insects, such as solitary wasps making return flights to the entrances of their underground burrows (Tinbergen, 1951; see Fig. 12.7).

The accuracy of bees' or wasps' search paths in these experiments shows that they have detected and learned the bearings and distances of nearby objects from the nest. There is some evidence that distance information is obtained from image motion, during a stereotyped pattern of flight on departure from the nest or food. By filming the departure flights of common wasps from a new source of food, Collett and Lehrer (1993) identified a distinct pattern of flight, in which the insects turned towards the food and flew in a series of arcs around it at increasing distances (Fig. 12.8). Similar "turn back and look" behaviour has also been observed in honey-bees (Lehrer, 1991), and in the solitary wasp *Cerceris* leaving its nest (Zeil, 1993). Although no direct evidence is yet available, these stereotyped flight patterns may be means of generating image motion over flight segments of roughly constant distance, speed, or both, and so of obtaining the approximate distances of nearby objects.

An interesting question for future research is how precisely flight speed and distance are constrained by these specialised forms of departure flight. It seems likely that air currents will introduce some variability into them, and this may be a reason why bees appear to use image motion to guide only their first few return flights to food, and then switch to using the angular sizes of nearby landmarks in later flights. Evidence for the use of angular size was obtained by Cartwright and Collett (1979) in experiments where bees were trained to visit a food source at a fixed distance from a dark, vertical cylinder in otherwise plain white surroundings. They were then tested by removing the food and changing the size of the cylinder. If the cylinder was made larger, bees searched further from it, whereas if it was reduced in size, they searched closer to it, implying that their flight was guided by stored information about the angular size of the landmark as seen from the food source. Cartwright and Collett (1983) interpreted these results in terms of a "snapshot" model, arguing that when bees find food they form a representation of the sizes of retinal images of surrounding landmarks, and use this to guide return flights.

An anomaly in Cartwright and Collett's (1979) results was that some bees continued to search at the correct distance from the landmark, after its size had been changed. It therefore seemed that some used the "snapshot" mechanism whereas others used image motion, and Lehrer and Collett (1994) suggested that the two groups had differed in the number of visits to food they had made. They tested this hypothesis by filming bees' responses to a change in landmark size after different numbers of training flights. After about six flights (the stage at which "turn back and look" flights no longer occur), bees searched at the correct distance from the changed landmark. After about 20 flights, however, the bees instead searched where the angular size of the landmark, and not its distance, was the same as in training. These results show that, after their first few visits to a food source, bees switch from using the angular speed of landmarks to using their angular size in order to find the food.

These discoveries about the visual control of bees' flight to familiar food sources have some

FIGURE 12.7

Top: Flight path of a digger wasp leaving the entrance to its burrow.
Below: Return to the nest is guided by nearby landmarks; if the circle of pine cones around the entrance is moved while the wasp is away, it returns to the wrong place. Reproduced from N. Tinbergen (1951), *The study of instinct,* by permission of Oxford University Press.

wider implications. At least two optical parameters—the angular sizes and velocities of landmarks—are potentially able to give bees the distance information they need to return to dishes of sugar solution or, in natural situations, nectar-bearing flowers. The flexibility that bees show in switching from one of these to the other after several flights is perhaps a means of minimising the risks involved in using only one parameter. The reliability of image motion is limited by the effect of unpredictable air currents on the control of speed during "turn back and look" flight, and the reliability of angular size can be compromised if animate objects near a food source change their distance from it, or disappear altogether. A bee may need to make several flights to a flower to "filter out" from its representation of the angular sizes of landmarks those of mobile

FIGURE 12.8

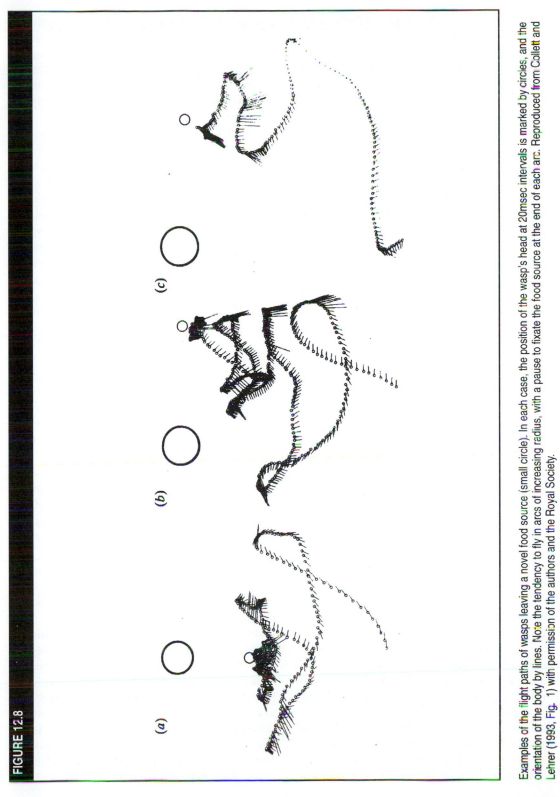

Examples of the flight paths of wasps leaving a novel food source (small circle). In each case, the position of the wasp's head at 20msec intervals is marked by circles, and the orientation of the body by lines. Note the tendency to fly in arcs of increasing radius, with a pause to fixate the food source at the end of each arc. Reproduced from Collett and Lehrer (1993, Fig. 1) with permission of the authors and the Royal Society.

objects, and to ensure that it describes the *stable* layout of the surroundings. The flexibility shown by bees in their use of different sources of distance information may therefore be an adaptation that achieves the best possible trade-off between different kinds of unpredictable events in the environment.

In general, it is likely to be difficult to achieve constant body speed during stereotyped patterns of locomotion, especially in airborne animals, and so the reliability of image motion in specifying absolute distance will often be limited. A more promising method, especially when an animal is resting on the ground surface and can keep its body still, is to make up-and-down or side-to-side movements of the head. The distance and speed of the resulting movement of the eyes will not be affected by wind or terrain, and will be predictable from motor output to neck muscles. Some animals exploit this possibility by using "peering" movements of the head to obtain distance information from image motion.

One example is the locust, which makes side-to-side swaying movements with its head before jumping from one surface to another. Sobel (1990) showed that the force of the jump is controlled by image motion generated by the swaying movement. When the target surface was moved artificially in the opposite direction to the swaying of a locust's head, the insect underestimated its distance and jumped with too small an initial velocity. In this case, the velocity of the image of the target was increased, and corresponded to that of a closer stationary surface. Conversely, movement of the target in the same direction as the head caused locusts to overestimate its distance.

Similar head movements are seen in gerbils, which make vertical "bobbing" movements of the head before jumping over a gap, and Ellard, Goodale, and Timney (1984) provide some indirect evidence that the behaviour enables image motion to be used to control the distance jumped. Goodale, Ellard, and Booth (1990) went on to discover an intriguing parallel with distance estimation in honey-bees, showing that gerbils prefer to use the angular size of a familiar target to gauge jumping distance, and under- or overshoot if its actual size

is changed. Only when the target is unfamiliar, or varies in size, does a gerbil bob its head to generate image motion, and Goodale et al. suggest that this preference for using angular size in familiar situations may be because a gerbil increases its risk of detection by a predator when it stops to head-bob.

Goodale et al. (1990) also found that the error in jumping caused by changing the size of a familiar target was not as large as predicted if angular size *alone* were used to give its distance. This implies that some other source, or sources, of information is used in combination with angular size to gauge the distance of a jump. It would be interesting to know how similar this integration of different sources of depth information by gerbils is to that which occurs when humans are presented with multiple depth cues (see Ch.7, pp.161–162). We will see other examples of the same process later in this chapter and in the next.

A well-known example of a stereotyped head movement is the head-bobbing of many bird species, including doves, pigeons, and chickens. During walking, the head moves backwards and forwards relative to the body, and there is a brief "hold" phase in each cycle in which the head is almost stationary relative to the surroundings, followed by a "thrust" phase in which the head moves forward more quickly than the body. Notice that a walking bird's head never actually moves backwards relative to the surroundings; the powerful illusion that it does is an example of how we see motion of a figure in relation to nearby, larger figures (see Ch.15, p.324).

It is known that head-bobbing in doves and pigeons is controlled by the optic flow produced by walking (Friedman, 1975; Frost, 1978), but its possible significance for vision is not fully understood. One possibility is that stabilisation of the head relative to the surroundings during the hold phase aids the detection of moving objects. However, this cannot be the only function of the behaviour, as pigeons maintain rhythmic head movement in fast running or slow flight without achieving stabilisation of the head (Davies & Green, 1988; Green, Davies, & Thorpe, 1994). The rapid forward movement of the head during the thrust phase will increase the velocities of texture patches over the retina, and so "amplify" relative motion between them; another function of head-bobbing may therefore be to aid the detection of small objects on the ground. Even so, the problem of obtaining absolute distances from optic flow remains, as the velocity of the head during the thrust phase is not predictable, but depends on walking or flight speed.

OPTIC FLOW AND TIME TO CONTACT

So far, we have restricted our discussion of how animals might obtain distance information from optic flow to one simple parameter, the angular velocity of a patch of optic texture. In an important theoretical advance, Lee (1980b) demonstrated that a more complex parameter of optic flow can yield depth information, and that it does so independently of the speed with which the eye is moving. In this section, we will first describe how this parameter specifies depth, and will then go on to discuss evidence that animals use it to time actions.

Consider an animal approaching a flat surface along a path perpendicular to it, with constant velocity. An equivalent situation is represented schematically in Fig. 12.9, in which a surface on the right is approaching an eye on the left with

velocity *V*. At time *t* it is a distance *Z(t)* away, in units of the diameter of the eye, for convenience. A texture element *P* on the surface has an image *P'* projected on the retina. At time *t*, *P'* is a distance *r(t)* from the centre of the expanding optic flow field and moving outwards with velocity *v(t)*.

From similar triangles,

$$\frac{1}{r(t)} = \frac{Z(t)}{r}$$

Differentiating with respect to time, and inverting,

$$\frac{r(t)^2}{v(t)} = \frac{R}{V}$$

As R = Z(t)r(t),

$$\frac{r(t)}{v(t)} = \frac{Z(t)}{V}$$

This ratio *r(t)/v(t)*, which Lee calls τ ("tau"), is the ratio at any instant of the distance of any point from the centre of an expanding optical pattern to its velocity away from the centre. It is equal to *Z(t)/V*, and therefore, if *V* is constant, to the time elapsing before the eye and surface collide. If an animal is able to obtain τ from the projection of the

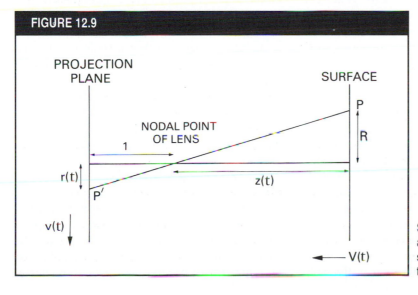

FIGURE 12.9

PROJECTION PLANE

SURFACE

NODAL POINT OF LENS

1

P

R

r(t)

z(t)

P'

v(t)

V(t)

Schematic representation of an animal's eye approaching a surface with velocity V(t). Adapted from Lee (1980b).

optic flow field onto its retina, it will have information about the depths of surrounding surfaces. Note that τ does not specify the distance of a surface, but time to contact with it—the time it would take to make contact with a surface if the animal continued to approach it with constant velocity. This is clearly valuable information for an animal to have in any situation where it needs to time an action, such as landing or jumping, as it closes with a surface. It also seems that the direct detection of time to contact will be a more efficient strategy than the detection of distance. In the second case, timing an action would require distance to be combined with some source of information about the animal's velocity, which would increase both delay and error in the control system.

In the derivation above, τ is the ratio of an optical variable (the distance between the images of a texture element and the centre of expansion) to the rate of change of the same variable. It has been shown that time to contact can also be specified by other variables of this form. For example, Lee and Young (1985) demonstrate that the ratio of the solid angle subtended at the eye by an object moving towards an observer to the rate of change of this angle also specifies time to contact. Tresilian (1991) has classified the different forms of the τ variable, and terms this an example of "local" τ, defined in relation only to local features of a flow field, in contrast to "global" τ, defined in relation to the centre of expansion of a flow field. We might expect these different τ variables to be useful in different situations, such as striking at airborne prey or jumping over a fence, respectively.

To summarise, there are powerful theoretical reasons to believe that the ability to detect τ variables can provide animals with a robust and efficient means of timing actions as they move about. Important evidence that τ is actually computed in visual pathways has been obtained by Wang and Frost (1992) from single-cell recordings in pigeons. They used computer graphics to produce a simulation on a television screen of a solid, patterned ball moving in depth, and found a group of cells in the midbrain that were strongly selective for the simulated direction of the ball,

responding only when the ball appeared to be on a course directly towards the eye. Furthermore, each of these cells began to fire when the simulated time to contact of the ball with the eye reached a specific value. This value remained constant over changes in both the size and approach speed of the ball, implying that each cell is tuned to a particular time to contact with an approaching object. It is not known how signals from motion-sensitive cells earlier in the visual pathway are processed to generate these responses, but the important question here is whether the information about time to contact provided by such cells is actually used in controlling the timing of actions. To answer this question, we must turn to behavioural evidence.

We described earlier (p.274) how a looming optic flow field causes a fly to initiate its landing manoeuvres, but does it use τ to detect the correct time in its approach at which to start landing? If landing is triggered when τ reaches some threshold value, then the distance from the target at which the landing manoeuvre begins will be greater for a fast approach than for a slow one (recall that τ is the ratio of the distance from a surface to the velocity of approach). Alternatively, if the fly detects the distance of the target and uses this to time its behaviour, then landing would be initiated at a *constant* distance from the target, whatever the velocity of approach.

Wagner (1982) analysed films of flies landing on small spheres in order to test the hypothesis that τ is used to time landing. He measured over many landings the variability of a number of parameters at the point when flies began to decelerate, and found that the parameter with the least variation was the ratio of the rate of expansion of the image of the sphere to its size. This parameter is the inverse of τ, and so the results support the hypothesis that flies directly obtain time to contact with a landing surface from optic flow, and not its distance.

In further research on the fly's landing response, Borst and Bahde (1988) question whether Wagner's (1982) results do demonstrate that τ is detected. They propose an alternative model, in which the outputs of motion detectors across the whole visual field are summed and then integrated over time. The fly begins landing when this integral reaches a threshold value. They point out that this is a more economical model of the fly's visual system, as it involves the same motion-processing mechanisms as those underlying the optomotor response, and avoids the need for a separate system computing values of τ.

Both the τ hypothesis and Borst and Bahde's (1988) model predict that the distance at which landing begins will increase with approach velocity, and so both account for Wagner's (1982) results. The latter model also predicts that landing distance will vary with the size of the target, its spatial structure, and the structure of the surroundings. In experiments with tethered flies presented with looming patterns, Borst and Bahde found that all these factors do influence the landing response, in the ways their model predicts. Their conclusion is that the fly uses a simple means of timing landing that does not achieve the ideal of triggering landing at a fixed distance or at a fixed time to contact, but which is none the less adequate for the fly's survival. Provided a fly's feet are extended and its velocity is within a low range, its exact velocity when it contacts a surface is probably not critical; we have all seen flies survive head-on collisions with windows!

The method of comparing the variability of different optical parameters used by Wagner (1982) was applied by Davies and Green (1990) to the landing flight of two bird species, the pigeon and the Harris hawk (*Parabuteo unicinctus*). During landings by hawks, τ varied less than did the distance between eye and perch at the point where the feet were extended, whereas in pigeons the opposite result was obtained. It may be that the two species use different optical information to time foot extension when they land, because pigeons head-bob during landing flight (see p.280), and this behaviour causes large fluctuations in the value of τ.

An important piece of evidence for the use of τ to time an action has been obtained from the gannet (*Sula bassana*), a seabird that hunts by flying over the sea at heights of up to 30m. When it detects a fish below the surface, a gannet dives almost vertically into the water to seize the fish in its beak. At the start of the dive, the bird assumes a swept-back wing posture (Fig. 12.10), which allows it to steer, presumably keeping the fish at a fixed point in its visual field. Gannets enter the water at speeds of up to 24m/sec (54mph) and would be injured if they kept their wings extended at this speed. When less than a second away from the water surface their wings are therefore stretched back into a streamlined posture. If the wings are streamlined too soon, steering accuracy will be lost, whereas if they are streamlined too late, the bird will be injured. It is therefore crucial to the bird's hunting success and survival that its streamlining is accurately timed.

As a gannet accelerates under the force of gravity during a dive, its velocity increases continuously, and therefore the value of τ at any instant does not specify time to contact but underestimates it by an amount dependent on the

FIGURE 12.10

Successive wing positions of a diving gannet. The wings are streamlined as the bird strikes the water. Drawing by John Busby, reproduced from Nelson (1978) with the permission of the publishers, A. & T.D. Poyser Ltd.

bird's current velocity. Even so, it is possible that by streamlining its wings when τ reaches a margin value the bird could achieve sufficiently accurate control of its dive. Lee and Reddish (1981) derived an expression for the time to contact with the water surface at which streamlining would occur on this hypothesis, in terms of the duration of the dive and the assumed values of τ and of the delay between its detection and streamlining. They then filmed gannets' dives and obtained values of time to contact and dive duration for each of a large number of dives. Figure 12.11 shows the data they obtained and the curve generated by their model that best fits the points. Lee and Reddish argue that strategies of timing streamlining that involve computation of the actual time to contact (from height, velocity, and acceleration), or streamlining at a particular velocity or at a particular height, would all give relationships between time to contact and dive duration that match the data less well than does the τ strategy.

All the experiments on detection of time to contact that we have discussed so far use an indirect method, in which the relationship between approach to a surface and the timing of some action is determined, and compared to the relationships predicted by various strategies, including the use of τ. This method can show that, of two or more alternative means of timing an action visually, the use of τ best explains the data. As Borst and Bahde's (1988) experiments illustrate, however, this does not necessarily imply that τ is actually used. The same problem arises in interpreting Lee and Reddish's (1991) findings from gannets. Wann (in press) argues that the results are equally consistent with the hypothesis that the birds fold their wings when they have fallen some fixed proportion of the height of their dive, and points out that testing this hypothesis against the τ strategy requires more records of dives from large heights than are available in Lee and Reddish's sample.

A more convincing case for the use of τ could be made if the parameter were manipulated during approach to a target, and the predicted effects on the timing of behaviour were observed. Sun, Carey, and Goodale (1992) report experiments in which gerbils were trained to run to a food dish in front of a television screen displaying a circle. The size of the circle, and its distance from the food, were varied to prevent the gerbils using the angular size of the circle as distance information. In test trials, the circle was changed in size while the gerbils were running towards it. When it expanded, the animals decelerated sooner than in the control condition, whereas when it contracted, their deceleration was delayed. These results imply that gerbils use τ to control their speed of approach to

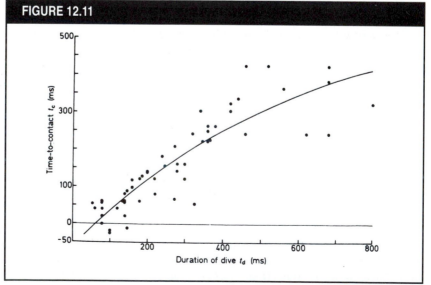

FIGURE 12.11

Relationship between the duration of a gannet's dive (t_d) and the time to contact at which it streamlines (t_c). The curve is the best fit generated by the model to the data. From Lee and Reddish (1981). Reprinted by permission of the author and publisher from *Nature*, Vol. 293, pp. 293–294. Copyright © 1981 Macmillan Magazines Ltd.

a goal. However, the effect of changing the size of the circle was smaller than would be predicted by a pure τ strategy, and so gerbils must integrate τ with other sources of depth information, in the same way as they integrate the angular size of a landmark with motion cues (Goodale et al., 1990; see p.280).

In conclusion, experiments investigating the use of τ to time animals' actions have yielded varying results, and it appears that the relative contributions of τ and other optical parameters vary from one situation to another, and also that τ may sometimes be used in combination with other optical information. This variation in control mechanisms is an interesting problem for further research. For example, we might expect τ to be useful in situations where the timing of actions is critical, as when a large animal jumps or flies towards a small target, or where approach velocity changes smoothly.

CONCLUSIONS

The experiments we have described in this chapter provide evidence that Gibson's analysis of the information available in the optic flow field is useful for understanding how animals obtain information needed to guide movement through the environment. We have seen, for example, how uniform lateral flow and centrifugal flow can be used by insects to stabilise flight and to initiate landing manoeuvres, and how τ variables can be used to time actions. In Chapter 13 we will see how these and other properties of optic flow are also important in the control of human movement, both in everyday situations and in skilled activities such as athletics.

As well as showing that Gibsonian principles are useful in understanding animal vision, these examples make two further points. The first is that it is misleading to think of an animal as constructing a metrically accurate representation of the three-dimensional layout of its surroundings. In many circumstances, animals will not need information about absolute distances of objects in order to control their actions successfully: a gannet does not need to know its height above the sea at each moment, but the optimum point at which to streamline its wings. We have seen that it is difficult to get absolute distance information from an optic flow field, because of the problem of independently gauging the animal's speed, but that heuristic strategies such as integration of velocity values, or computing τ, provide ecologically adequate means of timing approach to objects and surfaces.

The second point concerns a criticism often made of Gibson's theory, which is that it ignores the physiology of perception and is vague about how information available in light actually is detected. Although Gibson himself was not concerned with the physiology of vision, it would be mistaken to believe that his style of analysis of the information available in light is incompatible with neurophysiological analysis. As we have seen in this chapter and in Chapter 8, his emphasis on the information available for animals in the optic flow field has played a part in stimulating research on the physiological mechanisms by which optical motion is processed.

13

Visual Guidance of Human Action

In Chapter 12 we discussed how information obtained from patterns of optic flow is used to guide the flight paths of insects or the dives of gannets. In this chapter we discuss aspects of locomotor behaviour in higher animals, particularly man. We describe how research conducted within an ecological framework has helped us to understand aspects of human action that were largely ignored by traditional approaches to human perception.

Whereas the mental life of insects is presumably relatively uncomplicated, that of humans is complex and creative. We do not simply "respond" to the information that reaches our senses, but encode and reflect on it, and can describe our world to others. Nevertheless, just like lower animals, we must maintain posture and safe footing, and negotiate obstacles while moving around the world. We duck to avoid missiles, or move our arms and hands appropriately to catch them. We stop at the edge of a cliff, jump over puddles, or brake the car when an animal darts across the road.

Following Lee (1977) we can classify the types of information necessary for controlling such locomotor activities into three kinds— *exteroceptive*, *proprioceptive* and *exproprioceptive*.

Exteroceptive information about the layout of surfaces in the environment, and the positions of objects or course of events within the environment, is needed to guide action in the world. The most important source of exteroceptive information for humans and many other animals is vision. Proprioceptive information about the movement of body parts relative to one another is necessary for coordinated bodily actions, and is gained through mechanical receptors in joints and within the vestibular system, but also through vision (try bringing the tips of both your index fingers together with your eyes open and then with them closed). Exproprioceptive information about the position of the body or parts of it *relative* to the environment is also necessary for maintaining balance and guiding action through the world, and again vision provides powerful information of this kind.

Lee's classification departs from the traditional division of sensory systems into exteroceptors and proprioceptors, but his threefold system is more suitable for discussions of locomotor behaviour. In the examples of locomotor behaviour we discuss later we will show how vision provides important information of all three kinds. We will first discuss how vision guides gross postural adjustments that allow us to duck to avoid missiles, or to maintain our balance while standing. We then consider finer aspects of locomotion and describe how it is that we negotiate a smooth path through a variable terrain. These are activities that humans share with other land-living animals, but we will go on to consider the visual guidance of behaviour peculiar to humans, such as driving cars or catching and hitting balls in sport. We will see that several general principles, some of which we have already discussed in Chapters 11 and 12, apply to the visual control of this wide variety of activities.

POSTURAL ADJUSTMENTS

Avoiding objects on collision course

An object approaching an observer on a collision path needs to be avoided. A strong empiricist tradition might suggest that infants would need considerable experience of the tactile consequences of an approaching object before reacting to the visual information specifying collision. However, it appears that infants may have an innate appreciation of particular patterns of optic flow. Bower, Broughton, and Moore (1970) demonstrated that babies as young as eight days old would show defensive distress reactions when a foam rubber cube was pushed towards them. It appears that babies who are too young to have experienced the effects of colliding objects can respond appropriately to those apparently on collision course. Of course their reactions might be based on the change in air pressure created by the real approaching object rather than on the optical information specifying collision. However, Bower et al. (1970) and Ball and Tronick (1971) also tested young babies' reactions to dynamic optical displays in which no air pressure changes were present.

The displays were created by casting the shadow of a real object onto a screen in front of a supported infant. As the object was moved towards the light source, the shadow cast by it expanded in size, creating a "looming" image. Babies showed characteristic reactions to such displays. Their heads went back and their arms and hands were raised to cover their faces. Distress was also evident. Whereas Bower et al. reported that the reactions exhibited were somewhat less strong to an apparent than to a real object, Ball and Tronick reported no difference in the strength of the reactions in the two cases. The reactions given to these looming patterns were in marked contrast to those shown when the pattern cast specified an object that was approaching on a noncollision path, or when it specified an object receding from the child (a shrinking as opposed to a looming pattern). Schiff, Caviness, and Gibson (1962) reported similar responses in infant rhesus monkeys presented with looming patterns.

Adult humans are strongly influenced by knowledge of their surroundings, and do not show defensive responses to looming optic flow when they believe there are no sources of danger nearby. King, Dykeman, Redgrave, and Dean (1992) found that people would only respond to a looming object with a "flinching" movement of the head when they were concentrating hard on a distracting task (a computer game) and also believed that they were alone in a room. During the course of development, it seems that the simple defensive reactions to optic flow seen in babies come to be inhibited by conscious attention and by knowledge of the physical and social environment.

It may be that defensive responses are based on detecting τ, the optic variable that specifies time to contact (see Chapter 12). Schiff and Detwiler (1979) have shown that people are able to estimate when an object that had been approaching on a filmed collision course would have hit them, and that their judgements were influenced little by whether the object was filmed against a textured or a blank background. This suggests that people can use the rate of looming of the image of an obstacle to estimate τ, in the absence of information about the rate of background texture deletion. There is evidence that subjects systematically under-estimate time to contact in some simulations of looming objects (McCleod & Ross, 1983; Schiff & Detwiler, 1979), but the effect is not found with all displays (Freeman, Harris, & Tyler, 1994). It would be interesting to extend these findings by examining the timing of reactions by infant humans and monkeys to patterns looming at different speeds to see whether there is evidence that their behaviour is controlled by the detection of τ.

Maintaining balance

As adults (at least when sober) we take for granted our ability to remain upright on two feet. As every parent knows, however, the ability to stand and eventually to walk unsupported is an achievement that is gradually mastered by the infant, with months of unsteadiness and falls on the way. The gymnast on the narrow beam, the ballet dancer on points, or the circus artiste standing on a cantering horse must all learn to maintain balance in new and changing circumstances.

There are a number of different sources of information that may be used to control balance. These include information from receptors in the feet and ankle joints, information from the vestibular system—the organ of balance—and information received through the eyes. A simple demonstration suggests that visual information may be extremely important in maintaining posture. Try standing on one leg with eyes open and then with them closed. With eyes closed you will probably sway and perhaps even fall over, despite the information still being received from your feet, ankles, and vestibular system.

The importance of vision in maintaining balance has been more formally demonstrated by Lee and his colleagues (Lee & Aronson, 1974; Lee & Lishman, 1975; Lishman & Lee, 1973) in an experimental arrangement known as the "swinging room". The room essentially consists of a bottomless box suspended from the ceiling. The subject stands on a floor and the walls of the room can be moved backwards or forwards around the subject, without his or her knowledge. The walls of the room are covered with wallpaper to provide a visual texture. When the room is moved towards the subject, this produces the same expanding optic flow pattern that would be produced if the observer were in fact swaying towards the wall. If the room is moved away from the observer this produces a contracting optical flow pattern as though the observer were swaying away from the wall (see Fig. 13.1). Just as an optomotor experiment (Ch.12, p.268) simulates the optic flow produced when an insect turns, the swinging room simulates that generated by a person swaying.

Using this apparatus, Lee and his colleagues conducted a number of experiments in which they showed that vision could provide exproprioceptive information that could be used to control balance. In one experiment Lee and Aronson (1974) placed toddlers (aged 13–16 months) within the swinging

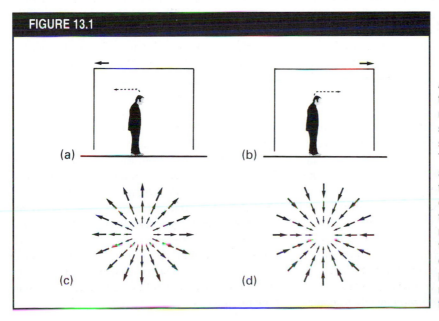

FIGURE 13.1

(a) (b) (c) (d)

An adult or child stands in the swinging room. (a) The room is moved towards the subject and the observer sways or falls backwards. (b) The room is moved away, and the observer sways or falls forwards. (c) The expanding optic flow pattern that would result from movement of the room towards the subject. (d) The contracting optical flow pattern that would result from movement of the room away from the subject.

room. After a period of acclimatisation in which the infant's normal stability while standing could be assessed, they tested the infant's reactions to movement of the wall of the room while the child was standing facing it. When the room was moved towards the subject the child was observed to sway, stagger, or fall in a direction away from the wall. This was not merely a defensive reaction to the "looming" pattern (cf. p.268) because the child staggered or fell towards the wall when it was moved away from it (see Fig. 13.1). Indeed, some of the children became distressed during the procedure and for them the experiment had to be prematurely terminated.

The responses shown by these children were entirely consistent with those that would be expected if the child interpreted the optic flow produced by movements of the room as resulting from its own postural sway. An outward flow, obtained when the room is moved towards the child, is consistent with sway towards the wall. The child then compensates for its apparent sway by moving backwards, and vice versa. It appears that in children acquiring the skill of balancing on two feet, visual information can override the veridical information about actual posture obtained from the feet, ankles, and vestibular system. Lee and Aronson suggest that it is vision that "tunes up" the sensitivity of these mechanical systems, and point out that vision is a better source of information for the child to rely on while the feet and ankles are maturing and growing.

Learning to stand upright is such an achievement for the child that we tend to forget earlier achievements, such as sitting upright. Vision seems to play a fundamental role in maintaining posture whether standing or sitting. Butterworth and Hicks (1977) showed that infants who have just learned to sit without being supported will sway with movements of the swinging room, and Butterworth (1983) showed that even two-month-olds will move their heads with the room.

Even for adults it appears that visual information may override that obtained from mechanical or vestibular receptor systems. A familiar example of this is when one experiences one's own stationary train as moving while another departs from the next platform, an example of induced movement (see Chapter 15). Lee and Lishman (1975) were able to affect body sway and stability in adults by small movements of the swinging room. Subjects' body sway was measured accurately with a sway meter when they stood with eyes open or eyes closed, or within the swinging room. Their body sway with eyes open could be "driven" by movements of the swinging room. Thus if the room was moved backwards and forwards in a regular, sinusoidal manner, the body was also seen to sway sinusoidally, linked to the movement of the walls. More recent experiments (e.g. Dijkstra, Schöner, & Gielen, 1994) have extended these findings, showing that large amplitudes of sway (up to several centimetres) can be induced in adults by oscillation of the visual surroundings.

Lee and Lishman (1975) also compared subjects standing normally, on a sloping ramp, on a pile of foam pads (a "compliant" surface), or on their toes. Although visual driving of sway was observed in all four conditions, it was greatest for subjects standing on the compliant surface, where the information from the foot and ankle receptors was the most impoverished. In a further experiment, Lee and Lishman had subjects adopt novel balancing postures such as the "Chaplin" stance (feet aligned at 180°) or the "pinstripe" stance (one foot angled behind the calf of the other leg while holding a weight in the hand opposite to the supporting leg). In such circumstances the adults, like the children in Lee and Aronson's study, could be made to stagger and fall by movements of the swinging room. They described the subject as like "a visual puppet; his balance can be manipulated by simply moving his surroundings without his being aware of it" (Lee & Lishman, 1975, p. 94).

We can conclude from these experiments that infants and toddlers learning to control their balance are strongly influenced by optic flow, which is used to tune other control systems relying on mechanical information from joints, muscles, and the vestibular system. As a result, adults are able to maintain balance using mechanical information alone, except in novel or demanding conditions, when the infant dependence on optic flow re-emerges.

The developmental interplay between mechanical and visual systems can be disrupted when people suffer from sensory impairments. If vision is absent altogether, mechanical systems cannot be tuned as accurately, and this may explain why congenitally blind children are slower than sighted ones in learning to stand and to walk, and blind adults show more body sway than sighted adults (Edwards, 1946). Conversely, if disease affects the vestibular system of the inner ear later in life, vision can regain its earlier role in controlling posture. People suffering from such disorders often complain of unusual sensitivity to movement in their surroundings, which may cause dizziness and loss of balance, and Redfern and Furman (1994) found that such patients also sway more strongly in response to sinusoidally oscillating optic flow than do controls.

The examples given monitored the forward and backward body sway of people facing the room as it moved towards or away from them. Lee and Young (1986) also describe studies by Anderson in which adults ran on a treadmill in the room, which was then unexpectedly tilted around a horizontal axis (see Fig. 13.2). The inclination of the room and of the subject's trunk was monitored using a Selspot movement-measuring system, where infra-red light-emitting diodes are attached to key spots and a film of their positions over time is recorded. Using this method, it was possible to compare the sideways movements of the trunk in the normal room with the movements that occurred as the room was tilted. The trunk clearly tilted with the room, as though the runner were compensating for his or her perceived tilt in the opposite direction. Owen and Lee (1986) went on to test 3–5-year-old children walking on a solid floor as the walls of the room tilted around them. Like the adults, the children also tilted their trunks with the room.

We have seen that vision appears to play an important role in affecting gross postural adjustments. Babies respond to the exteroceptive information in looming patterns and try to avoid the "objects" that are about to collide with them. Toddlers and adults make use of exproprioceptive information from vision when maintaining balance. We now turn to consider how we use vision when we are actively negotiating terrain during locomotion.

WALKING, RUNNING, AND JUMPING

It is obviously difficult to walk or run safely without adequate vision, but it is not necessarily obvious at how many different levels visual information is used to guide locomotion. At the coarsest level, vision can inform animals of their overall speed and direction of movement through the world, and we will take up this topic in the next section. Here, we will consider how visual information is used to control locomotion at a more fine-grained level, guiding steps or strides so as to avoid steep drops and to place the feet correctly on uneven terrain.

Detecting falling-off places

From the moment they are independently mobile, young animals must avoid falling off dangerous edges. Adult humans generally avoid accidentally stepping over the edge of a cliff, but would an unattended infant avoid crawling off? This was the question posed by E.J. Gibson, which led to her development of the "visual cliff" (Gibson & Walk,

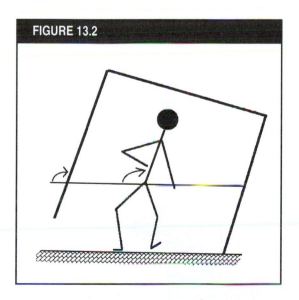

FIGURE 13.2

If the room is tilted as an adult or child walks or runs within it, their body tilts too. Adapted from Lee & Young (1986).

1960). The apparatus is shown in Fig. 13.3. It consists of a raised platform that divides two checkerboard surfaces (giving optical texture). One of these is at a similar level to the platform (the shallow side), the other is considerably lower (the deep side). Both sides provide surfaces of support, however, because the deep side is covered with a sheet of glass that is at the same level as that covering the shallow side. Thus both the shallow and deep sides have a surface that could safely support an animal or child, but the optical information given by the deep side specifies a sharp drop. Gibson and Walk showed that the young of all species that guide themselves mainly by vision, when placed on the central platform, would avoid venturing onto the glass covering the deep side. Human infants aged 6–14 months would not cross the glass even when encouraged by their mothers who were standing on the other side of it. Young

animals placed on the glass showed defensive reactions.

By manipulating the size of the texture elements on the surfaces, and the distances of these from the central platform, Gibson and Walk were able to explore which variables were important in guiding the behaviour of the animals tested. If the squares on the deep side were made larger, so that the perceived density of the squares as seen from each side of the platform was equivalent, the animals still avoided the deep side, suggesting that motion parallax, rather than texture density, was the important variable. However, if the actual depth of each surface was made the same (i.e. both shallow), but one was patterned with smaller sized squares than the other, there was still a slight tendency to prefer the optically shallow side, suggesting some role for texture density. These observations suggest that by the time they are mobile (immediately for

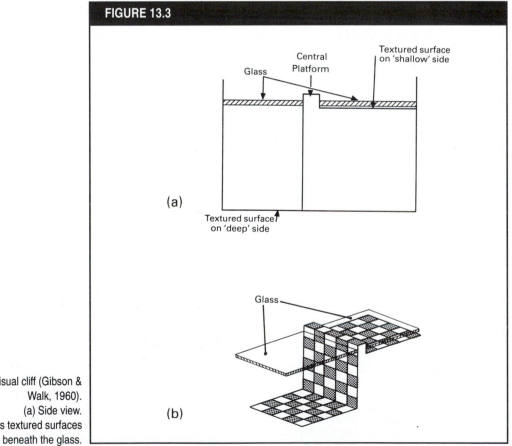

FIGURE 13.3

Glass

Central Platform

Textured surface on 'shallow' side

(a)

Textured surface on 'deep' side

Glass

(b)

The visual cliff (Gibson & Walk, 1960).
(a) Side view.
(b) Shows textured surfaces beneath the glass.

chicks and lambs, after six months or so for humans), young creatures can make use of motion parallax and also perhaps texture density changes in guiding themselves so that they remain on safe surfaces of support. The experiments on infant responses to looming patterns, along with those on the visual cliff, suggest that some appreciation of depth, or relative depth, may be inborn rather than learned in the way the Empiricist philosophers suggested (see Chapter 7). Bower (e.g. 1966, 1971) describes other observations of infants that are relevant to this issue.

Regulating gait

We have seen how vision may be used to detect gross aspects of layout, such as obstacles and cliffs, but vision is also necessary to guide finer aspects of locomotion. The movements of our limbs as we move through the world need to be tailored to the type of terrain we encounter, and the type of terrain needs to be anticipated and the limbs adjusted accordingly. To see why, we must briefly describe the nature of locomotor activity.

An animal or human walks or runs with a smooth and cyclically regular sequence of limb movements (Bernstein, 1967). It propels itself forwards by applying force backwards against the ground as each foot strikes it. When walking, one or more feet (depending on how many the walker possesses) remain in contact with the ground all the time; when running, the animal or human progresses by a series of leaps. The length of each leap ("flight") is determined by the speed at which the animal is travelling and the vertical thrust applied at each stride. Figure 13.4 illustrates this further for those familiar with vectors. For both walking and running it is important that the thrust being applied to the foot on contact is coordinated with the swing-through time of the foot that will next contact the ground, so that this meets the ground in the right way for maximum thrust. For example, if the foot is travelling forward relative to the ground when it contacts it, this will have a braking effect. Thus trained human runners try to lift their knees high so that they can thrust down hard and backwards relative to the ground as each foot strikes it just in front of the hips. The thrust applied at each stride must then give the runner sufficient vertical lift to ensure a long enough flight time so that the next foot can be swung through to its optimum strike position, and so on (Lee, Lishman, & Thomson, 1982).

FIGURE 13.4

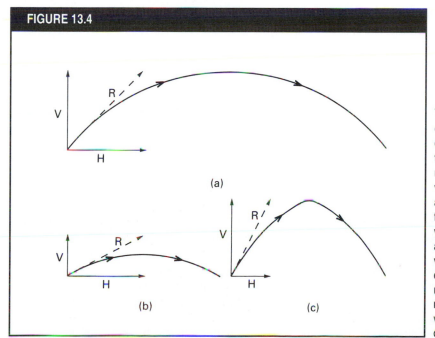

(a)

(b)

(c)

The distance travelled in each stride when running depends on the vertical thrust (V) and a force reflected in horizontal velocity (H). At (a), both V and H are large, and the flight is long. At (b) the vertical thrust is reduced, and at (c) the horizontal velocity is reduced. In both cases, flight length is reduced. The flight path is not the resultant (R) of vectors V and H, because other forces are operating.

The striking of the ground not only needs to be timed, but the force exerted needs to be modified according to the type of surface encountered. If the ground surface is slippery then a large force will produce skidding rather than the desired propulsion forwards. If the surface is compliant rather than firm then much of the force will be absorbed by the surface rather than moving the animal (try running fast on soft sand), and so more force must be applied in order to maintain speed. If the surface is uneven then the animal may fail to find adequate points of contact between its feet and the ground. Despite these difficulties humans and other animals can normally maintain fairly smooth progress through an environment of variable surfaces provided they can see properly. At night it can be an uncomfortably jarring experience to run across hilly or uneven ground, demonstrating how vision is needed to make fine adjustments to planned foot positions, postures, and forces (Lee, 1980a).

It is thus essential that gait is regulated to meet the demands of a particular terrain. Theories of action that stress the "blind" running off of programs of locomotor activity have little to say about this.

There will, in general, be unpredictable influences, both from within and without, which will deviate the activity from its intended course. The activity has, therefore, to be monitored in terms of the program and any deviation corrected by adjusting the ongoing program. It is in this continual process of formulating locomotor programs, monitoring their execution and adjusting them that sensory information plays its vital role (Lee & Lishman, 1977, p.226).

Lee et al. (1982) have illustrated this adjustment of locomotor programs by sensory information in their studies of the sport of long-jumping. A long-jumper needs to maximise his or her horizontal velocity and vertical thrust at the point of take-off (refer back to Fig. 13.4). Because the jump is measured to the take-off board, and is disqualified if the athlete steps over it, the athlete must try to reach maximum speed as the launching

foot strikes the board, with the body postured appropriately to give maximum lift. Athletic coaches encourage their students to develop a standard run-up, which they mark out in paces back from the board, and they may intersperse practice jumps with "run-throughs", where the athlete strikes the board but runs on through the sand without jumping. Such training procedures seem to be based on the assumption that some kind of run-up program can be set up, learned, and executed without further modification during the course of the action. Lee et al. (1982) set out to examine whether athletes did indeed maintain a standard run-up in accordance with training procedures.

They filmed the training sessions of three female athletes who ranged from club to Olympic standard. A striped marker strip was placed on either side of the track so that the athletes' foot placements could be accurately measured from single frames of the film. Their analysis revealed that the run-up consisted of two distinct phases. Until the athletes were a few strides from the board, their stride patterns were remarkably constant, which presumably reflected their training with standard run-ups. This consistency broke down over the last few strides, however. It appeared that the cumulative effect of the small inconsistencies during the first phase meant that the athlete had to adjust her final few strides in order to strike the board accurately. There was a dramatic increase in the variability of stride lengths for the last three strides, while the standard error (a measure of variability) of the footfall positions decreased dramatically over these same few strides, to reach 8cm at the board for the Olympic athlete.

Lee et al. (1982) went on to ask which parameter of the step cycle was being adjusted in order to regulate stride length so accurately in relation to distance from the board. Of the possible parameters, they found that flight time had the highest correlation with stride length, and therefore concluded that the runners were adjusting the vertical thrust of each take-off (see Fig. 13.4) in order to achieve the correct flight times on the last three strides. An economical means of doing this, Lee et al. propose, would be to detect time to contact with the board by means of the "local" τ

function of the angular size of the board (i.e. the ratio of the angle subtended by the board at the eye to the rate of change of the angle; see Ch.12, p.282), and then to adjust the vertical thrusts of the last three steps so that their flight times "just fill" this time.

Warren, Young, and Lee (1986) were able to obtain more direct evidence that strides are adjusted by varying flight length (and hence flight time) through modulating the vertical thrust (see Fig. 13.4) on each stride. In an ingenious analogue of the task of running over variable terrain, they used a Selspot recording system to film trained athletes who had to place their feet on irregularly spaced targets as they ran on a treadmill. Warren et al. confirmed that it was indeed flight length, rather than the trail and reach components of the stride length, that were adjusted by the athlete in such a situation. ("Trail" and "reach" refer to the extent to which the foot extends away from the body at take-off and landing respectively). Furthermore, as flight velocity was kept roughly constant, it appeared that flight distance was indeed primarily adjusted by varying flight time. Consistent with this, they found that most of the variation in the step time was due to variations in vertical step thrust. Again, visual detection of time to contact with the next target of foot placement seems a promising means of controlling vertical thrust.

The long-jumpers and athletes studied by Lee and his colleagues represent extreme examples of precisely timed locomotion, but those of us of meagre athletic ability are still able to run to catch a bus, jumping over puddles, and negotiating kerbs and other minor hurdles on the way. It may be that adjusting the flight times of strides is a general strategy that we all use for controlling our gait in relation to the terrain, and which is adapted by experts to particularly demanding tasks such as long-jumping. In support of this hypothesis, Berg, Wade, and Greer (1994) found that novice long-jumpers home in on the board by adjusting their strides in just the same way as Lee et al.'s (1982) experts did.

The hypothesis that the timing of strides in walking or running is controlled by using τ to obtain time to contact with the target of each footfall is an attractive one, although no evidence is yet available to support it directly. It has, however, been possible to identify the point in the step cycle at which visual information modulates stride length, by using a "visual denial" method. Laurent and Thomson (1988) asked subjects to walk towards a target and place either their left or their right foot on it. While walking, subjects were only able to see their surroundings during brief glimpses at specific points in the step cycle. Several interesting findings emerged from this experiment.

First, the adjustments that subjects made in order to place their feet accurately occurred in their last three strides, just as in long-jumpers (Lee et al., 1982), despite the large difference in speed in the two tasks. Second, and surprisingly, subjects showed no loss of accuracy in placing a foot on the target when they were only able to see for 300msec during each step cycle. These brief glimpses clearly provided enough visual information to carry out the task normally. Third, there was a subtle difference between conditions where the flash of light occurred while the foot aimed at the target was on the ground, and where it occurred while the foot was in mid-swing. Although the foot was placed accurately in both cases, the control of the last three strides was considerably less smooth in the second case, and was achieved in a series of irregular, variable stride lengths.

Laurent and Thomson's (1988) results suggest that, while a foot is on the ground, there is a "window" in which information needed to modulate the next stride with that foot is acquired, before the current stride (with the other foot) is completed. Hollands, Marple-Horvat, Henkes, and Rowan (1995) have obtained more evidence in support of this hypothesis. They recorded subjects' eye movements while walking from one irregularly spaced "stepping stone" to another and found a rhythm of saccadic eye movements tightly linked to the stepping rhythm. While one foot is on the ground, a saccade takes place towards its next target (not the target the other foot is currently swinging towards), and is completed before the foot leaves the ground or soon after. It seems that fixation of the target of each step, while the foot concerned is still on the ground, is important in obtaining whatever visual information is needed to adjust the vertical thrust of the step.

VISUAL CONTROL OF SPEED AND DIRECTION

In the previous section, we discussed the fine-grained control of walking or running, in which visual information is used to modulate each step or stride according to the terrain just ahead. As people walk or run, they also need information over a longer time scale, in order to control the speed and direction of their locomotion in relation to surrounding goals and obstacles. Next, we will consider how information in optic flow is used to control speed and direction, not only in natural locomotion but also when getting about with the help of cars or other vehicles.

Controlling speed

In principle, a walking person could use optic flow to maintain a particular speed by regulating the angular velocity of texture elements on the ground below. As these are at a known distance (the walker's eye-height), their angular speed specifies the walker's speed. Konczak (1994) observed people walking through a "swinging tunnel", to determine whether the altered speed of optic flow had any effect on their speed. As predicted, there was a tendency for subjects' speed to increase if the walls of the tunnel moved with the direction of walking (therefore slowing optic flow), although the effect was small, and inconsistent from one subject to another. Movement of the walls in the opposite direction had no effect on walking speed, and so overall there was no strong evidence that people adjust their walking speed by regulating optic flow, in the way that bees do when flying through the centre of an aperture (Ch.12, p.276). This is perhaps not surprising, because a walking person has many sources of mechanical information available about his or her gait, and provided that these do not signal any change, variations in optic flow are not needed to control speed.

In other situations it is likely that the visual control of speed will be more critical. One is where speed must be reduced so that a person comes to a stop at a target, as when a cricketer runs as fast as possible down the pitch and then brakes hard to stop just at the crease before turning to make another run. Another is where speed is reduced so as to collide with a target at a controlled speed, as when a person strides towards a swing door and slows down so that an outstretched hand strikes the door just hard enough to open it without jarring the wrist. In such cases, we need information to control our *deceleration*.

At first, the visual control of deceleration seems to involve detecting both the distance of the target and current speed in relation to desired speed, and then computing the deceleration required. Lee (1976) has argued that these steps may not be necessary, and that the detection and regulation of a single parameter of optic flow is sufficient to control deceleration. This parameter is the rate of change of τ (see Ch.12, p.281), denoted τ' (or "tau-dot") by Lee. Starting with the equations of motion relating distance, time, velocity, and acceleration, Lee (1976) calculated how τ' and deceleration vary during braking manoeuvres. If a person exerts a constant braking force, so that deceleration is constant, then τ' changes during braking (in other words, τ does not decrease at a constant rate). On the other hand, if braking is regulated to keep τ' constant (i.e. τ decreases at a constant rate), then deceleration varies.

Although constant deceleration may seem a simple strategy, it would require first computing the correct deceleration from velocity and distance. In a striking conclusion, Lee (1976) showed that this computation is made unnecessary by braking so as to keep τ' constant. With a constant value of τ' between 0 and –0.5, a person will stop precisely at a target, whereas with a value between –0.5 and –1 a person will collide with it at a particular speed (see Fig. 13.5, bottom). To stop just at a target by keeping τ' at a value between 0 and –0.5, braking force and thus deceleration must decrease during approach (see Fig. 13.5, top). Deceleration is constant only if τ' is kept at –0.5.

Although the detection and regulation of τ' could provide a simple means of controlling deceleration when approaching an obstacle, it is not easy to demonstrate conclusively that this method is used. The τ' hypothesis can be tested against the alternative hypothesis that deceleration is constant, by determining whether the

FIGURE 13.5

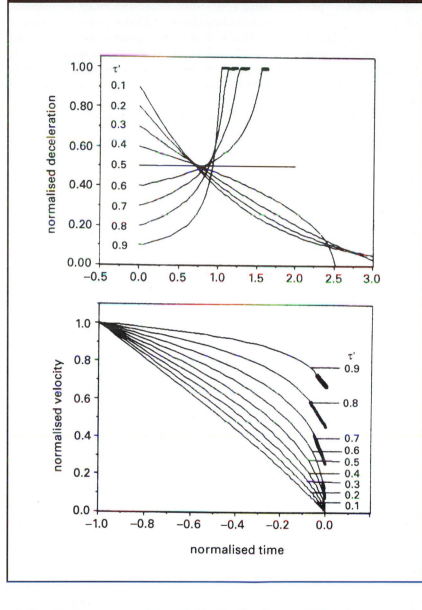

Top: Relationship between deceleration and time during approach to an obstacle, with braking controlled so as to keep τ' constant at various values between −0.1 and −0.9. Bottom: Relationship between velocity and distance from the obstacle for the same approaches. Note: for consistency with the text, the τ' values in these graphs should be multiplied by −1. Reproduced from Lee, Young, and Rewt (1992). Copyright © 1992 by the American Psychological Association. Reprinted with permission.

relationship between τ and time during braking is linear or not. During approaches of hummingbirds to a feeder (Lee et al., 1991), and of pigeons to a landing perch (Lee et al., 1993), the relationship is linear. In both cases, τ' remains constant at a value less than −0.5, implying that a controlled collision is achieved.

Lee's (1976) theory of braking has been tested for human locomotion by Wann, Edgar, and Blair (1993), who measured values of τ while people ran up to and stopped at a target. They found that, in some versions of the task, τ decreased linearly with a slope (i.e. τ' value) of −0.5 or a little less. In other tasks, particularly where people had to extend an arm to touch a target as they stopped, this pattern was followed by a brief second phase in which τ behaved differently. It appears that although the τ' theory explains some aspects of the control of speed as people slow down from a run, the overall organisation of braking is sometimes more complex than the theory predicts.

Lee, Young, and Rewt (1992) extended the theory of braking control by τ' to a case where angular velocity of approach is controlled, when a person performs a somersault. As a somersault is completed, the gymnast must reduce his or her angular velocity (speed of rotation), by extending the body from its curled up position in such a way as to come to rest in an upright, balanced posture. Lee et al. show that this angular braking problem can also be solved using τ' (in this case, the rate of change of the τ function of the angle between the body and the vertical). By filming trampolinists performing single forward somersaults, Lee et al. (1992) found that the change in angular velocity as they "unwound" to land fitted the predictions of the τ' theory better than alternatives. The evidence from both gymnasts and birds is indirect, however, and it is still an open question whether τ' is directly detected, or whether the same outcome is achieved in some other way.

Controlling direction

In order to reach particular goals or avoid obstacles as we move about, we must be able to control our *heading*, the point in the environment towards which we are moving. In his analysis of the optic flow produced by self-motion, Gibson (1966) argued that the centre of expansion of the flow field specifies an observer's heading (see Ch.11, p.260). It therefore seems that a simple means of controlling heading is to keep a goal aligned with the region of the optic flow field where there is no motion. There is a serious flaw in this argument, however. The direction of heading must be obtained from the projection of the optic flow field on to a *retinal* flow field, and this will be made up of two components: a linear flow field, which contains a centre of expansion specifying heading, and a rotary field generated by eye and head movements (cf. Ch.12, p.270). When these are added together, there is no simple relationship between heading and a centre of expansion of optic flow. The retinal flow field may contain no centre of expansion, and if it does, it may be some distance away from the direction of heading (see Fig. 13.6).

If the retinal flow field were analysed by the visual system into linear and rotary components, then heading could be obtained from the centre of expansion of the linear component of flow. One way of resolving the two components would be to use an "extraretinal eye position signal" to specify the direction and speed of the eye movement that caused the rotary component. As discussed in Chapter 7 (p.164), this could either be reafferent information from oculomotor commands, or signals from stretch receptors in the eye muscles. On the other hand, because rotary flow does not produce motion parallax, it is possible in principle to analyse retinal flow into linear and rotary components without any extraretinal information about eye movement (Longuet-Higgins & Prazdny, 1980).

Much effort has been devoted to finding out whether or not people use extraretinal information in detecting heading. The experiments concerned have used patterns of moving dots on a television screen that simulate the optic flow caused by movement with a particular heading through various kinds of environment. People watching such displays are able to estimate the simulated direction of heading with an accuracy of 1–2°. Warren and Hannon (1988) used this method to determine whether extraretinal information is needed to detect heading, by comparing heading judgements in two conditions. In the first, subjects watched a display similar to Fig. 13.6a that simulated forward movement over a ground surface, while making a smooth eye movement to track a moving fixation point. In the second condition, subjects fixated a stationary point but the display now contained an added rotary component simulating the effect of the eye movement in the first condition; this display resembled Fig. 13.6b. The retinal flow was therefore identical in the two cases, but extraretinal information to resolve rotary flow was only available in the first condition. Warren and Hannon found that judgements of heading were equally accurate in the two cases, implying that extraretinal information is not required.

Further experiments of this kind have sometimes obtained different results, finding poorer heading estimation with simulated than

FIGURE 13.6

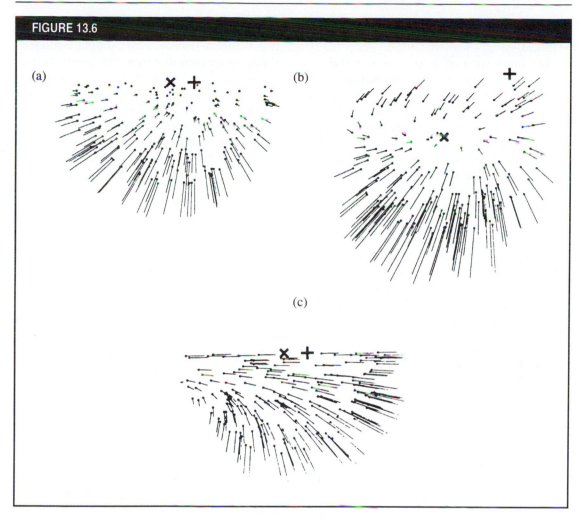

(a)

(b)

(c)

Three examples of retinal flow fields produced during forward movement over a ground plane. The lines attached to each dot show the speed and direction of optic motion at that point in the flow field. In each case, **+** denotes heading and **X** the direction of gaze. (a) No eye movement; there is a centre of expansion that coincides with heading. (b) Eye movement to fixate a point on the ground while moving forwards; there is a centre of expansion, but it does not coincide with heading. (c) Eye movement to track a moving object; there is no centre of expansion. Reprinted with permission from Lappe and Rauschecker (1994), *Nature*, Vol. 369, pp.712–713. Copyright © 1994 Macmillan Magazines Limited.

with real eye movements (see Royden, Crowell, & Banks, 1994). It seems likely that heading can be obtained in more than one way, and that extraretinal information is used in some circumstances but not in others. It is not entirely clear what factors are important, although extraretinal information is probably more important with faster eye movements. It is also likely that the nature of the fixation target is important, and that extraretinal information is needed if subjects move their eyes

to track a simulated moving object, but not if they track a point on a simulated ground surface (Lappe & Rauschecker, 1994; Van den Berg, 1993). It seems that we are able to obtain heading from the linear component of retinal flow, provided that the rotary flow has been generated by an eye movement tracking a stationary point on or near the ground. Theoretical models of heading estimation (e.g. Perrone & Stone, 1994) have made use of this constraint on eye movement during locomotion to simplify the processing problems involved.

The implication of these results is that eye movements made during walking and running are not always an arbitrary source of trouble for the detection of heading. Not surprisingly from a biological point of view, they instead appear to be organised in specific ways so as to contribute to solving the problem of obtaining heading from retinal flow. Cutting, Springer, Braren, and Johnson (1992) have followed this line of reasoning to a more radical conclusion about the role of eye movements, arguing that all approaches based on Gibson's analysis of optic flow are misconceived. They claim that the problem of resolving rotary and linear components of optic flow is an artificial one, created by the mistaken assumption that heading is obtained from the centre of expansion of linear flow.

Cutting et al.'s (1992) alternative theory begins not with a smoothly varying flow field produced by a flat ground surface (as a bird or an aeroplane pilot would experience; see Fig. 11.6), but with the optic flow produced by a cluttered environment containing objects and surfaces at many distances from an observer. They suggest that such a wood- or forest-like environment is more relevant to the evolution of human wayfinding abilities. If a person fixates an object while running or walking through cluttered surroundings, he or she will experience "differential motion parallax"; objects closer than the fixated one will move relative to the eye more quickly than, and in the opposite direction to, objects further away. The only exception will be for an object lying in the direction of the person's heading, where there will be no parallax. Thus, heading can be determined by repeated shifts of gaze controlled in a simple way by differential motion parallax, without any need to determine the centre of expansion of linear flow.

Cutting et al. (1992) describe experiments simulating movement through cluttered surroundings, and support for their theory is provided by the finding that failures of heading judgement occur specifically in situations where differential motion parallax is misleading. Even so, the fact remains that people are able to detect heading in displays simulating motion over a smooth surface, without making eye movements (e.g. Warren & Hannon, 1988), and this implies that shifts of gaze controlled by motion parallax cannot be the only mechanism involved. Cutting et al. (1992) suggest that in the more artificial tasks of steering cars or aeroplanes, where differential motion parallax is not useful, we do detect heading by using the centre of expansion of optic flow while adopting a tightly constrained pattern of gaze. Perhaps the same thing happens when people judge heading in simulations such as those used by Warren and Hannon.

Further progress towards understanding how we use vision to control our heading would be helped by two kinds of research. First, we need to know more about the eye movements that people actually make during different kinds of natural or simulated locomotion. Hollands et al.'s (1995) finding that people fixate their next-but-one footfall is a valuable starting point, and extensions of their methods to situations where people must alter course to negotiate obstacles would help in deciding between the different theories of heading detection discussed.

Second, we need to know whether results obtained in heading judgement tasks using small-screen displays would also be found in tasks where people must actively control their heading in relation to more natural visual stimulation. Wann, Rushton, and Lee (1995) describe a promising method of this kind, in which a wide-screen display of moving dots was used to simulate motion over an extended ground surface. Subjects were asked to use a steering wheel to direct their simulated motion towards a target in the display, which they fixated. They were able to control their "heading" with an accuracy of 1–2°, which suggests that estimation of heading in the presence of rotary flow (caused by rotation of the eye to maintain target fixation) is equally as good in this more natural task as in those using small-screen displays (Warren & Hannon, 1988).

Driving cars

Driving a car or other vehicle safely requires a great deal of knowledge of rules of the road, and skill in anticipating difficult situations and predicting the actions of other road users. All these things must, however, be built on the more basic skills of using visual information to steer and brake correctly, and so to stay on the road and avoid collisions. Because most people are able to acquire these skills, it is easy to overlook an obvious question: how is that we can learn to manoeuvre cars at all, when the speeds involved are so much higher than when we walk or run, and the movements of the limbs involved are so different? Is it because the same mechanisms of visual control transfer easily from walking to driving, or do we have to acquire entirely new ways of using visual information? The answers to these questions would tell us a good deal about the flexibility of the visual control of human action, and would also be of practical importance in helping to improve road safety.

We will begin our review of research on the role of vision in driving by considering the skill of accurate braking. A good driver will use the brake in good time, and with the correct force so that the car's speed can be reduced appropriately and smoothly. However, if brakes are applied too late (see unsafe driver 3 in Fig. 13.7), or too gently (unsafe driver 2 in Fig. 13.7), the driver will enter the "crash zone" shown in Fig. 13.7, which may be fatal.

There are thus two components to braking—knowing when to start and knowing how hard to brake. When following fairly closely behind another vehicle a driver is usually given a clear visual signal to start applying brakes when the brake-lights of the car in front light up. He or she still has to decide how hard to apply the brakes, however, as normal brake lights give no indication about how much the car in front is slowing. The driver must therefore respond to the optic information that specifies how quickly he or she is closing on the car in front. It is better to brake strongly at first, because this minimises the stopping distance, but the driver must also avoid braking too severely for the car behind to respond in turn. Good drivers drive safe braking distances apart, and this also requires adjustment according to speed and road conditions.

When brakes must be applied to negotiate an "obstacle" (e.g. traffic lights), the driver must decide when to start braking as well as how much pressure to apply. A potentially dangerous situation is encountered by the driver when leaving a fast highway where he or she may have adapted to travelling at a high constant speed, and may fail to brake sufficiently to negotiate a steeply curved exit road or a roundabout (traffic circle). The driver's ability to reduce speed accordingly can be enhanced by giving explicit advice on road signs about recommended exit or cornering speeds, or by

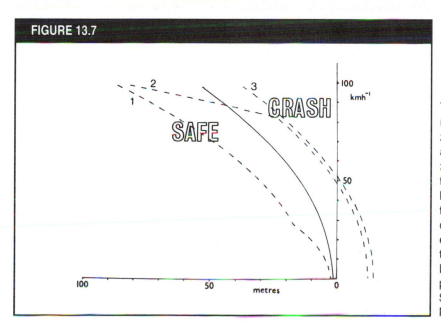

FIGURE 13.7

To stop safely, a driver must reduce speed (kmh^{-1}) to zero before the distance to an obstacle (metres) reaches zero. The safe driver (1) in this figure achieves this by braking strongly at first, and then more gently. Driver 3 does not start to brake soon enough, and driver 2 brakes too gently. Reprinted from Lee and Lishman (1977) with permission of the publishers, Scandinavian University Press.

augmenting the visual information that the driver responds to by constructing fences or painting lines across the road. One of the major through-routes in England, the A1, is particularly dangerous because it is almost of motorway (freeway) standard, hence people drive fast, but it is constantly interrupted by roundabouts (traffic circles), which must be taken slowly. Yellow lines have been painted across the road on the approach to some of these roundabouts, and the lines get closer together nearer the roundabout. The lines themselves give one a vivid impression of speed after the relatively featureless miles preceding them, and the gradual change in the spacing of the lines gives drivers visual information that suggests they are decelerating less quickly than they actually are. This causes drivers to brake harder than they might otherwise.

It would appear that good drivers must be constantly monitoring their distance from other cars and obstacles, and must know about their own and other cars' speeds, acceleration, and deceleration in order to brake effectively. However, Lee (1976) has argued that the control of braking can be more economically achieved if the driver responds directly to information about time to contact that is available in the optic flow field.

First, a driver could detect the τ function of the angular size of an obstacle such as the car ahead, which specifies time to contact (see Ch.12, p.282). When driving at night, the τ function of the angular separation of the two tail lights would provide the same information. Second, the rate of change of τ, or τ', could be used to control braking. As we saw earlier (p.296), a driver will stop at an obstacle without collision, provided τ' is kept between 0 and −0.5 during braking.

In support of the theory that drivers regulate τ' when braking, Lee (1976) cites results obtained by Spurr (1969), who measured the change in braking force (and therefore in deceleration) when drivers were asked to stop at a particular point from a normal driving speed. The drivers braked hard initially, and then slackened the brakes off steadily, as the τ' theory would predict (see Fig. 13.5). Lee (1976) and Lee and Lishman (1977) went on to propose a model (see Fig. 13.8) for the use of both τ and τ' to control acceleration and braking while driving in a stream of traffic, in such a way as to keep up with the car at front while maintaining a safe distance.

Following this theory, Lee suggests that road safety could be improved by amplifying or adding

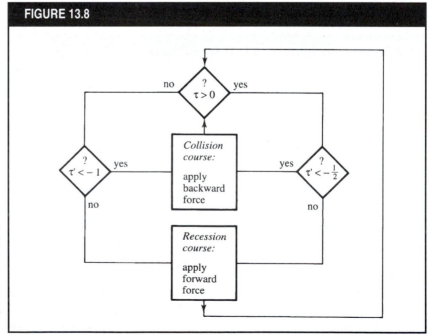

FIGURE 13.8

Lee's (1976) model illustrates how a driver can maintain a safe distance by maintaining τ and τ' at safe values. Redrawn from Lee and Lishman (1977) with permission of the publishers, Scandinavian University Press.

to the visual information gained from the rear ends of vehicles, particularly at night. By adding a reflectant strip so that the driver sees a progressively wider band of light the closer he or she approaches a vehicle at night, the information about rate of closure would be amplified, just as the yellow stripes painted across roads (see p.302) amplify information about speed. Information could be added by having an "imperative" brake signal, in addition to the normal brake lights, which would only operate when strong pressure was applied to the brake pedal by the driver in front.

Drivers must also control the direction of the vehicle by turning the steering wheel so as to keep heading aligned with the centre of the lane in which they are travelling, or with some other target. In simulated driving tasks, Land and Horwood (1995) found evidence for separate "near-road" and "far-road" systems in the control of steering. At low speeds, people can steer accurately as long as a segment of the road just ahead of the car is visible (as would be the case in fog). As driving speed increases, accurate steering requires a view of the road further (about 16m) ahead, presumably because at higher speeds approaching curves must be anticipated.

We have already seen evidence that fixation of gaze during locomotion plays an important role in the detection and control of heading (see p.299), and this seems to be true of the "far-road" system of steering control as well. Land and Lee (1994) recorded the direction of gaze and the angle of the steering wheel while drivers negotiated bends in a road, and found a remarkably close relationship between the two. Just before each turn of the steering wheel began, the gaze of the drivers "locked on" to the inside edge, or "tangent point", of the approaching curve in the road (see Fig. 13.9). The subjects were surprised by these results, and had been completely unaware of fixating the road in this precise way.

The regularity of drivers' gaze patterns when approaching bends suggests that fixation must play a role in controlling the heading of the car, but it is not yet clear what this role is. The tangent point may only be a convenient, arbitrary point on the ground surface on which to fixate, and so to facilitate the resolution of rotary and linear optic flow (Lappe & Rauschecker, 1994; Perrone & Stone, 1994). Alternatively, Land and Lee (1994) show that the angle between the tangent point and the direction of heading specifies the curvature of the road, which in turn determines the angle through which the steering wheel should be turned. Clearly, more research is needed to decide between these possibilities.

Drivers are not the only road-users who need to appreciate safe distances. Pedestrians crossing roads must also understand whether gaps between cars are large enough for safe crossing. This requires that pedestrians can perceive the difference between the times of arrival (time to contact) of the vehicles on either side of this gap, and can relate this difference to their own walking speed and distance across the road. Lee, Young, and McLaughlin (1984) have devised a "pretend road" crossing task for children to practise this skill safely, by pretending that a stretch of pavement beside a road is the road itself. Children practise crossing the pavement successfully so that they get to the other side of the pavement well before cars on the real road reach the same target point. Young and Lee (1987) evaluated a training programme based on the pretend road task extended to include two-way traffic. They found that after training, five-year-olds developed road-crossing competence at a level normally shown by considerably older children. Practice with the task led five-year-olds to set off to cross the pretend road more promptly when gaps were smaller, leading Lee and Young (1986) to suggest that five-year-olds have developed an improved ability to detect τ and to use this information to guide their actions. The pretend road-crossing task could thus prove an important component of road safety training, because it is at the ages of five and six that child pedestrian accidents are at a peak (Howarth, Routledge, & Repetto-Wright, 1974).

In conclusion, although most people are able to learn to use visual information so as to be safe drivers and pedestrians, the skills take some time to learn, and dangerous mistakes are occasionally made. One reason for both these problems may be that our natural mechanisms of controlling speed and direction are adapted to walking and running,

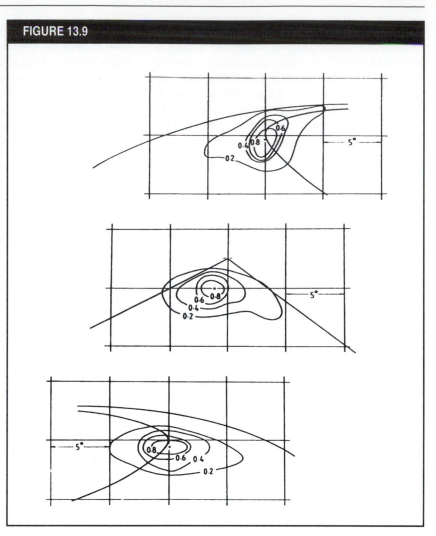

FIGURE 13.9

Distribution of drivers' fixation points relative to the road surface while negotiating right-hand bends (top) and left-hand bends (bottom), and when driving on a straight road (centre). When steering around bends, the distributions of fixations are closely centred on the tangent point. Reprinted with permission from Land and Lee (1994), *Nature*, Vol. 369, pp.742–744. Copyright © 1994 Macmillan Magazines Limited.

and do not transfer readily to the much higher speeds at which cars travel. For example, we outlined earlier (p.300) Cutting et al.'s (1992) argument that new patterns of controlling gaze must be adopted in order to detect heading when travelling in vehicles.

In a similar way, Stewart, Cudworth, and Lishman (1993) argue that our natural use of information in optic flow to obtain time to contact fails at the speeds characteristic of driving, and that we must therefore learn to use additional kinds of visual information to control braking. In particular, they suggest that drivers may estimate time to contact from the speed of their car and the distance of an obstacle, this distance being obtained by scaling its angular size against its known actual size. This could provide an explanation for the fact that children are victims of collisions with cars more frequently than are adults. If drivers use knowledge of the height of an "average" pedestrian to judge distance, and do so too quickly to bring any other information to bear, then they would overestimate the distance of a child and so begin braking later than they should. Stewart et al. (1993) support this theory with road accident statistics, and use it to suggest that child safety on roads could be improved by providing conspicuous railings or striped road markings of standard sizes at crossings, so as to give drivers a clear scale for judging distance.

INTERCEPTING OBJECTS

Crossing a road is only one of many situations where we must adjust our actions in response to things moving around us. We all have some ability to intercept moving objects by reaching, grasping, and hitting, and these skills are refined when we learn to play ball games. A crucial element in all these skills is the ability to control our body and limb movements *prospectively*, by predicting the path of a ball and bringing a hand, bat, or racquet to the correct point as the ball arrives there. In this section, we will first look at the early development of this ability, and then go on to see how it is achieved in various sports.

The development of reaching

As soon as infants first reach for stationary objects, at about 18 weeks of age, they are able to reach accurately for moving objects as well (von Hofsten & Lindhagen, 1979), and by the age of 9 months can achieve 50msec precision in grasping a moving target (von Hofsten, 1980, 1983). Over this period, infants' readiness to reach for fast-moving objects increases, and their ability to catch them improves. At all ages, those reaches that babies make are almost always accurate, suggesting that babies only initiate a reach when they are likely to be successful. We might expect that babies' reaching actions would be controlled in a simple way, perhaps by pursuing a target with the hand until it is caught. However, two sets of findings show that this is not so, and that the ability to control reaching *prospectively*, by extending the hand towards a predicted interception point, develops remarkably early in life.

First, a detailed film analysis of reaches made by babies (von Hofsten, 1980) revealed that they moved their arms in a series of ballistic movements (see p.275) to the point where contact would be made with the moving target. Babies at all ages were remarkably accurate at predicting the path of the target, but the older infants reached for it more "economically", using fewer ballistic steps.

Second, van der Meer, van der Weel, and Lee (1994) tested infants in a situation where a target could not be grasped simply by following it with the hand. They moved an attractive toy in a straight line behind a transparent screen, so that the infant subject could only grasp it as it passed a gap in the screen. Just before reaching this gap, the object disappeared briefly behind an opaque screen. Before the toy disappeared, infants aged 11 months both looked at and reached towards the "catching point" at the edge of the gap. Reaching movements with the hands were always directed towards the catching point, and never towards the toy. Together, these results show that the control of both eye and hand movements is prospective, and not based simply on the current position of the target. By varying the speed of the toy, van der Meer et al. also showed that both the gaze shift and the hand movement occurred when the toy reached a particular time to contact with the catching point, and not a particular position. In principle, these actions could be timed using the τ function of the angular separation of toy and catching point (see Ch.12, p.282).

By testing infants on this task from the age of 16 weeks onwards, van der Meer et al. (1994) went on to show that gaze is controlled prospectively as early as 20–24 weeks, and similar control of hand movement follows at 32 weeks. At first, infants initiate eye and hand movements when the toy reaches a particular point in its trajectory, but then switch to a time-to-contact strategy at about 40 weeks of age. As well as revealing strikingly sophisticated visual control of action in babies only a few months old, these results are also interesting in suggesting that the control of gaze may be necessary for subsequent development of limb control, and in showing that the visual information used to time an action can change during development.

Van der Meer, van der Weel, Lee, Laing, and Lin (1995) studied this developmental sequence in children born prematurely and so at risk of cerebral palsy, a form of brain damage that interferes with the control of movement. In relatively mild cases, cerebral palsy may not be diagnosed until a child is 1–2 years old, and this delay may cause problems for therapy. Van der Meer et al. (1995) found that all stages in the development of reaching occurred later in the group of premature children than in controls, and the difference was largest in the children who went on to show signs of cerebral palsy. Thus the experimental analysis of reaching in infants may provide a valuable new method of diagnosing this condition.

Catching

The basic ability to intercept a moving object with the hand seems to develop very early in life. What takes longer to acquire is the motor skill of getting to the target economically and of grasping or hitting it once there. In order to catch a moving ball, for example, the hand or hands must be oriented correctly and appropriate grasping movements must be initiated *before* the ball makes physical contact with the hand, while it is still in flight. Alderson, Sully, and Sully (1974) studied one-handed catching of tennis balls and found that the fine orienting movements of the hand began 150–200msec before the ball struck the palm and the grasping movement started 32–50msec before contact.

Although some vision is essential in order to assess the flight path and speed of a moving target and so to initiate these movements, it does not seem to be necessary to view the entire trajectory. Whiting and Sharp (1974) studied one-handed catching of tennis balls that were only illuminated for 80msec of their trajectory. The duration of the dark period that followed this brief illumination was varied from 125 to 445msec (which included a period of 125msec assumed to reflect CNS latency). They found that the function relating accuracy of catching and occlusion duration was U-shaped. Performance was poor if the occluded period was greater than 365msec or shorter than 205msec, peaking at 285msec. It appears that there is an optimal point in the trajectory during which to view the ball in order to predict its path, this being when the time to contact is about 250–300msec. If the ball is seen too early it gets "lost", possibly because of limitations on immediate memory. If it is seen too late there may be insufficient time to process the flight information and then begin the correct series of orienting movements.

Lee (1980a) has suggested that the 300msec time-to-contact interval is critical because catchers standardise the duration of their movements and therefore need only to initiate these movements at a specific time to contact. Standard movement durations have been observed in a study by Schmidt (1969) where subjects had to move a slider to hit an approaching target, and also in ball-hitting by baseball batters. Hubbard and Seng (1954) filmed baseball batters and observed that they always began to step forward when the ball was released by the pitcher, but geared the duration of the step to the speed of the ball. The duration of the bat swing was kept constant but its initiation was dependent on ball speed, occurring about 40msec after the forward foot was planted. Hubbard and Seng also tried to record the head and eye movements made by their sample of batters as they tracked the path of the ball. Though their methods were insensitive, their film analysis did suggest that batters did not track or fixate the ball during the final stage of its flight, nor when it actually made contact with the bat (contrary to the advice given in training manuals). Again it appears that it is information about time to contact picked up earlier in the flight path that is of more importance than the information gained in the final moments before contact occurs, just as when young children reach for a moving object.

What optical information is used during this 300msec "window" to control the movements of the hand so as to grasp or hit a ball accurately? Judge and Bradford (1988) showed that people use the vergence angle of the eyes, binocular disparity, or both (see Ch.7, p.138) to catch balls, at least when they are thrown slowly and on low trajectories. Their subjects were quite unable to catch balls thrown to them when they wore telestereoscopic spectacles, an optical device that exaggerates the disparity between the retinal images by mimicking the effect of increasing the distance between the eyes. Their catching accuracy returned to normal after about 20 attempts, presumably because the control of arm and hand movements by binocular information was recalibrated. In a control condition, subjects had no difficulty in catching balls while wearing spectacles that reduced their field of view to the same extent as the telestereoscope.

As we are able to catch balls with one eye closed, some other source (or sources) of information must be used together with binocular cues. There has been particular interest in the possibility that we use the parameter τ, in this case the ratio of the angular size of the ball to the rate of change of its angular size. In many situations, a problem with this "local" τ function as a means of timing interception is that it will change as the approaching object rotates relative to the observer (Tresilian, 1993). For a spherical ball, however, τ is not affected by rotation, and so this problem does not arise. Where a hitting or grasping action of standard duration needs to be performed, its initiation when τ reaches a particular value seems a straightforward and reliable strategy.

Lee, Young, Reddish, Lough, and Clayton (1983) have tested the τ hypothesis in a situation where subjects had to leap up and punch balls that were dropped from varying heights above them, as in volleyball. A ball dropping towards the ground accelerates at a constant rate under the influence of gravity. Its velocity thus increases continuously and the value of τ at any instant underestimates the actual time to contact (see Fig. 13.10), as when a gannet dives towards the surface of the sea (see Ch.12, p.284). Even so, τ could still provide an adequate means of initiating jumping and punching, as its value converges with time to

contact when the latter is less than 250msec, the period in which it is important to view a ball in flight.

Lee et al. (1983) measured the angles of the knee and elbow as these were flexed and extended in the punching act. When these angles were plotted against time to contact, the profiles of the flexion phase obtained with different drop heights did not coincide, as the actions began sooner and lasted longer the greater the drop height. When plotted against τ, however, they were more closely aligned, showing that a strategy of continuous control of flexion by τ accounts better for the data than one of computing time to contact from ball height and speed. Furthermore, subjects could not have geared their actions to the height of the ball above them, as this would yield the opposite relationship between drop height and initiation of the action to that observed.

Lee et al.'s (1983) results demonstrate that the τ hypothesis accounts for the data better than other specific alternatives, but as we have seen in other cases, such indirect evidence cannot prove the case. Other perceptual mechanisms could yield the same pattern of timing of an action. In this case, for example, subjects could have been using the height from which the ball was dropped together with

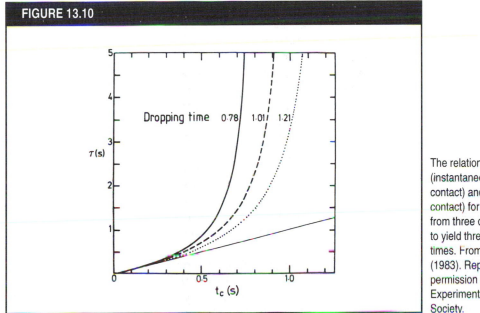

FIGURE 13.10

The relationship between τ (instantaneous time to contact) and t_c (actual time to contact) for balls dropped from three different heights to yield three different drop times. From Lee et al. (1983). Reprinted with permission of the Experimental Psychology Society.

learned knowledge of the acceleration of objects under gravity to time their jump (Tresilian, 1993; see also Wann, in press). Savelsbergh, Whiting, and Bootsma (1991) carried out a more direct test of the τ hypothesis by giving subjects a ball-catching task in which τ could be manipulated independently of speed and position, by deflating the ball as it approached. The shrinking ball optically mimics one of fixed size approaching more slowly, and so, if subjects used τ, their grasp should be delayed relative to a control condition in which the ball has a fixed size. Savelsbergh et al. found that the point at which the closing speed of the fingers reached a maximum was indeed delayed, by 5–6msec. Even so, subjects had no difficulty in grasping the deflated ball, suggesting that other sources of visual information must be used in parallel with τ. A further problem in interpreting the results is that the control of deflation was not accurate enough to allow the effect on timing to be predicted quantitatively, and the results cannot distinguish between the τ hypothesis and the possibility that grasp is modified in response to the changing size of the ball (Tresilian, 1994; Wann, in press).

τ specifies time to contact provided that a ball is approaching on a path straight towards the observer's eyes, as in Lee et al.'s (1983) ball-punching task. Usually, however, we catch balls on courses passing at varying distances from our eyes, and in this situation τ alone cannot specify time to contact with the hand. The hypothesis that τ is used to time catching would therefore seem to predict timing errors where the eyes are off the path of the ball, but Tresilian (1994) found that people could intercept a rolling ball at a particular point *more* accurately if their eyes were off its path than when it moved directly towards their eyes. These results provide evidence against the use of τ, and in favour of a role for the angular position and velocity of the target relative to the observer. Tresilian points out that these variables could be obtained either visually, or mechanically from changes in head and eye positions as the target is tracked.

To conclude, the experimental evidence that τ is used to time catching remains equivocal, and it is unlikely that the parameter provides a single, general-purpose explanation for the control of interceptive actions. Variables such as binocular disparity, vergence, and gaze direction can influence catching (Judge & Bradford, 1988; Tresilian, 1994) and so, if τ is used, it must be used together with other optical information, in combinations that probably vary from one task to another. As we have already seen in Chapter 12 (p.285), evidence from animals points to the same conclusion.

The interactions between τ and other cues have been studied by Heuer (1993), who showed that people's estimates of time to contact in displays simulating looming objects were influenced by both vergence angle and τ. Wann and Rushton (1995) provide similar evidence from a more natural task, which used a "virtual reality" display of an approaching ball, in which τ and binocular disparity could be manipulated independently to specify different times to virtual "contact" with a subject's hand. When subjects were asked to "grasp" the virtual ball, the timing of their grasp was affected by altering the value of τ. This effect was large when τ specified earlier arrival of the ball than did binocular disparity, but small when τ specified later arrival. These results show that τ and disparity are used together to time grasping, but that their relative contributions are not fixed.

Running to catch

In all the examples of reaching and catching that we have considered so far, we have assumed that a person is close enough to the path of the target to intercept it by moving arms and hands. In ball games it is often necessary first to run to a position close enough to where a ball will land in order to catch it. For most of the flight of the ball, the only information available to a fielder in cricket or baseball is its optical trajectory (i.e. that relative to the observer). Imagine standing still and watching a ball hit high into the air: it will rise above the horizon on an optical trajectory that will curve to one side or the other (unless it is hit straight towards you, when its trajectory will appear straight). By running fast enough in the right direction, it is possible to keep this trajectory straight, and McBeath, Shaffer, and Kaiser (1995) show that this simple strategy will automatically bring a fielder into the path of the ball and to the point on the ground where it will land (see Fig. 13.11).

FIGURE 13.11

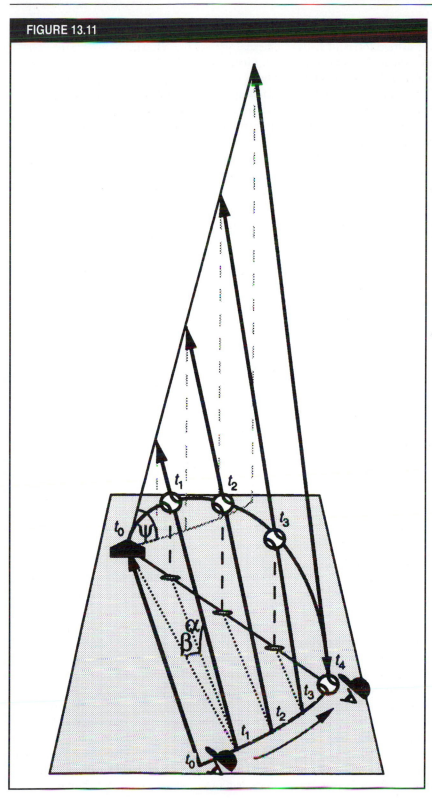

Perspective view of a baseball pitch. The ball is hit at the homeplate (top left of field) at time t_0 and follows the trajectory marked by its positions at times t_1 to t_4. The optical trajectory of the ball as seen by the fielder (denoted by a baseball cap) is the tilted line rising from the homeplate at an angle ψ. In order to keep this optical trajectory straight, the fielder must follow the curved path shown. This path will bring him or her to the point where the ball lands. Reprinted with permission from McBeath et al. (1995), *Science*, Vol. 268, pp.569–573. Copyright © 1995 American Association for the Advancement of Science.

Using films of fielders running to catch balls, and measurements of optical trajectories of balls obtained from shoulder-mounted cameras, McBeath et al. (1995) obtained evidence that people use this strategy. The implication is that a fielder does not compute where the ball will land from its trajectory, and then run there and wait for it. Instead, he or she follows a path that leads to the right place to catch the ball as it arrives there. This hypothesis also provides an explanation for three features of fielders' behaviour: they usually catch balls on the run, they sometimes collide with obstacles while running to catch balls going off the pitch, and they find balls heading straight towards them harder to catch.

A similar approach to the problem is taken by Dienes and McLeod (1993), who consider the more restricted case of a fielder running forwards or backwards to catch a ball struck in his or her direction. Here, interception can be achieved by keeping the rate of change of the tangent of the angular height of the ball constant. Although McBeath et al.'s analysis is broader in scope, and relies on the detection of a simpler optical parameter, further research is needed to test it against Dienes and McLeod's alternative. Even so, both theories provide good examples of how a problem may appear very difficult if treated analytically (by asking how a trajectory could be computed to predict a landing place), but can be more easily solved by using a simple rule governing the direction and speed of running.

CONCLUSIONS

The research we have described in this chapter is all prompted by a *broadly* Gibsonian outlook on visual perception, as it is concerned with the contribution of perception to the control of action, and bases explanations on the optical information available to people as they move about in natural surroundings. The knowledge obtained from this work attests to the value of such an outlook, but it is also worth mentioning some of its implications for more specific points in Gibsonian theory. We

will conclude by commenting briefly on three of these.

First, Gibson (1966) stressed that the world, not the retinal image, is the starting point for vision. This argument has led some Gibsonian theorists to regard eye movements as irrelevant to vision, on the grounds that they move the image relative to the retina but do not change optical structure. Although this is true in principle, it is none the less clear that eye movements actually do play a general role in the visual control of action. We have seen evidence for close relationships between the control of gaze and a variety of visually guided actions such as stepping, steering, reaching, and catching. Further evidence comes from research on the skill of hitting a ball accurately towards a particular target; in basket-ball, for example, expert players show earlier and longer fixation of gaze on the target than do novices (Ripoll, Bard, & Paillard, 1986). Rather than being an incidental means of sampling the optic array, the control of gaze appears to be closely integrated with the overall control of limb and body movements by optical information.

Second, a cornerstone of Gibson's theory is the proposition that changes in the spatial pattern of light reaching a person are sufficient to specify the nature of the surrounding world, and that knowledge or inference are therefore not needed for perception, except in contrived experimental situations. Hence perception requires only the "pick-up" of available information. Cutting (1986) has made an unorthodox challenge to this view, arguing that optic flow often *over-specifies* the world, as there are multiple sources of optical information to specify any particular property of the environment, such as distance, direction, size, or slant. Perception must therefore be active, or "directed", in order to select between these sources of information. We have seen several pieces of evidence supporting Cutting's case in this chapter and in Chapter 12, where distance, time to contact, and other variables appear to be detected from information in light in more than one way. Animals or people may combine different optical and other sources of information to give the most reliable estimate possible, or may shift between different combinations of these according to circumstances.

It is interesting to note the convergence between this evidence and the results from psychophysical experiments on the integration of multiple depth cues (see Ch.7, p.161).

Third, the proposition that optic structure is sufficient for vision gives the concept of "invariants" a central role in Gibsonian theory (Ch.11, p.257). An important reason for the great interest in the role of τ in timing actions has been its status as a possible concrete example of a high-level invariant of optic flow able to specify an important environmental property. Research has not supported such a straightforward view, however. Much of the empirical evidence relevant to τ is indirect and open to other interpretations, and there are important theoretical constraints on the accuracy of the time-to-contact information that τ can provide. Also, the evidence that τ is used in variable combinations with other sources of information about time and distance further illustrates Cutting's (1986) argument for perception as an active, selective process, and suggests that the strict Gibsonian formula of particular invariants sufficient to specify particular environmental properties is too simple a conception of the visual control of animal and human action.

14

Theories of the Control of Action

According to Gibson's ecological approach to visual perception, animals and people obtain information about their surroundings by directly detecting complex properties of optic flow, such as the centre of expansion of a flow field or τ. In this chapter, we turn to a second major theme in the ecological approach: its emphasis on the role of perception in controlling *actions*, such as landing from flight, steering a car, or catching a ball. Traditional theories assume that perception and action are entirely distinct processes, regarding perception as the processing of information in the retinal image to yield a symbolic representation of the world, and action as the generation of commands to the muscles. The implication is that each can be studied and understood without reference to the other.

In the ecological view, however, perception and action are tightly interlocked processes. Animals and people do not passively perceive the world but move about in it actively, picking up the information needed to guide their movement. There is a continuous cycle between organism and world. The consequence of this viewpoint is that the role of perception is to furnish the information needed to organise action, which in turn implies that an understanding of perception requires an understanding of the systems controlling action. In this chapter, we will outline the concepts developed by ecological theorists to describe how action is controlled and how it interacts with perception. We will begin by looking at the optomotor response of insects, in order to introduce some of the issues in a familiar context, before going on to discuss the more difficult problem of the control of human behaviour.

THE OPTOMOTOR RESPONSE

In Chapter 12, we described the turning response of a tethered insect in a rotating drum (p.268), and argued that the response keeps an insect on as straight a path as possible through the environment. Some components of the optomotor response are well understood at a physiological level, particularly the neural processing of optical motion in the visual pathway and the patterns of muscle activity that generate turns in flight. So far, however, direct physiological methods have not established how perceptual input and motor output are linked centrally, and we will go on to contrast two kinds of model that have been proposed to explain how this happens.

Von Holst (1954) proposed the model of the optomotor response shown in Fig. 14.1. A command to carry out a movement originates in a

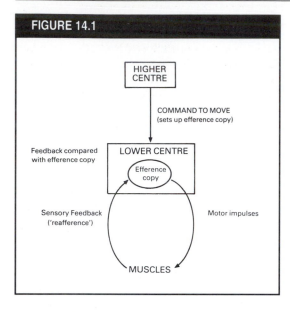

FIGURE 14.1

Von Holst's efference copy model.

"higher centre" of the nervous system and an "efference copy" of the commands to the muscles is retained in a "lower centre". As the movement is executed, there is a flow of optic texture over the eye, and this movement-induced input is called "reafference". The reafferent input is compared with the input expected from the commands stored as an efference copy in the lower centre. Note the similarity between this model and the one we discussed in Chapter 7 (p.164), which attempted to explain how the human nervous system compensates for "reafferent" effects of eye movement on the retinal image.

How does von Holst's "efference copy" model explain the optomotor response? If the insect is stationary, no optic flow over the eye is expected and so a discrepancy is registered if the drum rotates. The discrepancy indicates that the source of the movement is outside the insect and so it turns in order to reduce the discrepancy caused by relative movement. If, on the other hand, the insect initiates a movement in a stationary environment, the resulting reafference corresponds to that predicted from the efference copy and so there is no discrepancy. Von Holst argued that the efference copy model explains two important features of the optomotor response. First, it enables an insect to

discriminate between optical motion caused by its own active movement and that imposed on it by movement in the surroundings. Second, because an insect only tries to counteract optical motion that is not predicted from its own active movements, it is not locked into a fixed position by its own optomotor response.

These arguments for the efference copy model can be questioned on several grounds. First, as we saw in Chapter 12 (pp.268–269), the sensory information provided by a rotating drum would, in the insect's normal environment, unambiguously specify rotation of the insect. This rotation could be caused by some external force, such as an air current, or by an imbalance in the activities of flight muscles. If both these situations require the same motor output, then there is no need to discriminate them. At least in this context, the problem of distinguishing external and self-generated motion may not exist for an insect.

Second, von Holst's (1954) model is not the only way of explaining how insects can make spontaneous movements without being locked into position by the optomotor response. Reichardt and Poggio (1976) observed a semi-random fluctuation in a fly's torque as it fixated a visual pattern. In natural circumstances, where an airborne fly is surrounded by many objects competing for fixation, this instability in the optomotor response would result in occasional turns as the fly "jumped" from fixation of one object to another. Also, as we described in Chapter 12 (p.274), a small moving target can elicit a turn despite the opposing flow of background optic texture, because the mechanisms sensitive to local and global motion have different velocity sensitivities (Egelhaaf et al., 1989). In both cases, the stabilising effect of the optomotor response to global motion is briefly suppressed while a turn to fixate an object is made, but no "higher centre" is required to explain how this happens.

Finally, a third problem is that von Holst's efferent copy theory assumes that reafference *can* be predicted from motor commands. In the case of the human eye, this may well be so; given the mechanics of the muscles, inertia of the eyeball, and so on, a particular pattern of muscle contraction will yield a predictable rate, direction, and extent of movement over the retina. But this will not necessarily be so for a flying or walking animal. The same set of commands to the flight or leg muscles can generate quite different results depending on patterns of air flow around the animal or the terrain it is walking on. This problem is known as "context-conditioned variability", and we will return to it later in this chapter.

Given these arguments, could the "higher centre" and "efference copy" proposed by von Holst (1954) be superfluous? Is it possible that motion signals computed in the visual pathway are *directly* transduced into motor commands, without any comparison with an efferent copy? Reichardt and Poggio (1976) attempted to answer this question experimentally, by comparing the optomotor behaviour of houseflies under two conditions. In one, the normal effect of the fly's flight behaviour on optical motion was mimicked by measuring the torque exerted by the tethered fly and using this to control the rotation of the drum. This condition is termed "closed-loop", as the link between behaviour and its visual consequences is intact. In the other, "open-loop" condition, the fly is also tethered, but its torque has no effect on the movement of the drum.

A passive "transduction" model predicts that the same visual stimulation will yield the same yaw torque whether the fly is in closed- or open-loop conditions, whereas the efferent copy model predicts a difference between the two situations. Reichardt and Poggio (1976) determined the relationship between the position and motion of a target stripe and yaw torque under open-loop conditions (see Ch.12, p.271), and showed that it predicted behaviour under closed-loop conditions accurately. These results therefore appeared to show that, for this particular optomotor response, the "transduction" model is adequate (see Fig. 14.2).

More recent evidence has reopened the possibility that the efference copy model may still be correct, in at least some cases. Heisenberg and Wolf (1988) repeated Reichardt and Poggio's (1976) experiments, using the fruitfly *Drosophila* and a more accurate technique, which allowed single yaw torque traces in response to an oscillating drum to be obtained, rather than time-averaged traces. They found that, in closed-loop conditions, torque followed visual motion closely, whereas in open-loop conditions the torque response was weaker and showed much

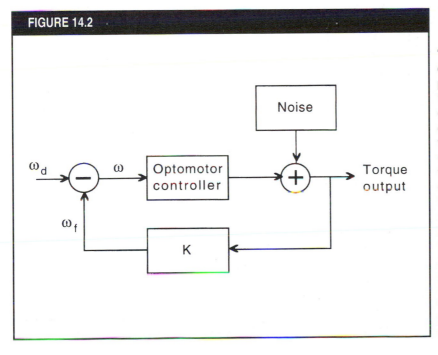

FIGURE 14.2

"Transduction" model of optomotor response proposed by Reichardt and Poggio (1976). The torque generated by the insect causes a rotation of the visual surroundings ω_f, determined by aerodynamic factors summarised in the coefficient K. The difference between ω_f and the imposed rotation of the drum ω_d is the image slip over the retina ω, which is transduced into torque output by the optmotor controller. Fluctuations in torque are assumed to arise from noise added to the controller output.

larger fluctuations. It therefore appears that the optomotor response becomes less stable under open-loop conditions.

Heisenberg and Wolf (1988) interpreted this result as showing that endogenous fluctuations in motor output cannot be treated just as a source of noise added to yaw torque, as in the transduction model (see Fig. 14.2), but instead must interact with the optomotor controller. In particular, Heisenberg and Wolf propose that these fluctuations block the response of the controller to motion in the opposite direction to the resulting turn. This is simply another way of expressing the central idea of the efference copy model, that the insect responds only to visual motion that is not predicted from its own actions.

It is not yet clear whether the discrepancy between the two sets of results arises from differences between insect species, or between measurement techniques, or from some other source. Some evidence that Heisenberg and Wolf's (1988) results reflect a general mechanism has been obtained by Möhl (1989), who recorded action potentials from the motor neurons driving the left and right wing muscles of locusts during tethered flight. The difference in timing of the bursts of potentials driving downstrokes of the wings was computed in real time and the result was used to control the rotation of the optomotor drum. This technique made it possible to set any arbitrary interval between the motor commands to the two sides to be the "correct" value that kept the drum stationary and so simulated stable flight.

We might expect that motor impulses to the right and left wing muscles would be closely synchronised, so that the downstrokes of the wings occur together and yaw torque is minimised. If this were true, then setting any other value of the interval between bursts of impulses to be "correct" would prevent the insect from stabilising the drum, and it would continue to rotate indefinitely. Instead, Möhl (1989) obtained a striking result. The interval between bursts of motor impulses to the left and right sides gradually shifted to the new "correct" value and the drum was stabilised. Each time the "correct" value was changed, the locust responded in the same way. Apparently, a locust is able to "learn" the correct timing of motor commands to

minimise visual motion. Möhl (1989) argues that this happens because the locust nervous system actively generates fluctuations in motor output and then detects correlations between output and the sensory feedback resulting from it. Those changes in motor output that cause "desirable" feedback, such as stabilisation of optical motion, are maintained. In this way, the nervous system can actively "search" for the parameters coupling sensory input to motor output that achieve the correct result.

It is easy to see why this flexibility in flight control should exist. The aerodynamic properties of a locust's wings and body are, to some extent, unpredictable over its lifetime. If the wings grow in a slightly asymmetric way, or are damaged by a predator, then the relative timing of flight muscle activity on the two sides of the body needed to prevent yawing will change, and the nervous system appears to be designed to modify motor output so as to compensate. As Möhl states (1989, p.81):

Fluctuations in motor patterns are not just an imperfect result but a clever strategy of evolution to explore permanently the exact function of each muscle for flight stability. By means of this strategy the system is able to adjust specifically the sensory input to different motor neurones, thus increasing precision of the genetically predetermined network of flight control.

The models of insect flight control proposed by Möhl (1989) and by Heisenberg and Wolf (1988) share the same basic principle as von Holst's (1954) efference copy model. In all three, changes in motor output are produced endogenously and the resulting change in visual input is compared in some way with an expected change. The important development in the more recent models is the new functional role they propose for the comparison of input and efference copy. Rather than being a means of discriminating self-generated and externally caused visual motion, this process has a deeper role in adjusting the functioning of sensorimotor systems to keep their performance optimal. A review of evidence for similar processes in other patterns of insect behaviour can be found in Wolf, Voss, Hein, and Heisenberg (1992), and an important question for the future is whether the same principles underlie flexibility in the visual control of movement in more complex animals.

THE CONTROL OF HUMAN ACTION

Most theorists are agreed that actions must ultimately be controlled at a high level in the nervous system where something like an "action plan" must be formulated and executed. When we consider the nature of action plans it is clear that at some level the representation must be sufficiently flexible and abstract to allow equivalent ends to be achieved in a variety of ways. Turvey (1977a) gives as an example the observation that we can draw a letter A with a pen on paper, with a finger on someone's back, or with a toe in the sand. At least some of these activities may be novel, but are not difficult for us. In the same way we can recognise a letter A drawn in different ways by different people (see Chapter 9). Some abstract representation of the letter perhaps allows for the way in which we can generalise both when perceiving and when acting.

Suppose then we wished to draw an A in the sand with a toe. Somehow the abstract representation that we wish to particularise must be translated into a specific pattern of motor (i.e. muscle) activity. It might be possible, in principle, to conceive of each muscle involved in this action being independently instructed by commands issued from a high level in the nervous system. Thus our abstract conception of the letter A might be translated into a series of independent commands to a variety of muscles in the leg, foot, and toes. This kind of "push-button" metaphor for the control of action has been criticised by Bernstein (1967), whose arguments have been summarised and extended by Turvey and his colleagues (Fitch, Tuller, & Turvey, 1982; Tuller, Turvey, & Fitch, 1982; Turvey, 1977a; Turvey, Fitch, & Tuller, 1982; Turvey, Shaw, & Mace, 1978).

There are two different, but closely associated problems with the push-button metaphor. The first

is known as the *degrees of freedom* problem. An "executive" issuing independent efferent commands to all those muscles involved in even the simplest of movements would have a very great deal of moment-to-moment computation to perform. This first problem is possibly compounded by the second—that of *context-conditioned variability* (Turvey et al., 1982). We have already met this problem in discussing the insect optomotor response, where we pointed out that the consequences of a particular pattern of commands to leg or wing muscles may not necessarily be predictable, but could depend on the external forces acting on the limbs. In the human case, the problem is even greater, as the context in which any particular muscle contraction occurs affects the actual limb movement achieved. The movement produced by a given contraction depends on the current configuration of the parts of the limb, the current motions of the adjoining limb segments, and the external forces against which each muscle must work. An executive pressing the buttons, in such a model, would have to have moment-to-moment information available about the external forces and the dynamic and static aspects of the current configurations of the limb segments.

Turvey et al. (1978) liken the problem of the push-button executive to that which an air pilot would face if he or she had to control individually each of the mechanical segments used to guide the flight of an aeroplane. At a minimum, an aeroplane has two ailerons at the back of the wings, which can be moved up or down to control roll; two elevators on the tail, which if moved up or down control pitch; and a rudder at the back, which can be moved left or right to control yaw (cf. insect flight in Chapter 12). There is thus one degree of freedom for each of these five hinged parts. If each of these parts had to be altered individually the pilot would be faced with an impossible informational load. Even if the mechanical parts could only be moved to one of eight positions the control system would still have to keep track of 8^5 (32,768) independent states.

Of course no air pilot actually has to cope with this task because the mechanical components of the guidance system are in fact linked. The ailerons are yoked so that when one moves up the other moves down. The rudder is linked to the ailerons so that it moves left when the right aileron goes down, and the elevators on the tail section move together—both up or both down. This linkage reduces the degrees of freedom to two, and the guidance of the aircraft can be achieved with a joystick, which also has two degrees of freedom (it can be moved forward or backward for ascent or descent and from side to side to bank or turn).

Turvey (1977a) and Turvey et al. (1978) suggest that combinations of muscles in animals are similarly linked and constrained to act together as *coordinative structures*. To some extent, these can function autonomously, without control from higher levels in the nervous system. Spinal reflexes can work in this way, even though they may involve quite complicated actions. For example, an animal with the upper part of the spinal cord completely sectioned will still repeatedly scratch an itch on its body with whichever foot can most easily reach it.

The concept of coordinative structures goes beyond simple reflex acts, however, to include patterns of inter-limb coordination in voluntary acts. An everyday example is given by the difficulty we experience if we try to beat out two quite different rhythms simultaneously with different hands. The hands seem constrained to act together in this situation. Kelso, Putnam, and Goodman (1983) have demonstrated this more formally. If two hands are required to make movements of different difficulties and directions, the movement of each hand is influenced by that of the other. Such patterns of mutual constraint and interaction would not be expected if an "executive" independently commanded each muscle. Instead, Turvey (1977a) suggests, the executive commands groups of muscles that function cooperatively together, and so the number of degrees of freedom can be greatly reduced.

Coordinative structures can also solve some of the problems of context-conditioned variability. For example, a coordinative structure can take care of the local context in which an action takes place if it behaves like a mass-spring system. The equilibrium point of a spring to which a mass is attached is not affected however the mass is pushed or pulled. The spring always returns to rest at the same length, without any executive monitoring its movements over time. Further models with similar properties have been developed to describe the behaviour of coordinative structures, using concepts from dynamical systems theory (for an introduction, see Abraham, Abraham, & Shaw, 1991). For example, some systems of muscles show the properties of *limit-cycle oscillators*, tending to return to a particular pattern of oscillation, rather than a set point, after being disturbed. It is possible to test models of this kind by measuring changes in rhythmic actions, such as finger tapping, after a perturbation.

A recent example of this approach can be found in Kay, Saltzman, and Kelso (1991), who provide evidence that finger tapping is driven both by a peripheral oscillator arising from a coordinative structure of arm and hand muscles and by a central neural oscillator. The interaction between the two oscillators appears to work in both directions: the peripheral system is not driven passively by the central one, but can also influence its activity. This two-way interaction underlying finger tapping provides one example of a more general argument made by Turvey et al. (1978) that motor control is not organised hierarchically, with the executive issuing commands that pass unidirectionally and without modification to lower levels. Rather they suggest that the system must be organised as a *heterarchy*, or, more radically, as a *coalition*. In a heterarchical organisation no one part of the system should be seen as dominating the others. All levels in a heterarchy contribute equally to hypothesis testing and decision making.

An important structure that contributes to the organisation and control of action is the segmental apparatus of the mammalian spinal cord. The spinal cord can be seen as a set of "segments" (marked out by the vertebrae), within each of which there are neuronal loops that control simple reflexes (like the knee jerk), without involving any "communication" with the brain. Complex voluntary activities may involve the recruitment, modification, and elaboration of these simple reflexes, which form the bases for coordinative structures. This may be achieved in part by *tuning* of the segmental apparatus prior to a movement occurring. Turvey (1977a) cites evidence from

Gurfinkel et al. (1971) in support of the notion of tuning. If a subject is asked to flex one leg, it typically takes about 170msec between the command and the flexion occurring. If, during this latency period, the knee-jerk reflex is elicited, its amplitude is enhanced relative to a control condition where no command is present. It therefore appears that an instruction issued from the brain to the leg involves the preparation or tuning of the segmental apparatus prior to the actual movement of the leg occurring.

If we continue to consider leg movements, in the more complex activity of walking or running, there is evidence that the organisation of the segmental apparatus of the spinal cord allows the initiation and maintenance of stepping movements of the limbs without sensory input. However, the form of the stepping pattern must be tailored to the external forces. This can be achieved by using afferent information obtained from reflex structures and also by tuning the segmental apparatus on the detection of relevant information obtained primarily through vision. In this way a basic pattern of activity can be attuned to the current contextual demands.

Implications for the role of perception

The traditional metaphor of a central executive controlling action in a push-button fashion complements the view that perception acts to provide a representation of the surrounding world for the central executive to use in making decisions. Having discussed the objections to such metaphors, what does the ecological approach outlined earlier imply about the role of perception? Turvey and his colleagues argue that visual information of particular kinds must be injected into unfolding activities at appropriate points, after which the coordinative structures that have been activated and tuned can take care of themselves to a large extent. They devolve the responsibility for these "injections" of visual information to the coordinative structures themselves (Fitch et al., 1982, p.272):

> We do not want a model in which the brain interprets the perceptual information, decides what portion of the information to

supply a given coordinative structure, and when to supply it. Instead, the organisation of the coordinative structure should be such as to accept only certain information at certain times.

Coordinative structures do seem to be organised so that a minimal change in one of their parameters has a maximum effect on behaviour. A person's speed of running is altered only by the thrust he or she applies to the ground, while other aspects of the step cycle remain constant, and the visual information needed to modify thrust is obtained at a specific point in the cycle (Ch.13, p.295). Another example is provided by Hubbard and Seng's (1954) demonstration that baseball batters keep the timing of their swings constant, and deal with balls of varying speed by altering only the speed with which they step forward (see p.306). Time to contact assessed during the ball's flight thus affects only a single parameter of a complex activity.

An implication of the ecological approach is that the information obtained through vision is not independent of the motor activity it controls. Consider someone catching a ball: as the action proceeds, the ball is tracked by head and eyes, the arms move, and the fingers open and then close on the ball. At each stage, the activity of coordinative structures is modulated by particular kinds of optical information specifying time to contact, ball size, or other features of the situation. In the ecological view, we should not assume that perception delivers a representation of the trajectory, speed, and size of the ball, and then leaves the rest to a motor system.

Evidence in support of the interdependence of perception and motor tasks comes from experiments showing that people use visual information differently when they are performing different actions. For example, Bootsma (1989) compared the behaviour of people hitting a falling ball with a bat, closing a switch to release an artificial arm holding a bat, and closing a switch to signal when the ball passed a marker. From a traditional point of view, all these tasks seem equivalent: in each one, the subject must detect when the ball reaches a particular point and then execute some action. From an ecological perspective, however, the different actions involved may use visual information in different ways. The results gave some support to the ecological view, as the timing of the natural batting movement was less variable than that of the switch-closing movements. The implication is that the control of the natural perception-action coupling is more accurate than that of a movement that may appear to be "simpler".

The most progress towards a detailed understanding of the links between perception and coordinative structures has been made in cases of rhythmic movements. Schmidt, Carello, and Turvey (1990) studied the synchronisation of limb movements between two people, by asking subjects to sit side-by-side with their legs crossed, and to each swing one lower leg up and down in time with the other. The interesting result from these experiments was that the coupled oscillations of the two legs of *different* people behaved in the *same* way as those of two fingers of the same person (Kelso et al., 1983; see earlier). Rhythmically varying visual information specifying the movement of the other person's leg therefore seems to become coupled to the observer's leg rhythm in the same way that different motor systems become coupled.

The coupling of perceptual and motor oscillations has been studied further by Schöner (1991) in the context of the "swinging room" effect, in which sinusoidal sway of the surroundings causes sway of body posture at the same frequency (see Ch.13, pp.289–290). A simple model of this behaviour would involve the transduction of optical motion detected at the retina into muscle activity causing sway, in the same way as Reichardt and Poggio's (1976) model of the optomotor response transduces optic motion into yaw torque (see Fig. 14.2). However, such a model neglects the *intrinsic* dynamics of posture control; in stationary surroundings, the body sways continuously, and this is the outcome of complex interactions between muscles of the feet, legs and trunk.

Schöner (1991) developed a dynamic model of postural sway, coupled in a linear fashion to optic flow. In experiments with a "virtual reality" version of the swinging room, Dijkstra et al. (1994) tested the model and found that it did not fully account for the effects of wall distance on sway. They suggest that the assumption of linear coupling of perceptual and motor oscillations is incorrect, and that the nervous system instead actively generates a sway rhythm matching that of the surroundings. In other words, it *anticipates* sway instead of responding to it. There is an important similarity between this proposal and models of the insect optomotor response (Heisenberg & Wolf, 1988; Möhl, 1989), in which turns are actively generated in order to learn their effect on visual feedback, and these ideas may represent an important emerging principle in perception-action coupling.

CONCLUSIONS

The analysis of the control of human action that we have discussed in this chapter is an important extension of Gibson's theory, and represents the achievements of ecological theorists in developing tools for understanding the mutual coupling of perception and action. The approach aims to understand the structure of action, and its modulation by environmental information, in terms of the behaviour of dynamical systems governed by physical laws, rather than the behaviour of a "central executive" controlling the muscles (see Kelso, 1995). The aim is clearly an ambitious one, and the progress made has so far been on a few specific problems such as the control of rhythmic limb movements and the coupling of the underlying dynamics to optical information.

The problems of the degrees of freedom in motor control, and of context-conditioned variability, have been tackled from other theoretical perspectives, and the reader may be interested in comparing these with the ecological approach sketched here. These include the analysis of the kinematics (trajectory and speed) of human movements to discover underlying invariants (e.g. Lacquaniti, 1989), and use of single-cell recording methods to determine how parameters of movement are coded in the activity of single cells in the spinal cord and brain (e.g. Bizzi,

Mussa-Ivaldi, & Giszter, 1991; Fetz, 1992; Georgopoulos, 1991). Connectionist modelling techniques (see Chapter 10) have also been applied to the problem, attempting to train a network to control a multi-jointed model person or limb without any explicit coding of movement parameters. A successful example is Hinton's (1984) model of reaching forward without losing one's balance, using a simple two-dimensional model person. The problem is to avoid swinging the arm out in a way that shifts the centre of gravity of the person as a whole to an unstable position—to avoid this, other limb and trunk movements must occur to compensate. Hinton found that a connectionist model could satisfy these two constraints (touch the object, while maintaining centre of gravity above the foot) simultaneously, and that the solution was much more elegant when combinations of joint angles were adjusted synergistically (cf. our earlier discussions of coordinative structures).

An important difference between the ecological approach and other approaches to understanding the control of action is that it treats perception and action as interlocked processes and tries to avoid separating out motor control as a distinct problem. Although it is possible to see how this principle could be carried through into more detailed models of those aspects of perception involved in the moment-by-moment control of movement—taking strides, hitting a ball, applying brakes, and so on—it does not seem directly relevant to understanding how perception yields information that is not used in the immediate control of activity but is instead stored in some way to influence activity later. The principle of perception being constrained by action is not obviously relevant to a person watching a television programme, for example. In the next chapter we follow up this point, and ask what the ecological approach has to offer the study of human perception outside the context of moment-by-moment control of movement.

15

Event Perception

In this part of the book we discuss ways in which a variety of animals, including humans, may detect specific patterns of flow or local change in the optic array in order to guide their actions in the world. The kind of perception that we have been discussing is that which demands immediate action—to locomote smoothly, to avoid collision, or to steer a straight course. However, a great deal of human perception results in comprehension and reflection rather than in immediate action. The film-goer, tennis umpire, the spectator at a football match, the air-traffic controller—all must interpret the complex dynamic visual information in the events they are viewing, although their immediate actions are not necessarily affected. We spent some time in Part II of this book discussing how it is that we recognise significant forms, from the conventional starting point of the static retinal image. We now turn to consider how it is that we interpret *dynamic* optical information, and thus consider event perception in terms of analysing transformations in optical flow.

In this chapter we will deal with human perception, as it is not clear to what extent animals contemplate in the way that we do the events in their world, although Humphrey and Keeble (1974) have shown that monkeys will work in order to be shown films, even when the films show events that monkeys find frightening. However, as

will become clear later on in the chapter, human perception of events may result in attributional processes that may at least in part be culturally and linguistically mediated.

We begin this chapter by describing how human observers interpret patterns of motion in fairly simple and artificial dynamic displays. Here we outline some of the principles that are needed to account for the perception of such displays, principles that we will find useful as we go on to consider the complex patterns of motion given by more natural events. As we will see later in the chapter, patterns of motion, in simple as well as more complex displays, give rise to causal interpretations and may even lead humans to attribute intentions and personality to the moving display elements. Thus the study of event perception builds the foundations for social perception, which we consider in Chapter 16.

THE PERCEPTION OF RELATIVE MOTION

People are more sensitive to relative motion than to absolute motion. Suppose a spot of light is moved very slowly in a dark room. There will be a particular threshold velocity at which the point is seen to be moving rather than stationary. Aubert

(1866; cited in Kaufman, 1974) found that this threshold velocity was between 10 and 20mins of arc per second if a luminous dot was moved in the dark. This is the threshold for *observer-relative* motion, which for a static observer corresponds to "absolute" motion. However, if a second spot of light is introduced, the velocity that the first must reach in order for movement to be seen in the display is lower. The threshold for *object-relative* motion is lower than that for observer-relative. Aubert showed that there was a tenfold decrease in the threshold for motion perception when a dot was moved against a pattern of lines, rather than a uniform field (Kaufman, 1974). In a situation where the velocity of one dot is below the observer-relative threshold, and a second, stationary dot is present, the perception of movement in the display is ambiguous. Either one, or the other, or both dots may appear to be moving.

When motions are above the observer-relative motion threshold, perceptions are rarely ambiguous, but they do seem to be dominated by the relative motions in the display. For example, if a stationary dot is surrounded by a rectangle that moves to and fro around it, the dot may appear to be moving in a direction opposite to that of the rectangle (see Fig. 15.1). This movement of the dot is *induced* by that of the rectangle. Induced motion can be seen in natural situations, when the moon appears to race in a direction opposite to that of the clouds on a windy night. On a cloudless night the moon appears perfectly still (its actual movement is too slow to be detected as it is below the threshold for observer-relative movement). It is

interesting that the moon's movement is seen relative to the clouds even if the stationary buildings nearby could provide an alternative frame of reference. The Gestalt psychologist Duncker (1929) suggested that there was a "separation of systems" in such perception. The movement of any one part of a display is seen relative to its immediate surrounding frame, but is not affected by more remote influences. A demonstration by Wallach (1959) supports this (see Fig. 15.2). Here a dot is surrounded by a rectangle that is in turn enclosed by a circle. The perceived motion of the dot is influenced only by the actual movement of the rectangle, and little by that of the circle. That of the rectangle in turn is influenced only by the circle.

A further demonstration of how differing perceptions are obtained depending on the relative motions present is given by the "rolling wheel" effect. If a light is placed on the rim of a wheel that is rolled along in an otherwise dark room, the light is seen to trace out its actual, cycloidal path (see Fig. 15.3). It appears to bounce, but no cyclical, wheel-like motion is perceived. If a second light is

FIGURE 15.2

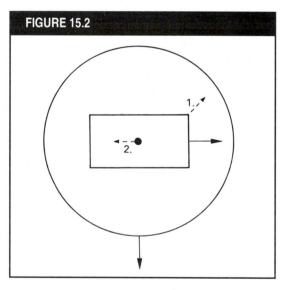

The circle is moved downwards and the rectangle is moved to the right (solid arrows). The perceived motion of the rectangle (1) is influenced by the actual movement of the circle. The perceived motion of the stationary dot (2) is influenced only by the actual movement of the rectangle. Adapted from Wallach (1959).

FIGURE 15.1

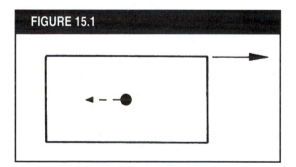

Induced movement. A stationary dot appears to move to the left as the rectangle surrounding it is moved to the right.

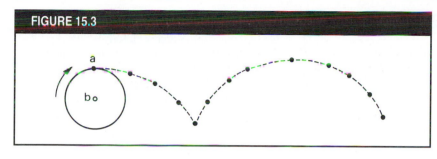

FIGURE 15.3

The cycloidal path traced out by a light (a) placed on the rim of a wheel that rolls in the dark. If only (a) is illuminated, this path is perceived. If the hub (b) is also illuminated, then (a) appears to cycle around (b).

illuminated on the hub, however, the one on the rim now seems to trace out a path that revolves around the hub, and the two lights now form a wheel-like configuration that translates across the field of view. The rolling wheel is one of a number of examples where the perceived configuration of the motion of one element is affected by the presence of another. A final example is shown in Fig. 15.4. The central dot, which moves on a diagonal path, is flanked by two dots, which move horizontally. The presence of these alters the way in which the central dot is seen to move. It appears to move vertically, between the flanking dots, while all three dots together move horizontally as a unit.

The perception of many such displays seems to conform to a "simplicity" or "minimum" principle. Of many possible interpretations of a display of separately moving elements, the simplest is made; that is, the one in which the motion components seen are minimised (Cutting & Proffitt, 1982). Johansson (1973, 1975) suggests in addition that the preferred perceptual interpretation of dynamic

displays is in terms of the motion of rigid structures. "Evidently it is obligatory that the spatial relation between two isolated moving stimuli be perceived as the simplest motion that preserves a rigid connection between the stimuli. The general formula is spatial invariance plus motion." (Johansson, 1975, p.73)

This preference for a rigid interpretation is demonstrated in the display in Fig. 15.5, where two dots each follow the same rectangular path. Under viewing conditions that minimise the impression that the screen on which the dots appear is flat, observers report the two dots as the end-points of a rigid stick that moves rather curiously in depth, rather than seeing them as "chasing" each other around the rectangle.

Such phenomena of relative motion perception were extensively investigated by Johansson (1973, 1975) who suggests that the perception of many such displays can be accounted for if it is assumed that the visual system performs some kind of *perceptual vector analysis*. Let us examine this

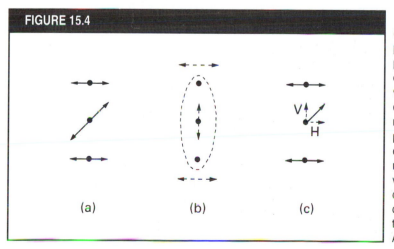

FIGURE 15.4

(a)   (b)   (c)

(a) Three dots move to and fro on the paths shown. In this situation the perception is as shown at (b). The central dot appears to travel on a vertical path between the two flanking dots, as the entire set of three dots moves from side to side. This perception can be explained in terms of vector analysis (c). The actual motion of the central dot is split into vertical (V) and horizontal (H) vector components. The horizontal component is in the same direction as the actual motion of the flanking dots. Adapted from Johansson (1975).

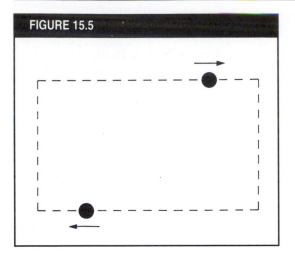

FIGURE 15.5

Two dots move on a rectangular path in the dark, as shown. The dots appear to form the ends of a stick that moves curiously in depth. Adapted from Johansson (1975). Copyright © 1975 by Scientific American, Inc. All rights reserved.

motion component of the whole display is partialled out, the motion that is "left over" (the residual) is a vertical motion of the central dot, which is what people report when shown such a display.

The same kind of analysis can be applied to the perception of the lights attached to a rolling wheel, described earlier. When a light is placed on the hub in addition to that on the rim, there is a common motion component shared by the two lights that corresponds to the direction in which the wheel is moving. This common-motion component completely accounts for the motion of the light on the hub, and when partialled out of the motion of the light on the rim, the residual left to this light is cyclical motion around the hub. This kind of description suggests that common motions are abstracted from a display first, leaving relative motions as the residual, although Cutting and Proffitt (1982) point out that Johansson has not always made such a strong claim.

Cutting and Proffitt (1982) argue that not all perceptions of such displays are consistent with the "common-motion-first" principle. For example, observers occasionally report the rolling wheel display with a single rim and hub light as appearing like a "tumbling stick" (Duncker, 1929). Here the two lights appear to be the end-points of a stick that rotates about a point halfway along its length. The stick is tumbling because the imaginary midpoint itself traces out a "hobbling" path (see Fig. 15.6). In such a situation relative motion analysis appears to take priority, with common motion left as residual.

There are thus two possible ways in which any given set of absolute motions can be resolved into a perception of relative and common motions. Either common motion can be detected first, in such a way as to minimise (give the simplest

notion by starting with one of Johansson's own displays. As we have already described, when the display in Fig. 15.4 is shown to human observers, they report seeing the central dot moving up and down a vertical path between the two horizontal "flanking" dots. Thus the resulting perception is of the vector that results after the components of *common motion* of the three display elements have been subtracted. To elaborate, the two horizontally moving flanking dots are moving together and therefore share a common horizontal translatory motion, against which other relative motions can be perceived. The diagonal motion of the central dot can be resolved into two vector components (see Fig. 15.4c), one in the direction of the common motion of the flanking dots, and the other perpendicular to this (i.e. vertical). If the common

FIGURE 15.6

The path traced out by the midpoint of an imaginary line joining lights on the rim and hub of a wheel. Observers occasionally report this display as like a stick tumbling along this path.

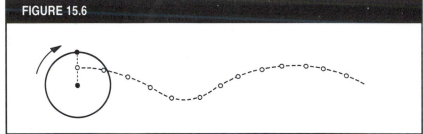

account of) the common motion present, and then, after abstraction of the common motion, the relative motions may be perceived as residual. Or relative motion can be detected and its components minimised, and after abstraction of this the common motion will be left as residual. These two possibilities make different predictions about the resulting perceptions of most displays of the "wheel-rolling" kind. As already mentioned, the "common-motion-first" theory predicts that a display with a hub light and a single rim light should appear wheel-like, whereas the "relative-motion-first" theory predicts that it should appear as a tumbling stick. Although the rolling wheel perception is preferred (Cutting & Proffitt 1982; Duncker 1929; Johansson 1975), the tumbling stick may be seen, particularly if subjects are not fixating on one of the lights (Duncker, 1929). For other displays the "relative-motion-first" theory gives a much better account of what is perceived. Consider the configuration of lights in Fig. 15.7. Here two lights are placed 90° apart on the rim of a wheel. The common motion in the display is again linear translation, and if this were abstracted first then we would expect observers to report both lights cycling around the imaginary centre of the wheel. However, if the relative motion were minimised, the two lights could be seen revolving around the midpoint of the imaginary line that joins them. After abstraction of this relative motion, the common motion left would be the prolate cycloidal motion of this midpoint—a kind of tumbling stick again. In fact, observers report the latter perception of such a display.

We seem to be left in a dilemma. For some displays it looks as though common motion is minimised and abstracted first, and for others it

seems that relative motions are first detected and common motion seen as residual. Cutting and Proffitt suggest that both processes may proceed simultaneously, with the one achieving solution first dominating the perception. That is, the perceptual system may seek to minimise both common and relative motions at the same time. The one that is solved first determines that the other be perceived as residual. This theory seems to give the best account of the perception of this type of display, and certainly reinforces the idea that absolute motions are rarely seen as such.

The patterns of relative motion before and after collisions can also be informative about other characteristics of the objects, for example their relative masses. When a heavy bowl hits a light skittle (or "pin" as in "ten-pin bowling"), the skittle is deflected by the bowl, but the path of the bowl is scarcely affected by the collision at all. A number of experiments have shown how people are able to make consistent judgements about the relative weights of objects represented by shapes moving in different ways. In Fig. 15.8a we see a schematic depiction of an object A striking B, with the result that B moves off at a relatively high speed and large angle to A, but A's path is deflected only very slightly. Shown an animated display in which the motions conform to this pattern, people will report that B appears to be a much lighter object than A. In Fig. 15.8b, in contrast, object A is deflected through a very large angle by the collision, but object B moves away very slowly after the collision. Under these conditions, subjects report that B appears to be a much heavier object than A. Gilden and Proffitt (1989, 1994) have analysed the way in which people make decisions about the relative mass of two objects like this from

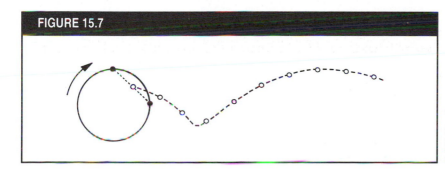

FIGURE 15.7

The path traced out by the midpoint of an imaginary line joining two lights placed 90° apart on the rim of a wheel.

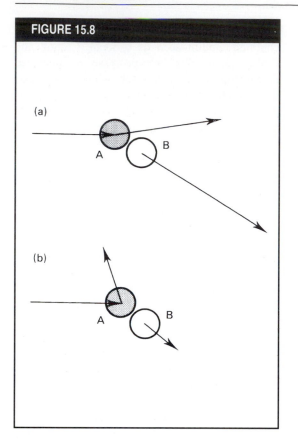

FIGURE 15.8

(a)

A

B

(b)

A

B

A schematic depiction of different relative motion patterns of objects A and B following a collision. In (a) A's path is deflected only slightly, and B moves a considerable distance following the impact, and observers will see A as much heavier than B. In (b) B moves only slightly following the impact, while A is deflected through a large angle by the impact. Observers here see B as much heavier than A. Adapted from Gilden and Proffitt (1994).

variations in their relative speed and angle of scatter after the collision. By examining their own and other researchers' data on what happens when the angle of deflection and the speeds of the objects post-collision are put into conflict, Gilden and Proffitt were able to gain support for their theory that people interpret such displays by using *two* judgemental heuristics, based on separate assessments of the speed and angle variables. Such a theory is in contrast to the more "direct" perception approach taken by Runeson (e.g. Runeson & Vedeler, 1993) who considers that kinematics (speeds and trajectories) directly

specify the object dynamics without mediation by inferential processes. Later in this chapter we will consider the spatial and temporal parameters that determine the perception of causality (i.e. that object A *caused* object B to move) in displays of this kind.

Thus we have seen that the visual system resolves simple dynamic displays into components of common and relative motions, and that the patterns of relative motion help specify other characteristics of the objects in motion. In the next section we consider a more elaborate example of the way in which patterns of relative motion specify the characteristics of objects-in-motion in the perception of *biological* motion.

BIOLOGICAL MOTION

The most dramatic demonstrations of the visual system's application of a "minimum" principle were produced by Johansson (1973) in his biological motion displays. Johansson produced films of people walking, running, and dancing in which the only visible features were lights attached to the actors' joints. Lights might be attached to the shoulders, elbows, wrists, hips, knees, and ankles, to form a total of 12 moving lights in the dynamic displays (see Fig. 15.9). Such a display is easy to produce by wrapping reflectant tape around the joints and filming with a video camera set up to pick up only high contrast. In the film that results, all information about the contour of the human figure has been removed, and if a still frame of such a film is shown it looks like a meaningless jumble of dots, or, at best, a Christmas tree. However, as soon as the actor is shown moving, the impression is immediately of a human figure. The perception of a moving human can be achieved with as little as 100msec of film, or with as few as six lights shown. Not only can the figure be clearly seen (with the invisible contours of arms and legs present in a ghostly way), but the posture, gait, and activities of the actor can be clearly described. It is clear from the displays whether the person is walking, running, jumping, limping, doing

FIGURE 15.9

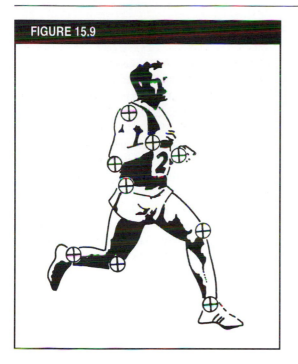

Lights are attached to the joints of an actor who runs in the dark. The changing pattern of lights is immediately interpreted as a human figure in motion.

push-ups, or dancing with a partner also portrayed by a set of moving lights. Mather and West (1993b) have more recently shown that adults are also quite accurate at recognising which of a number of species of animal is shown in a moving point-light display, but are quite unable to identify the creatures from static frames of the same displays.

Biological motion can exert significant top-down influences on low-level perceptual processes. For example, Bülthoff, Sinha, and Bülthoff (1995) showed that subjects' stereoscopic depth perception was distorted by their perception of the dynamic human figure. Subjects were presented stereoscopically with biological point-light displays and with control displays that could not be seen as biological forms. The depth positions of dots were systematically varied, and subjects were asked to report if specified dots lay in the same depth plane. Subjects were more accurate with the control than the biological sequences, where they tended to report dots as being in the same depth plane when they came from the same limb.

Sensitivity to the figural coherence of such displays of biological motion appears either to be innate, or to develop very quickly. Bertenthal, Proffitt, and Cutting (1984) found that three- and five-month-old infants were able to discriminate between upright and inverted walking point-light figures, although not between static frames from the upright and inverted conditions. Infants at this age were also able to discriminate a "coherent" point-light display of a person walking a treadmill from the same display with the dot motions scrambled to form what adults judged to look like "a swarm of bees".

Runeson and Frykholm (1981, 1983) demonstrated the extraordinary subtlety of perception possible by adults viewing moving point-light displays. In their experiments, they filmed the movements of actors throwing sandbags to targets at different distances. Runeson and Frykolm (1981) showed that observers can accurately judge differences in the weight carried by an actor, where both the actors and load together are depicted by a total of 21 points of light. In later experiments (Runeson & Frykholm, 1983), point lights were placed on the actors' joints, but no lights were placed on the bags, so that observers viewing the film had no information from the bags themselves about their motions. Nevertheless, observers were extremely accurate at judging how far the actors had been trying to throw the bag on each attempt.

Johansson considered the perception of biological motion in displays like these to be consistent with perceptual vector analysis, applied hierarchically. Let us take the case of an actor walking across a screen in front of the observer. The entire configuration of moving dots has a common motion component in the horizontal direction in which the actor is moving. Against this, the shoulders and hips make slight undulatory motions. Against this undulatory motion of the hips, the knee describes a pendular motion. Once the pendular motion of the knee has been partialled out, the ankle can be seen to describe a further pendular motion about this. Thus the dynamic configuration can be resolved into a set of hierarchical, relative motions of rigid limb segments. These walking figure displays again show how the visual system apparently "prefers" to interpret moving elements as representing the end-points of rigid structures in motion, even if the resulting *rigid* structures may then appear to have quite complex motions in depth. It should be stressed that Johansson considers the perceptual decoding principles of the vector analytic type, and the preference for rigid motions, to be "hard-wired" rather than derived from experience with real moving objects. We might note at this point a similarity with Ullman's theory (see Ch.8, p.198), who also made use of a rigidity assumption to interpret structure from moving point configurations.

However, Mather, Radford, and West (1992) have provided an alternative interpretation of the perception of these displays, by examining systematically the effects of omitting different dots from synthesised walking displays (see later for a discussion of possible limitations of the use of synthetic walking displays). According to the hierarchical "pendulum" approach, omitting dots at the hips and shoulders should cause most problems because these are needed to anchor the remaining residual motions. Alternatively, if the fixed end-points of rigid limb segments play a crucial role, then omitting points from the knees and elbows might create perceptual problems, as then neither the lower-limb nor upper-limb segments have their end-points specified. In contrast, however, Mather et al.'s (1992) results showed very clearly that omitting the shoulder/hip or elbow/knee points made virtually no difference to the accuracy with which walkers' motions could be detected, compared with full displays, whereas omitting the wrist and ankle points dramatically reduced performance. Mather et al. (1992) suggest that the perception of human biological motion in these displays arises not from a complex hierarchical analysis but from the recognition of characteristic patterns of motion in parts of the display. The extremities (wrists and ankles) move the furthest and thus provide better evidence than do other parts of the display. Given this, it would be interesting to establish how displays comprised *only* of wrist and ankle points compare with other possible combinations of only four points. According to Mather et al., wrist/ankle displays

should be perceived as very similar to full 12-point displays.

Cutting and his co-workers have investigated how observers may detect subtle differences in gait from biological motion displays. In preliminary work, Cutting and Kozlowski (1977) showed that observers performed well above chance at identifying themselves and their room-mates from such dynamic displays. In a number of subsequent experiments (Barclay, Cutting, & Kozlowski, 1978; Kozlowski & Cutting, 1977, 1978) they have gone on to show that observers are 60–70% accurate on average at detecting the *sex* of a walker from a display. In order to judge sex to this accuracy observers need to see about 2sec of the display, which corresponds to about two step cycles, suggesting that such judgements rely on some dynamic invariant rather than on static configurational cues. The detection of the sex of a walker does not seem to depend crucially on any particular elements in the display. Above chance level judgements can be made if only points on the upper body or lower body are illuminated (but see Kozlowski & Cutting, 1978, for a reinterpretation of the lower-body findings), although performance is best when joints on both upper and lower halves of the body are shown. Thus the information on which such judgements are made appears to be given by some *global* invariant, rather than by particular elements in the display.

Barclay et al. (1978) began the search for such an invariant with the observation that male and female bodies differ in the ratio of shoulder width to hip width. Men have broad shoulders and narrow hips compared with women. However, in the kinds of displays typically used, where the actor walks across the line of sight, only a single shoulder light and hip light are visible, so this ratio cannot be detected. Therefore the shoulder to hip width ratio cannot provide the basis for judgements of sex. This ratio does have consequences for other aspects of the relative motion in the display, however (Cutting, Proffitt, & Kozlowski, 1978). During locomotion, the hips and shoulders work in opposition to one another. When the right leg is forward in the step cycle, the right hip is also forward relative to the right shoulder which is back.

Likewise, when the left leg is forward, so too is the left hip, with the left shoulder back. The relative widths of the shoulders and hips should thus affect the relative side-to-side motion of the hip and shoulder joints when viewed from the side. A measure based on this relative swing was found to correlate reasonably well with the consistency with which different walkers were rated as male or female.

However, Cutting et al. (1978) went on to derive a more general invariant from their displays that correlated better with the ratings given to different walkers. This measure was the relative height of the *centre of moment* of the moving walkers. The centre of moment is the reference point around which all movement in all parts of the body have regular geometric relations: it corresponds to the point where the three planes of symmetry for a walker's motion coincide. Its relative location can be determined by knowing only the relative widths (or relative swings) of the hips and shoulders (see Fig. 15.10). The centre of moment for male walkers is lower than that for females, and therefore provides a possible basis for judgements of sex.

Cutting (1978) offered some support for the validity of the centre of moment as a determinant of gait perception by synthesising artificial dynamic dot displays that mimicked the movements of walkers. Using such displays it was possible to vary *only* the centre of moment in such displays, holding all other variables constant. The synthetic "male" and "female" walkers produced were correctly identified on 82% of trials, although if the lights corresponding to the hips and shoulders were omitted performance dropped to about 59%, still above chance. These results are compatible with those obtained with real walkers, where above chance, but reduced, performance was obtained when some of the lights were removed. However, the range of variation in the location of the centre of moment that Cutting incorporated into his synthetic displays was much greater than would be found in real walkers, limiting the generality of these results (see also Runeson, 1994). Nevertheless, this study did lend some support to the idea that a simple biomechanical invariant, the centre of moment, might be recovered from a display such as this and could be used to specify reasonably accurately the sex of the walking figure.

Mather and Murdoch (1994) have recently re-examined how people judge the sex of figures shown in moving point-light displays, using displays in which the walkers appear to walk towards or away from the camera, rather than across the line of sight as is more usual in such research. In these "front" and "rear" views, dynamic cues from shoulder and hip sways appear to be used to determine whether walkers seem male or female. Male upper bodies move more from side to side than female ones, whereas female hips move more from side to side than male ones. Mather and Murdoch varied both the amount of sway and the overall torso shape in their experiments, and showed that information about relative body sway

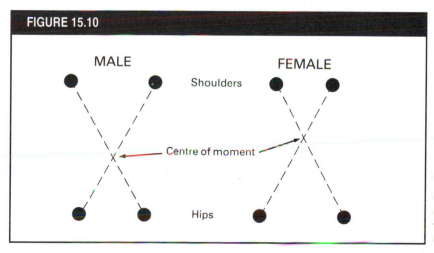

FIGURE 15.10

The relative location of the centre of moment for male and female walkers. Adapted from Cutting and Proffitt (1981).

dominated the structural cues arising from torso shape (centre-of-moment) when these were set into conflict. For example, a "male" body shape (wide shoulders, narrow hips) with female sway (hips moving from side to side more than shoulders) was categorised as female almost as often as a display in which the two sources of information were consistent. Mather and Murdoch suggest that in the side-views generally employed by other researchers, where lateral sway is not perceptible, it might still be the local velocity of the swing of shoulder and hip lights that underlies the perception of gender from such displays, rather than the more global invariant of "centre-of-moment".

Studies such as those of Cutting (1978), and Mather and Murdoch (1994), which use artificial point-light displays, would seem to provide a good means of testing hypotheses about the basis of our perceptions of such dynamic events. However, Runeson (1994) points out that to generate such displays often requires gross approximation, or even guess-work, about the movement patterns to which observers are sensitive. Unless the synthetic events are kinematically equivalent to real events, their usefulness in helping us to explain the perception of real dynamic events must be limited. One difference between synthetic point-light displays and those obtained from real walkers is that the former typically do not show any occlusion of one limb by another. Experiments using synthetic walkers have suggested that occlusion was an important ingredient that reduced the tendency of such synthetic displays to be seen as ambiguous in depth (Proffitt, Bertenthal, & Roberts, 1984). However, Runeson (1994) describes some unpublished experiments by Pardo (1992), which manipulated natural point-light displays to produce versions that lacked the usual clue of occlusion. He found no difference between the stability of the perceptions obtained from occluded compared to disoccluded natural point-light displays. This suggests that the dynamic properties of natural displays sustain perception of biological motion in a way that renders viewers insensitive to other properties such as occlusion. Such observations urge us to be cautious about automatically generalising from results obtained with "synthetic" walking displays to natural biological motion perception.

Although there seems to be some doubt about the adequacy of the centre-of-moment concept as an explanation of gender perception, it remains a useful candidate for a general invariant that can be found for other kinds of dynamic display. To return to the rolling wheel configurations (see p.325), the centroid—the centre of the configuration of lights—is directly analogous to the centre of moment. Proffitt and colleagues (Proffitt & Cutting, 1979; Proffitt, Cutting, & Stier, 1979) have shown that the relationship between the centroid and the centre of the wheel determines how wheel-like the motion observed is. When the two coincide (as when two lights are placed 180° apart on the rim), "perfect" wheel-like motions are seen. When the centroid and the centre of the wheel are far apart, as when the two lights are placed 90° apart on the rim (see Fig. 15.7), "hobbling" motions are seen.

We have seen (Chapters 11 and 13) that the centre of a radially expanding optical flow field is important in guiding locomotor activity, and this point is also the centre of moment for that dynamic display. Cutting and Proffitt (1981) have argued that the centre of moment is an even more widely useful concept, and can be applied to slow events, such as the ageing of a face (see Chapter 16) or the movement of stars in the night sky, which migratory birds use to steer their course. Cutting (1982) has demonstrated that viewers may be sensitive to alterations in *second-order* centres of moment (the centres of moment of component structures) when perceiving the bending motions present in "tree"- and "bush"-like configurations.

In all these examples, observers have viewed displays and have reported the *motions* present, or have identified or otherwise described the structures (e.g. human figures, objects of different masses) that give rise to these motions. One aspect of natural event perception that we have yet to consider is how we go beyond the motions present to attribute causality to the motions. It is to this topic that we turn next.

THE PERCEPTION OF CAUSALITY

When we watch a football match we are in no doubt about why the football suddenly speeds up and changes direction—it was kicked. That is, the change in the movement of the ball was *caused* by the action of one of the players' feet. Likewise, in boxing or judo, we see the action of one of the combatants as causing the other to fall to the floor. We might suggest that it is our previous experience of seeing footballs kicked, or opponents thrown, that allows us to make causal *inferences* in new situations. However, Michotte (1946, translated 1963) made the strong claim that causality is perceived *directly*.

Michotte experimented with simple displays. In one situation (Fig. 15.11a), subjects viewed a display in which a black square (A) moved towards a red square (B) at constant speed. At the moment when A came into contact with B, A stopped and B moved off, either at the same speed or at an appreciably slower one. After a short time B also came to rest. Michotte reports that in this situation observers see the black square bump into the red

square and set it into motion. "The impression is clear; it is the blow given by A that *makes B go*, which *produces* B's movement" (p.20). This has been termed the "launching effect".

In another demonstration (Fig. 15.11b) A again moves towards B, but continues its course without changing speed. When the two objects contact, B in turn moves off at the same speed as A until both objects finally come to rest together. In this situation Michotte describes the impression as of A carrying B along or pushing it ahead. This effect is known as "entraining".

Michotte backs up his claim that phenomenal causality is directly apprehended by demonstrating that the impression is critically dependent on the temporal, spatial, and structural properties of the display. In the first experiment described, if an interval is introduced between A contacting B and B moving off, the impression of causing, or launching, B's movement is eradicated. If B moves off faster than A then the impression is of B being "triggered" rather than launched, whereas if B moves off more slowly it appears to be launched rather than triggered. However, whether launching or triggering is seen also depends on the length of

FIGURE 15.11

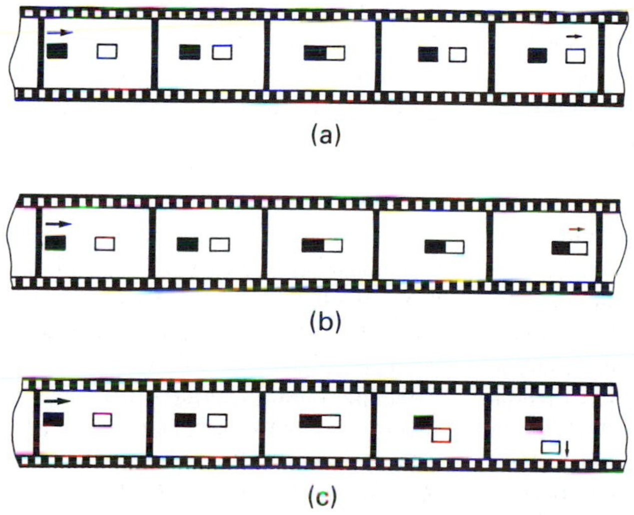

(a)

(b)

(c)

Frames of a film of the kinds of display used by Michotte. Black square A, Red square B (shown here in white). (a) Launching; (b) Entraining; (c) Display where B moves off at 90° and launching is not perceived.

the path that B subsequently follows as well as on the ratio of the objects' speeds, an observation that was confirmed by Boyle (1960).

According to Michotte, the launching effect depended not only on these spatial and temporal aspects but also on the similarity between the paths of the motion of the two objects. As object B's path was shifted in angle away from the direction of A's path, so the reported perceptions of launching declined. If B went off at a direction at right angles to A (Fig. 15.11c), Michotte claimed that launching was almost never observed. Whereas the impression of launching is thus crucially dependent on the temporal and spatial parameters, Michotte claimed that it was unaffected by the *nature* of the items used. If A was a wooden ball, and B a small, brightly coloured circle, Michotte reported that the launching effect was unchanged. Michotte regards this as important evidence for the "direct" perception of causality, because if previous experiences of cause and effect were responsible there should be no reason to see a causal relationship between two quite dissimilar items.

Although few would doubt that such causal impressions can be gained from displays of the types used by Michotte, there has subsequently been some doubt about the universality of observers' impressions. Michotte himself was often vague about the precise numbers of subjects he tested, or the instructions he gave them, and in places based strong claims on the results obtained with a very small number of highly practised subjects. Boyle (1960) reported having to discard 50% of his subjects on the basis of a pre-test in which these subjects failed to report "launching" or "entraining" from standard displays. Beasley (1968) assessed formally the extent of individual differences in the perception of these displays and reported that only 65% and 45% of his subjects responded respectively to "launching" and "entraining" displays in causal terms. Contrary to Michotte's claim, 45% did report causal impressions when object B departed at 90° from A in the launching display. In addition, and again contrary to claims made by Michotte, Beasley found that the nature of the objects used—squares, discs, or cars—did have an effect on the nature of

the responses elicited. Such variability appeared to cast doubt on Michotte's claims of the universality of such causal impressions, and on the idea that such effects are perceived "directly".

Recent research into the perception of causality has used more rigorous experimental techniques to investigate individual, experiential, and display factors affecting the perception of causality. Schlottman and Shanks (1992) have shown clear dissociations between factors that affect the perception of causality and those that affect *judgements* of contingency. In their experiments they showed that extensive experience during the experimental session did not affect the causal impressions gained from the impacts, which suggests that learning—at least within the limits of this experiment—does not affect causal impressions in adults. Moreover, in a second experiment they found that the predictiveness of a colour change did affect judgements of the *necessity* of one event for the occurrence of another, but that the causal impressions gained by the impacts themselves remained unaffected by their predictive validity within the experiment. For example, if on some trials object B moved away following a change in object A's colour, and on other trials object B moved away following an impact by object A *and* a change in its colour, and if object B never moved *unless* there was a change in colour, then clearly it is the colour change rather than the impacts that predict whether object B will move. Nevertheless, the causal impression given by "launching" trials that do include impacts is not affected by their reduced necessity for the production of B's movement. Schlottman and Shanks use these results to support the idea of a causality "module" that is impervious to subjects' beliefs or learned expectations in a particular situation. As we argue in Chapter 17, the notion of "cognitively impenetrable" computational modules is an important advance on that of "direct perception".

Leslie (1984; Leslie & Keeble, 1987) has investigated the "directness" of the perception of causality using a developmental approach and has shown that by 27 weeks infants can perceive causal relations such as launching. Leslie suggests that causal perception results from a visual mechanism that takes its input from lower-level motion processors, analyses the sub-movements to produce higher-level descriptions of the spatial and temporal properties of the event, and finally describes its causal structure. Thus according to Leslie the causality module can be reduced to elementary information-processing operations, but remains entirely impervious to higher-level beliefs or expectations. In contrast, however, Oakes (1994) provides more evidence of an influence of general information-processing skills than Leslie's analysis would predict. Oakes found that 7-month-olds are able to perceive causality in simple displays but not in ones containing complex objects, and that older (10 months) infants are unable to maintain causal impressions if the specific objects used change from trial to trial.

Thus there is some conflict in the research evidence over the extent to which causality perception is influenced by other information processing and by subjective beliefs or strategies. In an attempt to resolve these issues, Schlottmann and Anderson (1993) presented observers with displays in which one object, A, collided with another, B, and varied the spatial gap between A and B, the temporal delay at the point of impact between A and B, and the ratio of the speeds of the two objects' motions. They examined individual differences in the resulting causal impressions as well as impressions of the naturalness of the displayed launching events. They explain their data using an information-integration model in which there are two distinct processing stages—valuation and integration. "Valuation" determines the weights that people attach to different stimulus dimensions, and these may vary from one person to another. On the other hand, subjects' processes of integration across the different dimensions are remarkably invariant and agree with Michotte's original conclusions. Schlottmann and Anderson suggest that individual experience may affect the values placed on the different dimensions, and thus allow some reconciliation between Michotte and his critics.

An early computer model of causality perception by Weir (1978) interprets displays like those of Michotte in ways similar to human observers, and has the scope to incorporate individual differences alongside invariant perceptual processing mechanisms. Beyond this point, however, the details of Weir's (1978) model do not correspond closely with Schlottmann and Anderson's more recent statistical model. Weir's model is a transactionalist one, in which there is a continuous interaction between the stimulus pattern and stored internal representations in the form of action "schemata". It is thus nearer in conception to the kind of framework we presented in Part II of this book. Her computer program accepts a symbolic description of each of a sequence of static images, corresponding to different frames of a film of a Michotte display, so that the movement of each display element has to be computed by comparing elements from one frame to the next. This means that she has to tackle the "correspondence problem" (see Ch.8, p.196) in order to match the objects in each frame (Weir, 1978, p.249):

There will in general be more than one way of pairing the picture regions in two adjacent frames and a way of choosing which of the possible pairings correspond to an *enduring object in motion* must be provided.

Weir makes use of partial matches between incoming event sequences and stored action schemata to help solve this correspondence process, and so "top-down" processes (see Chapter 4) play a central role in her theory. This is unfortunate for our purposes here, as our emphasis in this part of the book is to explore perception within a framework which does not involve cognitive mediation. Nevertheless, some features of Weir's program are worth describing here as a modification of her theory could quite easily be applied to motions that had been computed without involving higher-level concepts.

The object motions are compared with stored "schemata" for different actions, which are dynamic descriptions for actions rather like the structural descriptions for objects that we considered in Chapter 9. An action schema contains units like "approaches" and "withdraws". The action schema for "Launching" is shown in Fig. 15.12a, and that for "Entraining" in Fig.

FIGURE 15.12

Schemas for Launching (a) and Entraining (b). Adapted from Weir (1978).

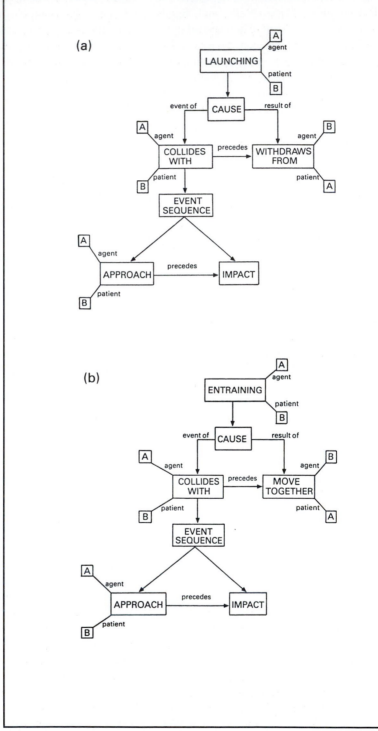

15.12b. For each action there is an *agent*, and an object on which the agent acts (here called the *patient*).

The schema consists of several components. Launching consists of collision followed by withdrawal, and the schema specifies the event sequence that defines a collision. Entraining consists of collision followed by movement together. If the first few frames of the film match the "collision" sequence, then both the launching and entraining schemas are activated. The subsequent actions in the display will allow a decision to be reached about which interpretation is correct.

Weir's simulation allows the possibility of anticipation of expected actions by the activation of "demons" that look out for expected sequences. It can also incorporate individual differences in perception. For example, some subjects may report launching only if B's speed after impact is substantially below A's before impact. This can be incorporated by restrictions in the definitions of actions like "withdraws from".

We have seen how causal impressions may be obtained from simple displays, and argued that such impressions are likely to be gained by a process of computation, rather than "directly" as Michotte claimed. We now turn to consider how *intentions* and *dispositions* may be perceived in the objects which move in simple dynamic displays.

PERCEPTION AND ATTRIBUTION

Observers who view displays of the type used by Michotte may describe the actions of the objects in animate terms. Thus A may be seen to "kick" or to "shove" B. B may be seen to "escape" from A who is "chasing" it. Therefore, in addition to perceiving causality, we may also perceive intentionality in the action of inanimate objects, just as in everyday life we interpret the actions of animate beings in terms of what they are trying to do. In addition, these momentary intentions that we observe may lead us to attribute enduring dispositional traits to the actors we observe. If person A kicks B, chases him, then kicks him again, A may be seen as a "bully".

The classic study of such attributional processes in perception was conducted by Heider and Simmel (1944) who showed observers a film in which two triangles of different sizes (the larger and smaller hereafter referred to as T and t, respectively) and a circle (c) were seen to move in the vicinity of a rectangular frame (the house) with a moveable flap in one side (the door) (see Fig. 15.13). The first few frames of the film sequence depicted the following movements (illustrated roughly in Fig. 15.13, and described here, as in the original article, in "anthropomorphic" terms for simplicity):

> T moved toward the house, opened the door, moved inside and closed the door. t and c appeared and moved around near the door. T moved out of the house towards t; the two fight, with T the winner; during the fight, c moved into the house.

Heider and Simmel showed the entire film to 34 subjects who were simply asked to "write down what happened in the picture". All but one of their subjects described the film in terms of the movements of animate beings. A typical subject's description of the first few frames was (pp.246–247):

> A man has planned to meet a girl and the girl comes along with another man. The first man tells the second to go; the second tells the first, and he shakes his head. Then the two men have a fight, and the girl starts to go into the room to get out of the way and hesitates and finally goes in. She apparently does not want to be with the first man.

In a second experiment Heider and Simmel asked their subjects to interpret the movements of the figures as actions of persons and then to answer a series of questions, which included such items as "what kind of a person is the big triangle". Such questions were answered with high consistency. Both triangles were usually perceived as male, with the larger one seen as "aggressive", a "bully", "bad-tempered", etc. The circle was seen as "frightened", "meek", or "helpless". Even in the first experiment, where no specific direction to see

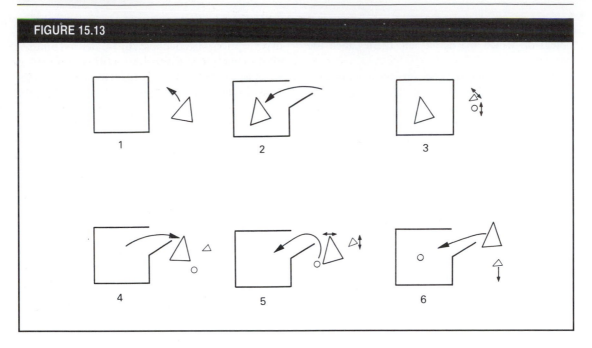

FIGURE 15.13

A sequence of events from the early part of Heider and Simmel's (1944) film. The film shows a big triangle, a small triangle, and a small circle moving around near a box with a moveable flap (the door). See text for a description of the event sequence.

the objects as people was given, subjects tended to describe the objects as being of different sex and with differing dispositions.

Heider and Simmel's original film confounded dynamic with structural properties of the displays. It is not clear, for example, how much of the perceptual interpretation is given by the relative sizes and shapes of the protagonists (small circles versus small and large triangles) as opposed to their movements. Berry and Misovich (1994) report using a quantisation technique to degrade the structural forms shown in the original Heider and Simmel film while preserving their dynamic aspects, and report that adults produced similar numbers of anthropomorphic terms in the structurally degraded as in the original condition. However, when static frames were shown from either the original or quantised versions then the number of anthropomorphic terms dropped substantially, suggesting that it is the dynamic characteristics of the displays that are critical for their perception. The same pattern of results was observed with young children, although in all conditions of the experiment young children

reported fewer anthropomorphic terms than did adults.

These recent investigations lend some support to Heider and Simmel's suggestion that causal impressions were given by the spatial, temporal, and figural aspects of the display. Thus when T is seen to "hit" t, the stimulus parameters are very similar to those in the "launching" experiment of Michotte. T approaches t until it comes into contact with it. Then T stands still while t starts to move in the same direction as T's earlier movement (p.253).

This phenomenal relationship is obviously determined by temporal succession and spatial proximity. The good continuation of the line—the fact that the direction of t's movement continues the direction of T's—probably plays a role in the convincing appearance of this apparent energetic movement.

The movements of T and the door, which result in the impression of T "opening" or "closing" the door, are similar to Michotte's "entraining" displays, as the movement of T is imparted to the door by prolonged contact rather than sudden impact. The question arises as to why it is always T who appears to push the door (rather than the door pushing T). Heider and Simmel suggest that here the interpretation is influenced by the context in which such movements occur. The door never moves *without* contact from T or one of the other shapes, whereas each of the shapes *is* seen to move in isolation. The shapes are therefore seen as "animate", the door as "inanimate", which resolves the ambiguity in the pushing action.

To resolve ambiguity in the interpretation of the movement in these displays, subjects may use a combination of the stimulus parameters and the personality characteristics that have been attributed to the display members. For example, if two objects move together at the same distance apart, the first may be seen to lead, with the second following, or the second may be seen to chase the first, which is fleeing. The interpretation given depends on the element that is seen as initiating the movement, and also on the power relationships that exist between the "people" who are moving. If T is seen as timid or cowardly, then t may seem to chase him (some such reports were obtained when the original film was shown in reverse). If T is seen as dictatorial or aggressive, then t may seem to follow him (p.254).

> If one sees two animals running in file through high grass, one will interpret these movements in accordance with other data. If the one in front is a rabbit and the one behind a dog, he will perceive a dog chasing a rabbit. If the first one is a big rabbit and the second a small one, he will not see "chasing" but "leading" and "following".

Thus Heider and Simmel see some aspects of the interpretation as given by the stimulus parameters, but other aspects, while *constrained* by these features, will additionally be influenced by the total context in which the individual action is embedded. Intention as well as action is involved in the interpretation of their film. If T is hitting t, then T wants to hurt t. If T chases t into the house, then t may be trying to hide from T. Such intentional attributions themselves influence the

dispositions that are accorded to the individual elements, and these dispositions may in turn influence how a new action sequence is interpreted.

These examples illustrate that even in the perception of the movements of simple shapes in a relatively neutral context, we see the application of quite complex and subtle attributional processes by humans. What we see happening will depend not only on the momentary motions in the display, but also on expectations built up over a sequence of actions, expectations that are derived from our broader social experiences. It would seem to be stretching the Gibsonian line too far to say that all the qualities imparted to these simple objects are specified in the light. The pattern of activity present doubtless constrains the range of possible interpretations, but cannot specify which interpretation will be given.

Nevertheless, it is still interesting to explore the ways in which different stimulus parameters influence the perception of such displays. Heider and Simmel's study was limited to a single film. Unlike Michotte, they made no attempt to vary spatial or temporal parameters systematically. Indeed, the film they constructed probably reflected their own intuitions about the phenomenological processes they wished to study. However, Bassili (1976) has conducted a study in which aspects of a Heider and Simmel type of display were systematically varied.

In Bassili's computer-generated displays, a black and a white circle were filmed undergoing various movements. Five different films were produced, ranging from a "chase" in which the temporal and spatial characteristics of the following (black) circle were tightly linked to those of the leading (white) one, down to a film in which both elements moved randomly and independently about the screen. Thus the temporal and spatial linking of the movements were progressively relaxed. Subjects who viewed the films were initially required to "Describe what you saw in one concise sentence" and then asked more specific questions about their perceptions of the film. The effect of temporal contingency was assessed by comparing the responses to two films, in both of which the directions of the motions were random. In one, however, a change in direction of one element was quickly followed by a change in direction of the other. In the other no such temporal contingency held.

It was found that temporal contingency between the changes in direction of the two figures was critical for the perception of an interaction between them, whereas the motion configuration (the spatial contingencies) were an important factor in the *kind* of interaction and the intentionality attributed to the figures. For example, subjects were much more likely to report that the black circle was chasing or following the white circle, and to ascribe intention to either or both of the circles, when the direction of the changes in the black circle's path were tightly linked to those of the white circle. When the directions were random, but temporally linked, subjects saw the circles as interacting in some unspecified way, but were less likely to describe this interaction in intentional terms.

It is interesting to contrast the *interactive* nature of the perception of these displays with the *relative motion* perceptions described earlier in this chapter. For example, Johansson (p.326) describes the perception of two white dots following one another around a rectangle (Fig. 15.5) as being of the dots forming the end-points of a rigid stick that itself moves in depth: in the work of Michotte, Heider and Simmel, and of Bassili, similar elements are seen as independent elements that influence the actions of each other. It seems likely that the nature of the elements, the viewing conditions, and the instructions given to subjects will all influence how such moving displays are interpreted. If the display elements are identical, as in Johansson's displays, they may be more likely to be grouped together as parts of a single object than if they are dissimilar as in Bassili's. If the display is viewed under conditions where the flatness of the screen, and the screen edges, are not apparent, then it is more likely that movement in depth will be seen. Finally, if subjects are requested to describe the *motions* in the display they may be less likely to respond in terms of animate interactions than if they are asked to state "what happened".

Dittrich and Lea (1994) produced simulations of biologically meaningful motion sequences using simple displays of moving letters in which subjects were asked to try to spot one letter acting as a "wolf" in pursuit of one of the other "sheep" letters, or in other conditions a letter was acting as a "lamb" trying to catch up with its mother "sheep". They found clear influences of dynamic variables on the perception of intentional motions of this kind, with intentionality appearing stronger when the "wolf/lamb" letter's path was more directly related to its target, and being more salient when its speed was relatively fast (wolf) rather than relatively slow (lamb). In these experiments Dittrich and Lea did not find significant effects of instruction— performance did not differ according to whether the task was described in intentional (wolf/sheep) or neutral (letters) terms. Despite the lack of effects of instructions, however, Dittrich and Lea discuss the perception of intentionality within a two-stage framework where perceptual motion variables are interpreted by activating intentional concepts, a framework that bears some resemblance to Weir's.

CONCLUSIONS

In this chapter we have examined how we perceive motion in relatively simple displays. We have concluded by considering how relatively simple display elements may be perceived in causal interrelationships, and endowed with "human" qualities of intention and personality. These complex attributional processes undoubtedly derive from our everyday social experiences, but the social attributions that we make in everyday life will themselves depend at least in part on information obtained from nonverbal aspects of a perceived interaction or situation. In the next chapter we turn to explore aspects of interpersonal perception in their own right, as we move from a discussion of event perception to social perception.

16

Perception of the Social World

In Chapter 15 we considered how people can perceive events by detecting complex transformations in patterns of light. In the case of Johansson's experiments, we described evidence that people are particularly sensitive to biological patterns of motion, such as those characteristic of a walking person. Johansson's evidence illustrates one way in which information in light about the animate world—the other people or other animals surrounding an observer—can be detected. In contrast, much of our discussion of the role of vision in guiding animals' and people's actions has so far been concerned with problems of manoeuvring through the inanimate world, such as those faced by diving gannets or by long-jumpers, which we considered in Chapters 12 and 13. In this chapter, we discuss more fully how vision guides action in the animate world, taking examples from both animal and human vision.

An animal needs information about the activities of other animals around it that in some way affect its chances of survival and reproduction. Carnivorous animals must detect, pursue, and capture *prey*. Most animals are themselves prey for other species, and must be able to detect and evade *predators*. Finally, most animals need information about the activities of other members of their own species, or *conspecifics*, with which they engage in various forms of social behaviour including courtship, mating, aggression, parental care, and play. In social insects and some mammals, it also includes elaborate forms of cooperative behaviour in which many individuals engage together in hunting, nest building, and other activities.

In all these situations, an animal must be able to perceive what other animals are doing and adjust its own behaviour accordingly. The ways in which people obtain food, protect themselves, and interact with other people involve many further complexities arising from culture and language, but, even so, human social interaction requires the same basic abilities to recognise other people and detect what they are doing. Our discussion in this chapter deals primarily with the role of vision in guiding animal and human *social* behaviour, although we also consider some examples of ways in which animals obtain information about prey or predators. We will discuss two main problems. First, how do animals detect the behaviour and identity of other animals? Second, how do people obtain information about other people from their faces, and particularly from their constantly changing facial expressions?

PERCEIVING OTHER ANIMALS' BEHAVIOUR

In Chapter 9 we saw examples of how insects, fish, and birds may use simple visual mechanisms to recognise other members of their species, relying on coloured markings, stereotyped movements, or other cues. Many animals need to do more than just recognise conspecifics, and must also make fine discriminations between the different patterns of behaviour they perform during a social interaction, such as courtship or a territorial dispute. One animal may need information about another's *posture*—the orientations of different parts of its body relative to each other. For example, the angles of a dog's ears relative to its head, and of its tail relative to its body, provide information about its aggressiveness. Similarly, gulls involved in aggressive encounters threaten other gulls by adopting an upright posture with the bill pointing downwards and the wings held forwards, and signal submission with the opposite, crouching posture (Fig. 16.1).

An animal may also need to be able to detect the *orientation* relative to itself of another animal's whole body or of a part of its body such as its head or a limb. An example is provided by the aggressive displays of Siamese fighting fish. In a threat display, a fish spreads its dorsal, tail, and anal fins (Fig. 16.2). It may turn broadside to its opponent and lower and twitch its pelvic fin (Fig. 16.2c). At the same time it may beat its tail and flashes of bright colour may occur on the tail and body.

Alternatively, it may face its opponent head-on and open its gill covers (Fig. 16.2d). Simpson (1968) analysed these encounters and discovered that a fish's behaviour is influenced by the orientation of its opponent relative to itself. A fish is more likely to turn to a broadside orientation if its opponent is facing it than if it is broadside, so that the two fish often take up a "T"-shaped configuration. Also, a fish is more likely to flicker its pelvic fin if the opponent is facing it than if it is broadside.

Many animals respond fearfully or aggressively if the head and eyes of another animal are oriented towards them. For example, when a group of jays feeds, the dominant bird eats first while the others mill about near the food. If a subordinate approaches closely, the dominant turns its head to fixate it either binocularly or monocularly. The subordinate often hops backwards when this happens, and is more likely to do so if the dominant bird fixates it binocularly (Bossema & Burgler, 1980). The same thing may happen with potential predators as well as with conspecifics. Ristau (1991) observed the alarm responses of plovers to human intruders walking near their nests, and found that these were more prolonged when the intruders looked in the direction of the nest than when they looked away from it.

There are two reasons why responses to being fixated by another animal's head and eyes are so widespread. First, predators as diverse as preying mantids and cats orient their heads towards prey before striking at it, presumably as part of a mechanism for controlling the direction of the

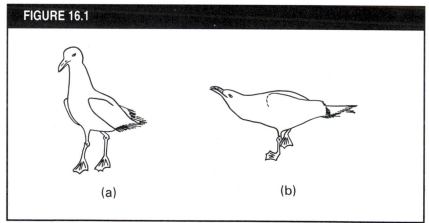

FIGURE 16.1

(a)   (b)

Threat (a) and appeasement (b) postures of the lesser black-backed gull. Drawn from photographs by N. Tinbergen in Manning (1978).

FIGURE 16.2

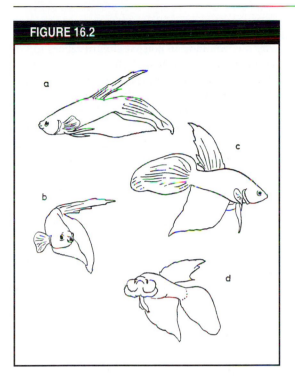

(a) and (b) Nondisplaying Siamese fighting fish, (c) Display posture with fins spread out and pelvic fin lowered, (d) Display posture with gill covers opened. Adapted from Simpson (1968).

strike. Eyes and head pointing towards an animal can therefore provide it with information that it is in immediate danger. Second, if an animal with a specialised retinal area such as a fovea fixates another, this signals to the second animal that the first is better able to obtain information about its identity or behaviour, which would be useful in an aggressive encounter.

There are various ways in which fixation by another animal could be specified by optical information. If both head and eyes are oriented towards the observer, the image of the face will be symmetrical, and this symmetry will be invariant with size, distance, and direction. Hampton (1994) tested this possibility in sparrows, observing their escape responses when presented with model human heads. He found that the birds responded more strongly to the heads when both eyes were visible to them than when only one was, but that breaking the symmetry of the model face by moving the nose had no effect. The implication is that sparrows are not sensitive to the symmetry of a face, but are alarmed just by the presence of a pair of eyes. This will sometimes lead to "false alarms", when a predator fixates an object to one side of the bird, but presumably natural selection has favoured a fast, simple perceptual mechanism in this vulnerable species.

Monkeys are able to detect small deviations from fixation, or "sideways" fixation with the eyes but not the head (Campbell, Heywood, Cowey, Regard, & Landis, 1990), and so clearly must be sensitive to more complex optical information specifying direction of gaze than are sparrows. The same is true of people, as we will see later in this chapter (p.357). Something is known of the physiological basis of gaze discrimination in primates; we mentioned in Chapter 3 (p.61) that cells in area STS of the temporal cortex of monkeys respond differently to a face seen in different views (full-face, three-quarters, etc). Perrett, Hietanen, Oram, and Benson (1992) have further tested these cells with stimuli in which both eye and head orientation vary, and have shown that they are best described as selective for another animal's direction of gaze relative to the perceiver. The activity of such a cell may signal, for example, that another monkey is directing its attention to the viewer's left, whatever combination of body, head, and eye orientation is involved.

Perceiving transformations of posture

In the aggressive interactions of gulls, fighting fish, and jays, the ability to detect the posture and the orientation of another animal, or a part of it, is crucial, and this is likely to be true of all but the simplest social behaviour. A question we can ask about the perceptual processes involved in cases like these is whether information about posture and orientation is obtained from a static retinal image, or whether animals detect transformations over time in these parameters. Does a Siamese fighting fish process a static retinal image to determine whether a particular configuration, such as a fish with extended fins, is present, or does it process a time-varying image to detect transformations in posture and orientation such as a flickering fin or a 90° turn?

To determine whether an animal detects static or dynamic properties of another animal's behaviour, we would need to compare behaviour towards appropriate stationary and moving models. This is technically difficult, but an example of such an experiment is provided by Turner (1964). Young chicks learn to feed by pecking at small objects on the ground and they have a strong tendency to peck close to the spot where the mother is pecking. Turner made a model hen (Fig. 16.3) that could be made to "peck" at the ground and found that chicks would approach it and peck around its bill as readily as they would approach a real hen. This only happened when the model made "pecking" movements, and the chicks were much slower to approach a stationary model in either an upright or head-down posture. It looks as if chicks may detect a simple change in optic structure—a downwards wiping of texture—which specifies a pecking action.

Less direct evidence suggesting that animals detect changes in posture and orientation of conspecifics is provided by experiments that demonstrate a close temporal relationship between such a change and some specific response, particularly if animals respond differently to different transformations of posture that lead to the same end result. Davis (1975) filmed the responses of small groups of pigeons when one of the group received a mild footshock. The alarmed bird immediately took flight, followed in most cases by the other birds in the group. The delay between the first bird and the next one starting to take off was very short, typically 100msec. Davis then asked why it is common in normal circumstances to see one pigeon in a group take flight whereas the others remain completely unaffected. He compared films of take-offs that did and did not induce flight in other pigeons and could find no visual or auditory differences between them. The differences turned out to lie in the pigeon's behaviour immediately before take-off: if the bird crouched, stretched its neck or looked upwards just before taking off, other birds rarely responded. If these movements did not occur, they did.

Davis' (1975) experiments demonstrate clearly that pigeons do not just recognise a snapshot-like configuration of a bird with outspread wings, and suggest that they can instead distinguish two patterns of transformation of another pigeon's posture. A similar response to other birds' behaviour occurs when birds flying in a flock all execute a turn in the same direction at the same time. Observed directly, the degree of synchrony of such turns is striking and has even inspired speculation about thought transference in birds!

Potts (1984) has provided an alternative explanation by filming turns made by large flocks of dunlin in response to an approaching object. The flock's turn begins with a turn by one bird, followed by a wave of turns in the same direction spreading in all directions through the flock. The first birds to respond to the initiator of the turn did so with a delay of 67msec, well above the reaction time of 38msec recorded to a startling stimulus in laboratory conditions. However, the average interval over the whole flock between a bird's turn and that of its nearest neighbour was only 14msec, which shows that the birds cannot simply be responding to their neighbour's turns. Potts (1984) proposed instead that each bird detects the *wave* of turns approaching it and times its turn to coincide with it, in the same way as dancers in a chorus line do. If this hypothesis is correct, it involves an ability to detect not just a transformation in one animal's posture, but a higher-order pattern of transformation in a number of animals.

We have seen examples from jays, pigeons, and dunlin where transformations in birds' postures are tightly locked to responses by other birds. In all these cases, the interaction involved is brief, as one

FIGURE 16.3

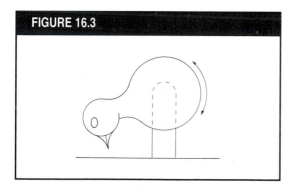

Flat cardboard model of a hen. "Pecking" movements of the model elicit pecking by chicks. Adapted from Turner (1964).

individual responds to another's movement by hopping back, taking flight, or turning. Some social interactions between animals involve longer periods of tightly meshed movement of two individuals, in which each individual's change in posture and orientation is closely followed by the other. An example can be seen in the mating behaviour of a tropical fish, the bluehead wrasse.

When a female wrasse enters the territory of a male, he performs a "circling display", swimming round and round in a tight circle above the female. Both fish then swim rapidly to the surface and spawn, releasing egg and sperm cells into the water. To fertilise the eggs, it is essential that both fish dash to the surface and spawn simultaneously, and Dawkins and Guilford (1994) examined videos of the circling display to find what information about the male's behaviour could be used by the female to time her own behaviour correctly. During the 10 seconds before he dashes to the surface, the rate of flickering of the male's pelvic fins increases steadily. As there is little variability in this rate at any one time, it provides reliable information for the female about "time to spawning", which could be used to time her own dash to the surface.

The mating behaviour of bluehead wrasse involves a relatively simple meshing of the swimming behaviour of two individuals. More complex situations, where many actions are coordinated simultaneously, can be found in mammals, and the rough and tumble play of two puppies provides a familiar example. Golani (1976) has analysed social interactions of this kind in more detail from film records, and Fig. 16.4 shows drawings he made from single frames of a film of two Tasmanian devils (dog-like marsupial mammals) play-fighting. In this sequence, the animals roll and tumble about in elaborate ways, but through much of the sequence a constant relative orientation of the animals' heads is maintained. Golani terms such a constant relative configuration a "joint", around which the animals move, and says (1976, p.117):

The heads of a pair of Tasmanian devils "wag" their bodies into a multitude of postures and movements. In a context of cheek-to-cheek joint maintenance, the two animals move in unison as one kinetic chain.

Another illustration comes from an analysis of wolf social interaction carried out by Moran, Fentress, and Golani (1981). They filmed "supplanting" interactions, in which a dominant wolf approaches a subordinate one; they interact for a period, and then the subordinate moves away. Moran et al. found that the relative orientations of the two wolves' bodies fell into four main categories. In each of these, as the animals moved, some aspects of their relative orientations remained constant.

Note that these patterns identified in the interactions of Tasmanian devils or wolves are not static displays such as the threat displays of gulls or fighting fish described earlier. Instead, they are descriptions of those aspects of the joint orientation of two animals that remain constant as the animals move. For such stability to occur, each animal must continually monitor the positions of parts of the other's body relative to its own and adjust its own movement to keep the appropriate variables constant. It is likely that senses of smell, sound, and touch play a role in achieving this, but likely too that it involves the use of vision to detect elaborate transformations of posture and orientation.

As well as raising questions about perceptual processes, the close meshing of movement in social interaction illustrated by Tasmanian devils and wolves poses interesting problems for theories of the control of movement (see Chapter 14). An indefinite number of different patterns of commands are sent to the Tasmanian devil's muscles, all with the effect that its head keeps the same joint orientation with the other animal's head. The concept of "coalitional organisation", which we outlined in Chapter 14, may be relevant to this problem.

Perceiving paths of travel

So far, we have discussed cases where an animal obtains information about another's behaviour that does not necessarily involve any movement of the other animal relative to the observer. Changes in posture and orientation can occur without any change in the relative positions of the two animals.

FIGURE 16.4

001   005   033

044   061   070

096   132   147

157   197   212

217   232   249

Drawings from single frames of a film of two Tasmanian devils in courtship play. Numbers refer to frames of film taken at 16 frames/sec. Until frame 249, the male (in the background until frame 147, in the foreground after frame 212) keeps the female's head adjacent to his right cheek. Reproduced from Golani (1976) with permission of the publishers, Plenum Publishing Corporation.

We therefore now turn to consider what information animals are able to obtain through vision about another animal's direction of movement.

Many simple forms of interaction between animals do not require one to detect the other's direction of movement. In order to pursue either prey or a conspecific, a simple tactic is to keep moving while orienting towards the target, as a fly does in pursuing a potential mate (Ch.12, pp.271–272). Similarly, an animal could escape from a predator by moving as fast as possible while orienting away from it. A more complex variant of this tactic has been described in blue crabs by Woodbury (1986). These animals swim in the shallow water of the inter-tidal zone, and, if a predator approaches, start to swim rapidly. Acting as a model predator, Woodbury walked towards crabs and recorded the bearing they took when they first responded to him. He discovered that they do not simply swim directly away from a predator, but that their bearing is an average of two component directions weighted differently. The stronger component is a directly offshore bearing carrying the crab into deeper and, presumably safer, water, and the weaker is a bearing away from the predator. Woodbury showed that the resulting escape route maximises the distance offshore the crab attains before being intercepted by the predator.

Woodbury (1986) always approached crabs directly, and so did not obtain any evidence whether they could discriminate different directions of a predator's movement relative to themselves. It is easy to see how this information could be useful: the predator moving directly towards an animal is more dangerous than one the same distance away but moving in some other direction. In order to make this discrimination between directions of motion relative to the observer, information from a static snapshot is not sufficient and some information about the transformation in the other animal's position is needed.

An experiment testing for the ability to discriminate direction of movement is reported by Burger and Gochfeld (1981), who compared the responses of nesting gulls to people either walking directly towards the nest or walking on a tangential route passing a minimum of one metre from the nest. Herring gulls nesting in the open showed alarm responses when the directly approaching person was at a greater distance than a person travelling tangentially. Clearly, the gulls did not detect just the instantaneous distance of the person, but unfortunately it cannot be firmly concluded that they detected direction of travel, as the directly approaching person looked straight at the gulls, but the tangentially walking person did not. It is therefore possible that the gulls discriminated different orientations or directions of gaze of the person relative to themselves, as Ristau (1991) showed that plovers do (see p.342).

A second way in which we might expect animals to use information about another animal's direction of travel is to intercept it. As we have already seen, a simple way for one animal to catch up with another is to move directly towards it, as a house-fly does in pursuing a potential mate. This would result in the approach path shown in Fig. 16.5a. In order to move straight to an interception point

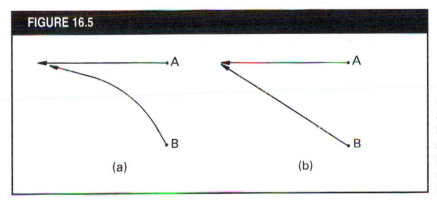

FIGURE 16.5

(a)   (b)

(a) Animal B approaches animal A by keeping its bearing at zero. (b) B moves straight to a point where it intercepts A's path of movement. Adapted from Menzel (1978).

(Fig. 16.5b), more complex control of the pursuer's movement is required, as when an infant reaches for a moving toy (Ch.13, p.305). If both animals are moving on straight paths at constant speeds, this can be achieved relatively easily. In these conditions, a pursuer can intercept another animal by moving so as to reduce its distance from the target, while keeping it at a constant angle to its own direction of movement. This tactic could be useful to some predators, although it is vulnerable to evasive manoeuvres made by the prey. In other situations, it may be necessary to use more complex means of extrapolating from a target animal's path to predict an interception point.

There are strong hints from the behaviour of some animals that they can move to intercept the paths of targets in the way shown in Fig. 16.5b. For example, dogs are strikingly accurate in jumping to intercept a ball and catch it in their jaws, and in running to intercept or head off the path of movement of a dog or person. They will also run on ahead of their owner, looking back to check the owner's path of travel and to adjust their own accordingly. Chimpanzees behave similarly (Menzel, 1978); if a number of chimps are travelling together and there is a clear leader of the group, who determines its direction of travel, other chimps will run on ahead and look back from time to time to adjust their direction to keep on the same route as the leader.

Why should the ability to intercept other animals' paths of movement be useful to a dog in catching prey or in social interaction? Dogs are closely related to wolves, which, like lions and other large carnivorous mammals, capture large prey by hunting in packs. An individual dog or wolf would have little success in catching large animals such as deer or caribou because it would be outdistanced or injured by a kick from the intended prey. A dog's abilities to move in relation to other animals' paths of movement are therefore likely to have evolved for more complex tasks than just running to intercept fleeing prey; in particular, for the task of cooperative pack hunting. What information about prey and conspecifics do dogs or wolves need to perform this task? Observations of pack-hunting predators have demonstrated a striking degree of coordination between individual animals. Lions fan out as they stalk their quarry (Schaller, 1972, Chapter 8), and Mech (1970, Chapter 7) describes wolves surrounding a caribou standing at bay or pursuing a running caribou in single file. Behaviour of this kind suggests that each animal in a pack is able to detect the positions and paths of movement of both the prey and the other members of the pack relative to itself, and to use this information to plan its own path. It is clearly difficult to determine the specific information used by pack-hunting animals, but some features of the behaviour of sheepdogs provide evidence for some of the processes involved.

The ways in which a shepherd and a sheepdog control a group of sheep draws on behavioural predispositions of dogs that evolved as part of pack-hunting behaviour, and Vines (1981) has described how the trainer builds on these predispositions when training a dog to respond to whistled commands. Our main interest is in the behaviour shown by a naive dog towards a group of sheep; the behaviour on which either pack-hunting skills or coordination with a shepherd is built. There are two particularly interesting features of this behaviour. First, an untrained dog tends to "herd" sheep, by circling around them, moving from side to side while keeping a roughly constant distance from them. The sheep draw closer together when a dog is near and move as a group, keeping beyond a minimum distance from the dog.

Second, a naive dog tends to position itself on the opposite side of a group of sheep from its trainer. If the trainer moves either to his right or to his left, the dog matches his move so as to keep the group of sheep directly between them. A shepherd exploits this tendency in training by giving the right or left turn whistle while the dog makes the appropriate turn relative to the sheep.

In these situations, the dog is moving so as to maintain its position relative to both the group of sheep and the trainer. On its own, it moves about a good deal but keeps a roughly constant distance from the sheep, while they keep a constant (and much smaller) distance from each other and a minimum distance from the dog. With the trainer present, the dog keeps the centre of the group of sheep on a line between itself and the trainer.

Are these rules regulating position relative to sheep and trainer part of a pack-hunting strategy? Predators such as dogs or wolves stand little chance of taking an animal such as a sheep from a group without risking injury from other prey. They therefore face the problem of splitting off one sheep from its group. Once this is done, they can move between it and the rest of the group and then attack it. To achieve this, however, they must overcome the sheep's strong tendency to keep close to other sheep.

The dog's tendency to keep a position opposite the trainer gives a clue as to how two dogs might be able to break up a group of sheep and split one off. The chances of this happening will be greater if they can make the sheep mill about and increase their distances from neighbouring sheep. Two dogs circling about a group of sheep in an uncoordinated way would not achieve this to any extent, as most of the time the sheep would be able to move as a group away from both dogs at once, maintaining close contact as they do so (Fig. 16.6).

If the dogs maintain positions opposite each other as they circle about, however, there will always be two directions in which each sheep could move to escape from the dogs (Fig. 16.7). The chances of splitting the group of sheep in two, or of splitting one off from the rest, will therefore be greater. All that needs to be added is for the dogs to detect a large gap between one sheep and the others and drive a wedge between them by running into the gap. A shepherd "singling" one sheep off from

a group works in this way, whistling a command to his dog to run towards him into a gap between one sheep and the rest.

These abilities to detect the positions and paths of movement of both prey and conspecifics provide one component of dogs' pack-hunting strategy, and no doubt abilities to detect further aspects of other animals' behaviour are also involved. Sheep are certainly able to detect the orientation and posture of dogs, keeping closer contact if a dog stares at them fixedly in a tense posture, and it is likely that dogs and other predators are able to recognise similar aspects of prey behaviour.

Perceiving other animals' goals

We have seen examples where animals show the ability to obtain more or less complex information about other animals' postures, orientations, and paths of travel. In none of these, however, have we seen any evidence that the orientation or movement of other animals *relative* to the environment is detected. This is an everyday human ability—we can readily detect what another person is looking at, pointing at, or walking towards—and there is evidence from the behaviour of some primates that they have the same ability.

Chimps show evidence of being able to detect the goal of another animal's movement; if a group of chimps approaches a piece of food, all but the one nearest it will turn away, as if each recognises the distance of the others from the goal. A band of

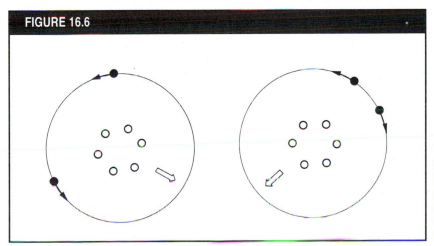

FIGURE 16.6

Two dogs (solid circles) circling a group of sheep (open circles) in an uncoordinated way. There is always a consistent direction in which the sheep can move to escape from both dogs.

FIGURE 16.7

Two dogs circling a group of sheep and maintaining positions diametrically opposite each other (a). As the dogs move, there are two possible escape routes for the sheep. In (b), one sheep moves in the opposite direction to the rest of the flock and is then pursued by the dogs (c, d).

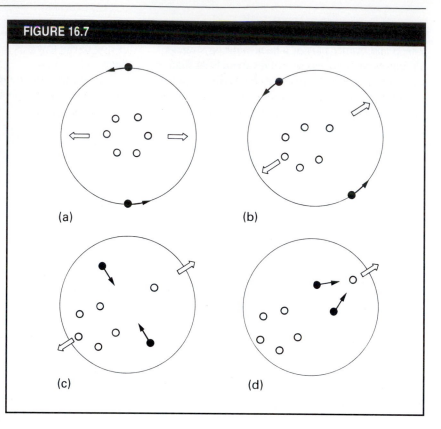

(a)

(b)

(c)

(d)

chimps hunting a small monkey in a tree spreads out to block its potential routes of escape along branches, suggesting that they are able to detect the layout of branches relative to the quarry as well as to themselves.

More conclusive evidence is available from experiments carried out by Menzel (1978). Chimps show a highly accurate memory for the locations of pieces of fruit scattered around a familiar enclosure. Menzel showed one chimp where a piece of fruit was hidden and then locked it with its companions in a hut adjoining the enclosure. On release, the group emerged from the hut and all the chimps set out together towards the food, some running on ahead to search along the knowledgeable chimp's line of travel. Control procedures showed that the other chimps were not simply finding the fruit by smell or sight, and so they must have been able to extrapolate from the knowledgeable chimp's path of travel.

As well as detecting the orientation of another animal's line of travel relative to the environment,

monkeys and apes seem able to detect the direction of gaze of another animal not only relative to themselves (see p.343), but also relative to objects in the environment. Packer (1977) describes how one male olive baboon will solicit the help of another in attacking a third male and driving him away from a female. This is done by alternately looking at the potential ally and looking at the rival, with a threatening expression. This suggests that the animal whose help is being solicited perceives the orientation of the head relative to the rival as well as to itself. Similarly, a subordinate chimp that knows the location of a piece of food will not approach it directly if a dominant chimp is present, but takes a roundabout route so that it approaches the food from a direction out of the dominant's line of sight.

Again, Menzel's (1978) experiments provide more conclusive evidence. In one, Menzel asked whether a chimp could tell where a piece of food was hidden by observing a person either taking a few steps towards it or pointing at it. In both cases, a chimp that had watched the person ran straight to the food. Furthermore, chimps were able to distinguish different kinds of goal according to how far the person had walked towards them. Presumably they are able to pick up information in the same way from the postures and gestures of other chimps.

In another experiment, Menzel and Halperin (1975) showed that other chimps' posture and movement can specify not only where an object is but also how interesting it is to chimpanzees. They hid a piece of fruit and a novel toy in an enclosure; of these two objects, chimps prefer the fruit. One chimp was shown the location of the fruit and another the location of the toy, before both were returned to the group. On release, all the group followed the individual that knew the location of the fruit, demonstrating that some subtle features of the chimp's behaviour must have indicated how desirable a goal they were approaching.

These observations raise interesting questions about the ability of animals to detect other animals' *intentions*, in the sense of the purpose or goal of another animal's actions. A simple form of detection of intention would be one chimp detecting the goal to which another is travelling, but Premack and Woodruff (1978) have argued that chimpanzees are capable of more elaborate perception of intention. They showed chimps videotapes of people attempting to solve various problems. These included trying to open a door or trying to get at bananas just out of reach. The chimp subject was given a set of photographs of various objects, such as a key or a pole, and almost always chose the object that would solve the person's problem. Premack and Woodruff argue that a chimp's natural mode of perceiving its animate environment is in terms of intentions; not simply the moment-by-moment behaviour of other chimps (or people) but where their behaviour is going in the world. Note the similarity between this argument and that of Heider and Simmel (1944) discussed in Chapter 15 (p.338) that people spontaneously attribute intentions to parts of artificial moving displays.

RECOGNITION OF INDIVIDUAL ANIMALS

All social behaviour relies on some means of recognising conspecifics, and of discriminating them from other objects or animals in the surroundings. We saw examples in Chapter 9 (pp.206–207) of how simple "key stimuli" are used by animals such as butterflies and sticklebacks to recognise their conspecifics. Some social animals have considerably greater powers of discrimination than these, and are able to recognise different members of their species as *individuals*. We see illustrations of this ability in cases where group-living birds and mammals discriminate between their own offspring and those of other animals in the group, or discriminate which individuals are dominant to them and which are subordinate.

Laboratory experiments can be devised to confirm that animals are able to discriminate between individual other animals on the basis of visual information. For example, Ryan (1982) has shown, using an operant conditioning procedure, that chickens can discriminate slides of one bird in a variety of poses from slides of other birds and could transfer this discrimination to novel sets of slides. Similarly, Rosenfeld and van Hoesen (1979) have shown that monkeys can easily learn to discriminate slides of one monkey's face seen from many angles from slides of other monkeys' faces. Any skepticism that chickens or monkeys vary enough in their appearance to make individual recognition possible is weakened by the fact that human observers are able, with sufficient experience, to discriminate individual members of these and similar species. Bateson (1977) provided evidence that an observer, familiar with a large colony of Bewick's swans, was able to recognise from photographs at least 52, and probably several hundred individual swans, using subtle differences in the markings on their bills.

The development of individual recognition

In order to study the processes involved in learning to recognise individual conspecifics, we need to find situations in which a young animal learns rapidly and reliably. A case that has been studied in some detail is that of young birds learning to recognise their mothers. The young of some bird species, such as chickens and ducks, are able to move about independently a short time after hatching, and, within a few days, to find their own food. For some time, however, the young birds are dependent on their mother as a source of warmth, protection from predators, and help in finding food. It is therefore essential for their survival that they keep close to her, which in turns means that they must recognise her and discriminate her from other adults of their species. This is achieved in part through recognition of the mother's calls, but there is evidence that vision is involved as well.

If a chick or duckling is hatched in an incubator, kept in darkness until it is about a day old, and then exposed to a conspicuous moving object, it approaches and follows it. After exposure to this object for an hour or so, it will later approach it in preference to any other object. This phenomenon is known as *imprinting* (for a recent review, see Bolhuis, 1991), and demonstrates that birds form some representation of the visual characteristics of a familiar object that enables them to recognise and keep close to it. Imprinting therefore provides a means by which a bird could learn to recognise its mother. In the first day or two after hatching, it will be exposed to her far more than to any other conspicuous, moving object, and so will learn to recognise and follow her.

The fact that young birds in the laboratory will imprint on a wide variety of artificial objects suggests that, at hatching, they have no representation of the visual properties of the mother bird and so will be equally likely to learn the characteristics of any object they are exposed to. Further research has demonstrated that this is not so. Dark-reared chicks with no previous visual experience follow a blue or red object more readily than a green or yellow one (Kovach, 1971), and this predisposition to avoid imprinting on green objects is presumably adaptive in a natural world full of moving foliage. Chicks' innate preferences between objects are even more specific than these, however. Johnson, Bolhuis, and Horn (1985) tested chicks' preferences between two moving objects: a rotating bright red box or a stuffed jungle fowl hen

moving with a rocking motion. They found that chicks not previously exposed to either of these objects showed a preference for the stuffed fowl, which, provided the chicks had some visual experience during their first day, emerged gradually over the second day after hatching.

The preference for a stuffed fowl observed by Johnson et al. (1985) develops *without* any exposure to the fowl. In experiments using artificial objects, in contrast, imprinting only occurs following exposure to an object. Clearly, chicks must have some representation of the visual properties of a fowl before they have any opportunity to learn them. In other experiments, Johnson et al. found that this developing preference for the stuffed fowl interacts with the process of acquiring a preference for a familiar object. They concluded that two processes are responsible for young birds' ability to recognise their mother. First, an initial representation of the visual characteristics of mother birds in general is built into the nervous system in some way that does not require experience of a mother bird. Second, exposure to one particular bird causes this representation to be refined, so that details specifying a young bird's own mother as distinct from others are incorporated.

Johnson and Horn (1988) went on to identify which features of a hen are specified in a chick's initial representation. They tested chicks' initial preference for a stuffed fowl over a variety of models in which some characteristics of a hen were removed and others maintained. Their results indicate that chicks do not recognise a hen on the basis of her overall outline or the colour and texture of her feathers, but recognise specifically the configuration of the head and neck region. Any model in which this part of the fowl was intact was equally as attractive to chicks as the complete fowl. Further experiments showed that chicks were equally attracted to a stuffed duck or polecat as to the fowl. These results indicate that the initial representation does not specify the head and neck shape of the young bird's own species precisely, but must instead be a cruder representation of a "generalised" head and neck.

HUMAN FACE PERCEPTION

So far in this chapter we have separated our discussion of the perception of what another animal is doing from our discussion of how its individual identity is recognised. In human perception such a separation can also be maintained to some extent. We may use some information such as overall posture and gait to inform us of another's actions or even intentions (e.g. Runeson & Frykholm, 1983; see Chapter 15), while recognising individual identity largely through other sources such as clothing, the voice, and particularly the face. However, both voice and face inform us not just about identity but also about a person's intentions, desires, and emotional state. Voice and face perception mediate social perception in a number of different ways, telling us about what a person is doing and feeling as well as telling us who they are. It is interesting to note that even within the very specific domain of human face processing the visual and cognitive system still seems to keep separate the perception of facial expressions and other facial gestures from the perception of facial identity (see Young & Bruce, 1991, for a discussion). In this final section we consider a range of different uses made of facial information within a broadly ecological framework. We will not, in this chapter, deal with the very large body of literature on how adults recognise familiar faces (although Chapter 9 introduced one aspect of this topic), nor can we do justice to the breadth of other literature on face perception and recognition. The interested reader is referred to the collection edited by Bruce, Cowey, Ellis, and Perrett (1992b) for a number of reviews of this rapidly growing area of research.

Development of face perception

There is now good evidence that face learning in the infant is guided by some innate specifications of what faces look like, in the same way as young birds possess an innate representation of the visual properties of hens. Goren et al. (1975) showed that new-born infants (with an average age of nine minutes) would track schematic face-like patterns more than control patterns with the same features rearranged, a result that has been replicated more recently by Johnson, Dziurawiec, Ellis, and Morton (1991). This result suggests that human infants may come equipped with knowledge of roughly what heads and faces look like, and this innate knowledge may allow them to attend selectively to such objects so that they can subsequently learn more about the appearance of their own caregivers.

A more controversial claim is that human neonates are able to discriminate and imitate facial expressions. Field, Woodson, Greenberg, and Cohen (1982) showed that infants aged 1–2 days looked less at faces whose expressions remained constant than at faces whose expressions changed, suggesting that the infants must have been able to discriminate between the different expressions. Meltzoff and Moore (1977) found that neonates would imitate facial expressions such as mouth opening and tongue poking. The facility to imitate requires that the infant is not only able to tell the difference between two different expressions, but is also able to map a particular seen expression onto a particular pattern of muscle activity. Such a mapping involves a rather sophisticated kind of expression-recognition ability. These demonstrations are not always replicated (e.g. McKenzie & Over, 1983), but they do remind us that face perception is not a unitary task but involves many different processes. As we elaborate later, identifying a particular person from the face is not the same as identifying an expression, and it would be quite possible, in principle, to have an innately specified facial expression system that was quite independent of the face identification system. Facial expressions (although not the rules for displaying them) appear to be culturally universal (Ekman, 1982; although see later) and thus the perception and production of expressions may develop uninfluenced by specific post-natal experience.

In contrast, it would seem absurd to suggest that an infant was born with a knowledge of the detailed appearance of its own particular family members, and instead it seems likely that learning of individual appearances occurs after birth. The ability to learn the appearances of strangers develops gradually over the first seven months of life (Fagan, 1979). Although there is evidence that one-month-olds (Sai and Bushnell, 1987) and even infants just a few days old (Bushnell, Sai, & Mullin, 1989; Pascalis, De Schonen, Moton, Deruelle, & Fabregrenet, 1995) can discriminate visually between their mother's and a stranger's face, their ability to do so seems likely to be based on hair-style and colour, rather than on internal facial features, as even infants aged 12 weeks cannot discriminate their mother's from a stranger's face when the hair region is concealed with a bathing cap (Bushnell, 1982). Nevertheless, the younger infants must be capable of rapid learning of quite subtle characteristics of hair and head outline: Bushnell et al. (1989) were careful to pair mothers with strangers who had broadly similar hair length and colour.

The human infant thus appears to have an innate knowledge of "faceness" plus, possibly, some innate knowledge of certain facial gestures and how to map these onto its own action patterns. Other face-processing abilities appear either to be more gradually learned during the first few months of life, and/or to rely on post-natal maturational processes (see Flin & Dziurawiec, 1989, for a review). A general theory of the development of face perception and recognition has been proposed by Johnson and Morton (1991; see also Morton & Johnson, 1991) who argue that the underlying processes are similar to those in imprinting in chicks. In both cases, initial attention to conspecifics (the following of mother hen by a chick, or of a human parent by an infant's head and eye movements) is mediated by midbrain mechanisms. In the case of humans, this initial attentional system then allows a cortical system to learn about the characteristics of particular individuals in the environment. However, the rapid learning of parental appearance within the first few days demonstrated by Bushnell et al.'s (1989) experiments is not easy to accommodate within this framework.

Adult face perception and identification

We now turn to consider what is known about the processes of face perception when fully developed in the adult. The dynamic configuration of the human face is endowed with a number of different kinds of meaning, all of which need to be extracted in the course of social interaction. The extraction of these different kinds of meaning must rely on the abstraction of different invariant and variant information. In addition to identifying familiar faces, we can derive other information even from unknown faces, and it is the information available from unfamiliar faces that forms the focus of this section. We can decide that a face looks young or old, male or female, hostile or friendly. We notice that someone looks happy, or angry, and their direction of gaze tells us to whom or to what they are directing their attention. This information is important in our social interaction—we may decide to go and talk to someone at a party because they look attractive or interesting to us, we take account of a child's apparent age when choosing topics of conversation, and so forth. Moreover, visual information from the face helps us to decipher what they are saying. Because the face and head are mobile, we may identify structural information from a face that remains invariant despite these transformations in pose and expression. Alternatively, or additionally, these dynamic patterns themselves may provide information. In this section we will review what is known about the dynamic and/or structural information that allows us to make such socially relevant judgements about faces.

Perceiving facial expressions

In the natural world the human face is in almost continuous motion. Some movements of the head involve rigid transformations, as when the head is turned from side to side, but expressive movements of the face, such as smiles and frowns, are not rigid. Such nonrigid motions include stretching and bulging of different parts of the face, produced by complex sets of muscles. Bassili (1978, 1979) has used a technique like Johansson's (see Ch.15, p.328), in which small illuminated spots are scattered over a face that is then filmed in the dark, to show that observers can identify a "face" from a moving configuration of lights without seeing any structural information about the facial features. Not only can a "face" be identified, but observers also have some success in identifying different emotions portrayed in such displays. Quite specific information about faces can be gleaned simply from the pattern of transformations present, without any need for information about the *form* of the face, just as human walkers can be identified in Johansson's displays, without any detail of the form of their limbs.

Despite the dynamic nature of facial expressions, most work in this area has used photographs of posed expressions to determine how accurately human observers can perceive the different emotions portrayed (for a review see Ekman, 1982; Russell, 1994). People are fairly accurate at assigning posed emotional expressions to one of a few fairly broad categories, such as happiness, surprise, anger, and disgust. There is some degree of universality in such judgements, as people from a variety of literate and some pre-literate cultures judge such displays in similar ways (Ekman & Oster, 1982; although see Ekman, 1994, and Russell, 1994, for debate). Although less is known about the accuracy with which observers can judge spontaneous expressive movements, there is evidence that, at the very least, positive and negative emotions can be distinguished in natural situations (Ekman, Friesen, & Ellsworth, 1982; Russell, 1994).

What processes might underlie our ability to judge emotional expressions? One possibility is that information about different facial "postures" is encoded and compared to some kind of stored catalogue, just as we suggested earlier in this chapter (p.344) that an animal might recognise another's posture by recognising different "snapshot" configurations. A particular emotion or group of related emotional states might be characterised by the relative dispositions and shapes of the component parts of the face, perhaps in respect to the major axis of symmetry, in a manner analogous to the part-based theories of object recognition we discussed in Chapter 9 (e.g. Biederman, 1987a; Marr & Nishihara, 1978).

However, it would be difficult to apply such a scheme in natural situations where there is continuous movement in the face. A better way to describe the information that underlies expressive judgements might be to make use of dynamic rather than static cues. Ekman and Friesen (1978, 1982b) have developed a Facial Action Coding System (FACS) to describe in detail the movements made by different parts of a face. The FACS consists of an inventory of all the perceptually distinct actions that can be produced by the facial muscles. Using such an inventory, we are in a position to ask whether unique combinations of actions (independent of who the actor is) underlie the perception of different emotions.

The kind of analysis is illustrated here for the eyebrows alone (Ekman, 1979). Figure 16.8 shows the distinguishable action units for the brows and forehead together, and the distinguishable combinations of these units. These patterns have been "frozen" for the purposes of illustration, and it is important to emphasise that Ekman and Friesen are concerned to code *actions* rather than configurations. Ekman has shown that different action units are indeed involved in different emotions. For example, action unit 1 alone, or with 4, indicates sadness, 4 alone yields anger or distress, 1 with 2 gives surprise, and 1 + 2 + 4 gives fear.

Ekman has thus shown that distinct patterns of activity are related to changes in emotional state, and it may be these patterns of activity that observers detect in the face. Momentarily frozen expressions might be compared with some stored catalogue of facial postures, but it may be more profitable to think of observers matching transformations in expression over time to dynamic emotion "schemata", like the action schemas in Weir's work that we described in Chapter 15 (pp.335–337). Expressions are never all-or-none, but are graded and blended. A person's momentary expression of faint surprise may represent a point of increasing or decreasing amazement, so we need to know its relationship both to prior and subsequent expressive movements and to concurrent events in the world, in order to interpret it properly.

Moreover, even when interpreting a single emotional category, the timing as well as the final posture of the face movements is important. Some expressions flicker rapidly across the face and last as little as 200msec. Ekman and Friesen (1982a) have analysed differences between spontaneous and deliberate, or "deceptive", smiles and shown that deceptive smiles are more asymmetrical in

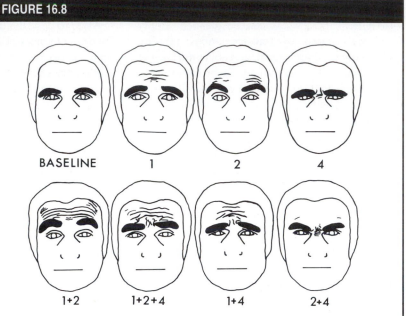

FIGURE 16.8

The different action units for the brow and forehead identified by the Facial Action Coding System (Ekman & Friesen, 1978). Action units 1, 2, and 4 may occur alone (top) or in combination (bottom). The drawings were obtained by tracing photographs. From Ekman, (1979), *About brows: Emotional and conversational signals.* In M. von Cranach, K. Foppa, W. Lepenies, & D. Ploog (Eds.), *Human ethology.* Reproduced with permission of the publishers, Cambridge University Press.

BASELINE   1   2   4

1+2   1+2+4   1+4   2+4

terms of the muscle movements involved and are also timed differently. Deceptive smiles have shorter onset times, irregular offset times, and are either relatively short or long in duration compared to spontaneous smiles. A more extensive investigation by Hess and Kleck (1990) suggested that differences in timing between spontaneous and posed expressions are clearer when actors are explicitly required to pose an expression that is deceptive about their underlying emotional state, for example, to smile while watching a disgusting video film. If there are physical differences between genuine and "deceptive" expressions, it is reasonable to enquire whether observers can distinguish one from the other. Preliminary evidence reported by Ekman (1992) suggests that observers can distinguish genuine from posed smiles from a series of face images, although it is not clear whether this judgement can be made when the smile is embedded in the richer context of everyday communication.

Perceiving facial speech

Face perception helps us to decipher speech. All of us lip-read, not just those who are hard of hearing. This can be demonstrated in a number of ways, but most directly by showing that speech can be deciphered at a much lower signal-to-noise ratio when the speaker's face can be seen than when only the vocal channel is available. Adding face to voice has an effect that allows a listener to tolerate an additional 4–6 decibels of noise to achieve the same level of intelligibility when seeing compared to only hearing a speaker (Summerfield, 1992), where each decibel of signal-to-noise ratio gained can improve intelligibility by 10–15%. These figures indicate that at certain levels of noise, seeing the face can allow a listener to "hear" otherwise unintelligible speech. Information from vision neatly complements that available from audition alone. Phonetic distinctions such as place of articulation, which are difficult to hear, are easy to see. Thus it is hard to hear the difference between "em" and "en", or "eff" and "ess", unless the speaker can be seen, explaining why it so often proves necessary to spell out postal codes when giving an address via telephone, and why such information is often misheard. A more dramatic demonstration that lip-reading is an obligatory component of speech perception is given by the "McGurk" effect, where conflicting speech information presented via the face and voice may be "heard" in a way that appears to combine information from both channels (McGurk & MacDonald, 1976). For example, if lips say "ga" and voice says "ba" the percept is commonly of "da".

What information from the face is required to confer the usual benefits of audio-visual speech perception? McGrath (1985; discussed by Summerfield, 1992) compared the accuracy of identifying vowels by lip-reading under different conditions. In one condition, subjects could see the whole face, whereas in others a moving schematic face including the main facial features was shown (Brooke & Summerfield, 1983). Using a schematic face in which the teeth were not shown, vowels could be identified on 51% of trials, whereas with the teeth shown, performance rose to 57% correct. Performance was similar in comparison conditions using a real face in which only the lips (shown with luminous lipstick) or lips plus teeth (lipstick plus ultra-violet illumination) were shown to observers. This suggests that the schematic face provides the same information to observers as the isolated information from lips and teeth in a real face. However, these levels of performance are well below those obtained from a real face, where 78% of vowels can be recognised. This suggests that information additional to that from the lips and teeth contributes to "lip"-reading. Summerfield (1992) suggests that this additional information may include perception of the tongue or wrinkling and protrusion of the lips.

The synchrony of voice and face is crucial if audio-visual speech benefits are to be obtained. Summerfield (1992) reviews evidence that shows that integration of audio and visual channels can occur up to delays of about 80msec. Longer delays can be tolerated if the audio channel lags behind the visual channel rather than vice versa, probably because the response latencies in the retina are considerably longer than in the cochlea. Summerfield suggests that a delay of up to 80msec is tolerated so that the sight and sound of events occurring at some distance from the observer are perceived as synchronous, given that sound takes longer to reach the observer than light. We can therefore see that the parameters within which audio-visual synchrony is achieved may arise as a result of a rather complex set of constraints from the physical properties of the signals and the biological properties of the observer.

Perception of gaze

In addition to information from the lips and mouth, a number of other facial gestures convey information important for mutual understanding in conversation, for example nodding and shaking of the head. Gaze patterns provide an extremely important and rich set of social signals that help to regulate conversation as well as expressing intimacy and social control (see Kleinke, 1986). The timing as well as direction of such facial gestures may be crucial for their interpretation. A prolonged stare means something different from a brief glance, for example. Conversants signal their "turns" within a conversation by gaze, and gaze patterns may also reveal to an observer where other persons are attending, and whether they are attending to things in the world or to their own thoughts. Even very young children are able to interpret a face with eyes rolled upwards as a person who is "thinking", and are able to use direction of gaze to understand what a person may be thinking about (Baron-Cohen, 1994).

Humans are very accurate at detecting changes in gaze direction. For example, Watt (1992) describes studies by Gibson and Pick (1963) and Cline (1967) that showed that people could reliably discriminate deviations in gaze of approximately 1 minute of arc of visual angle. Detecting gaze direction from a full-face image might seem relatively straightforward, as it could be achieved by assessing the degree of deviation of the pupils from the axis of facial symmetry, but such a task becomes much more complex when head angle also varies, particularly as perceived gaze direction must take account of head angle in a rather subtle way. There is evidence that head direction influences the perceived direction of eye gaze (Gibson & Pick, 1963; Vecera & Gilds, submitted). Moreover, Vecera and Johnson (1995) showed that sensitivity to a deviation in gaze (of 0.1° of visual angle) was much greater for an upright schematic than for an inverted or scrambled schematic face display, suggesting that even a task that could be performed by examining the symmetry of the eyes alone seems to make use in some way of the frame of reference provided by the whole face.

Categorising faces

In Chapter 9 we discussed theories of the representations underlying our ability to recognise individual faces, and here we will consider how we categorise faces in ways that are important for our social interactions with people whom we may not know. How do we decide whether a face is old or young, male or female, European or Japanese?

The most extensively researched example of an ecological approach to face perception has examined the information that underlies *ageing*. Shaw and Pittenger (1977) examined the nonrigid transformation that the profile of a human head undergoes while it ages, and have identified information that remains invariant under this transformation.

Shaw and Pittenger have shown that people are very consistent at rank-ordering profile outlines according to their apparent relative age, suggesting that head shape provides at least one of the sources of information that we use when establishing a person's age. Consider the set of profiles shown in Fig. 16.9. You will probably agree that the one on the right looks "young" and the one on the left looks "old". How can we describe the nature of the transformation that relates the older to the younger profiles? Shaw and Pittenger have demonstrated that the growth process transforms the human head in a similar way to that which occurs in dicotyledonous plants. The profile of a human head is very similar in shape to a dichotyledonous structure (see Fig. 16.10). Ignoring facial detail, the shape is like an inverted heart with a rounded top—a *cardioid*.

Shaw, McIntyre, and Mace (1974) demonstrated that a single transformation, if applied to the outline of the skulls of infant, child, and adult, could map one skull continuously onto the other. They hypothesised that there might be a cardioidal shape invariant for growth space, with ageing representing cardioidal strain. Strain is imposed on the bones of the skull by stresses produced by growth of softer, highly elastic tissues. Pittenger and Shaw (1975) tested the extent to which perceived changes in relative age level are captured by a strain transformation as opposed to a shear transformation (which modifies the angle of the facial profile). Subjects were shown a series of profiles produced by modifying a single outline profile over seven levels of strain and five levels of shear (Fig. 16.11). They found that 91% of the relative age judgements made by their subjects were consistent with the hypothesis that a strain transformation was responsible for these perceived age changes, whereas only 65% of the judgements were consistent with a shear transformation, which confirmed their intuition that it was strain that was the important determinant. In further experimental work they demonstrated that observers were consistent in perceiving a profile with larger strain as "older" than a different one with smaller strain, and that they showed a high sensitivity in these judgements even when the pairs of profiles differed to a very small degree.

Finally, they showed that sufficient structural invariants are preserved during growth to permit the identification of heads at different age levels, despite the remodelling produced by ageing. They asked subjects to select the age-transformed skull profile that matched a target profile, from a set of two in which the "foil" was the profile of a different head transformed to the same degree (see

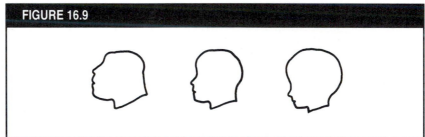

FIGURE 16.9

The profile on the right looks younger than the one on the left, and the central one appears intermediate in age.

FIGURE 16.10

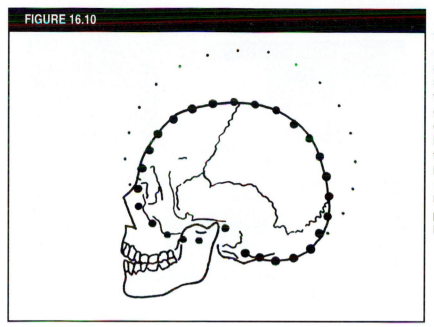

The small dots show a regular cardioidal shape lying above a profile of a human skull. Appropriate transformation of this shape gives a good fit to the shape of the skull, as shown by the large black dots. Reprinted from Shaw, McIntyre, and Mace (1974). Copyright © 1974 by Cornell University. Used by permission of the publisher, Cornell University Press.

Fig. 16.12). Subjects performed this task considerably better than chance. It thus appears that the ageing transformation preserves invariant information that might specify individual identity. We are indeed able to match pictures of people taken at different ages, provided the age spans are not too great (Seamon, 1982), and Shaw and his colleagues have shown how one source of information—skull profile shape—might contribute to these judgements.

FIGURE 16.11

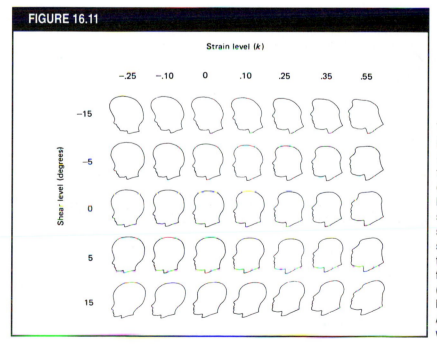

The series of profiles used by Pittenger and Shaw (1975). The profiles were all formed from the same original, which was modified by five different levels of shear (vertical axis) and seven different levels of strain (horizontal axis) to give this set of 35. Reproduced from Shaw and Pittenger (1977). Copyright © 1977 Lawrence Erlbaum Associates Inc. Reprinted with permission.

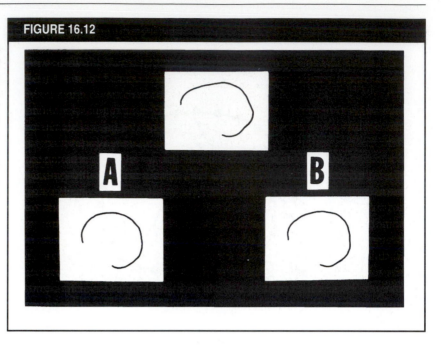

FIGURE 16.12

The skull outline at the top is the same as B, but age-transformed to a different extent. Skull A is a different individual, at the same transformational level as B. Reproduced from Shaw and Pittenger (1977). Copyright © Lawrence Erlbaum Associates Inc. Reprinted with permission.

We have omitted all the mathematical detail from this account of Shaw and Pittenger's work, and you are referred to their articles for a full discussion of this (see also Todd, Mark, Shaw, & Pittenger, 1980). It is worth pointing out here that the invariant they claim accounts for age transformations is *topological* rather than *metrical*. The former requires a different kind of geometry from the familiar Euclidean geometry we learn at school. The concept of "shape" that emerges from a weaker (nonmetrical) geometry is qualitative rather than quantitative, but may provide the right way to handle the changes in shape provided by nonrigid transformations.

The early work on cardioidal strain that we have just reviewed was rather restricted in its application of the growth transformation to simple, line-drawn cranio-facial profiles, and as such said rather little about the perception of age from normal faces. Mark and Todd (1983) published an interesting extension of this work in which the cardioidal strain transformation was applied in three dimensions to a representation of the head of a 15-year-old girl (see Fig. 16.13). A computer-sculpted bust of the girl is shown to the right of Fig. 16.13, and to the left is a bust that was cut from the same data-base, age-transformed in a direction that

should render it younger in appearance. The vast majority of subjects indeed saw the transformed version as younger, which led Mark and Todd to conclude that the strain transformation could be perceived from more realistic, three-dimensional heads.

Bruce, Burton, Doyle, and Dench (1989) have examined this claim more carefully, using computer-aided design techniques, which allow a three-dimensional model to be constructed in wire-frame form and displayed as a smooth surface using standard lighting models (e.g. see Fig. 16.14). Bruce et al. obtained a data-base of 3-D head measurements from a laser-scan of an adult head and age-transformed this to different extents in a direction that should have rendered the resulting head younger in appearance. Subjects were asked to judge which member of each of a pair of heads looked the younger, and their ability to do this was assessed as a function of the amount of difference in age levels between the two heads shown, and the views in which these were shown (two profiles, two three-quarter views, or one profile and one three-quarter view). Subjects made relative age judgements equally accurately when shown two different views (a profile and a three-quarter view) and when shown two identical

FIGURE 16.13

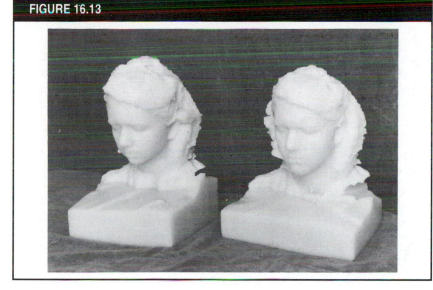

Right: a computer-sculpted bust of a girl aged about 15 years. Left: the bust that was cut after age-transforming the data-base in a direction that should make the girl appear younger in age. From Mark & Todd (1983), reprinted by permission of Psychonomic Society Inc.

views (e.g. two profiles) that allowed comparison between the shapes of the occluding contours; these results were consistent with Mark and Todd's (1983) conclusion that subjects can detect the strain transformation in three dimensions.

However, Bruce et al. (1989) also found that many subjects did not spontaneously see the supposedly "younger" versions of the head as younger, but needed to be given some information about the range of ages that were to be anticipated. Without this guidance, some subjects saw the "younger" heads, for example, as belonging to "little old ladies who had lost their teeth". It seems, then, that richer data structures such as 3-D models of heads present wider opportunities for interpretation. Cardioidal strain level is only one possible route to judging age and does not necessarily lead to the "direct" perception of age

FIGURE 16.14

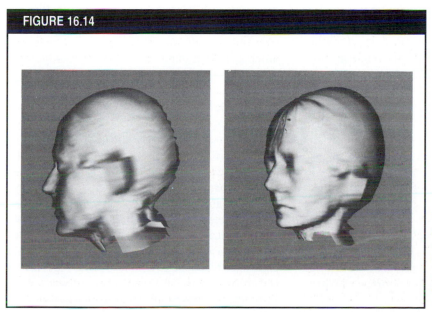

Left: a three-dimensional data-base of a head obtained from laser-scanning. Right: the same head, age-transformed in a direction that should make it appear younger.

level. Our argument here is similar to that used against the "direct" perception of causality in the displays used by Michotte (see Ch.15, p.333). Because naive subjects are not consistent in the impressions formed of heads with varying levels of cardioidal strain, we would argue that this is only one of a number of cues that constrain the judgement of age.

Such an interpretation would be consistent with some recent experiments by Burt and Perrett (1995), who examined the separate contributions of surface colouration and head shape to the perception of the relative age of faces. By using a morphing technique they were able to average together faces in a way that did not result in blurred images. In this way, they produced composite colour images of faces of different chronological age bands, and found that the resulting composites appeared to be of similar, although somewhat younger, age range to the component faces. An "older" composite could be made to look older still if the differences in colouration between it and a "younger" composite were exaggerated, confirming the contribution of superficial colour information about skin and hair colour to the perceived age of faces.

The ecological approach to face perception has also been extended in a different way by Berry and McArthur (1986; see also the collection edited by Alley, 1988) who have argued that invariant structural information leads to the "direct" perception of subtle social attributes. This work has also concentrated on the effect of cardioidal strain on the face, and has shown, for example, that "baby-faced" adults, whose facial features are relatively low down the face, are seen as more weak and submissive than adults whose features are placed relatively higher up the face. Similarly, the orthodontist Enlow (1982) suggested that the difference between female and male faces was related to the difference between immature and mature heads, with female faces having somewhat more "babyish" proportions. In particular, Enlow claimed that because males have greater lung capacities than females, their nose region develops more, so that males have larger noses and more protruberant brow regions than females, who have more concave profiles.

To what extent can we explain impressions of masculinity and femininity in terms of such simple geometric variables? Roberts and Bruce (1988) obtained evidence for the importance of the configuration of the nose relative to the rest of the face in making *sex judgements*. Masking the nose had a large detrimental effect on sex judgements, and a much greater effect than masking eyes or mouths. A different pattern was found with the same masks on a familiarity judgement task, where, consistent with other results on feature saliency in identification, masking the noses had no observable effect on performance but masking the eyes had a significant detrimental effect. Bruce et al. (1993) showed that altering the shape of the noses of 3-D head models (like the one shown in Fig. 16.14) can have a reliable effect on the rated masculinity and femininity of the heads. Making the nose more concave in shape makes the head look more feminine, and making it more protruberant in shape makes it look more masculine.

However, in two extensive investigations, Burton, Bruce, and Dench (1993) and Bruce et al. (1993) investigated more closely how the sex of faces could be discriminated. Human performance at the task of deciding whether faces are male or female is impressive—people are over 95% accurate at this task even when faces have their hairstyles concealed, when faces are clean-shaven, and when cues from cosmetics are absent. Burton et al. (1993) conducted an investigation in which a large number of measurements were made on different face features and other aspects of face shape, and the statistics of these measures were investigated to see which ones distinguished male from female faces. Burton et al. (1993) found that in order to approach the 95% success rate achieved by human vision, discrimination requires a combination of a large set of local cues (e.g. width and spacing of eye-brows), and 3-D cues (e.g. nose shape). A parallel set of experiments conducted by Bruce et al. (1993) were consistent with the multiple determination of face sex by a range of different cues. For example, when faces were displayed as 3-D surfaces devoid of their usual pigmented features and texture (such as Fig. 16.14) performance at a sex-decision task was considerably above chance, at least when angled viewpoints were shown. On the other hand, discrimination of sex from these displays was much less accurate than was possible with photographs in which hairstyle was concealed. These results suggest that features such as the eyebrows give important clues about face gender, and that other aspects of face shape also contribute to performance.

The conclusion therefore appears to be that perception of both the sex and the age of faces does not rely on a single, or simple, "invariant", but rather a very large and complex set of cues derived from different aspects of a face's appearance. Such a conclusion is reinforced by some recent experiments by Hill, Bruce, and Akamatsu (1995), in which it was possible to examine the relative contributions of the underlying shape of the face alongside the superficial surface colour and texture (as is picked up by a colour camera taking a picture of the face). Using computer image-processing techniques it was possible to combine the surface colour information from one face with the underlying shape of another. Volunteers were asked to make categorical decisions about the sex of the faces (half were female) or the race of the faces (half were Japanese, half Caucasian), from the shape information alone, from colour information alone, or from shape-colour combinations. As in Bruce et al.'s (1993) results, people were about 75% accurate at deciding the sex of faces from shape alone, but much more accurate when given the colour information that presented such local features as eye-brows and face texture (e.g. visible stubble in some male faces). When face shape and colour were combined, decisions were dominated by colour, but there was some influence of shape as well; for example, a female colour image mapped to a male face shape was more likely to be seen as male than if it were mapped onto a female face shape. For decisions about the *race* of faces, subjects were considerably more accurate when presented with shape alone, and more influenced by the shape—particularly in angled views—when the shape was combined with colour from a different race. Thus these studies also confirm the use of multiple information sources in the determination of simple categories of facial appearance.

A final example of the way in which adults categorise unfamiliar faces lies in our judgements about facial attractiveness. There is reasonable agreement between individuals, and even across different racial groups (e.g. see Perrett, May, & Yoshikawa, 1994), about which faces look more and which less attractive, but what visual information forms the basis of such judgements? Since Galton's work on facial composites, (see Ch.7, p.143) it has been reported that blending faces produces faces that are more attractive than the individuals contributing to the blend. Such observations have led to the suggestion that attractiveness *is* averageness. However, early studies used photographic composites, which suffer from the blurring arising from averaging together different shapes, and it may be the softening that results from blurring that gives rise to the increased attractiveness. Modern digital blending reduces these problems, and using this technique, Langlois and Roggman (1990) showed that the average of a set of faces was indeed rated as more attractive than the contributing individual faces. However, in a clever follow-up study, Perrett et al. (1994) showed that the average of a sub-set of female faces that were rated as attractive was seen as more attractive than the average of the whole set of faces (including the attractive sub-set). Moreover, if the "attractive" average was compared with the "overall" average and its difference exaggerated using caricaturing techniques, it became more attractive still. This study found consistent findings using both male and female observers, from Japanese and Caucasian populations, and using both Japanese and Caucasian faces. Thus the study shows that there is considerable cross-cultural universality in attractiveness judgements, but that these judgements cannot solely be based on how average a face looks.

Use of dynamic cues for categorising faces

The theme of this part of our book emphasises how additional information may arise from dynamic patterns of transformation. Most research into the processes of face perception and recognition, and most of the work we have considered earlier on the categorisation of unfamiliar faces, has made use of pictures of static faces. To what extent is information important for categorising people or for identifying them conveyed by dynamic patterns?

In Chapter 15, we described research by Cutting and colleagues that suggested that the dynamic patterns of human gait may convey information about whether the walker is male or female, or even which friend is shown in the display. What information about face category or identity is carried by patterns of facial movement? For example, is any information about an individual's identity preserved in patterns of expressive movement? Strong evidence to support such an idea would be provided if observers could identify their friends from the Bassili "point-light" displays we described earlier (p.354). Bruce and Valentine (1988) examined this by filming expressive facial movements (smiling, frowning, and gasping) and rigid head movements (e.g. nodding, shaking, and rocking) of three male and three female colleagues whose faces were displayed using Bassili's technique. Subjects in the experiment were told whose heads might appear (all the actors were known to subjects) and what motions they might make, and were asked to decide on each trial how the face was moving, whether it was male or female, and whose face it was. Like Bassili, we found that subjects identified rigid movements perfectly and were highly accurate at identifying expressive movements from these dynamic displays.

When subjects were asked to give the sex and identity of faces in point-light displays, however, Bruce and Valentine (1988) found that performance levels were very low compared to the identification of expressions. It appears that patterns of expressive movement in isolation convey rather little invariant information to specify identity. This is not to argue that useful *information* is not extracted from a moving sequence to allow the identification of faces. A film or video of a moving face will contain very much more information about the appearance of that face at different viewpoints and expressions, and such additional information will help to build an enduring representation of a novel face (see Bruce, 1994) and will provide more opportunities to access an existing representation of a familiar one. However, it is not clear that motion *per se* is very useful in the process of identifying faces (Christie & Bruce, submitted).

CONCLUSIONS

This chapter has briefly surveyed the perceptual bases of social perception, suggesting ways in which the ecological approach to perception might be applied to problems as diverse as hunting in packs and judging a person's age. We concluded with a more detailed survey of some of the processes of face perception in humans, and examined how an ecological approach has contributed to this research area. We have deliberately used a broad definition of the term "ecological" here, rather than confining our discussion to research conducted by those taking a "direct" perception stance. As we have seen in some of the examples in this chapter, there can be much in common between the "computational" level of theory and the "ecological" approach that we have explored in this part of the book. Indeed we have implicitly treated the "ecological" level as a "higher" level of theory, which can guide the details of an algorithmic specification of some process. However, in making this assumption we have glossed over some important theoretical and philsophical issues that have sustained deep divisions between researchers of perception. In our final chapter, we return to consider these issues in more detail.

Part IV

Conclusions

17

Contrasting Theories of Visual Perception

We have now considered the current state of knowledge of visual perception as it has been built up from research within three traditions. The physiological tradition, which we introduced in the first part of this book, studies the nervous system directly, seeking to establish how the pattern of light falling on receptor cells is transformed by networks of nerve cells into patterns of electrical activity. The second approach, which we described in Part II, moves away from this physiological level and asks what processes operate on the retinal image to yield perceptual experience. The third, "ecological" approach, which we introduced in Part III, also seeks explanation at a more abstract level than physiology, but differs from the second in taking the starting point for vision as the spatiotemporal pattern of light in the optic array.

So far, we have treated these different traditions as frameworks for research and have asked what knowledge has been gained within each. In fact, there is a great deal more to the difference between the second and third approaches than simply whether it is more useful to treat the input for vision as an image or as an optic array. This issue is only one aspect of a much wider theoretical debate concerning the nature of perception and the proper ways to explain it, and it is time now to deal with this debate. For simplicity, we will contrast two positions, which we will call "traditional" and "ecological," although there is much diversity of opinion within each viewpoint. By "traditional" theorists we mean psychologists and computational theorists of the tradition that emphasises the inferential and constructive nature of perception. By "ecological" theorists we mean those theorists who claim that perception involves the direct pick-up of information from the time-varying optic array. In Chapters 4 and 11 we introduced these two theoretical positions before going on to describe the research they have each inspired. In this chapter we try to summarise the important differences between them and ask where reconciliation is and is not possible. Our discussion falls under two headings: the nature of the input for vision and the question of whether perception is direct or indirect.

THE NATURE OF THE INPUT

First, we sum up and clarify the issues at stake in choosing the retinal image or the optic array as the starting point for visual perception. Obviously, there is no argument over the facts that a single-chambered eye forms an image on the retina and that the image has to be there for vision to occur. The image is a projection of a segment of the optic array and the spatiotemporal pattern of light is reproduced in it, within limits imposed by the eye's acuity. For many practical purposes, image and optic array are interchangeable. As we saw in Chapter 12, for example, the optical parameter τ can be equally well used to describe a pattern of flow in the optic array or in its projection on a retina.

So, what difference does it make to introduce the concept of the optic array? One advantage is in the comparative study of vision, where it helps us to understand that image-forming eyes are not the only light-sensitive structures that can achieve a degree of directional selectivity (Chapter 1). A more significant consequence of Gibson's concept of the optic array is that it leads to a quite different conception of the information available in light to a perceiver. The traditional view took the input to be nothing more than a mosaic of points of light on the retina, each characterised by its intensity and wavelength. Gibson attacked this belief on several grounds, but particularly because it makes the mistake of describing the input for a perceiver in the same terms as the input for a single photoreceptor.

The input for a receptor is a stream of photons, but the input for a perceiver is a *pattern* of light extended over space and time. Gibson therefore argued that ways of describing this pattern should be devised, and examples of the terms he introduced are gradients and rates of flow of optic texture. Although descriptions of spatial structure can be applied equally easily to an optic array or to a retinal image, it is important to avoid artificially "freezing" the retinal image and losing sight of the temporal pattern of light in the changing optic array.

Once the possibility of describing the input for vision in terms of structure is accepted, it becomes possible to ask what relationships hold between a perceiver's environment and the structure of the optic array. Gibson's "ecological optics" sets out to explore these relationships, and we have seen examples of them throughout the third part of this book. In the traditional view, there was no obvious place for such questions; input was made up of elements of point intensity, and the intensity of light falling on a single receptor provides no information about the environment.

That said, we would note that the contrast between these two positions has weakened considerably over the years, in part because of technical advances. Forty years ago, psychophysical investigations of human vision worked with points of light or simple line figures as stimuli, and this perhaps encouraged theorists to treat such things as the real "elements" of the visual world. Modern computer graphic techniques allow the use of enormously more sophisticated stimuli—consider for example the displays described in Chapter 7 used to analyse how disparity, shading, occlusion, and motion contribute to our perception of depth. The use of displays such as these rests easily with the view that the input for vision is the dynamic structure of light reaching the eyes, and not elements such as dots and lines.

Gibson might therefore have had little quarrel with modern psychophysics about the nature of the input for vision, and about the ability of spatiotemporal structure in light to provide useful information about the environment. Where conflict would certainly still arise is over the answer to another question: are *all* objects and events in the environment fully specified by the pattern of light in the optic array, or only a limited class of simple properties such as the distances, slants, and textures of surfaces? We shall see later that Gibson's answer to this question is more difficult to accept.

DIRECT AND INDIRECT THEORIES OF PERCEPTION

As well as defining the nature of the input for vision, a theory of perception must also have something to say about how it is that the structured light reaching a perceiver gives rise to perceptual experience and to visually guided action. The answers given by traditional and ecological theories diverge sharply at this point, and are far less easily reconciled than the differences we have considered so far. The roots of the difference can be found in the history of Gibson's theory.

Gibson's early work was concerned with the perception of the layout and distances of the surfaces surrounding an observer. Since the time of Helmholtz, traditional theory had argued that such perception required processes of *inference* to supplement the supposedly impoverished nature of the flat, static retinal image. These processes of inference were held to *mediate* between retinal image and perception. From his analysis of the structure of the optic array and optic flow, Gibson argued that the problem was wrongly conceived and that processes of inference are required only if a restricted kind of description of the input for vision is adopted.

Gibson therefore argued that, as the structure of light directly specifies surface layout, mediating processes of the kind proposed by Helmholtz are not necessary for perception of "distance". From this conclusion, he went on to argue against *any* role for mediating or inferential processes in perception and to claim that invariant properties of the optic array specifying structures and events in the environment are detected *directly*.

The claim that perception is direct and unmediated has been taken up by "ecological" theorists, but strongly criticised by others, and in the remainder of this chapter we will set out the points at issue between them. First, however, it is worth mentioning the points where there is no disagreement between the two approaches. At a philosophical level, both direct and indirect theorists subscribe to *realism*, maintaining that we are in sensory contact with a real world and that perception reveals this world to us. Both positions also agree that visual perception is mediated by light reflected from surfaces and objects in the world, and both agree that some kind of physiological system is needed to perceive this light. Finally, there is also agreement that perceptual experience can be influenced by learning.

The issue that divides the direct from the indirect accounts of perception is the question of how physiological systems must be organised to perceive the world. The traditional approach to visual perception maintains that the world of objects and surfaces that we see must be reconstructed by piecing together more primitive elements such as edges or blobs. To carry out this reconstruction, knowledge of the world is needed, and various kinds of knowledge have been proposed in different "indirect" theories. Examples are knowledge of the sizes of objects in order to detect their distance, or knowledge that natural objects approximate to generalised cones. The process of reconstruction can, the traditional approach maintains, be broken down into stages and analysed both physiologically (as we saw in Part I) and psychologically (as we saw in Part II).

In contrast, the ecological approach maintains that qualities such as surface slant or object shape are perceived directly. An object's shape is not perceived by adding up a set of "features" like edges or blobs, using knowledge of the world to do so. There is information to specify shape in higher-order invariants in the light, and it is not necessary, or even possible, to decompose such processes into more primitive psychological operations or "computations". It may be a task for physiologists to unravel the complexities of how nervous systems are attuned to such higher-order invariants, but the ecological psychologist need enquire no further once invariant information has been described.

Now, any theory of indirect perception must allow *something* to be detected "directly", and traditionally it is assumed that photoreceptors detect changes in light intensity directly. A biochemist would wish to decompose the process of intensity detection further, but traditional theorists would treat it as an elementary process closed to further analysis, and certainly would not claim that the detection of changes in intensity involved "mediation" by knowledge of the world. They would, however, claim that higher-order properties of the world must be reconstructed by making use of those properties that *are* directly detected, and "gluing" them together by making use of knowledge of the world. In contrast, a direct theory of perception maintains that the perception of *all* properties of the world is like the detection of light intensity. The system is attuned to higher-order variables, and the only task for psychology is to discover what these higher-order variables are.

What are the important issues dividing these two positions and is there any possibility of reconciling them? We see two important senses in which perception is regarded as "mediated" in the traditional view, and we will consider the objections of ecological theorists to each in turn. The first is the sense that perception of higher-order variables is mediated by processes of computation from low-level properties, and the second is the sense that perception must involve the formation, matching, and storage of representations of the world.

Mediation of perception by computational processes

The first issue between direct and indirect theories of perception concerns the levels at which perception can be properly explained. For a direct theory of perception, there are two: the ecological and the physiological. The ecological level is concerned with the information an animal needs from the environment in order to organise its activities, and with the ways in which the changing optic array can provide the information needed. The physiological level is concerned with how networks of nerve cells are organised so as to detect invariants in the optic array. Gibson was concerned to work at the first of these levels, and had little to say about the second, speaking simply of an animal being "attuned" or "resonating" to invariants. Taking the case of the parameter τ as an example, an explanation at the ecological level would be concerned with how τ specifies time to contact with a surface, and with the evidence showing that the timing of animals' and people's actions relies on detection of τ. A direct theory of perception would say that there is nothing more for psychology to ask about this situation, but would accept as valid a physiological investigation of how nerve cells are organised so as to "resonate" to τ.

We would agree with "direct" theorists that the control of action by information in the structure of light can be studied without reference to physiological processes, but we differ with their assertion that there is no level of explanation lying between the ecological and the physiological. Consider what is actually involved in determining how an animal's nervous system is built to detect τ. The discovery that cells selective for values of τ exist (see Ch.12, p.282) is important, but still only a first step. A physiologist's goal would be to establish what interactions between neurons in the visual pathway yield a value of τ as output, given a fluctuating pattern of light intensities as input. To achieve this, models of the computation of τ from the responses of motion-sensitive cells (see Chapter 8) must be tested against neuro-physiological evidence. The modelling required for this physiological analysis would be an algorithmic level of explanation, to use Marr's terminology discussed in Chapter 4.

Ullman (1980) argues that the "direct" theory is mistaken in believing that there are two distinct levels of explanation, the ecological and the physiological, and concurs with Marr in believing that an algorithmic theory must come between the two in order to organise physiological knowledge. We agree with Ullman's position, and feel that "direct" theorists have not paid sufficient attention to the problem of the relationship between ecological and physiological levels of explanation.

Marr (1982) makes a similar argument, accepting the value of ecological optics but asserting the need for algorithmic explanations of how properties of the optic array are detected. Marr suggested that (1982, p.29):

> In perception, perhaps the nearest anyone came to the level of computational theory was Gibson (1966).

This is not at all a paradoxical claim, as Marr's notion of a "level one" or "computational theory" is an abstract understanding of the structure and constraints of the visual information-processing problem and must not be confused with the algorithmic level that spells out actual computations. It is Gibson's denial of the algorithmic level with which Marr quarrels:

> Gibson's important contribution was to take the debate away from the philosophical consideration of sense-data and the affective

qualities of sensation and to note instead that the important thing about the senses is that they are channels for perception of the real world outside, or, in the case of vision, of the visible surfaces. He therefore asked the critically important question, How does one obtain constant perceptions in everyday life on the basis of continually changing sensations? This is exactly the right question, showing that Gibson correctly regarded the problem of perception as that of recovering from sensory information "valid properties of the external world" (Marr, 1982, p.29).

Although one can criticise certain shortcomings in the quality of Gibson's analysis, its major, and, in my view, fatal shortcoming lies at a deeper level and results from a failure to realise two things. First, the detection of physical invariants, like image surfaces, is exactly and precisely an information-processing problem, in modern terminology. And second, he vastly underrated the sheer difficulty of such detection (Marr, 1982, p.30).

If Ullman's and Marr's arguments are accepted, we can then go on to ask how the variables of optic flow that Gibson and others have identified are computed from a fluctuating pattern of light intensities in a time-varying image. We cannot agree with the radical Gibsonian argument that analyses of this kind are irrelevant to the explanation of perception, and that matters must be left at the assertion that any information available in light is "directly" perceived. For the purposes of an ecological level of analysis, they can be left at that point, but if links to a physiological level are to be made, they cannot.

Perhaps some common ground between the two positions can be found by agreeing with the "direct" position that properties of the world can be detected without "cognitive" processes of inference, interpretation, and judgement, but arguing, with "indirect" theorists such as Marr and Ullman, that such processes of detection none the less rely on computation. The term *cognitively impenetrable* (Fodor & Pylyshyn, 1981; Pylyshyn, 1981) has been used to refer to perceptual processes that cannot be influenced by beliefs, expectations, and the like. Examples of such processes might be the analysis of optic flow, or the elaboration of forms in the primal sketch in Marr's theory (see Chapter 6).

Cognitive impenetrability does not necessarily imply direct detection in the sense that no computational explanation is possible. Indeed, Fodor (1983) suggests that it is the data-driven, cognitively impenetrable sensory modules that will be most profitably explored with current computational techniques, and is much more pessimistic about our prospects for understanding more central cognitive processes. Fodor and Pylyshyn's (1981) notion of *compiled detectors* is a useful one here, referring to computational processes that run in an autonomous, data-driven way. At a higher level of analysis, compiled detectors can be regarded as detecting properties of the world directly, but at a lower level of analysis their operations can be unpacked. At a behavioural level, it does not matter whether one argues that τ, for example, is perceived directly, or whether it is computed by compiled detectors. What does matter is that its detection need not rely on inferences of the hypothesis-testing variety.

For the purposes of ecological analysis we can proceed simply by saying that τ is detected, and leave others to work out the details of how this detection is accomplished. Much of the research we described in Part II of this book can be seen as attempts by researchers such as Marr to work out these details, whereas much of that in Part III asks simply what the ecologically relevant variables are, and how they are used, but does not address the issue of how they can be recovered.

Does perception require representations?

We have concluded that the problem of whether perception is mediated by computational processes should be understood in terms of levels of explanation. At an ecological level, structures in light can be regarded as directly detected, and at a physiological level, light intensity can be regarded as directly detected. The two levels are not neatly separable, however, and to explore perception at a physiological level requires theories of algorithms that enable the detection of structures in light, and which are implemented by the nervous system.

There is a second sense in which traditional theory regards perception as mediated, however, and this raises issues that extend beyond problems of perception to questions of the nature of our knowledge of the world. The argument is that in order to perceive the world an animal or person must form an internal representation of it. We have seen examples of representations of the world that theories of perception have postulated; Marr's $2\frac{1}{2}$-D sketch (see Chapter 7) represents the layout of the surfaces surrounding an observer, whereas theories of object recognition (see Chapter 9) have postulated catalogues of stored descriptions of objects held in memory. The term "representation" is used in a wide variety of senses. It is used to refer to any symbolic description of the world—whether this is the world as it has been in the past (as in stored "memories"), as it is now (the $2\frac{1}{2}$-D sketch, or structural descriptions), or as it might be in the future (as in certain kinds of imagery). It is also used by "connectionist" theorists (see Chapter 10) to refer to nonsymbolic patterns of activation in simple networks, which, nevertheless, *represent* some object, feature, distance, or other property of the surroundings.

Direct theories of perception completely reject *all* such representations as further examples of mediating processes standing between the world and the perceiver. The counter-argument would run as follows. Just as sizes, slants, and distances of surfaces surrounding an observer are specified by invariant properties of optic flow patterns, so any object we can recognise, from a pencil to a painting, is specified by as yet unidentified "high-level" invariants. Therefore, just as we can, at an ecological level, regard detection of distance specified by a texture gradient as direct, so we can equally well regard perception of a pencil or painting as direct. There is no need for any processes of constructing or matching representations.

A further argument against a role for representation in perception is that the direct fit between perception and action is broken. The invariants to which an animal is attuned are those specifying the actions it must perform to ensure its survival, and Gibson (1979) devised the term

affordance to express this point. An affordance is an opportunity for action provided by an object, such as support by a firm surface, grasping by a limb of a tree, or mating by an animal of the opposite sex. Gibson claimed that affordances such as these are specified by the structure of the light reflected from objects, and are directly detectable. There is therefore no need to invoke representations of the environment intervening between detection of affordances and action: one automatically leads to the other.

We have already argued in similar terms (see Chapter 12) that an insect's vision does not work to build up a representation of its surroundings, but instead to provide just the information required to modulate its flight. A female fly (or anything resembling one) could be said to afford pursuit, and the fly to detect the information in the optic array specifying this affordance. In these terms, where is the need for a representation of a female fly to which input is matched?

It is clear that if an algorithmic level of explanation is allowed (as we have argued it must be), then "representations" of some sort are inevitably involved, for the purpose of an algorithm is to transform one representation into another. Thus, Marr (1982, p.34) states that the algorithms involved in fly vision:

> deliver a representation in which at least three things are specified: 1) whether the visual field is looming sufficiently that the fly should contemplate landing; 2) whether there is a small patch—it could be a black speck or, it turns out, a textured figure in front of a textured ground—having some kind of motion relative to its background, and if there is such a patch; 3) ψ and ψ' for this patch are delivered to the motor system.

> [ψ is the angular bearing and ψ' the angular velocity of the patch; see Ch.12, p.271].

What Marr is doing here is to analyse the link between the fly's perception and action into a series of algorithms and representations, and we would argue that such an explanation is not only legitimate but necessary if a physiological analysis is to be undertaken. It is not at all the same as saying that a conceptual representation of the world is built up that a "little fly in the head" consults before taking action, although by using the word "contemplate" Marr could mislead us into thinking that this is what he intends. The representations are patterns of activity in networks of neurons.

In this situation, it becomes difficult to distinguish the ecological and representational positions. The first states that the tuning of the fly to the invariances in the light reaching it fits it to its environment, and the second states that properties of the fly's environment are represented in the neural networks detecting the structure of light. If the term representation is used in this sense, it seems there is really nothing to argue about. It is only if we wanted to claim that the fly had a "concept" of something to pursue that there should be any dispute. If we allow algorithms we must allow representations, but for many examples of animal vision in particular, we should consider these to be nonsymbolic patterns of activity in the nervous system rather than "concepts" or "memories". We return to consider the issue of nonsymbolic representations a little later.

By choosing the example of a fly's visual perception, however, we have avoided more difficult issues raised by the "representation" debate. In this example, we are dealing with the *direct* control of activity by a known invariant in the light *currently* reaching the fly's eyes. Let us consider an example from animal perception not meeting these criteria: Menzel's demonstration of chimpanzees' memory for the location of pieces of food (Ch.16, p.350). If a chimp is carried around a familiar field, shown the locations of 20 pieces of food, and then released, it will move around the field gathering up all the pieces. Control experiments show that the locations of food cannot be detected by a chimp that has not previously been shown them. What are we to make of this phenomenon?

The first difference from the fly example is that control of activity is not direct; information obtained from light specifying where food is hidden is used later to guide travel around the field. The second is that there is no information in the light reaching the chimpanzee while it is gathering

up the food to specify where food is. In an indirect theory of perception, these facts are accommodated by saying that the chimp forms a representation of the information specifying the locations of food, and this representation is later used to guide travel around the field.

A direct theorist would reply that the representational explanation makes the mistake of putting over-narrow bounds on the sample of light in which information can be detected. If we take the sample of light to be that stretching over both sessions of the experiment, then there are invariants specifying the locations of food and there is no need to invoke representations. There is no difference in principle, to a "direct" theorist, between this situation and one in which a chimpanzee's view of a piece of food while approaching it is briefly interrupted by an obstacle. In both cases, activities extended over time are guided by directly detected invariants in a sample of light extended over time. The difficulties many have in accepting this formulation are typified by Menzel's comment that (1978, p.417):

> I am an ardent admirer of Gibson, and I don't doubt that his theory could explain much of the data cited in this chapter; but when he starts talking about how animals can "see" things that are hidden from sight or even located in a different room he loses me.

The disagreements become sharper when we move to human perception. The Gibsonian position is that anything we perceive must be specified by invariant properties of stimulation, directly detected without any need for representation of information. There are invariants specifying a friend's face, a performance of *Hamlet*, or the sinking of the *Titanic*, and no knowledge of the friend, of the play, or of maritime history is required to perceive these things. Gibson also applied the concept of affordance to human perception; a pen, he argued, affords writing and a letterbox the posting of a letter. No knowledge of writing or of the postal system needs to be represented in memory, as invariants specifying these affordances are directly detected.

An important difference between these examples and those we used earlier is that we are now dealing with situations where no invariants specifying objects, events, or affordances have been demonstrated or seem likely to be demonstrated. The calm with which Gibsonian theorists contemplate this difficulty is captured in Michaels and Carello's (1981) reply to the question:

> How can the ecological approach account for experiential dimensions of hedonic tone (humor, pleasure, amusement) that appear to have no physical stimulus referent?

with the answer:

> The invariants must be very higher-order indeed (Michaels & Carello, 1981, p.178).

Critics of the Gibsonian position do not accept that this answer is adequate, and we will outline the objections made to it by Fodor and Pylyshyn (1981). Their principal criticism is that the terms "invariant" and "directly detected" are left so unconstrained in their meanings in Gibsonian theory as to be meaningless. They take the example of an art expert detecting the fact that a painting was executed by da Vinci and not by an imitator. To explain this by stating that the expert has directly detected the invariant property "having been painted by da Vinci" is, they argue, to use the term "invariant" in a trivial way. For any percept, if a sufficiently large sample of available light is considered, there can in principle be some invariant to specify a property of this sort; here, a sample including the light reflected from all da Vincis, imitations of da Vincis, books on da Vinci, and so on.

Fodor and Pylyshyn argue that the notions of invariant and direct detection can be constrained by what they term a "sufficiency criterion". The pattern of light reflected from a looming surface is sufficient to cause the perception of impending collision, as shown by experiments with artificial simulations of such a pattern. Therefore, it makes sense to speak of an invariant property of this pattern being detected directly. In contrast, we have no reason to believe that a sample of light reflected from a da Vinci is sufficient to cause recognition of

it. Rather, Fodor and Pylyshyn argue, further information beyond that in the light is necessary, and this must be information about the properties of da Vinci's paintings represented in memory.

This sufficiency criterion therefore restricts the notion of direct perception to situations where structured patterns of light with particular invariant properties can be shown to be sufficient to explain perception and behaviour (although, as we argued earlier, the processes involved in detecting them can be analysed at an algorithmic level). On this criterion, perception of other people, familiar objects, and almost everything we perceive falls on the da Vinci rather than the looming surface side of the boundary, and therefore requires additional kinds of representation of the perceived object.

Thus, for most of human perception we must advocate that information in light is compared with stored knowledge of the world. There are some compelling demonstrations to testify to this, such as the "hollow face" illusion (Fig. 7.10, p.151). There is sufficient information here to see the mask as hollow, but we stubbornly fail to do so. If we move our head from side to side the face appears to follow us, in blatant disregard for the actual motion perspective present. The hollow face is not an example of an illusion that involves static observers or monocular viewing, and is a difficult one for the ardent Gibsonian to dismiss as a laboratory trick. We must invoke a memory of some sort here to explain why we see what we are used to seeing despite useful information to the contrary.

However, we do feel that the ecological psychologists make some very pertinent criticisms of current conceptions of memory, and it is worth examining these here. First, the kinds of representational schemes used in research into object recognition, which we discussed in Chapter 9, are not easy to adapt to the recognition of dynamic configurations like moving human figures. Marr and Nishihara's axis-based representations are derived from the occluding contours in static images, and it may be that different representational schemes could be constructed that are based on information in a transforming optic array. Two rather different approaches to this problem were introduced briefly in Chapter 15, where we talked about Cutting's analysis of the centres of moment in moving displays, and Weir's action "schemas", in which temporal relations such as "approach" and "withdrawal" were specified. These kinds of ideas seem worth pursuing.

Second, and more generally, ecological psychologists (e.g. Bransford, McCarrell, Franks, & Nitsch, 1977) object to the notion of memory as a set of associated locations that must be searched through. This particular metaphor for memory is ingrained in our everyday language (we talk of trying to "find" a name that we have forgotten) and entrenched in many contemporary models of memory (Roediger, 1980). Ecological psychologists object that such conceptions of memory often imply that we must search exhaustively through our memories to discover that something is novel, and make it difficult to articulate the nature of the novelty once this is discovered.

They point instead to the subtle interactions between the context in which something is perceived and the meaning attributed to it. To take one of Bransford et al.'s examples, consider an outstretched hand. This could mean "come with me", "I have five children", "read my palm", etc, and Bransford et al. consider it absurd that every possible meaning for this configuration should be stored as a different potential association, yet this is precisely how many models of memory are described. We feel that these are important points, and that it is well worth seeking alternative formulations for memory. However, although the criticisms made by direct theorists are valid, they have yet to present any adequate alternative.

Perhaps, though, the connectionist movement that we discussed in Chapter 10 may provide a computational metaphor more acceptable to the Gibsonian ecological theorist, by avoiding the necessity for *symbol* processing and *symbolic* representations, even for longer-term "concepts" and "memories". At first glance, the connectionists (e.g. McClelland, Rumelhart, & Hinton, 1986) seem to make a number of points that echo those of the Gibsonians. *Symbolic* representations of the world are replaced by *patterns* of activity, in networks whose operation is (roughly) like the activity of neurons. Memories are *content addressable*—a fragment of a known pattern as input will lead to the restoration of the whole pattern of activity, without any process of *search*. Contextual sensitivity is built into connectionist models because the co-activation of two or more units will tend to recur again in the future. Memory is not a set of explicit traces stored at identifiable addresses, but, particularly in distributed memory models, is more a set of potentialities of the entire network. Given one cue, one "memory" will be retrieved, given some other cue, a quite different memory will be retrieved from the same set of connections between the same set of units. To the extent that parallel distributed processing models provide alternative explanations of the same psychological phenomena, perhaps here is a computational metaphor for the Gibsonian notions of "resonance" and "attunement"?

Connectionist models are certainly geared to action, but Fodor and Pylyshyn (1988) have argued that they suffer from the same short-comings as other purely *associative* (S-R) accounts of cognitive phenomena. Because of this, Fodor and Pylyshyn (1988) suggest that connectionist models *cannot* provide an alternative to traditional symbol-processing models because they cannot embody syntactic constraints to which cognition is sensitive. Many of the arguments that they level against the connectionist revival are similar to the arguments levelled by Chomsky (1959) against the behaviourist account of language acquisition and we will not repeat these arguments here. Their conclusion, however, is that connectionism should only be an *implementation*-level theory, not an algorithmic-level theory. Connectionist models may show us how, for example, the brain maps from a viewer-centred to an object-centred coordinate system (cf. Chapter 10), but they do not do away with the *psychological* level of theory at which the brain must be seen as constructing and manipulating symbolic representations.

The distinction between algorithm and implementation is important, and there is much debate over which of these levels connectionist models are tackling (e.g. Broadbent, 1985; Rumelhart & McClelland, 1985). Whereas connectionist theorists might disagree with Fodor and Pylyshyn (1988), they do generally agree that they are tackling cognitive processes at a different level from that of traditional theories. Rumelhart and McClelland (1985), for example, contrast traditional "macrostructural" level theories with the "microstructural" level addressed by parallel distributed processing models, and Smolensky (1987, 1988) suggests that connectionist models operate at the "sub-symbolic" level, from which representations emerge that have properties approximately the same as those of symbolic representations at a higher level. Thus even for committed connectionists, in contrast to the Gibsonians, there is a level of theory at which it may be legitimate, and possibly more convenient, to consider the construction, manipulation, and storage of explicit "symbolic" representations.

Although connectionist models appear to provide a different metaphor for memory, it is important to note that many of the attractive properties of these models are neutral in respect to the connectionist/traditionalist contrast (cf. Fodor & Pylyshyn, 1988). For example, a compelling feature of PDP memory models is that they can abstract the prototype of a category *and* retain sensitivity to recent instances, yet traditional nonconnectionist models can show similar properties (e.g. Hintzman, 1986). Traditional models can be instance-based or abstractive in their learning properties, and so can connectionist models.

We have implicitly agreed with Fodor and Pylyshyn (1988) by assigning connectionist models to a subordinate role in Part II of this book, where we introduced them as a means of achieving particular levels of description discussed elsewhere in more traditional terms. This is not to imply that these models will play a subordinate role in the development of visual science—on the contrary, some of the most exciting developments in theoretical and applied vision may be driven by this school. However, we agree with Fodor and Pylyshyn's argument that such models do not provide an *alternative* to traditional accounts at the *psychological* level of theory.

"SEEING" AND "SEEING AS"

Our aim in this chapter has not been to review thoroughly the debate between Gibsonian and traditional theories, or to offer new insights, but rather to organise and sift the issues, and to offer our own resolution of them. The debate is a furious one, and the reader is referred to the papers by Fodor and Pylyshyn (1981), Turvey (1977b), Turvey, Shaw, Reed, and Mace (1981), and Ullman (1980), and even to reviews of the first edition of this book (Pittenger & Mace, 1985; Sutherland, 1985) for further detail of it. In some respects current arguments about the status of connectionist models are concerned with the same, central debate about the necessity for a cognitive or psychological level of theory to stand between the "stimulus" and the "response" (see the collection edited by Pinker & Mehler, 1988). Some points of argument are, we feel, relatively easily settled, particularly by recognising the different levels at which perception can be explained and the relationships between them. We have argued that Gibson's early insights into the nature of the input for vision, and the ecological optics he formulated, have been of enormous value, and the insights into perception we have discussed in the third part of the book testify to their productivity.

On the other hand, we find that the Gibsonian approach is not helpful in dealing with the relationship between ecological optics and physiological levels of explanation. Gibson's concern to avoid mediation and inference led him to shy away from these problems, and we find their clearest treatment in discussions such as Ullman's (1980) and Marr's (1982). We must stress that Marr's work shares a good deal with Gibson's views. He places great emphasis on understanding the relationship between the structures in the world that a perceiver needs to detect and the ways in which they structure light, just as Gibson's ecological optics does. In Marr's approach, assumptions about the world are built into algorithms for perceiving it, and explicit forms of "inference" avoided wherever possible. In comparison, Marr's use of an image, rather than optic flow, as a starting point is no important barrier between them.

In addition, we find it difficult to accept that Gibson's formulation does away with any role for memory in understanding perception. We find it unconvincing to explain a person returning after 10 years to their grandparents' home and seeing that a tree has been cut down as having detected directly an event specified by a transformation in the optic array. At this point, we concur with Fodor and Pylyshyn (1981) that the terms of Gibson's theory are being extended to the point of becoming empty. Even so, we believe that Gibsonian criticisms of traditional views will continue to be valuable in forcing a re-examination of the models of the role of memory in perception.

A further comment we have on the debate between direct and indirect theorists is that the examples in which their arguments carry most force are quite different. The Gibsonian concept of affordance, for example, is at its most powerful in the context of simple visually guided behaviour such as that of insects. Here it does indeed make sense to speak of the animal detecting the information available in light that is needed to organise its activities, and the notion of a conceptual representation of the environment seems redundant.

For more intelligent creatures, and for people, we can make the same kinds of argument about detection of distance, falling-off places, and so on in the guidance of locomotion. It is in these contexts where Gibsonian arguments carry most conviction. Indeed, some "direct" theorists, such as Turvey et al. (1981), seem to claim that it is only these kinds of activities that fall within the scope of an "ecological" theory of perception, and with this we would have no argument. It is only if they wished to argue that these activities alone constitute perception that we would be unhappy.

Proponents of the representational view, however, challenge Gibsonian theory by invoking human abilities to perceive objects, events, and meanings that are bound up in a rich cultural context. Fodor and Pylyshyn's (1981) discussion of the recognition of a genuine da Vinci is an example. Here, two aspects of Gibsonian ideas become a good deal less convincing. First, the mere assertion that there are high-level invariants in the structure of light that allow the direct perception of

such objects dilutes the concept of invariant. Second, the argument of animal-environment mutuality, which was so useful when we considered the classes of information a fly might need to survive and reproduce, becomes vague and even trivial when we consider human beings perceiving and acting in a cultural rather than a physical environment.

We feel that a distinction made by Fodor and Pylyshyn (1981) between "seeing" and "seeing as" captures the difference between the two kinds of situation (1981, p.189):

What you see when you see a thing depends upon what the thing you see *is*. But what you see the thing as depends upon what you know about what you are seeing . . .

Here is Smith at sea on a foggy evening, and as lost as ever he can be. Suddenly the skies clear, and Smith sees the Pole Star. What happens next? In particular, what are the consequences of what Smith perceives for what he comes to believe and do? Patently, that depends upon what he sees the Pole Star *as*. If, for example, he sees the Pole Star as the star that is at the Celestial North Pole (plus or minus a degree or two), then Smith will know, to that extent, where he is; and we may confidently expect that he will utter "Saved!" and make for port. Whereas, if he sees the Pole Star but takes it to be a firefly, or takes it to be Alpha Centauri, or—knowing no astronomy at all—takes it to be just some star or other, then seeing the Pole Star may have no particular consequences for his behaviour or his further cognitive states. Smith will be just as lost after he sees it as he was before.

The successes of the ecological approach have been in understanding *seeing*—how we use information in light to walk upright or catch a ball—but its attempts to explain *seeing as* have not progressed beyond general assertions. Most human activity takes place within a culturally defined environment, and we see no alternative to the assumption that people may see objects and events as what they are in terms of a culturally given conceptual representation of the world.

It is interesting to speculate that the emphasis of the traditional approach to "seeing as", and of the ecological approach to "seeing", may not just be a matter of historical accident, but may reflect a real distinction between two ways in which the brain operates in using visual information. In Chapter 3 (p.44) we mentioned "blindsight"—the ability of some people with damage to the striate cortex to point towards or even identify targets in a region of the visual field in which they are convinced that they are blind. This ability to use visual information to guide actions, without any conscious awareness of doing so, has been discovered in other patients suffering from neurological damage. One intriguing case is that of a person who was completely unable to discriminate between objects on the basis of their size, and yet, when filmed while reaching out to pick up the same objects, was found to adjust the gap between her finger and thumb just as accurately as normal subjects (Goodale, Milner, Jakobson, & Carey, 1991).

Reviewing findings such as these, Goodale and Milner (1992) argue that two distinct brain pathways process visual information. One is responsible for conscious awareness of objects and events, and one for controlling movement in relation to the surroundings. (This theory is an extension of the model of two processing streams in extrastriate cortex; see Ch.3, p.56). Although the distinction between these pathways will probably not turn out to be so clear-cut, there is strong evidence that some visual processes can operate independently of consciousness, whereas others do not. As the roots of the traditional approach to visual perception are in the philosophical analysis of seeing, and more recently in psychophysical methods, its theories and findings may reflect the operation of the visual pathways responsible for the conscious awareness of objects and events that is required to communicate with another person about the outcome of a perceptual task. Conversely, through its emphasis on the direct control of action, the ecological approach has perhaps helped us to understand the previously neglected pathways responsible for the unconscious tuning of limb movements by visual information.

One specific implication of this point of view is that we cannot always assume that different perceptual tasks are actually tapping the same underlying visual processes, however similar they may appear to be. For example, quite different perceptual processes may be involved in an everyday visual task, and in what appears to be a straightforward laboratory analogue of it. This turned out to be the case when Ebbesen, Parker, and Konĕcni (1977) examined how drivers decided whether to cross an intersection depending on the speed and distance of an oncoming car. In a laboratory task, using model cars, it appeared that "drivers" were making a complex decision about when to cross, based on the estimation of the distance and velocity of the approaching car. These subjects made 9% errors. In the field, with real cars, and real risks, it seemed that drivers simply made use of temporal headway (time to contact) with the approaching car, which does not require the separate computation of distance and velocity. These drivers made no errors.

Tresilian (1995) cites other evidence of this kind showing that people estimate time to contact in quite different ways in different tasks. Drawing on Goodale and Milner's (1992) theory, Tresilian concludes that fast interceptive acts, such as catching a ball, are timed by a "motor" visual system, whereas laboratory tasks such as estimating time to collision with a simulated looming object can involve the operation of a separate "cognitive" visual system. The relative contribution of the two systems in such tasks varies according to the detailed conditions, and so interpretation of the results obtained is a complex and difficult problem.

CONCLUSIONS

In these pages we have set down our own reasons for rejecting the strong claim that perception is *direct*, as ecological psychologists would have it. We have argued that perception involves computations and that it involves representations, and that it is a legitimate task of psychology to enquire into the nature of these computations and representations. However, it is clear that the nature of these computations may be different once one considers a dynamic pattern of light and not a retinal image as the input to visual processing, and the successful control of action and not conscious awareness as its goal. Different kinds of computations require different sorts of representation, and many of the traditional ideas may need rethinking in the light of the findings of ecological psychologists.

Although the theories inspiring the kinds of research described in Parts II and III of this book differ strongly on fundamental issues, we therefore feel that there is considerable scope for using the insights of both to solve smaller, more defined problems in visual perception. It is in understanding how simple animals such as flies perceive their surroundings that a combination of the two approaches has achieved most success, specifying the ecological problems vision must solve for the animal, devising appropriate algorithms, and unravelling their implementation by nervous systems. In human beings, this enterprise is vastly more difficult, particularly because human perception operates in a cultural as well as a physical environment. The formulation and testing of algorithmic theories, and the investigation of their physiological bases, is therefore a difficult task, but none the less a fascinating one.

References

Abraham, F.D., Abraham, R.H., & Shaw, C.D. (1991). *A visual introduction to dynamical systems theory for psychology*. Santa Cruz, CA: Aerial Press.

Adelson, E.H., & Bergen, J.R. (1985). Spatiotemporal energy models for the perception of motion. *Journal of the Optical Society of America, A2*, 284–299.

Adelson, E.H., & Bergen, J.R. (1991). The plenoptic function and the elements of early vision. In M.S. Landy & J.A. Movshon (Eds.), *Computational models of visual processing*. Cambridge, MA: MIT Press.

Adelson, E.H., & Movshon, J.A. (1982). Phenomenal coherence of moving visual patterns. *Nature, 300*, 523–525.

Albright, T.D. (1992). Form-cue invariant motion processing in primate visual cortex. *Science, 255*, 1141–1143.

Alderson, G.H.K., Sully, D.J., & Sully, H.G. (1974). An operational analysis of a one-handed catching task using high-speed photography. *Journal of Motor Behaviour, 6*, 217–226.

Aleksander, I. (1983). Emergent intelligent properties of progressively structured pattern recognition nets. *Pattern Recognition Letters, 1*, 375–384.

Alley, T.R. (Ed). (1988). *Social and applied aspects of perceiving faces*. Hillsdale, NJ: Lawrence Erlbaum Associates Inc.

Allman, J., Miezin, F., & McGuinness, E. (1985). Stimulus specific responses from beyond the classical receptive field: Neurophysiological mechanisms for local-global comparisons in visual neurons. *Annual Review of Neuroscience, 8*, 407–430.

Andersen, R.A., Essick, G.K., & Siegel, R.M. (1985). Encoding of spatial location by posterior parietal neurons. *Science, 230*, 456–458.

Anderson, B.L. (1994). The role of partial occlusion in stereopsis. *Nature, 367*, 365–368.

Anderson, B.L., & Nakayama, K. (1994). Toward a general theory of stereopsis: Binocular matching, occluding contours and fusion. *Psychological Review, 101*, 414–445.

Anderson, S.J., & Burr, D.C. (1985). Spatial and temporal selectivity of the human motion detection system. *Vision Research, 25*, 1147–1154.

Anstis, S.M. (1980). The perception of apparent movement. *Philosophical Transactions of the Royal Society of London, B, 290*, 153–168.

Anstis, S.M. (1990). Motion aftereffects from a motionless stimulus. *Perception, 19*, 301–306.

Anstis, S.M., & Duncan, K. (1983). Separate motion aftereffects from each eye and from both eyes. *Vision Research, 23*, 161–169.

Attneave, F. (1971). Multistability in perception. *Scientific American, 225*, December, 63–71.

Bair, W., Koch, C., Newsome, W., & Britten, K. (1994). Power spectrum analysis of bursting cells in area MT of the behaving monkey. *Journal of Neuroscience, 14*, 2870–2892.

Baizer, J.S., Ungerleider, L.G., & Desimone, R. (1991). Organization of visual inputs to the inferior temporal and posterior parietal cortex in macaques. *Journal of Neuroscience, 11*, 168–190.

Baker, C.L., & Braddick, O.J. (1982). Does segregation of differently moving areas depend on relative or absolute displacement? *Vision Research, 22*, 851–856.

Baker, C.L., & Braddick, O.J. (1985). Temporal properties of the short-range process in apparent motion. *Perception, 14*, 181–192.

Ball, W., & Tronick, E. (1971). Infant responses to impending collision: Optical and real. *Science, 171*, 818–820.

Ballard, D.H., Hinton, G.E., & Sejnowski, T.K. (1983). Parallel visual computation. *Nature, 306*, 21–26.

Barclay, C.D., Cutting, J.E., & Kozlowski, L.T. (1978). Temporal and spatial factors in gait perception that influence gender recognition. *Perception and Psychophysics, 23*, 145–152.

Barlow, H.B. (1972). Single units and sensation: A neuron doctrine for perceptual psychology? *Perception, 1*, 371–394.

Barlow, H.B., & Hill, R.M. (1963). Selective sensitivity to direction of motion in ganglion cells of the rabbit's retina. *Science, 139*, 412–414.

Barlow, H.B., & Levick, W.R. (1965). The mechanism of directionally selective units in rabbit's retina. *Journal of Physiology, 178*, 477–504.

Barlow, H.B., & Mollon, J.D. (1982). *The senses*. Cambridge, UK: Cambridge University Press.

Barnes, R.D. (1968). *Invertebrate zoology* (2nd edn.). Philadelphia, PA: W.B. Saunders.

Barnes, R.D. (1974). *Invertebrate zoology* (3rd edn.). Philadelphia, PA: Saunders College Publishing/Holt, Rinehart & Winston.

Baron-Cohen, S. (1994). How to build a baby that can read minds—cognitive mechanisms in mindreading. *Cahiers de Psychologie Cognitive—Current Psychology of Cognition, 13*, 513–552.

Bartfeld, E., & Grinvald, A. (1992). Relationships between orientation-preference pinwheels, cytochrome oxidase blobs, and ocular dominance columns in primate striate cortex. *Proceedings of the National Academy of Sciences of the USA, 89*, 11,905–11,909.

Bartlett, J.C., & Searcy, J. (1993). Inversion and configuration of faces. *Cognitive Psychology, 25*, 281–316.

Bassili, J.N. (1976). Temporal and spatial contingencies in the perception of social events. *Journal of Personality and Social Psychology, 33*, 680–685.

Bassili, J.N. (1978). Facial motion in the perception of faces and of emotional expression. *Journal of Experimental Psychology: Human Perception and Performance, 4*, 373–379.

Bassili, J.N. (1979). Emotion recognition: The role of facial movement and the relative importance of upper and lower areas of the face. *Journal of Personality and Social Psychology, 37*, 2049–2058.

Bateson, P.P.G. (1977). Testing an observer's ability to identify individual animals. *Animal Behaviour, 25*, 247–248.

Baylis, G.C., Rolls, E.T., & Leonard, C.M. (1985). Selectivity between faces in the responses of a population of neurons in the cortex in the superior temporal sulcus of the monkey. *Brain Research, 342*, 91–102.

Beasley, N.A. (1968). The extent of individual differences in the perception of causality. *Canadian Journal of Psychology, 22*, 399–407.

Beck, J. (1972). Similarity grouping and peripheral discriminability under uncertainty. *American Journal of Psychology, 85*, 1–20.

Beck, J., & Gibson, J.J. (1955). The relation of apparent shape to apparent slant in the perception of objects. *Journal of Experimental Psychology, 50*, 125–133.

Becker, S., & Hinton, G.E. (1992). Self-organizing neural network that discovers surfaces in random-dot stereograms. *Nature, 355*, 161–163.

Bennett, A.T.D., & Cuthill, I.C. (1994). Ultraviolet vision in birds: What is its function? *Vision Research, 34*, 1471–1478.

Berg, W.P., Wade, M.G., & Greer, N.L. (1994). Visual regulation of gait in bipedal locomotion: Revisiting Lee, Lishman and Thomson (1982). *Journal of Experimental Psychology: Human Perception and Performance, 20*, 854–863.

Bergen, J.R., & Adelson, E.H. (1988). Early vision and texture perception. *Nature, 333*, 363–364.

Bergen, J.R., & Landy, M.S. (1991). Computational modelling of visual texture segregation. In M.S. Landy & J.A. Movshon (Eds.), *Computational models of visual processing*. Cambridge, MA: MIT Press.

Berkeley, G. (1709). An essay towards a new theory of vision. In *A New Theory of Vision and other writings*, Intro. A.D. Lindsay. London: J.M. Dent and Sons Ltd (1910).

Berkley, M.A., DeBruyn, B., & Orban, G. (1994). Illusory, motion and luminance-defined contours interact in the human visual system. *Vision Research, 34*, 209–216.

Berns, G.S., Dayan, P., & Sejnowski, T.J. (1993). A correlational model for the development of disparity selectivity in visual cortex that depends on prenatal and postnatal phases. *Proceedings of the National Academy of Sciences of the USA, 90*, 8277–8281.

Bernstein, N. (1967). *The coordination and regulation of movements*. Oxford: Pergamon Press.

Berry, D.S., & McArthur, L.Z. (1986). Perceiving character in faces: The impact of age-related cranio-facial changes on social perception. *Psychological Bulletin, 100*, 3–18.

Berry, D.S., & Misovich, S.J. (1994). Methodological approaches to the study of social event perception. *Personality and Social Psychology Bulletin, 20*, 139–152.

Bertenthal, B.I., Proffitt, D.R., & Cutting, J.F. (1984). Infant sensitivity to figural coherence in biomechanical motion. *Journal of Experimental Child Psychology, 37*, 213–230.

Beverley, K.I., & Regan, D. (1979). Separable aftereffects of changing-size and motion-in-depth: Different neural mechanisms? *Vision Research, 19*, 727–732.

Biederman, I. (1987a). Recognition by components: A theory of human image understanding. *Psychological Review, 94*, 115–147.

Biederman, I. (1987b). Matching image edges to object memory. *Proceedings of the First International Conference on Computer Vision*. IEEE Computer Society, London.

Biederman, I. (1995). Some problems of visual shape recognition to which the application of clustering mathematics might yield some potential benefits. *DIMACS Series in Discrete Mathematics, 19*, 313–329.

Biederman, I., & Cooper, E.E. (1991). Priming contour-deleted images: Evidence for intermediate representations in visual object recognition. *Cognitive Psychology, 23*, 393–419.

Biederman, I., & Cooper, E.E. (1992). Size invariance in visual object priming. *Journal of Experimental Psychology: Human Perception and Performance, 18*, 121–133.

Biederman, I., & Gerhardstein, P.C. (1993). Recognizing depth-rotated objects: Evidence and conditions for three-dimensional viewpoint invariance. *Journal of Experimental Psychology: Human Perception and Performance, 19*, 1162–1182.

Biederman, I., & Ju, G. (1988). Surface versus edge-based determinants of visual recognition. *Cognitive Psychology, 20*, 38–64.

Bizzi, E., Mussa-Ivaldi, F.A., & Giszter, S. (1991). Computations underlying the execution of movement: A biological perspective. *Science, 253*, 287–291.

Bjorklund, R.A., & Magnussen, S. (1981). A study of interocular transfer of spatial adaptation. *Perception, 10*, 511–518.

Blake, R., & Overton, R. (1979). The site of binocular rivalry suppression. *Perception, 8*, 143–152.

Blakemore, C. (1970). The representation of three-dimensional visual space in the cat's striate cortex. *Journal of Physiology, 209*, 155–178.

Blakemore, C.B., & Campbell, F.W. (1969). On the existence of neurones in the human visual system selectively sensitive to the size and orientation of retinal images. *Journal of Physiology, 203*, 237–260.

Blasdel, G.G. (1992). Orientation selectivity, preference and continuity in monkey striate cortex. *Journal of Neuroscience, 12*, 3139–3161.

Blondeau, J., & Heisenberg, M. (1982). The three-dimensional optomotor torque system of *Drosophila melanogaster*. *Journal of Comparative Physiology, 145*, 321–329.

Boden, M. (1987). *Artificial intelligence and natural man* (2nd edn.). Hassocks, UK: Harvester Press.

Bootsma, R.J. (1989). Accuracy of perceptual processes subserving different perception–action systems. *Quarterly Journal of Experimental Psychology, 41A*, 489–500.

Bolhuis, J.J. (1991). Mechanisms of avian imprinting: A review. *Biological Reviews, 66*, 303–345.

Bonds, A.B. (1991). Temporal dynamics of contrast gain in single cells of the cat striate cortex. *Visual Neuroscience, 6*, 239–255.

Boring, E.G. (1942). *Sensation and perception in the history of experimental psychology*. New York: Appleton-Century-Crofts.

Born, R.T., & Tootell, R.B.H. (1991). Spatial frequency tuning of single units in macaque supragranular striate cortex. *Proceedings of the National Academy of Sciences of the USA, 88*, 7066–7070.

Born, R.T., & Tootell, R.B.H. (1992). Segregation of global and local motion processing in primate middle temporal area. *Nature, 357*, 497–499.

Borst, A., & Bahde, S. (1988). Spatio-temporal integration of motion. *Naturwissenschaften, 75*, 265–267.

Bossema, I., & Burgler, R.R. (1980). Communication during monocular and binocular looking in European jays (*Garrulus garrulus glandarius*). *Behaviour, 74*, 274–283.

Boulton, J.C., & Baker, C.L. (1993). Dependence on stimulus onset asynchrony in apparent motion: Evidence for two mechanisms. *Vision Research, 33*, 2013–2019.

Bovik, A.C., Clark, M., & Geisler, W.S. (1990). Multichannel texture analysis using localized spatial filters. *IEEE Transactions PAMI, 12*, 55–73.

Bower, T.G.R. (1966). The visual world of infants. *Scientific American, 215*, December, 80–92.

Bower, T.G.R. (1971). The object in the world of the infant. *Scientific American, 225*, October, 30–38.

Bower, T.G.R., Broughton, J.M., & Moore, M.K. (1970). Infant responses to approaching objects. An indicator of response to distal variables. *Perception and Psychophysics, 9*, 193–196.

Boyle, D.G. (1960). A contribution to the study of phenomenal causation. *Quarterly Journal of Experimental Psychology, 12*, 171–179.

Braddick, O.J. (1974). A short-range process in apparent motion. *Vision Research, 14*, 519–527.

Braddick, O.J. (1980). Low-level and high-level processes in apparent motion. *Philosophical Transactions of the Royal Society of London, B, 209*, 137–151.

Braitenberg, V., & Ferretti, C.L. (1966). Landing reaction of *Musca domestica* induced by visual stimuli. *Naturwissenschaften, 53*, 155.

Bransford, J.D., McCarrell, N.S., Franks, J.J., & Nitsch, K.E. (1977). Toward unexplaining memory. In R. Shaw & J. Bransford (Eds.), *Perceiving, acting and knowing: Toward an ecological psychology*. Hillsdale, NJ: Lawrence Erlbaum Associates Inc.

Braunstein, M.L. (1968). Motion and texture as sources of slant information. *Journal of Experimental Psychology, 78*, 247–253.

Breitmeyer, B.G. (1984). *Visual masking: An integrative approach*. Oxford: Oxford University Press.

Brennan, S.E. (1985). The caricature generator. *Leonardo, 18*, 170–178.

Bressler, S.L., Coppola, R., & Nakamura, R. (1993). Episodic multiregional coherence at multiple frequencies during visual task performance. *Nature, 366*, 153–156.

Brindley, G.S., & Merton, P.A. (1960). The absence of position sense in the human eye. *Journal of Physiology, 153*, 127–130.

Broadbent, D.E. (1985). A question of levels: Comment on McClelland and Rumelhart. *Journal of Experimental Psychology: General, 114*, 189–192.

Brooke, N.M., & Summerfield, A.Q. (1983). Analysis, synthesis and perception of visible articulatory movements. *Journal of Phonetics, 11*, 63–76.

Bruce, C., Desimone, R., & Gross, C.G. (1981). Visual properties of neurons in a polysensory area in superior temporal sulcus of the macaque. *Journal of Neurophysiology, 46*, 369–384.

Bruce, V. (1988). *Recognising faces*. London: Lawrence Erlbaum Associates Ltd.

Bruce, V. (1994). Stability from variation: The case of face recognition. The M.D. Vernon memorial lecture. *Quarterly Journal of Experimental Psychology, 47A*, 5–29.

Bruce, V., Burton, A.M., Carson, D., Hanna, E., & Mason, O. (1994). Repetition priming of face recognition. In C. Umilta & M. Moscovitch (Eds.), *Attention and performance XV*. Cambridge, MA: MIT Press.

Bruce, V., Burton, A.M., Doyle, A., & Dench, N. (1989). Further experiments on the perception of growth in three dimensions. *Perception and Psychophysics, 46*, 528–536.

Bruce, V., Burton, A.M., Hanna, E., Healey, P., Mason, O., Coombes, A., Fright, R., & Linney, A. (1993). Sex discrimination: How do we tell the difference between male and female faces? *Perception, 22*, 131–152.

Bruce, V., Hanna, E., Dench, N., Healy, P., & Burton, A.M. (1992a). The importance of "mass" in line drawings of faces. *Applied Cognitive Psychology, 6*, 619–628.

Bruce, V., Cowey, A., Ellis, A.W., & Perrett, D.I. (1992b). Processing the facial image. Proceedings of a Discussion Meeting at the Royal Society of London. *Philosophical Transactions of the Royal Society, B, 335*, 1–18. Clarendon Press: Oxford Science Publications.

Bruce, V., & Humphreys, G.W. (1994). Recognising objects and faces. *Visual Cognition, 1*, 141–180.

Bruce, V., & Langton, S. (1994). The use of pigmentation and shading information in recognising the sex and identities of faces. *Perception, 23*, 803–822.

Bruce, V., & Morgan, M.J. (1975). Violations of symmetry and repetition in visual patterns. *Perception, 4*, 239–249.

Bruce, V., & Valentine, T. (1985). Identity priming in the recognition of familiar faces. *British Journal of Psychology, 76*, 373–383.

Bruce, V., & Valentine, T. (1988). When a nod's as good as a wink: The role of dynamic information in facial recognition. In M.M. Gruneberg, P.E. Morris, & R.N. Sykes (Eds.), *Practical aspects of memory: Current research and issues* (Vol. 1). Chichester, UK: Wiley.

Bruner, J.S., & Goodman, C.C. (1947). Value and need as organising factors in perception. *Journal of Abnormal and Social Psychology, 42*, 33–44.

Bülthoff, H.H., & Edelman, S. (1992). Psychophysical support for a two-dimensional view interpolation theory of object recognition. *Proceedings of the National Academy of Sciences of the USA, 89*, 60–64.

Bülthoff, H.H., & Mallot, H.A. (1988). Integration of depth modules: Stereo and shading. *Journal of the Optical Society of America A, 5*, 1749–1758.

Bülthoff, I., Sinha, P., & Bülthoff, H.H. (1995). *Top-down influence of recognition on stereoscopic depth perception.* Paper presented at ARVO '95.

Burbeck, C.A., & Kelly, D.H. (1984). Role of local adaptation in the fading of stabilized images. *Journal of the Optical Society of America, A1*, 216–220.

Burger, J., & Gochfeld, M. (1981). Discrimination of the threat of direct versus tangential approach to the nest by incubating herring and great black-backed gulls. *Journal of Comparative and Physiological Psychology, 95*, 676–684.

Burr, D. C., Holt, J., Johnstone, J. R., & Ross, J. (1982). Selective depression of motion sensitivity during saccades. *Journal of Physiology, 333*, 1–15.

Burr, D.C., & Morrone, M.C. (1990). Feature detection in biological and artificial visual systems. In C. Blakemore (Ed.), *Vision: Coding and efficiency.* Cambridge, UK: Cambridge University Press.

Burr, D.C., Morrone, M.C., & Ross, J. (1994). Selective suppression of the magnocellular visual pathway during saccadic eye movements. *Nature, 371*, 511–513.

Burr, D.C., Ross, J., & Morrone, M.C. (1986). Seeing objects in motion. *Proceedings of the Royal Society of London, B, 227*, 249–265.

Burt, D.M., & Perrett, D.I. (1995). Perception of age in adult caucasian male faces—computer graphic manipulation of shape and colour information. *Proceedings of the Royal Society of London, B, 259*, 137–143.

Burt, P., & Julesz, B. (1980). Modifications of the classical notion of Panum's fusional area. *Perception, 9*, 671–682.

Burton, A.M. (1994). Learning new faces in an interactive activation and competition model. *Visual Cognition, 1*, 313–348.

Burton, A.M., Bruce, V., & Dench, N. (1993). What's the difference between men and women? Evidence from facial measurement. *Perception, 22*, 153–176.

Bushnell, I.W.R. (1982). Discrimination of faces by young infants. *Journal of Experimental Child Psychology, 33*, 298–308.

Bushnell, I.W.R., Sai, F., & Mullin, J.T. (1989). Neonatal recognition of the mother's face. *British Journal of Developmental Psychology, 7*, 3–15.

Butterworth, G. (1983). Structure of the mind in human infancy. In L.P. Lipsett (Ed.), *Advances in infancy research* (Vol. 2). Norwood, NJ: Ablex.

Butterworth, G., & Hicks, L. (1977). Visual proprioception and postural stability in infancy: A developmental study. *Perception, 6*, 255–262.

Cameron, D.A., & Pugh, E.N. (1991). Double cones as a basis for a new type of polarization vision in vertebrates. *Nature, 353*, 161–164.

Camhi, J.M. (1970). Yaw-correcting postural changes in locusts. *Journal of Experimental Biology, 52*, 519–531.

Campbell, F.W., & Robson, J.G. (1968). Application of Fourier analysis to the visibility of gratings. *Journal of Physiology, 197*, 551–566.

Campbell, F.W., & Wurtz, R.H. (1978). Saccadic omission: Why do we not see a grey-out during a saccadic eye movement? *Vision Research, 18*, 1297–1303.

Campbell, R., Heywood, C.A., Cowey, A., Regard, M., & Landis, T. (1990). Sensitivity to eye gaze in prosopagnosic patients and monkeys with superior temporal sulcus ablations. *Neuropsychologia, 28*, 1123–1142.

Cannon, M.W., & Fullenkamp, S.C. (1993). Spatial interactions in apparent contrast: Individual differences in enhancement and suppression effects. *Vision Research, 33*, 1685–1695.

Canny, J. (1986). A computational approach to edge detection. *IEEE Transactions PAMI, 8*, 679–698.

Carey, S. (1992). Becoming a face expert. *Philosophical Transactions of the Royal Society of London, B, 335*, 95–103.

Carpenter, R.H.S. (1988). *Movements of the eyes* (2nd edn.). London: Pion Press.

Cartwright, B.A., & Collett, T.S. (1979). How honey-bees know their distance from a nearby visual landmark. *Journal of Experimental Biology, 82*, 367–372.

Cartwright, B.A., & Collett, T.S. (1983). Landmark learning in bees: Experiments and models. *Journal of Comparative Physiology, 151*, 521–543.

Cavanagh, P. (1991). Short-range vs long-range motion: Not a valid distinction. *Spatial Vision, 5*, 303–309.

Cavanagh, P. (1992). Attention-based motion perception. *Science, 257*, 1563–1565.

Cavanagh, P., & Mather, G. (1989). Motion: the long and short of it. *Spatial Vision, 4*, 103–129.

Cave, C.B., & Kosslyn, S.M. (1993). The role of parts and spatial relations in object identification. *Perception, 22,* 229–248.

Chomsky, N. (1959). Review of verbal behaviour by Skinner. *Language, 35,* 26–58.

Christie, F., & Bruce, V. (submitted). *The role of movement in unfamiliar face recognition.* Paper presented to the Experimental Psychology Society, Bristol, UK, April 1996.

Chubb, C., & Sperling, G. (1988). Drift-balanced random stimuli: A general basis for studying non-Fourier motion perception. *Journal of the Optical Society of America, A5,* 1986–2006.

Clarke, P.G.H., & Whitteridge, D. (1977). A comparison of stereoscopic mechanisms in cortical visual areas V1 and V2 of the cat. *Journal of Physiology, 272,* 92–93.

Cleland, B.G., & Levick, W.R. (1974). Properties of rarely encountered types of ganglion cells in the cat's retina and an overall classification. *Journal of Physiology, 240,* 457–492.

Cline, M.G. (1967). The perception of where a person is looking. *American Journal of Psychology, 80,* 41–50.

Clowes, M.B. (1971). On seeing things. *Artificial Intelligence, 2,* 79–112.

Collett, T.S. (1977). Stereopsis in toads. *Nature, 267,* 349–351.

Collett, T.S. (1980). Some operating rules for the optomotor system of a hoverfly during voluntary flight. *Journal of Comparative Physiology, 138,* 271–282.

Collett, T.S., & Lehrer, M. (1993). Looking and learning: A spatial pattern in the orientation flight of the wasp *Vespula vulgaris. Proceedings of the Royal Society of London, B, 252,* 129–134.

Cooper, E.E., & Biederman, I. (1993). *Metric versus viewpoint-invariant shape differences in visual object recognition.* Poster presented at the Annual Meeting of the Association for Research in Vision and Opthalmology. Sarasota, FL, May.

Cooper, L.A., Schacter, D.L., Ballesteros, S., & Moore, C. (1992). Priming and recognition of transformed three-dimensional objects: Effects of size and reflection. *Journal of Experimental Psychology: Learning, Memory and Cognition, 18,* 43–57.

Cornsweet, T.N. (1970). *Visual perception.* New York: Academic Press.

Cott, H.B. (1940). *Adaptive coloration in animals.* London: Methuen.

Croner, L.J., & Kaplan, E. (1995). Receptive fields of P and M ganglion cells across the primate retina. *Vision Research, 35,* 7–24.

Croze, H. (1970). Searching image in carrion crows. *Zeitschrift für Tierpsychologie, Supplement 5.* Cited in M. Edmunds (1974). *Defence in animals.* New York: Longman.

Cumming, B. (1994). Motion-in-depth. In A.T. Smith & R.J. Snowden (Eds.), *Visual detection of motion.* London: Academic Press.

Cumming, B.G., Johnston, E.B., & Parker, A.J. (1993). Effects of different texture cues on curved surfaces viewed stereoscopically. *Vision Research, 33,* 827–838.

Cutting, J.E. (1978). Generation of synthetic male and female walkers through manipulation of a biomechanical invariant. *Perception, 7,* 393–405.

Cutting, J.E. (1982). Blowing in the wind: Perceiving structure in trees and bushes. *Cognition, 12,* 25–44.

Cutting, J.E. (1986). *Perception with an eye for motion.* Cambridge, MA: MIT Press.

Cutting, J.E., & Garvin, J.J. (1987). Fractal curves and complexity. *Perception and Psychophysics, 42,* 365–370.

Cutting, J.E., & Kozlowski, L.T. (1977). Recognizing friends by their walk: Gait perception without familiarity cues. *Bulletin of the Psychonomic Society, 9,* 353–356.

Cutting, J.E., & Millard, R.T. (1984). Three gradients and the perception of flat and curved surfaces. *Journal of Experimental Psychology: General, 113,* 198–216.

Cutting, J.E., & Proffitt, D.R. (1981). Gait perception as an example of how we may perceive events. In R.D. Walk & H.L. Pick, Jr. (Eds.), *Intersensory perception and sensory integration.* New York: Plenum.

Cutting, J.E., & Proffitt, D.R. (1982). The minimum principle and the perception of absolute and relative motions. *Cognitive Psychology, 14,* 211–246.

Cutting, J.E., Proffitt, D.R., & Kozlowski, L.T. (1978). A biomechanical invariant for gait perception. *Journal of Experimental Psychology: Human Perception and Performance, 4,* 357–372.

Cutting, J.E., Springer, K., Braren, P.A., & Johnson, S.H. (1992). Wayfinding on foot from information in retinal, not optical flow. *Journal of Experimental Psychology: General, 121,* 41–72.

Dartnall, H.J.A., Bowmaker, J.K., & Mollon, J.D. (1983). Human visual pigments: Microspectrophotometric results from the eyes of seven persons. *Proceedings of the Royal Society of London, B, 220,* 115–130.

Davies, G.M., Ellis, H.D., & Shepherd, J.W. (1978). Face recognition accuracy as a function of mode of representation. *Journal of Applied Psychology, 63*, 180–187.

Davies, M.N.O., & Green, P.R. (1988). Head-bobbing during walking, running and flying: Relative motion perception in the pigeon. *Journal of Experimental Biology, 138*, 71–91.

Davies, M.N.O., & Green, P.R. (1990). Flow-field variables trigger landing in hawk but not in pigeons. *Naturwissenschaften, 77*, 142–144.

Davis, J.M. (1975). Socially induced flight reactions in pigeons. *Animal Behaviour, 23*, 597–601.

Dawkins, M.S., & Guilford, T. (1994). Design of an intention signal in the bluehead wrasse (*Thalassoma bifasciatum*). *Proceedings of the Royal Society of London, B, 257*, 123–128.

DeAngelis, G.C., Ohzawa, I., & Freeman, R.D. (1991). Depth is encoded in the visual cortex by a specialized receptive field structure. *Nature, 352*, 156–159.

de Monasterio, F.M. (1978). Properties of ganglion cells with atypical receptive-field organization in retina of macaques. *Journal of Neurophysiology, 41*, 1435–1449.

de Monasterio, F.M., & Gouras, P. (1975). Functional properties of ganglion cells of the rhesus monkey retina. *Journal of Physiology, 251*, 167–195.

de Monasterio, F.M., & Schein, S.J. (1982). Spectral bandwidths of colour-opponent cells of geniculocortical pathway of macaque monkeys. *Journal of Neurophysiology, 47*, 214–224.

De Valois, R.L., Abramov, I., & Jacobs, G.H. (1966). Analysis of response patterns of LGN cells. *Journal of the Optical Society of America, 56*, 966–977.

De Valois, R.L., Albrecht, D.G., & Thorell, L.G. (1982). Spatial frequency selectivity of cells in macaque visual cortex. *Vision Research, 22*, 545–559.

De Valois, R.L., & De Valois, K.K. (1990). *Spatial vision*. Oxford: Oxford University Press.

De Valois, R.L., Thorell, L.G., & Albrecht, D.G. (1985). Periodicity of striate cortex cell receptive fields. *Journal of the Optical Society of America, A2*, 1115–1123.

Derrington, A.M., Badcock, D.R., & Henning, G.B. (1993). Discriminating the direction of second-order motion at short stimulus durations. *Vision Research, 33*, 1785–1794.

Derrington, A.M., & Henning, G.B. (1994). Implications of motion detection for early non-linearities. In *Higher order processing in the visual system* (Ciba Foundation Symposium 184, pp.211–220). Chichester, UK: Wiley.

Derrington, A.M., Krauskopf, J., & Lennie, P. (1984). Chromatic mechanisms in lateral geniculate nucleus of macaque. *Journal of Physiology, 357*, 241–265.

Derrington, A.M., & Lennie, P. (1984). Spatial and temporal contrast sensitivities of neurones in lateral geniculate nucleus of macaque. *Journal of Physiology, 357*, 219–240.

Derrington, A.M., Lennie, P., & Wright, M.J. (1979). The mechanism of peripherally evoked responses in retinal ganglion cells. *Journal of Physiology, 289*, 299–310.

Desimone, R., & Duncan, J. (1995). Neural mechanisms of selective visual attention. *Annual Review of Neuroscience, 18*, 193–222.

Desimone, R., & Schein, S.J. (1987). Visual properties of neurons in area V4 of the macaque: Sensitivity to stimulus form. *Journal of Neurophysiology, 57*, 835–868.

DeYoe, E., Knierem, J., Sagi, D., Julesz, B., & van Essen, D. (1986). Single unit responses to static and dynamic texture patterns in macaque V2 and V1 cortex. *Investigative Ophthalmology and Visual Science, 27*, 18.

DeYoe, E.A., & van Essen, D.C. (1985). Segregation of efferent connections and receptive field properties in visual area V2 of the macaque. *Nature, 317*, 58–61.

Diamond, R., & Carey, S. (1986). Why faces are and are not special: An effect of expertise. *Journal of Experimental Psychology: General, 115*, 107–117.

Dienes, Z., & McLeod, P. (1993). How to catch a cricket ball. *Perception, 22*, 1427–1439.

Dijkstra, T.M.H., Schöner, G., & Gielen, C.C.A.M. (1994). Temporal stability of the action-perception cycle for postural control in a moving visual environment. *Experimental Brain Research, 97*, 477–486.

Dittrich, W., Gilbert, F.S., Green, P.R., McGregor, P.K., & Grewcock, D. (1993). Imperfect mimicry: A pigeon's perspective. *Proceedings of the Royal Society of London, B, 251*, 195–200.

Dittrich, W.H., & Lea, S.E.G. (1994). Visual perception of intentional motion. *Perception, 23*, 253–268.

Douglas, R.H., Collett, T.S., & Wagner, H.-J. (1986). Accommodation in anuran amphibia and its role in depth vision. *Journal of Comparative Physiology, 158*, 133–143.

Dowling, J.E. (1968). Synaptic organization of the frog retina: An electron microscopic analysis comparing the retinas of frogs and primates. *Proceedings of the Royal Society of London, B, 170*, 205–228.

Duffy, C.J., & Wurtz, R.H. (1991). Sensitivity of MST neurons to optic flow stimuli. I. A continuum of response selectivity to large-field stimuli. *Journal of Neurophysiology, 65*, 1329–1345.

Duncker, K. (1929). Über induzierte Bewegung (Ein Beitrag zur Theorie optisch wahrgenommener Bewegung). *Psychologische Forschung, 12,* 180–259. Translated and abridged as "Induced Motion" in W.D. Ellis (Ed.), *A source book of Gestalt psychology.* London: Routledge and Kegan Paul (1955).

Eagle, R.A., & Rogers, B.J. (1996). Motion detection is limited by element density not spatial frequency. *Vision Research, 36,* 545–558.

Ebbesen, E.B., Parker, S., & Konĕcni, V.J. (1977). Laboratory and field analyses of decisions involving risk. *Journal of Experimental Psychology: Human Perception and Performance, 3,* 576–589.

Edelman, S. (1995). Representation, similarity and the chorus of prototypes. *Minds and Machines, 5,* 45–68.

Edelman, S., & Bülthoff, H.H. (1992). Orientation dependence in the recognition of familiar and novel views of three-dimensional objects. *Vision Research, 32,* 2385–2400.

Edwards, A.S. (1946). Body sway and vision. *Journal of Experimental Psychology, 36,* 526–535.

Edwards, D.P., Purpura, K.P., & Kaplan, E. (1995). Contrast sensitivity and spatial frequency response of primate cortical neurons in and around the cytochrome oxidase blobs. *Vision Research, 35,* 1501–1523.

Egelhaaf, M. (1985). On the neuronal basis of figure-ground discrimination by relative motion in the visual system of the fly. III. Possible input circuitries and behavioural significance of the FD-cells. *Biological Cybernetics, 52,* 267–280.

Egelhaaf, M., Hausen, K., Reichardt, W., & Wehrhahn, C. (1989). Visual course control in flies relies on neuronal computation of object and background motion. *Trends in Neuroscience, 11,* 351–358.

Eisner, T., Silberglied, R.E., Aneshansley, D., Carrel, J.E., & Howland, H.C. (1969). Ultraviolet video-viewing: The television camera as an insect eye. *Science, 146,* 1172–1174.

Ekman, P. (1978). Facial signs: Facts, fantasies and possibilities. In T. Sebeok (Ed.), *Sight, sound and sense.* Bloomington, IN: Indiana University Press.

Ekman, P. (1979). About brows: Emotional and conversational signals. In M. von Cranach, K. Foppa, W. Lepenies, & D. Ploog (Eds.), *Human ethology.* Cambridge, UK: Cambridge University Press.

Ekman, P. (1982). *Emotion and the human face* (2nd edn.). Cambridge, UK: Cambridge University Press,.

Ekman, P. (1992). Facial expressions of emotion: An old controversy and new findings. *Philosophical Transactions of the Royal Society of London, B, 335,* 63–69.

Ekman, P. (1994). Strong evidence for universals in facial expressions: A reply to Russell's mistaken critique. *Psychological Bulletin, 115,* 268–287.

Ekman, P., & Friesen, W.V. (1978). *Facial action coding system.* Palo Alto, CA: Consulting Psychologists Press.

Ekman, P., & Friesen, W.V. (1982a). Felt, false and miserable smiles. *Journal of Nonverbal Behaviour, 6,* 238–252.

Ekman, P., & Friesen, W. (1982b). Measuring facial movement with the Facial Action Coding System. In P. Ekman (Ed.), *Emotion in the human face* (2nd edn.). Cambridge, UK: Cambridge University Press.

Ekman, P., Friesen, W.V., & Ellsworth, P. (1982). Does the face provide accurate information? In P. Ekman (Ed.), *Emotion in the human face* (2nd edn.). Cambridge, UK: Cambridge University Press.

Ekman, P., & Oster, H. (1982). Review of research, 1970–1980. In P. Ekman (Ed.), *Emotion in the human face* (2nd edn.). Cambridge, UK: Cambridge University Press.

Ellard, C.G., Goodale, M.A., & Timney, B. (1984). Distance estimation in the Mongolian gerbil: The role of dynamic depth cues. *Behavioural Brain Research, 14,* 29–39.

Ellis, A.W., Young, A.W., Flude, B.M., & Hay, D.C. (1987). Repetition priming of faces recognition. *Quarterly Journal of Experimental Psychology, 39A,* 193–210.

Emerson, R.C., Bergen, J.R., & Adelson, E.H. (1992). Directionally selective complex cells and the computation of motion energy in cat visual cortex. *Vision Research, 32,* 203–218.

Enlow, D.H. (1982). *Handbook of facial growth.* Philadelphia, PA: W.B. Saunders.

Enroth-Cugell, C., & Robson, J.G. (1966). The contrast sensitivity of retinal ganglion cells of the cat. *Journal of Physiology, 187,* 517–552.

Erkelens, C. (1988). Fusional limits for a large random-dot stereogram. *Vision Research, 28,* 345–353.

Ewert, J.P. (1974). The neural basis of visually guided behaviour. *Scientific American, 230,* March, 34–49.

Fagan, J. (1979). The origins of facial pattern recognition. In M.H. Bornstein & W. Keesen (Eds.), *Psychological development from infancy: Image to intention.* Hillsdale, NJ: Lawrence Erlbaum Associates Inc.

Fechner, G.T. (1860). *Elemente der Psychophysik.* Leipzig, Germany: Brechtkopf and Härtel.

Feldman, J.A. (1985). Four frames suffice: A provisional model of vision and space. *Behavioural and Brain Sciences, 8*, 265–289.

Fender, D.H., & Julesz, B. (1967). Extension of Panum's fusional area in binocularly stabilized vision. *Journal of the Optical Society of America, 57*, 819–830.

Ferrera, V.P., Nealey, T.A., & Maunsell, J.H.R. (1992). Mixed parvocellular and magnocellular geniculate signals in visual area V4. *Nature, 358*, 756–758.

Ferster, D. (1981). A comparison of binocular depth mechanisms in areas 17 and 18 of the cat visual cortex. *Journal of Physiology, 311*, 623–655.

Ferster, D., & Koch, C. (1987). Neuronal connections underlying orientation selectivity in cat visual cortex. *Trends in Neuroscience, 12*, 487–492.

Fetz, E.E. (1992). Are movement parameters recognizably coded in the activity of single neurons? *Behavioural and Brain Sciences, 15*, 679–690.

Field, D.J. (1987). Relations between the statistics of natural images and the response properties of cortical cells. *Journal of the Optical Society of America, A4*, 2379–2394.

Field, D.J., Hayes, A., & Hess, R.F. (1993). Contour integration by the human visual system: Evidence for a local "association field". *Vision Research, 33*, 173–193.

Field, T.M., Woodson, R., Greenberg, R., & Cohen, D. (1982). Discrimination and imitation of facial expressions by neonates. *Science, 281*, 179–181.

Fishman, M.C., & Michael, C.R. (1973). Integration of auditory information in the cat's visual cortex. *Vision Research, 13*, 1415–1419.

Fitch, H.L., Tuller, B., & Turvey, M.T. (1982). The Bernstein Perspective. III. Timing of coordinative structures with special reference to perception. In J.A.S. Kelso (Ed.), *Human motor behaviour: An introduction.* Hillsdale, NJ: Lawrence Erlbaum Associates Inc.

Flanagan, P., Cavanagh, P., & Favreau, O.E. (1990). Independent orientation-selective mechanisms for the cardinal directions of colour space. *Vision Research, 30*, 769–778.

Fleet, D.J., Jepson, A.D., & Jenkin, M.R.M. (1991). Phase-based disparity measurement. *Computer Vision, Graphics and Image Processing: Image Understanding, 53*, 198–210.

Flin, R., & Dziurawiec, S. (1989). Developmental factors in face processing. In A.W. Young & W.D. Ellis (Eds.), *Handbook of research on face processing.* Amsterdam: North Holland.

Fodor, J.A. (1983). *The modularity of mind.* Cambridge, MA: MIT Press.

Fodor, J.A., & Pylyshyn, Z.W. (1981). How direct is visual perception? Some reflections on Gibson's "Ecological Approach". *Cognition, 9*, 139–196.

Fodor, J.A., & Pylyshyn, Z.W. (1988). Connectionism and cognitive architecture: A critical analysis. *Cognition, 28*, 3–71.

Foley, J.M. (1980). Binocular distance perception. *Psychological Review, 87*, 411–435.

Foley, J.M., & Boynton, G.M. (1993). Forward pattern masking and adaptation: Effects of duration, inter-stimulus interval, contrast, and spatial and temporal frequency. *Vision Research, 33*, 959–980.

Fox, R., Lehmkuhle, S.W., & Westendorff, D.H. (1976). Falcon visual acuity. *Science, 192*, 263–265.

Freeman, R.D., & Ohzawa, I. (1990). On the neurophysiological organization of binocular vision. *Vision Research, 30*, 1661–1676.

Freeman, T.C.A., Harris, M.G., & Tyler, P.A. (1994). Human sensitivity to temporal proximity: The role of spatial and temporal speed gradients. *Perception and Psychophysics, 55*, 689–699.

Friedman, M.B. (1975). Visual control of head movements during avian locomotion. *Nature, 255*, 67–69.

Frisby, J.P. (1979). *Seeing: Illusion, brain and mind.* Oxford: Oxford University Press.

Frisby, J.P., & Mayhew, J.E.W. (1980). Spatial frequency tuned channels: Implications for structure and function from psychophysical and computational studies of stereopsis. *Philosophical Transactions of the Royal Society of London, B, 290*, 95–116.

Frisch, H.L., & Julesz, B. (1966). Figure-ground perception and random geometry. *Perception and Psychophysics, 1*, 389–398.

Frost, B.J. (1978). The optokinetic basis of head-bobbing in the pigeon. *Journal of Experimental Biology, 74*, 187–195.

Frost, B.J., & Nakayama, K. (1983). Single visual neurons code opposing motion independent of direction. *Science, 220*, 744–745.

Frost, B.J., Scilley, P.L., & Wong, S.C.P. (1981). Moving background patterns reveal double opponency of directionally specific pigeon tectal neurons. *Experimental Brain Research, 43*, 173–185.

Galton, F. (1907). *Inquiries into human faculty and its development.* London: J.M. Dent and Sons Ltd.

Garnham, A. (1987). *Artificial intelligence: An introduction.* London: Routledge and Kegan Paul.

Gaudiano, P. (1994). Simulation of X and Y retinal ganglion cell behaviour with a nonlinear push-pull model of spatiotemporal retinal processing. *Vision Research, 34,* 1767–1784.

Georgeson, M.A. (1980). The perceived spatial frequency, contrast and orientation of illusory gratings. *Perception, 9,* 695–712.

Georgeson, M.A. (1992). Human vision combines oriented filters to compute edges. *Proceedings of the Royal Society of London, B, 249,* 235–245.

Georgeson, M.A. (1994). From filters to features: Location, orientation, contrast and blur. In *Higher order processing in the visual system* (Ciba Foundation Symposium 184, pp.147–165). Chichester, UK: Wiley.

Georgeson, M.A., & Georgeson, J.M. (1987). Facilitation and masking of briefly presented gratings: Time-course and contrast dependence. *Vision Research, 27,* 369–379.

Georgeson, M.A., & Harris, M.G. (1984). Spatial selectivity of contrast adaptation: Models and data. *Vision Research, 24,* 729–741.

Georgeson, M.A., & Harris, M.G. (1990). The temporal range of motion sensing and motion perception. *Vision Research, 30,* 615–619.

Georgopoulos, A.P. (1991). Higher order motor control. *Annual Review of Neuroscience, 14,* 361–378.

Gibson, E.J., Gibson, J.J., Smith, O.W., & Flock, H.R. (1959). Motion parallax as a determinant of perceived depth. *Journal of Experimental Psychology, 58,* 40–51.

Gibson, E.J., & Walk, R.D. (1960). The "visual cliff". *Scientific American, 202,* April, 64–71.

Gibson, J.J. (1947). *Motion picture testing and research.* AAF Aviation Psychology Research Report No 7. Washington, DC: Government Printing Office.

Gibson, J.J. (1950a). *The perception of the visual world.* Boston, MA: Houghton Mifflin.

Gibson, J.J. (1950b). The perception of visual surfaces. *American Journal of Psychology, 63,* 367–384.

Gibson, J.J. (1961). Ecological optics. *Vision Research, 1,* 253–262.

Gibson, J.J. (1966). *The senses considered as perceptual systems.* Boston, MA: Houghton Mifflin.

Gibson, J.J. (1975). *The implications of experiments on the perception of space and motion.* Final Report to Office of Naval Research, Arlington, VA.

Gibson, J.J. (1979). *The ecological approach to visual perception.* Boston, MA: Houghton Mifflin.

Gibson, J.J., & Cornsweet, J. (1952). The perceived slant of visual surfaces—optical and geographical. *Journal of Experimental Psychology, 44,* 11–15.

Gibson, J.J., & Dibble, F.N. (1952). Exploratory experiments on the stimulus conditions for the perception of a visual surface. *Journal of Experimental Psychology, 43,* 414–419.

Gibson, J.J., & Pick, A.D. (1963). Perception of another person's looking behaviour. *American Journal of Psychology, 76,* 386–394.

Gibson, J.J., & Radner, M. (1937). Adaptation, aftereffect and contrast in the perception of tilted lines. I. Quantitative studies. *Journal of Experimental Psychology, 20,* 453–467.

Gibson, J.J., & Waddell, D. (1952). Homogeneous retinal stimulation and visual perception. *American Journal of Psychology, 65,* 263–270.

Gilbert, C.D. (1995). Dynamic properties of adult visual cortex. In M. S. Gazzaniga (Ed.), *The cognitive neurosciences.* Cambridge, MA: MIT Press.

Gilbert, C.D., & Wiesel, T.N. (1990). The influence of contextual stimuli on the orientation selectivity of cells in primary visual cortex of the cat. *Vision Research, 30,* 1689–1701.

Gilbert, C.D., & Wiesel, T.N. (1992). Receptive field dynamics in adult primary visual cortex. *Nature, 356,* 150–152.

Gilden, D.L., & Proffitt, D.R. (1989). Understanding collision dynamics. *Journal of Experimental Psychology: Human Perception and Performance, 15,* 372–383.

Gilden, D.L., & Proffitt, D.R. (1994). Heuristic judgment of mass ratio in two-body collisions. *Perception and Psychophysics, 56,* 708–720.

Gluhbegovic, N., & Williams, T.H. (1980). *The human brain: A photographic atlas.* Hagerstown, MD: Harper & Row.

Golani, I. (1976). Homeostatic motor processes in mammalian interactions: A choreography of display. In P.P.G. Bateson & P.H. Klopfer (Eds.), *Perspectives in ethology* (Vol. II, pp.69–134). New York: Plenum.

Goodale, M.A., Ellard, C.G., & Booth, L. (1990). The role of image size and retinal motion in the computation of absolute distance by the Mongolian gerbil (*Meriones unguiculatus*). *Vision Research, 30,* 399–413.

Goodale, M.A., & Milner, A.D. (1992). Separate visual pathways for perception and action. *Trends in Neuroscience, 15,* 20–25.

Goodale, M.A., Milner, A.D., Jakobson, L.S., & Carey, D.P. (1991). A neurological dissociation between perceiving objects and grasping them. *Nature, 349,* 154–156.

Goodman, L.J. (1965). The role of certain optomotor reactions in regulating stability in the rolling plane during flight in the desert locust *Schistocerca gregaria*. *Journal of Experimental Biology, 42*, 385–407.

Goren, C.C., Sarty, M., & Wu, R.W.K. (1975). Visual following and pattern discrimination of face-like stimuli by newborn infants. *Pediatrics, 56*, 544–549.

Graham, N., & Nachmias, J. (1971). Detection of grating patterns containing two spatial frequencies: A comparison of single-channel and multiple-channel models. *Vision Research, 11*, 251–259.

Graham, N.V.S. (1989). *Visual pattern analyzers*. Oxford: Oxford University Press.

Gray, C.M., König, P., Engel, A.K., & Singer, W. (1989). Oscillatory responses in cat visual cortex exhibit inter-columnar synchronization which reflects global stimulus properties. *Nature, 338*, 334–337.

Green, D.G. (1986). The search for the site of visual adaptation. *Vision Research, 26*, 1417–1429.

Green, P.R., Davies, M.N.O., & Thorpe, P.H. (1994). Head-bobbing and head orientation during landing flights of pigeons. *Journal of Comparative Physiology, 174*, 249–256.

Gregory, R.L. (1972). *Eye and brain* (2nd edn.). World University Library.

Gregory, R.L. (1973). The confounded eye. In R.L. Gregory & E.H. Gombrich (Eds.), *Illusion in nature and art*. London: Duckworth.

Gregory, R.L. (1980). Perceptions as hypotheses. *Philosophical Transactions of the Royal Society of London, B, 290*, 181–197.

Griffin, D.R. (1958). *Listening in the dark*. New Haven, CT: Yale University Press.

Grimson, W.E.L. (1981). *From images to surfaces*. Cambridge, MA: MIT Press.

Grinvald, A., Lieke, E.E., Frostig, R.D., & Hildesheim, R. (1994). Cortical point-spread function and long-range lateral interactions revealed by real-time optical imaging of macaque monkey primary visual cortex. *Journal of Neuroscience, 14*, 2545–2568.

Grosof, D.H., Shapley, R.M., & Hawken, M.J. (1993). Macaque V1 neurons can signal "illusory" contours. *Nature, 365*, 550–552.

Grusser, O.-J., Krizic, A., & Weiss, L.-R. (1987). Afterimage movement during saccades in the dark. *Vision Research, 27*, 215–226.

Gulick, W.L., & Lawson, R.B. (1976). *Human stereopsis: A psychophysical analysis*. New York: Oxford University Press.

Gurfinkel, V.S., Kots, Ya.M., Krinsky, V.I., Pal'tsev, Ye, I., Feldman, A.G., Tsetlin, M.L., & Shik, M.L. (1971). Concerning tuning before movement. In I.M. Gelfand, V.S. Gurfinkel, S.E. Fomin, & M.L. Tsetlin (Eds.), *Models of the structural-functional organisation of certain biological systems*. Cambridge, MA: MIT Press.

Guzman, A. (1968). Decomposition of a visual scene into three-dimensional bodies. *AFIPS Proceedings of the Fall Joint Computer Conference, 33*, 291–304.

Hailman, J.P. (1977). *Optical signals: Animal communication and light*. Bloomington, IN: Indiana University Press.

Hammett, S.T., & Smith, A.T. (1992). Two temporal channels or three? A re-evaluation. *Vision Research, 32*, 285–291.

Hammond, P., Mouat, G.SV., & Smith, A.T. (1986). Motion after-effects in cat striate cortex elicited by moving texture. *Vision Research, 26*, 1055–1060.

Hampton, R.R. (1994). Sensitivity to information specifying the line of gaze of humans in sparrows (*Passer domesticus*). *Behaviour, 130*, 41–51.

Hancock, P.J.B., Burton, A.M., & Bruce, V. (1996). Face processing: Human perception and principal components analysis. *Memory and Cognition, 24*, 26–40.

Harkness, L. (1977). Chameleons use accommodation cues to judge distance. *Nature, 267*, 346–349.

Harris, J.P., & Gregory, R.L. (1973). Fusion and rivalry of illusory contours. *Perception, 2*, 235–247.

Harris, M.G. (1980). Velocity sensitivity of the flicker to pattern sensitivity ratio in human vision. *Vision Research, 20*, 687–691.

Harris, M.G. (1986). The perception of moving stimuli: A model of spatiotemporal coding in human vision. *Vision Research, 26*, 1281–1287.

Harris, M.G. (1994). Optic and retinal flow. In A.T. Smith & R.J. Snowden (Eds.), *Visual detection of motion*. London: Academic Press.

Hartline, H.K., & Graham, C.H. (1932). Nerve impulses from single receptors in the eye. *Journal of Cellular and Comparative Physiology, 1*, 227–295.

Hartline, H.K., Wagner, H.G., & Ratliff, F. (1956). Inhibition in the eye of *Limulus*. *Journal of General Physiology, 39*, 651–673.

Haxby, J.V., Grady, C.L., Horwitz, B., Ungerleider, L.G., Mishkin, M., Carson, R.E., Herscovitch, P., Schapiro, M.B., & Rapoport, S.I. (1991). Dissociation of object and spatial visual processing pathways in human extrastriate cortex. *Proceedings of the National Academy of Sciences of the USA, 88*, 1621–1625.

He, Z.J., & Nakayama, K. (1994). Apparent motion determined by surface layout not by disparity or three-dimensional distance. *Nature, 367*, 173–175.

Hebb, D.O. (1949). *The organisation of behaviour*. New York: Wiley.

Heckenmuller, E.G. (1965). Stabilization of the retinal image: A review of method, effects and theory. *Psychological Bulletin, 63*, 157–169.

Heeger, D.J. (1992a). Normalization of cell responses in cat striate cortex. *Visual Neuroscience, 9*, 181–197.

Heeger, D.J. (1992b). Half-squaring in responses of cat striate cells. *Visual Neuroscience, 9*, 427–443.

Heider, F., & Simmel, M. (1944). An experimental study of apparent behaviour. *American Journal of Psychology, 57*, 243–259.

Heiligenberg, W. (1973). Electrolocation of objects in the electric fish *Eigenmannia*. *Journal of Comparative Physiology, 87*, 137–164.

Heisenberg, M., & Wolf, R. (1988). Reafferent control of optomotor yaw torque in *Drosophila melanogaster*. *Journal of Comparative Physiology, 163*, 373–388.

Heitger, F., Rosenthaler, L., von der Heydt, R., Peterhans, E., & Kubler, O. (1992). Simulation of neural contour mechanisms: From simple to end-stopped cells. *Vision Research, 32*, 963–981.

Helmholtz, H. von (1866). *Treatise on physiological optics, Vol. III* (trans. 1925 from the third German edition, ed. J.P.C. Southall). New York: Dover (1962).

Hendry, S.H.C., & Yoshioka, T. (1994). A neurochemically distinct third channel in the macaque dorsal lateral geniculate nucleus. *Science, 264*, 575–577.

Hertz, M. (1928). Figural perception in the jay bird. *Zeitschrift für vergleichende Physiologie, 7*, 144–194 (trans. and abridged in W.D. Ellis, *A source book of Gestalt psychology*). London: Routledge and Kegan Paul (1955).

Hertz, M. (1929). Figural perception in bees. *Zeitschrift für vergleichende Physiologie, 8*, 693–748 (trans. and abridged in W.D. Ellis, *A source book of Gestalt psychology*). London: Routledge and Kegan Paul (1955).

Hess, R.F., & Holliday, I.E. (1992). The coding of spatial position by the human visual system: Effects of spatial scale and contrast. *Vision Research, 32*, 1085–1097.

Hess, R.F., & Snowden, R.J. (1992). Temporal properties of human visual filters: Number, shapes and spatial covariation. *Vision Research, 32*, 47–59.

Hess, U., & Kleck, R.E. (1990). Differentiating emotion elicited and deliberate facial expressions. *European Journal of Social Psychology, 20*, 369–385.

Heuer, H. (1993). Estimates of time to contact based on changing size and changing target vergence. *Perception, 22*, 549–563.

Heywood, C.A., & Cowey, A. (1987). On the role of cortical area V4 in the discrimination of hue and pattern in macaque monkeys. *Journal of Neuroscience, 7*, 2601–2617.

Hildreth, E.C. (1984a). Computations underlying the measurement of visual motion. *Artificial Intelligence, 23*, 309–354.

Hildreth, E.C. (1984b). *The measurement of visual motion*. Cambridge, MA: MIT Press.

Hildreth, E.C., & Koch, C. (1987). The analysis of visual motion: From computational theory to neuronal mechanisms. *Annual Review of Neuroscience, 10*, 477–533.

Hill, H., & Bruce, V. (1993). Independent effects of lighting, orientation, and stereopsis on the hollow-face illusion. *Perception, 22*, 887–897.

Hill, H., & Bruce, V. (1994). A comparison between the hollow-face and hollow-potato illusions. *Perception, 23*, 1335–1337.

Hill, H., & Bruce, V. (in press). Effects of lighting on the perception of face surfaces. *Journal of Experimental Psychology: Human Perception and Performance*.

Hill, H., Bruce, V., & Akamatsu, S. (1995). Perceiving the sex and race of faces: Role of shape and colour. *Proceedings of the Royal Society of London, B, 261*, 367–373.

Hinton, G.E. (1981). A parallel computation that assigns canonical object-based frames of reference. In *Proceedings of the International Joint Conference on Artificial Intelligence*. Vancouver, Canada.

Hinton, G.E. (1984). Parallel computations for controlling an arm. *Journal of Motor Behaviour, 16*, 171–194.

Hinton, G.E. (1986). Learning distributed representations of concepts. In *Proceedings of the Eighth Annual Conference of the Cognitive Science Society*. Amherst, MA.

Hinton, G.E. (1989). Connectionist learning procedures. *Artificial Intelligence, 40*, 185–234.

Hinton, G.E., & Anderson, J.A. (Eds.). (1981). *Parallel models of associative memory*. Hillsdale, NJ: Lawrence Erlbaum Associates Inc.

Hinton, G.E., & Sejnowski, T.J. (1986). Learning and relearning in Boltzmann machines. In D.E. Rumelhart, J.L. McClelland, & The PDP Research Group (Eds.), *Parallel distributed processing: Explorations in the microstructure of cognition, Vol. 1: Foundations*. Cambridge, MA: MIT Press.

Hintzman, D.L. (1986). "Schema abstraction" in a multiple-trace memory model. *Psychological Review, 93*, 411–428.

Hochberg, J. (1950). Figure-ground reversal as a function of visual satiation. *Journal of Experimental Psychology, 40*, 682–686.

Hochberg, J. (1968). In the mind's eye. In R.N. Haber (Ed.), *Contemporary theory and research in visual perception*. London: Holt, Rinehart & Winston.

Hochberg, J. (1978). *Perception* (2nd edn.). Englewood Cliffs, NJ: Prentice Hall.

Hochberg, J., & Brooks, V. (1960). The psychophysics of form: Reversible perspective drawings of spatial objects. *American Journal of Psychology, 73*, 337–354.

Hoffman, D.D., & Richards, W.A. (1984). Parts of recognition. *Cognition, 18*, 65–96.

Hollands, M.A., Marple-Horvat, D.E., Henkes, S., & Rowan, A.K. (1995). Human eye movements during visually guided stepping. *Journal of Motor Behaviour, 27*, 155–163.

Holliday, I.E., & Anderson, S.J. (1994). Different processes underlie the detection of second-order motion at low and high temporal frequencies. *Proceedings of the Royal Society of London, B, 257*, 165–173.

Honda, H. (1991). The time courses of visual mislocalization and of extraretinal eye position signals at the time of vertical saccades. *Vision Research, 31*, 1915–1921.

Honda, H. (1993). Saccade-contingent displacement of the apparent position of visual stimuli flashed on a dimly illuminated structured background. *Vision Research, 33*, 709–716.

Horn, B.K.P., & Brooks, M.J. (Eds.) (1989). *Shape from shading*. Cambridge, MA: MIT Press.

Horn, B.K.P., & Schunck, B.G. (1981). Determining optical flow. *Artificial Intelligence, 17*, 185–203.

Horn, G., & Hill, R.M. (1969). Modification of receptive fields of cells in the visual cortex occurring spontaneously and associated with bodily tilt. *Nature, 221*, 186–188.

Horton, J.C., & Hubel, D.H. (1981). Regular patchy distribution of cytochrome oxidase staining in primary visual cortex of macaque monkey. *Nature, 292*, 762–764.

Howard, I.P., & Rogers, B.J. (1995). *Binocular vision and stereopsis*. Oxford: Oxford University Press.

Howarth, C.I., Routledge, D.A., & Repetto-Wright, R. (1974). An analysis of road accidents involving child pedestrians. *Ergonomics, 17*, 319–330.

Hubbard, A.W., & Seng, C.N. (1954). Visual movements of batters. *Research Quarterly, 25*, 42–57.

Hubel, D.H., & Wiesel, T.N. (1959). Receptive fields of single neurons in the cat's striate cortex. *Journal of Physiology, 148*, 574–591.

Hubel, D.H., & Wiesel, T.N. (1962). Receptive fields, binocular interaction and functional architecture in the cat's visual cortex. *Journal of Physiology, 160*, 106–154.

Hubel, D.H., & Wiesel, T.N. (1968). Receptive fields and functional architecture of monkey striate cortex. *Journal of Physiology, 195*, 215–243.

Hubel, D.H., & Wiesel, T.N. (1970). Stereopsis vision in the macaque monkey. *Nature, 225*, 41–42.

Hubel, D.H., & Wiesel, T.N. (1974). Sequence regularity and geometry of orientation columns in the monkey striate cortex. *Journal of Comparative Neurology, 158*, 267–294.

Hubel, D.H., & Wiesel, T.N. (1977). Functional architecture of macaque monkey visual cortex. *Proceedings of the Royal Society of London, B, 198*, 1–59.

Huffman, D.A. (1971). Impossible objects as nonsense sentences. In B. Meltzer & D. Michie (Eds.), *Machine intelligence 6*. Edinburgh: Edinburgh University Press.

Hummel, J.E., & Biederman, I. (1992). Dynamic binding in a neural network for shape recognition. *Psychological Review, 99*, 480–517.

Humphrey, G.K., & Jolicoeur, P. (1993). An examination of the effects of axis foreshortening, monocular depth cues, and visual field on object identification. *Quarterly Journal of Experimental Psychology, 46A*, 137–159.

Humphrey, G.K., & Khan, S.C. (1992). Recognizing novel views of three-dimensional objects. *Canadian Journal of Psychology, 46*, 170–190.

Humphrey, N.K., & Keeble, G.R. (1974). The reactions of monkeys to "fearsome" pictures. *Nature, 251*, 500–502.

Humphreys, G.W. (1984). Shape constancy: The effects of changing shape orientation and the effects of changing focal features. *Perception and Psychophysics, 35*, 361–371.

Humphreys, G.W., & Bruce, V. (1989). *Visual cognition: Computational, experimental and neuropsychological perspectives*. Hove, UK: Lawrence Erlbaum Associates Ltd.

Ikeda, H., & Wright, M.J. (1972). Functional organization of the periphery effect in retinal ganglion cells. *Vision Research, 12*, 1857–1879.

Ittelson, W.H. (1952). *The Ames demonstrations in perception*. Princeton, NJ: Princeton University Press.

Jackson, J.F., Ingram, W., & Campbell, H.W. (1976). The dorsal pigmentation pattern of snakes as an antipredator strategy: A multivariate approach. *American Naturalist, 110*, 1029–1053.

Jacobs, G.H. (1986). Cones and opponency. *Vision Research, 26*, 1533–1541.

Jacobs, G.H. (1993). The distribution and nature of colour vision among the mammals. *Biological Reviews, 68*, 413–471.

Jain, R., Kasturi, R., & Schunk, B.G. (1995). *Machine vision*. New York: McGraw-Hill.

Johansson, G. (1973). Visual perception of biological motion and a model for its analysis. *Perception and Psychophysics, 14*, 201–211.

Johansson, G. (1975). Visual motion perception. *Scientific American, 232*, June, 76–89.

Johnson, M.H., Bolhuis, J.J., & Horn, G. (1985). Interaction between acquired preferences and developing predispositions during imprinting. *Animal Behaviour, 33*, 1000–1006.

Johnson, M.H., Dziurawiec, S., Ellis, H., & Morton, J. (1991). Newborns' preferential tracking of face-like stimuli and its subsequent decline. *Cognition, 40*, 1–19.

Johnson, M.H., & Horn, G. (1988). Development of filial preferences in dark-reared chicks. *Animal Behaviour, 36*, 675–683.

Johnson, M.H., & Morton, J. (1991). *Biology and cognitive development: The case of face recognition*. Oxford: Blackwell.

Johnston, A., & Clifford, C.W.G. (1995). A unified account of three apparent motion illusions. *Vision Research, 35*, 1109–1123.

Johnston, A., McOwan, P.W., & Buxton, H. (1992). A computational model of the analysis of some first-order and second-order motion patterns by simple and complex cells. *Proceedings of the Royal Society of London, B, 250*, 297–306.

Johnston, E.B., Cumming, B.G., & Landy, M.S. (1994). Integration of stereopsis and motion shape cues. *Vision Research, 34*, 2259–2275.

Johnston, E.B., Cumming, B.G., & Parker, A.J. (1993). Integration of depth modules: Stereopsis and texture. *Vision Research, 33*, 813–826.

Jones, J.P., & Palmer, L.A. (1987). An evaluation of the two-dimensional Gabor filter model of simple receptive fields in cat striate cortex. *Journal of Neurophysiology, 58*, 1233–1258.

Jones, R.K., & Lee, D.N. (1981). Why two eyes are better than one: The two views of binocular vision. *Journal of Experimental Psychology: Human Perception and Performance, 7*, 30–40.

Jones, R.M., & Tulunay-Keesey, U. (1980). Phase selectivity of spatial frequency channels. *Journal of the Optical Society of America, 70*, 66–70.

Judge, S.J., & Bradford, C.M. (1988). Adaptation to telestereoscopic viewing measured by one-handed ball-catching performance. *Perception, 17*, 783–802.

Julesz, B. (1965). Texture and visual perception. *Scientific American, 212*, February, 38–48.

Julesz, B. (1971). *Foundations of cyclopean perception*. Chicago: University of Chicago Press.

Julesz, B. (1975). Experiments in the visual perception of texture. *Scientific American, 232*, April, 34–43.

Julesz, B. (1981). Textons, the elements of texture perception, and their interactions. *Nature, 290*, 91–97.

Julesz, B. (1984). A brief outline of the texton theory of human vision. *Trends in Neurosciences, 6*, 41–45.

Julesz, B., Frisch, H.L., Gilbert, E.N., & Shepp, L.A. (1973). Inability of humans to discriminate between visual textures that agree in second-order statistics—revisited. *Perception, 2*, 391–405.

Julesz, B., & Miller, J. (1975). Independent spatial-frequency-tuned channels in binocular fusion and rivalry. *Perception, 4*, 125–143.

Kalmus, H. (1949). Optomotor responses in *Drosophila* and *Musca*. *Physiologia Comparata et Oecologia, 1*, 127–147.

Kanade, T. (1981). Recovery of the three-dimensional shape of an object from a single view. *Artificial Intelligence, 17*, 409–460.

Kanisza, G. (1976). Subjective contours. *Scientific American, 234*(4), 48–52.

Kaplan, E., & Shapley, R.M. (1986). The primate retina contains two types of ganglion cells, with high and low contrast sensitivity. *Proceedings of the National Academy of Sciences of the USA, 83*, 2755–2757.

Kaufman, L. (1974). *Sight and mind: An introduction to visual perception*. New York: Oxford University Press.

Kay, B.A., Saltzman, E.L., & Kelso, J.A.S. (1991). Steady-state and perturbed rhythmical movements: A dynamical analysis. *Journal of Experimental Psychology: Human Perception and Performance, 17*, 183–197.

Kayargadde, V., & Martens, J.B. (1994a). Estimation of edge parameters and image blur using polynomial transforms. *CVGIP: Graphical Models and Image Processing, 56*, 442–461.

Kayargadde, V., & Martens, J. B. (1994b). Estimation of perceived image blur. *IPO Annual Progress Report, 29,* 66–71. Institute for Perception Research, Eindhoven, Holland.

Kelly, D.H. (1979a). Motion and vision. I. Stabilized images of stationary gratings. *Journal of the Optical Society of America, 69,* 1266–1274.

Kelly, D.H. (1979b). Motion and vision. II. Stabilized spatio-temporal threshold surface. *Journal of the Optical Society of America, 69,* 1340–1349.

Kelly, D.H., & Burbeck, C.A. (1980). Motion and vision. III. Stabilized pattern adaptation. *Journal of the Optical Society of America, 70,* 1283–1289.

Kelso, J.A.S. (1995). *Dynamic patterns: The self-organization of brain and behaviour.* Cambridge, MA: MIT Press.

Kelso, J.A.S., Putnam, C.A., & Goodman, D. (1983). On the space-time structure of human inter-limb coordination. *Quarterly Journal of Experimental Psychology, 35A,* 347–375.

Kennedy, J.M. (1978). Illusory contours and the ends of lines. *Perception, 7,* 605–607.

Kettlewell, B. (1973). *The evolution of melanism.* Oxford: Oxford University Press.

Kilpatrick, F.P. (Ed.). (1952). *Human behaviour from the transactionalist point of view.* Princeton, NJ: Princeton University Press.

King, S.M., Dykeman, C., Redgrave, P., & Dean, P. (1992). Use of a distracting task to obtain defensive head movements to looming visual stimuli by human adults in a laboratory setting. *Perception, 21,* 245–259.

Kirchner, W.H., & Srinivasan, M.V. (1989). Freely flying honeybees use image motion to estimate object distance. *Naturwissenschaften, 76,* 281–282.

Kirschfeld, K. (1976). The resolution of lens and compound eyes. In F. Zettler & R. Weiler (Eds.), *Neural principles in vision.* Berlin: Springer.

Kleinke, C.L. (1986). Gaze and eye contact: A research review. *Psychological Bulletin, 100,* 78–100.

Knill, D.C. (1992). Perception of surface contours and surface shape: From computation to psychophysics. *Journal of the Optical Society of America, A9,* 1449–1464.

Koenderink, J.J. (1986). Optic flow. *Vision Research, 26,* 161–180.

Koenderink, J.J., & van Doorn, A.J. (1976). Local structure of movement parallax of the plane. *Journal of the Optical Society of America, 66,* 717–723.

Koenderink, J.J., & van Doorn, A.J. (1987). Representation of local geometry in the visual system. *Biological Cybernetics, 55,* 367–375.

Koffka, K. (1935). *Principles of Gestalt psychology.* New York: Harcourt Brace.

Köhler, W. (1947). *Gestalt psychology: An introduction to new concepts in modern psychology.* New York: Liveright Publishing Corporation.

Kohonen, T., Oja, E., & Lehtio, P. (1981). Storage and processing of information in distributed associative memory systems. In G.E. Hinton & J.A. Anderson (Eds.), *Parallel models of associative memory.* Hillsdale, NJ: Lawrence Erlbaum Associates Inc.

Konczak, J. (1994). Effects of optic flow on the kinematics of human gait—a comparison of young and older adults. *Journal of Motor Behaviour, 26,* 225–236.

Kovach, J.K. (1971). Interaction of innate and acquired: Colour preferences and early exposure learning in chicks. *Journal of Comparative and Physiological Psychology, 75,* 386–398.

Kozlowski, L.T., & Cutting, J.E. (1977). Recognizing the sex of a walker from a dynamic point-light display. *Perception and Psychophysics, 21,* 575–580.

Kozlowski, L.T., & Cutting, J.E. (1978). Recognizing the gender of walkers from point-lights mounted on ankles: Some second thoughts. *Perception and Psychophysics, 23,* p.459.

Kuffler, S.W. (1953). Discharge patterns and functional organization of mammalian retina. *Journal of Neurophysiology, 16,* 37–68.

Kulikowski, J.J., & King-Smith, P.E. (1973). Spatial arrangement of line, edge and grating detectors revealed by subthreshold summation. *Vision Research, 13,* 1455–1478.

Lacquaniti, F. (1989). Central representations of human limb movement as revealed by studies of drawing and handwriting. *Trends in Neuroscience, 12,* 287–291.

Land, E.H. (1977). The retinex theory of colour vision. *Scientific American, 237*(6), 108–128.

Land, M.F. (1968). Functional aspects of the optical and retinal organization of the mollusc eye. *Symposia of the Zoological Society of London, 23,* 75–96.

Land, M.F. (1981). Optics and vision in invertebrates. In H. Autrum (Ed.), *Comparative physiology and evolution of vision in invertebrates. B: Invertebrate visual centres and behaviour I.* Berlin: Springer.

Land, M.F., & Collett, T.S. (1974). Chasing behaviour of houseflies (*Fannia canicularis*): A description and analysis. *Journal of Comparative Physiology, 89*, 331–357.

Land, M.F., & Horwood, J. (1995). Which parts of the road guide steering? *Nature, 377*, 339–340.

Land, M.F., & Lee, D.N. (1994). Where we look when we steer. *Nature, 369*, 742–744.

Langley, K., Atherton, T.J., Wilson, R.G., & Larcombe, M.H.E. (1990). Vertical and horizontal disparities from phase. Proceedings of the first ECCV. *Springer Verlag Lecture Series in Computer Science, 427*, 315–325.

Langlois, J.H., & Roggman, L.A. (1990). Attractive faces are only average. *Psychological Science, 1*, 115–121.

Lappe, M., & Rauschecker, J.P. (1994). Heading detection from optic flow. *Nature, 369*, 712–713.

Laurent, M., & Thomson, J.A. (1988). The role of visual information in control of a constrained locomotion task. *Journal of Motor Behaviour, 20*, 17–37.

Lawson, R., & Humphreys, G.W. (1996). View-specificity in object processing: Evidence from picture matching. *Journal of Experimental Psychology: Human Perception and Performance, 22*, 395–416.

Lawson, R., Humphreys, G.W., & Watson, D. (1994). Object recognition under sequential viewing conditions: Evidence for viewpoint-specific recognition procedures. *Perception , 23*, 595–614.

Ledgeway, T. (1994). Adaptation to second-order motion results in a motion aftereffect for directionally-ambiguous test stimuli. *Vision Research, 34*, 2879–2889.

Ledgeway, T., & Smith, A.T. (1994). Evidence for separate motion-detecting mechanisms for first- and second-order motion in human vision. *Vision Research, 34*, 2727–2740.

Lee, D.N. (1976). A theory of visual control of braking based on information about time-to-collision. *Perception, 5*, 437–459.

Lee, D.N. (1977). The functions of vision. In H.L. Pick & E. Saltzman (Eds.), *Modes of perceiving and processing information*. Hillsdale, NJ: Lawrence Erlbaum Associates Inc.

Lee, D.N. (1980a). Visuo-motor coordination in space-time. In G.E. Stelmach & J. Requin (Eds.), *Tutorials in motor behaviour*. Amsterdam: North-Holland.

Lee, D.N. (1980b). The optic flow field: The foundation of vision. *Philosophical Transactions of the Royal Society of London, B, 290*, 169–179.

Lee, D.N., & Aronson, E. (1974). Visual proprioceptive control of standing in infants. *Perception and Psychophysics, 15*, 529–532.

Lee, D.N., Davies, M.N.O., Green, P.R., & van der Weel, F.R. (1993). Visual control of velocity of approach by pigeons when landing. *Journal of Experimental Biology, 180*, 85–104.

Lee, D.N., & Lishman, J.R. (1975). Visual proprioceptive control of stance. *Journal of Human Movement Studies, 1*, 87–95.

Lee, D.N., & Lishman, J.R. (1977). Visual control of locomotion. *Scandinavian Journal of Psychology, 18*, 224–230.

Lee, D.N., Lishman, J.R., & Thomson, J.A. (1982). Regulation of gait in long-jumping. *Journal of Experimental Psychology: Human Perception and Performance, 8*, 448–459.

Lee, D.N., & Reddish, P.E. (1981). Plummeting gannets: A paradigm of ecological optics. *Nature, 293*, 293–294.

Lee, D.N., Reddish, P.E., & Rand, D.T. (1991). Aerial docking by hummingbirds. *Naturwissenschaften, 78*, 526–527.

Lee, D.N., & Young, D.S. (1985). Visual timing of interceptive action. In D. Ingle, M. Jeannerod, & D.N. Lee (Eds.), *Brain mechanisms and spatial vision* (pp.1–30). Dordrecht: Martinus Nijhoff.

Lee, D.N., & Young, D.S. (1986). Gearing action to the environment. *Experimental Brain Research Series 15*. Berlin: Springer.

Lee, D.N., Young, D.S., & McLaughlin, C.M. (1984). A roadside simulation of crossing behaviour. *Ergonomics, 27*, 1271–1281.

Lee, D.N., Young, D.S., Reddish, P.E., Lough, S., & Clayton, T.M.H. (1983). Visual timing in hitting an accelerating ball. *Quarterly Journal of Experimental Psychology, 35A*, 333–346.

Lee, D.N., Young, D.S., & Rewt, D. (1992). How do somersaulters land on their feet? *Journal of Experimental Psychology: Human Perception and Performance, 18*, 1195–1202.

Legge, G.E., & Gu, Y. (1989). Stereopsis and contrast. *Vision Research, 29*, 989–1004.

Lehrer, M. (1991). Bees which turn back and look. *Naturwissenschaften, 78*, 274–276.

Lehrer, M., & Collett, T.S. (1994). Approaching and departing bees learn different cues to the distance of a landmark. *Journal of Comparative Physiology, 175*, 171–178.

Lehrer, M., & Srinivasan, M.V. (1993). Object detection by honeybees: Why do they land on edges? *Journal of Comparative Physiology, 173*, 23–32.

Lehrer, M., Srinivasan, M.V., & Zhang, S.W. (1990). Visual edge detection in the honeybee and its spectral properties. *Proceedings of the Royal Society of London, B, 238,* 321–330.

Lehrer, M., Srinivasan, M.V., Zhang, S.W., & Horridge, G.A. (1988). Motion cues provide the bee's visual world with a third dimension. *Nature, 332,* 356–357.

Lekhy, S.R., & Sejnowski, T.J. (1988). Network model of shape-from-shading: Neural function arises from both receptive and projective fields. *Nature, 333,* 452–454.

Lennie, P., Krauskopf, J., & Sclar, G. (1990). Chromatic mechanisms in striate cortex of macaque. *Journal of Neuroscience, 10,* 649–669.

Leslie, A.M. (1984). Spatiotemporal continuity and the perception of causality in infants. *Perception, 13,* 287–305.

Leslie, A.M., & Keeble, S. (1987). Do six-month-old infants perceive causality? *Cognition, 25,* 265–288.

Lettvin, J.Y., Maturana, H.R., McCulloch, W.S., & Pitts, W.H. (1959). What the frog's eye tells the frog's brain. *Proceedings of the Institute of Radio Engineers, 47,* 1940–1951.

LeVay, S., Hubel, D.H., & Wiesel, T.N. (1975). The pattern of ocular dominance columns in macaque visual cortex revealed by a reduced silver stain. *Journal of Comparative Neurology, 159,* 559–576.

LeVay, S., & Voigt, T. (1988). Ocular dominance and disparity coding. *Visual Neuroscience, 1,* 395–414.

Leventhal, A.G., Rodieck, R.W., & Dreher, B. (1981). Retinal ganglion cell classes in the Old World monkey: Morphology and central projections. *Science, 213,* 1139–1142.

Levinson, E., & Sekuler, R. (1975). The independence of channels in human vision selective for direction of movement. *Journal of Physiology, 250,* 347–366.

Levinson, E., & Sekuler, R. (1976). Adaptation alters perceived direction of motion. *Vision Research, 16,* 779–781.

Lindsay, P.H., & Norman, D.A. (1972). *Human information processing.* New York: Academic Press.

Linsker, R. (1986a). From basic network principles to neural architecture: Emergence of spatial opponent cells. *Proceedings of the National Academy of Sciences of the USA, 83,* 7508–7512.

Linsker, R. (1986b). From basic network principles to neural architecture: Emergence of orientation-selective cells. *Proceedings of the National Academy of Sciences of the USA, 83,* 8390–8394.

Linsker, R. (1986c). From basic network principles to neural architecture: Emergence of orientation columns. *Proceedings of the National Academy of Sciences of the USA, 83,* 8779–8783.

Lishman, J.R., & Lee, D.N. (1973). The autonomy of visual kinaesthesis. *Perception, 2,* 287–294.

Liu, L., Stevenson, S.B., & Schor, C.M. (1994). Quantitative stereoscopic depth without binocular correspondence. *Nature, 367,* 66–69.

Livingstone, M.S., & Hubel, D.H. (1983). Specificity of cortico-cortical connections in monkey visual system. *Nature, 304,* 531–534.

Livingstone, M.S., & Hubel, D.H. (1984). Anatomy and physiology of a colour system in the primate visual cortex. *Journal of Neuroscience, 4,* 309–356.

Livingstone, M.S., & Hubel, D.H. (1988). Segregation of form, colour, movement and depth: Anatomy, physiology and perception. *Science, 240,* 740–749.

Locke, J. (1690). *An essay concerning human understanding.* Edited from the fourth (1700) and fifth (1706) editions by P.H. Nidditch. Oxford: Oxford University Press (1975).

Longuet-Higgins, H.C., & Prazdny, K. (1980). The interpretation of moving retinal images. *Proceedings of the Royal Society of London, B, 208,* 385–397.

Lowe, D.G. (1987). Three-dimensional object recognition from single two-dimensional images. *Artificial Intelligence, 31,* 355–395.

Lu, Z.-L., & Sperling, G. (1995). The functional architecture of human visual motion perception. *Vision Research, 35,* 2697–2722.

Lund, J.S. (1988). Anatomical organization of macaque monkey striate cortex. *Annual Review of Neuroscience, 11,* 253–288.

Mach, E. (1914). *The analysis of sensations.* Republished 1959. Dover Publications.

MacKay, D.M. (1970). Elevation of visual threshold by displacement of retinal image. *Nature, 225,* 90–92.

Maier, E.J., & Bowmaker, J.K. (1993). Colour vision in the passeriform bird, *Leiothrix lutea*: Correlation of visual pigment absorbance and oil droplet transmission with spectral sensitivity. *Journal of Comparative Physiology, 172,* 295–301.

Malach, R., Amir, Y., Harel, M., & Grinvald, A. (1993). Relationship between intrinsic connections and functional architecture revealed by optical imaging and in vivo targeted biocytin injections in primate striate cortex. *Proceedings of the National Academy of Sciences of the USA, 90,* 10469–10473.

Malik, J., & Perona, P. (1990). Preattentive texture discrimination with early vision mechanisms. *Journal of the Optical Society of America, A7,* 923–932.

Malik, J., & Perona, P. (1992). Finding boundaries in images. In H. Wechsler (Ed.), *Neural networks for perception. Vol. I: Human and machine perception* (Chap. II.7). London: Academic Press.

Malonek, D., Tootell, R.B.H., & Grinvald, A. (1994). Optical imaging reveals the functional architecture of neurons processing shape and motion in owl monkey area MT. *Proceedings of the Royal Society of London, B, 258,* 109–119.

Malpeli, J.G., Schiller, P.H., & Colby, C.L. (1981). Response properties of single cells in monkey striate cortex during reversible inactivation of individual lateral geniculate laminae. *Journal of Neurophysiology, 46,* 1102–1119.

Mandelbrot, B.B. (1982). *The fractal geometry of nature.* San Francisco, CA: Freeman.

Mandler, M.B., & Makous, W. (1984). A three channel model of temporal frequency perception. *Vision Research, 24,* 1881–1887.

Manning, A. (1978). *An introduction to animal behaviour* (3rd edn.). London: Edward Arnold.

Mark, L., & Todd, J.T. (1983). The perception of growth in three dimensions. *Perception and Psychophysics, 33,* 193–196.

Marr, D. (1976). Early processing of visual information. *Philosophical Transactions of the Royal Society of London, B, 275,* 483–524.

Marr, D. (1977). Analysis of occluding contour. *Proceedings of the Royal Society of London, B, 197,* 441–475.

Marr, D. (1982). *Vision: A computational investigation into the human representation and processing of visual information.* San Francisco, CA: Freeman.

Marr, D., & Hildreth, E. (1980). Theory of edge detection. *Proceedings of the Royal Society of London, B, 207,* 187–217.

Marr, D., & Nishihara, H.K. (1978). Representation and recognition of the spatial organization of three-dimensional shapes. *Proceedings of the Royal Society of London, B, 200,* 269–294.

Marr, D., & Poggio, T. (1976). Cooperative computation of stereo disparity. *Science, 194,* 283–287.

Marr, D., & Poggio, T. (1979). A computational theory of human stereo vision. *Proceedings of the Royal Society of London, B, 204,* 301–328.

Marr, D., & Ullman, S. (1981). Directional selectivity and its use in early visual processing. *Proceedings of the Royal Society of London, B, 211,* 151–180.

Martin, G.R. (1985). Eye. In A.S. King & J. McClelland (Eds.), *Form and function in birds* (Vol. 3, pp.311–374). London: Academic Press.

Martin, G.R. (1994a). Visual fields in woodcocks *Scolopax rusticola* (Scolopacidae; Charadriiformes). *Journal of Comparative Physiology, 174,* 787–793.

Martin, G.R. (1994b). Form and function in the optical structure of bird eyes. In M.N.O. Davies & P.R. Green (Eds.), *Perception and motor control in birds* (pp.5–34). Berlin: Springer.

Martin, K.A.C. (1988). From enzymes to visual perception: A bridge too far? *Trends in Neuroscience, 11,* 380–387.

Mather, G. (1994). Motion detector models: Psychophysical evidence. In A.T. Smith & R.J. Snowden (Eds.), *Visual detection of motion.* London: Academic Press.

Mather, G., & Morgan, M.J. (1986). Irradiation: Implications for theories of edge localization. *Vision Research, 26,* 1007–1015.

Mather, G., & Murdoch, L. (1994). Gender discrimination in biological motion displays based on dynamic cues. *Proceedings of the Royal Society of London, B, 258,* 273–279.

Mather, G., Radford, K., & West, S. (1992). Low-level visual processing in biological motion. *Proceedings of the Royal Society of London, B, 249,* 149–155.

Mather, G., & West, S. (1993a). Evidence for second-order motion detectors. *Vision Research, 33,* 1109–1112.

Mather, G., & West, S. (1993b). Recognition of animal locomotion from dynamic point-light displays. *Perception, 22,* 759–766.

Matin, L. (1976). Saccades and extra-retinal signal for visual direction. In R.A. Monty & J.W. Senders (Eds.), *Eye movements and psychological processes.* Hillsdale, NJ: Lawrence Erlbaum Associates Inc.

Maturana, H.R., & Frenk, S. (1963). Directional movement and horizontal edge detectors in the pigeon retina. *Science, 142,* 977–979.

Maunsell, J.H.R., Nealey, T.A., & DePriest, D.D. (1990). Magnocellular and parvocellular contributions to responses in the middle temporal visual area (MT) of the macaque monkey. *Journal of Neuroscience, 10,* 3323–3334.

Maunsell, J.H.R., & Newsome, W.T. (1987). Visual processing in monkey extrastriate cortex. *Annual Review of Neuroscience, 10,* 363–401.

Mayhew, J.E.W., & Frisby, J.P. (1981). Psychophysical and computational studies towards a theory of human stereopsis. *Artificial Intelligence, 17,* 349–385.

McBeath, M.K., Shaffer, D.M., & Kaiser, M.K. (1995). How baseball outfielders determine where to run to catch fly balls. *Science, 268,* 569–573.

McClelland, J.L., & Rumelhart, D.E. (1985). Distributed memory and the representation of general and specific information. *Journal of Experimental Psychology: General, 114*, 159–188.

McClelland, J.L., & Rumelhart, D.E. (1986). *Parallel distributed processing: Explorations in the microstructure of cognition. Vol II: Applications.* Cambridge, MA: Bradford Books.

McClelland, J.L., Rumelhart, D.E., & Hinton, G.E. (1986). The appeal of parallel distributed processing. In D.E. Rumelhart & J.L. McClelland (Eds.), *Parallel distributed processing: Explorations in the microstructure of cognition. Volume I: Foundations.* Cambridge, MA: MIT Press.

McCleod, R.W., & Ross, H.E. (1983). Optic-flow and cognitive factors in time-to-collision estimates. *Perception, 12*, 417–423.

McGurk, H., & MacDonald, J. (1976). Hearing lips and seeing voices. *Nature, 264*, 746–748.

McIlwain, J.T. (1964). Receptive fields of optic tract axons and lateral geniculate cells: Peripheral extent and barbiturate sensitivity. *Journal of Neurophysiology, 27*, 1154–1173.

McKee, S.P., Silverman, G.H., & Nakayama, K. (1986). Precise velocity discrimination despite random variations in temporal frequency and contrast. *Vision Research, 26*, 609–619.

McKenzie, B., & Over, R. (1983). Young infants fail to imitate facial and manual gestures. *Infant Behaviour and Development, 6*, 85–89.

McLean, J., & Palmer, L.A. (1989). Contribution of linear spatiotemporal receptive field structure to velocity selectivity of simple cells in area 17 of the cat. *Vision Research, 29*, 675–679.

McLean, J., & Palmer, L.A. (1994). Organization of simple cell responses in the three-dimensional (3-D) frequency domain. *Visual Neuroscience, 11*, 295–306.

McLean, J., Raab, S., & Palmer, L.A. (1994). Contribution of linear mechanisms to the specification of local motion by simple cells in areas 17 and 18 of the cat. *Visual Neuroscience, 11*, 271–294.

Mech, L.D. (1970). *The wolf: The ecology and behaviour of an endangered species.* Garden City, NY: The Natural History Press.

Meltzoff, A.N., & Moore, M.K. (1977). Imitation of facial and manual gestures by human neonates. *Science, 198*, 75–78.

Menzel, E.W. (1978). Cognitive mapping in chimpanzees. In S.H. Hulse, F. Fowler, & W.K. Honig (Eds.), *Cognitive processes in animal behaviour.* Hillsdale, NJ: Lawrence Erlbaum Associates Inc.

Menzel, E.W., & Halperin, S. (1975). Purposive behaviour as a basis for objective communication between chimpanzees. *Science, 189*, 652–654.

Merigan, W.H., Byrne, C.E., & Maunsell, J.H.R. (1991). Does primate motion perception depend on the magnocellular pathway? *Journal of Neuroscience, 11*, 3422–3429.

Merigan, W.H., & Eskin, T.A. (1986). Spatio-temporal vision of macaques with severe loss of Pb retinal ganglion cells. *Vision Research, 26*, 1751–1761.

Merigan, W.H., Katz, L.M., & Maunsell, J.H.R. (1991). The effects of parvocellular lateral geniculate lesions on the acuity and contrast sensitivity of macaque monkeys. *Journal of Neuroscience, 11*, 994–1001.

Merigan, W.H., & Maunsell, J.H.R. (1993). How parallel are the primate visual pathways? *Annual Review of Neuroscience, 16*, 369–402.

Metzger, W. (1930). Optische Untersuchungen in Ganzfeld II. *Psychologische Forschung, 13*, 6–29.

Michael, C.R. (1978). Color vision mechanisms in monkey striate cortex: Simple cells with dual opponent-color receptive fields. *Journal of Neurophysiology, 41*, 1233–1249.

Michael, C.R. (1981). Columnar organization of color cells in monkey's striate cortex. *Journal of Neurophysiology, 46*, 587–604.

Michaels, C.F. (1978). *The information for direct binocular stereopsis.* Unpublished manuscript (cited in Michaels & Carello).

Michaels, C.F., & Carello, C. (1981). *Direct perception.* Englewood Cliffs, NJ: Prentice Hall.

Michotte, A. (1963). *The perception of causality.* Trans. by T. & E. Miles from French (1946) edition. London: Methuen.

Mignard, M., & Malpeli, J.G. (1991). Paths of information flow through visual cortex. *Science, 251*, 1249–1251.

Miller, E.K., Li, L., & Desimone, R. (1993). Activity of neurons in anterior inferotemporal cortex during a short-term memory task. *Journal of Neuroscience, 13*, 1460–1478.

Millott, N. (1968). The dermal light sense. *Symposia of the Zoological Society of London, 23*, 1–36.

Minsky, M. (1977). Frame-system theory. In P.N. Johnson-Laird & P.C. Wason (Eds.), *Thinking: Readings in cognitive science.* Cambridge, UK: Cambridge University Press.

Minsky, M., & Papert, S. (1969). *Perceptions.* Cambridge, MA: MIT Press.

Möhl, B. (1989). "Biological noise" and plasticity of sensorimotor pathways in the locust flight system. *Journal of Comparative Physiology, 166*, 75–82.

Mollon, J.D. (1982). Colour vision and colour blindness. In H.B. Barlow & J.D. Mollon (Eds.), *The senses* (pp.165–191). Cambridge, UK: Cambridge University Press.

Mollon, J.D. (1989). "Tho' she kneel'd in that place where they grew...": The uses and origins of primate colour vision. *Journal of Experimental Biology, 146,* 21–38.

Moran, G., Fentress, J.C., & Golani, I. (1981). A description of relational patterns of movement during "ritualized fighting" in wolves. *Animal Behaviour, 29,* 1146–1165.

Moran, J., & Desimone, R. (1985). Selective attention gates visual processing in the extrastriate cortex. *Science, 229,* 782–784.

Morgan, M.J. (1992). Spatial filtering precedes motion detection. *Nature, 355,* 344–346.

Morgan, M.J. (1996). Visual illusions. In V. Bruce (Ed.), *Unsolved mysteries of the mind: Tutorial essays in cognition* (pp.29–58). Hove, UK: Erlbaum (UK) Taylor & Francis

Morris, R.G.M. (Ed.). (1989). *Parallel distributed processing: Implications for psychology and neuroscience.* Oxford: Oxford University Press.

Morrone, M.C., & Burr, D.C. (1986). Evidence for the existence and development of visual inhibition in humans. *Nature, 321,* 235–237.

Morrone, M.C., & Burr, D.C. (1988). Feature detection in human vision: A phase-dependent energy model. *Proceedings of the Royal Society of London, B, 235,* 221–245.

Morrone, M.C., Burr, D.C., & Maffei, L. (1982). Functional significance of cross-orientational inhibition, Part I. Neurophysiology. *Proceedings of the Royal Society of London, B, 216,* 335–354.

Morrone, M.C., & Owens, R.A. (1987). Feature detection from local energy. *Pattern Recognition Letters, 6,* 303–313.

Morrone, M.C., Ross, J., Burr, D.C., & Owens, R.A. (1986). Mach bands are phase-dependent. *Nature, 324,* 250–253.

Morton, J., & Johnson, M. (1991). Conspec and Conlern: A two-process theory of infant face recognition. *Psychological Review, 98,* 164–181.

Moulden, B. (1980). After-effects and the integration of patterns of neural activity within a channel. *Philosophical Transactions of the Royal Society of London, B, 290,* 39–55.

Movshon, J.A., Adelson, E.H., Gizzi, M.S., & Newsome, W.T. (1985). The analysis of moving visual patterns. In C. Chagas, R. Gattass, & C. Gross (Eds.), *Pattern recognition mechanisms* (pp.117–151). Vatican City: Vatican Press.

Movshon, J.A., & Blakemore, C.B. (1973). Orientation specificity and spatial selectivity in human vision. *Perception, 2,* 53–60.

Movshon, J.A., Thompson, I.D., & Tolhurst, D.J. (1978). Receptive field organization of complex cells in the cat's striate cortex. *Journal of Physiology, 283,* 79–99.

Nakayama, K., & Loomis, J.M. (1974). Optical velocity patterns, velocity-sensitive neurons and space perception: A hypothesis. *Perception, 3,* 63–80.

Nakayama, K., & Shimojo, S. (1990). Da Vinci stereopsis: Depth and subjective occluding contours from unpaired image points. *Vision Research, 30,* 1811–1825.

Nakayama, K., Shimojo, S., & Silverman, G.H. (1989). Stereoscopic depth: Its relation to image segmentation, grouping and the recognition of occluded objects. *Perception, 18,* 55–68.

Nalbach, H.-O., Wolf-Oberhollenzer, F., & Remy, M. (1993). Exploring the image. In H.P. Zeigler & H.-J. Bischof (Eds.), *Vision, brain and behaviour in birds* (pp.25–46). Cambridge, MA: MIT Press.

Nawrot, M., & Sekuler, R. (1990). Assimilation and contrast in motion perception: Explorations in cooperativity. *Vision Research, 30,* 1439–1451.

Nayar, S. K., & Oren, M. (1995). Visual appearance of matte surfaces. *Science, 267,* 1153–1156.

Neisser, U. (1967). *Cognitive psychology.* New York: Appleton-Century-Crofts.

Nelson, B. (1978). *The gannet.* London: T. & A.D. Poyser.

Nelson, J.I., & Frost, B.J. (1985). Intracortical facilitation among co-oriented, co-axially aligned simple cells in cat striate cortex. *Experimental Brain Research, 61,* 54–61.

Newsome, W.T., & Paré, E.B. (1988). A selective impairment of motion perception following lesions of the middle temporal visual area (MT). *Journal of Neuroscience, 8,* 2201–2211.

Nilsson, D.E. (1988). A new type of imaging optics in compound eyes. *Nature, 332,* 76–78.

Nishida, S., Ashida, H., & Sato, T. (1994). Complete interocular transfer of motion aftereffect with flickering test. *Vision Research, 34,* 2707–2716.

Nishida, S., & Sato, T. (1995). Motion aftereffect with flickering test patterns reveals higher stages of motion processing. *Vision Research, 35,* 477–490.

Normann, R.A., & Werblin, F.S. (1974). Control of retinal sensitivity. I. Light and dark adaptation of vertebrate rods and cones. *Journal of General Physiology, 63*, 37–61.

Nothdurft, H.C. (1985). Sensitivity for structure gradient in texture discrimination tasks. *Vision Research, 25*, 1957–1968.

Nothdurft, H.C. (1991). Texture segmentation and pop-out from orientation contrast. *Vision Research, 31*, 1073–1078.

Nothdurft, H.C. (1993). The role of features in preattentive vision: Comparison of orientation, motion and colour cues. *Vision Research, 33*, 1937–1958.

Oakes, L.M. (1994). Development of infants' use of continuity cues in their perception of causality. *Developmental Psychology, 30*, 869–879.

Obermayer, K., & Blasdel, G.G. (1993). Geometry of orientation and ocular dominance columns in monkey striate cortex. *Journal of Neuroscience, 13*, 4114–4129.

Obermayer, K., Sejnowski, T., & Blasdel, G.G. (1995). Neural pattern formation via competitive Hebbian mechanisms. *Behavioural Brain Research, 66*, 161–167.

Ogle, K.N. (1964). *Researches in binocular vision*. New York: Hafner.

Ohzawa, I., De Angelis, G. C., & Freeman, R.D. (1990). Stereoscopic depth discrimination in the visual cortex: Neurons ideally suited as disparity detectors. *Science, 249*, 1037–1041.

Olson, R.K., & Attneave, F. (1970). What variables produce similarity grouping? *American Journal of Psychology, 83*, 1–21.

O'Toole, A.J., Deffenbacher, K.A., Valentin, D., & Abdi, H. (1994). Structural aspects of face recognition and the other-race effect. *Memory and Cognition, 22*, 208–224.

Owen, B.M., & Lee, D.N. (1986). Establishing a frame of reference for action. In M.G. Wade & H.T.A. Whiting (Eds.), *Motor development in children: Aspects of coordination and control*. Dordrecht: Martinus Nijhoff.

Packer, C. (1977). Reciprocal altruism in *Papio anubis. Nature, 265*, 441–443

Palmer, S.E. (1992). Modern theories of Gestalt perception. In G.W. Humphreys (Ed.), *Understanding vision*. Oxford: Blackwell.

Palmer, S.E., Rosch, E., & Chase, P. (1981). Canonical perspective and the perception of objects. In J. Long & A.D. Baddeley (Eds.), *Attention and performance IX*. Hillsdale, NJ: Lawrence Erlbaum Associates Inc.

Paradiso, M.A., Shimojo, S., & Nakayama, K. (1989). Subjective contours, tilt aftereffects, and visual cortical organization. *Vision Research, 29*, 1205–1213.

Pascalis, O., De Schonen, S. , Moton, J., Deruelle, C., & Fabregrenet, M. (1995). Mother's face recognition by neonates—a replication and an extension. *Infant Behaviour and Development, 18*, 79–85.

Pearson, D.E., Hanna, E., & Martinez, K. (1986). Computer-generated cartoons. *Proceedings of the Rank Prize Funds Symposium on Images and Understanding*. Cambridge, UK: Cambridge University Press.

Pearson, D.E., & Robinson, J.A. (1985). Visual communication at very low data rates. *Proceedings of the IEEE, 73*, 795–812.

Pelz, J.B., & Hayhoe, M.M. (1995). The role of exocentric reference frames in the perception of visual direction. *Vision Research, 35*, 2267–2275.

Pentland, A. (1986a). Local shading analysis. In A.P. Pentland (Ed.), *From pixels to predicates*. Norwood, NJ: Ablex.

Pentland, A. (1986b). Perceptual organisation and the representation of natural form. *Artificial Intelligence, 28*, 293–331.

Pentland, A.P. (1987). A new sense for depth of field. *IEEE Transactions PAMI, 9*, 523–531.

Pentland, A.P. (1989). Shape information from shading: A theory about human perception. *Spatial Vision, 4*, 165–182.

Perrett, D.I., Hietanen, J.K., Oram, M.W., & Benson, P.J. (1992). Organization and function of cells responsive to faces in the temporal cortex. *Philosophical Transactions of the Royal Society of London, B, 335*, 23–30.

Perrett, D.I., May, K.A., & Yoshikawa, S. (1994). Facial shape and judgements of female attractiveness: Preferences for non-average characteristics. *Nature, 368*, 239–242.

Perrett, D.I., Mistlin, A.J., Potter, D.D., Smith, P.A.J., Head, A.S., Chitty, A.J., Broennimann, R., Milner, A.D., & Jeeves, M.A. (1986). Functional organisation of visual neurones processing face identity. In H.D. Ellis, M.A. Jeeves, F. Newcombe, & A. Young (Eds.), *Aspects of face processing*. Dordrecht: Martinus Nijhoff.

Perrett, D.I., Rolls, E.T., & Caan, W. (1982). Visual neurones responsive to faces in the monkey temporal cortex. *Experimental Brain Research, 47*, 329–342.

Perrone, J.A., & Stone, L.S. (1994). A model of self-motion estimation within primate extrastriate cortex. *Vision Research, 34*, 2917–2938.

Peterhans, E., & von der Heydt, R. (1989). Mechanisms of contour perception in monkey visual cortex. II. Contours bridging gaps. *Journal of Neuroscience, 9,* 1749–1763.

Pheiffer, C.H., Eure, S.B., & Hamilton, C.B. (1956). Reversible figures and eye movements. *American Journal of Psychology, 69,* 452–455.

Phillips, R.J. (1972). Why are faces hard to recognise in photographic negative? *Perception and Psychophysics, 12,* 425–426.

Phillips, W.A. (1974). On the distinction between sensory storage and short-term visual memory. *Perception and Psychophysics, 16,* 283–290.

Pietrewicz, A.T., & Kamil, A.C. (1977). Visual detection of cryptic prey by blue jays. *Science, 195,* 580–582.

Pinker, S. (1984). Visual cognition: An introduction. *Cognition, 18,* 1–63.

Pinker, S., & Mehler, J. (Eds.). (1988). *Connections and symbols.* Cambridge, MA: MIT Press.

Pittenger, J.B., & Mace, W.M. (1985). Visual perception as a text [Scientific correspondence] *Nature, 317,* 22.

Pittenger, J.B., & Shaw, R.E. (1975). Aging faces as viscal-elastic events: Implications for a theory of non-rigid shape perception. *Journal of Experimental Psychology: Human Perception and Performance, 1,* 374–382.

Poggio, G.F., & Fischer, B. (1977). Binocular interaction and depth sensitivity in striate and prestriate cortex of behaving rhesus monkeys. *Journal of Neurophysiology, 40,* 1392–1407.

Poggio, G., & Poggio, T. (1984). The analysis of stereopsis. *Annual Review of Neuroscience, 7,* 379–412.

Polat, U., & Sagi, D. (1993). Lateral interactions between spatial channels: Suppression and facilitation revealed by lateral masking experiments. *Vision Research, 33,* 993–999.

Polat, U., & Sagi, D. (1994). The architecture of perceptual spatial interactions. *Vision Research, 34,* 73–78.

Pollard, S.B., Mayhew, J.E.W., & Frisby, J.P. (1985). PMF: A stereo correspondence algorithm using a disparity gradient limit. *Perception, 14,* 449–470.

Pollen, D.A., Gaska, J.P., & Jacobson, L.D. (1988). Responses of simple and complex cells to compound gratings. *Vision Research, 28,* 25–39.

Pollen, D.A., & Ronner, S.F. (1981). Phase relationships between adjacent simple cells in the visual cortex. *Science, 212,* 1409–1411.

Potts, W.K. (1984). The chorus-line hypothesis of manoeuvre co-ordination in avian flocks. *Nature, 309,* 344–345.

Premack, D., & Woodruff, G. (1978). Does the chimpanzee have a theory of mind? *Behavioural and Brain Sciences, 4,* 515–526.

Price, C.J., & Humphreys, G.W. (1989). The effects of surface detail on object categorization and naming. *Quarterly Journal of Experimental Psychology, 41A,* 797–828.

Pringle, J.W.S. (1974). Locomotion: Flight. In M. Rockstein (Ed.), *The physiology of insects* (2nd edn., Vol III, pp.433–476). London: Academic Press.

Pritchard, R.M. (1961). Stabilized images on the retina. *Scientific American, 204,* June, 72–78.

Proffitt, D.R., Berthenthal, B.I., & Roberts, R.J. (1984). The role of occlusion in reducing multistability in moving point-light displays. *Perception and Psychophysics, 36,* 315–323.

Proffitt, D.R., & Cutting, J.E. (1979). Perceiving the centroid of configurations on a rolling wheel. *Perception and Psychophyics, 25,* 389–398.

Proffitt, D.R., Cutting, J.E., & Stier, D.M. (1979). Perception of wheel-generated motions. *Journal of Experimental Psychology, 5,* 289–302.

Pugh, E.N., & Cobbs, W.H. (1986). Visual transduction in vertebrate rods and cones: A tale of two transmitters, calcium and cyclic GMP. *Vision Research, 26,* 1613–1643.

Purple, R.L., & Dodge, F.A. (1965). Interaction of excitation and inhibition in the eccentric cell in the eye of *Limulus. Cold Spring Harbor Symposia on Quantitative Biology, Vol. 30.*

Pylyshyn, Z.W. (1981). The imagery debate: Analog media versus tacit knowledge. *Psychological Review, 88,* 16–45.

Pylyshyn, Z.W., & Storm, R.W. (1988). Tracking multiple independent targets: Evidence for a parallel tracking mechanism. *Spatial Vision, 3,* 179–197.

Quinlan, P.T., & Humphreys, G.W. (1993). Perceptual frames of reference and 2–dimensional shape recognition—further examination of internal axes. *Perception, 22,* 1343–1364.

Ramachandran, V.S. (1988). Perception of shape from shading. *Nature, 331,* 163–166.

Ramachandran, V.S., & Cavanagh, P. (1985). Subjective contours capture stereopsis. *Nature, 317,* 527–531.

Rauschecker, J.P., von Grünau, M.W., & Poulin, C. (1987). Centrifugal organization of direction preferences in the cat's lateral suprasylvian visual cortex and its relation to flow field processing. *Journal of Neuroscience, 7*, 943–958.

Redfern, M.S., & Furman, J.M. (1994). Postural sway of patients with vestibular disorders during optic flow. *Journal of Vestibular Research: Equilibrium and Orientation, 4*, 221–230.

Reed, E., & Jones, R. (Eds.). (1982). *Reasons for Realism: Selected essays of J.J. Gibson.* Hillsdale, NJ: Lawrence Erlbaum Associates Inc.

Regan, D. (1989). Orientation discrimination for objects defined by relative motion and objects defined by luminance contrast. *Vision Research, 29*, 1389–1400.

Regan, D., & Beverley, K.I. (1978). Looming detectors in the human visual pathway. *Vision Research, 18*, 415–421.

Regan, D., & Beverley, K.I. (1979). Binocular and monocular stimuli for motion in depth: Changing disparity and changing size feed the same motion-in-depth stage. *Vision Research, 19*, 1331–1342.

Regan, D., & Hamstra, S. (1991). Shape discrimination for motion-defined and contrast-defined form: Squareness is special. *Perception, 20*, 315–336.

Regan, D., & Hamstra, S.J. (1992). Dissociation of orientation discrimination from form detection for motion-defined bars and luminance-defined bars: Effects of dot lifetime and presentation duration. *Vision Research, 32*, 1655–1666.

Reichardt, W. (1969). Movement perception in insects. In W. Reichardt (Ed.), *Processing of optical data by organisms and by machines.* New York: Academic Press.

Reichardt, W., & Poggio, T. (1976). Visual control of orientation behaviour in the fly. Part I. A quantitative analysis. *Quarterly Review of Biophysics, 9*, 311–375.

Reichardt, W., & Poggio, T. (1979). Figure-ground discrimination by relative movement in the visual system of the fly. *Biological Cybernetics, 35*, 81–100.

Reichardt, W., Poggio, T., & Hausen, K. (1983). Figure-ground discrimination by relative movement in the visual system of the fly. Part II: Towards the neural circuitry. *Biological Cybernetics, 46*, 1–30.

Rhodes, G., Brake, S., & Atkinson, A. (1993). What is lost in inverted faces? *Cognition, 47*, 25–57.

Richards, W. (1971). Anomalous stereoscopic depth perception. *Journal of the Optical Society of America, 61*, 410–414.

Riggs, L.A., Merton, P.A., & Morton, H.B. (1974). Suppression of visual phosphenes during saccadic eye movements. *Vision Research, 14*, 997–1010.

Riggs, L.A., Volkmann, F.C., & Moore, R.K. (1981). Suppression of the black-out due to blinks. *Vision Research, 21*, 1075–1079.

Ripoll, H., Bard, C., & Paillard, J. (1986). Stabilisation of head and eyes on target as a factor in successful basketball shooting. *Human Movement Science, 5*, 47–58.

Ristau, C.A. (1991). Before mindreading: Attention, purposes and deception in birds? In A. Whiten (Ed.), *Natural theories of mind: Evolution, development and simulation of everyday mindreading* (pp.209–222). Oxford: Blackwell.

Roberts, A.D., & Bruce, V. (1988). Feature salience in judgements of sex and familiarity of faces. *Perception, 17*, 475–481.

Roberts, L.G. (1965). Machine perception of three-dimensional solids. In J.T. Tippett, D.A. Berkowitz, L.C. Clapp, C.J. Koester, & A. Vanderburgh (Eds.), *Optical and electro-optical information processing.* Cambridge, MA: MIT Press.

Robson, J.G. (1966). Spatial and temporal contrast sensitivity functions of the visual system. *Journal of the Optical Society of America, 8*, 1141–1142.

Robson, J.G. (1983). Frequency domain visual processing. In O.J. Braddick & A.C. Sleigh (Eds.), *Physical and biological processing of images* (pp.73–87). Berlin: Springer.

Robson, J.G., Tolhurst, D.J., Freeman, R.D., & Ohzawa, I. (1988). Simple cells in the visual cortex of the cat can be narrowly tuned for spatial frequency. *Visual Neuroscience, 1*, 415–419.

Rodman, H.R., & Albright, T.D. (1989). Single-unit analysis of pattern-motion selective properties in the middle temporal visual area (MT). *Experimental Brain Research, 75*, 53–64.

Roediger, H.L. (1980). Memory metaphors in cognitive psychology. *Memory and Cognition, 8*, 231–246.

Rogers, B., & Graham, M. (1979). Motion parallax as an independent cue for depth perception. *Perception, 8*, 125–134.

Rogers, B., & Graham, M. (1982). Similarities between motion parallax and stereopsis in human depth perception. *Vision Research, 22*, 261–270.

Rolls, E.T. (1987). Information representation, processing and storage in the brain: Analysis at the single neuron level. In J.-P. Changeux & M. Konishi

(Eds.), *The neural and molecular bases of learning* (pp.503–540). Wiley.

Rolls, E.T. (1992). The processing of face information in the primate temporal lobe. In V. Bruce & M. Burton (Eds.), *Processing images of faces*. Norwood, NJ: Ablex.

Rosenfeld, S.A., & Van Hoesen, G.W. (1979). Face recognition in the rhesus monkey. *Neuropsychologia, 17*, 503–509.

Ross, J. (1976). The resources of binocular perception. *Scientific American, 234*, March, 80–86.

Ross, J., Morrone, M.C., & Burr, D.C. (1989). The conditions under which Mach bands are visible. *Vision Research, 29*, 699–715.

Rossel, S. (1983). Binocular stereopsis in an insect. *Nature, 302*, 821–822.

Roth, G., & Wiggers, W. (1983). Responses of the toad *Bufo bufo* to stationary prey stimuli. *Zeitschrift für Tierpsychologie, 61*, 225–234.

Royden C.S., Crowell, J.A., & Banks, M.S. (1994). Estimating heading during eye movements. *Vision Research, 34*, 3197–3214.

Rumelhart, D.E., Hinton, G.E., & Williams, R.J. (1986). Learning internal representations by error propagation. In D.E. Rumelhart & J.L. McClelland (Eds.), *Parallel distrubuted processing: Explorations in the microstructure of cognition. Volume 1: Foundations.* Cambridge, MA: MIT Press.

Rumelhart, D.E., & McClelland, J.L. (1985). Levels indeed! A response to Broadbent. *Journal of Experimental Psychology: General, 114*, 193–197.

Rumelhart, D.E., & McClelland, J.L. (1986). *Parallel distributed processing: Explorations in the microstructure of cognition. Volume I: Foundations.* Cambridge, MA: MIT Press.

Rumelhart, D.E., & Zipser, D. (1986). Feature discovery by competitive learning. In D.E. Rumelhart & J.L. McClelland (Eds), *Parallel distributed processing: Explorations in the microstructure of cognition, Volume I. Foundations.* Cambridge, MA: MIT Press.

Runeson, S. (1994). Perception of biological motion: The KSD-Principle and the implications of a distal versus proximal approach. In G. Jansson, S.S. Bergstrom, & W. Epstein (Eds.), *Perceiving events and objects* (pp.383–405). Hillsdale, NJ: Lawrence Erlbaum Associates Inc.

Runeson, S., & Frykolm, G. (1981). Visual perception of lifted weights. *Journal of Experimental Psychology: Human Perception and Performance, 7*, 733–740.

Runeson, S., & Frykolm, G. (1983). Kinematic specifications of dynamics as an informational basis for person-and-action perception: Expectation, gender-recognition and deceptive intention. *Journal of Experimental Psychology: General, 112*, 585–615.

Runeson, S., & Vedeler, D. (1993). The indispensability of precollision kinematics in the visual perception of relative mass. *Perception and Psychophysics, 53*, 617–633.

Russell, J.A. (1994). Is there universal expression of emotion from facial expression? A review of cross-cultural studies. *Psychological Bulletin, 115*, 102–141.

Ryan, C.M.E. (1982). Concept formation and individual recognition in the domestic chicken (*Gallus gallus*). *Behaviour Analysis Letters, 2*, 213–220.

Sai, F., & Bushnell, I.W.R. (1987). The perception of faces in different poses by 1-month-olds. *British Journal of Developmental Psychology, 6*, 35–41.

Salzman, C.D., Murasugi, C.M., Britten, K.H., & Newsome, W.T. (1992). Microstimulation in visual area MT: Effects on direction discrimination performance. *Journal of Neuroscience, 12*, 2331–2355.

Sanger, T.D. (1988). Stereo disparity computation using Gabor filters. *Biological Cybernetics, 59*, 405–418.

Sary, G., Vogels, R., & Orban, G.A. (1994). Orientation discrimination of motion-defined gratings. *Vision Research, 34*, 1331–1334.

Savelsbergh, G.J.P., Whiting, H.T.A., & Bootsma, R.J. (1991). Grasping tau. *Journal of Experimental Psychology: Human Perception and Performance, 17*, 315–322.

Schaeffel, F. (1994). Functional accommodation in birds. In M.N.O. Davies & P.R. Green (Eds.), *Perception and motor control in birds* (pp.35–53). Berlin: Springer.

Schaeffel, F., & Howland, H.C. (1987). Corneal accommodation in chick and pigeon. *Journal of Comparative Physiology, 160*, 375–384.

Schalkoff, R.J. (1989). *Digital image processing and computer vision*. New York: Wiley.

Schaller, G.B. (1972). *The Serengeti lion: A study of predator-prey relations*. Chicago: Chicago University Press.

Schiff, W., Caviness, J.A., & Gibson, J.J. (1962). Persistent fear responses in rhesus monkeys to the optical stimulus of "looming". *Science, 136*, 982–983.

Schiff, W., & Detwiler, M.L. (1979). Information used in judging impending collision. *Perception, 8*, 647–658.

Schiller, P., Finlay, B.L., & Volman, S.F. (1976). Quantitative studies of single-cell properties in monkey striate cortex. I. Spatiotemporal organization of receptive fields. *Journal of Neurophysiology, 39*, 1288–1319.

Schiller, P.H., & Lee, K. (1991). The role of primate extrastriate area V4 in vision. *Science, 251*, 1251–1253.

Schiller, P.H., & Logothetis, N.K. (1990). The colour-opponent and broad-band channels of the primate visual system. *Trends in Neuroscience, 13*, 392–398.

Schiller, P.H., Logothetis, N.K., & Charles, E.R. (1990). Functions of the colour-opponent and broad-band channels of the visual system. *Nature, 343*, 68–70.

Schlottman, A., & Anderson, N.H. (1993). An information integration approach to phenomenal causality. *Memory and Cognition, 21*, 785–801.

Schlottman, A., & Shanks, D.R. (1992). Evidence for a distinction between judged and perceived causality. *Quarterly Journal of Experimental Psychology, 44A*, 321–342.

Schmidt, R.A. (1969). Movement time as a determiner of timing accuracy. *Journal of Experimental Psychology, 79*, 43–47.

Schmidt, R.C., Carello, C., & Turvey, M.T. (1990). Phase transitions and critical fluctuations in the visual co-ordination of rhythmic movements between people. *Journal of Experimental Psychology: Human Perception and Performance, 16*, 227–247.

Schöner, G. (1991). Dynamic theory of action-perception patterns: The "moving room" paradigm. *Biological Cybernetics, 64*, 455–462.

Schor, C.M., & Tyler, C.W. (1981). Spatio-temporal properties of Panum's fusional area. *Vision Research, 21*, 683–692.

Schor, C.M., & Wood, I. (1983). Disparity range for local stereopsis as a function of luminance spatial frequency. *Vision Research, 23*, 1649–1654.

Schor, C.M., Wood, I., & Ogawa, J. (1984). Binocular sensory fusion is limited by spatial resolution. *Vision Research, 24*, 661–665.

Scott-Samuel, N.E., & Georgeson, M.A. (1995). Does early nonlinearity account for second-order motion? *Perception, 24* (Suppl.) p.104.

Seamon, J.G. (1982). Dynamic facial recognition: Examination of a natural phenomenon. *American Journal of Psychology, 95*, 363–381.

Sedgwick, H.A. (1973). *The visible horizon*. PhD thesis, Cornell University, Ithaca, NY.

Sekuler, R.W., & Ganz, L. (1963). After-effect of seen motion with a stabilized retinal image. *Science, 139*, 419–420.

Selfridge, O.G. (1959). Pandemonium: A paradigm for learning. In *The mechanisation of thought processes*. London: HMSO.

Shapley, R., & Lennie, P. (1985). Spatial frequency analysis in the visual system. *Annual Review of Neuroscience, 8*, 547–583.

Shapley, R., & Perry, V.H. (1986). Cat and monkey retinal ganglion cells and their visual functional roles. *Trends in Neuroscience, 9*, 229–235.

Sharpe, C.R., & Tolhurst, D.J. (1973). Orientation and spatial frequency channels in peripheral vision. *Vision Research, 13*, 2103–2112.

Shaw, R.E., & Bransford, J. (1977). Introduction: Psychological approaches to the problem of knowledge. In R.E. Shaw & J. Bransford (Eds.), *Perceiving, acting and knowing: Toward an ecological psychology*. Hillsdale, NJ: Lawrence Erlbaum Associates Inc.

Shaw, R.E., McIntyre, M., & Mace, W. (1974). The role of symmetry in event perception. In R.B. MacCleod and H.L. Pick (Eds.), *Perception: Essays in honour of James J Gibson*. Ithaca, NY: Cornell University Press.

Shaw, R.E., & Pittenger, J.B. (1977). Perceiving the face of change in changing faces: Implications for a theory of object recognition. In R.E. Shaw & J. Bransford (Eds.), *Perceiving, acting and knowing: Toward an ecological psychology*. Hillsdale, NJ: Lawrence Erlbaum Associates Inc.

Sherrington, C.S. (1906). *Integrative action of the nervous system*. New Haven, CT: Yale University Press (reset edition, 1947).

Shimojo, S., & Nakayama, K. (1990). Real world occlusion constraints and binocular rivalry. *Vision Research, 30*, 69–80.

Shirai, Y. (1973). A context sensitive line finder for recognition of polyhedra. *Artificial Intelligence, 4*, 95–120.

Sillito, A.M., Jones, H.E., Gerstein, G.L., & West, D.C. (1994). Feature-linked synchronization of thalamic relay cell firing induced by feedback from the visual cortex. *Nature, 369*, 479–482.

Silverman, M.S., Grosof, D.H., DeValois, R.L., & Elfar, S.D. (1989). Spatial frequency organization in primate striate cortex. *Proceedings of the National Academy of Sciences of the USA, 86*, 711–715.

Simpson, J.I. (1984). The accessory optic system. *Annual Review of Neuroscience, 7,* 13–41.

Simpson, M.J.A. (1968). The display of the Siamese fighting fish *Betta splendens. Animal Behaviour Monographs, 1,* 1–73.

Singer, W., & Gray, C.M. (1995). Visual feature integration and the temporal correlation hypothesis. *Annual Review of Neuroscience, 18,* 555–586.

Sivak, J.G. (1978). A survey of vertebrate strategies for vision in air and water. In M.A. Ali (Ed.), *Sensory ecology: Review and perspectives.* New York: Plenum.

Sivak, J.G., Hildebrand, T., & Lebert, C. (1985). Magnitude and rate of accommodation in diving and nondiving birds. *Vision Research, 25,* 925–933.

Skottun, B.C., De Valois, R.L., Grosof, D.H., Movshon, J.A., Albrecht, D.G., & Bonds, A.B. (1991). Classifying simple and complex cells on the basis of response modulation. *Vision Research, 31,* 1079–1086.

Smallman, H.S., & MacLeod, D.I.A. (1994). Size-disparity correlation in stereopsis at contrast threshold. *Journal of the Optical Society of America, A11,* 2169–2183.

Smith, A.T. (1994). Correspondence-based and energy-based detection of second-order motion in human vision. *Journal of the Optical Society of America, A11,* 1940–1948.

Smith, A.T., & Edgar, G.K. (1994). Antagonistic comparison of temporal frequency filter outputs as a basis for speed perception. *Vision Research, 34,* 253–265.

Smith, A.T., & Over, R. (1975). Tilt aftereffects with subjective contours. *Nature, 257,* 581–582.

Smith, A.T., & Over, R. (1977). Orientation masking and the tilt illusion with subjective contours. *Perception, 6,* 441–447.

Smolensky, P. (1987). Connectionist AI, symbolic AI and the brain. *Artificial Intelligence Review, 1,* 95–110.

Smolensky, P. (1988). On the proper treatment of connectionism. *Behavioural and Brain Sciences, 11,* 1–74.

Snowden, R.J. (1992). Orientation bandwidth: The effect of spatial and temporal frequency. *Vision Research, 32,* 1965–1974.

Sobel, E.C. (1990). Depth perception by motion parallax and paradoxical parallax in the locust. *Naturwissenschaften, 77,* 241–243.

Sperling, G. (1960). The information available in brief visual presentations. *Psychological Monographs, 74,* whole no. 498.

Spurr, R.T. (1969). Subjective aspects of braking. *Automobile Engineer, 59,* 58–61.

Srinivasan, M.V., Lehrer, M., & Horridge, G.A. (1990). Visual figure-ground discrimination in the honeybee: The role of motion parallax at boundaries. *Proceedings of the Royal Society of London, B, 238,* 331–350.

Srinivasan, M.V., Lehrer, M., Kirchner, W.H., & Zhang, S.W. (1991). Range perception through apparent image speed in freely flying honeybees. *Visual Neuroscience, 6,* 519–535.

Stevens, J.K., Emerson, R.C., Gerstein, G.L., Kallos, T., Neufield, G.R., Nichols, C.W., & Rosenquist, A.C. (1976). Paralysis of the awake human: Visual perceptions. *Vision Research, 16,* 93–98.

Stevens, K., & Brookes, A. (1988). Integrating stereopsis with monocular interpretations of planar surfaces. *Vision Research, 28,* 371–386.

Stewart, D., Cudworth, C.J., & Lishman, J.R. (1993). Misperception of time-to-collision by drivers in pedestrian accidents. *Perception, 22,* 1227–1244.

Stone, J., & Fukuda, Y. (1974). Properties of cat retinal ganglion cells: A comparison of W cells with X and Y cells. *Journal of Neurophysiology, 37,* 722–748.

Stoner, G.R., & Albright, T.D. (1994). Visual motion integration: A neurophysiological and psychophysical perspective. In A.T. Smith & R.J. Snowden (Eds.), *Visual detection of motion.* London: Academic Press.

Stonham, J. (1986). Practical face recognition and verification with WISARD. In H.D. Ellis, M.A. Jeeves, F. Newcombe, & A. Young (Eds.), *Aspects of face processing.* Dordrecht: Martinus Nijhoff.

Sumby, W.H., & Pollack, I. (1954). Visual contribution to speech intelligibility in noise. *Journal of the Acoustical Society of America, 26,* 212–215.

Summerfield, Q. (1992). Lipreading and audio-visual speech perception. *Philosophical Transactions of the Royal Society of London, B, 335,* 71–78.

Sumner, F.B. (1934). Does "protective coloration" protect? Results of some experiments with fishes and birds. *Proceedings of the National Academy of Science of the USA, 10,* 559–564.

Sun, H.-J., Carey, D.P., & Goodale, M.A. (1992). A mammalian model of optic-flow utilization in the control of locomotion. *Experimental Brain Research, 91,* 171–175.

Sutherland, N.S. (1973). Object recognition. In E.C. Carterette & M.P. Friedman (Eds.), *Handbook of perception: Volume III. Biology of perceptual systems.* London: Academic Press.

Sutherland, N.S. (1985). Vision as a guide to action. [Book review] *Nature, 315,* 258.

Sutherland, N.S., & Williams, C. (1969). Discrimination of checkerboard patterns by rats. *Quarterly Journal of Experimental Psychology, 21,* 77–84.

Tanaka, H., & Saito, H. (1989). Analysis of motion of the visual field by direction, expansion/contraction and rotation cells clustered in the dorsal part of the medial superior temporal area of the macaque monkey. *Journal of Neurophysiology, 62,* 626–641.

Tanaka, J., & Farah, M.J. (1993). Parts and wholes in face recognition. *Quarterly Journal of Experimental Psychology, 46A,* 225–246.

Tanaka, K. (1993). Neuronal mechanisms of object recognition. *Science, 262,* 685–688.

Tarr, M.J. (1995). Rotating objects to recognize them: A case study on the role of viewpoint dependency in the recognition of three-dimensional objects. *Psychonomic Bulletin and Review, 2,* 55–82.

Tarr, M.J., & Bülthoff, H.H. (1995). Is human object recognition better described by geon-structural-descriptions or by multiple views—comment on Biederman and Gerhardstein (1993). *Journal of Experimental Psychology: Human Perception and Performance, 21,* 1494–1505.

Tarr, M.J., & Pinker, S. (1989). Mental rotation and orientation-dependence in shape recognition. *Cognitive Psychology, 21,* 233–282.

Terzopoulos, D. (1986). Integrating visual information from multiple sources. In A. Pentland (Ed.), *From pixels to predicates.* Norwood, NJ: Ablex.

Thayer, G.H. (1918). *Concealing coloration in the animal kingdom.* New York: Macmillan.

Thompson, P.G. (1981). Velocity aftereffects: The effects of adaptation to moving stimuli on the perception of subsequently seen moving stimuli. *Vision Research, 21,* 337–345.

Thompson, P.G. (1984). The coding of velocity of movement in the human visual system. *Vision Research, 24,* 41–45.

Thorell, L.G., De Valois, R.L., & Albrecht, D.G. (1984). Spatial mapping of monkey V1 cells with pure colour and luminance stimuli. *Vision Research, 24,* 751–769.

Tinbergen, N. (1951). *The study of instinct.* Oxford: Clarendon Press.

Todd, J.T., Mark, L.S., Shaw, R.E., & Pittenger, J.B. (1980). The perception of human growth. *Scientific American, 242,* February, 106–114.

Tolhurst, D.J. (1973). Separate channels for the analysis of the shape and the movement of a moving visual stimulus. *Journal of Physiology, 231,* 385–402.

Tononi, G., Sporns, O., & Edelman, G.M. (1992). Re-entry and the problem of integrating multiple cortical areas: Simulation of dynamic integration in the visual system. *Cerebral Cortex, 2,* 310–355.

Tootell, R.B.H., Silverman, M.S., Hamilton, S.L., Switkes, E., & DeValois, R.L. (1988). Functional anatomy of macaque striate cortex. V. Spatial frequency. *Journal of Neuroscience, 8,* 1610–1624.

Toyama, K., Komatsu, Y., Kasai, H., Fujii, K., & Umetani, K. (1985). Responsiveness of Clare-Bishop neurons to visual cues associated with motion of a visual stimulus in three-dimensional space. *Vision Research, 25,* 407–414.

Treisman, A. (1988). Features and objects. The Fourteenth Bartlett Memorial Lecture. *Quarterly Journal of Experimental Psychology, 40A,* 201–237.

Tresilian, J.R. (1991). Empirical and theoretical issues in the perception of time to contact. *Journal of Experimental Psychology: Human Perception and Performance, 17,* 865–876.

Tresilian, J.R. (1993). Four questions of time to contact: A critical examination of research on interceptive timing. *Perception, 22,* 653–680.

Tresilian, J.R. (1994). Approximate information sources and perceptual variables in interceptive timing. *Journal of Experimental Psychology: Human Perception and Performance, 20,* 154–173.

Tresilian, J.R. (1995). Perceptual and cognitive processes in time-to-contact estimation: Analysis of prediction-motion and relative judgement tasks. *Perception and Psychophysics, 57,* 231–245.

T'so, D.Y., & Gilbert, C.D. (1988). The organization of chromatic and spatial interactions in the primate striate cortex. *Journal of Neuroscience, 8,* 1712–1727.

Tuller, B., Turvey, M.T., & Fitch, H.L. (1982). The Bernstein Perspective. II. The concept of muscle linkage or coordinative structure. In J.A.S. Kelso (Ed.), *Human motor behaviour: An introduction.* Hillsdale, NJ: Lawrence Erlbaum Associates Inc.

Tulunay-Keesey, U. (1982). Fading of stabilized retinal images. *Journal of the Optical Society of America, 72,* 440–447.

Tulunay-Keesey, U., & Jones, R.M. (1980). Contrast sensitivity measures and accuracy of image stabilization systems. *Journal of the Optical Society of America, 70,* 1306–1310.

Turner, E.R.A. (1964). Social feeding in birds. *Behaviour, 24,* 1–46.

Turvey, M.T. (1977a). Preliminaries to a theory of action with reference to seeing. In R. Shaw & J. Bransford (Eds.), *Perceiving, acting and knowing:*

Toward an ecological psychology. Hillsdale, NJ: Lawrence Erlbaum Associates Inc.

Turvey, M.T. (1977b). Contrasting orientations to the processing of visual information. *Psychological Review, 84*, 67–89.

Turvey, M.T., Fitch, H.L., & Tuller, B. (1982). The Bernstein Perspective. I. The problems of degrees of freedom and context-conditioned variability. In J.A.S. Kelso (Ed.), *Human motor behaviour: An introduction.* Hillsdale, NJ: Lawrence Erlbaum Associates Inc.

Turvey, M.T., Shaw, R.E., & Mace, W. (1978). Issues in the theory of action: Degrees of freedom, coordinative structures and coalitions. In J. Requin (Ed.), *Attention and performance VII.* Hillsdale, NJ: Lawrence Erlbaum Associates Inc.

Turvey, M.T., Shaw, R.E., Reed, E.S., & Mace, W.M. (1981). Ecological laws of perceiving and acting: In reply to Fodor and Pylyshyn (1981). *Cognition, 9*, 237–304.

Tynan, P., & Sekuler, R. (1975). Moving visual phantoms: A new contour completion effect. *Science, 188*, 951–952.

Ullman, S. (1979). *The interpretation of visual motion.* Cambridge, MA: MIT Press.

Ullman, S. (1980). Against direct perception. *Behavioral and Brain Sciences, 3*, 373–415.

Ullman, S. (1989). Aligning pictorial descriptions: An approach to object recognition. *Cognition, 32*, 193–254.

Ungerleider, L.G., & Mishkin, M. (1982). Two cortical visual systems. In D.J. Ingle, M.A. Goodale, & R.J.W. Mansfield (Eds.), *Analysis of visual behaviour* (pp.549–586). Cambridge, MA: MIT Press.

Uttal, W.R. (1981). *Taxonomy of visual processes.* Hillsdale, NJ: Lawrence Erlbaum Associates Inc.

Valentin, D., Abdi, H., O'Toole, A.J., & Cottrell, G.W. (1994). Connectionist models of face processing. *Pattern Recognition, 27*, 1209–1230.

Van den Berg, A.V. (1993). Perception of heading. *Nature, 365*, 497–498.

van der Meer, A.L.H., van der Weel, F.R., & Lee, D.N. (1994). Prospective control in catching by infants. *Perception, 23*, 287–302.

van der Meer, A.L.H., van der Weel, F.R., Lee, D.N., Laing, I.A., & Lin, J.P. (1995). Development of prospective control of catching in premature at risk infants. *Developmental Medicine and Child Neurology, 37*, 145–158.

van der Zwan, R., & Wenderoth, P. (1994). Psychophysical evidence for area V2 involvement in the reduction of subjective contour tilt aftereffects by binocular rivalry. *Visual Neuroscience, 11*, 823–830.

Van Essen, D.C. (1985). Functional organization of primate visual cortex. In A. Peters & E.G. Jones (Eds.), *Cerebral cortex. Vol. 3: Visual cortex* (pp.259–329). New York: Plenum.

Van Essen, D.C., Anderson, C.H., & Felleman, D.J. (1992). Information processing in the primate visual system: An integrated systems perspective. *Science, 255*, 419–423.

van Santen, J.P.H., & Sperling, G. (1984). Temporal covariance model of human motion perception. *Journal of the Optical Society of America, A1*, 451–473.

Vautin, R.G., & Berkley, M.A. (1977). Responses of single cells in cat visual cortex to prolonged stimulus movement: Neural correlates of visual aftereffects. *Journal of Neurophysiology, 40*, 1051–1065.

Vecera, S.P., & Gilds, K.S. (submitted). *What are you looking at? Visual mechanisms underlying gaze perception.* Paper presented at the Object Perception and Memory (OPAM) conference, St. Louis, Missouri, November 1994.

Vecera, S.P., & Johnson, M.H. (1995). Gaze detection and the cortical processing of faces. Evidence from infants and adults. *Visual Cognition, 2*, 59–87.

Victor, J.D., & Shapley, R.M. (1979). The nonlinear pathway of Y ganglion cells in the cat retina. *Journal of General Physiology, 74*, 671–689.

Vines, G. (1981). Wolves in dogs' clothing. *New Scientist*, September 10th.

Volkmann, F.C., Riggs, L.A., Moore, R.K., & White, K.D. (1978). Contrast sensitivity during saccadic eye movements. *Vision Research, 18*, 1193–1199.

von der Heydt, R., & Peterhans, E. (1989). Mechanisms of contour perception in monkey visual cortex. I. Lines of pattern discontinuity. *Journal of Neuroscience, 9*, 1731–1748.

von der Heydt, R., Peterhans, E., & Baumgartner, G. (1984). Illusory contours and cortical neuron responses. *Science, 224*, 1260–1262.

von der Heydt, R., Peterhans, E., & Dursteler, M.R. (1992). Periodic pattern-selective cells in monkey visual cortex. *Journal of Neuroscience, 12*, 1416–1434.

von Hofsten, C. (1980). Predictive reaching for moving objects by human infants. *Journal of Experimental Child Psychology, 30*, 369–382.

von Hofsten, C. (1983). Catching skills in infancy. *Journal of Experimental Psychology: Human Perception and Performance, 9*, 75–85.

von Hofsten, C., & Lindhagen, K. (1979). Observations of the development of reaching for moving objects. *Journal of Experimental Child Psychology, 28*, 158–173.

von Holst, E. (1954). Relation between the central nervous system and the peripheral organs. *British Journal of Animal Behaviour, 2*, 89–94.

Wagner, H. (1982). Flow-field variables trigger landing in flies. *Nature, 297*, 147–148.

Wagner, H., & Schaeffel, F. (1991). Barn owls use accommodation as a distance cue. *Journal of Comparative Physiology, 169*, 515–521.

Wallach, H. (1959). The perception of motion. *Scientific American, 201*, July, 56–60.

Wallach, H., & O'Connell, D. N. (1953). The kinetic depth effect. *Journal of Experimental Psychology, 45*, 205–217.

Walls, G.L. (1942). *The vertebrate eye and its adaptive radiation*. New York: Hafner.

Waltz, D.L. (1975). Generating semantic descriptions from scenes with shadows. In P.H. Winston (Ed.), *The psychology of computer vision*. New York: McGraw-Hill.

Wang, Y., & Frost, B.J. (1992). Time to collision is signalled by neurons in the nucleus rotundus of pigeons. *Nature, 356*, 236–238.

Wann, J.P. (in press). Anticipating arrival: Is the tau-margin a specious theory? *Journal of Experimental Psychology: Human Perception and Performance*.

Wann, J.P., Edgar, P., & Blair, D. (1993). Time-to-contact judgement in the locomotion of adults and preschool children. *Journal of Experimental Psychology: Human Perception and Performance, 19*, 1053–1065.

Wann, J.P., & Rushton, S.K. (1995). Grasping the impossible: Stereoscopic virtual balls. In B.G. Bardy, R.J. Bootsma, & Y. Guiard (Eds.), *Studies in perception and action III* (pp.207–210). Hillsdale, NJ: Lawrence Erlbaum Associates Inc.

Wann, J.P., Rushton, S.K., & Lee, D.N. (1995). Can you control where you are heading when you are looking at where you want to go? In B.G. Bardy, R.J. Bootsma, & Y. Guiard (Eds.), *Studies in perception and action III* (pp.171–174). Hillsdale, NJ: Lawrence Erlbaum Associates Inc.

Warren, C., & Morton, J. (1982). The effects of priming on picture recognition. *British Journal of Psychology, 73*, 117–129.

Warren, W.H. (1984). Perceiving affordances: Visual guidance of stair climbing. *Journal of Experimental Psychology: Human Perception and Performance, 10*, 683–703.

Warren, W.H., & Hannon, D.J. (1988). Direction of self-motion is perceived from optical flow. *Nature, 336*, 162–163.

Warren, W.H., Young, D.S., & Lee, D.N. (1986). Visual control of step length during running over irregular terrain. *Journal of Experimental Psychology: Human Perception and Performance, 12*, 259–266.

Watson, A.B., & Ahumada, A.J. (1985). Model of human visual-motion sensing. *Journal of the Optical Society of America, A2*, 322–341.

Watson, A.B., Ahumada, A.J., & Farrell, J.E. (1986). Window of visibility: A psychophysical theory of fidelity in time-sampled visual motion displays. *Journal of the Optical Society of America, A3*, 300–307.

Watson, A.B., & Eckert, M.P. (1994). Motion-contrast sensitivity: Visibility of motion gradients of various spatial frequencies. *Journal of the Optical Society of America, A11*, 496–505.

Watson, A.B., Thompson, P.G., Murphy, B.J., & Nachmias, J. (1980). Summation and discrimination of gratings moving in opposite directions. *Vision Research, 20*, 341–347.

Watson, J.B. (1913). Psychology as the behaviourist views it. *Psychological Review, 20*, 158–177.

Watson, J.B. (1924). *Psychology from the standpoint of a behaviourist*. Philadelphia, PA: Lippincott.

Watt, R.J. (1988). *Visual processing: Computational, psychophysical and cognitive research*. London: Lawrence Erlbaum Associates Ltd.

Watt, R.J. (1991). *Understanding vision*. London: Academic Press

Watt, R.J. (1992). Faces and vision. In V. Bruce & M. Burton (Eds.), *Processing images of faces*. Norwood, NJ: Ablex.

Watt, R.J., & Morgan, M.J. (1983). The recognition and representation of edge blur: Evidence for spatial primitives in human vision. *Vision Research, 23*, 1457–1477.

Watt, R.J., & Morgan, M.J. (1984). Spatial filters and the localisation of luminance changes in human vision. *Vision Research, 24*, 1387–1397.

Watt, R.J., & Morgan, M.J (1985). A theory of the primitive spatial code in human vision. *Vision Research, 25*, 1661–1674.

Weir, S. (1978). The perception of motion: Michotte revisited. *Perception, 7*, 247–260.

Weiskrantz, L. (1986). *Blindsight*. Oxford: Clarendon Press.

Welch, L. (1989). The perception of moving plaids reveals two motion processing stages. *Nature, 337*, 734–736.

Werblin, F.S., & Dowling, J.E. (1969). Organization of the retina of the mudpuppy *Necturus maculosus*. II. Intracellular recording. *Journal of Neurophysiology, 32*, 339–355.

Wertheimer, M. (1923). Untersuchungen zur Lehre von der Gestalt, II. *Psychologische Forschung, 4*, 301–350. Translated as "Laws of organisation in perceptual forms" in W.D. Ellis (1955). *A source book of Gestalt psychology*. London: Routledge and Kegan Paul.

Wheatstone, C. (1838). Contributions to the physiology of vision. Part I: On some remarkable and hitherto unobserved phenomena of binocular vision. *Philosophical Transactions of the Royal Society of London, B, 128*, 371–394.

Whiting, H.T.A., & Sharp, R.H. (1974). Visual occlusion factors in a discrete ball-catching task. *Journal of Motor Behaviour, 6*, 11–16.

Wigglesworth, V.B. (1964). *The life of insects*. London: Weidenfeld & Nicolson.

Williams, D.W., & Sekuler, R. (1984). Coherent global motion percepts from stochastic local motions. *Vision Research, 24*, 55–62.

Wilson, H.R. (1983). Psychophysical evidence for spatial channels. In O.J. Braddick & A.C. Sleigh (Eds.), *Physical and biological processing of images* (pp.88–99). Berlin: Springer

Wilson, H.R. (1994a). The role of second-order motion signals in coherence and transparency. In *Higher order processing in the visual system* (Ciba Foundation Symposium 184, pp.227–244). Chichester, UK: Wiley.

Wilson, H.R. (1994b). Models of two-dimensional motion perception. In A.T. Smith & R.J. Snowden (Eds.), *Visual detection of motion*. London: Academic Press.

Wilson, H.R., Ferrera, V.P., & Yo, C. (1992). A psychophysically motivated model for two-dimensional motion perception. *Visual Neuroscience, 9*, 79–97.

Wilson, H.R., & Kim, J. (1994a). A model for motion coherence and transparency. *Visual Neuroscience, 11*, 1205–1220.

Wilson, H.R., & Kim, J. (1994b). Perceived motion in the vector sum direction. *Vision Research, 34*, 1835–1842.

Wilson, H.R., McFarlane, D.K., & Phillips, G.C. (1983). Spatial frequency tuning of orientation selective units estimated by oblique masking. *Vision Research, 23*, 873–882.

Winston, P.H. (1973). Learning to identify toy block structures. In R.L. Solso (Ed.), *Contemporary issues in cognitive psychology: The Loyola symposium*. Washington, DC: Hemisphere Publishing Corp.

Winston, P.H. (1975). Learning structural descriptions from examples. In P.H. Winston (Ed.), *The psychology of computer vision*. New York: McGraw-Hill.

Winston, P. H. (1984). *Artificial intelligence*. London: Addison-Wesley.

Wittreich, W.J. (1959). Visual perception and personality. *Scientific American, 200*, April, 56–75.

Wohlgemuth, A. (1911). On the after-effect of seen movement. *British Journal of Psychology Monographs 1*.

Wolf, R., Voss, A., Hein, S., & Heisenberg, M. (1992). Can a fly ride a bicycle? *Philosophical Transactions of the Royal Society of London, B, 337*, 261–269.

Wong-Riley, M.T.T. (1979). Changes in the visual system of monocularly sutured or enucleated cats demonstrable with cytochrome oxidase histochemistry. *Brain Research, 171*, 11–28.

Wood, D.C. (1976). Action spectrum and electro-physiological responses correlated with the photophobic response of *Stentor coeruleus*. *Photochemistry and Photobiology, 24*, 261–266.

Woodbury, P.B. (1986). The geometry of predator avoidance by the blue crab *Callinectes sapidus* Rathbun. *Animal Behaviour, 34*, 28–37.

Wundt, W. (1896). *Grundriss der Psychologie*. Translated by C.H. Judd (1907) as *Outlines of psychology*. New York: G.E. Stechart & Co.

Wurtz, R.H., & Albano, J.E. (1980). Visual-motor function of the primate superior colliculus. *Annual Review of Neuroscience, 3*, 189–226.

Yo, C., & Wilson, H.R. (1992). Perceived direction of moving two-dimensional patterns depends on duration, contrast and eccentricity. *Vision Research, 32*, 135–147.

Young, A.W., & Bruce, V. (1991). Perceptual categories and the computation of grandmother. *European Journal of Cognitive Psychology, 3*, 5–50.

Young, A.W., Hellawell, D.J., & Hay, D.C. (1987). Configural information in face perception. *Perception, 16*, 747–759.

Young, D.S., & Lee, D.N. (1987). Training children in road crossing skills using a roadside simulation. *Accident Analysis and Prevention, 19*, 327–341.

Young, M.J., Landy, M.S., & Maloney, L.T. (1993). A perturbation analysis of depth perception from combinations of texture and motion cues. *Vision Research, 33*, 2685–2696.

Young, M.P. (1992). Objective analysis of the topological organization of the primate cortical visual system. *Nature, 358*, 152–155.

Young, M.P., Tanaka, K., & Yamane, S. (1992). On oscillating neuronal responses in the visual cortex of the monkey. *Journal of Neurophysiology, 67,* 1464–1474.

Young, M.P., & Yamane, S. (1992). Sparse population coding of faces in the inferotemporal cortex. *Science, 256,* 1327–1331.

Young, R. A. (1985). *The Gaussian derivative theory of spatial vision: Analysis of cortical cell receptive field line-weighting profiles.* Technical Report GMR 4920, General Motors Research Labs. Warren, MI.

Young, R. A. (1987). The Gaussian derivative model for spatial vision. I. Retinal mechanisms. *Spatial Vision, 2,* 273–293.

Young, R.A., & Lesperance, R.M. (1993). *A physiological model of motion analysis for machine vision.* Technical Report GMR 7878, General Motors Research Labs. Warren, MI.

Yuille, A.L., & Grzywacz, N.M. (1988). A computational theory for the perception of coherent visual motion. *Nature, 333,* 71–74.

Zanker, J.M., Egelhaaf, M., & Warzecha, A.-K. (1991). On the co-ordination of motor output during visual flight control of flies. *Journal of Comparative Physiology, 169,* 127–134.

Zeil, J. (1993). Orientation flights of solitary wasps (Cerceris; Sphecidae; Hymenoptera). II. Similarities between orientation and return flights and the use of motion parallax. *Journal of Comparative Physiology, 172,* 207–222.

Zeki, S.M. (1978). Uniformity and diversity of structure and function in rhesus monkey prestriate visual cortex. *Journal of Physiology, 277,* 273–290.

Zeki, S. (1980). The representation of colours in the cerebral cortex. *Nature, 284,* 412–418.

Zeki, S. (1983). Colour coding in the cerebral cortex: The reaction of cells in monkey visual cortex to wavelength and colours. *Neuroscience, 9,* 741–765.

Zeki, S., Watson, J.D.G., Lueck, C.J., Friston, K.J., Kennard, C., & Frackowiak, R.S.J. (1991). A direct demonstration of functional specialization in human visual cortex. *Journal of Neuroscience, 11,* 641–649.

Zhou, Y.-X., & Baker, C.L. (1993). A processing stream in mammalian visual cortex neurons for non-Fourier responses. *Science, 261,* 98–101.

Zipser, D., & Andersen, R.A. (1988). A back-propagation programmed network that simulates response properties of a subset of posterior parietal neurons. *Nature, 331,* 679–684.

Glossary

This glossary gives definitions of technical terms, particularly physiological and mathematical ones, not defined in the text, and also of terms used in sections of the book distant from those in which they are explained. Terms *italicised* are defined elsewhere in the glossary.

Absorption spectrum The relationship between the wavelength of light striking a *pigment* and how strongly the light is absorbed.

Accommodation Adjustment of the optics of an eye to keep an object in focus on the retina as its distance from the eye varies. In the human eye this is achieved by varying the thickness of the lens.

Action potential The interior of a nerve cell has a negative electrical charge relative to the exterior. If the axon of a nerve cell is stimulated electrically, the membrane allows current to cross it and the charge is momentarily reversed. This change in membrane behaviour spreads rapidly down the axon and the wave of change in voltage across the membrane that it causes is called an action potential.

Acuity See *visual acuity*.

Adaptation A change in the sensitivity to light of either a *photoreceptor* or of the visual system as a whole, so as to match the current average light intensity. Adaptation to bright light (e.g. when you wake up and switch on a light) occurs rapidly, whereas dark adaptation (e.g. when you walk from daylight into a dark cinema) is a slower process.

Affordance A term introduced by Gibson, which refers to a possibility for action afforded to a perceiver by an object. The affordances of an object depend on the perceiver as well as on the characteristics of the object. For example, a stream affords such actions as jumping and paddling to a person, but to a frog it affords swimming.

Algorithm A specified procedure for solving a problem.

Amacrine cell A type of cell in the vertebrate retina (see Fig. 2.4).

Ambient optic array See *optic array*.

Area centralis Area in a vertebrate retina rich in *cones*, with little pooling of receptor outputs. In the human eye, the area centralis corresponds to the *fovea*, but this is not so in all species.

Axon The long, slender process of a nerve cell leading away from the cell body and ending at *synapses* with other cells.

Bandwidth A measure of the frequency tuning of the response of a cell or other device. The smaller a cell's bandwidth, the narrower the range of frequencies to which it responds (see Fig. 3.10).

Bipolar cell   A type of cell in the vertebrate retina (see Fig. 2.4).

Bottom-up process   See *data-driven process*.

Centre-off response   A cell with a *concentric receptive field* that responds to a reduction of light intensity in the centre of its field relative to that in the surround is said to have a centre-off response.

Centre-on response   A cell with a *concentric receptive field* that responds to an increase in light intensity in the centre of its field relative to that in the surround is said to have a centre-on response.

Closed-loop control   A control system in which the output is continuously modified by feedback from the environment. An example is a person maintaining balance on a surfboard; their posture (the output) is continually adjusted in response to movement of the board (feedback).

Colour-opponency   Cells with this property are excited by light in one region of the spectrum and inhibited by light in another region (see Fig. 2.10).

Complex cell   Cell in the *visual cortex* responding either to an edge, a bar, or a slit stimulus of a particular orientation falling anywhere within its *receptive field*.

Computational theory   A term introduced by Marr. Computational theories of vision are concerned with how, in principle, particular kinds of information such as the shapes of objects or distances of surfaces can be extracted from images. Solutions to such problems involve consideration of the constraints that apply to the structures of natural objects and surfaces and the ways in which they reflect light. An example is the demonstration that the shape of an object can be recovered from its silhouette if the shape approximates to a *generalised cone*.

Concentric field   A *receptive field* divided into an inner circular region and an outer ring-shaped region. Light falling in each of the two regions has opposite effects on the response of the cell.

Conceptually driven process   A process of extraction of information from sensory input that relies for its operation on prior knowledge of the properties of objects or events to be detected. For example, a conceptually driven process for recovering the structures of solid objects represented in an image would require prior information about the geometrical properties of objects (such as the nature of cubes and cylinders) that could be present.

Cone   Vertebrate *photoreceptor* with short outer segment, which does not respond to light of low intensity.

Connectionist model   Model of the operation of the nervous system or some part of it made up of a large number of units, each taking input from many of the others as well as from external sources. Inputs and outputs of units are numerical values—not symbols—and the operations performed by units on their inputs are relatively simple.

Contrast   Difference between maximum and minimum intensities in a pattern of light expressed as a proportion of the mean intensity.

Cue invariance   A cell shows cue invariance if its selectivity for, say, orientation is the same when the pattern orientation is defined by different spatial cues such as variation in *luminance*, colour, texture, or motion.

Cytochrome oxidase (CO)   An enzyme. The level of CO in a cell reflects its metabolic activity.

Data-driven process   A process of extraction of information from sensory input that relies only on information available in the input. For example, a data-driven process for recovering the structures of solid objects represented in an image would require no knowledge of the geometrical properties of particular kinds of object.

Dendrites   The processes of nerve cells that carry *slow potentials* from *synapses* to the cell body.

Depolarisation   A change in the *membrane potential* of a nerve cell such that the interior becomes less negatively charged relative to the exterior. If the membrane of an axon is depolarised, *action potentials* are generated with increased frequency.

Derivative The result of differentiating a function to find its slope or rate of change. A time derivative is obtained if a function relating some quantity to time is differentiated with respect to time. For example, the time derivative of a function relating the volume of water in a bath to time expresses how the rate of emptying or filling of the bath varies with time. See also *partial derivative*.

Diffraction The scattering of rays of light by collision with particles of matter as they pass through a medium such as air or water.

Direction preference An alternative term to *direction selectivity*.

Direction selectivity A difference in the response of a cell to a pattern of light moving through its *receptive field* according to the direction of movement.

Directional sensitivity A single *photoreceptor* is stimulated by light arriving through a segment of the *optic array*. In this book, we have used the term directional sensitivity to refer to the size of this segment. The smaller it is, the greater the directional sensitivity of the photoreceptor. In order to achieve a high degree of directional sensitivity, some means of forming an image is required. The term is used by some authors as a synonym of *directional selectivity*.

Eccentricity Angular distance of a point on the retina from the centre of the *fovea*.

Edge segment In Marr's theory of early visual processing, a token in the *raw primal sketch* formed where *zero-crossing segments* from $\nabla^2 G$ *filters* of adjacent sizes coincide.

Electrotonic spread The spread of a *slow potential* over the membrane of a *dendrite* or nerve cell body.

End-inhibition A property of some cells in the *visual cortex* that respond strongly to either an edge, a bar, or a slit that ends within the *receptive field* but that are inhibited by longer contours.

Endothermic Term describing an animal which can maintain its body temperature at a fixed level above that of its surroundings.

Exothermic Term describing an animal which cannot maintain its body temperature above that of its surroundings.

Exproprioceptive information Information about the position of a perceiver's body, or parts of the body, relative to the environment. Lee (1977) introduced this term to give a threefold classification of types of sensory information, along with the traditional classes of *exteroceptive* and *proprioceptive* information.

Exteroceptive information Information about surfaces, objects, and events in a perceiver's environment.

Extrastriate cortex Region of primate cerebral cortex anterior to *striate cortex* (see Fig. 3.12).

Fibre See *axon*.

Filter, $\nabla^2 G$ An *algorithm* that smooths an array of light intensity values in an image with a *Gaussian filter* and then applies a *Laplacian* operator to each region of the smoothed image. The wider the filter, the greater the degree of smoothing of the image by the Gaussian part of the filter.

Firing rate The frequency at which *action potentials* pass down the *axon* of a nerve cell.

First-order Term used to describe the structure of an image formed by local variation (*modulation*) in the intensity (or wavelength) of a uniform field of light.

Fixation In the case of an animal with mobile eyes, alignment of the eyes so that the image of the fixated target falls on the *area centralis*. Otherwise, alignment of the head to point towards the fixated target.

Fourier analysis Fourier's theorem proves that any one-dimensional pattern can be fully described as the sum of a number of sine waves of different frequencies, amplitudes, and phases. The same is true of a two-dimensional pattern provided that horizontal and vertical components of each sinusoid are analysed. Fourier analysis is a procedure for breaking down a pattern into its sinusoidal components.

Fourier transform   The description of a pattern in terms of the frequencies, amplitudes, and phases of its sinusoidal components that is obtained by applying *Fourier analysis*.

Fovea   Pit-shaped depression in a vertebrate retina, usually in an *area centralis*.

Gabor function   A sinusoidal wave-packet, i.e. a smoothly tapered segment of a sinusoidal wave, formed by multiplying together a sine-wave and a *Gaussian* function. Named after scientist Denis Gabor. A Gabor patch is the 2-D image formed in this way, as shown in Fig. A.1 (p.420). The *phase* of the sinusoid, relative to the peak of the Gaussian, determines the symmetry of the Gabor patch, which may be odd or even (Fig. 3.5) or asymmetric. Widely used in vision, because it has a fairly well-defined spatial frequency and orientation, and a fairly well-defined location in space.

Ganglion cell   A type of cell in the vertebrate retina (see Fig. 2.4). The *axons* of ganglion cells are packed together in the *optic nerve* and carry information from retina to brain.

Gaussian filter   Algorithm smoothing spatial or temporal variation in an image by averaging neighbouring values of light intensity, the contribution of values to the average being weighted according to a Gaussian (normal) function.

Generalised cone   The surface created by moving a cross-section of constant shape but variable size along an axis (see Fig. 9.15).

Gradient   A vector that defines the slope of a function at a given point, and the direction in which the function slopes. An image $I(x,y)$ has *partial derivatives* $\partial I/\partial x$ and $\partial I/\partial y$, and these are the x- and y-components of the gradient vector: $\text{Grad}(I) = (\partial I/\partial x, \partial I/\partial y)$. $\text{Grad}(I)$ is also written as ∇I. The slope at any point is thus given by the magnitude of the gradient vector, $\sqrt{[(\partial I/\partial x)^2 + (\partial I/\partial y)^2]}$.

Grating   A pattern of parallel dark and bright bars. In a sinusoidal (or sine wave) grating, brightness varies sinusoidally across the pattern, so that the stripes are blurred (see Fig. 2.6).

Horizontal cell   A type of cell in the vertebrate retina (see Fig. 2.4).

Hypercomplex cell   A *simple* or *complex cell* with the property of *end-inhibition*.

Hyperpolarisation   A change in the *membrane potential* of a nerve cell such that the interior becomes more negatively charged relative to the exterior. If the membrane of an axon is hyperpolarised, *action potentials* are generated with lower frequency.

Impulse   See *action potential*.

Interneuron   Nerve cell in the central nervous system that is neither a *receptor* nor a *motor neuron*.

Intracellular recording   Recording the *membrane potential* of a nerve cell by means of an electrode penetrating the membrane.

Invariant   In Gibson's use of the term, some measure of the pattern of light reflected from an object, event, or scene that remains constant as other measures of the pattern vary. An invariant therefore provides information for a perceiver about some aspect of his/her surroundings. For example, the size of elements of optic texture in the light reflected from a surface varies with the nature of the surface and with its distance from the perceiver, and therefore does not provide information to specify the slant of the surface relative to the perceiver. For a particular slant, however, the rate of change of the size of texture elements is invariant for different surfaces and different distances.

IT (inferotemporal area)   Visual area in *extrastriate cortex* (see Fig. 3.12).

LGN (lateral geniculate nucleus)   The part of the mammalian brain where the axons of retinal *ganglion cells* terminate, and from which *axons* run to the *visual cortex* (see Fig. 3.1).

Laplacian ($\nabla^2 G$)   If a quantity such as light intensity varies along one dimension, then the second derivative of that quantity describes the rate at which its gradient is changing at any point. For example, a positive value of the second derivative would indicate that the gradient of light intensity is becoming steeper. Where light intensity varies in two dimensions (as it does in an image), the Laplacian is the sum of the second derivatives of intensity taken in two orthogonal directions (i.e. at right angles).

Thus $\nabla^2 = (\partial^2/\partial x^2 + \partial^2/\partial y^2)$.

Linearity   A device with a single input and output is said to operate in a linear fashion if the relationship between the value x of the input and and the value y of the output has the form y = mx + c (and therefore can be represented graphically as a straight line). For a linear device with multiple inputs, the relationship between output and the values x1, x2, . . . of the inputs has the form y = m1x1 + m2x2 . . . + c. Examples of nonlinearities are where the output is a function of a higher power of x (e.g. x^2), log x, or the absolute value of x.

Luminance   Light intensity.

M cell   Cell in a magnocellular layer of the *LGN*, or a *retinal ganglion cell* making synaptic contact in one of these layers.

Masking   General term for the loss of visibility of a test pattern caused by the presence of another pattern (the masker) that is either superimposed on the test pattern or adjacent to it in space and/or time. There are many varieties of masking, and many different visual processes contribute to it.

Membrane potential   The difference in electrical potential between the interior and the exterior of a nerve cell. In the resting state, the interior is always negative relative to the exterior.

Modulation   One signal modulates another if the values of the first signal directly control some aspect or quantity in the second signal. Thus radio signals are amplitude-modulated (AM) or frequency-modulated (FM) if the audio signal imposes a corresponding variation in the local amplitude or frequency of a high frequency carrier wave. In vision, contrast modulation is produced when a low frequency wave (the envelope) is used to vary the local contrast of a high frequency carrier grating (Fig. 8.8) or noise pattern (Fig. 8.9). The task of the radio receiver, and the visual system, is to recover the modulating signal

from the modulated carrier—a process known as "demodulation".

Motion parallax   Movement of the image of an object over the retina. The rate of movement depends on the velocity of the object relative to the eye, and its distance from the eye.

Motor neuron   A nerve cell that synapses with a muscle cell. *Action potentials* passing down the axon of the motor neuron cause the muscle to contract.

MST (medial superior temporal area)   Visual area in *extrastriate cortex* (see Fig. 3.12).

MT (middle temporal area)   Visual area in *extrastriate cortex* (see Fig. 3.12).

Neuron   Nerve cell.

Nonlinearity   See *linearity*.

Ocular dominance   Cells in the *visual cortex* that respond more strongly to a stimulus presented to one eye than to the other are said to show ocular dominance.

Off-centre cell   Cell with a *centre-off response*.

Ommatidium   Unit of the compound eye containing a light-sensitive rhabdom (see Fig. 1.8).

On-centre cell   Cell with a *centre-on response*.

Open-loop control   Control system in which the output is not continuously modified by feedback from the environment. An example is a person swatting a fly: once the swing of the arm begins, it is completed whatever the fly does.

Operant conditioning   A term introduced by Skinner. In an operant conditioning procedure, an animal's behaviour is changed by pairing a piece of behaviour (the operant) with reinforcement. For example, if a rat receives food each time it presses a bar, it will come to press the bar more frequently. Such methods can be used to determine whether an animal can discriminate two stimuli. For example, if a rat can learn to press a bar when it hears a tone of one pitch and not to press when it hears one of another pitch, then it must be able to discriminate the tones.

Opponent-colour response   See *colour-opponency*.

Opsins   A group of *pigments* found in *photoreceptor cells*.

Optic array   Term introduced by Gibson, to refer to the instantaneous pattern of light reaching a point in space from all directions. In different regions of the optic array, the spatial pattern of light will differ, according to the nature of the surface from which it has been reflected.

Optic flow field   The fluctuating patterns of light intensity reaching an observer caused by any relative movement between observer and environment.

Optic nerve   Nerve running from retina to brain.

Optic texture   The spatial pattern of light reflected from a textured surface.

Optomotor response   The turning response of an animal presented with uniform flow of *optic texture*, in the direction that minimises rate of flow relative to the animal.

Orientation preference (or selectivity)   Variation in the response of a cell with the orientation of an edge, bar, or slit. The preferred orientation is that giving the greatest response.

P cell   Cell in a parvocellular layer of the *LGN*, or a *retinal ganglion cell* making synaptic contact in one of these layers.

Partial derivative   Given a quantity (e.g. image intensity, I) that is a function of several variables (x, y, t...) the slope of the function in the x-direction is given by the partial derivative with respect to x, denoted $\partial I/\partial x$; and similarly for the other variables (y, t, ...). Using calculus, it is obtained by holding the other variables constant. Thus if $I = x^2 + y^2$, then $\partial I/\partial x = 2x + y^2$, and $\partial I/\partial y = x^2 + 2y$. See also *gradient*.

Peak spectral sensitivity   The wavelength of light to which a *photoreceptor* responds most strongly.

Perpendicular component   The component of the velocity of motion of an edge that is perpendicular to the edge.

Phase   The position of a sine wave relative to a given fixed point (the origin). Expressed either in degrees or radians. Thus a 90° phase shift ($\pi/2$ radians) displaces the sine wave through one-quarter of a cycle, equal to half a bar width. A 180° phase shift (π radians) shifts the wave through half a cycle. This is equivalent to reversing the contrast of the dark and light bars.

Photon,   Unit of energy in electromagnetic radiation.

Photopic vision   Vision in light sufficiently bright to excite *cones*.

Photoreceptor cell   A *receptor cell* sensitive to light.

Pigment   A chemical substance which absorbs light. Pigment molecules change in shape as they absorb light and, in a *photoreceptor*, this change begins a series of biochemical processes that lead to the *receptor potential*.

Pitch   Rotation of a flying insect or bird in a "head-up" or "head-down" manner (see Fig. 12.1).

Plexiform layer   Layer of nerve cell processes and *synapses* in the vertebrate retina (see Fig. 2.4).

Poles (of optic flow field)   These are the two points in the *optic flow field* surrounding an observer moving through the environment at which there is no flow of *optic texture*. One is the point towards which the observer is moving (see Fig. 11.6) and the other is the point away from which the observer is moving.

Prestriate cortex   See *extrastriate cortex*.

Projection   Light rays are said to be projected to the image plane when an image is formed. The word also has a quite different meaning in neurophysiology, to refer to the region where the *axons* of a group of nerve cells in the brain terminate and make *synaptic* contact.

Proprioceptive information   In Lee's use of the term, information about the positions of parts of the body relative to one another.

Psychophysics   The analysis of perceptual processes by studying the effect on a subject's experience or behaviour of systematically varying the properties of a stimulus along one or more physical dimensions.

Quadrature   Two signals or images are "in quadrature" if the frequency components of one signal are shifted in *phase* by 90° from the other signal. Thus sin(x) and cos(x) are in quadrature, since sin(x) = cos(x–90).

Raw primal sketch   In Marr's theory of vision, a rich representation of the intensity changes present in the original image.

Receptive field   The area of the retina in which light causes a response in a particular nerve cell.

Receptor cell   A nerve cell sensitive to external energy.

Receptor potential   The change in *membrane potential* of a *receptor cell* caused by external energy impinging on it.

Refraction   The bending of rays of light as they cross a boundary between two transparent media of different optical densities.

Retinal ganglion cell   See *ganglion cell*.

Retinotopic map   An array of nerve cells that have the same positions relative to one another as their *receptive fields* have on the surface of the retina.

Retinula cell   A *photoreceptor* in the eye of an insect or other arthropod (see Fig. 1.8).

Rod   Vertebrate *photoreceptor* with long outer segment, sensitive to light of low intensity.

Roll   Rotation of a flying insect or bird around the long axis of the body (see Fig. 12.1).

Saccade   Rapid movement of the eye to fixate a target.

Scalar   A quantity that has magnitude only.

Scotopic vision   Vision in dim light, sufficiently bright to excite *rods* but not *cones*.

Second-order   Term used to describe the structure of an image formed by local variation (*modulation*) in some higher-order property of the image, such as its local contrast, texture density, element orientation, flicker rate, etc.

Sensitivity spectrum   The relationship between the wavelength of light striking a *photoreceptor* and the size of the *receptor potential*.

Simple cell   Cell in the visual cortex showing linear *spatial summation* of light intensities in parts of its *receptive field* separated by straight line boundaries.

Sinusoidal grating   See *grating*.

Slow potential   A small change in the *membrane potential* of a nerve cell, such as a *receptor potential*, which decays as it spreads passively over the membrane. In contrast, an *action potential* is propagated by an active change in membrane properties and does not decay in amplitude as it is transmitted.

Spatial frequency   The frequency, expressed as cycles per unit of visual angle, of a periodic pattern of light such as a *grating*. At a particular viewing distance, the spatial frequency of a grating depends on the width of its bars; the narrower these are, the higher the frequency.

Spatial frequency tuning   A nerve cell in a visual pathway that responds more strongly to sinusoidal *gratings* that have *spatial frequencies* in a particular range than to gratings of other frequencies is said to show spatial frequency tuning.

Spatial summation   If the response of a cell to a pattern of light is a function of the difference in the amounts of light falling in different regions of its *receptive field*, then it is said to show linear spatial summation.

Stereopsis   Perception of depth dependent on disparity in the images projected on the retinas of the two eyes.

Stereoscopic fusion   The process whereby the two disparate retinal images are combined to yield a single percept in depth.

Striate cortex   See *visual cortex*.

Superior colliculus   Structure in mammalian midbrain where some *retinal ganglion cell axons* terminate.

Synapse   A point where the membranes of two nerve cells nearly touch and where electrical activity in one cell influences the *membrane potential* of the other cell.

3-D model representation   An object-centred representation of shape, organised hierarchically (see Fig. 9.16).

Top-down process   See *conceptually driven process*.

Topology   A branch of geometry describing the properties of forms that are unaffected by continuous distortion such as stretching. For example, a doughnut and a record have the same topology.

Torque   Turning force, equal to force applied multiplied by the distance of its point of application from the centre of rotation.

Transduction The process by which external energy impinging on a *receptor cell* causes a change in its *membrane potential*.

2½-D sketch A viewer-centred representation of the depths and orientations of visible surfaces (see Fig. 7.19).

V1 Primary *visual cortex* of a primate.

V2, V3, V4 Visual areas in *extrastriate cortex* (see Fig. 3.12).

Vector A quantity that has both magnitude and direction.

Velocity field A representation of the velocity of image motion at any instant in each of many small regions of a time-varying image.

Vergence movements Binocular movements of the eyes making their direction of gaze either more or less convergent.

Vestibular system The organ in the inner ear involved in the *transduction* of angular acceleration of the body into nerve impulses.

Visual acuity An observer's visual acuity is measured by the angle between adjacent bars in the highest frequency *grating* that they can distinguish from a plain field of the same average brightness as the grating.

Visual angle The angle which an object subtends at the eye (see Fig. 1.13).

Visual cortex, primary Region of the mammalian cortex in the occipital lobe receiving input from the *LGN*. Cells in the primary visual cortex respond to light falling on the retina and are arranged in a *retinotopic map*. In primates, this region is also known as the striate cortex or V1.

W cells The *ganglion cells* of the mammalian retina that do not have *concentric fields*.

X cells *Ganglion cells* that show linear *spatial summation* of light intensities in centre and surround areas of the *receptive field*.

Y cells *Ganglion cells* that show nonlinear responses to changes in light intensity.

Yaw Rotation of a flying insect or bird around the vertical axis (see Fig. 12.1).

Zero-crossing A point where values of a function change sign.

FIGURE A.1

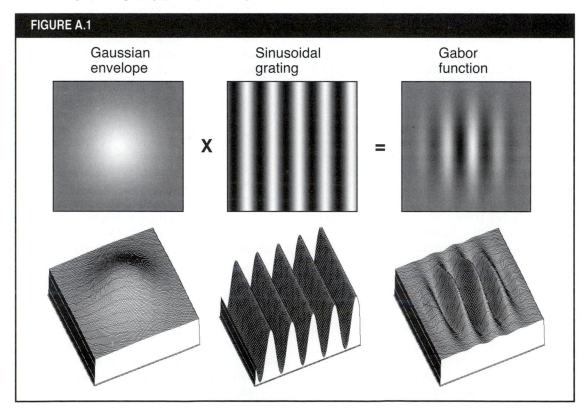

Gaussian envelope X Sinusoidal grating = Gabor function

Author Index

Subject Index